D1715790

Cultural Memory
in
the
Present

Mieke Bal and Hent de Vries, Editors

J. HILLIS MILLER; OR, BOUSTROPHEDONIC READING

Manuel Asensi

Translated by Mabel Richart

BLACK HOLES

J. Hillis Miller

In memory of Bill Readings

STANFORD UNIVERSITY PRESS

STANFORD, CALIFORNIA

1999

Stanford University Press
Stanford, California
© 1999 by the Board of Trustees of the
Leland Stanford Junior University

Printed in the United States of America

CIP data appear at the end of the book

Like unicorns and gargoyles, black holes seem more at home in the realms of science fiction and ancient myth than the real Universe. Nonetheless, well-tested laws of physics predict firmly that black holes exist. In our galaxy alone there may be millions, but their darkness hides them from view. Astronomers have great difficulty finding them.

—KIP S. THORNE,
  Black Holes and Time Warps: Einstein's Outrageous Legacy

Preface

Why write a book with a graphic arrangement in which the two texts of the two authors face one another? Is it a fancy? Is it a hazardous choice? Is it the classical "modernism" or "vanguardism" of criticism and theory today? Of course, it is neither a fancy nor a hazardous choice. It would be necessary to discuss the question of "vanguardism" somewhere else. What we propose is justified by reasons I shall explain briefly:

At first what we see is Hillis Miller making an analysis, for example, of some aspects of Marcel Proust's work; we also see, face to face with that, Manuel Asensi analyzing Hillis Miller's general work. However, this is only an appearance of what really happens. My writing on Miller's work could be classified as "discordant," "strange," "anomalous." Why?

In the first place because this writing is carried out by someone belonging to a cultural tradition (the European) different from the American. If we take into account that literary theory bloomed, above all, in European movements (from "Russian Formalism" through "Glossematics" or "nouvelle critique"), this will permit us to see Miller's work in a broad perspective. Up until now, it has perhaps been possible to consider Miller's work in relation to New Criticism or criticism of consciousness, but what happens with the connection or disconnection between Miller

Preface

"Boustrophedonic": the word means turning back and forth, as an ox ploughs a field. It comes from the Greek *bous*, "ox," and *strophe*, "turn," as in the strophes and antistrophes of the choruses in Greek tragedies. These were so called because the chorus paused at one end of the stage or the other, turned, and delivered the next "strophe" of its speech. Certain early forms of written language were inscribed in boustrophedonic form, neither from left to right, like English, nor from right to left, like one way of writing Chinese, but back and forth in alternate lines, so the eye could follow from left to right and then back again from right to left across the page. Whether or not my criticism or my way of thinking generally is boustrophedonic I do not know. I must leave it to the reader to follow through Manuel Asensi's part of this book and decide. I am not sure that I even want to know. Could there even possibly be a joke at my expense in Manuel Asensi's choice of that word to name my movement back and forth between my consciousness and the other consciousness, between the text written by the other and the text I write as a "reading" of it? I work my way back and forth, like a dumb ox. I am not sure I want to know either whether that joke is meant. Though I am greatly honored by Asensi's careful attention to my work, I do not, as might have been expected, wholly recognize myself in his portrait, though I must admit it is probably me. The experience is the uncanny one of looking in the mirror and seeing a not wholly familiar face reflected there that must nevertheless be my own face.

In any case, my part of this book was drafted before I was able to read Asensi's part. While he was writing his analysis, he asked me to contribute something new that might accompany it. I set to work. *Black Holes* was the ultimate result, though I did not initially foresee the shape it would take. My first instinct, like an ox turning its head in the gesture

and Shklovsky, Jakobson, Bakhtin, Greimas, Barthes, Petofi, Eco, and so forth?

In the second place, my analysis of Miller's work is heterodox in two senses. On the one hand, my discourse is far from the approaches usually followed in order to classify Miller's criticism. (Critics have shown us Miller changing "movements" and translating ideas of Wimsatt, Poulet, Derrida, de Man, Lacan, etc.) Nevertheless, my writing wants to prove the opposite: all these authors and movements, all their works, have translated Miller's essential concerns. Miller has always been "beyond" "method" and "school"—perhaps this explains his connection with deconstruction and Derrida. On the other hand, my writing does not move among "generalities" as a strategy for approaching Miller's work. It analyzes his analyses. It is not a question of using the formula "Miller's literary criticism is X," but of penetrating into some texts into which he has already penetrated and, of course, into the writing he has created

William Faulkner calls "refraining," was to try to write something so discontinuous with the work I had already published, that is, the work Asensi was then able to read, that it would disqualify whatever Asensi might say about me. That has remained a strong part of my motivation for writing *Black Holes*. I do not think, however, that I have been wholly successful in my attempt to escape Asensi's reading. Why should I want to escape it? To avoid being monumentalized, as by a tombstone. Life, so it seemed to me, means change, and I wanted to show that I was going on changing.

The initial donnée for *Black Holes* was the notion of the other, or rather of "others," since the other is always plural. That notion or problem was the track I was then following, and am still following, in my teaching and writing. It seemed to me something genuinely new in my work. I was, I believe, to some degree mistaken in thinking that, as Asensi's book has persuaded me. What I have to say now about the "others" is more a making explicit of something latent or implicit all along than an irruption of the wholly new. So much for my attempt to derail Asensi's project, to get his plow out of the furrow.

The reader will see how fundamental the question of otherness remains in *Black Holes*, but my interest in that became crossed with two other strong motivations. Partly instigated by my reading in manuscript of Bill Readings's brilliant *The University in Ruins*, partly moved by my own experience of the unusually rapid changes in literary study in the United States research university, I found myself wanting to understand those changes, to account for them in my own way, and in relation to that idea of the "others." The first half of this book does that. The second motivation was an example of what is most abiding in all my teaching and writing from the beginning: the desire to account for, to understand, to "read" in the sense of seeing through, the strangeness of particular literary works. In this case the works were Anthony Trollope's *Ayala's Angel* and Marcel Proust's *A la recherche du temps perdu*. Another book in progress, to be called *Others*, will investigate otherness in other works. Though Trollope and Proust are two dead white males (one straight, one gay, apparently), I do not see any reason to apologize for that. Reading such "canonical" works has always been, and still remains, my vocation. That vocation has been from the beginning defined by my sense that the Western tradition is other to itself, inhabited by its own otherness. I call that otherness the "strangeness" of canonical works.

Just as my attempt to think out what is happening to United States

about these texts. This strategy implies the superimposition of different
texts in which the differences and dissonances between them can be perfectly seen. (Asensi gets into a book by Thomas De Quincey and into
Miller's analysis of De Quincey; at the same time, Asensi underlines the
methodology used, its achievements and its limits.)

In the third place—and as something that follows from the two
previous points—it is possible to assert that my discourse goes beyond
the assumptions and beliefs of Miller's work itself. Deep down, the question is: to what extent does Miller recognize his own work in my words?
No doubt, he will or won't agree with me, but can he really recognize
his words in my words, his discourse in my discourse, his criticism in
my criticism of his criticism? The reading I claim to accomplish wants
to interrupt and disturb not only what the history of criticism and philosophy have said about Miller (the reader will find a sharp discussion
with Rodolphe Gasché and Suzanne Gearhart), but also the presupposi-

literary study took its own to some degree unforeseen course once I got started with it, so the readings of *Ayala's Angel* and *A la recherche du temps perdu* took over my interest and assumed their own form. I became more interested in the questions of how Ayala knows she is in love or why Proust has Marcel hear the Venetian boatman sing "O sole mio!" than in abstract questions about the "others." For me initial conceptual questions, far from being answered, are always distorted, deformed, changed so much that they become almost unrecognizable, by each act of reading. That might be one meaning of saying that the other is always plural, always "others." Those others always make their demand on the one who encounters them. Both *Ayala's Angel* and *A la recherche du temps perdu* center on intuitions of otherness, but each intuition is special, sui generis, not fully able to be subsumed under a common concept. That is one reason why I need to go on reading and re-reading literature, even works that seem most familiar, most predictable. Each such reading to some degree remakes me, in a version of the back and forth Manuel Asensi calls "boustrophedonic."

Bits and pieces of this book or alternative expressions of ideas that went into it have been published in preliminary form in various places and in various languages. All have now been reworked to fit the argument of this book and to conform to my present understanding of its topics. I am grateful to the editors of books and journals and to sponsors of conferences that gave me a chance to try out my ideas on diverse audiences. I am grateful also for comments, oral and printed, including resisting ones, on various lectures and essays drawn from this work. See, for example, Graham Bradshaw's review of the English Language and Literature Association of Korea volume listed below. This appeared in *Studies in English Literature*, a publication of The English Literary Society of Japan, English Number 1998, 149–54. These opportunities and responses have greatly helped me in the further development of my ideas. I am grateful also for permission to re-use the material listed below in revised form.

"Return, Dissenter," *The Times Literary Supplement*, July 15, 1994, 10.
"Literary Study in the University Without Idea," *English Studies in Korea: Retrospect and Prospect*, Proceedings of the 1994 ELLAK (English Language and
Literature Association of Korea) International Symposium (Seoul: ELLAK,
1994), 283–302.

tions and statements of Miller himself. It is like becoming immersed in the black holes of his texts. For these reasons, if we were to publish two separate books, we would lose an essential part of the project: the interference that is not only readable and audible, but also and above all visible. It is necessary that my words be juxtaposed to Miller's words, because through this arrangement the reader will perceive in the form something that comes from the content: the instability of two strange and alien discourses. Only from the perspective of that strangeness and that otherness is it possible to illuminate one of the main works within the field of twentieth-century literary criticism and philosophy: the work of J. Hillis Miller. Therefore what we see in the format is the dialogue, the discussion (even the breaking up) of diverse traditions, of diverse critical viewpoints, and of two discourses that light up in their juxtaposition. This format brings into the open something disturbing and uncanny that is essential for us.

"Wangji wang lu yinhezhongde hetong: Meiguo wenxue yanjiu xin quxiang," trans. Chen Dongrong, *Zhongwai wenxue* 24, no. 1 (June 1995): 72–89.

"The University of Dissensus," *The Oxford Literary Review*, issue on *The University in Ruins* 17, nos. 1–2 (1995): 121–43.

"Daxue renwen yanjiude quan qiu yitihua qingxiang," trans. Chen Dongmei, *Guowai wenxue* 3 (1995): 3–9.

"What Is the Future of the Print Record?," *Profession 95*, 33.

"Hypertekstens etik," trans. Karen-Margrethe Simonsen, *Passage* 20/21 (1995), 241–63.

"The Ethics of Hypertext," *Diacritics* 25, no. 3 (Fall 1995): 27–39.

"The Other's Other: Jealousy and Art in Proust," *Skrift* 16 (1/96): 52–67.

"Governing the Ungovernable: Literary Study in the Transnational University," *Between the Lines* 2, no. 2 (Winter 1995), 2–3.

"Literary Study in the University Without Idea," *ADE Bulletin* 113 (Spring 1996): 30–33.

"Wangjiwanglu yinhezhong de hetong: Meiguo wenxue yanjiu xin quxiang," trans. Chen Dongrong, in Francis K. H. So and Hsiao-yu Sun, eds., *Modern Literature and Literary Theory Revisited* (Kaohsiung: Dept. of Foreign Languages and Literature, National Sun Yat-sen University, 1996), 17–41.

"Literary Study in the Age of Reproduction," in Rüdiger Ahrens and Laurenz Volkmann, eds., *Why Literature Matters: Theories and Functions of Literature* (Heidelberg: Universitätsverlag C. Winter, 1996), 297–310.

" 'Le Mensonge, le Mensonge Parfait': Théories du mensonge chez Proust et Derrida," trans. Yasmine Van den Wijngaert, with Chantal Zabus and Cécile Hayez, in Michel Lisse, ed., *Passions de la littérature* (Paris: Galilée, 1996), 405–20.

"Literary Study in the Transnational University," *Profession 1996* (1996), 6–14.

"Ideology in Trollope's *Ayala's Angel*," *Journal of Literary Criticism* 1 (June 1996): 1–6.

"Los estudios literarios en la universidad transnacional," trans. Mabel Richart, *Eutopías, 2° Epoca* 142 (1996): 1–23.

"English Literature in the United States Today," in Loesley Marx, Loes Nas, and Lara Dunwell, eds., *Fissions and Fusions*, Vol. III, Proceedings of the First Conference of the Cape American Studies Association (Bellville: University of the Western Cape, January 1997), 4–20.

"Cultural Studies and Reading," *ADE Bulletin*, no. 117 (Fall 1997), 15–18.

Contents for 'J. Hillis Miller; or, Boustrophedonic Reading'

Contents for 'Black Holes'

Abbreviations for Works by J. Hillis Miller

AT   *Ariadne's Thread: Story Lines.* New Haven: Yale University Press, 1992.

CD   *Charles Dickens: The World of His Novels.* Cambridge: Harvard University Press, 1958.

DG   *The Disappearance of God.* Cambridge: Harvard University Press, 1963.

ER   *The Ethics of Reading.* New York: Columbia University Press, 1987.

FR   *Fiction and Repetition.* Cambridge: Harvard University Press, 1982.

FVF   *The Form of Victorian Fiction.* Notre Dame: University of Notre Dame Press, 1968.

HH   *Hawthorne and History.* Oxford: Basil Blackwell, 1991.

I   *Illustration.* Cambridge: Harvard University Press, 1992.

ITER   "Is There an Ethics of Reading?" In James Phelan, ed., *Reading Narrative: Form, Ethics, Ideology.* Columbus, Ohio: Ohio State University Press, 1989. 79–101.

LM   *The Linguistic Moment.* Princeton: Princeton University Press, 1985.

PR   *Poets of Reality.* Cambridge: Harvard University Press, 1966.

RN   *Reading Narrative.* Norman: University of Oklahoma Press, 1999.

T   *Topographies.* Stanford: Stanford University Press, 1995.

TH   *Thomas Hardy: Distance and Desire.* Cambridge: Harvard University Press, 1970.

TNT   *Theory Now and Then.* London: Harvester Wheatsheaf, 1991.

TPP   *Tropes, Parables, Performatives.* London: Harvester Wheatsheaf, 1991.

VP   *Versions of Pygmalion.* Cambridge: Harvard University Press, 1990.

VS   *Victorian Subjects.* London: Harvester Wheatsheaf, 1990.

J. Hillis Miller; or, Boustrophedonic Reading | *Black Holes*

I.

Prolegomena, Connection, and Disconnection

Matrix: A Rhapsodic Criticism

The position J. Hillis Miller adopts toward literary criticism begins with a problem both salient and complex: the relation between the critic and the author, between the critic and the text, between the critic's language and the text's language. What does "relation" mean here? Miller has assured us on several occasions that "literary criticism is language about language" or "a recreating in the mind of the critic of the consciousness inscribed in the texts studied" (TH, vii). But reading his vast work, one immediately realizes that, in spite of outward appearances, such a relation with the other can by no means be expounded on the model of Emmanuel Levinas (1968, 1969), for whom the answer of the "I" to the other, by means of language, merges the world that is named with the world of the one who names. Nor is it possible to consider it in the manner of a scientific metalanguage protected by a hypothetical deductive system. But if this relation is neither a merging nor a movement of objectivity, how can it be defined, assuming we accept its existence?

Literary Study in the Transnational University

The Fractal Mosaic

Something drastic is happening in the university. Something drastic is happening *to* the university. The university is losing its idea, the guiding mission that has sustained it since the early nineteenth century.[1] It was then, in Germany, that the modern research university was invented. John Henry Newman's *The Idea of a University* (1852, 1859, 1873) expounded for English readers both this concept of the university and, among other things, the place of literary study in it.[2] Idea—the word has a Platonic resonance. It names a transcendent form—presiding, generative, paternal—on which particular material embodiments are modeled. The university governed by an idea is rapidly being replaced by what Bill Readings calls the university of "excellence." Whatever a given discipline defines at the moment as important work is "excellent." Excellence does not refer to an ahistorical transcendent model operating above the university to determine what it should be and do, giving it a mission and a goal. Excellence is, as Readings observes, a tautological self-definition.

What is the use of literary study now, in this new university without idea? Should, ought, or must we still study literature? What is the source now of the obligation to study literature? Who or what addresses to us a call to do so? Why should we do it? To what purpose? Can literary study still be defended as a socially useful part of university research and teaching or is it just a vestigial remnant that will vanish as other media become

Miller's work generally has been treated as a series of abrupt transitions from one critical methodology to another. Recently, Vita Fortunati and Giovanna Franci have asserted that toward the end of the sixties his rhetoric of consciousness was replaced by a rhetoric of textuality and by devotion to the diffusion of Derrida and the deconstructionist doctrine (Fortunati and Franci, 1989: 194). Earlier, Donald Pease spoke of "conversions" (Pease, 1983: 77). Does this mean we confront an individual who dismisses logical contradiction, "who mixes every language, even those said to be incompatible; who silently accepts every charge of illogicality, of incongruity" (Barthes, 1975: 3)? Should we believe Miller himself when, on being asked about his changes of critico-literary perspective by Martin Heusser, he replied: "It would be boring, I think, if you didn't change" (Heusser and Schweizer, 1991: 155). Is this a question of capricious and gratuitous boredom? Why would someone get bored doing literary criticism? What does Miller mean by that? Is this sentence literal or ironic? How can we read it, or how should we read it? That will be one of the central problems of this essay.

I will not question the advisability, much less the necessity, of establishing chronological periods or proving particular facts, even through discontinuities, that might contribute to a historiography of the humanities. Nor will I claim that Miller's work is coherent from beginning to end. To do this would be more problematic than problem solving. In my opinion, one of the values of Miller's entire oeuvre is that it grows precisely out of the contradictory, oxymoronic, and paradoxical nature of his writing.

If any thesis is going to be defended here, it will be that the contradictions are not a result of simple external influences whose change

more dominant in the new global society that is rapidly taking shape? My part of this book attempts to confront and answer these questions.

A provocative passage toward the end of Marcel Proust's *A la recherche du temps perdu*, that huge assemblage of provocative passages, proposes an analogy between understanding individual people and understanding politics. Literature, for the most part, deals with imaginary characters. It usually approaches larger political, social, religious, or philosophical issues only through these characters' stories. The passage I shall cite from Proust makes this connection explicit. It might therefore serve as a defense of literary study at a time when its social utility is not always evident to everyone. Some students these days in literature programs seem more at ease when they are reading works of theory, more confident that they are doing something important, than when they are reading the literature those works theorize. That is understandable. The political import of literary works is indirect. It has to be worked out through a laborious process of reading and deciphering, while contemporary theoretical works talk directly about race, class, gender, and other urgent political or social issues. Reading theory, so it may appear, saves one the hard work of reading literature.

In 1871 George Eliot was already worrying uneasily about the apparent triviality, provinciality, and lowness of the characters in *Middlemarch*. Do not be anxious, she tells her readers, in an admirably ironic passage, you may take my narrative of middle-class people as a parable. You can then transfer what I say to higher and more important levels of society: "Since there never was a true story which could not be told in parables where you might put a monkey for a margrave, and *vice versa*—whatever has been or is to be narrated by me about low people, may be ennobled by being considered a parable. . . . Thus while I tell the truth about loobies, my reader's imagination need not be entirely excluded from an occupation with lords."[3] I have discussed this passage in detail elsewhere.[4] What is important here is the contingency and reversibility of the analogies affirmed in parables. "Monkey" just happens to sound like "margrave," as "looby" alliterates with "lord." These accidental and senseless linguistic similarities justify putting one of either pair in the place of the other, but in either direction: margrave for monkey, lord for looby, and vice versa. Reading the political import of literature is like decoding a parable or an allegory. It takes special training to do so, since it depends on certain cryptological assumptions. Proust indicates what those might be.

(Wimsatt, Poulet, Derrida, de Man) is immediately reflected in the receiver, but reflect a matrix—Millerian—that existed before those differences, schools, and methodologies. This matrix is contradictory and
plural in itself. It makes use of different critical discourses in order to circulate throughout literature and to interrogate its own concerns. It is a
matrix to which such discourses adapt themselves, of course transforming
it, but also, and above all, receiving its particular trace. Because deconstruction (Derrida or Miller himself) has already reflected on translation,
we hardly need raise such questions as the following: What would it mean
to affirm that Miller translates Derrida or de Man? What does the accli-
matization of deconstruction in the United States or in other countries
mean—in Spain or China for instance? Why do some, such as Gasché,
say that someone has "mistranslated" or displaced Derrida's work from
its "real" field when he or she uses it in literary criticism? The answers to
these questions will be found throughout this book, though it is basically
devoted to analyzing the (contradictory, plural and split) "matrix" that I
consider fundamental in understanding what Miller brings to twentieth-
century literary criticism.

In fact, Miller has sometimes referred to that matrix: "I do not
think this commitment to close reading is 'an inheritance from the New
Criticism.' It springs rather from an initial and persistent fascination with
local strangeness in literary language. This fascination possessed me before I ever heard of the New Criticism, much less of Freud, Lacan, and
Abraham and Torok. It was my motivation for turning from physics
to literature in about 1946" (TPP, vii). Further, he has said, "literature
continually exceeds any formulas or any theory with which the critic is
prepared to encompass it. The hypothesis of possible heterogeneity of

Proust makes a use of analogy somewhat analogous to Eliot's. It would seem to confirm the choice of those who prefer literature to theory. Marcel has been talking about the way "life with Albertine and with Françoise had accustomed [him] to suspect in them thoughts and projects which they did not disclose." This experience of deception has led him, transferring personal experience to a national level, to doubt assertions of "pacific intentions" by Germany, Bulgaria, or Greece. These nations are here personified as like single living persons, that is, as having a unity like that of an organism or a consciousness. Moving from this, as Marcel often does, to a high level of generalization, expressed by means of a brilliant metaphor, he asserts that individual life is to national life as a single cell is to the large living body of which it is a part:

Of course my quarrels with Françoise or with Albertine had been merely private quarrels, of interest only to the life of that little cell, endowed with a mind [*cette petite cellule spirituelle*], that a human being is. But just as there are animal bodies and human bodies, each one of which is an assemblage of cells as large in relation to a single cell as Mont Blanc, so there exist huge organised accumulations of individuals and their life does no more than repeat on a larger scale [*répéter en les amplifiant*] the lives of their constituent cells, and anybody who is incapable of comprehending the mystery, the reactions, the laws of these smaller lives, will only make futile pronouncements [*ne prononcera que des mots vides*] when he talks about struggles between nations.[5]

This is wonderfully reassuring to a lover of literature. If you want to understand national politics and the conflicts between nations, study individual human lives, such as the endlessly proliferating details Marcel gives about his affair with Albertine or the stories about loobies George Eliot tells in *Middlemarch*. If you do not understand people you will never understand politics. Why? Because they can be counted on to correspond exactly. The study of people is easier, closer to home, and more immediate than the seemingly more abstract study of politics. Happily, each repeats the other on a different scale, so that to study one is indirectly to study the other. To adopt George Eliot's language, each is the parable of the other or, to use a word more active in Proust's lexicon, each is the allegory of the other. The claim is that an understanding of nations cannot be approached directly, whereas individual human lives can be comprehended in themselves. If anyone tries to approach national politics without a detour through the analogy with individual lives, she will be sure to

form in literary works has the heuristic value of preparing the reader to confront the oddnesses of a given novel, the things in it that do not 'fit.' The seven readings here have attempted to identify the anomalous" (FR, 5). Or, even more recently (1992), posed here in the manner of a retropro-gression, Miller has said that deconstruction, for him, "was also the return to an indigenous, abiding fascination with local linguistic anomalies in literature. This was my original motivation for the study of literature long before I had heard of Jacques Derrida, or of Kenneth Burke either, for that matter. This fascination has remained the chief constant throughout all my work" (AT, xv). Not long before that, he stated that the "odd" and "anomalous" dimension is a part of literature's power to resist any expla-nation, because its voice "is something unpredictable, savage, violent, without ascertainable cause or explanation, irrational" (LM, 13).

This matrix begins therefore with a "sublime" conception of lit-erature, not so much in the Kantian sense of the representation of the infinite, the colossal, and the unbounded, inaccessible to conceptual knowledge, but in the sense, affirmed in pseudo-Longinus's treatise "On the Sublime," of what leads the listener not to persuasion but to ecstasy by means of language. This mixture of oddness, ecstasy, and language was the first thing that attracted Miller's attention to literature and, accord-ing to him, was his motivation for turning from physics to literature. We might thus presume that his starting point is the distinction, as defined by Samuel Johnson and De Quincey, between rhetoric, or the litera-ture of power, and logic, or the literature of knowledge. If this is indeed the starting point, then Miller's literary criticism could be seen as mov-ing away from its inception within the framework of the New Criticism toward a contrast between a poetic, emotive, nonconceptual language and a scientific, impersonal, and conceptual one.

speak hollow words. Such pronouncements are not only false but ineffectual, "empty." They have no performative purchase on the real world. The study of literature will allow readers to intervene successfully in society and to deflect the course of history. An example is how the diplomat Norpois, in a splendid comic episode late in *A la recherche*, succeeds, through his understanding of individual psychology, in getting a man he casually names to Prince Foggi appointed prime minister of Italy: "And has no one mentioned the name of Signor Giolitti?" (F 4: 215; E 3: 650).

The passage in Proust is a little less reassuring, however, to the reader who notices that what Marcel says one must learn about individuals in order to understand nations is not just "the laws of these smaller lives," but their "mystery" and the fact that most of the time they are lying. *Comprendre le mystère* may mean to penetrate it, but it may also mean understanding that it is impenetrable. The phrase may be an oxymoron. Marcel's account of his life with Albertine is perhaps the best account in literature of the impenetrable mystery of the lie. Just why a lie, for Proust, can never certainly be found out is a complex matter, to which I shall return in the section on Proust at the end of this book. Such clarification of the impenetrable will go by way of a discussion of Marcel's life with Albertine. It can be said here, however, that a lie, contrary to what seems the case, is a matter of bearing false witness, not just a contrary-to-fact statement. It is therefore as much a performative use of language as a constative one. To the degree it is a speech act it is not open to cognition. It belongs to another domain of language. It dwells in the domain of doing things with words rather than in the domain of conveying true or false knowledge. If Germany, Greece, and Bulgaria characteristically lie, as do Albertine and Françoise, then what we may need to know about international politics is that understanding them is based on the science of the lie, another oxymoron.

In what follows the passage I have been discussing, Proust proposes another striking figure for the relation between individuals and nations. A strong, current resonance ties that figure to two main topics of this book: the effects of the Cold War's end on the university and the effects of new communication technologies on university study of national literatures. I call this figure the "fractal mosaic." Just as an organic body repeats on a larger scale the life of each cell that makes it up, and vice versa, so, says Marcel, "la grande figure France" is like a huge geometric shape "filled to its perimeter with millions of little polygons of various shapes," while Germany is "another figure filled with an even greater number of polygons"

However, as we shall see later, the power Miller accords to literature has very little to do with the rhetoric De Quincey talks about. Indeed, the words Miller uses to describe De Quincey's "deconstruction" (*avant la lettre*) of the pair rhetoric/logic are perfectly applicable to what has happened in Miller's own case: "Logic seems neatly set in opposition to rhetoric. In De Quincey's descriptions of logical thought, however, there is a curious reversal, in which logical discourse comes to be praised for possessing just those qualities which make the literature of power so precious" (DG, 150). What attitude does Miller take before the object-other, which is at once odd, anomalous, logical, and rhetorical?

In one of the passages from the Platonic dialogue *Ion*, Socrates says to his interlocutor:

This gift you have of speaking well on Homer is not an art; it is a power divine, impelling you like the power in the stone Euripedes called the magnet, which most call "stone of Heraclea." This stone does not simply attract the iron rings, just by themselves; it also imparts to the rings a force enabling them to do the same thing as the stone itself, that is, to attract another ring, so that sometimes a chain is formed, quite a long one, of iron rings, suspended from one another. . . . Just so the Muse. She first makes men inspired, and then through these inspired ones others share in the enthusiasm [*ēnthousiazōnton*], and a chain is formed. (Plato, 1963: 219–20; 533, d–e)

The idea of an interpretative chain of rings is very close to Miller's thought, but in principle this chain means that the rhapsodist, by virtue of the inspiration (*ēnthousiazōnton*), becomes himself a "conductor" of Homeric poetry, just as we say metal is a good conductor of electricity. As a result, those who listen to the rhapsodist feel themselves contaminated and overcome by the current reaching them through that conductor.

(F 4: 350; E 3: 795). A nation, France or Germany, is a huge spatial array with the integrity of a certain geometric shape, outlined with definite borders. This spatial pattern is filled up from border to border with millions of little polygons similar in shape. It is like a mosaic made of many small tesserae set side by side to make a pattern. Each of these little polygons is what we today would call a subjectivity, a subject, a subject of the nation-state in which it is located. France is filled to the edges with Frenchmen, Germany with Germans. The peculiarity of this mosaic, as Marcel tells the reader, is that the total pattern of the nation, the slightly irregular hexagon that outlines France, repeats "on a larger scale" all those smaller polygons, even though the repetition is always repetition with a difference. It follows that if you understand one or more of the smaller polygons, you will understand the large one.

The figure Proust describes is like a spatial design of which he could have had no knowledge, the fractal. Fractals are characterized by what the mathematicians call "self-similarity." Smaller parts, at whatever scale, repeat the larger pattern of the whole, though in the most interesting fractals never exactly or predictably. The unpredictability, approaching that studied in chaos theory, occurs if an aleatory element is included in the generating formula. An example of a fractal is the way the general design of a coastline is repeated, on a statistical average of irregularity, at ever smaller and smaller segments, down to the outline made by a few feet of beach, with its rocks, sand, and pools. The coastline of the state of Maine, where I spend my summers, is a case of this. My 420 feet of shore repeat, with a difference, the general irregularity of bays, islands, necks, and peninsulas characteristic of the whole Maine coastline many hundreds of miles long. Or rather the coastline of Maine, like all fractal borders, is in a sense infinitely long, since any segment of it can always be inspected at a smaller scale and further refined in its irregularity. Each new level of irregularity makes it longer.[6]

Proust's two figures—the body made of many cells and what I am calling the fractal mosaic—not only justify the study of literature as politically useful. They also indicate presuppositions that would allow the rational organization of such study. A nation, Proust's figures suggest, is a living, organic unity, with definite edges. It is the embodiment of a unified national culture. This culture is as definite and unique as the biology of a single species. Each citizen of a given state is a unity that mirrors in a special way the singular configurations of that nation. The validity of the

That is why Socrates notes: "Well, do you see that the spectator is the last of the rings I spoke of, which receive their force from one another by virtue of the loadstone? You, the rhapsodist and actor, are the middle ring" (Plato, 1963: 221; 535, e). Heidegger, in "A Dialogue on Language (Between a Japanese and an Inquirer)," pointed out that the word "hermeneutics" is related to the god Hermes' name, so that the *epmeneuin* is "that exposition which brings tidings because it can listen to a message" (Heidegger, 1971: 29). The rhapsodist is the one in charge of bringing messages and news, the one placed in a "hearing" position.

A fundamental difference between two kinds of interpretation is taking shape here. On the one hand, there is the *rhapsodic* position—represented by Ion—whose aim is to "listen" and let the poetic text speak through the bard's body and word. As Socrates observes, his means is ecstasy. On the other hand, there is the *technical* position, which attempts to study, to classify, and to prescribe what poetry is and what poetry must be. Its model would be Aristotle, who does not actually *listen* to Sophocles but embodies his work, *Oedipus the King*, for instance, within a prescriptive or descriptive framework inside a conceptual scheme. Miller refers to this specifically when he writes: "One important goal of the *Poetics* is to make tragedy a natural growth and to provide its taxonomy. Tragedy is, as it were, one more animal or plant determined by nature for which the rational and encyclopedic philosopher needs to account" (RN, 6). This attitude is analogous to Hegel's when he required philosophical study to renew the work of the concept. Miller has also referred to this when he tells us about the "strong critic" who "takes possession of the poem," "puts it aside," and "puts himself in its place" (LM, 53).

Therefore, fascination with the strangeness and the irrationality of literature makes Miller adopt, like a distinguished contemporary of

trope of synecdoche, part for whole, allows the study of the whole by means of the part, as in the ocean, according to Will Ladislaw in *Middlemarch*, "the little waves make the large ones and are of the same pattern."[7] If a work of literature may be assumed to be like a human individual, if it is the fractal image of its author, as Proust repeatedly and eloquently argues in *A la recherche*, then the study of literature, it would follow, should be organized as the separate study of each national literature's most important works. These would be the works that most directly embody that culture's self-understanding of its tradition. Each major national author is a little polygon mirroring in a special way the whole nation. The work of each author will echo in fractal self-similarity the unity and specificity of the national culture—what makes France France, Germany Germany, the United States the United States. Moreover, the law of fractal self-similarity means that study of a limited number of carefully chosen representative works from different historical periods will allow the reader to understand the unified culture of a whole nation. I shall discuss later what is problematic about these assumptions.

A further support for the current applicability of the mosaic figure comes from the way this image is often proposed these days by scholars of United States multiculturalism. It is used as an appropriate replacement for the traditional figure of the United States as a melting pot transforming immigrants from many lands, cultures, and languages into homogeneous, monolingual "Americans" (as by metonymy we habitually call them, forgetting that the United States is only one part of America). The United States, in the now outmoded figures, is filled, after the melting pot has done its work, with millions of little polygons repeating with a difference the national culture's unified shape. In a multicultural nation, on the contrary, the tesserae remain distinct, the side by side juxtaposition of elements that are never assimilated to universal sameness. Nevertheless, the notion of ethnic groups repeats in a different way the nationalist assumptions of Proust's fractal polygon. The implication is that all African Americans or Native Americans or Chicanos and Chicanas are essentially defined by their participation in their ethnic group. Each group is a nation within the nation. The term "mosaic" is a focus for the battle between differing notions of what United States culture is or ought to be.

"Mosaic," in addition, is the name of a once widely used browser program for navigating the World Wide Web of the Internet. The figure invites us to think of the Internet as a spatial array of contiguous fields

his, Roland Barthes, an interpretative *rhapsodic* position (which does not mean a passive position) toward literature. The initial problem of the relation between the critic('s language) and the text('s language) should be understood in light of this perspective. For this reason, on several occasions Miller has expressed himself in an almost mystical terminology. For instance, in 1963 he asserted: "Criticism demands above all that gift of participation, that power to put oneself within the life of another person, which Keats called negative capability" (DG, ix). Criticism has to do with gift, participation, power, and with negative capability, that is to say, with unusual elements in the scientific tradition of our century's literary theory. Curiously, such terminology had not disappeared from Miller's lexicon by 1984, during his "deconstructivist" period: "The reader of 'The Torn Letter' becomes not so much, through a familiar kind of negative capability, the self of the speaker-writer of the poem, the 'I' who has received the letter and is haunted by it, as, by a far stranger form of metamorphosis, the 'you' to whom the poem is spoken or written" (TPP, 180). Miller tells us this in an essay entitled "Hardy, Derrida, and the 'Dislocation of Souls.'" Although "negative capability" is denied in this case, it is replaced by a "metamorphosis" which corresponds to the same process from the opposite direction. The reader is not transformed into the sender but into the receiver. Nevertheless, the reading remains connected with that mechanism by which the reader or the critic yields to the movement of the other.

While Miller speaks of "negative capability" in 1963 and of "metamorphosis" in 1984, the concept he uses in 1990 is that of "analogy." At the end of his magnificent essay on "Bartleby, The Scrivener," he states: "In the case of Melville's story, the narrator's inability to fulfill his re-

that may be explored by multiple hypertext links, since each tessera in the mosaic is adjacent to many others. A user can advance through such an array in many different ways to reach the same goal. "Mosaic" functions as a program for finding things in the World Wide Web. It does this by allowing its user to move efficiently by a series of choices out of many possible routes from link to link to reach the desired goal. About the Internet and the World Wide Web I shall have more to say later, but the image imbedded in the name of the Mosaic program implies the timeliness for us today of Proust's figure and of his work.

"*Get 'Geist'*": The Crisis in Representation

The passage by Proust gives an apparently natural inevitability to the way the study of Western literature has traditionally been organized in our universities. United States universities characteristically have a number of discrete departments, each devoted to the separate study of a single national literature. The dominant department is the one representing our nation's language and literary tradition. Does this well-established paradigm still hold? Can we accept the figure of the fractal mosaic both as a true description and as a heuristic pattern indicating not only how the study of literature ought to be organized in the university but also what use such study is? What is happening today with the study of national literatures? By "today" I mean not only the time when new communication technologies—computers, e-mail, faxes, VCRs, videos, CD-ROMs, hypertexts, and "surfing on the Internet"—are fundamentally changing the ways humanistic scholars interact and do their work. I mean also the time when the Cold War has ended, when the power and integrity of nation-states are weakening, when economic and cultural systems are being globalized, and when as a consequence the university's mission is being transformed.[8]

Vincent Cable, in "The Diminished Nation-State,"[9] emphasizes how new technologies have globalized business. He distinguishes two different technological drives: "First, and more sedate, transport costs have fallen with improved physical communications: better cars; jet aircraft; containerization; motorways. Second, and more spectacular, advances in computing power and in telecommunications—digital systems, satellite technology, and, more recently, fiber optics—have transformed the ease, speed, quantity, and quality of international information flows."[10] One

sponsibility to Bartleby is analogous to our inability to read this text in
the sense of providing a satisfactory interpretation based on what the
text says. . . . Here the reader, like the narrator in the story, is put in the
position of Galatea" (VP, 175). The concept of "analogy" gives rise to a
long tradition of uses going from Plato, Aristotle, Saint Thomas Aquinas,
and Nicholas of Cusa to Hegel. Furthermore it is related to the difficult
problem of mimesis, copy, and repetition, and to the uses Freud, Marx,
Nietzsche, Deleuze, Derrida, and others make of these terms. In any case,
analogy has to do with participation, *sym-pathy* (from *sim-pathos*, "feeling with") among people, objects, and ideas. For this reason, Plato will
claim in *Theaetetus* that every single act of knowing is made *ana tōn lōgon*,
that is, by means of the *eidōs* in which every sentient individual being
participates (Plato, 1963: 891; 186, a–c).

Naturally, this is not Miller's use of "analogy." (I shall return to this
later on.) He does, however, retain from it the ideas of "participation"
(going back to the "gift of participation") and "model" that function in
an important way in his writing. In "The Minister's Black Veil" (1991)
he concludes: "He [Hooper] turns the living spectators into ghosts with
dead stares. This exposes the way the whole system of displacements is
figurative. We realize that we are ourselves living corpses, spirits imprisoned within a body that will be our tomb, as Socrates long ago said. We
readers of 'The Minister's Black Veil' may even glimpse for a moment the
fact that we are after all reading an inscription, the text of the story, black
marks on the pages" (HH, 90).

The reader (this reader, Miller, or the reader-narrator, paper silhouette, who talks to us in Miller's writings) occupies the same position as
the spectators who view the concealment of the Minister's face behind
a veil. Between the "outside" of Hawthorne's tale (the reader, the read-

result is what Cable calls "the end of geography." This end is particularly conspicuous in the globalizing of international finance and therefore of the flow of capital that funds transnational corporations. Especially interesting is how Cable, citing Richard O'Brien, sees money as transformed in the computer age into "an information product": "'The essence of money is . . . the information it conveys, whether as a store of value or medium of exchange.'[11] Thus, Richard O'Brien begins his explanation of the ways in which computerization and advanced telecommunications (involving almost instantaneous linkages) have transformed international finance. There are now global markets for currency transactions and all forms of marketable securities. Competition is intense and capital is highly mobile."[12] Banking used to be, with unconscious irony, called an "industry," as though it actually produced something of use value. Now money is "information," and banking is an information service. Money flows back and forth at the speed of light on the Internet along with all the other cultural information, including, but of course by no means limited to, all the works of literature available "on line" as electronic texts. Money and literature or other cultural artifacts become no more than somewhat different forms of information, available at any point where there is an appropriate computer terminal. This new ubiquity ends geography in the sense of penetrating all borders and local enclosures. It does not matter where I am so long as I have a computer connected to the Internet. When both money and literature, along with other cultural artifacts, are turned into information, Wallace Stevens's somewhat enigmatic aphorism in the "Adagia," "Money is a kind of poetry,"[13] is fulfilled in an unexpected, hyperbolic way. If money is a kind of poetry, "poetry," in the broad sense of cultural forms generally in various media, is also a kind of money. Vincent Cable stresses the new value assigned to intellectual property and telecommunication rights: "Information, per se, has become tradable: management consultancy; films, records, and compact discs; television news; telecommunications services; software systems, design, and programming. It is no coincidence that the Uruguay Round [an international economic "summit" meeting held in Uruguay] had some of its most testing moments over 'information' issues that were scarcely thought of five years earlier: intellectual property protection, market access for films, and telecommunications."[14]

Many curious signs abound of the way globalization is changing our cultural and practical life. The Public Broadcasting System in the United States, until recently still to such a degree funded by Federal money that

ing) and the "inside" (the protagonist and the rest of the characters) there takes place an analogical event in which the narration foreshadows its future readings. To foreshadow means, in this particular context, to contaminate rather than to anticipate a future behavior. It is not unwarranted at all that in an essay of 1982 entitled "Parable and Performative in the Gospels and in Modern Literature" Miller expresses himself as follows: "The language of parables contaminates, or perhaps it might be better to say inseminates, impregnates, its commentators. Such language forces them to speak parabolically" (TPP, 138). Sometimes metamorphosis or analogy has to do with a process of "exemplarization." In an early work of 1957, "Franz Kafka and the Metaphysics of Alienation," we read, on the one hand, that "his heroes are like Kafka himself" (TPP, 19) and, on the other, that Kafka is "the most truly exemplary figure of our time" (TPP, 30). The *conduction* that holds together the rings in the interpretation alludes not only to the text and to the reader but also to the author and to the character, to the character and to the reader.

In fact, there is a phase in Miller's work in which this complex "analogical" conception comes to a climax. Of course I am speaking of *The Ethics of Reading* (1987). In its introductory chapter, "Reading Doing Reading," Miller wonders if there is a correspondence between the character's ethical act inside the book and the ethical acts the reading engenders outside the book. He later answers: "My assumption . . . is that there are analogies among all four of these ethical moments, that of the author, the narrator, the character, and the reader, teacher, critic" (ER, 9). Evidently, as Miller himself recognizes, the point of reference for the existence of those analogies is unknown factor that must be interrogated. However, that does not prevent him from using a schema of "participation" that persists even in the more apparently "formalist"

it seemed almost an arm of the government, one of the state apparatuses under the rubric of "media," has now changed its name, no doubt for good commercial and ideological reasons, to "Public Radio International." Presumably this means they sell some of their programs abroad. A shop in Camden, Maine, advertises that it "unconditionally guarantees everything it sells to be 'Made on Earth.' " This is a globalizing joke, of course, a play on "Made in the USA" or "Made in Japan." Our shops are full of things that are "Made on Earth," that is, designed in one country, their parts manufactured in many different countries, assembled in another, and sold in many more.

Analogous changes are occurring in our universities. Though some of these are being imposed from the outside, most obviously in the reduction of funding, the changes are also happening from the inside, with the conscious or unconscious complicity of university teachers and administrators. The traditional word "crisis" is not appropriate for this change. That word suggests the possibility of going beyond the crisis and returning to a new form of the previous condition, as a sick person weathers a crisis and gets well. The change in the university going on now is irreversible. It affects all branches and departments of the research university, but in different ways. Its effect on the teaching of national literatures is especially strong. Those who teach and do research in departments of national literatures have hardly begun to be aware of the way these changes alter their work. They have only begun to develop the conceptual figurations necessary to grasp the changes. A growing number of books and essays, however, are addressing this task from many different perspectives.[15]

I want here to identify what these changes are and how they alter the vocation of literary study. When something traumatic is happening, the academic's response is to try to understand it, as the hero of Poe's "A Descent into the Maelstrom" saved himself by detached observation. In this case, it may be, knowledge is not enough. By the time we are aware of it, the change has already occurred and it is too late, as a parallel with trauma suggests. Apparently we have walked away unharmed from what has been done to the university. The old departments are still there, seemingly doing what they have always done. We have survived unscathed. Only later do the symptoms of post-traumatic stress syndrome begin. They often take the form of a painful repetition of the events whose traumatic power we did not notice at the time. They were events that in a sense did not take place when they took place, since they were not experienced as traumatic.

stages of his work. It will suffice to recall that when he tries to define what he understands by "linguistic moment," he resorts to the Aristotelian notion of rhythm as one of the two fundamental sources of the pleasure taken from poetry. The other is the pleasure of learning by imitation. Rhythm is at the beginning of *poiesis*—that is, in mimesis—and at its end, in the impression (or catharsis) on the receiver. "The paradox is that transport in the sense of ecstasy is a vertical movement interrupting the forward rhythmical movement of the action. Transport in one sense contradicts transport in the other sense. Transport, as ecstasy, vertical going over, transcendence or transascendence, is caesura, the breaking of the rhythm" (LM, 39–40). That caesura, or linguistic moment, of the literary text "affects" the reader, placing him in a position of "undecidability" programmed by the text itself. This way, the reader participates in the atonal and fissured rhythm imposed by the poetic work.

Everything said until now makes clear that our critic's point of departure could not be completely in agreement with the following words of Paul de Man: "The reading is not 'our' reading, since it uses only the linguistic elements provided by the text itself; the distinction between author and reader is one of the false distinctions that the reading makes evident" (de Man, 1979: 17). For Miller the first part of this statement, referring to the negation of "our" reading, is not something obvious that can be guaranteed in the way de Man describes. It is rather a cause of perennial interrogation, since that identification can never be taken for granted. As for the second part of the statement, Miller might say the same or the opposite. In other words, he might say that the identification between author and reader is one of the false identifications the reading makes evident. In a sense Miller's hesitation disrupts de Man's confidence, though he agrees more than once with de Man.

They take place as traumatic only now, in retrospect, after the fact, when it is already too late and the old university we thought we were still inhabiting is in ruins. Far from liberating us, moreover, as the hero of Poe's story was liberated from the maelstrom by thoughtful observation, in this case trying to take stock of what is happening to the university, for example my effort here, may only accelerate the process of globalization and denationalization it describes.

I take the study of English literature in the United States as my example, since it is my field. It should be recognized from the start, however, that the choice is hardly innocent. English literature is not just one national literature among others. A main feature of globalization is that the English language, primarily by way of the United States, is gradually becoming, for better or for worse, a universal language. English is already spoken everywhere in the world as the second language of millions and millions of people for whom it is not the mother tongue. With the study of the English language goes the study of its literature, as one of the most potent instruments of the spread of capitalist ideologies. Or at least we used to be confident that this is the case. It is not quite clear, when you think of it, how the study of Shakespeare or Hardy will aid the economic imperialism of the United States.

What is happening, as a result of these societal changes, to the study of English literature in the United States? For one thing, it is gradually being swallowed up by increased offerings in American, that is, United States, literature. Most United States universities now have departments of English and American literature, whatever they may be called. United States literature has become more and more dominant within such agglomerations. Moreover, a "crisis in representation," as Brook Thomas terms it,[16] exists for writing, teaching, and curricular design in departments of the national literatures. Most teachers in American colleges and universities used to believe in the validity of a part for whole relation in literary study, on the model of Proust's fractal mosaic. A good literary work was presumed to be an organic whole, so the study of a part could be a means of understanding or teaching the whole. Teachers could use with a clear conscience the detailed study of a passage. Such a procedure was brilliantly exploited as a method of reading by Erich Auerbach in *Mimesis*.[17] The whole work, carefully chosen and explicated on the assumption that each part of it mirrored its totality and also the totality of the culture around it, could then be used as a way of understanding what was

To summarize, the matrix I have been talking about shows that what "leads" and "articulates" J. Hillis Miller's discourse from the end of the 1940's to the 1990's is the problem of the bond between the (language of the) critic or reader and the (language of the) text or author, that of the "meeting" between two different spaces. To put this point another way, it is the problem of literature as alterity, "surd," irrationality, silence, *alogos*, inexpressivity, abyss (LM, 394). In saying "problem," I am using the correct word, because that relation or bond never ceases to be interrogated or questioned in the context of the readings and by the readings themselves, and, moreover, because this matrix must not be understood as an immutable concept that has remained identical from "The Creation of the Self in Gerard Manley Hopkins" (1955, VS, 1–23) to *Illustration* (1992), but rather as the opposite, that is, as an interrogation open to the adventure of contact with an endless number of textualities for which Hillis Miller has or had a truly passionate feeling: Plato, Dickens, Hardy, Meredith, Stevens, Browning, Shelley, Wimsatt, Poulet, Borges, de Man, Derrida, etc. Using Derridean terminology, it might be said that those textualities contaminate, "parasitize," corrupt the Millerian matrix at the same time as they are contaminated, parasited, and corrupted by it. This book intends to follow, as far as possible, the traces of that adventure.

From the outset of this essay, I have asserted that Miller's writing is contradictory and oxymoronic. Although I shall come back to this point, it is appropriate to mention now that, though our critic has an irrational, ecstatic, and abyssal conception of literature, he is not seeking a force acting beyond or before language, but rather a power present in language or transmitted through language. Language is that irrationality, the place where metaphysics and nihilism collide. For this reason, one should not be surprised that in 1958 he wrote: "A poem or novel is indeed the world

assumed to be a homogeneous surrounding culture. For Auerbach, one citation from Virginia Woolf's *To the Lighthouse* could illustrate the entire modernist practice of realistic representation. It was possible for other scholars to imply that study of *Moby-Dick* and a few other canonical works would give readers something approaching a full understanding of mid-nineteenth-century American culture. Of course, such claims were often made with careful qualification, but some version of the synecdochal assumption operated widely as an unquestioned ideologeme. An ideological element is by definition unquestioned, since it is an unconscious assumption, a cultural artifact taken as a fact of nature. This particular ideologeme may have had all the more power for being an unspoken presupposition that guided the choice of the canon and the devising of curricula. To translate this ideologeme into Proust's figure, it is the assumption that all the little polygons are like one another and that all are equally images of the whole, the one big polygon.

Few people have any longer an unshaken confidence in this paradigm, even those who most stridently assert it. We recognize that the United States is a multicultural and multilingual nation. A given work or canon represents only one part of a complex, nontotalizable whole. To choose to teach *Moby-Dick* rather than *Uncle Tom's Cabin* or even to choose to teach both of them together, is not the result of a proof that either work is objectively representative of its culture. The choice is motivated and unjustifiable—which does not mean that it is necessarily bad. It means that those who devise syllabi and curricula must take responsibility for their choices, not defend them by pointing to universal criteria of exemplarity. Nor do we any longer have recourse to some standard of intrinsic superiority allowing us to say that *Moby-Dick* is a better work than *Uncle Tom's Cabin*, or vice versa. That standard too is the result of ideological bias. This loss of confidence in the possibility of justifying a syllabus on the basis of its verifiable representative status is almost as much of a disaster for those trained in the old ways of teaching literature (me for example) as would be, for citizens of the United States, a loss of confidence in the power of their elected representatives to represent them.

The "crisis" of representation in the humanities leads to enormous problems in establishing curricula, in the practical work of teaching and writing about literature, in making decisions about appointments and programs. One reason that so much time is spent these days in theoretical speculation is that we have no consensus about just how we should pro-

refashioned into conformity with the inner structure of the writer's spirit given, through words, a form and substance taken from the shared solidity of the exterior world. It is in this sense that the words of the work are themselves the primary datum, a self-sufficient reality beyond which the critic need not go" (CD, x). Those who, like Donald Pease, have seen a "recalcitrant formalism" (Pease, 1983: 77) in Miller's work are mistaken. The fact that Hillis Miller has combined elements from "New Criticism" and "criticism of consciousness," or from "criticism of consciousness" and "psychocriticism," or from "criticism of consciousness" and "deconstruction" responds to a paradoxical conception of language that is not solved by an orientation toward form, or toward consciousness, or toward divine Platonic force. Rather it tries to put these all into play—at once.

Furthermore, in 1972, in an essay later incorporated in *The Linguistic Moment*, Miller had already replied to the "formalist" label: "The notion of form has always presupposed a bifurcation between shape and substance, origin and result, cause and effect, model and copy, mold and molded. . . . The paradox lies in the fact that the English word *form*, like the Greek *tupos*, is used to name both the model and its copy. This paradox is not accidental. It brings into the open an intrinsic undecidability in the concept of form" (LM, 60–61). Miller's literary criticism cannot be understood if one applies to his writing a criterion of *identity* with itself and does not realize that it is made of differences with regard to itself, like the texts he reads. For this reason an analysis of his work, his language, and his rhetoric (that is to say, of his work as *text*), will show us that beyond the declarations of principles, beyond the abrupt transitions, multiple writings are superimposed in it, a process of "grafts" similar to what Derrida has called "the principle of taxonomical disorder" (1992b: 67). It is not advisable then, to oversimplify here.

ceed. Many feel they must reinvent the whole institution of teaching literature from the ground (or lack of ground) up. Bernard Bergonzi has written a polemical book about this change as it affects the discipline of English literature. The title of his book tells what he feels about the changes: *Exploding English*.[18]

For literature departments the so-called crisis of representation accompanies a larger crisis of representation for the humanities as an element in a new kind of university in a different world. This change accompanies a recognition, in the United States at least, that we are not and never have been a nation-state with a unified culture, as least not as that concept has supervised the European sense of citizenship since the Renaissance or, in its more modern form, since the eighteenth century. That concept is still strongly present, as my citations have shown, in Proust's work.

The loss of a special role for the study of English literature puts English departments especially under stress in the new university that is developing. Professors of English have been deprived of their traditional role as preservers and transmitters of a nation-state's unified culture. There was always something of an anomaly in basing the cultural ideals of the United States on the study of English literature, that is, on the study of a foreign literature that happens to be written in a version of our dominant language. English literature has had a role in United States education parallel to that of Greek and Latin literature in eighteenth- and nineteenth-century English education, before the university study of English literature had been formally institutionalized. A British citizen and a United States citizen, whatever their class, gender, or race, are likely to read Shakespeare, Milton, or Dickens in quite different ways. These authors do not belong to United States citizens or express our national values or even the values of our hegemonic class in the same ways that they belong to or express such values for British citizens. This does not mean that English literature is not of great importance as an influence on the developing United States literature. Reading Shakespeare in order to understand *Moby-Dick* better is not the same thing, however, as reading it as a primary expression of your own native heritage. A parallel might be made between the function *Oedipus the King* had for Athenians and the importance knowing it and other Greek tragedies has for understanding A. C. Swinburne's *Atalanta in Calydon*. Shakespeare's ringing affirmation of England's island unity and his patriotic depiction of victory at Agincourt have a hollow sound in a country that established itself in a revolutionary war by defeat-

One might think that a critic who takes a rhapsodic stance toward a literature understood as "surd" would himself need to use an irrational language, full of folds, labyrinthine and almost unintelligible; a language about which one might wonder, as Sarah Kofman did concerning Derrida, how someone could dare to write a meaningful discourse about a writing that presents itself as meaningless play. She concludes that if one wants to write about Derrida, one should do so without attempting to understand either what he means or of what his texts give knowledge (1984: 25). On several occasions Derrida's "manner" has been described as "Gongoran," that is, as over-ornate, baroque (Leitch, 1983). I do not share such views. They seem erroneous to me when applied to Derrida, and they by no means define Miller's style. To all appearances his language is organized according to a logical model of argumentation in which, just as in the works of Aristotle (the *Poetics*, for instance), one finds from the very outset the goals pursued, the means, the methodological presuppositions, the *tabulae*, the *jusjurandum*, the *quis*, the *quid*, the *cur*, the *quomodo*, and the *quibus auxiliis* (the tables, the sworn promise, the who, the what, the why, the how, and the by what means). One often finds in his prefaces or introductions sentences like the following: "Literary criticism may focus on a single poem, play or novel, on the total body of a writer's work, or on the unity made up of all the writings of an age" (DG, ix); "My book will explore the ethics of narrative in its connection with the trope of prosopopoeia" (VP, 11); "I propose to argue . . . that there is a necessary ethical moment in that act of reading as such, a moment neither cognitive, nor political, nor social, nor interpersonal, but properly and independently ethical" (ER, 1).

Miller usually also adopts a narrative morphology in which the reader seems to witness a plot which creates "horizons of expectations"

ing the British. The names "Lexington," "Bunker Hill," "Yorktown," and "Valley Forge" have more resonance for us than "Agincourt." Nevertheless, English literature was the basis of a literary education in the United States when I got my undergraduate and graduate degrees not all that many decades ago. My graduate qualifying examination for the Ph.D. in English stopped with Thomas Hardy and included no United States literature at all, much less any theory.

The study of English literature in the United States is in one major way like its study in Korea, Norway, Taiwan, Germany, or Italy. In another major way it is unlike. To study English literature in the United States, Korea, Spain, or Norway, to take it seriously as a source of values and humanistic understanding, is to study the literature of a foreign country, a small island nation off the west coast of Europe. The difference of course is that a version of English also happens to be the dominant, one might even say "official," language of the United States, whereas it is a second language in Korea, Norway, Taiwan, Spain, Germany, and the rest. The dominance of the American version of the English language in the United States, however, perhaps only makes it harder for us to see what is problematic about basing United States training in humanistic values on a literature that is not native to our soil. United States literature and British literature are by no means parts of one homogeneous whole, even though United States literature has traditionally been taught as a subordinate part of English literature, as at my own university now and at the other two universities at which I have taught: Johns Hopkins and Yale. At Harvard, where I got my Ph.D., it was, in 1952 at least, not necessary to know anything at all about United States literature, any more than about Australian or Canadian literature, in order to get a Ph.D. in English. The difference between United States literature and British literature would have been more obvious all along if they had happened to have been written in different languages. Training in British literature is still the basis of literary education in the United States. At the University of California at Irvine, where I now teach, there are between six and seven hundred English majors. It is the most obvious choice for undergraduates who want to concentrate on literature, even though almost half of the students at Irvine are Asian Americans, many of whom have English as a second language. Chaucer, Shakespeare, Milton, Wordsworth, Dickens, Woolf—these still play a large role in determining the way citizens of the United States with a higher education think and behave.

These days, however, radical changes in society, in the university's

and then frustrates them, a plot which "deceives" and "undeceives" and most of the time tells the story of a failure. "Franz Kafka and the Metaphysics of Alienation" (1957, TPP, 15–31), for instance, is organized around two sequences that originate in the same nucleus: our age (our age and Kafka's) can only experience God in a negative way, "as a terrifying absence." The first sequence opens with Kafka's attempt to be close to God by means of an integration into the human and social world (to be a good son, to have a wife and children, to have a job, etc.). However, that first attempt fails, for Kafka finds out that all human community "is in the desert, attempting to build an impious tower of Babel to scale heaven, but really cutting itself off more and more from God" (TPP, 18), placing itself outside the law. He finds now within his own society the emptiness he had felt in isolation.

The second sequence, which springs from the fiasco of the first, begins with Kafka's attempt to rescue himself by means of writing, since it, Kafka thinks, has the power of transforming things into words and also of halting the endless fall into the abyss. Euphoria is radicalized: "Literature was not simply the salvation of his own poor identity; it was also the salvation of the world itself" (TPP, 26). But Kafka is disappointed again—and we are also disappointed—because he realizes that the space of literature is identical to the place of exile in which he began: "The space of literature is, *par excellence*, the place of separation" (TPP, 27), since the fissure between the thing and the image is accomplished in it.

Miller's style is clear, perspicuous, economical, canonical, almost as economical and canonical as the style of an Argentinean writer he often cites, Jorge Luis Borges. In both, an apparently synthetic and logical language thematizes contradictory, ambiguous, and inexplicable spheres. In Borges, we have "The Aleph"; "The Library of Babel"; "Funes, the

relation to society, and in the study of literature are putting in question the traditional English major. By traditional English major I mean the more or less sequestered study of major canonical works by British authors from "*Beowulf* to Virginia Woolf," organized in courses devoted to historical "periods": Medieval literature, the Renaissance, the eighteenth century, Romanticism, the Victorian period, modernism, and postmodernism. Such a division makes many problematic assumptions about the canon, about the unity of works and periods, about the linear continuity of literary history, and so on. Just what changes are dismantling those assumptions, and just why have they occurred?

The Western research university in its modern form originated with the founding in the early nineteenth century of the University of Berlin, established according to a plan devised by Wilhelm von Humboldt. Such universities had as their primary role service to the nation-state, still nascent at that time in Germany. The nation-state was conceived as an organically unified culture with a single set of ideals and values enshrined in a unified philosophical tradition and national literature (or in a certain way of appropriating Greek and Latin literature). The university was to serve the nation-state in two ways: (1) as the place of critical thinking and research, of finding out the truth about everything, of giving everything its rationality, according to the Leibnizian formula that says nothing is without its reason; (2) as the place of education, formation, or *Bildung*, where male citizens (they were all male then in the university) are inculcated, one might almost say "inoculated," with the basic values of a unified national culture. It was the business of the university to produce subjects of the state, in both senses of the word *subject*: as subjectivities and as citizens accountable to state power and capable of promulgating it. For Humboldt and his colleagues, following Kant, the basis of *Bildung* was the study of philosophy. People with a higher degree are still, for the most part, called "doctors of philosophy," whatever the discipline in which they received the degree. This practice is something of an absurdity these days, since philosophy proper does not, to say the least, still have the role it did in German universities in the days of Kant, Fichte, and Hegel, while most Ph.D.'s in other fields know little or nothing about philosophy.

With some support from Schiller's *Letters on Aesthetic Education*, Anglo-Saxon countries in the mid-nineteenth century, first England and then the United States, deflected this paradigm in an important way by substituting literature for philosophy as the center of cultural indoctri-

Memorious"; "Pierre Menard, Author of Don Quixote"; or "The Garden of the Forking Paths." In Miller, we find opium, the impossibility of identifying a character like Bartleby, the caesura of rhythm, the mystery of the parable, or the irrationality of Stevens's poetry. Borges adopts (parodies) the patterns of the essay. Miller uses the resources of narrative or those coming from logical or enthymemetic argumentation. But both always put before us a language moved by a desire for conceptual accuracy. Notwithstanding this, the relation between what is said and the way of saying it brings into the open a complication: what was apparently clear and perspicuous, economical and canonical, becomes dark and double, complex and avant-garde. Suddenly, the reader/Miller becomes, in Barthes's words, fetishistic (because he singles out quotations), obsessive (because of the voluptuousness of secondary and eccentric languages), paranoiac (because he perceives sophisticated texts and stories as secret demands), and even hysterical (because he enters into the groundless comedy without truth of language) (Barthes, 1975: 63).

In other words, according to Miller, language does not need to be extended or complicated because language itself, in its synchronico-diachronic crossing, is a complication where, by way of an irresolute antithesis, light and darkness, logic and rhetoric, metaphysics and nihilism, rule and deconstruction are interlaced. The prison of language will go on being an infinite number of hexagonal galleries on whose shelves one finds everything that can be expressed and in all languages, "the minute history of the future, the autobiographies of the archangels, the faithful catalogue of the Library, thousands and thousands of false catalogues, a demonstration of the fallacy of these catalogues, a demonstration of the fallacy of the true catalogue" (Borges, 1962: 83). At this point, we begin to observe two paradoxes within Miller's literary criticism that we shall

nation. Grounds for this shift already existed in the centrality granted to literary education by many German theorists: the Schlegels, Schelling, and Hegel, for example. The shift occurred in England and in the United States to a considerable degree under the aegis of Matthew Arnold's formulations about culture and anarchy, about the study of poetry, and about the function of criticism. The modern United States research university has inherited the double mission of Humboldt's university. This continuity was evident in the founding of The Johns Hopkins University in Baltimore in 1876. The Hopkins was based explicitly and self-consciously on the German university rather than on the English university, though Thomas Henry Huxley, an advocate for the new scientific English university, spoke at the inauguration of Johns Hopkins. An admirable proliferation of both public and private research universities in the United States followed soon after or was already under way.

The combination of gathering scientific knowledge (which includes knowledge of history, cultural history, and literary history, as well as knowledge of anthropology, physics, biology, and other social and physical sciences) while at the same time teaching a nation's unifying values seems coherent enough. Nevertheless, a tension has always existed between these two goals as charges to the department responsible for doing research and teaching in a country's national literature. On the one hand, the charge is to teach students by way of literature the central ideas and values of a national culture. These are presumed to be enshrined in the nation's canonical works—in *Beowulf*, Chaucer, Shakespeare, and the rest. On the other hand, scientific research is supposed to be critical and "disinterested" (in a way different from Arnold's use of the word), a search for truth independent of subjective bias. Research is value free, *wertfrei*. It is organized according to a universal methodology of verifiable research applicable mutatis mutandis to the human sciences as well as to the physical, social, and life sciences.

A touching confidence that these two enterprises would achieve the same results for a long time made it possible for those in departments of national literatures to believe they were fulfilling both missions and reconciling the two contradictory charges the university had given them. A professor of English could simultaneously pursue research of the most positivistic kind into the minutiae of an author's life, or do the most mind-numbing bibliographical or editorial work, and at the same time teach undergraduate classes extolling the ethical virtues contained in works by

have the opportunity to analyze in detail. First, there is a rhapsodic stance toward literature, but one that does not lead to a "passivity" on the part of the critic (think about the well-known dialectics, closely studied by Miller, of the parasite and its host, or of knowledge and the performative). Second, there is a "transparent" language, close to the traditional mode of a technical approach to literature, which nevertheless reveals itself to be an accomplice in the process whereby there is no conceptual expression without figure, no "intertwining of concept and figure without an implied narrative" (TNT, 148).

Throughout the course of this discussion, the reader will find topics which I have already sketched in this chapter; but before moving on, let me provide some clarification, which may be useful in reading the pages which follow. First, I do not seek to reduce Miller's work to a series of concepts or themes that make this work into something familiar to the reader. Unlike Geoffrey Bennington in his book on Derrida, I have not sought to compile a dictionary or a data base. It would have been absurd to do so, among other reasons, because the strategy of Miller's work is absolutely different from that of Derrida. Miller is not a theorist who creates concepts, but one who utilizes concepts created by others to speak of concrete literary texts. This does not mean that he has not created concepts, simply that his creation arises from a practice of literary criticism (with all the conflicting associations attached to the term "practical"). I hope to put into relief the concepts, ideas, and paths which Miller's essentially practical literary criticism has opened up. It would be absurd to seek to systematize what has already been presented systematically. This does not imply that the presentation of his work is not laden with difficulties, however. On the contrary: a close reading demonstrates its complexity. I

Milton, Johnson, Browning, Arnold, and the rest. The first activity made him (they were almost all male) feel he was doing something useful to support his university's scientific devotion to truth seeking. He was adding to the archives of achieved knowledge. The second made him feel he was fulfilling his responsibility to *Bildung*. This combination was, for example, strongly institutionalized as the ethos of Johns Hopkins when I taught there in the fifties and sixties. We knew exactly what we were doing. Our assumptions seemed permanently in place, impossible to question.

The Culture Evermore About to Be

The use of a foreign country's literature in the formation of United States citizens is a symptom of a fundamental change in the Humboldtian research university that took place when the model was adopted in the United States. Bill Readings is right when he says that the concept of a unified national culture in the United States has always been a promise or hope for the future. It is something always yet to be created by contractual agreement among the free citizens of a republic rather than something inherited as an inescapable tradition from the nation's historical past.[19] It always remains up for grabs. English literature was co-opted by American schools and universities as the basic tool for the creation of a national culture that remains about to be, rather than something that is. Recent books have demonstrated that the creation of English literature as a pedagogical discipline occurred in the eighteenth and nineteenth centuries as part of British imperialism, whether in Scotland or in India. Franklin Court and Robert Crawford have shown how in Scotland English studies were devised as a way of putting down the Scots dialect and making Scotland more a part of a unified Great Britain.[20] Gauri Viswanathan has shown how the study of English literature was used as an instrument of colonial domination in nineteenth-century India.[21] The United States, however, did not need to be coerced into still acting like a colony, at least in the sense of taking its cultural ideals from English literature.

Some might argue that over the past fifty years United States citizens have come to recognize that they have an indigenous national literature which unifies them and makes them all Americans, little polygons all like the big polygon of the whole United States. But the rise of "American literature" and "American studies" as separate disciplines in universities and colleges demonstrates just the opposite. The important books on United

have sought to recognize a complexity in Miller's texts that lies beneath their appearances. This, I believe, is the only way to do them justice.

Second, the path I have followed in presenting Miller's work is that of a careful reading of the readings Miller has carried out throughout his career. This book analyzes his analyses. It could be considered another practical text which mimes the procedure of what it reads.

The book is divided into three chapters: (1) "Prolegomena, Connection, and Disconnection," (2) "A Human Head with an Equine Neck," and (3) "Narrativity, Example (Exemplarity), Endlessness, Uncontrolled Performatives." Each of these is divided, in turn, into three sections. The book begins by examining Miller's reading of Thomas De Quincey in *The Disappearance of God* and its problematization of the identification of the reader's consciousness with that of the text. If we take at face value the methodologies and theoretical suppositions Miller claims to follow, we cannot appreciate how, in his discourse and its encounter with De Quincey's words, the contact between critic and author forms part of a contradictory and paradoxical process of "touching" and "not touching," or how the apparent "reflexivity" of the literary text is put into question by the fact that the object of the "reflexivity" is subject to the dynamic of infinite divisibility.

This discussion of the "reflexivity" of the literary text leads to the third section in Chapter 1, "Dirty Mirrors and Deconstructions," whose objective is to study, taking Miller's work as a starting point, the conflicts that a deconstructive theory and/or literary criticism present. I take issue with Rodolphe Gasché's thesis in *The Tain of the Mirror: Derrida and the Philosophy of Reflection* and seek to demonstrate that, despite the necessity and pertinence of Gasché's work, the accusations it directs against deconstructive literary theory in general arise from, among other things,

States literature, from those by F. O. Matthiessen, Charles Feidelson, Jr., R. W. B. Lewis, and Perry Miller down to more recent work by Roy Harvey Pearce, Sacvan Bercovitch, and Harold Bloom,[22] have been devoted not so much to describing as to attempting to create the unified national culture we do not have. They characteristically do this by a complex, performative scholarly ritual that masquerades as objective scholarship. They appeal to such general concepts as the frontier ("Go west, young man"), the American Renaissance, the American Adam, a certain use of symbolism, a certain use of romance, the Puritan ideal, the unity of a canonical poetic tradition from Emerson, Dickinson, and Whitman through Crane and Stevens to Ammons and Ashbery, and so on, in incoherent multiplicity. Different figurative paradigms for totalizing American literature appear and disappear like shadows in the mist. Each scholar makes up his or her own idea about the unity of American literature, and each idea is incompatible with the others. Readings says that the interest in canon formation in the United States arises from the fact that we do not have an inherited traditional canon and have tried to create one by fiat. This is another form of that future-anterior speech act characterizing United States culture generally. We project into the future what we need to have already in order to do the projecting. If one has a canon that can be taken for granted, as to a considerable degree the educated classes do in England, one does not need to worry about it or theorize about it. Only the somewhat maverick F. R. Leavis in England has in our time engaged in the sort of declarations about canon that in the United States are made by the scholars mentioned above.[23] This does not mean that the canon of English literature has always remained absolutely fixed. Samuel Johnson's high valuation of Edmund Waller over John Donne is not shared by modern readers. T. S. Eliot— originally an American, of course—participated decisively in giving the Metaphysical poets a new importance in the English canon, though in the long run he was unsuccessful in lowering Milton's status. These changes, nevertheless, were readjustments in a canon that has remained relatively stable, though it perhaps especially seems so from a United States perspective.

All canon forming in the United States, however, is manifestly partial and invidious. An example is Bloom's central canon of American writers listed above. Not only are the chief authors in the canon all, with the exception of Dickinson, men and all from the Northeast, his canon also leaves out T. S. Eliot, William Carlos Williams, Robert Lowell, Adrienne

an inadequate interpretation of the proposals of the Jena Romantics, in particular the concept of "transcendental poetry" introduced by Friedrich Schlegel. Above all, I attempt to demonstrate that the possibility of a deconstructive literary criticism depends on the operation of a third notion of "writing," which is not fully identified with either a transcendental notion of "writing" or an empirical notion of writing corresponding to the traditional and vulgar concept of "text." This argument is a sine qua non for understanding the work of a literary critic such as J. Hillis Miller and, I could add, much "deconstructive" theory and literary criticism.

Once we have established that Miller's preoccupations as a follower of Poulet are not alien to his later concerns as a reader of Derrida and de Man, we must continue to individuate his work in relation to other deconstructions. To this end, I have noted in the first part of Chapter 2, "Viruses, Heterosemes, and Heterographs," that Miller's work does not take the deconstruction of a hierarchical opposition, a polarity or duality, as its point of departure. Rather, through an analysis of "The Critic as Host," we see that Miller's deconstruction is a deconstruction of oneness, of the possibility of, at a given moment, reducing a text to essential or indivisible components, whether these be semantic, syntactical, morphological, or phonological. The one is dissolved in a contradictory multiplicity of particles. This allows us to see how Miller's work diverges from that of Derrida or de Man, and also how his work is now unfolding within a specific form of literary and linguistic philology.

As a philological literary critic, Miller's objectives are close to the German philological tradition, to structuralism, to semiotics, and, of course, to a certain form of New Criticism. I have sought to show the individuality of Miller's work, its similarities to and above all its differ-

Rich, Sylvia Plath, Robert Frost, Theodore Roethke, and many others who from other perspectives would have a claim to be included in the canon of United States poets.[24] Any attempt to unify United States literature, however, will be biased and political—in short, ideological. I mean by "ideology" here the mistaking of a linguistic reality for a phenomenal one. Recent work, for example by Carolyn Porter, calls for a disunified and multilingual American Studies, a discipline more reflective of the actual state of things,[25] and recognizes that these claims of unity were all along ideological, not real, or rather that they were performative, not constative. Their aim was to create by a speech act the unified culture we do not yet have. Such claims do this by appealing to a certain selective way of reading the past as though it were a tradition we all in the United States share in the way Germany, France, or England each might appear to have a unified national culture participated in by all its citizens. Or at any rate Germany, France, and England have sometimes thought they have a unified culture, while we are uneasily uncertain.

Of course the cultural oneness of Germany, France, or England was built on the exclusion of minority cultures, on the subordination of women, and on many other unjust acts of power. England achieved cultural unity through savage violence toward the Scots and Irish, through the suppression of Cornish, Gaelic, Scots, and Welsh languages, and so on. German cultural unity was to a considerable degree a fabrication of poets and philosophers: from Kant, Hegel, Fichte, Schiller, Goethe, the Schlegels, Hölderlin, and others on down to Heidegger and the poets of the Stefan George school. This German culture was built on two weird ideas, or ideas that at any rate seem weird to anyone outside the German tradition. One was Fichte's assertion that anyone anywhere can think philosophically —as long as he or she does it in the German language, though of course not all Germans think philosophically.[26] The other was the notion of a continuity between Greek and German culture, leaving Latin and Latinate or romance cultures out of the loop, so to speak, of cultural transmission. Both these strange but immensely productive notions are still fundamental in Martin Heidegger's thinking.[27] Linguistic nationalism has great power to determine national sentiment generally. It is as important as race or blood, as crucial as attachment to a single territory with sharp borders, the one-colored patch on the map. Nationalist sentiment in European countries has depended on extremely problematic and dangerous assumptions,

ences from these traditions. The second section of Chapter 2, entitled "Boustrophedonism: The Text as Surd," is written with this aim. This section is central to the study as a whole, since it begins to introduce concepts Miller has been creating throughout his literary critical career and thus allows us to contemplate his critical universe. I have sought to enable such a contemplation via contrast with principal European textual critics, emphasizing, for example, how Miller's use and theorization of "intertextuality" contrasts with its treatment by Greimas, Bakhtin, Kristeva, Jenny, Barthes, Derrida, Compagnon, and Eco. Mindful of such contrasts, and taking as a guiding thread Miller's reading of Wallace Stevens's poem "The Rock" in *The Linguistic Moment*, we begin to distinguish the concepts that characterize the Millerian reading: the "linguistic moment," "boustrophedonism," the "textual gene," the "semiotic polysystem," and the "hieroglyphic" or "critical painting." Above all, we notice how this conceptualization correlates with the personal project I refer to throughout this study as the "Millerian matrix." The third part of Chapter 2, "J. Hillis Miller: Who Is He?," opens a parenthesis in the midst of the analysis of his work. This chapter considers a crucial aspect both of his work and of this study of his work: Miller's testimonial, autobiographical mark. Here, by introducing the term "auto(veil)graphy," I recount Miller's response to the problem of autobiographical narration which the project of this double and crossed book has raised.

This takes the reader to Chapter 3, which attempts to reunite the themes of the first two (which cover, essentially, the Millerian matrix and the concepts which arise from his literary criticism) with concerns centered on the notion of narrativity and the narrative text. The first section, entitled "Theory Out of Place: A Strange 'Literariness,'" examines how Miller has come to understand narrative analysis through a close look

and therefore has contained its own vulnerability within it. Yet it has been even harder to sustain the idea of cultural unity in the United States.

"The University in Ruins"

Humboldt's concept of literary study within the university lasted until quite recently, at least as an ideal, in the United States. It is now rapidly losing its force. We are entering an era in which new paradigms for the university, as well as new justifications for literary study, will need to be found. The changes are occurring simultaneously outside and inside the university.

On the outside, many forces are weakening the unity and borders of the nation-state. The end of the Cold War, along with economic and technological globalization, are, as I have said, more and more replacing separate nations with transnational corporations as centers of power. Bill Gates is perhaps more powerful than Bill Clinton. The European Union and the North American Free Trade Agreement are striking examples of the blurring of national borders and concurrent weakening of individual countries' self-determining autonomy. The development of "the Pacific Rim" is another example. This means that California belongs both to the United States and to an economic entity that includes companies in Japan, Korea, Taiwan, Singapore, Hong Kong, Australia, and New Zealand, and will more and more include mainland China as well, especially now that it has repossessed Hong Kong. These changes by no means make nationalist sentiment vanish. In fact they often exacerbate it. An example is England's resistance to using the Euro, in part because it would mean giving up coins engraved with the queen's effigy, though there are also deeper economic reasons. Other examples are the return to isolationist policies in the United States, nationalist wars in Eastern Europe after the collapse of the Soviet Union, similar civil wars in postcolonial Africa, and nationalist imperialism in Iraq and North Korea. Such forms of nationalism more and more appear inappropriate to present economic realities. The way to prosperity, to put it ironically, is to learn English and to get as many international corporations as possible to set up factories in one's area and make capital investments there. As the nation-state's existence as a unified entity weakens through one form or another of globalization and the consequent eroding of national boundaries, it will be harder and harder to tell where France ends and Germany begins, even where the United States ends and

at his reading of Hardy's *The Well-Beloved* in *Fiction and Repetition*. I concentrate here on two principal foci of interest: (1) Miller's particular understanding of the notion of "literariness"—which serves me as a springboard in responding both to critics who claim that Miller's work is merely a repetition of formalist proposals of the beginning of the century (Jakobson, Eichenbaum, Shklovsky, etc.) and to criticisms from the field of cultural studies; and (2) his differences with the theoretical-literary subdiscipline known as narratology. I outline, for example, how Miller's treatment of narration differs from theories of reception such as those of Iser and Jauss, or from structuralist theories such as Greimas's actantial system or Barthes's linguistics.

The second and third parts of Chapter 3, "As if . . ." and "J. Hillis Miller's Galatea," are dedicated to what Miller has referred to as the "ethics of reading." This notion, according to which in all narration there is a necessarily ethical moment which allegorizes the reader's position before the text, returns to the theme of the rhapsodic matrix in its handling of the concept of analogy between text and reader, but does so with a new perspective and force. The second section reflects on Miller's reading of Kant's *Foundations of the Metaphysics of Morals* in *The Ethics of Reading*. This chapter, in fact, serves as a pretext for reactivating the problem of narrativity and the problem of "giving an example." Above all, however, the chapter seeks to comprehend Miller's understanding of "narration" as the "entry of literature"—that is, his questioning of the existence of something called "literature" in favor of a more tangential notion of this "entry." Finally, the last section centers on Miller's *Versions of Pygmalion*, more specifically on his analysis of Melville's "Bartleby, The Scrivener." This chapter demonstrates how other fundamental concepts of Miller's criticism (catachresis, prosopopoeia, undecidability, etc.) enter into his

Mexico begins. We shall all come to feel ourselves living on some margin, fringe, or borderland, at the periphery.

At the same time the integrity of the nation-state is weakening in another way. The United States is a striking example. In spite of energetic attempts by conservative politicians and educationists to impose a single language and a single literary curriculum, United States cultural life is made up of diverse, interpenetrating cultural communities speaking and writing in many different languages. These communities cannot easily be reconciled. Their sites are the loci of mutually incompatible goods. These values would be impossible to unify by some overarching idea of universal human "culture." Nor does any individual belong unequivocally to any one of these communities. In a few years more than half the citizens of California will have English as a second language. A poll taken recently of kindergarten classes in Irvine, California, an upper-middle-class and homogeneous-looking city (though not really a city in the traditional sense, since it has no center), found that over twenty different languages were spoken in the homes of these children. They will grow up, like most Chicanos and Chicanas, or like most Asian Americans, divided within by participation in at least two incompatible cultures. A more recent study claimed that no fewer than sixty different languages are spoken in Orange County. The frequently used figure of hybridity to describe this situation is misleading. It implies that the hybrid individual participates in a mixed culture made by mating stable genes from the two sources. In fact, the original cultures that are hybridized were by no means as stable or unified as an animal or plant species is. In any case, the melting pot is no longer hot enough or capacious enough to melt all this difference down. The larger polygon is not a whole. It is divided and subdivided within itself. Nor does it have definite borders. The little polygons are also each divided within. Each self is inhabited by its other or by an indeterminate number of "others," in plural swarming. No Habermasian dialogue, conversation, or communicative discourse could or should bring all this diversity back to consensus. The traditional single set of values transmitted by aesthetic education is now seen as what it always was: an ideological fabrication made to serve primarily the power of educated white middle- or upper-class heterosexual males.

What possible role can literary study have in the new technological, transnational university? In the United States and, in one degree or another, in many other Western nations those responsible for funding

matrix. The chapter also discusses the significance of his notion of the "ethics of reading"—now an "ethic of narration"—in the context of the polemics with New Historicism and cultural studies.

One might ask, with reason, why this route through Miller's work stops at *Versions of Pygmalion* (1992), without continuing up to, for example, *Topographies* (1996). There are two reasons for this. First, in practical terms, the manuscript was written for the most part during the spring and summer of 1993. Consequently, I could not write about books which had not yet been published and which I only later discovered through my contacts with Miller during my visits to the University of California, Irvine, as a visiting professor. The second reason is methodological. Miller's writings are under continual formation and transformation, and so the desire for exhaustivity in comprehending them is doomed to failure, because with each new publication a new element irrupts into the constellation of his work. There is no way to avoid the necessary fragmentariness of this study. Yet it was necessary to configure a series of units which would provide a global vision of some kind, although taking into account, again, that this is a work of reading readings carried out by Miller. This is why this work has assumed the fragmentary form of a jumping from text to text. As has been said before, may each reader add or take away what he or she sees fit.

Opium

In a work to which I shall return throughout this book, Boris Eichenbaum asserts that what characterized the two groups that formed Russian Formalism was "the attempt to create an independent science of literature which studies specifically literary material" (Eichenbaum, 1965:

higher education no longer believe that their nation needs the university in the same way as it once did. The primary evidence has been the cutting off of funds, almost always justified by budget constraints, as has happened in the past few years at the University of California. That university was until recently arguably the greatest research university in the world. Now it has been weakened by budget cuts and through early retirements made irresistibly attractive for many professors by "golden handshake" offers of retirement benefits. About two thousand professors have taken early retirement. This procedure is borrowed from the corporate world. Those who pay for the university no longer have the same confidence they once had in the need for basic research as something directly funded by the nation (that is, the federal government) or by its subdivisions, the separate states of the United States. Basic research was in any case always largely supported as ancillary to the military buildup. With the end of the Cold War came the end of the apparent need for many kinds of basic research. It is difficult for most humanities professors to accept the fact that their prosperity in the 1960's, 1970's, and 1980's was as much a result of the Cold War as was the prosperity of aircraft and weapons manufacturers, or as was the space race that put men on the moon. Nevertheless, we were part of the military-industrial complex. The expensive development of humanities programs was an ancillary part of our need to be best at everything, including the humanities, in order to defeat the Soviet Union in the Cold War. This goal was made explicit in the legislation establishing the National Endowment for the Humanities. Now that the Cold War is over, humanities programs are being "downsized" along with scientific parts of university research and teaching. The NEH survives today with greatly reduced funding and is threatened with extinction. The job situation for newly trained physicists is nearly as bad as it is for new Ph.D.'s in English. For the latter, it is extremely bad.[28] What those in charge (legislators, trustees, granting agencies, university administrators, foundation officers, and corporate executives) need, or think they need, and therefore demand, is immediately applicable technology. The weakening of our space program and the killing of the superconducting supercollider project are salient demonstrations of this. Much applied research can be done just as well or better by computer or pharmaceutical companies and the like. These have been increasingly funding applied research inside the university, co-opting the university's scientific skills and laboratory facilities (often originally paid for by federal money) for research oriented toward

103). With this, the foundation for what would be the prevailing tendency of literary criticism, at least until the 1970's, was laid: the attempt to endow humanistic studies—literary studies, in this particular case—with a scientific status. Russian Formalism continued the Kantian tradition of considering the work of art and aesthetics to be free from metaphysical and ethical implications and to shape an autonomous domain. Other schools resisted, for one reason or another, what they perceived as "simplification," that is, the sequestering of literature from human life and from history. Marxism in its different forms demanded a study of literature that took into account the conditions of social production; existentialism focused on the nexus between being in the world and literature; and so on. Yet with the exception of certain individual critics, these modes of literary study did not pose, as did the Jena Romantics, the problem of the "alterity" of literature as an insoluable riddle, at least a mystery of the unnamable nonreading about which Blanchot speaks (Blanchot, 1959: 207). To put this another way, they did not pose the problem—in my opinion the key problem—of literature as an alterity absolutely other. But what can be the meaning of an alterity of literature that always remains "absolutely other"? I shall try to answer this by following Miller's texts. For the moment, I will simply note that neither Gadamer (1960; 1988), with his insistence on the aesthetic experience, nor Ricœur (1975; 1977), with his metaphoric reference, nor pragmatists and aestheticists of reception, with their emphasis on the possibility of a decodification programmed by the text (Iser, 1972; 1974 and 1976; 1978), have taken this direction. Instead, they have understood the "alterity" of literature in terms of an assimilable "object" or, at best, in terms of a dialogue between subject and object.

"Criticism of consciousness"—George Poulet's, for instance—also did not understand literature as an "alterity" that constantly remains

the discovery of patentable procedures that will make the companies rich. In response to these radical changes, the university is becoming more and more like a bureaucratic corporation itself, for example by being run by a corps of proliferating administrators whose bottom-line business, as in any bureaucracy, is to perpetuate themselves efficiently, even if this sometimes means large-scale "administrative cutbacks." The analogy between a university and a corporation is imperfect, however, since universities do not need to show a profit to shareholders. The university's primary "product," in addition to applicable research, is students who have earned degrees.

The lack of a unified national culture in the United States has made it especially easy for educators to shift with the global decline in the nation-state's importance to a university modeled to some degree on the bureaucratic corporation. The answer to the question "Who now governs our universities?" is that universities are more and more coming to be governed, however invisibly or indirectly, by corporations. This major change will have incalculable effects on university teaching and research. Money is power, in this area as in others. As federal and state sources of funding are greatly reduced, both public and private universities are turning to corporations for funding. At my own university, the University of California at Irvine, corporate support means seeking money from pharmaceutical companies, computer companies, medical technology companies, parts of the so-called financial industry, media companies, and the like. These companies may be owned by Japanese, English, French, German, Korean, or Taiwanese corporations, or they may do much of their manufacturing or much of their sales outside the United States. In any case, they do not owe primary allegiance to a single nation-state. Moreover, they are not just any kind of corporation. They are participating in the worldwide transformation we call the coming of the information age or, more negatively, the age when everything is turned into spectacle.

Today, money is information, passed around like other bytes on the Internet, just as information is money. An unbroken continuum binds pharmaceutical companies that deal in medical prostheses controlled by computer chips or that depend on genetic research to computer companies that invent the hardware and software making it possible to store and circulate information (for example, in genetic research), to banking and investment companies that exchange the sort of information we call money, to media companies that turn everything into spectacle in film, television, and video, influencing thereby what people think, what they buy, and

"absolutely other." In 1966, during a colloquium in Cérisy-la-Salle, Poulet began his lecture: "The new critique . . . is above all a critique of participation, or rather, of identification. There is no true criticism without the coinciding of two ways of thinking or conceiving" (Poulet, 1967: 11, my trans.).

Logically, understanding literature as absolute "alterity" would mean that true criticism could not exist without an "unmeeting" between two different ways of conceiving, or at least without their coincidence in difference. In the last three decades there have been at least three "critics" who have, each in his own way, developed such a way of seeing literature, philosophy, or criticism itself: Jacques Derrida, Paul de Man, and J. Hillis Miller. My focus is on Miller, who at the start of his career—in 1963, the year of *The Disappearance of God*, and 1965, that of *Poets of Reality*—sided with criticism of consciousness: "If literature is a form of consciousness the task of the critic is to identify himself with the subjectivity expressed in the words" (DG, ix). Everything begins, therefore, with a hermeneutic conception in the nineteenth-century mode of Schleiermacher: to avoid the lack of understanding between interpreter and author, interpreter and text by reconstructing a construction and by an immediate sympathetic and congenial comprehension. The idea of "participation" appears, then, at the beginning of Miller's work.

Miller has never understood literary criticism as a science modeled on the method of the natural sciences, precisely because of "sym-pathos," which renders obsolete or at least problematic the subject/matter distinction: "It is impossible to make the same distinction between humanistic study and its subject-matter that can be made more or less unequivocally between nature and the sciences investigating it. The arts and their interpretation have been inextricably connected throughout history" (TPP,

how they vote. These days an event does not "happen" unless it happens on television. The media formats determine what happens, even in the literal sense of transforming the way military "interventions" are conducted today, for example, in Somalia and Bosnia.[29] The new global economy is not an economy in the old-fashioned sense of the production and distribution of goods. Theory's opponents lament the falsely supposed suspension of language's referential function in "deconstruction," but that suspension actually characterizes the new global economy in all its features. Giorgio Agamben, in a terrifying passage in *The Coming Community*, describes the way the new "society of spectacle" is transforming humankind everywhere and putting an end to the old securely founded and authorized nation-state:

In this extreme nullifying unveiling, however, language (the linguistic nature of humans) remains once again hidden and separated, and thus, one last time, in its unspoken power, it dooms humans to a historical era and a State: the era of the spectacle, or of accomplished nihilism. This is why today power founded on a presupposed foundation is tottering all over the globe and the kingdoms of the earth set course, one after another, for the democratic-spectacular regime that constitutes the completion of the State-form. Even more than economic necessity and technological development, what drives the nations of the earth toward a single common destiny is the alienation from linguistic being, the uprooting of all peoples from their vital dwelling in language. . . . Contemporary politics is this devastating *experimentum linguae* that all over the planet unhinges and empties traditions and beliefs, ideologies and religions, identities and communities.[30]

So what's the difference? As long as we get funding, can we in the humanities not go on about our business of teaching and research in more or less the same old way? Do the faculty and the administration not still govern the university, determining its curricula and its research priorities? Are we not skilled in taking the money and doing more or less what we want with it? Have not humanists always benefited from the affluence of scientific colleagues? To some degree the answer to all these questions is yes. Nevertheless, the shift from state and federal funding to transnational corporate funding is altering the research university and its governance more radically than many people yet recognize. Agamben does not mention the university, but it is easy to see that as the state loses its foundation so does the university that served the state. The university is transformed from being an educational state apparatus, in Althusser's term,[31] or, to put it more benignly, a place of critical and innovative thinking, into being

79). This position does not exclude rigorous reading, even though we are as far from a techno-scientific criticism as from an aesthetic or impressionistic one. But where are we exactly, in a starting point that assures the necessity of immediate adherence to another's thought (as in the criticism of the French scholar Albert Thibaudet [1874–1936])? We are, rather, in an uncertain and insecure place. The call to identify with the subjectivity expressed in the text already delivers a warning. "Criticism demands above all that gift of participation, that power to put oneself within the life of another person, which Keats called negative capability. If literature is a form of consciousness the task of the critic is to identify himself with the subjectivity expressed in the words" (DG, ix). Whom is Miller translating with these words? Whom is he reading? Is it Proust, with whom he begins his preface? Gabriel Marcel, from whom he has taken the term "intersubjectivity" some lines before? Poulet, who resounds in the "task of the critic"? Keats, from whom he borrows the expression "negative capability"? Are all of them in agreement with one another? Do they remain in peaceful contact?

"When the work of Jacques Derrida and Paul de Man, or my own work, is reduced to abstract theoretical formulations, it is often forgotten that those formulations in every case are attained by an act of reading" (T, 323). Let us choose two references of reading: Poulet and Keats. We have already referred to Poulet's suggestion that one explore from within the most secret coherences of a given work. (Criticism is the vision of a vision, Ramón Fernandez told us.) What happens in Keats? He talks about "negative capability" in a letter sent to his brothers George and Tom on December 22, 1818: "I had not a dispute but a disquisition with Dilke, on various subjects; several things dovetailed in my mind, & at once it struck me, what quality went to form a Man of Achievement espe-

one site among many others, perhaps an increasingly less important site, for the production and transfer of globally exchanged information.

If the secrecy demanded by university military research during the Cold War was deplorable, a new kind of secrecy is invading our universities, the secrecy demanded by corporations as a quid pro quo for their support of research. Two senior scientists in a department of biology, for example, each with his or her team of junior faculty, post-doctoral researchers, graduate students, and technicians, may each be funded by a different pharmaceutical company. Each scientist is accountable to the funding company. This means a subtle shift from basic research toward doing research that will result in marketable products, even though the companies probably tell the scientists to go on doing what they have been doing but to promise them first development rights if anything patentable happens to be discovered. It is also in the interest of the funding company to keep the results of research secret as long as possible, at least until the results are patented. This may delay the publication of research results, whereas research funded by the National Science Foundation or the National Institutes of Health has as a condition timely publication and universal access to the results of research. In the new situation two graduate students or two post-docs in the same department may be inhibited from discussing with one another or from using in teaching what they are doing in their research work, in fundamental violation of basic assumptions about academic freedom. The measure of research accomplishment will be more and more not the acquisition of new knowledge but productivity as defined by the companies to whom the university is accountable. Almost the first thing the new president of the University of California, Richard C. Atkinson, did when he took office in the fall of 1995 was to hire consultants from the corporate world to advise him on how to make the central administration more "productive." It is easy to see that the president's having applied the business-world model of productivity to his own bailiwick will justify his later applying it also to the teaching and research activities that are the university's reason for being.

Individual professors in this new kind of university belong as much to international communities of those working in the same areas as they do to local research communities within their own universities. I shall discuss later the role of new communications technologies in creating these transnational research "teams." These technologies mean you can stay put in your own university and still be working on a research project with

cially in Literature & which Shakespeare possessed so enormously—I mean *Negative Capability*, that is when man is capable of being in uncertainties, mysteries, doubts, without any irritable reaching after fact & reason" (Keats, 1970: 43). Later on in the letter, Keats reproaches Coleridge for "being incapable of remaining content with half knowledge."

It is difficult to relate this definition of "negative capability" to the gift of identification, because in identification we necessarily approach a type of knowledge of the author and/or the text, whereas negative capability implies a state of nonknowledge and doubt that does not seek to go beyond itself. This not seeking to go beyond mysteries is inconsistent with any movement of transcendence from the critic to the text, or from the author to his characters. At most, it is connected with negative knowledge. In an earlier letter, addressed to Benjamin Bailey, Keats opposes "Men of Genius," characterized by a lack of individuality, to "Men of Power," whose main characteristic is having a proper self. Keats, being a man of genius and thus lacking in individuality, can for this very reason go beyond himself and participate in the world surrounding him: "If a Sparrow come before my Window I take part in its existence and pick about the Gravel" (Keats, 1970: 36–38). This is an empathetic and non-epistemological participation, an identification that does not lead to any kind of knowledge. Though this lack of individuality favors an ethereal circulation within the world, negative capability aims basically at knowing how to remain in doubts and shadows, that is to say, oriented in a direction opposite to a literary criticism that looks for understanding and explanation. Therefore, when criticism appropriates the lack of individuality or negative capability to which Keats refers, it carries out two displacements. The first displacement is from literature to criticism. (Keats speaks about the man of genius, about Shakespeare, and not about the

colleagues from many countries thousands of miles away. Another globalizing factor is the constant migration of professors and students from one country to another. This migration is a small-scale version of the unprecedented migration these days of large groups from one country to another, as work patterns change. In one academic year alone (1994–95) a professor I know had as colleagues working under his sponsorship scholars from Spain, Rumania, Bosnia, Japan, and Switzerland. Like many of his colleagues he lectured in many countries, in this case in England, Norway, Italy, the Netherlands, Denmark, Korea, Taiwan, and the People's Republic of China. This professor was doing his bit in these two ways to make his university part of a global organization detached from its local and national roots.

In a concomitant change, "society" (in the concrete form of legislators, regents, and corporations that manage and give money to public universities and of trustees who manage and corporations that support private ones) also no longer needs the university in the old way to transmit national cultural values. This is true however much such authorities may still pay lip service to this traditional role of humanities departments. The work of ideological indoctrination and training in consumerism, it is tacitly understood, can be done much more effectively by the media, by newspapers and magazines, by television and cinema. Moreover, these academic bureaucrats and legislators are not stupid. After what has happened in humanities departments from the 1960's on, they now no longer trust professors of literature to do what they used to do or even, the bureaucrats might claim, what they are hired to do. The cat is out of the bag. Whatever may be the protestations of those running the universities about the eternal values embodied in the Western canon, the news has got through to them that the actual culture of the United States is multifarious and multilingual. Moreover, they know now that you can no longer trust professors to teach Chaucer, Shakespeare, Milton, and the rest in the old ways. New ways of reading them have shown that these authors, read from a certain angle, as professors seem inclined to do and to teach their students to do, are what some governing the university consider to be dynamite that might blow up the social edifice. So the more or less unconscious strategy is to welcome the transformations of traditional literature departments as they shift to cultural studies and then perhaps gradually cut off the money. In public universities this deed is done in the name of financial stringency and the need to build more prisons and fund welfare

critic.) The second displacement is from nonknowledge to knowledge. (Keats never talks about these processes as epistemological activities.) Criticism "mis-interprets" Keats's text.

This should teach us something about the functioning of "critical" discourse. Its composition is anything but a homogeneous model oriented by linguistic consciousness or intention. We might propose as a working hypothesis that the critical text, like the literary text, does not know what it does or what it says. In this sense, the weave of Miller's text shows two layers, oriented quite differently. The first concerns the relation between the critic and the states of mind embodied in the literary text, where what the critic intends, according to criticism of consciousness, is to achieve the highest knowledge, via identification, of those states of mind. The second is the domain of literature in relation to knowledge, where what one looks for, according to Keats, is just the opposite, that is, the way the literary subject is able to remain in mystery and doubt, unaware of facts and reason. In one way or another, literature responds to criticism and criticism responds to literature. How can we relate "intersubjectivity" to doubts and uncertainties, or how can we relate mysteries and uncertainties to a possible identification? These two references clash, are antithetical, probably as antithetical as the relation between word and mind.

This clashing is not only a paradox, that is, a semantic relation in which, for instance, a logical sense and a grammatical one or a declaration and a factual practice exclude each other (de Man, 1979); it also indicates the presence of codes that have not been completely sutured, whose fissure establishes a significant and nondialogical game (Bakhtin, 1981; 1984b). Poulet himself writes that the subject we find in the work is not the author but something inside the work itself (Poulet, 1967: 319). Miller

programs. In private universities the attempt to control what is taught in the humanities is sometimes more direct and blatant. An example is the twenty-million-dollar gift to the humanities at Yale by Lee Bass, a member of a wealthy United States oil family. He thought his gift would entail the right to choose the professors his money would endow and the curriculum they would teach. What is most sinister about this dark episode, from which Yale admirably extricated itself by ultimately returning the gift, is the possibility that Bass's naïveté was not in assuming that his money would give him some right to govern the university but in being so up-front about it. Most such control is exercised in more tactful, subtle, and indirect ways. In a related change, professors have less and less importance as public affairs experts, no doubt because the media that allow those authorities to speak no longer have confidence that the experts from within the university will say what they want to hear, just as Bass did not trust Yale to make appointments of which he would approve. The experts on public television panels, for example, are often drawn from conservatively funded think tanks rather than from universities.

Robert Atwell, president of the American Council on Education, asserted in 1992 that American colleges and universities will be leaner and meaner by the year 2000: "Higher education is in its most dire financial condition since World War II." [32] This "slenderizing" is happening not because universities want to be smaller and dumber, but because the money supply is being cut off. The articles discussing this bleak future recognize that many valuable programs are being eliminated. During the recession in the early 1990's, faculty at the University of California were told that state funding would never rise again to the levels of the 1980's. This could not have been because the state would never again have enough money to return to those levels. In 1995 California was out of its recession and becoming prosperous again, with surplus tax revenues. The annual state budget of the University of California now has regained the level it had before the recession. This increase in funding must not, however, be misunderstood as a return to the prosperity of the 1980's. The increase is necessary to support salaries and student aid in the new down-sized university. Funding for individual divisions is still sharply down from historical levels. [33] Less than one quarter of the total revenue of the University of California at Irvine in 1994–95 came from the State of California, whereas 52 percent was from state funding in 1984–85. [34] In the latest information I have (1998), it is 24 percent. The assertion that funding will never rise to the old

will insist on that strange connection: mental writing, mind scattered by writing. Do "mind," "subjectivity," and "identification," on the one side, go hand in hand with "writing," "uncertainty," and "nonknowledge," on the other? If they do, we find ourselves with a contradiction. Precisely this antithesis governs *The Disappearance of God*, a book that is representative of Miller's supposed "phenomenological" stage. Let me examine in detail the chapter dedicated to Thomas De Quincey.

The introduction to *The Disappearance of God* already makes clear that the author is concerned about two specific aspects of the literary works he is going to study: their themes and their implications for life. In fact (though I assert this with all possible caution), the introduction is about two constants that will never disappear from his discourse. Contrary to the Kantian tradition, Miller does not view literature as an autonomous domain beyond good and evil, but sees it as inextricably linked to metaphysical and ethical topics. To a certain extent (and this "certain extent" is very important), there is something traditional in this. It is present already in Aristotle's *Poetics* and in classical commentaries on literature from Plato on: the need to treat myths and fables in the same way as a real "fact." Speaking very schematically, Aristotelian poetics does not distinguish between text and world, since everything ends up as an effect on the world or as catharsis. An equation joins the book to the world, in a direction opposite to the one Hans Blumenberg (1981) points out for the tradition that includes Flaubert, Mallarmé, and Valéry. Flaubert's comment in a letter addressed to Mlle. Leroyer de Chantepie — "the only way to bear existence is to stupefy or intoxicate oneself by way of literature, as if in a perpetual orgy" (September 4, 1858; Flaubert, 1980: 852, my trans.) — clearly opposes Plato, who in the *Republic* wants to introduce himself even into the privacy of people's homes in order to watch over

levels can have only one meaning. It means that the State of California, in the form of its governor and legislature, will not promise to give quite the old level of funding to the University of California even when the money again becomes available. They do not need the old university enough to pay for it. They do not need its basic research in the same way. It is not yet clear whether or not they even need the university for the primary, stated purpose of giving a higher liberal education to all young citizens of California who have grade averages in high school above a certain level. The latter commitment was to some degree a cover for another mission of the university, namely, to do Cold War research. It remains to be seen whether that commitment will be maintained in the new circumstances.

The return of funding now is based on a new image of the university's mission: to aid the economic prosperity of the State of California as it becomes a big player on the global stage. It took those in charge only five years to figure out a new use for the university. This change is strikingly clear in statements by Pete Wilson, governor of California, and Richard C. Atkinson, University of California president. In presenting his proposals for the California 1996–97 budget, Wilson said, "California universities and colleges have long been revered as the finest institutions in the world. Like the pioneers, entrepreneurs, and innovators who made California a land where any dream is possible, our institutions of higher learning are carrying on that tradition by preparing our students to compete and win in the global marketplace." Atkinson echoed Wilson almost word for word: "I applaud the governor's recognition of the important role higher education plays in preparing a skilled workforce for competition in the global marketplace and the important role UC plays in a healthy California economy." Atkinson again stressed this new orientation in a more recent policy statement issued in January 1997. "We must have substantial economic growth," he said. "This requires investments in university-based research and a highly educated workforce." Atkinson mentions the humanities only once in his six-page statement: "Lyric poetry and magnetic resonance imagery may be very different, but both are ways of giving us access to information that would be otherwise inaccessible."[35] "Information" here is the key word, as in the term "Informatics" used to name new required undergraduate courses at my university designed to make all the students computer literate. Lyric poetry is, for Atkinson, valuable if, like magnetic resonance imagery, it gives us information available in no other way. It is kind of President Atkinson to include lyric poetry along

the impressions myths make on them: "We must begin, then, it seems, by a censorship over our story-makers, and what they do well we must pass and what not, reject. And the stories on the accepted list we will induce nurses and mothers to tell to the children and so shape their souls by these stories far rather than their bodies by their hands" (Plato, 1963: 624; II, 377 b–c). Plato, like Stendhal, Nietzsche, and Miller, worries about the "performativity" of the fable insofar as he is conscious that it is a way of doing things more effectively than with one's own hands. For this reason, Miller quotes Kierkegaard's *Repetition* when he expresses himself in existential terms: Where am I? Who am I? How did I come here? What is this thing called the world? What does this world mean? (DG, 9).

But with what subject does the book deal? It deals with the disconnection between man and God, "between man and nature, between man and man, even between man and himself" (DG, 2). It develops Hölderlin's vision: "But, my friend, we have come too late. Though the gods are living / Over our heads they live, up in a different world" ("Brot und Wein," stanza 7; Hölderlin, 1980: 249). There is an explicit reference to baroque poetry, "the crucial moment of the change from a poetry of presence to a poetry of allusion and absence" (DG, 7). This assertion is entirely appropriate when we think about the transitional literature between the Middle Ages and the Enlightenment. However, baroque poetry (Gongora, for instance) supposes that the text becomes cloistered within itself when referentiality and the interpretative task appropriate to it are attenuated or lost. In this sense, baroque art expresses the moment of the separation not only between man and God, but also between the sign and its signification. It is not gratuitous that Miller, citing Valéry on the subject of the modern historical sense, writes: "Like Babylon, Nineveh, and Elam, our civilization will become mere heaps of broken artifacts, frag-

with magnetic resonance imaging. I suppose there is a sense in which lyric poetry gives "information," but that is hardly the right way to name the most important thing it does. To say Tennyson's "The Lady of Shallott" gives information about England's canals in the 1830's or about Tennyson's state of mind when he wrote it is true, but trivial. "The Lady of Shallott" gives knowledge, of an exceedingly peculiar kind, but that is not the same thing as information. That poem is also a speech act, a way of doing things with words, something not allowed for in the reigning paradigm of "information." We should probably capitalize on such generous analogies in defending the humanities. Nevertheless, the analogy is clearly a false one.

The question that haunts me, that has haunted me ever since I first read Bill Readings's *The University in Ruins*, but haunts me even more when I read statements like President Atkinson's, is this: What is now the function of literary study, if any, in the new technologized, globalized, post-colonial research university, the university whose mission is to produce an educated workforce to make the region where it is located "competitive in the global economy"? I do not think that question is at all easy to answer, particularly if we try to follow Readings in not fooling ourselves into thinking that the old ways and old justifications can continue. Hand-wringing will accomplish little. Some other justifications for the humanities and for literary study within the humanities must be found.

The Department of English and Comparative Literature at the University of California at Irvine, where I teach, is perhaps the strongest department in the whole university, as measured by the quality of those who apply to do graduate work, the scholarship of its faculty, its national ranking, and so on. Its reward for this accomplishment was to lose seven of its senior faculty to the enticements of early retirement and to have its budget for graduate fellowships cut back to the point where smaller numbers of graduate students can be accepted each year. It is difficult not to draw the conclusion that the State of California (in the form of voters, legislators, and university administrators) did not need what we were doing enough to be willing to pay for it at previous levels. Now that funding has increased again, new positions are being allotted to replace some of the ones lost to early retirement. The new mission for the university justifies these restorations of funding. Our claim on more graduate fellowships is weakened, I am bound to say, by the fact that it is not easy to justify the production of more and more Ph.D.'s in English or Comparative Literature if there will be fewer and fewer jobs for them. My department is at present a

ments whose very use, it may be, will have been forgotten." This Babelian sense of history is very familiar to Gongora. It alludes, above all, to a confusion of disordered pieces whose order cannot be guessed. The same happens in Kafka: "The people are as depthless as the walls: we see their gestures and expressions with extraordinary distinctness, but the meaning of these gestures and these glances is precisely that they have no meaning. They are simply there before us" (TPP, 20).

The Other, whether nature or the sign or man or his own consciousness, presents itself before me like a thick wall, impossible to penetrate, perturbing, destabilizing. This should prevent us from speaking of a kind of identification between the critic and the subjectivity supposedly implied in the text. The impossibility of this identification keeps us from misunderstanding Miller's use of Keats's set phrase "negative capability." To borrow Ortega y Gasset's words, the misery and the splendor — that is to say, the contradiction — of the critic who risks himself in attempting an identification consists in a "meeting" with "undecidability" (Ortega y Gasset, 1962a: 122). For this reason, "To Don Quixote the windmills are giants, to Emma Bovary Rodolphe is the fulfillment of her romantic dreams, and for Henry James the novel presents not facts but someone's interpretation of them" (DG, 12). For this reason, also, already in this significant introductory chapter Thomas De Quincey is presented to us as someone for whom "the gap between man and the divine power" appears in the most extreme and extravagant way (DG, 15). When at the end of the Introduction Miller writes, "each section tries to identify the meaning of one mode of experience in the writer" (DG, 16), how should we interpret this? As the identification of a textual meaning, or as the identification of a textual meta-meaning that indicates the impossibility of identifying a textual meaning? As Poulet wants to? Or as Keats wants to? Let us

strange mixture of a traditional English department, a large component of up-to-date American studies, a comparative literature program focusing on literary theory along with Renaissance and post-Enlightenment European literature, an internationally famous program in creative writing, a program in English composition, plus courses in women's studies, cultural studies, film studies, African American studies, Native American studies, postcolonial studies, Chicano/Chicana studies, and so on. It might be difficult to formulate the unifying rationale for all this or even the rationale for why it is disunified in just this way. We might be hard put to it to explain to someone, let us say a state legislator or a corporation CEO, what it is we do so well and why we ought to be doing just this and not some other thing, what good it is for the State of California and its citizens. This book is an attempt to provide such a rationale.

How We Got from There to Here

So far I have discussed some of the external forces that are changing the study of English literature in the United States. How, looked at from the inside, did departments of English evolve from a relatively coherent program into the not easily defensible mixture that now characterizes many of them? The changes began just after the Second World War. The evolution occurred in a number of distinct phases: from the triumph of the New Criticism in the 1950's and 1960's, to the dominance of language-based theory in the 1970's and early 1980's, to the inclusion of cultural studies in the 1980's and in the 1990's. Each of these has been a stage in the dismantling of the old idea that the humanities should teach the values of a unified culture.

Current accounts of the rise of literary theory over the last half century tend to be organized around a certain narrative. This story is an example of what Jean-François Lyotard has called a metanarrative or a grand narrative. He has told us we postmodernists do and should distrust such stories.[36] The story about literary theory's rise and fall, however, is so taken for granted that it is hard to see how it is in part an ideologically motivated fabrication. Ideology is by definition unconscious. It is therefore difficult or impossible to eradicate it by demonstration that it is erroneous. Ideology arises as a phantasmal reflex of our real material conditions of existence in the world, including the institutions within which we live and work. It would be a mistake to hope to change that ideology merely by exposing

see what Hillis Miller tells us about De Quincey or, perhaps, what De Quincey tells us about Hillis Miller.

In his writing—which we do not know whether to call "literary," "autobiographical," or "essayistic"—De Quincey seeks in an orderly and continuous fashion to set out exhaustive knowledge of the object he is treating at any moment. To attain this knowledge, we need to think through a system of oppositions: "One state cannot be known unless we also know its opposite. This notion (which De Quincey may possibly have learned from John Paul Richter, his favorite German writer) is given the widest extension in De Quincey's thought" (DG, 43). This system of oppositions is a law of the semiotic perception of reality insofar as it explains phenomena of worldly experience as well as experiences coming from literature itself. It would almost be possible to say that De Quincey's writing is about a *transcendental* system of oppositions. It maintains, for instance, that the death of those whom we have loved is more affecting in midsummer than on any other occasion. This is because an antagonism exists between the prodigality of life in that season and "the wintry sterility of the grave." This very fact makes us understand "chiaroscuro" as a law governing poetic style, since the antithesis between images revivifies them reciprocally. Just as Jakobson makes metaphor and metonymy two mental processes of perception of reality and of linguistic expression, so De Quincey ascribes a fundamental epistemological place to the system of oppositions. Miller tells us that for De Quincey there are "two very distinct kinds of mental building" (DG, 45): rhetoric, or the literature of power, and logic, or the literature of knowledge. If already in the preface to *The Disappearance of God* the terms "mind" and "word," "subjectivity" and "writing" are mingled, now with regard to De Quincey, that strange mixture continues. Is this mental building? Or a type of writing

it. Ideology critique does not change ideologies. That requires a different kind of work. Nevertheless, an ideological story, however ghostly, is by no means without its effects on our collective life and behavior. Far from it. Being infatuated by an ideology is like being in love as Proust describes it. You can fall out of love, just as you can lose an ideological mystification, but that does not happen because someone has patiently explained how wrong you are about your beloved or how mystified your understanding of institutional changes is. Why have we needed to tell ourselves just this story about our recent disciplinary history? I think I can specify at least part of the answer.

Once upon a time, so the story goes, were those primitive days before the Second World War when a single canon was firmly in place. Professors did biography, philology, literary and intellectual history, character description, and impressionistic evaluation without any conscious need for theory. They had little awareness of the implicit theoretical presuppositions of their work. What they did was a naive form of extrinsic criticism. It was also the United States version of Humboldtian *Bildung*, the Arnoldian study of the best that has been thought and said in the world. When I entered Oberlin College in 1944, just before the end of the Second World War and just before the introduction of the New Criticism, the required freshman course in English was a composition class. The textbook was a series of readings about the ideals of a liberal education by nineteenth-century English authors: Newman, Arnold, Huxley, and others. This book had first been published in 1914, but was still being used as a required text for all students at Oberlin in 1944.[37] The writings of Arnold, Newman, and the rest were not only presented as models of good prose. Reading them also provided the inculcation in basic cultural ideas that was still considered a primary function of higher education. I doubt if many such courses are taught anywhere in the United States today as a requirement for all undergraduates.

Then came the epoch of the New Criticism. The New Criticism was in part a response to the need to teach literature to veterans of World War II. They could now go to college because of the "GI Bill," but many were almost wholly ignorant of the Western tradition. The New Criticism did not respond to this, as might have been expected, by devising crash courses in that tradition. Quite the contrary. In a politically and pedagogically brilliant move, the New Criticism presumed that it is not necessary to have any special knowledge of literary or intellectual history in order to

appearing in a concrete and historical text? At first Miller seems to understand well enough the direction toward which everything is headed: "De Quincey's style is an exact mirror of his mental space" (DG, 48). This assertion faithfully reproduces the Romantic principle of expressivity: that is, mind is a lamp that gives light, and literature is the mirror in which that light is reflected. Literature is the mimesis of an inner space (Abrams, 1953). Rhetoric is musical, expansive, and ascending; it dances around and around its object. By contrast, logic is linear, discursive, and horizontal; it goes directly to its objective. Here we have a clear and important example of antithesis.

However, only an ingenuous reading would find in Miller's or in De Quincey's text such a clear and easy exposition. Like Plato, who inveighs against mimesis while writing mimetic discourses, De Quincey claims the virtues of rhetoric, or the literature of power, while writing by means of logic, or the literature of knowledge. This he does probably because it "defends him from the powers of darkness outside, and also from . . . the power of incoherence . . . within" (DG, 49). Nevertheless, this literature of knowledge ends up showing features that specifically belong to the literature of power: its discontinuity and its development by "reverberations, permutations and combinations of a primitive germ" (DG, 50). Logic, like rhetoric, "dances." For that reason, "logic has turned out to be strictly analogous to rhetoric." Some important implication, as we will demonstrate, can be inferred from this statement.

The antithesis between the literature of knowledge and the literature of power both is cancelled and still stands, because at least one of the antithetical positions shares some features of the other. What Miller discovers in his reading of De Quincey is a form of "arch-rhetoric," a quality of writing whose borders are difficult to draw insofar as it drama-

read a poem. One could be a good reader and a good citizen without ever learning that history. The poems in Cleanth Brooks and Robert Penn Warren's *Understanding Poetry*, the bible of the New Criticism, are detached from their original cultural contexts. They are given dates and authors, but that is about all. A good dictionary is the only required tool of explication. Each poem is found by accident, so to speak, written on a loose sheet of paper blown by the wind. The poem is then given the powerful context of *Understanding Poetry* itself. The New Criticism, according to the usual story, was an extreme form of atheoretical intrinsic criticism. It claimed to be so commonsensical as not to need theoretical presuppositions. At the same time it insinuated into students' minds a set of theoretical presuppositions about the superiority of lyric poetry, the autonomy of the literary work, the organic unity of good works, the importance of metaphor over other figures, and so on. The New Criticism, as its critics have observed, also smuggled in a good many conservative political and ethical ideas by way of an apparent formalist objectivity. The New Criticism was a mode of what has recently been called "aesthetic ideology." Aesthetic ideology means asserting the role for literature in supporting the organic nation-state that is claimed for it in Schiller's *Letters on Aesthetic Education*. In the New Criticism version aesthetic ideology also meant asserting a large degree of self-enclosed autonomy for literature. The "organic unity" of the good literary work justified cutting it off from its biographical and historical contexts. The work could be studied as a self-enclosed formal monad that could be "analyzed" and appreciated in isolation. Such a work is its own end. It should be appreciated as such, in detachment from any vulgar instrumental use, and largely in detachment from its historical conditions. It is no accident that John Crowe Ransom, one of the founders of the New Criticism, was a Kantian of sorts. The New Critics' presumptions about literature explain why for them the short lyric was the paradigmatic example of a literary work. It is much more difficult to make claims for the novel of contextlessness and a self-enclosed, unified autonomy in which each minute element contributes to the whole.

Such an account of the New Criticism fails to see that attention to how meaning is generated by words as opposed to discussion of thematic meaning is already a more than rudimentary theoretical move. Such a move has far-reaching consequences.[38] The move subverts the conservative agenda many New Critics had. The political effect of the New Criticism can by no means be summed up by identifying the politics of its founders.

tizes a constant self-referentiality. This arch-rhetoric is a kind of unlimited semiosis (using Peirce's well-known terminology), in which "any one part of a logical system presupposes all the others" (DG, 51), and it organizes itself like a fugue. In addition, such constant self-referentiality adopts another form: that of infinite divisibility. It is impossible to fix the arch-rhetorical "dance" at a concrete spatial or temporal point because "any finite entity in time and space is infinitely divisible" (DG, 53). If logic shows within it features that are specific to its opposite, rhetoric, this means that any unity not only opposes its counterpart but reproduces in itself that law of opposition. A superficial glance easily uncovers that Miller is already testifying to what I shall later call "deconstruction of one-ness." He would express it in 1977 as follows: " 'Parasite' is one of those words which calls up its apparent 'opposite.' It has no meaning without that counterpart. There is no parasite without its host. At the same time both word and counterword subdivide. Each reveals itself to be fissured already within itself" (TNT, 144). This, of course, does not mean that the opposition between parasite and host necessarily disappears. In any event, its disappearance could have a varied range of meanings.

In the essay on De Quincey, Miller tells us something similar: "The rhetorical style, the style of musical reverberation, degenerates into a series of sentences, each one of which is a maze, and, in its echoing 'laby-rinth of clauses,' contains its own infinity" (DG, 56), and "Every subject, however small, is inexhaustible" (DG, 52). Where does all this lead us? It leads to a specific form of negative capability, that is to say, to a perma-nence in the midst of doubts, mysteries, and uncertainties, born of the impossibility of reaching the other, whether it be an object in the world, an object in literature, or even God. In effect, everything in De Quincey implies a nearly mystical reach. Opium dreams had revealed to him that

Whatever those founders intended, the New Criticism in its attention to textual details endangered the traditional idea that literary study transmits a single culture's permanent values. In place of that, the New Criticism put, more or less in spite of itself, technical training in the skills of "close reading." Such skills were detached from any fixed cultural values. They could be applied to any text of any time. The New Critics asserted certain universal cultural values while at the same time teaching an ahistorical, technologized form of reading antipathetic to those values.

The New Criticism, the story continues, was superseded in the 1960's, 1970's, and early 1980's by the heyday of theory—theory structuralist, semiological, phenomenological, reader response, Marxist, Lacanian, or Foucauldian, but especially and quintessentially deconstructionist theory. Deconstruction was the model of exigent and rigorous theory. Like the New Criticism, so the story goes (but in this case the story lies, just as it to some degree falsifies the New Criticism), deconstruction was a form of intrinsic criticism, but an intrinsic criticism supported by subtle theoretical reflection. Deconstruction, so this false story goes, is apolitical, ahistorical, turns everything into language, suspends reference, and so on, according to a familiar apotropaic litany. Most educated people have encountered this story not only in journalism but also in academic discourse of both the right and the left.

Everything in this widely accepted account of deconstruction is distorted, often by asserting the exact opposite of what is actually the case. Jacques Derrida, not only in the manifest orientation of his work, but also in patient argument in many interviews, has demonstrated repeatedly the error of these false characterizations. "Deconstruction," he says in "Mochlos," "is also, and at the least, the taking of a position [*une prise de position*], in the work itself [*dans le travail même*], toward the politico-institutional structures that constitute and regulate our practice, our competences, and our performances."[39] The important words here are "work" and "position taking." Deconstruction is work. It works. It works by taking a position, by an active intervention in the university and in the political field within which the university is situated. This book is a taking of a position.

Paul de Man, in the late interview (1983) with Stephano Rosso published in *The Resistance to Theory*, responded to Rosso's question about the "frequent recurrence of the terms 'ideology' and 'politics'" in de Man's recent work by saying: "I don't think I ever was away from these problems, they were always uppermost in my mind."[40] It can easily be demonstrated

"the infinite powers of the mind match its infinite depths, and give [him] a brief possession of the omnipresence and simultaneity of God" (DG, 51). The possibility of reaching that goal fails, however, because of the infinite divisibility of any object taken as a focus. It is not possible to write a definitive history of any period or fact, since facts themselves constantly generate smaller and bigger facts that can be combined in an infinite number of possible ways. That is not all. There is not only a problem of continuous divisibility, but also of "singularity": "Not only can any entity be subdivided ad infinitum, but for De Quincey each of its parts is unique, and cannot be satisfactorily subsumed under some more general law" (DG, 54). This is the law of the law of genre (Derrida, 1980a). Each particular entity participates in, although it does not belong to, the general law. "No leaf is the copy of another leaf" (DG, 54). Miller's reading of De Quincey is in line with the reading Borges does of the same author in "Funes, The Memorious": "Funes not only remembered every leaf on every tree of every wood, but even every one of the times he had perceived or imagined it" (Borges, 1962: 114). Consequently "it was not only difficult for him to understand that the generic term *dog* embraced so many unlike specimens of differing sizes and different forms; he was disturbed by the fact that a dog at three-fourteen (seen in profile) should have the same name as the dog at three-fifteen (seen from the front)" (1962: 114).

Evidently we are inside a properly Nietzschean theme. When speaking of Nietzsche, Miller insists on the "leaf": "This 'making equal' of what is unequal is registered in the primordial act of naming. Man makes up the name 'leaf' for what does not exist, since no two leaves are the same, nor does any one remain the same from moment to moment" (AT, 40). Even more than De Quincey, Funes neither sleeps nor forgets any-

that this is the case. De Man's work is always concerned with ideology, politics, and history, with the social effect of literary study's institutionalized ideological errors, and with developing alternative forms of active intervention in history.

These forms of intervention, however, were no more compatible with transmitting the fixed values of a national culture than was the New Criticism. The rise of theory was the next stage after the New Criticism in undoing the traditional role of national literature departments as the place where citizens are imbued with a national culture. Those who have seen theory as inimical to this traditional role of the humanities are right. It needs to be added, however, that this model was in the United States and in the West generally already much weakened at the time theory became dominant. The rise of theory was more a symptom than a cause. It arose, as I have suggested, out of the necessity of understanding rapid historical and ideological change. The error has been to see theory as causing what it registered and attempted to confront. It responded in part by fulfilling with a clear conscience that other half of the university's mission: to comprehend everything rationally. Literary theory is conceptual reflection on how meaning is generated by words. Theory is intrinsically transnational. It is no accident that European theory, especially as transformed and extended within the United States university, is being appropriated by universities all over the world. This diffusion parallels the global spread of Western technology and capitalist economic organization. That does not mean it is the same thing.

Today, as so-called cultural studies becomes more and more important, in some universities and colleges at least, theory of the 1960's, 1970's, and 1980's goes on being carefully read, appropriated, and used in ever-new and diverse ways. Moreover it is constantly being extended in new theoretical work. By the new importance of "cultural studies" I mean the shift in the 1980's and 1990's within literature departments in United States colleges and universities, as well as in other countries around the world, to a new interest in the social contexts of literature. This has meant, among other things, a turn to the study of popular culture, minority discourses, non-Western literatures and cultures, hitherto marginalized literature by women, gays, and lesbians, as well as attention to media like film, television, and video. What was once the Department of Comparative Literature at the University of Minnesota has been renamed to include the phrase "Cultural Studies." The Critical Theory Institute at the University

thing. He says to the narrator: "*I have more memories in myself alone than all men have had since the world was a world.* . . . And again, toward dawn: *My memory, sir, is like a garbage disposal*" (Borges, 1962: 112). In regard to De Quincey, Miller notes that those things that took place in the past "fill up the reservoir of the past, and form themselves into a perdurable block from which man can never escape" (DG, 59).

Underlying De Quincey's initial project, like the projects of Miller or Funes, is the idea that it is possible to reconstruct the past. For De Quincey, reconstructing the past via opium presupposes the disappearance of pain and the discovery of an artificial paradise similar to the paradise of infancy, now lost. For Funes, reconstructing the past is an obligatory and painful exercise produced by memory itself. For both, ambivalent lucidity arrives as a result of a "satori," that is, a sudden and dazzling discovery of *something* through a gratuitous event. A toothache leads at random to a friend who, in turn, leads to a druggist who sells a *tincture* of opium for a penny, or, as with St. Paul or Funes, a fall from a horse is transformed into a fall into the abysses of memory. This memory is an unknown ramification of the subject's psychic geography. De Quincey's and Funes's exercises seem to be easier than Miller's, because for the former the exercise concerns self-knowledge, a descent into the depths of their own psyches, whereas the latter seeks an approach to, and possible identification with, the consciousness of the other. In any event, all these projects end in failure, or better, a strange failure.

It does not seem gratuitous that De Quincey talks about a *pharmakon nepenthé*, that is, about a "remedy for pain," because the figure of *pharmakon*, a key term in Derrida's reading of Plato's *Phaedrus*, appears in the history of writing. De Quincey begins by praising opium for its medicinal value and for its ability to make pain disappear and bring

of California at Irvine, originally founded to study such topics as mimesis and representation, spent three years during the early 1990's attempting, not with complete success, to define and understand what is meant by cultural studies. The Institute then shifted to the topic of "globalization." A full inventory of programs, departments, scholarly journals, teaching, and research projects that now use the term "cultural studies" would make a long list. Duke University Press, Oxford University Press, Princeton University Press, and the University of Minnesota Press all use the term as a rubric in their catalogues, though other university presses do not yet do so. A recent issue of *New Literary History* (28, no. 1 [Winter 1997]) was entitled "Cultural Studies: China and the West."

The exasperating vagueness of the term "cultural studies" and the heterogeneity of things included within it should not keep one from recognizing that the widespread use of the term shows we witness and participate in "a sea change in special circumstances." That is the phrase J. L. Austin, silently citing Shakespeare's *The Tempest* in *How to Do Things with Words*, uses to name what happens when a performative utterance is transferred to a different context and use.[41] Naming this widespread new orientation "cultural studies" is, like any act of naming, a speech act, a performative not constative utterance. It makes a claim for the existence and unity of what it names. This does not mean, however, that the phrase does not create or reveal something that is really there. This speech act has been felicitous. It has worked. It has had effects in the real world, for example to lead those distinguished university presses to reorganize their book lists and to publish new kinds of books.

In many, but by no means all, cases the reorientation to cultural studies has meant a return to mimetic, representationalist assumptions about the relation of a work to its context. Though the modern concept of culture has nationalist origins, as in Proust's assumptions that France is filled with French men and women who have the same shape, the new cultural studies tends to recognize the existence of an indefinitely large number of subcultures within a given dominant culture. An individual is likely to be "hybrid" or to belong to several different cultures simultaneously. The United States, for example, is seen as multicultural, multilingual, multiracial, and multiethnic. The new cultural studies is by no means homogeneous in its presuppositions and practices, nor has the shift to doing cultural studies taken place at the same rhythm or to the same degree in all departments, institutions, or countries. It is different in England,

back paradise: order, legislation and harmony, the erasing of spatial and temporal barriers, and the restoration, as if in the present, of wonderful moments with his sister. But bliss soon gives way to the other side of the *pharmakon*, to its painful and poisonous aspect. Opium turns the mind not only into a source of happiness, but also into the fearsome book of the Last Judgment, because, as De Quincey admits, such a book "is, in fact, the mind itself of each person." Suddenly, De Quincey finds himself before the infinite divisibility the "Piranesi effect" describes: "Creeping along the sides of the walls, you perceived a staircase; and upon it, groping his way upwards, was Piranesi himself: follow the stairs a little further, and you perceive it come to a sudden abrupt termination, without any balustrade, and allowing no step onwards to him who had reached the extremity, except into the depths below. Whatever is to become of poor Piranesi, you suppose, at least, that his labours must in some way terminate here. But raise your eyes, and behold a second flight of stairs still higher: on which again Piranesi is perceived, but this time standing on the very brink of the abyss" (De Quincey, 1985: 70).

In these words we witness a process that has neither beginning nor ending, a version of eternal repetition. The problem of "time" is faced in a concrete way. The following words especially attract our attention: "Even the first experience of anything is never really the first, but is only another repetition of something we have done innumerable times before" (DG, 70). De Quincey and Miller are saying something similar to what Derrida will say in chapter 4 of *Speech and Phenomena*, that is, that "The presence-of-the-present is derived from repetition and not the reverse" (Derrida, 1991: 12). Miller writes: "De Quincey's experience of *déjà vu* ties together past, present, and future. The present is suddenly experienced as a mysterious repetition of some half-remembered past, and this lightning-

Australia, South Africa, or the People's Republic of China from what it is in the United States. Lively debates among those doing such work in all those countries indicate not only cultural studies' heterogeneity, the way it is a site of dissensus, but also the way something serious is at stake. People in general do not fight so hard about something that is trivial. Scarcely a literature department, in the United States at least, has not been marked in one way or another by what we call cultural studies. Such orientations have been around for a long time in literature departments. They are to some degree a return to practices and attitudes that prevailed before the advent of the New Criticism and subsequent language-oriented theory. In many ways, however, contemporary cultural studies is different from its predecessors, for example, in the sharp attention to gender, race, and ethnicity. Moreover, cultural studies comes after the New Criticism and theory. Its historical position as post-post-structuralist marks and distinguishes it — for example, its assimilation of previous theory or resistance to it.

Rey Chow expresses the connection between theory and cultural studies elegantly and succinctly: "One of the strongest justifications for studying the non-West has to do precisely with the fundamental questioning of the limits of Western discourse which is characteristic of deconstruction and poststructuralist theory. The question of the sign as such leads logically to the opening up of the study of other signs and other systems of significations, other disciplines, other sexualities, other ethnicities, other cultures. Thus, against the arguments of many, I would say that deconstruction and poststructuralist theory have very close ties with cultural studies, gender studies, gay and lesbian studies, and ethnic studies, in that the investigations of disciplines, class, race, gender, ethnicity, and so forth, however empirical, must always already contain within them the implicit *theoretical* understanding of the need to critique hegemonic signs and sign systems from without as well as from within."[42] Wherever cultural studies is effective both in getting new knowledge and in making institutional or political change it will have done this by appropriating or reinventing, whether consciously or not, the theory it sometimes denigrates. Why this is so I shall explain later.

Nevertheless, as Rey Chow recognizes when she says that what she asserts is "against the arguments of many," the mistaken characterization of deconstruction, as a synecdoche for "theory" generally, along with its energetic repudiation, has seemed to some scholars necessary to clear a space for cultural studies. Since "high theory" was done primarily by white males

like revelation is a guarantee that the present will be repeated yet again in the future" (DG, 70). Literary criticism becomes at the present time a philosophical criticism, and De Quincey's "literature" hesitates between literariness (we shall see what this means in Miller's work) and the philosophical at the moment the problem of time arises. One must remember that this paradoxical structure is equally to be found in "literary," "philosophical," and "critical literary" discourses and that De Quincey himself assures us on several occasions that he is reading Kant (although in his own way).

If the critic's task is to identify with the subjectivity expressed in words, what does it mean, given this process of infinitude, that his task has failed, that he has encountered the opacity of language? Does it happen this way "because in this implicit linking of the opacity of language with the resistance of the critical consciousness to total submission, Miller begins to draw a connection between the self-consciousness of the critic and the self-reflexivity of the text" (Pease, 1983: 77–78)? What the critic faces is not really the failure of an identification, or the discovery of a linguistic thickness, but quite the opposite, an effective contact (how is the existence of a critical discourse without an effective contact possible?) between himself and the text-consciousness that leads him to an experience of impossibility and of the other.

As a result, we are not authorized to talk about self-reflexivity in the usual sense in Miller's critical discourse on De Quincey, since this reflexive turn takes place in an abyssal way and, as we saw, by means of entities that reproduce themselves ad infinitum. Nor do De Quincey and Miller collide with the opacity of language. They encounter, rather, crocodiles that kiss with cancerous kisses ("I was kissed, with cancerous kisses, by crocodiles" [De Quincey, 1985: 73]). If linguistic opacity

in elite institutions, it must, such scholars assume, be complicit with the status quo that cultural studies wants to contest. Even to read it might be to be contaminated by the conservative ideology it presumably supports. Theory bashing is an intrinsic part of cultural studies. This is especially true wherever such studies are an antitheoretical return to extrinsic criticism.

It was in reaction to the supposed dead end of formalist criticism in deconstruction, so the story goes, that in the mid-1980's, or even earlier, there was a swing back to extrinsic criticism, to a new desire to politicize and rehistoricize the study of literature, to make such study socially useful, to make it an instrument of the liberation and intellectual enfranchisement of women, minorities, and the once-colonized in a postcolonial, posttheoretical epoch. "Culture," "history," "context," and "media"; "gender," "class," and "race"; "the self" and "moral agency"; "multilingualism," "multiculturalism," and "globalization"—all have now become in different mixes watchwords of the new historicism, of neo-pragmatism, of cultural studies, of popular culture study, of film and media studies, of women's studies and gender studies, of gay studies, of studies of various "minority discourses," and of studies in "postcolonialism."[43] The list is by no means homogeneous. What we call "cultural studies" today, as I have said, is a heterogeneous and somewhat amorphous space of diverse institutional practices. These practices can hardly be said to have a common methodology, goal, or institutional site. In spite of their diversity, however, all these new projects have an interest in the historical and social contexts of cultural artifacts. They tend to presume the context is explanatory or determining. The author is back in. His or her death was prematurely announced. The subject, subjectivity, the self is back in, along with personal agency, identity politics, responsibility, dialogue, intersubjectivity, and community. A new or renewed interest has developed in biography and autobiography, in popular literature, in film, television, advertising, in visual culture as opposed to linguistic culture, and in the nature and role of "minority discourses" within the hegemonic discourse.

For cultural studies literature is no longer the privileged expression of culture, as it was, say, for Matthew Arnold, or for the United States university until recently. Literature is just one symptom or product of culture among others, to be studied side by side not only with film, video, television, advertising, magazines, and so on, but also with the myriad habits of everyday life that ethnographers investigate in non-Western cultures or in our own. As Alan Liu observes, "literature" is "a category that

means the abyss of traces from which it is impossible to escape, or the ambiguity between mind and word, term and thing, if opacity means touching the alterity of a literature that disperses in a vertiginous writing, then Miller has found an "opacity." But if "linguistic opacity" alludes to a way of understanding the impossibility of going beyond language as "formalism," then the term does not describe Miller's thought. These lines explain it: "This horror is the endpoint of De Quincey's long exploration of his plight after the death of his sister and the withdrawal of God. Opium dreams are no permanent escape from suffering. They only make it possible for him to experience the true nature of his situation. He is an infinitesimal speck of consciousness an infinite distance from its own inner depths. Those depths are the mirror image of the external infinities of space and time, astronomical abysses where God is present only as an ungraspable absence, and where the benign Memnon head has been transmuted into the frightful face in the nebula of Orion" (DG, 71–72).

The Orion myth narrates the story of a failure. First Orion is deceived by King Enopion, who promised to leave his daughter Merope to Orion and instead winds up putting out Orion's eyes. Later on, Orion is murdered by Artemis because of a mistake committed by Apollo. In the end, Artemis puts Orion's image among the stars, eternally persecuted by a scorpion. There is little difference between the crocodile's persecution of De Quincey and the scorpion's persecution of Orion. In both cases, something is lost, specifically the possibility of reaching paradise. Miller verifies the distance between consciousness and its object in De Quincey's texts, or, to put it more conveniently, the existence of a disseminated consciousness ("an infinitesimal speck of consciousness") that does not match its own inner depths because these cannot be centered

has increasingly lost its distinction on the unbounded plane of cultural 'discourse,' 'textuality,' 'information,' 'phrase regimes,' and 'general literature.' " Cultural studies, as Liu puts it, "make literature seem just one of many equipollent registers of culture and multiculture—no more or less splendid, say, than the everyday practices of dressing, walking, cooking, or quilting." [44]

Though people in this new field tend to be defensive about the relation of cultural studies to the social sciences, it seems evident that if cultural studies becomes more dominant in the humanities, the humanities will approach closer to a merger with the social sciences, especially with anthropology. Just as anthropologists have learned much from colleagues in the humanities, so training at the graduate level in protocols of anthropology and sociology would be helpful for those going into cultural studies, for example training in statistical analysis, in the relation between data and generalization, in the university's obligations when human subjects are used, in the need to learn by hook or by crook the languages necessary for the work undertaken, and so on. A traditional Eurocentric literary education is not much help for many of the projects of cultural studies.

Those in cultural studies will be quick to point out that the social sciences in the United States are complicit in many ways with American imperialism, just as Rey Chow observes that the study of non-Western languages and cultures is already institutionalized in the university as another part of that imperialist project.[45] This is true, but anthropology has been struggling to confront this problem since at least Lévi-Strauss's *Tristes Tropiques*. Cultural studies has much to learn from anthropology's procedures and strategies, including those devised to deal with its ingrained Eurocentrism. Moreover, the fact that the social sciences have done cultural studies in the wrong way does not make cultural studies any the less in many of its features a social science. There is no reason to be scandalized by this. The present standard division of the disciplines in United States universities is just one arrangement among others. It could be different. In the People's Republic of China, literary studies are part of the mission of the Chinese Academy of Social Sciences. Disciplinary divisions and affiliations in the humanities and social sciences in United States universities are in any case now rapidly changing.

or identified, and because they are immediately divided and separated in relation to themselves. Gasché's comment that "indeed the dominant misconception of Derrida is based on the confusion by many literary critics of deconstruction with reflexivity" (Gasché, 1986: 5–6) is by no means applicable either to this text by Miller or to the texts of his "deconstructive" period. Contrary to appearances, Miller denies the possibility of self-reflection in De Quincey. From Descartes and German Idealism to Husserl, self-consciousness has had an emancipatory force. To express this in a very schematic way: if the subject or the object knows himself/itself, he/it is free and finds a center for his/its uncertainties.

We can argue, therefore, that in De Quincey's literary space we witness the *deconstruction* of self-consciousness. To follow further what has already been said, what can be the significance of a self-consciousness split in itself, ungraspable, infinitely divided? This consciousness is a movement in which reflexivity is impossible, as impossible as the discovery of Ann after her disappearance or as Orion's escape from the scorpion. To all appearances, what De Quincey anticipates up to a point, and what Miller confirms, is the Nietzschean criticism of reflection and self-consciousness as it had been expounded from Descartes to Hegel. For De Quincey, as for Nietzsche, self-consciousness cannot become a foundation because it is incommensurable with itself and thus not subject to reflexive appropriation. What Miller verifies in De Quincey (a fact that will have important consequences in his future criticism) is not only the Nietzschean hiatus between knowledge, on the one hand, and self-cognition, on the other, but something more radical, which later we shall also find in Nietzsche: the impossibility of any kind of knowledge, if we understand by "knowledge" getting to some form of basis that cannot be split into a thousand more pieces. Naturally, this must lead us to

Comparing Everything

The displacement of language-based theory by cultural studies is evident everywhere in humanities departments of Western universities. One place where it can be clearly seen is in the 1993 "Bernheimer Report" of the American Comparative Literature Association, "Comparative Literature at the Turn of the Century." This report proposes that a new discipline of comparative literature should replace both (1) the old-fashioned, Eurocentric, pre-1975 form of comparative literature that set canonical works from European and United States national literatures side by side to "compare" them, and also (2) the theory-based and reading-based comparative literature of the 1970's and 1980's. For these should be substituted a form of cultural studies that will compare cultures by juxtaposing many kinds of artifacts and forms of behavior—works verbal, visual, and aural, as well as dress, habits of walking, and so on. Comparative literature will now study film, popular literature, popular music, advertising, et al., alongside examples of what has traditionally been thought of as "literature." The Bernheimer Report has accepted so completely one form of the current project of cultural studies that it might be taken as an excellent description of that project, with a slight emphasis on the comparative aspect. Comparison, however, is always a part of cultural studies, even outside comparative literature departments. Here is what the report says about "the space of comparison today":

The space of comparison today involves comparisons between artistic productions usually studied by different disciplines; between various cultural constructions of those disciplines; between Western cultural traditions, both high and popular, and those of non-Western cultures; between the pre- and postcontact cultural productions of colonized peoples; between gender constructions defined as feminine and those defined as masculine, or between sexual orientations defined as straight and those defined as gay; between racial and ethnic modes of signifying; between hermeneutic articulations of meaning and materialist analyses of its modes of production and circulation; and much more. These ways of contextualizing literature in the expanded fields of discourse, culture, ideology, race, and gender are so different from the old models of literary study according to authors, nations, periods, and genres that the term "literature" may no longer adequately describe our object of study.[46]

"The term 'literature' may no longer adequately describe our object of study"! You can say that again. This explosion of the discipline of

conclude that De Quincey's reading of Kant (under the hallucinogenic effects of opium) is obviously a perverse one. With voluntary or involuntary irony, he writes: "Now, then, I was again happy: I now took only 1000 drops of laudanum per day: and what was that? A latter spring had come to close up the season of youth: my brain performed its functions as healthily as ever before: I read Kant again; and again I understood him, or fancied that I did" (De Quincey, 1985: 55).

De Quincey's writing footnotes within other footnotes or a syntax of cloisterings ad infinitum (DG, 56) is another version of this cryptic structure ("the shyest nooks, watery cells and crypts," says De Quincey [1985: 179]) without center that, just when it turns on itself, has already redoubled. There is no possibility of self-reflexivity either on the part of consciousness or on the part of the text. Miller has encountered, not the opacity of language, but its absolute and infinite depth, that is, a prolongation that always refers to the other of itself and in itself. Indeed, De Quincey's metaphor of the palimpsest, applied to the human brain, illustrates this phenomenon quite accurately: "They expelled the writing sufficiently to leave a field for the new manuscript, and yet not sufficiently to make the traces of the elder manuscript irrecoverable for us" (De Quincey, 1985: 141). This passage employs a very common metaphor within the history of philosophy and literary criticism, but here the figure insists on the abyssal character of the written marks. A mark or a trace— and the role this notion plays in De Quincey's discourse is evident— allows us to see past marks and traces, while at the same time the last ones have not erased all those that went before, and the first will not be extinguished by future inscriptions. It is difficult not to relate all this to a particular version of Derridean *écriture*, even though what Miller says

comparative literature, leaving it commissioned to study just about everything human, therefore nothing definite, parallels the similar explosion of English departments. By including everything listed here ("and much more"), the new comparative literature will marginalize literature, to say the least. It will compare everything that can be labeled "culture," in a self-enclosed circling, just as Diogenes Teufelsdröckh, in Carlyle's *Sartor Resartus*, was, in Carlyle's quaint spelling, a professor of *Allerley-Wissenschaft* at the University of Weissnichtwo.[47]

What is disappearing in the new comparative literature, as in many other forms of cultural studies, is the emphasis on reading that was so important a feature in theory of the 1970's and 1980's. In place of an exigent theoretical attention to reading is put an assumption of the "translatability," without significant loss, of cultural meanings from one language to another, one medium to another, one discipline to another. A strenuous rejection of translation was a keystone of the older comparative literature. This was the case even though the rejection of translation was to a considerable degree bogus. Comparative literature as a discipline has tended to express the linguistic imperialism of one or another single language: American English, for example, in the United States, or French in the case of the comparative literature of René Etiemble in Paris. The comparatist knows many languages, but can translate them all into the dominant language he or she uses. This is the case, for example, with René Wellek's "monumental" history of modern criticism.[48] The implicit claim is, "Trust me. I know all these languages and can translate texts from all into English for you. You can forget that they were originally written in German, Russian, Polish, Czech, or whatever. I have given the originals in a subordinate place in case you want to look them up, but problems of untranslatability have largely been circumvented by my own mastery of all these languages. I am the relay station within which all these other languages are turned into English."

For the new cultural studies form of "comparative literature," however, translation has a new meaning. It has to do not so much with finding equivalents in one language for expressions in another but rather with the carrying over of an entire other culture or discipline into one's own. About turning the other into the same I shall say more later. Here is what the Bernheimer report says about translation:

While the necessity and unique benefits of a deep knowledge of foreign languages must continue to be stressed, the old hostilities toward translation should be miti-

about this figure in De Quincey was written before *Of Grammatology* was published, a fact that should make us think about Miller's work.

At what place does the critic of consciousness arrive? De Quincey answers this question when he notes: "What else than a natural and mighty palimpsest is the human brain? Such a palimpsest is my brain; such a palimpsest, O reader! is yours. Everlasting layers of ideas, images, feelings, have fallen upon your brain softly as light. Each succession has seemed to bury all that went before. And yet in reality not one has been extinguished" (De Quincey, 1985: 144). The critic has arrived at the place of a savage intertextuality. Because, indeed, the critic *has arrived* at the text (though for the moment it is impossible to know whether it is a *written* or a *mental* text). For the act of reading to be accomplished, the critic must touch the literary text and what is expressed in it; or, to put it in other words, the critic must touch the "surface" of the text, since, to a certain extent, there is nothing but textual surface (Derrida 1991: 194). For that reason, it is not possible to say about Miller what de Man says, in talking about the problem of identification, concerning Poulet: "Nevertheless, this relationship exists first of all in the form of a radical questioning of the actual, given self, extending to the point of annihilation. And the medium within which and by means of which this questioning can take place can only be language, although Poulet hardly ever designates it explicitly by that name. What was here being described as a relationship between two subjects designates in fact the relationship between a subject and the literary language it produces" (de Man, 1983: 98). This interpretation by de Man turns around Poulet's proposal of a "criticism of consciousness," whereas the proposal we are outlining here obviously requires the different strategies put forward by Miller. For him, it is not

gated. In fact, translation can well be seen as a paradigm for larger problems of understanding and interpretation across different discursive traditions. Comparative Literature, it could be said, aims to explain both what is lost and what is gained in translations between the distinct value systems of different cultures, media, disciplines, and institutions. Moreover, the comparatist should accept the responsibility of locating the particular place and time at which he or she studies these practices. Where do I speak from, and from what tradition(s), or counter-traditions? How do I translate Europe or South America or Africa into a North American cultural reality, or, indeed, North America into another cultural context?[49]

Just by being who and where we are, the Bernheimer report assumes, we translate all the time. Remembering vigilantly my own "subject position" will more or less handle whatever lingering problems of translation may remain.

Comparative Literature in the Age of Multiculturalism, the volume that contains the Bernheimer report and a series of essays in response to it, registers the agony, in the sense of death throes, of the traditional discipline of comparative literature as it melts into being just another form of cultural studies. This change may also help to explain the precipitous decline in foreign language study, especially of European languages. According to Modern Language of America statistics, from 1991 to 1997 United States French departments lost almost 25 percent of previous enrollments, while German lost 27.8 percent. I doubt if this process can be stopped. It constitutes a necessary moment of evolution in the United States university. It testifies to worldwide changes that prohibit a return to older forms of literary study. The old Eurocentric comparative literature, like the traditional separate study of European national literatures, will continue for a time, overlapping with the new work in cultural studies and with the various regional studies disciplines into which cultural studies may and ought to evolve, but its death knell is ringing. The Bernheimer report is an obituary only slightly premature. Nostalgia for the old privileged place of literature is expressed in some of the essays in the volume containing the Bernheimer report, those, for example, by Peter Brooks, Michael Riffaterre, and Jonathan Culler—all older white males, like me. Nostalgia, however, will in this case butter no parsnips.

a question of turning around, but of keeping open the contradiction between "the touching" and "the not touching" of the critic with regard to
the literary text.

The critic of consciousness is right when he talks about the necessity
of identification, as long as that identification is related to evidence the
text gives us. But what that encounter finds is the "other" of the surface,
that is to say, a writing that, because of its depth, cannot be revealed,
just as De Quincey finds himself incapable of reaching his own abysses,
or just as the new writing cannot erase previous writing that, in its turn,
comes back in order, in its dissemination, to get lost again. The process
created by opium foreshadows the double function of touching and not
touching: "The palimpsest of the human brain contains indelibly our
early happiness, and opium dreams bring back this happiness, but also
bring back, and just as necessarily, 'the deep, deep tragedies of infancy,
as when the child's hands were unlinked for ever from his mother's neck,
or his lips for ever from his sister's kisses'" (DG, 63). According to Miller,
"opium" is the word that reveals in De Quincey's text the true process
that the critic or reader intending to reach the literary text has experienced: beyond decontextualizing as reading's condition of possibility, the
critic touches the text (its center, its paradise); he encrypts himself inside
the text. De Quincey's text is the opium of the critic, the medium which
transports the critic to a region where in a given space and time he or she
is no longer himself or herself and from which the critic is transported
to other spaces and other times, places where the critic can inhabit other
personalities, consciousnesses, or words distinct from the critic's own. In
this sense, the critic is what Keats denominates a person of "Genius," but
the critic is furthermore the place of an identification, the identification
of the meaning of a concrete work, of a group of works, or of an age: "Lit-

Abjecting Theory

Though "theory" continues to play a subsidiary role in cultural studies, as in the disciplinary names "film theory" or "queer theory," it has sometimes been superseded, in the Bernheimer report and in many other places, by a return to precritical or pretheoretical assumptions about the way literature, along with other arts, mirrors its historical and social contexts. The rejection of language-based theory on the basis of the false characterization of it I sketched above has, for some scholars, been an essential part of this shift to a new form of extrinsic criticism. Why is this the case? Just why has it seemed necessary to some to "abject" theory, as Tom Cohen puts it,[50] to tell a false story about it in order to clear a space for these new developments? How does this mistake about theory vitiate some work in cultural studies? Deconstruction never rejected the referentiality of language. Far from it. But it saw the inescapable referential vector of language as a problem to be interrogated, not a solution that can be taken for granted. Insofar as cultural studies still depends on the traditional idea of culture as the production in a subject or subjectivity of an identity produced through indoctrination by a nation-state or by a subculture such as an ethnic or gender community, for example, the presumed community of African Americans, Chicanos and Chicanas, gays, or lesbians, it was necessary to resist the questioning by deconstruction of all the key concepts necessary to this idea of culture. These include identity, agency, the homogeneity of a given culture, whether hegemonic or minority, the definition of the individual by his or her participation in a nation or community, the unbreakable tie of a text or any other assemblage of signs to its context. The questioning by theory of these concepts often needed to be sidestepped in order for the project of cultural studies and related new disciplines to get going. These key concepts are glued together by a re-installed referentiality that can no longer afford to be put in question and remain a question. An example is the presumed specular relation between a culture as a whole and any subject identity within it, in another version of the fractal polygon. Hence the need to abject "theory," among some, at least, of those in cultural studies.

The term "cultural studies" itself suggests the degree to which this new discipline has in its own self-definition accepted one side of the traditional mission of the nation-state university that it would transform. That mission, you will remember, was double: (1) to amass and archive critical

erary criticism may focus on a single poem, play, or novel, on the total body of a writer's work, or on the unity made up of all the writings of an age" (DG, ix). Opium, the person of Genius, the critic of consciousness, all find signification in the sense of Hjemslev or Barthes: the meeting of a signifier and a signified, the sign, in short, as logic.

However, opium also designates absolute and radical change: "The waters now changed their character, — from translucent lakes, shining like mirrors, they now became seas and oceans. And now came a tremendous change, which, unfolding itself slowly like a scroll, through many months, promised an abiding torment" (De Quincey, 1985: 72). Through that change, the critic finds himself taken aside from the text, because it loses its unity by way of an infinite divisibility, a characteristic De Quincey will project into the whole of space and time. There is no procedure capable of exerting secure control: logic seemed, at first, to keep itself at a distance from the rhetorical dance, but soon it shows its hidden side, that is, it shows that it also contains an infinitude of echoes. This way, the critic, who intended to encrypt himself inside the literary text and the consciousness expressed in it, recognizes that the text itself is a labyrinthine and profound crypt that constantly confuses him and leaves him at the door. The text he touches has been created for him, just as the door-keeper at the end of Franz Kafka's parable "Before the Law" bellows in the peasant's ear: "No one but you could gain admittance through this door, since this door was intended only for you. I am now going to shut it" (Kafka, 1955: 237). The critic of consciousness, unlike the peasant in Kafka's parable, has touched the surface of the textual door, only to realize that he himself is being encrypted at the door of a crypt into which he can penetrate only on the condition that he disintegrate into infinite specks of consciousness or signification.

knowledge, knowledge both of physical or biological nature and of culture, including literary history as a key form of culture, and (2) to form subjects of the state by inculcating in them the national culture through the process the Germans call *Bildung* and we in the United States have traditionally called a "liberal education." Cultural studies has tended to repudiate the second mission. To fulfill it would be to fall into the hands of the conservatives who want a single canon and the values of a single national culture taught in schools and universities. Those in cultural studies have, however, embraced a form of the first mission by making culture itself an object of study, understanding, and archival storage. The second word in the term "cultural *studies*" expresses this. Rather than being what determines the subject as who he or she is, after a lengthy process of education by the educational state apparatus, culture in all its diversity is now an object of study like any other, like astrophysics and the human genome. It may be less an eagerness to give minority cultures representation in the university than a recognition that cultural studies can easily be co-opted that explains the suspicious ease with which it has been institutionalized in American universities. Turning minority cultures into objects of university study like elemental particles and genomes may be a way of destroying those cultures, not preserving their vitality.

Opposition to cultural studies might be stronger if it were understood that all these diverse cultures are going to be inculcated in students, not just studied. Most celebrations of cultural studies, such as the Bernheimer Report and other essays in that volume, carefully avoid defining the new project as performative or activist. On the contrary, cultural studies is characteristically defined as the gathering of new knowledge, as "studies." This is necessary to gain legitimacy within the research university. Whenever the shift from *Wissenschaft* to *Bildung* has overtly happened for minority or subordinate cultures, the university has tended to respond with violence, by calling in the police, as in the late 1960's. In any case the project of *Bildung* by the university depended on the notion of a nation-state with a single unified culture. It does not seem to make sense to interpellate students to be subjects of many cultures simultaneously. Or it makes sense only through a radical redefinition of culture along the lines of the global consumerist economy that is reshaping the university these days. Culture then becomes a surface matter of fashion and dress. This is just the way the new global capitalism may want it—a whole world full of people in vestigial native costumes wearing blue jeans underneath and

Identification turns contradictory. Unless it can escape being so, it can only accede to the endless play of the signifying scattering: "De Quincey can never stop. All his works are fragments, full of unfilled gaps, failures in scale (in which one part of the paper is in far greater detail than other parts), or incomplete at the end, either with a huddled conclusion, or with no conclusion at all, a meander which ends in the air" (DG, 55–56). This is precisely the problem of the critic placed before a text. Strictly speaking, he can never stop either his reading or his commentary. To inhabit otherness means, therefore, to change constantly without the possibility of attaining knowledge, to remain in the "negative capability" Keats talks about, in uncertainties, mysteries, doubts. The critic, Miller in this case, reads De Quincey and develops a metacommentary which points out the impossibility of accomplishing an act of signification in which expression and content meet. Or, to put it another way, the critic has found a rhetoric dancing laterally between the Man of Genius, without self-identity, and the Man of Power, with a specific personality. It is not gratuitous that Miller writes (regarding both De Quincey and himself): "The result of all these modes of inexhaustibility is that no essay of De Quincey's can be satisfactorily finished" (DG, 55). Suddenly the critic has seen himself introduced inside De Quincey's Funes-like mind. This means he has been projected into a labyrinthine space and time in which the search for similarities becomes, thanks to an interminable self-division, Sisyphean.

　　Miller's text shows itself to be ironic because it moves between two poles impossible to reconcile. On the one hand, it states—in the classical manner of an assertion—that the critic's task must be to identify with the subjectivity expressed in the words of the text (this is what we have

listening to transistor radios. This is sometimes called "glocalization." The question is how to live within a multicultural situation without succumbing to this superficiality.

The goals of the new developments—cultural studies, women's studies, studies in various minority discourses, and so on—are laudable. Who could oppose giving a voice to the heretofore voiceless, to women and minorities, to those defined as gays and lesbians, to the economically disadvantaged? Who could oppose giving a place in the university to all the ethnic varieties that characterize both our national society and the new global society that is more omnipresent every day?[51] Who could oppose using such transformation of the university to help create the democracy to come, that horizon of all our political and intellectual effort? Who could oppose the careful study of popular culture and of the media—television, video, cinema—that shape our minds and behavior far more than books do these days? A fundamental part of scholarship in cultural studies has been descriptive and archival. Works in different media and from different cultures, works by women and minorities, need to be identified, categorized, edited, republished, brought into the open, made available in the university and to the general public so they can be effective there. This work is essential and necessary. This present book is, in its own small way, in part an effort in cultural studies, since historical investigation of literary study's institutionalization has been an important aspect of cultural studies, as in books and articles already mentioned above. I am fearful, however, that the efforts of cultural studies, the desire of those in that field to change the university and through that to help create a more just society, may be thwarted by features in what they do that will allow cultural studies to be recuperated by conservative forces within the university.

Putting neglected works in the classroom, in the curriculum, in books, articles, conferences, and study groups is only the beginning of the work. Knowledge is not enough. These works must be put to work. Only what might be called a materialist reading will accomplish that. "Materialist" here does not mean displacing attention from the work to its historical context, but attention to the materiality of the work's inscription in its original language. Archiving multiculturalism, expanding the curriculum to include works from all over the world hitherto little read in United States universities, may even, as I have suggested, negate the power such works have to effect cultural change. The university has a formidable

been denominating the *code of touching*). On the other hand, the type of language he uses to prove the former assertion leads him to recognize that this identification means throwing oneself into an abyss of particles that cannot be fixed (what we have called the *code of not touching*). These two textual codes or strata do not operate separately, but one leads to the other and vice versa. To choose an image familiar to Miller himself, it would be as if the semic notion of *symbol*, as the Greeks understood it (as half a given object which joins together with the other half in order to seal a commitment), were to lead to an anasemic notion of *symbol* in which the other half remains irrevocably lost forever ("Derrida's Topographies," T: 306–7). The semic or code of contact leads to the anasemic or code of not touching, and vice versa. What happens within Miller's discourse is equivalent to what happens between his text and De Quincey's. The codes of touching and not touching represent what happens in the act of reading: what literary criticism calls a second language or metatext belongs to the same sphere as the first language or text. The metatext or second language cannot take place in some supposed outside of textuality, given that it too is inscribed in a concrete language and tradition. In this sense, the metatext identifies with and participates in the text on which it comments.

At the same time, the metatextuality, being a second language, experiences—as do those of Miller and De Quincey—all the possible modes of inexhaustibility of the text as first language. Critical language never comes into contact with the text as a delimiting object. In tropological terms, we could say that a metaphorical model of similitude, equivalence, and participation leads to an antithetical model of difference and exclusion, and vice versa. The following question is not idle. What exactly does Miller do in this essay or in the rest of *The Disappearance of*

power of neutralization. I shall suggest in more detail later how this might be resisted.

Literature in Cyberspace

Why did the shift to cultural studies from language-based theory begin when it did, around 1980? The reorientation was no doubt overdetermined and even contradictory. Many factors contributed to it, such as the Vietnam War, the student movement in the 1960's, and the civil rights movement. Those creating cultural studies had been decisively marked by those events. Moreover, literature in the old-fashioned sense of canonical master works, the evidence suggests, plays a smaller and smaller role in the emerging global multiculture. It is natural that young scholars should not wish to spend their time on something that seems increasingly marginal. The large numbers of women and minority scholars who now do graduate work in the humanities or have joined humanities faculties have certainly contributed much to the change. Such people are unable or unwilling to draw their sense of themselves from works in the old white male canon read in the old way. It is natural that they should look elsewhere to find works that will help them establish a sense of cultural identity, just as it is natural that sooner or later American citizens in general will come to recognize that English literature is the literature of a foreign country, a literature no doubt deeply linked to our own self-development, but foreign nevertheless. As Wallace Stevens puts this in the "Adagia": "Nothing could be more inappropriate to American literature than its English source since the Americans are not British in sensibility." [52]

A fear or resentment of literature's ungovernable force may also operate to marginalize literature in cultural studies. This may work in a double way to generate a double bind. On the one hand, if literary works—for example, English novels from Defoe to Forster—are assumed to be among the most powerful expressions of capitalism, patriarchy, and imperialism, then reading English literature might contaminate the reader with the ideology he or she is trying to contest. Popular literature, advertising, subliterary pamphlets, and so on, toward which the scholar can safely condescend, might be less dangerous to read. No one today is likely to take seriously the Renaissance writings about hermaphroditism Stephen Greenblatt discusses in one of his essays,[53] whereas Shakespeare is a writer of such power that his complicity in Jacobean ideologies of gender difference, social hier-

God? We hazard the following hypothesis: by having set forth in the preface the problem of identification and by having explored that problem by way of an example, namely, De Quincey's textuality, Miller literally and allegorically (as does De Quincey) develops the metatheoretical problem of reading. Probably Miller's interest (his "subject matter," as I said at the beginning) lies not so much in De Quincey, Browning, Brönte, and the disappearance of God as in what those authors and that subject matter allegorically represent. This is the enigma of reading as enigma or, what is the same, the enigma of literature as an alterity absolutely other: "Only in a confrontation of the incomprehensible otherness of another person can I bring into the open my own hidden otherness" (FVF, 45).

If this is so, Loesberg's statements (Loesberg, 1991: 106, 116) that neither Derrida nor de Man is truly interested in reading literary works because they use them to delineate the theoretical, philosophical, or ideological problems of reading would apply equally to Miller. Perhaps he is also using De Quincey, for instance, to understand the theoretical or metatheoretical problem of reading. He is not basically doing any type of practical criticism. What can one say about this? Is it feasible to establish a sharp difference between practical criticism and theoretical interests, no matter whether they be philosophical, scientific, political, psychoanalytic, and so forth? To begin with, such a difference only makes sense if we start from a conception in which doctrine and learning are installed in watertight compartments. It is true that, pragmatically, each doctrine knows its limits and when it is crossing a border. But this is quite a different thing from giving them ontological limits.

If Loesberg's (1991) or Gasché's (1986) claims were valid, then we would be forced to accomplish two movements of thought:

archy, and nascent English imperialism might even today be "catching." On the other hand (this is the double bind), the literary theory against which some younger scholars have "revolted" has had as one of its lessons the complexity and individuality of literary works,[54] their heterogeneity and polyvalence, the way they are other to the culture that surrounds them. If this is true, it endangers the presumption that the products of a given culture can be fully explained by the ideology of their circumambient contexts. Again, but for a different reason, reading "canonical" literature may endanger the project of cultural studies. It might be better to leave literature alone, or to devote much effort, as cultural studies has done, to disqualifying canonical works by showing that they are the expression of some malign aspect of the hegemonic culture that is being contested. The danger is that the power such works have might inadvertently seep through and be transmitted even by way of the effort cultural studies or new historical studies makes to disempower them through critique. D. A. Miller's putdown of Trollope in *The Novel and the Police* might lead someone to read Trollope and be influenced by that author's view of things, even though this is the opposite of the effect Miller apparently intends.

Cultural studies is intertwined in the immense network of economic, ideological, and political forces within which the university is embedded today. Moreover, cultural studies itself, as I have said, cannot be justly summarized under a single set of conceptual presuppositions. Its relation to the language-oriented theory that preceded it is particularly complex and diverse. One major force, however, leading to the rise of a cultural studies that tends to marginalize literature has been the growing impact of new communication technologies. Technology has been changing society throughout the nineteenth and twentieth centuries. No one doubts that. The rate of change, however, has much accelerated in recent years with the advent of the electronic age. The younger United States scholars who have turned to cultural studies are the first generation of university teachers and critics brought up with television and with new forms of commercialized popular music. Many of them as children and teenagers spent as much time watching television or listening to popular music as they did reading books. I do not say these activities are bad. They are just different. Reading books can be bad for you, as Flaubert's Emma Bovary and Conrad's Lord Jim show. The critics of this new generation have been to a considerable degree formed by a new visual and aural culture. "Culture" has a somewhat new meaning now. It names in part the media component of a global

1. To reduce the literary text to its aesthetic function without recognizing other types of function within it, for instance, theoretical, philosophical, or deconstructive. Applied to de Man, this movement would mean the following. De Man bases his reading of Rousseau's *Julie* on the presupposition that "philosophers of science like Bachelard or Wittgenstein are notoriously dependent on the aberrations of the poets" (de Man, 1979: 17) and affirms that "the paradigm for all texts consists of a figure (or system of figures) and its deconstruction. . . . Allegorical narratives tell the story of the failure to read whereas tropological narratives, such as the *Second Discourse*, tell the story of the failure to denominate" (de Man, 1979: 205). Yet we must not believe him, since if the literary text were theoretically concerned about reading, then it would be no longer literary and would become a philosophical discourse that uses the literary mode to delineate its theoretical, philosophical, or ideological concerns. That is to say, neither Rousseau, nor Proust, nor Rilke, nor Nietzsche should be considered literary authors, but theoreticians. This would mean denying that literary texts involve a knowledge (however aberrant it is), as well as denying that they have allegorical concerns in relation to reading as a theoretical question. In other words, by applying Gasché's rule we would say that no literary text is interested in reading. Neither Cervantes, nor Schlegel, nor Dante, nor Wallace Stevens put in their texts anything more than an aesthetic function of beauty. Gasché and Loesberg should have taken into account the long history of this problem, but it suffices to read de Man (or the Jena Romantics) to recognize that every literary text entails in one way or another both an aesthetic force and a theoretical force, two components that are practically indissoluble and that are independent of the type of relation the two forces have between themselves.

consumerist economy. The new media include of course some counter-hegemonic elements. This new electronic culture is fast replacing the culture of the book. It is not surprising that these young scholars should wish to study what has largely made them what they are, in spite of their participation in the culture of the book. Clear evidence of literature's weakening force in the United States is the way many young scholars trained in literary study should now feel so great a call to study popular culture that they more or less abandon canonical literature or even literature in toto.

However we might wish it were not the case, the sad fact is that literature in the old-fashioned sense is playing a smaller and smaller role worldwide in the new globalized cultures. This fact is particularly distressing to me, since I have already spent fifty years in the study of literature and plan to go on studying it. It is painful to have a lifelong vocation for something that has diminishing importance. Nevertheless, the facts must be faced. If someone is watching television, or a movie on VCR, or surfing on the Internet, he or she cannot at the same time be reading Shakespeare or Emily Dickinson, though some schoolchildren and even some university students claim to be able to do both at once. All the statistics show that more and more people are spending more and more time watching television and cinema. Now there has been a rapid shift even from those to the computer screen. The cultural function once served, for example in nineteenth-century England, by novels is now being served by movies, by popular music, and by computer games. There may be nothing intrinsically wrong with this, unless you happen to have, as I do, a big investment in the old printed-book culture. Though many works of literature are available on line, ready to be downloaded into anyone's computer, I believe relatively few people are using that wonderful new resource. Certainly the new "digital young" Jon Katz describes, in an essay in *Wired*, are not using the Internet to get access to Shakespeare. One strong point made by Katz about the citizens or "netizens" of the new Digital Nation is their commitment to popular culture and their disdain for those who still live outside it and want to lecture them about the shallowness of popular music, cinema, etc.

"The digital young," says Katz, "share a passion for popular culture —perhaps their most common shared value, and the one most misperceived and mishandled by politicians and journalists. On Monday mornings when they saunter into work, they are much more likely to be talking about the movies they saw over the weekend than about Washington's issue

It was Derrida who pointed out the existence of literary texts that have a formalizing power higher than some explicitly theoretical discourses.

2. To reduce literary-critical discourse to a mere practical, descriptive, or prescriptive function without theoretical or philosophical scope. Or, at the other extreme, to reduce each philosophical text to a discourse cloistered in its own lucubrations without contact with empirico-textual reality. Quoting and paraphrasing de Man again, I would say that the first would be a kind of resistance to theory, and the second a kind of resistance to practice. In both cases, the error consists in thinking that either theory or practice can occur without the other. Let me choose two examples: Barthes, in *S/Z* (1974), arbitrarily divides Balzac's narrative into a series of short fragments in which he identifies five types of codes. Once he arrives at section 331 ("— *'What are you afraid of?' asked Vitagliani, the company's most famous singer. 'Go ahead; you need fear no rivals here'* "), Barthes breaks up Vitagliani's discourse, focusing on the expression "You have no rival." He writes: "The tenor says: *'You have no rival,'* because: (1) you are loved (Sarrasine's understanding); (2) you are wooing a castrato (understanding of the accomplices and perhaps, already, of the reader). According to the first understanding, there is a snare; according to the second, a revelation. The braid of the two understandings creates an equivocation. And in fact the equivocation results from the two voices, received on an equal basis: there is an interference of two lines of destination" (Barthes, 1974: 144–45).

Is this an example of practical criticism? The answer is strongly affirmative, since Barthes analyzes in a fragment the particular significative functioning of the whole text. Any reader of Barthes would have already recognized the motif of "castration" around which, according to the

of the week [or, I might add, about what a wonderful poem Milton's *Paradise Lost* is]. Music, movies, magazines, some television shows, and some books are elementally important to them—not merely forms of entertainment but means of identity."[55] Poems and novels used to be means of identity. Now it is the latest rap group. "As much as anything else," Katz continues, "the reflexive contempt for popular culture shared by so many elders of journalism and politics has alienated this group, causing its members to view the world in two basic categories: those who get it, and those who don't. For much of their lives these young people have been branded as ignorant, their culture malignant. The political leaders and pundits [one might add: the educators] who malign them haven't begun to grasp how destructive these perpetual assaults have been, how huge a cultural gap they've created" (ibid.). The colophon page of *Wired* not only lists the "Zines [that is, magazines] of Choice," but also "music that helped get this magazine out." The April 1997 issue of the latter lists, among others, Matthew Sweet, *100% Fun*; Arvo Pärt, *De Profundis Clamavi, Psalm 130*; Melvins, *Interstellar Overdrive*; Steven Jesse Bernstein, *Prison*; *Miami Vice*; Mari Boine, *Radiant Warmth*. What does this have to do with globalization? This popular culture is disseminated all over the world as films, tapes, CDs, radio broadcasts, and now through the Internet as the latter becomes more and more a multimedia operation. This media culture has immense power to drown out the quiet voice of the fading book culture and also to drown out the specificities of local cultures everywhere, though these are often deliberately appealed to and encouraged by global media corporations in their search for "niche" local markets. This is one thing meant by "glocalization."

At the same time the new communication technologies are rapidly transforming the way research and teaching are carried on in the humanities. These transformations have accompanied and to some degree brought about the replacement of the Humboldtian university by the new technologized, transnational university that serves the global economy. This new kind of university is an important feature of the weakening of the nation-state. Some of the claims for the revolutionary effect of computers and the Internet on the humanities have been exaggerated or wrongly formulated. Seen from a certain perspective, a computer, even one connected by modem or Ethernet to the World Wide Web, is, as many people would claim, no more than a glorified typewriter. One should not, however, underestimate the changes this glorification makes, for example, the

French critic, all *Sarrasine* is organized. We are ourselves immersed in the "infinite paradigm of difference" of this particular text. Is this an instance of theory that gives an example in order to delineate its own concerns about the methodologies of textual analysis? No doubt, because it would be impossible to understand why Barthes says what he says about the expression "*You have no rival*" if we did not take into account the following: (1) his distance from structuralist positions and thus from a metatheory that intends to equalize texts "under the scrutiny of an in-different science" (Barthes, 1974: 3); (2) his expanding theory; and (3) the necessity of cutting up the original signifier into a series of brief fragments he proposes to call *lexias* (Barthes, 1974: 13), a fact that should not imply any methodological responsibility. While anyone is reading Barthes's essay, he or she is reproducing his or her own theoretical and metatheoretical concerns. However, in order to expound his or her own (this adjective, strictly speaking, should mean a plurality of codes or a "perspective of quotations") theoretical and metatheoretical concerns, he or she needs at all costs and as an unavoidable step to read a text.

My second example has to do with de Man. In the last chapter of *Allegories of Reading*, entitled "Excuses (*Confessions*)," de Man chooses to discuss the episode in which Rousseau confesses the theft of the pink ribbon. Though Rousseau does not want to exculpate himself, he pleads the fact of being madly in love with Marian as the only reason for his misdemeanor. De Man perceives an anacoluthon, however, in that architectonic construction. The sentence "Je m'excusai sur le premier objet qui s'offrit" (I excused myself on the first object that offered itself) is "a foreign element that disrupts the meaning, the readability of the apologetic discourse, and reopens what the excuse seemed to have closed off. How

new ease of revision, the facility with which things can be added, deleted, or moved from one place to another in a computer file as opposed to a typed manuscript. Such ease gradually encourages the adept in computer composition to think of what he or she writes as never being in quite finished form. Whatever is printed is always just one stage in a potentially endless process of revision, deletion, addition, and rearrangement. This present book is an example of that. It has been more or less continuously revised, augmented, reduced, and rearranged over a four-year period. The revision has in part been necessitated by changes in the university and its social context just during the years since I began writing this book, not to speak of changes in my own ideas. Parts of the book have been given as lectures or published in many different overlapping forms all over the world, including publication on the Internet. A hypertext version of *Black Holes* might contain links to all those other previously distributed parts, since they often differ significantly from the final version here. A hypertext version might also include links to relevant parts, in digitized form, of the material referred to in footnotes.

Nothing, however, prevents using the computer and the Internet for quite conventional work in humanities research or teaching. Certain programs, "hypertext" and multimedia though they may be, encourage traditional notions about the relation of a work to its author and to its historical and cultural contexts. The Brown University IRIS (Institute for Research in Information and Scholarship) project in Victorian literature is to some degree an example of that. It presumes that a Victorian work like Tennyson's "The Lady of Shallott" is to be understood by more or less traditional placement of the poem in its socio-economic and biographical context, by reference, for example, to the building of canals in England at the time.[56] The apparent freedom for the student to "browse" among various "links" may hide the imposition of predetermined connections. These may reinforce powerful ideological assumptions about the causal force of historical context on literary works. It depends on what links have been set up or on the user's inventiveness in creating new ones. Hypertext can also be a powerful way to deploy what Kenneth Burke called "perspective by incongruity," that is, a way to break up conventional assumptions about explanatory context.

Hypertexts of whatever sort, moreover, are powerful solvents of the assumption that proper meaning fits into the traditional printed book's linear continuity. On the one hand, the significance of the computer, as

are we to understand the implications of this sentence and what does it do to the very idea of understanding which we found to be so intimately bound up with and dependent upon the performative function itself?" (de Man, 1979: 289–90). Is this a case of practical criticism? According to a tradition of commentators going back to Quintilian, a rhetorical analysis of a text is a way of doing criticism of the text in question. De Man is showing us the way in which the signification of this work by Rousseau is generated. Although the results are different, what de Man does is not distinct from what Barthes called literary theory in opposition to literary criticism, that is to say, not to give a particular sense but to analyze the conditions under which sense is possible. In both cases, however, it is necessary to do practical criticism.

Is de Man's essay on Rousseau a text that delineates its own theoretical and metatheoretical concerns? Yes, because such concerns are implicit in the way he does practical criticism. In order to understand what de Man does, it is essential to take into account: (1) his notions of grammar and rhetoric; (2) his idea that the literary text entails self-knowledge and, for this reason, its own self-deconstruction; (3) his insistence on the fact that the literary text "prefigures" its readings and illustrates in itself certain concrete linguistic phenomena. Therefore de Man can assert: "The interest of Rousseau's text is that it explicitly functions performatively as well as cognitively, and thus gives indications about the structure of performative rhetoric" (de Man, 1979: 282). It happens in the same way as in Barthes: in order to read, it is essential to develop the appropriate theoretical and metatheoretical concerns; in order to set forth those concerns, it is necessary to read the text and to do practical criticism.

It follows that, far from being able to distinguish between *use* and

of the typewriter, the linotype machine, or any other technological device, depends on what use is made of it. On the other hand, neither the
computer nor the typewriter nor the linotype machine is just one technological device among others. Each belongs to the special class of prostheses
to the hand, voice, ears, and eyes in the generation, projection, reception,
and exchange of signs. As one such device, the computer is quite different
from the typewriter. It imposes its own new matrix on the process of sign
generation, reception, and exchange. It would be a mistake to minimize
the changes this will make in the way humanists do research and teaching and in the intellectual space within which they are rapidly coming to
live. Just what are these changes? They are hard to define and understand,
partly because we are in the midst of them. The digital revolution now
going on, however, is clearly as radical and as irreversible as the move from
a manuscript to a print culture. E-mail, faxes, computerized library catalogues, composition on the computer rather than in longhand or on the
typewriter, the increasing use of computers and networks in instruction,
often as a commercial venture, the availability online of more and more
material, the move from linear print media to multimedia hypertext, on-
line publishing of articles and monographs that is altering the way research
results are disseminated—all these are rapidly and irrevocably transforming the way teachers and students of literature (and of other disciplines)
do their work.

The most dramatic and spectral effect, however, is the hardest to see,
understand, and gauge. This is the change effected in the objects of our
study by their digitizing. What is the difference between reading Henry
James's *The Golden Bowl* in a printed copy and as a cybertext downloaded
into my desktop or laptop? At first there might seem to be little difference
beyond the not unimportant one of the ability to "search," extract from,
and otherwise manipulate the cybertext version. I claim, on the contrary,
that the difference is radical and profound, no less than a transformation
of the literary object's mode of existence. Understanding, even in a preliminary way, this change may help to see why the information model does
not apply to all those literary works that are circulating through cyberspace at the speed of light, located everywhere and nowhere as so many
black holes in the presumed transparency of information networks. Much
is made these days of problems of security on the Internet and of the need
for strong cryptography as against the government's desire to have the keys
to all encrypting programs. Literary works continue to hide their secrets,

interpretation of a text, as Richard Rorty and Umberto Eco do, literary criticism is a type of discourse that both interprets and uses literary texts. Indeed, in order to use a text—that is to say, in order to bring into the open its theoretical, philosophical, political, and other concerns—one must interpret it, that is, read it. And in order to interpret a text, or, to put it another way, do practical criticism, one must use that text to clarify the theoretical or metatheoretical questions it raises. Use and interpretation are two activities so intimately bound up with one another that we can never be completely sure whether we are dealing with use or dealing with interpretation. When the narrator of Borges's "Pierre Menard, Author of Don Quixote" compares Menard's Quixote with that of Cervantes and notices that "the text of Cervantes and that of Menard are verbally identical, but the second is almost infinitely richer" (Borges, 1962: 52), he is doing two things (not easily distinguished, as has already been said). He *uses* Cervantes' text in order to pose the theoretical problem of reading in relation to the delicate matter of decontextualizing, and he *interprets* it, since he establishes the encyclopedic contents of both texts (history, the truth, rhetorical eulogy, etc.). He also sums up a stylistic analysis: "Equally vivid is the contrast in styles" (Borges, 1962: 53).

This use and interpretation are not free from irony. If the reader takes into account the ninth chapter of Don Quixote, he will notice in what sense the expression "ingenious layman" is ironical. Contrary to Eco, Borges would hardly maintain that "the sememe presupposes the co-text and the text is nothing else but the expansion of the sememe" (Eco, 1979b: 25), since this presupposes the existence of a textual programming projected into the figure of the Model Reader. Borges is closer to Miller than to Eco. He does not see in the text a programming of

however, secrets as dark as death, even if they are totally exposed and made public, universally available all over the world to anyone with a computer, a modem, and a service provider. Paradoxically, the new digitized existence only makes more evident, if we have eyes to see it, eyes to see what cannot be seen, what was perhaps more hidden in print versions, that is, the way literary works hide what I call black holes.

Walter Benjamin recognized that new media are radically transformative. He applied this insight to the analysis of photography and cinema under the name "the age of technical reproducibility." Print, too, as we perhaps tend to forget, is also a form of technical reproducibility, but the effects of reproducibility are, it may be, more evident in the instantaneous flash of the camera shutter that produces a negative, giving a spectral, endlessly repeatable life to what is already dead in the instant it is preserved. What is photographed is killed and given an indefinite afterlife of survival in the act of clicking that camera shutter. Eduardo Cadava, in a brilliant book on Benjamin and photography, *Words of Light*, has identified the political and social implications of photography for Benjamin. Speaking of Benjamin's figure of a "caesura in the movement of thought" in the "Theses on the Concept of History," Cadava says, "This caesura—whose force of immobilization not only gives way to the appearance of an image but also intervenes in the linearity of history and politics—can be understood in relation to what we might call the photograph's Medusa effect."[57] Our time of computers, of an unimaginable chaos of digitized images and texts accessible on the Internet, is the age of technological reproducibility with a vengeance, that age squared or cubed, hyperbolically or exponentially expanded and so transformed, taken beyond a threshold or limit of *technischen Reproduzierbarkeit*. Digitizing, which melts down the distinction between image and text, produces image/texts that are much more fleeting and ubiquitous than a photograph. They bring even more into the open the other side of Benjamin's sense of the photograph as instantaneous: its way of giving a ghostly and spectral persistence, everywhere and nowhere, a life after death to what has been "shot." Literature has always had a strange connection to ghosts, to death, and to survival after death, but this has tended to be sidestepped in much literary study. To read *The Golden Bowl* is to encounter the traces of James's dictating voice, a little like Tennyson's voice or Browning's on one of those primitive phonograph records, voices that truly sound as if they were coming from the grave, voices of the shuttle weaving a shroud. The new digitized mode of exis-

future readings or interpretations, but quite the opposite. He sees a de-programming, as a result of the distinct rearrangement of the textuality in a particular period. For this reason, when Eco writes:

Naturally, a text can also be read as an uncommitted stimulus for a personal hal-lucinatory experience, cutting out levels of meaning, placing upon the expression "aberrant" codes. As Borges once suggested, why not read the Odyssey as writ-ten after the *Aeneid* or the *Imitation of Christ* as written by Céline? . . . I think, however, that it is possible to distinguish between the free interpretative choices elicited by a purposeful strategy of openness and the freedom taken by a reader with a text assumed as a mere stimulus. (Eco, 1979b: 40)

It is not difficult to observe that he is using Borges's text to delineate his theoretical and metatheoretical concerns about interpretation.

If we read (now in order to *interpret*) the last paragraph of "Pierre Menard, Author of Don Quixote," we realize that Borges, by referring to the possibility of attributing *The Imitation of Christ* to James Joyce, is not talking about taking a text "as an uncommitted stimulus for a personal hallucinatory experience," but purely and simply about reading, about what happens when *in fact* one reads. Here is the fragment: "Menard (perhaps without wishing to) has enriched, by means of a new technique, the hesitant and rudimentary art of reading: the technique is one of delib-erate anachronism and erroneous attributions" (Borges, 1962: 54). Can one infer from this that Borges proposes both a correct and an incor-rect reading, or does he mean that reading responds to the technique of anachronism? Nowhere is the first possibility considered. Instead, the second possibility is present explicitly: reading is the technique of anach-ronism. Here lies the force of this "fiction." Although it may seem that

tence for literary works in databases and on the Internet turns those works into an innumerable, murmurous swarm of ghosts that return and can return again at our command, like the shades from the underworld that rise for Ulysses in Book Eleven of *The Odyssey*, or like the recorded sounds of Glenn Gould playing Bach's *The Well-Tempered Clavier* back in the 1960's, which I am listening to on my computer at this moment. (I leave it to you to establish the referent of "at this moment" and "I" in that sentence.)

My claim is that this new digitized existence will change literature and literary study in manifold and as yet unforeseen ways. I would go so far as to say that it will transform, is already transforming, the concept of literature or of literarity, killing literature and giving it a new existence as the survivor of itself. Students of literature will and should remain as the guardians and surviving witnesses of previous historical epochs, just as classicists bear witness to what was the nature and function of Greek tragedy within a vanished classical culture. Literature as we know it, as Derrida has argued, is inextricably associated with democracy, that is, with freedom of speech, the freedom to say or to write anything and everything (never completely obtained, of course). Even the concept of free speech, I would add, is being changed by the electronic revolution. "Literature" is also, I further claim, concomitant with industrialization prior to the electronic revolution, with the age, now coming to an end, of the printed book, and with Cartesian and post-Cartesian conceptions of selfhood, along with associated notions of representation and of "reality." All these are intertwined and mutually self-sustaining factors. Literature as a distinctive way to use language arises not from any special way of speaking or writing, but from the possibility of taking any piece of language whatsoever as fictional or, on the other hand, as possibly truthtelling, as referential in the ordinary sense. This "taking" happens according to complex historically determined conventions, codes, and protocols. That neat opposition between fiction and truth telling is a feature of print culture. In the digitized world of the Internet the distinction breaks down or is transformed, just as it has already been transformed by television. On television, advertising cannot always be distinguished from news, and wars like Somalia and the Gulf War are presented as a media spectacles, not all that different from war movies.

Let me try to specify the difference between literature in print form and literature in cyberspace with an example. I am writing this in Deer Isle, Maine,[58] far from any research library, but I have a computer connection through the World Wide Web to the Internet by way of programs

there are both a correct and an incorrect reading, the latter takes place starting from the literal repetition of the text that is read. Could there be a more radical challenge to correct reading?

The reader recognizes the subtlety of this Borgesian narration when he or she realizes that even the literal interpretation of the narrator, when he establishes content, is not free from doubt. The interpreter repeats, emphasizes, and comments: "History, *mother* of truth; the idea is astounding" (Borges, 1962: 53). But can we take for granted that in the ninth chapter of the first part of *Don Quixote* Cervantes is talking purely and simply about truth and its connection with history? It does not seem probable, since, shortly before, the narrator has written: "If any objection can be made against the truth of this history [he is referring to the Arabic narration that will be translated into Spanish], it can only be that its narrator was an Arab—men of that nation being ready liars" (Cervantes, 1950: 78). The context could not be more telling. Don Quixote's history was interrupted, and the narrator finds some manuscripts containing the continuation in Arabic. Cervantes brings into play the problem of the relation author–translation–truth. This problem does not, of course, allow the reduction of reading to reading the history that is the mother of truth. Borges ironically suggests that there is no interpretation that does not imply keeping semiosis active. Borges's theoretical force opposes Eco's. Furthermore, Borges's theoretical force deconstructs Eco's theory even before Eco himself speaks, since Borges foresees it. Eco uses the Borgesian narrative as an example of his own theory, however, by attributing to Borges intentions he never had. So, in order to explain to us the difference between the use and the interpretation of a text, Eco finds himself

called Turbogopher, Mosaic, and MacWeb, a modem in my Macintosh Powerbook, and a courtesy connection to the Internet through Colby College. The World Wide Web is a hypertext-based system for finding and acquiring access to Internet resources. "Internet" is the name for the whole international assembly of interconnected databases.

I have been reading, as part of a long-term project, Marcel Proust's *A la recherche du temps perdu*. One of the resources available to anyone with an academic connection to the Internet is the huge database of works in French literature and philosophy called ARTFL, the acronym of "American and French Research on the Treasury of the French Language." The URL is http://humanities.uchicago.edu/ARTFL/ARTFL.html. This is a cooperative project of the University of Chicago and the Institut National de la Langue Française of the Centre National de la Recherche Scientifique. It is not possible to "download" the works in this database, but complex Boolean word searches can be made in any work or works included in it. You may ask for all the examples of a given word or a given word in proximity to another word, and so on. Among the works in ARTFL is the first Pléiade edition of Proust's *Recherche* (1954). It is possible, for example, to ask for all the examples of the word *soleil* ("sun") in one or another or in all of the separate sections of Proust's *Recherche*. These will appear on the screen with up to three hundred words of surrounding context. They can then be saved in your computer and manipulated in any way you wish. A mouseclick on the word "page" will give you the full page on which the word appears. A search of the section of the *Recherche* called *La fugitive* produces thirty-three "hits," that is, thirty-three examples of the word *soleil* in context. What you do with these passages is entirely up to you, but ARTFL puts an enormous treasure of French works at your fingertips. My example is not fortuitous, since *Black Holes* ends with a discussion of Proust's *Recherche*, and that in turn ends with an analysis of two solar passages in *La fugitive*. How does having this search capability change the way I read *A la recherche du temps perdu*? I shall return later to this question.

I am also re-reading here on Deer Isle a novel by Anthony Trollope, *Ayala's Angel* (1881). I brought with me my old copy of the Oxford World's Classics reprint of this novel. This reprint was originally published in 1929 and reissued several times thereafter. My copy is dated 1960. It was part of a more or less comprehensive edition of Trollope's novels. These were included over fifty years ago in the World's Classics series (in which *Ayala's*

caught in the universal web of all literary criticism or theory: in using and interpreting a text, one cannot always delimit clearly what one is doing. One thing is certain: Eco, among other things, is making use of a text to explain to us the difference between use and interpretation. It follows that the opposition between use and interpretation is a use—and not an interpretation—required by the theory of the Model Reader. Strange entanglement.

After this brief interruption, I can answer the question that generated it: What does Miller do in his essay on De Quincey and in the rest of *The Disappearance of God*? On the one hand, he brings into the open the problem of reading by means of a possible identification with the consciousness or subjectivity expressed in the words of the text. On the other hand, he interprets De Quincey from the viewpoint of a literature that attends the loss of a fundamental center: God. As we have seen, these two vectors conflict. The desired identification (the one) has led to a loss of contact (to a "bringing into the open" of the other). As Miller puts it: "The death of De Quincey's sister has transformed the one into the other" (DG, 22). The unity has ended up in fragmentation: "What was an indissoluble unity has been fragmented" (DG, 22). At first this seems to have consequences going from the psychological or from the inner world of the author to the textual or external world: "The representation of De Quincey's inner world is the fourteen and more volumes of his collected work" (DG, 27). In all this collected work one does not find any type of architectonic building, or orientation, or structuring around a beginning, a middle, and an end. On the contrary, his texts are digressive, ambiguous ("any direction is both right and wrong"; DG, 29), nonstructured, and without any central point of reference. In addition, they break

Angel was number 342), long before personal computers were invented. A note at the end of the book tells me it was "set in Great Britain at the University Press, Oxford, and Printed by J. W. Arrowsmith Ltd, Bristol." It cost "10s 6d. net in U.K. only," and I bought it in London in the late 1960's. I first read the novel in this edition. It is a quasi-sacred object for me, an object with which I have a long personal association. I have carried it from place to place as part of my library. My relation to this object is an example of the way so many readers of my generation and of many generations before mine have participated in a more or less benign fetishism of the book.

My *Ayala's Angel* is a little book in small but readable type, six inches by a little less than four inches by one inch in size. It still has its pink paper dust-jacket. On the front of this is a black and white print of a bewhiskered Victorian gentleman in top hat, black coat, and white spats facing an elegant Victorian lady with black hat, scarf, and muff. Her eyes are modestly downcast. Her narrow dress reaches the ground. He faces her boldly, with his hand on his hip, elbow akimbo. The other hand leans on a walking stick. The cloth binding of the book is blue, Oxford blue, like almost all the books in the World's Classics series. The seal of Oxford University is embossed in the cloth. All the prestige and authority of one of the world's great universities are present in that blue binding and in the seal. To read the book almost makes me feel like a member of the university, as if I had fulfilled Jude Fawley's dream in Hardy's *Jude the Obscure* and had moved from outside to inside of Oxford for the small sum of 10s. 6d. The little book feels comfortable in my hands. I could carry it in my pocket and have done so. It not only feels familiar. It also smells familiar. It has that faint smell of paper, printer's ink, glue, cardboard, and cloth those who belong to the book culture know so well. I know how to read it (word after word in linear sequence from page one to the end), and how to find my way around in it.

Ayala's Angel, however, is also available to me here on my island in another way: as an electronic book, part of the Oxford Text Archive collection of such books. A group of Trollope novels have been made available in this collection in "machine readable" form, as the phrase has it, by David Skilton of the University of Cardiff. "Machine readable"! It sounds as if the machine were doing the reading. The Oxford collection of electronic books is a subset of the large and rapidly growing set of electronic text databases available through the World Wide Web.

What is the difference between reading *Ayala's Angel* in book form

promises the author himself makes in certain moments of his writing. Furthermore, "De Quincey's style is an exact mirror of his mental space" (DG, 48). As I have already said, these assertions reproduce a romantico-expressionist conception of art strongly in agreement with the postulates of criticism of consciousness. However, the truth is that we do not know whether, for instance, the collapsed opposition between logic and rhetoric is a feature of the material written text or of a mental process or of both. Where exactly does it take place?

The reader of Miller's essay would expect those two spaces, the space of the mind and the space of literary writing, to remain clearly distinguished. Nevertheless, from the very beginning they are uneasily mingled: "Though literature is made of words, these words embody states of mind" (DG, ix). The word, despite being a word, expresses something else: consciousness, subjectivity. But what are those mental states, that consciousness or subjectivity? Does Miller understand them in the Aristotelian way, that is, as a soul that transmits itself through phonemes? The distinction between rhetoric, or the literature of power, and logic, or the literature of knowledge, should, in principle, correspond to the field of writing that expresses or embodies mental states: "There are for De Quincey two very distinct kinds of mental building. One he calls, in a famous distinction, rhetoric, the literature of power; the other logic, the literature of knowledge" (DG, 45). Why does Miller pose it in this way? If we are dealing with literature, that is, with material and empirical writing, verifiable and tangible in the particular works of concrete authors (for instance, John Milton), why does Miller give the name "mental building" to the model De Quincey chooses for explaining to us that we obtain from him not knowledge but power? Does he refer to the fact that

and in electronic text form? At first sight it would seem that there might be little difference. In both cases the novel is made up of the same words in the same order. The electronic text can be "downloaded," as they say, into my computer and printed out if I wish to do so, so that I could have a physical object in my hands, something to read not wholly unlike my little Oxford World's Classics book.

Nevertheless, reading *Ayala's Angel* in one form is quite different from reading it in the other. I have stressed the physical embodiment of *Ayala's Angel* in its World's Classics form. Not only is the text of the novel caught in the materiality of the book. It is also tied by way of its paper, cardboard, ink, and glue to the historical and economic conditions of its production, distribution, and consumption. It was printed in such and such a place at such and such a time. It was part of a moment in English publishing history when one of the great academic and commercial English publishers made "classic" books in Western literature available in inexpensive form. This was preceded by earlier moments, first by the initial publication of the book in 1881, then by subsequent cheap editions. Many of Trollope's novels were reprinted in yellow-bound paperback editions sold in railway stations in the late nineteenth century. The twentieth-century World's Classics version belonged to a later stage in English publishing history. It depended on the existence of a large, literate, middle-class reading public in Britain at the time. It also depended to some degree on the fact that television was not yet available. Though the Oxford World's Classics series, as its name implies, was by no means all made up of works in English literature, such works to a considerable degree dominated, along with other works primarily from Western literature, in English translation of course. The World's Classics series defined what was a world classic. Since these books were widely available and cheap, it can be said that the Oxford University Press exercised a large power of canon formation, no doubt in reflection of received opinion at Oxford about what ought to go in such a series both for educational and for economic reasons. A parallel and rather different exercise in canon formation is performed today by Penguin Books. Just what gets included and what gets left out in such a series would merit a long literary and sociological study. People read what is available, or, to put it another way, you cannot so easily read what is not available in cheap, widely distributed form. Including *Ayala's Angel* along with the other books in the World's Classics series gave that novel an unmistakable authority as "literature," as a classic of world literature.

literature is produced by the mind? Or do these forms inhabit the mind before existing in the materiality of a written text? Given that an opposition responding to a necessity of knowledge ("law of the mind," says Miller; DG, 43) is at stake, it seems clear that the opposition should exist a priori in the subject's mind. In fact, in "On the Knocking at the Gate in Macbeth," De Quincey writes: "Here I pause for one moment to exhort the reader never to pay any attention to his understanding when it stands in opposition to any other faculty of his mind" (De Quincey, 1985: 81). In this case, the opposition, one belonging to the field of material writing, is dangerous. Does it place inside what should be outside, or is what it expresses perhaps at the same time the expression?

Yet another possibility exists: that, basically, there is nothing left to do in speaking about mind and material writing other than to mix both spaces.

Some pages before, Miller writes: "All of De Quincey's writing, in one way or another, is modeled on the characteristics of his dreams. In writing it is not a question of the dreams themselves, but of the deliberate representation of them, or of something like them, in words" (DG, 37). This does not answer the question of whether the dreams are a question of writing. He has already told us that writing is not the dream. What about the dream? Does it have anything to do with writing? And what about the mind? Does it have anything to do with writing? This is the question Derrida identifies in 1967 when, with regard to Freud, he writes: the question is "not if the psyche is indeed a kind of text, but: what is a text, and what must the psyche be if it can be represented by a text? For if there is neither machine nor text without psychical origin, there is no domain of the psychic without text. Finally, what must be the relationship

In 1960 the Oxford University Press was, moreover, an international operation. Its books were marketed all over the world, especially by way of cities once British colonies or parts of the British Empire. The globalization of the English language did not occur by accident or because that language has some intrinsic superiority. The list of cities where the Oxford University Press (on the page facing the title page of *Ayala's Angel*) asserts itself as being located reads like a litany of sites associated with British colonialism and imperialism: "Glasgow, New York, Toronto, Melbourne, Wellington, Bombay, Calcutta, Madras, Karachi, Kuala Lumpur, Cape Town, Ibadan, Nairobi, Accra." The sun never sets on the Oxford University Press. My analysis of history's presence in this book when it is seen as a physical object marked with signs could be further refined, for example, by investigation of the typeface, the paper used, the question of why this particular item in the Oxford World's Classics series was printed in Bristol, that is, farmed out, while my Oxford World's Classics edition of Trollope's *An Autobiography*, dated 1961, was printed "at the University Press, Oxford, by Vivian Ridler, Printer to the University." In all these ways, the little book that I hold in my hand is embedded in history, embodies that history in material form, and gives me access to that history.

The electronic text version of *Ayala's Angel* is cut off from these signs of historical context. Or rather, it is given a strange new historical placement in today's "cyberspace." A date of original publication is indicated, and that is about all. We are told that the Oxford Text Archive version is made from tapes that were prepared for the recent Folio Edition of *Ayala's Angel*. The novel does not exist as embodied in material form, or at least not as material in the same fixed way as a printed book. It exists as a large number of "bits" of information, zeroes or ones inscribed as magnetic differences on a hard disk or on magnetic tape or as minute scratches on an optical disk or as electrical pulses on the wires and wireless transmissions of the Internet. The computer chip knows only on or off, yes or no. When "read" by machine, these zeroes and ones are assembled into bytes of information that may easily be transferred electronically to any place in the world where there is a computer with a modem or an Ethernet connection to the Internet. A "byte" usually consists of a series of eight bits, zeroes and ones arranged in a certain order that represent one character, a letter, numeral, or punctuation mark expressed, for example, though it is only one example, in ASCII code. "ASCII" stands for "American Standard Code for Information Interchange." When an appropriate machine "reads" those

between psyche, writing, and spacing for such a metaphoric transition to be possible, not only, nor primarily, within theoretical discourse, but within the history of psyche, text, and technology?" (1978b: 199). This same issue is present in De Quincey when he uses the metaphor of the palimpsest to refer to the human brain. Let me quote it again: "What else than a natural and mighty palimpsest is the human brain? Such a palimpsest is my brain; such a palimpsest, O reader! is yours" (De Quincey, 1985: 144).

Is the equation "human brain = palimpsest" a real metaphor in De Quincey, a "metaphorical step," or what? In truth, Miller gets carried away by the semantic field of writing when, after quoting the passage just cited from *Suspiria*, he explains: "The countless images of the buried past have inscribed themselves *successively* on the brain, and it seems as if their resurrection too will be successive. De Quincey more than once emphasizes the processional character of dreams, the way they consist of an endless succession of images following one another, as parts of a theatrical procession are substituted for one another on a vast stage" (DG, 35). Miller tackles the writing character of the brain and dreams by means of three features:

1. that of inscription, and thus its iterability;
2. that of successivity or spacing ("the traces of each successive handwriting," DG, 142);
3. that of the theatrical image.

In all of these, Miller cannot avoid a conception of De Quincey's inner world as a writing that, though it does not identify itself with material or empirical writing, shares the main attributes of material inscrip-

bytes, they can, by another series of relays, be projected on a computer screen that you and I can read if we know the language—usually, but by no means always, English.

"Read" means, apparently, something quite different for a machine and for a human being. A machine can "read" a file if it has the ability to transfer it as it is or to translate it into another form, as the zeroes and ones are turned into those letters on the screen or are translated from one operating system to another, so the file can be read in turn by Macintosh, PC, or UNIX machines. For a human being to read a text means something quite different—or does it? Perhaps even the most active, interventionist, and engaged human comprehension is only another form of translation. The possibility that the human brain is no more than an extraordinarily powerful, complex, and compact computer haunts us these days like a bad dream that we cannot quite remember. Turned into "machine-readable" form, *Ayala's Angel* becomes angelic indeed, a subtle, impassable, and disembodied information messenger that can move so fast it is almost ubiquitous. It is ubiquitous because though the source code may be stored in one place, in this case in the Oxford Text Archive (though it is also available in the database of electronic books called "Wiretap"), that source may be approached on any one of thousands and thousands of the World Wide Web's filaments. *Ayala's Angel* may be moving at the speed of light, as "packets of information," anywhere on this vast Internet at any time as one or another "client" of the web calls it up like a ghostly revenant on his or her computer screen. On the screen *Ayala's Angel* appears as a fragile shade that would disappear in an instant if the power were to fail. It is sustained on the screen only so long as it is suspended within the RAM or "random access memory" of one or more of the computer's memory chips, each one itself a miniature Internet of etched transistor gateways holding anywhere from 1,000,000 to 128,000,000 or more bytes of information. *Ayala's Angel* itself is 1,321,000 bytes long. The whole system of the Internet and the 6.8 pound Macintosh Powerbook that connects me to it by the slender umbilical of a telephone cord is an amazing technological accomplishment.

The Internet, as is well known, had its beginning as something called ARPANET, created by the United States military as a redundant system to forestall the threat of nuclear catastrophe by ensuring that at least parts of the communication network and essential databases would remain functional even if some command posts were destroyed. If Washington, D.C., were "nuked," other military centers would survive and have the same

tion. De Quincey and Miller do not express themselves in the same way on this question, since the former speaks of "handwriting," whereas the latter speaks of "images." This divergence is only relative, however, because everything aims in the same direction after all: toward the indelible traces that, as in Funes's case, follow their own logic. All this makes Miller's reading proposal more complex. The consciousness expressed in words, with which the critic attempts to identify, is not a domain prior to material writing. It is another form of writing that, although not identified with material inscription, has all its attributes. How, then, should we understand a sentence like "De Quincey's style is an exact mirror of his mental space" (DG, 48)? *Exact* in what sense? Exact in the sense that an original or mental space is re-produced in detail by the instrumental use of writing in the form of style or literature, or exact in the sense that both spaces copy one another mutually because they share a quality called "writing"?

Miller's position here cannot be reduced to the thesis that opposing elements cannot be differentiated. He claims the need for mimetologism, although this concerns imitation of mental interiors, of minds, dreams, or consciousnesses. In this Miller, at least in this early essay, places himself at the antipodes of the great antireferentialist tradition of the twentieth century. Of course, one must read all the antireferentialist ideas of contemporary literary theory in a sophisticated way. But the definition Todorov (1965), following formalist and structuralist trends, gives of literary language—namely, that such language lacks a referent, was widely assumed within the framework of continental theory. In Miller's work the impossibility of literary criticism's escaping absolutely from a *mimetic* reading of literary works is manifest. In *The Disappearance of God* and

information. The transformation of that limited military network into today's immense worldwide cyberspace generates a double paradox. On the one hand, cyberspace may easily be thought of as a postapocalyptic survival. It is as though when we enter cyberspace we are living virtually beyond the end of the world. We are using what would survive if all the books, manuscripts, and other material archives were destroyed in a nuclear holocaust. Jacques Derrida, in "No Apocalypse, Not Now (full speed ahead, seven missiles, seven missives),"[59] speaks of the nuclear holocaust as "the possibility of an irreversible destruction, leaving no traces, of the juridico-literary archive—that is, total destruction of the basis of literature and criticism. . . . Here we are dealing hypothetically with a total and remainderless destruction of the archive. This destruction would take place for the first time and it would lack any common proportion with, for example, the burning of a library, even that of Alexandria, which occasioned so many written accounts and nourished so many literatures" (26–27). As more and more of the "juridico-literary" archive comes "on line" and dwells in cyberspace, however, it will be as capable of surviving the rain of nuclear bombs as the military information would have done on the original ARPANET. The remainderless destruction Derrida names will not happen, and the Internet is like the survivor of a nuclear war that has not yet occurred. We enter the millennium when we open a link to the Internet. The other side of the paradox is that apparently a nuclear holocaust would create such intense magnetic fields that all the hard disks all over the world would be erased, bringing about an evacuation of cyberspace. The military were not so smart as they thought. Derrida's vision of the archive's "remainderless destruction" may be a danger we still face after all.

It might still be argued that once a given client has *Ayala's Angel* on the computer screen, reading it is not all that different from reading it in that little book I can hold in my hand. On the contrary, I think it differs greatly in two ways, one having to do with the external and to some degree determining context of the electronic version of *Ayala's Angel*, the other having to do with its internal organization and forms of accessibility. Not only does that familiar historical embedding, inscribed in the printed book version of *Ayala's Angel* in the ways I have specified, disappear in the electronic book form. It is also replaced by a new, quasi-historical context, the context of today's cyberspace. I say "quasi" because this new historical placement does not correspond very well to any of the traditional notions of historical context for a literary work. These have characteristically in-

in *Poets of Reality*, one might say that we encounter a discourse that is *tendentiously* mimetic, although not *simply* mimetic.

For this reason, the problem of the literary referent should be carefully analyzed. Gasché, for instance, attempting to differentiate between the notions of "text" in Derrida and in literary theory, argues that "the absence of an extra-text is affirmed in the case of the general text only and not of the traditional, reassuring because totalizing, concepts of text. The novel, the poem, the short story, and so forth may depend on the preexistence of a totalizing referent or signified outside the text, especially if they are conceived within the perspective of mimetologism" (Gasché, 1986: 282). At first one must agree with Gasché, but immediately afterward disagree. One agrees because Miller never speaks, either in "phenomenological" or in "deconstructive" essays, of an absence of reference in literary texts. One disagrees because Gasché reproaches deconstructive literary criticism for maintaining an antireferential conception of the literary text via a mistranslation of Derrida's thought. I do not know what deconstructive literary criticism Gasché is referring to. He cannot be referring to Miller's or to de Man's, which assume a referential crisis, not a dogmatic antireferentialism, a crisis based on other traditions within the history of literary theory. One also disagrees because Gasché presupposes that in the field of literary criticism one can tacitly assume that a work depends on the preexistence of a totalizing referent or signified outside the text. Although Gasché's theses are much more complex (I shall discuss them in the following chapter), his assertion is extremely problematic, especially if one has examined the theories of Felix versus Vodička, Ingarden, Barthes, Genette, Derrida, and many others. None of these assumes that a literary work is ever straightforwardly mimetic or referential. It

volved specific location in one place, time, nation, class, socio-economic condition, language, genre, author of a certain gender, and so on. The electronic *Ayala's Angel* is wrested free of all that. It is put in a new, transnational space, to whose strangeness the common figures (World Wide Web, Internet, mosaic, information superhighway or "Infobahn," galaxy, netscape, and so on) hardly do justice. Such figures suggest a comprehensible spatial array in which each thing is in one place. Such an array is extremely complex. Nevertheless it is still open to understanding as a visible pattern. The figures of the web, net, mosaic, galaxy, and so on attempt, perhaps instinctively, to reduce to familiar and comprehensible patterns, something visible to eyesight as a spatial array, what does not exist like that at all. "The Internet isn't a single, identifiable entity," says an article by Joe Clark in *MacUser*, "it's a network of networks, a multitude of computers all around the world, communicating via phone lines, Ethernet, and any other media that can support *IP* (Internet Protocol), the Internet's special protocol, or language." [60] Having said the Internet is not definable, Clark proceeds to define it in a variant of the network image, and in the figure of "language" as a name for the code computers use to "talk" to one another. Nevertheless, the Internet is not really a net and what passes around within it is not really a language in the sense of a natural language.

The rhetorical name for such figures is "catachresis." "Catachresis" means "against usage" in Greek. "Catachresis" names the "abusive" transfer of what names something known—here, a visible net, mosaic, web, or galaxy—to something unnamed and not an "identifiable entity," something unknown. It is, properly speaking, unknowable, if "knowable" means direct apprehension by the senses. All the common names for the Internet and its programs are catachreses. [61] The Internet is not a "space," if one means by that a Euclidean manifold in which each thing is in one place and has identifiable relations by coordinates to all other things and to the borders that define regions within the volume. In the nonspaced space or spaced-out space of the Internet, everything is in a sense everywhere at all times. Everything is juxtaposed to everything else, in pell-mell confusion. This confusion takes the concrete form of the difficulty of remembering from one time to another just how you found a given item, since there are so many ways to get from here to there in cyberspace. [62]

Many different programs, with strange names like Gopher, Wais, Mosaic, Veronica, MacWeb, EI Galaxy, Netscape, Explorer, Telnet, Archie, Anarchie, Lycos, Yahoo, HotBot, and so on, exist to accomplish essentially

is also problematic when applied without further discussion to Miller's work.

In addition, Miller makes evident that at the point where "writing" raises the mimetic question, it acquires a different nuance. At that point it is no longer a question of imitating something distinct from literary writing, but of imitating something that shares the same attributes, its character of inscription and repetition, plus the need for spacing. Although at first the direction of the creative and interpretative process seemed clear, that is, from the subject's inside to the outside or vice versa, a problem now arises. De Quincey's theory of writing is modeled on a strong notion of palimpsest. When in *Palimpsestes* (1982) Genette gives the name "hypertext" "to every text generated by a former text through a simple transformation . . . or through an indirect transformation" (17), he presupposes the possibility of identifying hypertexts and the possibility of narrativizing them. However, we must remember that this would be impossible in De Quincey's work, since every text is subject to the law of infinite divisibility and plunges into its own abyss. Miller states, "If De Quincey wishes to exhaust each subject before moving on to the next, then it is impossible ever to get from one to another, however close together the two may be, for he can never finish enumerating the infinite number of parts into which even a moment or a drop of dew may be divided. Even if Achilles will catch the tortoise, it is impossible to find words for the infinite degrees of his approach" (DG, 53–54). The writing De Quincey speaks of does not circulate but rather falls into its own endlessly repetitive abyss, so that language never catches up with it. This raises two important questions. First, how might it be possible to reflect, mirror, or imitate what is not identifiable or finite? Second, are De Quincey and Miller setting forth a theory of writing prior to language?

the same ends of locating and calling up a given file. To reach *Ayala's Angel* in the summer of 1994, I used MacWeb to go first to Colby College, then to the list of electronic books at Carnegie Mellon University, then to the Oxford Text Archive in Oxford, England. I say "I went" from one of those places to another, but of course I did not "go" anywhere. I sat in my study in Deer Isle watching my computer screen and manipulating my keyboard and trackball. The "movement" was invisible and inaudible except for some whirrs and clicks, accompanied by the spinning of a little icon of the earth's globe on the screen and the appearance of various filenames on my screen. These indicate, if you can decode them, just where in the world I "virtually" am and by what route I got there. Eventually the first page of *Ayala's Angel* appeared on the screen, with the remainder held in suspension in my random access memory ready to be called forth, like a spirit from the vasty deep. Though I could have reached the same end by a bewildering number of different routes, each stage in the route I chose to take has a barbarous file name or URL, "Universal Resource Locator," for example, "http://www.cs.cmu.edu:8001/Web/books.html" for the list of electronic text collections at Carnegie Mellon, "http://black.ox.ac.uk/TEI/ota.html" for the Oxford Text Archive within that list, and "file://black.ox.ac.uk/ota/english/Trollope/ayala.1873" for *Ayala's Angel* itself. "Http" stands for "hypertext transfer protocol" and "html" for "hypertext markup language." About hypertext I shall say more later.

I have used a number of the strange new terms that have been devised for "navigating" the Internet to indicate the way cyberspace depends on a new language within English. These terms are part of the verbarium of a new international culture or subculture in which the network surfer comes to participate. This language is a weird combination of technical jargon, based on strange acronyms and abbreviations, and many witty, often irreverent figures of speech. The monthly magazine *Wired* is perhaps the purest expression of this new international culture. It is, of course, available on-line as well as in printed form. The URL is http://www.hotwired.com. *Wired* is distinctive in its use of striking graphics and typefaces. These are printed in garish pinks, yellow-greens, and other such colors. This magazine shows how the computer world overlaps with the world of popular music, the media, and with such venerable expressions of the counter-culture as *Mad Magazine*.

If somewhere always here and there in the Internet one may still catch a whiff of the military-industrial complex that initially developed it,

In answer to the first question, one must admit that it concerns a process of contamination rather than a "reflex." Literary writing, instead of functioning like a "mirror," will superimpose itself on prior writing without erasing it entirely. To put it another way, the relation between the material writing of the literary text and the mental writing of consciousness is equal to the relation between the superimposed writing in a palimpsest and earlier identifiable writing beneath it. Given that the literary text cannot coincide with the mental traces, as a result of the latter's eternal capacity to divide themselves, the literary text will launch into a repetition in which its every fragment and particle will constantly subdivide. It thereby attains a degree of particularity that cannot be subsumed under any type of general law. In a significant footnote Miller recognizes that De Quincey's thought, even though it is his "own" thought, is a tissue of quotations, translations, and adaptations of other authors who, we suspect, would lead to other authors who, in their turn, would lead to others (DG, 27–28). Complete knowledge turns out to be impossible. De Quincey's writing does not know. It merely acts, since, as the Borgesian narrator writes: "To think is to forget a difference, to generalize, to abstract. In the overly replete world of Funes there were nothing but details, almost contiguous details" (Borges, 1962: 115). Literary writing is not a reflex of "inner" mental writing because this mental writing is already a "reflex" or contamination from the "outside." If, in a particular moment of his reading, Miller tells us that De Quincey's style is the exact mirror of his inner world, he assures us somewhere else that "gradually, through the experience of wandering, he comes to discover that the infinity is also within, and that his inner spiritual depths are the exact mirror of the empty sky, or the desert, or the labyrinth of London" (DG,

that original purpose has been appropriated and transformed by a world-wide collection of computer users. These adepts are insubordinate spirits skilled at fighting any hierarchy. Much has been made of the inherent de-mocratization of the Internet. Whether or not it is democratic is a complex and problematic question, but for those who have access to the Internet a levelling no doubt occurs. Anyone anywhere in the world who has such access can more or less freely use the vast resources of the Web for any pur-pose. If you happen to have access, for example, by being a student, faculty member, or administrator at almost any college or university, it will seem to you that the Internet is entirely free. Of course someone is paying for it or has paid for its construction, but once you are "wired," almost every-thing on the Internet seems free. I did not pay 10s. 6d. for the electronic version of *Ayala's Angel*. I did not pay anything at all beyond the telephone charges for my connection from Deer Isle to Colby.

In all these ways the electronic *Ayala's Angel* is not contextless. It has a strange and disorienting new context that tears it further and further away from the familiar context of the little book in the Oxford World's Classics. The World Wide Web abounds in indexes. Each tends to be in-complete, odd, or grotesque in one way or another, by the juxtaposition of incompatibles, like the bizarre Chinese encyclopedic system of classi-fying animals Borges lists.[63] *Ayala's Angel* jostles side by side in cyberspace with weather maps, satellite images, bulletin boards on every imaginable subject, the latest information about the human genome project, recent pictures from the Hubble Space Telescope, free software, games, agricul-tural information, millions of e-mail messages flitting to and fro, and so on and on, in an amazing richness and unordered profusion.

Even the indexes of electronic books, a relatively orderly, familiar-looking corner in the Internet, are in the end not so reassuringly famil-iar. Something strange has happened to the canon. The "info" file for the Oxford Text Archive explains firmly that it has nothing to do with the Oxford University Press but is a function of the Oxford Computing Cen-ter. It stores whatever texts someone happens to have turned into machine-readable form. It measures itself by its size (a gigabyte is a thousand mil-lion bytes), rather than by its inclusiveness or by any established canon of "classics." It contains just whatever it happens to contain:

WHAT IS THE OXFORD TEXT ARCHIVE?

The Oxford Text Archive is a facility provided by Oxford University Com-puting Services. It has no connexion with Oxford University Press or any other

27). One might add here, "or of the palimpsest," since, if we attentively take note, we shall see that the labyrinth of London is not distinct from the labyrinth of images from the past (or the palimpsest) that is contemplated through horrible opium dreams. To inquire into the outside and thus into the materiality of writing means to become aware of the inside: "The exploration of the outer space . . . turns out to be at the same time an act of self-discovery, the exploration of inner space" (DG, 27).

Without a doubt, here one is talking about "mimesis," but a mimesis that, as in De Quincey, has lost its center and finds itself in a labyrinth without origin or ending. This indication of the nonexistence of an archaeology or teleology seems of great importance. Writing imitates the inside. It is the exact reflex of the writer's inner world. Up to now, we have what we can call a classical conception of the relation of the subject to the artwork, a conception that never fades from the text, that is even necessary for the functioning of the text as text. However, it is equally true that the inside imitates writing or at least functions in the same manner as material writing. From the perspective of this second approach, there is no copy any more, unless we mean the copy of a copy. Nevertheless, to speak of the copy of a copy should lead us to erase the concept of copy in order to supersede it with a concept of "contamination" or "participation." The act of copying is only possible if we start with a model. Otherwise, we return to the Millerian matrix of "participation," now related not to the reader and the text, but to the two types of writing: material writing (real and tangible) and mental writing (imaginary and nonempirical).

Reality and imagination have a palimpsestlike relationship. One is inscribed on the other, and the other is inscribed on the first, without either of them erasing the other—hence the possibility of a mimetic read-

commercial organisation and exists to serve the interests of the academic community by providing archival and dissemination facilities for electronic texts at low cost. The Archive offers scholars long term storage and maintenance of their electronic texts free of charge. It manages non-commercial distribution of electronic texts and information about them on behalf of its depositors.

WHAT TEXTS DOES IT CONTAIN?

The Archive contains electronic versions of literary works by many major authors in Greek, Latin, English and a dozen or more other languages. It contains collections and corpora of unpublished materials prepared by field workers in linguistics. It contains electronic versions of some standard reference works. It has copies of texts and corpora prepared by individual scholars and major research projects worldwide. The total size of the Archive exceeds a gigabyte and there are over 1500 titles in its catalogue.

A gigabyte sounds like a lot, but many desktop computers these days have hard disks that hold several gigabytes, that is, the equivalent of the entire Oxford Text Archive stored in just part of a mechanism you can hold in the palm of your hand. No doubt the Oxford Text Archive by now contains much more than a gigabyte. Whatever may remain of traditional Oxford in the description just cited (for example the words "major" and "standard" as well as putting Greek and Latin before English, but English before other vernaculars) tends to have vanished in other lists of electronic books that also include *Ayala's Angel*, for example, the list by authors of "Books On-line" at "cmu.edu," that is, Carnegie Mellon University, also reachable through MacWeb, Mosaic, Netscape, or Microsoft's Internet Explorer. In that list many more books by Edgar Rice Burroughs and Arthur Conan Doyle are included than books by Anthony Trollope. Though Aeschylus, Shakespeare, Milton, and many other canonical authors are included, so are many not in the old canon. *Zen and the Art of the Internet*, by Brendan Kehoe, is placed side by side with Kant's *Critique of Pure Reason*, since both authors' names begin with "K." Many books about non-Christian religions are included. Lots of children's books are included.

The databases of electronic books are not chaotic or senseless. They indicate a new process of canon formation. This new canon will include many books from the old canon where someone has an interest in preserving them, but it will pointedly omit many others. Lyric poetry, the poetry of Wordsworth, Emily Dickinson, T. S. Eliot, or Wallace Stevens, has a relatively small place in this new canon, whereas it is the backbone of the traditional canon: for example the Bloomian canon, in Harold

ing. However, one also replaces the other—hence the impossibility of a mimetic reading. The one touches the other, but does not identify with it. Both enter into a game of traces. One might say of mental writing or the psychic image generally what Derrida writes in *Of Grammatology*: "The psychic image of which Saussure speaks must not be an internal reality copying an external one" (Derrida, 1976: 64). That is why, in 1968, Miller writes: "This interaction tends to blur the distinction between real and unreal, nonfictive and fictive. The various levels in their play of reflection, mind within mind—mind within mind within mind, or metaphor within metaphor, or narrator within narrator—come to appear equally real, equally imaginary . . . both sides of the mirror have the same reality" (FVF, 37). What in 1963 was, on the subject of the "disappearance of God," a rustle of codes careening among themselves, each interfering with the others, becomes in 1968, in *The Form of Victorian Fiction*, with regard to the "death of God," a point of reference that already acquires the status of a presupposition or working hypothesis. Note that in the quoted passage the preposition "within" indicates a constant process of interiorization, a movement going from the outside toward the inside. But also note that Miller comes to the conclusion, not that everything is language, but that in the midst of language it is not possible to decide on its real or imaginary character, or, what is the same, to the conclusion that in the text there is a play of differences that cannot be reduced. This would also explain why Miller, throughout this short book, expresses himself constantly in paradoxical terms. He notes that "a novel is made of words and in that sense is unreal or imaginary. There are no physical objects, no real people in any novel." Immediately after, he specifies that "the words of a novel embody a structure of related minds" (FVF, 29).

Bloom's book on the Western canon.[64] For Bloom, literature is essentially and quinessentially poetry, including of course dramatic and epic poetry as well as lyrics. For the new readers of electronic books it is chiefly novels, along with Greek and Renaissance drama, especially Shakespeare. The new canon will include many books that people are actively interested in now but that would not have made it into the old Oxford World's Classics series. The Oxford Text Archive statement says nothing about "World's Classics," by which was meant almost exclusively Western works from the Greeks on. It boasts rather of including "copies of texts and corpora prepared by individual scholars and major research projects worldwide." The OTA is part of a process of globalization quite different from the old British imperial project that had branches of the Oxford University Press in Calcutta, Kuala Lumpur, and all those other places.

Ayala's Angel as an electronic book takes on a novel meaning when it is placed in this new context, when it floats in cyberspace. It is detached from its local historical context. It becomes a "text" in the context of an enormous and incoherent abundance of artifacts of all kinds — verbal, pictorial, and auditory. As such, it might now be the object of a globalized "cultural studies" by scholars who are themselves more and more cut off, in part by their use of the computer and by their inhabitation of cyberspace, from participation in any local culture of their own.

The Ethics of Hypertext

I said reading *Ayala's Angel* in electronic form is different from reading the printed version. Just what is the difference? For one thing, as I have suggested, the electronic version has a much more fragile, fleeting, and insubstantial existence. *Ayala's Angel* appears and disappears page by page on my computer screen as I call it up. A book in cyberspace feels much more mutable and insolid, quite unlike the fixed linear form of the printed book. This is true even though it could be argued that *Ayala's Angel* is more permanent on the Internet, since so many copies exist safely stored in different places. Electronic storage of books may allow them to escape the fragility Wordsworth lamented in Book Five of *The Prelude*:

> Oh! why hath not the mind
> Some element to stamp her image on
> In nature somewhat nearer to her own?

In relation to the second question—Is Miller setting forth a theory of writing prior to language?—one should reply, with all possible caution, that it seems logical to admit that Miller is not identifying "writing" with literature or with the current concept of "writing." In this sense, he is closer to Derrida than to the supposed mistranslation of the latter's thought in the field of literary criticism. Yet the field of literary criticism, as a privileged discipline, has made it possible to pose those problems about the inside/outside relation. With Derrida—for instance, in *Of Grammatology*—we are dealing with a discourse explicitly oriented toward the production of a third term ("arche-writing" or "arche-trace") that would result from the deconstruction of the pair speech/writing or, what comes to the same thing, would arise from setting Saussure against himself. What Miller writes is not explicitly oriented toward a deconstruction. Instead, he produces a discourse whose internal composition and encounter with "De Quincey" bring about its self-deconstruction. Miller's work remains much more undecidable than *Of Grammatology*, more in connection with Saussure than with Derrida, for it is not radically guided in a particular direction, though it seeks to be. One must understand that, all things considered, Miller and Derrida presuppose two completely different contexts of reading, despite their sharing of "thematic" similarities.

In truth, Miller, when he speaks of literature and dreams, mind, or brain, has been led to a notion of writing that has more to do with "general inscription" than with the materiality of the concrete text. He contends that "the countless images of the buried past have *inscribed* themselves successively on the brain" (DG, 35, my italics), letting it be known that: (1) literature arises at the moment when material writing

Why, gifted with such powers to send abroad
Her spirit, must it lodge in shrines so frail?[65]

Though the figure of "stamping" is not quite appropriate for the new kind of inscription in ghostly zeroes and ones, the Internet, it could be argued, is to some degree a "shrine" less frail than a printed book. *Ayala's Angel* comes from the Oxford Text Archive carrying some of the marks of the beast upon it in the form of odd coded instructions in place of typesize and formatting and in place of certain marks of punctuation. These are Hypertext Markup Language instructions to the computer printer for the Folio edition. A dash, for example, becomes "—." I can, by suitable instructions to my computer or by a suitable "browser," change these into the "correct" text. The need to do this, however, reminds me of the way all texts must be embodied in some kind of marks in order to be readable, though all textual embodiments are to some degree arbitrary codes. They could be otherwise. Some electronic texts arrive at the desktop computer in compressed form. They may then appear on the screen in incomprehensible code, unless you have appropriate decompression software, "unzip," for example, if the file has been compressed in "zip."

This sense of the text's fragility is reinforced by another feature of electronic texts. Once I have got the file in my computer I can easily change it in many ways, ways that would be impossible with a printed book. I can alter the typeface into any one of several dozen I have in my computer. Hundreds of other typefaces would be easily available. I can extract citations from anywhere in the novel and insert them anywhere else, for example, in an essay on the novel. I could also easily deface the text in any way I might want. I could scramble the chapters, substitute a new word for every example of a given word, remove all examples of a given word or words, and so on. I could change every example of "Ayala" to "Susan" and turn the book into *Susan's Angel*. I do not know why I would want to do that, but I could. My sense of the text is changed by my awareness of this vulnerability. It is a fragility quite different from a printed book's liability to having pages torn out or burned.

More important for research, however, is my ability, if I have the right software, to apply various search techniques to the electronic *Ayala's Angel*. I can almost instantly call up on screen every example of a given word or short string of words. Using a "Boolean search engine," I can find all places where any two words or strings are nearby. What I would do

embodies a mental writing, and (2) one is not possible without the other. Does that not amount to saying that literature and mental processes depend as possibilities on an "inscription" that is prior to them? If the brain and everything related to it, especially memory, functions as a non-empirical materiality, and if literature depends on a concretization of that nonempirical materiality in the outer world, then is one not perhaps recognizing that there is an inscription without inscription prior to inscription, as Blanchot might put it, which offers the possibility of every writing, whether mental or material?

Curiously, what we are now discovering in Miller is similar to what he describes apropos Wordsworth in an essay of 1972 entitled "The Stone and the Shell: The Problem of Poetic Form in Wordsworth's Dream of the Arab," incorporated in the Wordsworth chapter of *The Linguistic Moment* (LM, 59–113). In effect, Wordsworth first appears as the paradigm of the poet who defends the primacy of consciousness and speech over writing. A detailed analysis, however, reveals that things are not so simple. Insofar as the proem and the dream in Book V of *The Prelude* are dominated by the metaphor of the mind as writing (book, inscription, etc.), it is no longer easy to distinguish between the two fields. Miller ends by saying: "The speaking face of nature is necessary for the 'intercourse' of the sovereign intellect with man. The deathless spirit behind nature would be invisible or inaudible if it were not for its articulation in natural types and symbols. In an analogous way man must have books in order to maintain the "commerce of [his] nature with herself' . . . , in a kind of continuous internal dialogue. Wordsworth's phrasing recalls the use by Plato in the *Philebus* of the image of the book to describe that inner conversation that

with the results of such searches would be up to me, but it is clear that they facilitate certain kinds of critical analysis. When I find a passage that is especially interesting, I can call up in a few seconds all the other passages that contain the key words of that passage. If Georges Poulet, when he was writing *The Metamorphoses of the Circle*,[66] had possessed electronic texts and search programs, he would not have had to be the extraordinarily fast reader he was to find all the passages about circles, centers, peripheries, and so on that are the basic data of his admirable book.

Such search capabilities do not yet quite turn *Ayala's Angel* into a hypertext, though it would be possible to do so. A hypertext, as its name suggests, is a hyperbolic text, a text to a higher power, squared or cubed. A hypertext invites the reader to break down the usual linear way of reading from the first word through to the end, word by word. It does this by creating links between one part of the text and another or between one text and other texts or other databases. The latter may contain visual or auditory as well as textual material. The hypertext link is indicated on the computer screen by underlining, by highlighting, by a color change, or all three. The chief methods for exploring the Internet I mentioned above (MacWeb, Mosaic, Netscape, and Navigator) are hypertext-based "browsers." The user moves from one location to another by clicking on a hypertext link. An invisible mechanism then magically activates the connection to call up the text, graphic, or sounds to which that word or phrase is linked. I say it is invisible, but it may be made visible by simply clicking on "Page Source" in the pull-down Menu named "View" of "Netscape," now one of the most widely used World Wide Web browsers. Then all the hidden Hypertext Markup Language markers appear on the screen along with the words of the text.

Hypertexts are commonly multimedia assemblies of signs. Hypertext expansion can turn a linear verbal text into a vast indeterminate assemblage that mixes sounds and pictures with words. These can be navigated in innumerable different ways, as each link leads to further links, and as you choose or do not choose to click on a given marked element or on some object in a hypertext graphic that will open up to a new world. A hypertext version of *Ayala's Angel* could have links connecting one part of the novel to other parts associated by some principle of relation. The reader might have many different ways to read the novel—for example, by reading all the chapters in which Ayala encounters Jonathan Stubbs, leaving out all

takes place for a man when there are no other men with whom to talk. The mind of man in order to communicate with itself must separate itself from itself, project itself into the external and mediate form of books" (LM, 86–87). Not only do Miller's words here belong to an essay written in a Derridean key, but he comes back to the problem already posed in his essay on De Quincey, that is, the problem of the relation between mind and writing, between mental writing and material writing. This is and is not the same question Derrida deals with when discussing the opposition speech/writing. Nowhere in this brief essay does Miller reduce everything to literature or pure writing. Rather, he echoes again a notion of "inscription" that belongs completely neither to the field of the mind nor to the field of writing. I will not attempt to assert that this concept of inscription is equivalent *mutatis mutandi* to that of "arche-writing" or "arche-trace" formulated by Derrida, not least because I would not know how to ascertain what one means by saying "this is equivalent to that." Nonetheless, one cannot infer from Miller's discourse that he is exclusively talking about literature in the sense of ordinary writing. Since there now seems to be a return in literary theory to imaginary, anthropological, or thematic aspects (not only in the United States, but also in European countries such as Spain or France), one should remember that Miller was talking in 1963 about an "embodiment" of imaginary contents in the literary word. These contents, without ceasing to be imaginary, are also, and above all, inscription or participation in the trace process of the general palimpsest.

the rest, or by following separately all the chapters involving Tom Tringle. A hypertext *Ayala's Angel* might also have links connecting this or that passage in the novel to passages in the rest of Trollope's other novels and prose works that are related in some way. Hypertext links in the foxhunting chapters could connect the reader to all the other foxhunting passages in other novels and prose works by Trollope. Other links could take the reader outside Trollope's work to Victorian books about foxhunting, to pictures of fox hunts, and to sounds of hounds, hunting horns, and the cries of the hunters. The fact that the reader has to choose or not choose to click on a given link is what justifies the word "interactive" for this kind of reading.

The possibility of such hypertext explosions of the linear continuity of older texts is intrinsic to the new electronic media. Hypertext links could make *Ayala's Angel* approach but not quite reach the deliberate exploitation of hypertext and multimedia possibilities in current creations made especially for computer use. Often these are stored on CD-ROM and require a CD-ROM player for their access. An example is "the first CD-ROM smash hit," *Myst*, a creation of the brothers Rand and Robyn Miller. It was developed by Cyan, Inc., and is sold by Brøderbund Software, Inc. The advertisement for *Myst* says it has "5 complete worlds to explore" and "over 2,500 photorealistic images," as well as an "original sound track," and "QuickTime [a trademark of Apple Computer] video and animation." *Myst*, says an article by Jon Carroll in *Wired*, "may also be the first interactive artifact to suggest that a new art form may well be plausible." It is "a kind of puzzle box inside a novel inside a painting— only with music. Or something."[67] The object of this strange game or novel is to reconstruct a story by clicking on various objects in the pictures that appear on the screen. This game, if that is what it is, was "designed to be played in 40 hours by the 'average' first-time player" (72). Several different endings to the story may be reached when the forty hours are up. *Myst* is a free country. You can choose the ending you like best, though with a shadowy awareness of the others. This is not possible with *Ayala's Angel*, which definitely has a single ending. As the advertisement for *Myst* says, "Only you can untangle the web of lies and deceit that shrouds the 5 worlds of Myst" (67), whereas in *Ayala's Angel* the untangling is done for the reader by the narrator and by the straightforward narrative sequence. In the article about *Myst* in *Wired* Carroll writes somewhat portentously (and in the language of unconscious romanticism characteristic of such pronouncements) about the social significance of this "new art form":

Dirty Mirrors and Deconstructions

What will deconstructive literary criticism have been? What is deconstructive literary criticism? What will deconstructive literary criticism be? What is the effect of the adjective "deconstructive" on the syntagm "literary criticism"? To deny or to state the possibility of a *deconstructive* literary criticism can take several things for granted—for instance, that literary criticism is one thing or another, or that deconstruction means doing one kind of work and not another. That is to say, denying or stating the viability of a deconstructive literary criticism implies granting both literary criticism and deconstruction specific identities. Without attempting to simplify Gasché's thesis, even while agreeing with it in some respects, I would point out that to suggest that "Derrida's analyses pursue a different goal, aiming to establish the law that governs the 'contradictions' of philosophical discourse, the law that explains why and how what is supposedly pure, ideal, transcendental, and so on is unavoidably contaminated by its opposite, and why speech in its purity cannot be thought except by referring to writing" (Gasché, 1986: 273) or that "the importance of Derrida's thinking for the discipline of literary criticism is not immediately evident" (ibid., 255) makes no sense if we do not presuppose in one way or another a fairly strong line of demarcation between literary criticism and philosophy.

Gasché had asserted such a boundary in 1979 when he asked, rather abruptly, "What does theory mean in this context except the all too often naive and sometimes even, for its uncontrolled and unwanted side-effects, ridiculous application of the results of philosophical debates to the literary field?" (Gasché, 1979: 178). Gasché responded to this question by

I thought that things keep changing, that the engine of democratization sitting on so many desktops is already out of control, is already creating new players in a new game. It's not just Silicon Valley anymore; it's not just MIT and Berkeley; it's not just anything. Anyone with guts and talent can be a player; lines of code don't ask about religion, political opinions, taste in clothing or music. We are used to the idea that rebels can find cracks in the new systems; we are not used to the idea that rebellion doesn't matter anymore. It's pure imagination now, unfettered by trend or anti-trend; it can happen anywhere the hardware lives.

Moral co-evolution; that's one thing that's happening. Like others before them (Dante, Milton, Blake), the Millers encountered their dark sides even while searching for the light. They discovered the fascination of danger and disgrace. The universe of Myst may be miraculous, but it is not benign. The tale embedded in the game of Myst has several endings, the official right ending "represents the triumph of The Good Father," but it is ultimately not very interesting. The "wrong" ending is much more fun and much more cathartic. Soon there will be another world to create, and the lesson of Dante will still apply: Paradise can get tiresome; Inferno is where the action is. Was there art in Eden before the apple was eaten? Maybe not. (73)

Carroll has certainly been reading his Milton and Dante by way of Blake. He is of the devil's party by choice, not, as Blake said of Milton, "without knowing it." One should be suspicious about the novelty so enthusiastically affirmed by Carroll. *Myst* would presumably not be such a best-seller if, for all its novelty and originality, it did not fit certain ideological presuppositions, including those inherited from a certain romanticism. These presuppositions prepare its users or readers or players (whatever they should be called) to take pleasure from putting in those forty hours of hard interactive work.

It could be argued that hypertext does no more (though that is quite a lot) than make more easily available through a new technological mechanism what has always been the case about linguistic assemblages and perhaps about the "life" with which they are intertwined. In a passage almost at the end of Proust's *A la recherche du temps perdu*, Marcel, meditating on the form the great work he is about to write will have to take, describes the way any of his encounters with a person involves everything else in his life and can lead to it. Therefore, says Marcel, he realizes he needs a new technique of narration, a three-dimensional technique not all that different from what we would now call hypertext:

saying that such mixing of philosophy and literary theory means "the (in-stitutionally motivated) absence of all rigorous formation in pilot sciences such as anthropology, linguistics, psychoanalysis, and especially philoso-phy" (1979: 178–79). In *The Tain of the Mirror: Derrida and the Philosophy of Reflection*, Gasché again attacks "some uninformed readers" of Der-rida's thought (Gasché, 1986: 164). Gasché does not stand alone in this thinking. Georges Mounin, in *Introduction à la sémiologie*, had expressed himself in similar terms when he accused Barthes of misusing concepts from Saussurian linguistics and glossematics by applying them to the field of literature or of general semiology. Mounin's tone is similar to Gasché's: "The use Barthes makes of the concepts of present-day linguistics is . . . neither satisfactory nor convincing" (Mounin, 1970: 220). Camille Schu-wer (1949), Roger Ayrault (1961–76), and V. Manuel de Aguiar e Silva (1969) similarly assert that the early German Romantics take advantage of Fichte's philosophy, misinterpreting it by turning Fichte's abstract "I" into a concrete "I."

It would be interesting to write a history of the kinds of accusations that are normally directed from a restrictively defined disciplinary area toward a more inclusive one, with the aim of trying to explain what is hidden behind or motivates these accusations. This would imply neither a need for surveillance nor a plea for rigor. Moreover, *The Tain of the Mirror: Derrida and the Philosophy of Reflection* is unquestionably one of the most important works published in the last decade on the "topic" of deconstruction. It has, although not uniquely, the virtue of framing problems in a context that is usually, if not always, the correct one. Given that it is one of the most serious and rigorous attacks on "deconstructive literary criticism," we must pause to discuss some of its premises.

I have said that it would be impossible to depict our relationship with anyone whom we have even slightly known without passing in review, one after another, the most different settings of our life. Each individual therefore—and I was myself one of these individuals—was a measure of duration for me, in virtue of the revolutions which like some heavenly body he had accomplished not only on his own axis but also around other persons, in virtue, above all, of the successive positions which he had occupied in relation to myself. And surely the awareness of all these different planes within which, since in this last hour, at this party, I had recaptured it, Time seemed to dispose the different elements of my life, had, by making me reflect that in the book which tried to tell the story of a life it would be necessary to use not the two-dimensional psychology [*la psychologie plane*] which we normally use but a quite different sort of three-dimensional psychology [*une sorte de psychologie dans l'espace*], added a new beauty to those resurrections of the past which my memory had effected while I was following my thoughts alone in the library, since memory by itself, when it introduces the past, unmodified, into the present—the past just as it was at the moment when it was itself the present—suppresses the mighty dimension of Time which is the dimension in which life is lived [*cette grande dimension du Temps suivant laquelle la vie se réalise*].[68]

I began this book by speaking of *A la recherche du temps perdu* as a huge database of memories. Marcel treats his memories as though he had a hypertext program for moving around within them. Anywhere he begins will lead ultimately by a series of links everywhere else in that vast storage disk of recollections, but not according to any predetermined pathways. We readers must do the same. We are constantly coached into doing the same by the narrator's intricate system of cross-references. These are not entirely unlike hypertext links, though the reader must have stored the whole enormous text in his memory and do the work a hypertext does for its user. Something of the same sort could be said of *Ayala's Angel*. The good reader of this novel will connect whatever passage he or she is reading with similar earlier passages. The reader will create a virtual hypertext without the aid of any machine other than the printed pages and his or her own memory.

Nevertheless, in the period now coming to an end, when the printed book dominated as the chief means of storing and retrieving information, it was still possible to be beguiled into thinking of a work like *Ayala's Angel* or even like *A la recherche du temps perdu* as a stable and unmoving organic unity, on the model of a spatial array. Northrop Frye, for example, habitually spatialized literature in this way. Joseph Frank's "Spatial Form in

In "Some Statements and Truisms about Neo-logisms, Newisms, Postisms, Parasitisms, and Other Small Seismisms," Derrida criticizes Gasché's book: "When Gasché . . . reproaches certain literary deconstructionists for not being radical enough because they fail to reexamine the premises of or even the kind of priority given to the deconstruction of philosophy, his gesture seems to me at the same time necessary and risky. Necessary, because to reconstitute the deconstructive jetty into theory, into a theory, into a deconstructionist jetty, runs the risk of loosing the essential force and excess which consists in unsettling the entire philosophical foundation. . . . But conversely, the equivocal risk that Gasché's book runs—not necessarily in the texture and in the careful and cautious details of his analysis, which are subtle enough to avoid this risk, but in the global and massive effect to which books are unfortunately reduced once they have been closed and once they start being discussed— the risk would be to reconstitute the deconstructive jetty as a *philosophy of deconstruction*, with . . . its 'infrastructures,' its systemacity, etc. One would then be faced with a deconstructionist philosophy or metaphilosophy, with a theory of theories, a deconstructionist supertheory" (Derrida, 1992b: 89).

Derrida is referring to the risk of delimiting specific discourses, levels, and areas of knowledge, a delimitation that poorly tallies with what in the same article he calls "the principle of taxonomic disorder" (1992b: 67). This has to do with the constitution of identities (for instance, of Marxism, structuralism, psychoanalysis, poststructuralism, etc.) that incorporate other identities "by contamination, parasitism, grafts, organ transplants, incorporation" (Derrida, 1992b: 66). It seems to me that the problem with Gasché's book lies not only in its effects once the book has

Modern Literature" was an influential codification of this presupposition. T. S. Eliot's "Tradition and the Individual Talent" invited a generation of literature students to think of all Western literature as such a spatial array.[69] A fixed, spatialized text imposed on its readers a single unified meaning generated by a linear reading from the first word through to the end, in Proust's case more than three thousand pages later. The reader who accepted this model could think of the act of reading as a purely cognitive matter. I as reader do not create a meaning that did not exist before I engaged myself, "interactively," in the text. The meaning was there, waiting to be generated in me in an experience of passive reception. A hypertext that is overtly organized as such, on the contrary, offers the reader the necessity of deciding which path to follow through the text, or of letting chance choose for him or her. Nor is there any "right" choice, that is, one justified objectively, by a pre-existing meaning. A hypertext demands that we choose at every turn and take responsibility for our choices. This is the ethics of hypertext. Hypertext brings into the open the way the generation of meaning in the act of reading is a speech act, not a passive cognitive reception. As a doing things with words it is not fully authorized or justified by the text. The text makes a demand on me to read it. My reading is a response to that demand. It is a response to an irresistible obligation to read all the books, and now all those texts on the Internet too. Whether or not I have fulfilled this obligation in a given case can never be confirmed. I am, in the end, responsible for what I make of a text.

Hypertexts on computers expose this uneasy situation. They teach us to see earlier works of literature in a different way. We come to see them as already proto-hypertexts that invite or allow many different pathways of reading. All reading, even the most linear, involves the constant to and fro of cross-referencing memory inside the text and out that Proust describes as the structure of human time. For this mobile, ungrounded, and unmasterable vibration fixed visual spatial images like "Internet" or even "fractal mosaic" are not adequate. They do not do justice to the semiotic structure that is possessed, in their different ways, both by *Myst* and by novels from the age of the printed book like *Ayala's Angel* and *A la recherche du temps perdu*. Works of literature are black holes in the Internet Galaxy. The presence of literature and the literary on the Internet forbids thinking of the Internet as a transparent electronic highway system on which "information" passes back and forth freely, without interruption, as an open secret. Concerning this blocking of information transfer by what might be

been closed and the discussion started but also, and above all, in its internal texture and development. I shall limit myself to pointing out and discussing the three most problematic aspects of this work.

1. The first has to do with a poor and inappropriate interpretation of the Jena Romantics' "postulates," especially those of Friedrich Schlegel.

2. The second is related to what I will call "the triple notion of text or writing" in Derrida. Although, inadvertently, Gasché names the "third" notion of text or writing, he confines himself to speaking only of two, to text or writing in its vulgar empirical sense as present reality and to the general text or arche-writing as a (present and absent) condition of possibility of writing, speech, and other metaphysical oppositions. The consequence constitutes the aim of the book. In other words, this double notion of writing either places us in a sphere of philosophical discussion or turns us back to the field of traditional literary criticism. It leaves specific disciplines, above all, literary theory, forbidden to "use" Derridean distinctions because literary works, according to Gasché, are texts only in the empirical sense, not in the general sense.

3. Finally, the third aspect concerns the effects deconstruction has already had on literary criticism and on its internal debates, effects that Gasché does not take into account.

This last aspect, as well as the first one, put into question the habit of invoking the name of Derrida as the sole, homogeneous point of reference for deconstructive literary criticism. When one speaks of deconstruction, is one talking about "translating" Derrida, just as the old com-

called the "literary" or "rhetorical" element in any sign system, even the most transparently "scientific," there would be much more to say. I shall return to this later.

Cultural Studies and the Ontopolitopological

One effect of globalization and the new telecommunications technologies is the way they are leading to many new forms of constructive and potentially powerful social organization, new kinds of communities. These include research and university communities. An example is the sense of lively and often contentious solidarity among those who interact with one or another website or chatgroup, those, for example, devoted to a theorist like Derrida, or to canonical writers like Shakespeare, Henry James, or Proust, or to special interest groups like feminists or those in minority studies.

The new forms of transnational organization by way of the Web are going beyond that, however, to new forms of political groupings. A recent essay by Jon Katz in *Wired*, cited already, describes and celebrates what is going on, in the United States at least, as not only "the slow death of the current political system" but also "the rise of postpolitics and the birth of the Digital Nation." Surfing the Net during the recent presidential election, Katz claims that he "saw the primordial stirrings of a new kind of nation—the Digital nation—and the formation of a new postpolitical philosophy. This nascent ideology," he continues, "fuzzy and difficult to define, suggests a blend of some of the best values rescued from the tired old dogmas—the humanism of liberalism, the economic opportunity of conservatism, plus a strong sense of personal responsibility and a passion for freedom." Whether this new, postpolitical community will come to anything remains to be seen. I think Katz is right, however, to say that a new form of dynamic change or even a disquieting fluidity characterizes interaction on the Web. "Ideas," says Katz, "almost never remain static on the Web. They are launched like children into the world, where they are altered by the many different environments they pass through, almost never coming home in the same form in which they left." Katz is hopeful that these postpolitical communities can lead to a better world, if those belonging to them choose to use their power in the right way. "The ascending young citizens of the Digital nation can, if they wish," he says, "construct a more civil society, a new politics based on rationalism, shared

parative literature once spoke of the reception of Goethe in England? In fact, the three aspects I have named are interrelated. The first leads to the second, and the second unavoidably leads to the third. Here I will address the first and second, since the third coincides with the unfolding of this book.

As for the first aspect, the problem can be outlined in the following way. Gasché puts on the same level deconstructive literary criticism (thus from the outset presupposing the existence of *a* deconstructive literary criticism) and an activity that consists in the neutralization or reciprocal repeal of opposing concepts or textual strata. To understand deconstruction in this way means, according to Gasché, that literary criticism, in appropriating some specific strategies, has misinterpreted it: "This misconception has informed most deconstructive literary criticism, whether of literary, philosophical, or critical texts, and it has come to be known as the theory of self-reflection or self-deconstruction of texts" (Gasché, 1986: 138). That mistake of literary criticism is, according to Gasché, a double mistake. First, it leads the discussion to the field of literature, when its real field is that of philosophy. Gasché assures us that Derrida's discourse arises from a particular philosophical problem, "namely, the criticism of the notion of reflexivity" (Gasché, 1986: 5). Second, having once entered within that philosophical problem, he identifies deconstructive literary criticism with attention to reflexivity, when "reflection and reflexivity . . . are precisely what will not fit in Derrida's work—not because he would wish to refute or reject them in favor of a dream of immediacy, but because his work questions reflection's unthought, and thus the limits of its possibility" (Gasché, 1986: 6). Gasché's demonstration begins with a historical revision of the problem of reflexivity, by way of two fundamental

information, the pursuit of truth, and new kinds of community."[70] We shall see about that. It might go the other way. It all depends—on many unpredictable factors. Certainly tremendous efforts of various sorts are now being made in the United States both to control or censor the Web and to commercialize it.

Another effect of globalization is even more problematic and also closer to accounting for the radical changes in literary study and humanistic study generally that are currently occurring, at least in the United States. Walter Benjamin long ago argued that new technologies, new modes of production and consumption, all the changes made by nineteenth-century industrialization, had already created a radically new human sensibility and therefore a new way of living in the world. "As the entire way of being changes for human collectives over large historical periods so also change their modes of sensual perception [*die Art und Weise ihrer Sinneswahrnehmung*]."[71] All the changes brought about by industrialization, the rise of great cities, and the development of new communications technologies like photography and cinema produced, according to Benjamin, a new way of being human, the nervous, solitary Baudelairean man of the crowd, hungry for immediate experience while at the same time obsessed with the sense of a faraway, unattainable horizon that undermines every immediacy. Benjamin's most often cited essay on this topic is "The Work of Art in the Age of Technical Reproducibility."[72] One would do well to be sceptical about such claims for a mutation in sensory experience. These claims are associated, in Benjamin's formulations, with the rise of new collectivities. We still have the same five senses that our ancestors had. Evolutionary mutations usually take thousands and thousands of years, not a mere two centuries. Nevertheless, the human sensory, emotional, and cognitive apparatus is unusually flexible among those possessed by different life forms. It may be that a man or woman today sitting before a computer screen or watching a film on a VCR or watching television has a radically different sense of being in the world from that once possessed by the inhabitant of an eighteenth-century village. Reading works of literature from the past is one way to find out about that. This is one strong defense of reading literature. The evidence, I must say, is ambiguous. Shakespeare's people, or even Chaucer's, seem in many ways more like us than they seem radically different, in spite of the fact that they had no television. Nevertheless, the differences are important too. They need to be studied carefully in order to be identified accurately.

steps, Kant and Hegel. Hegel, through the concept of "speculation" and "absolute reflection," comes to *solve* the antinomies that were pending in Kantian philosophy: "To sum up: Speculation, or absolute reflection, is a critique of reflection and, particularly, of philosophical reflection insofar as its mirroring function permits the overcoming of the major antinomy of reflection, that between the empirical, formal, or transcendental self-reflection of cognition (the thinking being) and the reflected object of this epistemological endeavor (what is thought)" (Gasché, 1986: 45).

Why, then, is it not possible to compare deconstructive literary criticism with Derridean deconstruction? The answer is that, whereas Derrida's discourse is situated further on or on the fringe of reflexivity— in a line going from Nietzsche, Dilthey, and Husserl to Heidegger, with whom he has a conflictive relationship—deconstructive literary criticism remains anchored as close as possible to reflexivity, even in its center. There is a clear antecedent here, according to Gasché, in the Jena Romantics, that is, the young Friedrich Schlegel and the rest of the members of the periodical *Athenaeum*. Gasché refers to them in several passages of his book, but in the chapter entitled "Deconstructive Methodology" he points particularly to the link between them and deconstructive literary critics as well as to the obstacles arising from the attempt to incorporate such critics into Derridean deconstruction. On the one hand, he argues, a crucial relationship is ignored or put aside: "The suspicion that antagonistic positions or opposite concepts are identical arises from a neglect of the historical and pragmatic aspects of the contexts in which they are expressed" (Gasché, 1986: 139). Study of historical context reveals the origins of this kind of literary criticism: Romantic philosophy. On the other hand, one has to take into account that Romantic philosophy and

Jacques Derrida, in an eloquent passage in a recent seminar, stresses the strange combination of solitude and a new kind of being with others of the person using a computer to reach the World Wide Web, as well as the breakdown of traditional boundaries between inside and outside brought about by new telecommunications. As this epochal cultural displacement from the book age to the hypertext age has accelerated, we have been ushered ever more rapidly into a threatening living space. This new electronic space—the space of television, cinema, telephone, videos, fax, e-mail, hypertext, and Internet—has profoundly altered the economies of the self, the home, the workplace, the university, and the nation-state's politics. These were traditionally ordered around the firm boundaries of an inside-outside dichotomy, whether those boundaries were the walls between the home's privacy and all the world outside or the borders between the nation-state and its neighbors. The new technologies invade the home and confound all these inside/outside divisions. On the one hand, no one is so alone as when watching television, talking on the telephone, or sitting before a computer screen reading e-mail or searching an Internet database. On the other hand, that private space has been invaded and permeated by a vast, simultaneous crowd of verbal, aural, and visual images existing in cyberspace's simulacrum of presence. Those images cross national and ethnic boundaries. They come from all over the world with a spurious immediacy that makes them all seem equally close and equally distant. The global village is not out there, but in here, or a clear distinction between inside and out no longer operates. The new technologies bring the *unheimlich* "other" into the privacy of the home. They are a frightening threat to traditional ideas of the self as unified and as properly living rooted in one dear, particular culture-bound place, participating in a single national culture, firmly protected from any alien otherness. They are threatening also to our assumption that political action is based in a single topographical location, a given nation-state with its firm boundaries, its ethnic and cultural unity. Derrida calls this set of assumptions the *ontopolitopologique.* It is not surprising that there should be strong reactions to what Derrida calls "a new and powerful advance in the technological prosthesis that, in a thousand ways, ex-propriates, de-localizes, de-territorializes, *extirpates,* that is to say, in the etymological and therefore radical sense of this word, uproots, therefore *de-etymologizes,* dissociates the political from the topological, separates from itself what has always been the very concept of the

Romantic poetics propose a notion of discourse (the sym-philosophy, sym-poetry or transcendental poetry) that, because of its self-reflexive tendency toward the elimination of all differences, represents the realization of metaphysics' so-called *telos*.

Here is the passage in Gasché's book: "Let us remember that this kind of criticism originated in early German Romanticism. The reciprocal dissolution of opposing concepts or contradictory strata within a text, which this criticism promotes, must be traced back to the Romantics' attempt at a transcendental poetry that was to represent an amalgam not only of all different genres but also of all the hitherto separate disciplines. Such a poetry was to be created through a fluidization or liquefaction (*Verflüssigung*) of all oppositions and particularities by means of objective irony. The result was to be a *medium of reflexivity*, in which all individual, and thus opposite, stands would achieve total reciprocity" (Gasché, 1986: 139). Gasché tells us, immediately afterward, that the criticism of those premises was already carried out by Hegel and that, in conclusion, "deconstruction has nothing in common with this sort of philosophical or critical practice, although it is often confused with it. Deconstruction does not engage in the annulment or neutralization of opposites" (Gasché, 1986: 142). Unlike Gasché's earlier "Deconstruction as Criticism," which openly engages Paul de Man and his followers (including perhaps J. Hillis Miller), *The Tain of the Mirror* contains no mention of them, save several footnotes, in one of which he comments that Paul de Man was conscious of the distance between his work and Derrida's. In short, Gasché discusses deconstructive literary criticism without mentioning, except in passing, either its representatives or their works.

Why, in this book, should Gasché risk disguising the facts? If I

political, that is, what links the political to the topical, to the city, to the
territory, to the ethno-national frontier."[73]

One reaction to this uprooting, dislocation, and blurring of borders, also discussed by Derrida, is the violent return to the nationalisms,
ethnic purities, and fanatical, militarized religions that are leading to such
horrible bloodshed around the world these days. Another reaction is the
hysterical return to isolationism in the United States. Yet another very different response, it may be, is the rapid switch in university humanities
departments, beginning around 1980, from literary study, organized primarily around the separate study of national literatures, to cultural studies.
Though nothing could be more different from ethnic cleansing in Rwanda
or Bosnia than a program in cultural studies, the development of such
studies may to some degree be another very different reaction to the transformations in daily life new communications technologies bring about.
Cultural studies can function as a way to contain and tame the threat of
the invasive otherness the new technologies bring across the thresholds of
our homes and workplaces.

This containing and taming takes a double, contradictory form. On
the one hand, it tends to reestablish firm boundaries between one nation
and another, one ethnic group and another, one gender or sexual orientation and another. It may sometimes assume that a given individual can be
defined by his or her participation in an ethnic group, and can therefore be
understood by understanding the ethos of that ethnicity. The tradition of
dividing university disciplines along national, linguistic, generic, or ethnic
lines remains to a considerable degree intact after the introduction of cultural studies, in spite of much talk about interdisciplinarity and much
recognition of what is problematic about defining identity through membership in a given group or community. Often the traditional divisions are
now simply expanded to include separate programs in women's studies, gay
and lesbian studies, Native American studies, African American studies,
Chicano and Chicana studies, Asian American studies, film studies, visual
culture studies, and so on. All these "others" are now given a place in the
university, but they are fenced off in a firm re-establishment of the in-
side/outside dichotomy that the new technologies threaten. The "others"
are still kept safely outside. Interdisciplinarity still presupposes the separate
integrity of the disciplines that interact, just as "hybridity" presupposes the
fixed nature of the two genetic strains that are hybridized. Joint appointments (say in English and African American studies) may cause scholars

were to use de Man's terminology, I would say that Gasché suffers from a blindness in consequence of his intent to preserve the philosophical character of Derrida's discourse. Such blindness forces him to read the proposals of the Jena Romantics and, consequently, those of the deconstructive critics (I imagine he is speaking of Paul de Man and J. Hillis Miller, among others) in a way that shifts and hides the main questions. Therefore, when he quotes the concept of transcendental poetry, for instance, he refers exclusively to the elimination of all oppositions and differences which takes place inside such a genre. Something similar happens when he incorporates the notion of the medium of reflexivity. But is this the only perspective from which both transcendental poetry and the medium of reflexivity can be contemplated? Is this a suitable perspective for dealing with them? On the basis of my reading works by Benjamin (1973), Blanchot (1969), Lacoue-Labarthe and Nancy (1978), Derrida (1980a), and Marike Finlay (1988), among others, I would say no. The first thing to attract our attention is that as soon as the figure of Schlegel is introduced into a discussion of the problem of "reflexivity," it is no longer possible to know just where we are. Are we in a philosophical space or, on the contrary, are we in the field of art and literature?

In order to answer these questions it is necessary to recall Benjamin's thesis concerning what separates Fichte from the Romantics. For Fichte, "reflexivity" has to do with the transforming reflecting of a form, with the self-knowledge of a method, and, above all, with a spiritual attitude represented by a thought whose function is to limit the infinite process of reflection. Without this, it would be impossible to accede to an effective (self-)consciousness. The Romantics accepted the infinity of reflection Fichte had rejected. They felt a true reverence for the infinite. For them

to lead a double, hybrid life, subject to the presuppositions and protocols of two different disciplines. One should not, however, underestimate the longterm transformative effect on national literature departments the presence of such scholars within those departments will cause.

On the other hand, the return, wherever it happens, to a mimetic, representational, descriptive methodology tends to turn those threatening others into something that in theory (for this is a theory too) can be easily understood, "translated," and appropriated. This happens, or is presumed to happen, along the lines proposed for intercultural translation in the Bernheimer report. The universalizing idea of culture in cultural studies, just because it is a term so all-inclusive as to be virtually empty, may be a place of exchange, of turning the other back into the same. This might be the case even though all cultures and all individuals may be seen as to some degree hybrid, not as fixed, univocal essences. Individual works may be seen as unproblematically representative of the culture they reflect. A few carefully chosen examples can stand for a whole culture and give us a means of understanding it and taking it in. This procedure depends on a thematic way of interpretation that sees texts or other cultural artifacts as directly reflective of a historical or social context that is open to understanding by way of the work, though of course separate study of the context is also necessary. This form of study also sometimes depends on uncritical acceptance of the extremely dubious trope of synecdoche, part for whole, just as does taking "deconstruction" as standing for the whole of theory.[74] The historical context can then by way of the representative work be easily transposed into the terms of the university discipline assigned to assimilate it. That translation can occur without essential loss is the key presupposition here. Such forms of archival appropriation have been in place in the university since the Humboldtian research university was first established. They are part of the foundational heritage of the university, which says that everything has its reason, can be brought to light, known, understood, and appropriated. This double, contradictory gesture says at once that the other is really other and may be kept safely outside the traditional literary disciplines and that the other is not really other and may be made a *heimlich* member of the family.

Such a double disabling gesture is by no means universal in cultural studies. As I have said, theory of the 1960's, 1970's, and 1980's has gone on being effective, even in those who are overtly hostile to it. This includes the deep understanding of culture by Raymond Williams and others in Brit-

reflection spreads without limits, and the thought formed in reflection becomes a thought devoid of form heading for the absolute. It is obvious that that "absolute" is not understood as effectivity or completion. For this reason Blanchot writes that it is a matter of "at the same time affirming the absolute and the fragmentary; affirming totality, but in a form that, being all forms—that is, at the limit, being none at all—does not realize the whole, but signifies it by suspending it, even breaking it" (Blanchot, 1993: 353).

Blanchot recognizes in the proposals of the *Athenaeum* what Gasché does not perceive, that is, their essential paradox. If we turn to fragment 116 of the *Athenaeum*, we shall observe that if at first Schlegel speaks of Romantic poetry as a space that tends to "unify all genres," toward the end he notes: "The romantic type of poetry is still in the state of becoming; that, in fact, is its real essence: that it should forever be becoming and never be perfected. It can be exhausted by no theory and only a divinatory criticism would dare to characterize its ideal. It alone is infinite, just as it alone is free; and it recognizes as its first commandment that the will of the poet can tolerate no law above itself" (Schlegel, 1991: 32). The poetry that cannot be exhausted by any theory might not admit its own (self-)exhaustion. It shows, therefore, a kind of reflexivity that takes place only as a process without ultimate foundation. This is why the young Schlegel is as far from Fichte as from Hegel. What separates him from Fichte is his worship of infinity. This, according to Fichte's own words, leads to the impossibility of attaining an "effective consciousness." Several things separate Schlegel from Fichte, but it suffices to say that, whereas in Hegel the "absolute reflection" supposes a work of overcoming all the aporias and antinomies that leads toward a situation of foundation and

ain,[75] as well as the understanding of ideology in Louis Althusser and other continental Marxists. An advocate of cultural studies and a practitioner of postcolonial studies like Rey Chow, as I have shown, strongly affirms the continuity of poststructuralist theory and cultural studies. Wherever the rejection of theory occurs, however, whether it is made explicitly under the aegis of the "revolt against theory" or just spontaneously, as a defensive reflex against a perceived threat, it may disable the project of cultural studies, just as it would disable any other discipline that intended to alter the status quo. It will prevent cultural studies from reaching its goal of political and institutional change toward the democracy to come which most people desire.

The acceptance by the university of cultural studies has been relatively rapid and easy, though no doubt it has not seemed that way, for example, to those who have had to fight for years for the institutionalizing of women's studies. The firm establishment of cultural studies in the university has nevertheless taken only fifteen years or so, a relatively short time for such a genuinely revolutionary change. This may be because cultural studies is unconsciously assumed by those in charge to be non-threatening, to leave the old institutional structures more or less intact. If so, I think university administrators may have misjudged cultural studies' power to transform the university. Nevertheless, the university may even think of cultural studies as a way of policing minority groups. Once these new disciplines have been set up, at least the authorities will know where to find members of those groups.

The rise of cultural studies has accompanied the technologizing and globalizing turn in the university and, where it is an antitheoretical return to mimetism, is a concomitant of that turn. Why does this antitheoretical turn, when it occurs, disable cultural studies? For one thing it is a regression to just the conservative hegemonic ideology cultural studies would contest. The right and certain components of the left are sometimes similar in their basic presuppositions about cultural forms. Both sometimes accept, for example, the notion that cultural artifacts unproblematically reflect their cultural contexts. You cannot use the ideology of those you would displace to displace their ideology. Wherever cultural studies deploys precritical notions of the self and its agency, of referentiality, of cultural artifacts' transparency, or wherever it assumes that history can be narrativized unproblematically or that cultural artifacts can be exhaustively described by a repertoire of themes, its work will be politically ineffective.

closure, in Schlegel, as we have already seen, the act of putting differences in touch with one another is carried out in an interminable, infinite, and unfinished way.

This is, I maintain, because Friedrich Schlegel cannot be sequestered in the philosophical field to which Gasché apparently wants to restrict the discussion of "reflexivity." By introducing the Romantics' proposals into the debate, Gasché is already in the field of literature, at least in the field of literature as theory, or theory as literature. Benjamin is very attentive to this transition and emphasizes that the center of reflection in early German Romanticism is art and not the self. What Gasché seeks to avoid—the transition in Derrida's thought from the philosophical (regarding the problem of reflexivity) to the literary—*has already taken place* in the historical moment he cites. It is true enough that "with the exception of certain rare examples, literary writing has subjugated itself to the constraints of the concept and to the ethos of philosophy. Literature, then, speaks the voice of philosophy. It is a mere proxy, stillborn. There has hardly ever been any literature, if literature is supposed to mean something other than philosophy" (Gasché, 1986: 256). But this idea, with all the truth it reveals, establishes what it tries to avoid. Gasché states that when the differences between philosophy and literature are resolved by what might be called a general "literaturizing," this is a metaphysical gesture. He hastens to assure us, however, that both philosophy and literature speak in the voice of philosophy. He ignores what is closer to the truth, what Lacoue-Labarthe and Nancy announce in a very precise way: early German Romanticism and its exposition of a "literary absolute" supposes the introduction of a radical instability, a break within philosophical discourse. Apart from that, one might have to wonder whether

Fortunately much work in cultural studies has great theoretical so-
phistication and is able, through interventionist acts of "reading," to pass
on the dislocating energy of the cultural artifacts it discusses. "Reading"
here names a transaction not just with literary or exclusively verbal texts
but "readings" of works in other media: visual or aural media like film,
television, popular music, or advertising. "Reading," however, must be
distinguished from "theory." Though theory may facilitate reading and
should ideally have arisen from acts of reading, the two are not the same
thing, nor are they by any means always in harmony. Genuine acts of reading are always to some degree sui generis, inaugural. They always to some
extent disable or disqualify the theory that may have been the motivating
presupposition of the reader. It is easy enough to sprinkle a text in cultural studies with cogent, correct, and forceful appeals to "theory" — for
example, references to Foucault, Benedict Anderson, Bhabha, Fanon, Said,
or Irigaray — while performing acts of reading that are precritical, pretheoretical, and predominantly thematic. Simple tests make possible a distinction between the two kinds of reading. A thematic reading summarizes
plots, describes characters as if they were real people, and, where the work
is in a language other than the language of the reader, can cite a translation
without needing to go back to the original language. What I am calling a
"genuine reading" always must have recourse to the original language of
the work, however awkward and time-consuming this may be, and however much it may go against the powerful ideology of journals and both
university and commercial presses. This ideology assumes that everything
can be translated without loss into English. This recourse to the original
language is necessary because the force of the original work, its happening
as a cultural event that to some extent exceeded the social context from
which it arose, lies in its unique use of its own vernacular idiom.

I call this unique use the irreducible otherness of the work, even its
otherness to the culture that apparently "generated" it. Use of a translation
uproots the work, denatures it, transforms it into a *hortus siccus* or dried,
specimen flower ready to be stored in the bottomless archives of a transnational university system that is more and more dominated by the English
language as a global language. This argument for return to the original
languages in acts of reading is, however, only the most visible version of
a need, even in studying works in the same language as that of the critic,
to get behind thematic reading and pay attention to what might be called
the materiality of the work. The work's force as an event bringing cultural

the work of Cervantes, for instance, is an example of text that speaks with the voice of philosophy.

The controversy between Hegel and the Romantics takes place not only in the technical space of philosophy, but also, above all, in the technical space of poetics. In this sense, as Marike Finlay (1988) has proved, the controversy between Hegel and the Romantics concerns both the problem of reflexivity and the function of art. Moreover, the polemic of the Romantics takes place in relation to the great ideals of classical poetics. Speaking in a very schematic way, one might say that from the outset of the Renaissance—through the re-reading of Plato's and Aristotle's *corpora*—until about the middle of the eighteenth century, we witness a conception of literature that is essentially the same in 1750 as in 1550. That conception can be summed up in four principles:

1. the principle of mimesis or the priority of *res*;
2. the principle of the finality of art as an element linked to ethics and metaphysics;
3. the principle that links the creative process to (a) the mechanical conception of mind, (b) wit, and (c) the technique necessary for poetic composition;
4. the principle of the rules and divisions of arts and genres, as well as the principle of identity governing the idea of "genre."

I wish to focus on two of these four principles, the first (mimesis) and the fourth (the rules, divisions, and identity of genres). As a result of the logic and the economy of his interests, Gasché fails to note that in Schlegel's texts the notion of "transcendental poetry" links up with other notions like "irony," "wit," and "parabasis." As Marike Finlay has noticed:

value or meaning into existence depends on a certain performative use of language or other signs. Such a reading must attend to what is internally heterogeneous, contradictory, odd, anomalous about the work, rather than presupposing some monolithic unity that directly reflects a cultural context. Only such a reading can hope to transmit or preserve some of the force as an event the original work had or can still have. This might even make the reading, as recorded in an essay or lecture, a new event helping to bring about social change.

Many people working in cultural studies have assimilated the theory of the 1960's, 1970's, and 1980's—Foucault, Lacan, Bakhtin, de Man, Derrida, Lyotard, and the rest—and are going forward with new, urgent tasks on that foundation. This is true for the work of Judith Butler or Diane Elam,[76] to mention two among many others. Butler's work is of course strengthened by her professional training as a philosopher. The ideology of an unreflective representationalism is so powerful, however, that many others, even if they are theoretically sophisticated, may instinctively succumb to it when doing the actual work of reading. The critic may revert to a merely thematic description of works, and begin, for example, talking about the characters in a novel as if they were real people and about the novel as a direct reflection of historical conditions as distorted by the class ideology of its author. This is a particular temptation when so much new work in so many media, so much work neglected by the white male traditions of scholarship, needs to be assimilated into the university—described, inventoried, and stored there. It is also a particular temptation when a primary assumption is that a given work may to a considerable degree be explained by its relation to the transindividual historical and ideological context that is embedded in it.

Nostalgia for the old Humboldtian university or even the hope that we might turn it into a new, unified, multicultural university to replace the monocultural one will not reverse the changes now taking place. The old university is "in ruins," as Readings puts it, and cannot be reconstructed. The responsibility of those who teach and do research now is to see as clearly as possible what has happened (no easy task) and to figure out what to do now. This present situation must be the object of our transformative praxis. Such work will be extremely difficult. Nostalgia for the old university of consensus devoted to the promulgation of a single culture will not easily die. The very idea of a university depends on that project. Moreover, in the new transnational university it will be hard to keep the humanities

"As we allow these models to interrelate, certain contradictions and oppositions will be seen to arise, which place the representational model in a state of crisis" (Finlay, 1988: 40). Here is the nucleus of the controversy between Hegelian phenomenology and Schlegelian irony. Hegel conceives art as expression (*Vorstellung*), that is to say, under a model basically mimetic, although the mimesis is not of nature or human subjectivity but of the *Geist*.

Gasché is clearly inclined to follow Hegel's position, as seen from the perspective of Derridean deconstruction as he understands it. He writes: "Yet that which authorizes the commentary—the metaphysics of the commentary—does minimal violence to the works of literature because this metaphysics already governs the works commented upon. The critical commentary seems to be commensurate with traditional literary works. Literary criticism, then, is a philosophy of a literature which has from the outset yielded to the categories of philosophy, or in other words to literature as such. The critical enterprise is, as its name reveals, a philosophical enterprise. It is linked to the possibility of the *krinein*—that is, to the possibility of decision—of a mastery of the meaning or signified of the literary text. . . . One of the more specific names for such a critical approach to literature is *thematic* criticism" (Gasché, 1986: 262). He concludes, "Thematic criticism of all shades is undoubtedly a very legitimate approach to such writing" (Gasché, 1986: 263).

To say that metaphysics governs the works commented upon by literary criticism is just what is put in question by Derrida. In Paul de Man or in J. Hillis Miller we also find a demonstration of the opposite thesis. When Hegel conceives art as a medium for representing something alien to himself, the Absolute Spirit (*Geist*) that expresses itself, he is rejecting

from becoming vestigial, no more than an assembly of programs teaching communication skills. Such a university would be devoted primarily to the production, transfer, and exchange of economically valuable information. Rather than forming citizens of one nation-state, its humanities programs would be charged with training people for service in a global economy and with making them expert consumers of that economy's products. How can humanists effectively resist this and in the name of what alternative goal?

The Other Other

The concept of otherness has great importance both in recent theoretical thinking and as an indispensable term in cultural studies, women's studies, African American studies, and so on. A single hegemonic culture, cultural studies tends to presume, needs to define all other cultures as "other" in order to establish its own integrity and power. The word or the concept of "the other" is used, however, in many different, incompatible ways in current humanistic discourse. Just what are those ways? They are easiest to think of as personified in a series of well-known names. These are names to conjure with in current theory and criticism, personifications of positions that exceed any one person and that do not themselves have the unity we associate with personhood. I give these names pell-mell, in no particular order.

For Emmanuel Levinas "the other" is an absolute transcendence, "beyond being," who leaves traces of itself or himself in the face of the other person. Levinas says *traces*, not signs. A sign presupposes the existence and availability of its referent. A trace is a catachresis (though Levinas does not use this word) for something or someone I can never confront directly, something truly "other." These traces belong to "a past absolutely bygone." The other never was present and can never be made present.[77]

For Jacques Lacan, in a celebrated formulation, "the unconscious is the discourse of the other." This presence of the other within my depths, out of my sight, sets up those triangular Lacanian relations in which a message circulates among three persons. Lacan has expressed this circulation as the law of the three ostriches: one with its head buried in the sand, the second thinking he or she is therefore invulnerable, while the third ostrich calmly plucks the tailfeathers of the second. This law is investigated in Lacan's essay on Poe's "The Purloined Letter." That story is a letter that has been passed from critic to critic in contemporary theory: from Poe to

what Schlegel understands by "transcendental poetry." Transcendental poetry is, according to fragment 238 of the *Athenaeum*, the ability to produce a poetic theory of the poetic faculty and in its presentations also to present itself (*selbst mit darstellen*) — that is, to "always be both poetry and the poetry of poetry" (Schlegel, 1991: 51). One must keep in mind that Schlegel uses the expression *Darstellung*, presentation, and not *Vorstellung*, representation. The representational vision of art (Hegel) opposes the presentational vision of it (Schlegel). As Finlay writes, "Hegel criticizes romantic irony for emptying the world of all content and reducing existence and art to isolated, capricious, accidental form" (Finlay, 1988: 148). Derrida in *Glas* (1974b: 14, left column) and Miller himself in the chapter from *The Linguistic Moment* devoted to Hopkins (LM, 235 and following) have also paid attention to this opposition.

Transcendental poetry presents itself and does not limit itself to representing either an external reality or an internal one. The work of art will have destructive moments in which it will refer only to itself. It will be symbolic (opaque) and not allegorical (transparent). This is the key to the dispute between Hegel and Schlegel: "While the artistic could never qualify as the Absolute, Hegel's *Phenomenology* does. This is the key to the Hegelian dispute with irony. Irony, contrary to the *Phenomenology*, remained within the dialectical tensions as opposed to transcending these antitheses of representation and arriving at the level of the philosophical Idea" (Finlay, 1988: 154). But why irony? According to Gasché, irony is the means by which the "fluidization or liquefaction (*Verflüssigung*) of all oppositions and particularities" is attained (Gasché, 1986: 139). When Schlegel tells us in fragment 69 from the set of fragments called "Ideas," however, that "irony is the clear consciousness of eternal agility,

Baudelaire to Lacan to Derrida to Barbara Johnson to others, in a ceaseless dissemination.[78] What is most problematic about Lacan's writing might be economically phrased by asking whether the "other" is really "other" for Lacan, or whether, for him, in Derrida's phrase, the letter always reaches its destination, that is, can be brought out in the open, pinned down to a definite meaning, for all to read, or at least for its destined recipient to read, and therefore is no longer radically other. When this happens the other is assimilated, becomes the same, or returns to the same after its circuit is complete.[79]

For Jacques Derrida, on the other hand, the letter never reaches its destination, even though, like a postcard, it is exposed where all can read it. The letter is condemned to wander interminably, not so much in its plurisignificance as in its aporetic indeterminacy of meaning and addressee.[80] For Derrida, as he says, "Tout autre est tout autre," which means, among other things, "Every other is wholly other."[81] The notion of otherness has fundamental importance from one end of Derrida's work to the other, even when it is given other names or is glimpsed in different ways, for example, in the relay of *la différance* to a past that never occurred, or in the exploration in "Fors" of what it means to speak of an event that took place without ever having taken place and that has brought the Wolf Man to be haunted by a dead-alive body in a crypt in his unconscious. It would be a long trek to track the Protean other through all the diversity of Derrida's work. Four recent essays confront the question of the other directly: an interview with Jean-Luc Nancy; the title essay in *Psyche: Inventions of the Other*; Derrida's book on death (*Aporias*); and the chapter entitled "Tout autre est tout autre" in *The Gift of Death*.[82] In *Aporias* Derrida patiently demonstrates that Heidegger's thought about death in its relation to Dasein is undermined by an aporia. If the otherness of death is wholly other, it cannot be used as a distinguishing feature of Dasein. If death is the possibility of an impossibility, then it is impossible to say anything more about it than that. Even to say that is too much, since as an aporia it is an impasse in speech and thought. This aporia marks all the way in thought that has been traversed to get to it with the sign not of a *Holzweg*, a "forest path," as in the title of one of Heidegger's books, but of a "Dead End."

Richard Kearney asked Derrida in an interview in 1981: "What then of the question of language as reference? Can language as mutation or monstrosity refer to anything other than itself?" To this Derrida answered:

of an infinitely teeming chaos" (Schlegel, 1991: 100) or in fragment 48 of the "Critical Fragments" that "irony is the form of paradox" (Schlegel, 1991: 6), he is aiming not so much at the union of two irreconcilable ideas, of two opposites (which would only reproduce the classical conception of irony), as at the meeting of heterogeneous and chaotic materials in the same space. Gasché misses this in his analysis of the supposed historical antecedents of "deconstructive" literary critics. Irony is not just a question of collecting and mixing, as fragment 116 of the "*Athenaeum* Fragments" announces, but of making the collected material oscillate between union and destruction. For this reason, in the novel *Lucinde* the narrator advises: "Create, discover, transform, and retain the world and its eternal forms in the perpetual variation of new marriages and divorces" (Schlegel, 1971: 58).

In light of these words, we must recognize that irony supposes a semiotic tension, which produces an infinity of signs ("hierographies," according to Schlegel), which can never be fixed in a signified, in an opposing pair of signifieds, or in a constant substitution of signifier for signifier. From the viewpoint of textual constitution, irony identifies itself with parabasis, that is, with the interaction between the mimetic and the nonmimetic or fantastic. As a result, mimetic continuity is broken by diegetics, that is, by the sequencing of narrative, and vice versa. Schlegel understands the meeting of opposites as an interaction and not as a fusion. Irony is the constant suspended flow between self-creation and self-destruction that Schlegel calls "a permanent parabasis" (Schlegel, 1958–95: 18: 85). It might be characterized—if it can really be characterized at all—as a type of modalization that multiplies perspectives in order to disrupt the narrative voice's unity, thereby making ambiguous the se-

It is totally false to suggest that deconstruction is a suspension of reference. Deconstruction is always deeply concerned with the "other" of language. I never cease to be surprised by critics who see my work as a declaration that there is nothing beyond language, that we are imprisoned in language; it is, in fact, saying the opposite. The critique of logocentrisim is above all else the search for the "other" and the "other of language." . . . Certainly deconstruction tries to show that the question of reference is much more complex and problematic than traditional theories supposed. It even asks whether our term "reference" is entirely adequate for designating the "other." The other, which is beyond language and which summons language, is perhaps not a "referent" in the normal sense which linguists have attached to this term. But to distance oneself thus from the habitual structure of reference, to challenge or complicate our common assumptions about it, does not amount to saying that there is *nothing* beyond language. . . . I totally refuse the label of nihilism which has been ascribed to me and my American colleagues. Deconstruction is not an enclosure in nothingness, but an openness towards the other.[83]

The Wolf Man's Magic Word, the book by Nicolas Abraham and Maria Torok on Freud's patient the "Wolf Man," is the occasion of Derrida's inventive commentary in "Fors."[84] Abraham and Torok characteristically associate the other with ghosts, melancholy, and haunting. In another essay they propose the provocative possibility that Hamlet is haunted, not by his father's ghost, but by his dead father's unconscious.[85] The latter goes on living as a cryptic inhabitant, neither dead nor alive, in Hamlet's own unconscious. It causes much perturbation in his conscious thoughts and feelings. Each of us, it may be, is haunted by the unconscious of the other.

For Frantz Fanon, Edward Said, and innumerable other cultural studies experts today, the term "other" names the racial, class, gendered, or national other. This cultural other is necessarily posited as the ground for the dominance of the hegemonic culture. This other that I posit in order to assert my own superiority is always a caricature or parody, shot through with ideological lies, just as is the sense of myself or of my nation, culture, or society. Nevertheless, this ideological image of the other's otherness has great power. It is used to justify the most inhuman acts of cruelty—ethnic cleansing in Bosnia, for example, or the horrors of the Shoah.[86]

Jean-François Lyotard's term "differend" names an irreducible difference between one person or group and another. As opposed to Jurgen Habermas, for whom dialogue has as its horizon a reconciling consensus, Lyotard presupposes a personal or social heterogeneity that can never be

mantic values of mimetic and poetic illusion. *Lucinde* is a good example of this. What will hardly be found in its "practice" and in its "theory" is *a* position, whether in the sense of eliminating definite antinomies or oppositions, or in the sense of sustaining those same oppositions and antinomies.

This logically affects the other great principle of classical poetics: the generic and textual identity that constitutes our second focus of interest. Classical writings use the organism as a metaphor to conceptualize the literary text (Asensi, 1990). Aristotle, dealing with the "fable" (*muthos*), writes: "Now, according to our definition, Tragedy is an imitation of an action that is complete, and whole, and of a certain magnitude. . . . A whole is that which has a beginning, a middle, and an end. . . . A well constructed plot, therefore, must neither begin nor end at haphazard, but conform to these principles. Again, a beautiful object, whether it be a living organism or any whole composed of parts, must not only have an orderly arrangement of parts, but must also be of a certain magnitude" (Aristotle, 1951: 31). Tragedy (although not only tragedy) is subject to a classical theory of beauty that is linked with notions of rhythm, symmetry, and harmony among parts, that is to say, with the general formula of unity in variety (Bosanquet, 1910: 30–33). Or, in the words Plato uses in the *Phaedrus*, "any discourse ought to be constructed like a living creature, with its own body, as it were; it must not lack either head or feet; it must have a middle and extremities so composed as to suit both each other and the whole work" (Plato, 1963: 264c, 510). Any specialist in the history of poetics knows that the hegemony of the metaphor of the organism was transmitted through Horace to modernity. With the Jena Romantics, precisely this conception of the text as organism is in

negotiated or talked out of existence. For Lyotard the social other—for example, the racial, class, gendered, or political other—is truly other. My values cannot by any means be reconciled with the values of someone who is "other" in one of these ways, nor can they be subsumed at some higher level that will encompass them both. Only a democracy based on dissensus and on some idea of radical heterogeneity in different persons and groups within a single polity could recognize and protect this radical otherness. "It seems to me," says Lyotard, "that the only consensus we ought to be worrying about is one that would encourage this heterogeneity or 'dissensus.'"[87] Maurice Blanchot and Jean-Luc Nancy have tried to imagine what such an "unworked" community might be like, while Bill Readings, in his brilliant diagnosis of the university in *The University in Ruins*, and Diane Elam, in an admirable book, *Feminism and Deconstruction*, have explored in different areas what a community of dissensus might be like.[88] I shall return later to the topic of dissensus.

The "dialogical" in Mikhail Bakhtin's thought at first perhaps appears to be a confrontation through conversation's give and take of one person with another. The term names, rather, an incongruity within language that can never be smoothed out in some monological discourse. Just as Bakhtin appears to have been not just one person, Bakhtin, but at the same time also Voloshinov and Medvedev, or perhaps, after all, three different persons, so a dialogic discourse, or what might be called heteroglossolalia, has two or more "logoi," two or more irreconcilable centers of emission and control of meaning. It verges on a heterogeneous speaking in tongues. An extraordinary passage in the essay "Discourse in Life and Discourse in Art (Concerning Sociological Poetics)"[89] suggests that dialogue is actually a triadic relation in which the motivating pole is the muteness and inhuman alienation of a material other.

Paul de Man does not seem to have much patience with portentous terms like "the other" or "others." His radical concept of irony, however, presupposes the encounter with an otherness within language that generates a permanent suspension of meaning. In de Man's last essays this otherness is given the strange, quasi-Marxist name "materiality." Examples are phrases in his work that are by no means easy to understand, phrases about "the materiality of language," "the materiality of inscription," or "the materiality of history." "Materiality," in de Man's last essays, does not name the solid substance of physical materiality, open to the senses and to our manipulation. It names a radical alterity that is not phenomenal, that

crisis. The general coherence of the work collapses as a result of a fragmentary practice that must not be confused with a fragmentary variety of expression (as in Shaftesbury, La Rochefoucauld, Pascal, Montaigne, and others).

Transcendental or Romantic poetry is theorized (and practiced) as fragment. Furthermore, the dialogue and the novel are theorized in the same way, so that the theory of the fragment becomes a basis for a theory of the text in general, a constitutive principle of discourse and writing (Asensi, 1991). This theory announces the failure to achieve an organically unified work, or, in Blanchot's words, the work of the absence of the work, poetry affirmed in the purity of the poetic act, assertion without duration, liberty without realization. Still more important, by assuming the meeting of different types of discourses that do not arrive at a complete fusion, transcendental poetry conceives the text as contradictions among the different levels, strata, codes, and intertextualities that constitute it. This conception of the concrete and empirical text is the starting point of proposals made by both Derrida and the deconstructive literary critics, although the conception leads to different results for each. As we shall see below, it is not so much that de Man and Miller *translate* Derrida, as that Derrida, de Man, and Miller employ (in a conscious or unconscious way) a notion of text that arises, obviously in contradictory forms, among the Jena Romantics. The text is an object essentially impure and illegitimate. It constitutes itself from a mixture of matters and materials that affects both utterance and form of enunciation. The term "text," for the Jena Romantics, as for Derrida, de Man, and Miller, includes assemblages of words dealing with a variety of topics extending from poetry, philosophy, and general aesthetics to politics, music, gender difference, and current anecdotes.

is not the object of a representable intuition, that cannot be confronted directly, that cannot be named referentially or literally. Other displaced names for this de Manian other are "death" and "the impossibility of reading." This material other is the unintelligible and imperceptible base of all meaning, something not a part of what de Man calls "phenomenality." It vitiates and undermines clear sensemaking, as the contingency of puns causes language to escape the control of the person who uses it. An inadvertent pun (and language is full of inadvertent puns) makes the user say something different from what he or she intended to say. This something may nevertheless have performative effects in the real world, since it is only the materiality of words, beyond perspicuous meaning, that, for de Man, can make language be a historical event. Speaking in the lecture "Kant and Schiller" about the "event" of Kant's *Critique of Judgment*, de Man described "a movement, from cognition, from acts of knowledge, from states of cognition, to something which is no longer a cognition but which is to some extent an *occurrence*, which has the materiality of something that actually happens, that actually occurs . . . , that occurs materially, that leaves a trace on the world, that does something to the world as such," and he went on to say that "this notion of occurrence is not opposed in any sense to the notion of writing."[90] De Man's revision of speech act theory sees language, in particular the machinelike operations of grammar and the aporias of tropes, as detached from the control of the consciously willing "I." For de Man, language acts on its own to posit effective performatives. These enter the human world and make history through just those features of language that present a stubborn otherness to any efforts of control. That otherness de Man calls the "materiality" of language.[91]

In these different notions of otherness, a single problematic may be observed. On the one hand, the other is seen as part of a dialectical dyad either allowing for an *Aufhebung* or presupposing some "one" of which the two are derivatives, as all particular cultures may be seen as examples of culture in general. Such an alterity does not lead to aporias. If the other is really another form of the same, powerful machines of thinking, saying, and doing are not impeded in their working. Understanding and reconciliation are possible. The various sides can talk, perhaps reach a consensus. The concept of multiculturalism, for example, often, though by no means always, presupposes a notion of culture that is common to all the cultures juxtaposed in rainbow bands. However strange the other culture is, however different is the minority culture within the hegemonic culture, it is still

Schlegel's theory of the fragment is even more radical, however. The theory of the fragment as impurity implies that discourse constitutes itself from other preexisting discourses. Discourse exists as repetition, parody, quotation, paronomasia, and so on. The study Reinhold Münster devotes to Schlegel's *Lucinde* (Münster, 1987) shows how that work exemplifies its author's theory. Novalis expresses it another way by saying that the art of writing books has not yet been discovered and that fragments are literary seeds. Schlegel speaks of a new era for the arts and thinks of the theory of the fragment as an as yet unfulfilled desire. In fragment 77 of the "*Athenaeum* Fragments," he writes, "But as yet no genre exists that is fragmentary both in form and content" (Schlegel, 1991: 27). Schlegel's theoretico-practical fragmentarism must not be identified with the practice of the traditional fragment in the style of Chamfort. The fragment in this other sense is certainly one of Schlegel's favorite forms of expression, but the most relevant and most interesting point for my argument is that the fragment presupposes a theory of general writing applicable to the totality of genres. More exactly, it presupposes the desire of a future writing. We read in the *Athenaeum*, fragment 116, for instance, that the romantic genre, rather than being identified with the novel, does not yet exist and will not exist, since it is a constant process without end (Schlegel, 1991: 31–32). This future writing will disturb the traditional generico-textual order. It will begin with a mixing and a differential linguistic energy that the Jena Romantics call irony. I want to emphasize again that this general theory of fragmentary writing has nothing to do with the concrete, generic practice of the fragment, which, as Gasché well observes, "is itself dependent on the possibility of apprehending totality and system in a pointlike, punctual, and immediate intuition" (Gasché, 1986: 179). Yet Gasché once more incompletely reads the Romantic proposal.

a culture. "Culture" can be a universal concept making possible a horizon of reconciling coexistence, which the terms "pluralism" and "multiculturalism" name. This universalism means I may assume I can understand the alien culture, put myself within it, negotiate with it, in one way or another assimilate it, absorb it within sameness, as the Bernheimer report suggests those in comparative literature should do. I do not need to be a Native American in order to understand and teach Native American literature and culture, just as I do not need to be a British citizen to teach English literature. The institutionalization of the humanities in the United States (and in many other countries too) depends on such assumptions. These are the basic presuppositions, for example, of comparative literature as a discipline, the older kinds as well as the new project that will make comparative literature a branch of cultural studies. New programs in cultural studies or in "multiculturalism" do not consistently put that presupposition in question, in spite of their respect for the singularity of cultures.

On the other hand, the other may be entirely other, the *tout autre* Derrida names. In the dialogue with Richard Kearney, Derrida defines deconstruction as a response to this wholly other: "I do not mean that the deconstructing *subject* or *self* affirms. I mean that deconstruction is, in itself, a positive response to an alterity which necessarily calls, summons, or motivates it. Deconstruction is therefore vocation—a response to a call."[92] If the other is wholly other, then no negotiation will reach consensus. All that can occur is some speech act inventing, inaugurating, or instituting what might be called a fiction of the other. This alternative possibility is intertwined, necessarily, with the first. If the other is the wholly other, that does not mean there is nothing there. The nonconcept of the wholly other is as far as can be from any nihilism. In fact it may be a prejudice or habit that leads us to speak of the other in the singular. Perhaps it might be better to speak of the "wholly others." I call the wholly others a "nonconcept" because a concept forms part of a thought system open to logical or dialectical synthesis, whereas the wholly others cannot be assimilated into any such system. The evidence that something inassimilable is making a demand on me is the way the wholly others perturb every speech-act-instituted fiction, for example, the fiction of personal, group, or national identity. The wholly others divide such unities within themselves, make them nontotalizable.

A parallel, though it is only a figurative one, a juxtaposition of incommensurables, may be drawn between the wholly others and the black holes

Derrida's "The Law of Genre" (1980a) reveals his consciousness of these questions. This essay takes as its starting point Philippe Lacoue-Labarthe and Jean-Luc Nancy, *The Literary Absolute* (1978; 1988). The hypothesis of Derrida's essay is: "To formulate it in the scantiest manner—the simplest but most apodictic—I submit for your consideration the following hypothesis: a text cannot belong to no genre, it cannot be without or less a genre. Every text participates in one or several genres, there is no genreless text; there is always a genre and genres, yet such participation never amounts to belonging. And not because of an abundant overflowing or a free, anarchic and unclassifiable productivity, but because of the *trait* of participation itself, because of the effect of the code and of the generic mark. Making genre its mark, a text demarcates itself. If remarks of belonging belong without belonging, participate without belonging, then genre-designations cannot be simply part of the corpus" (Derrida, 1980a: 212). If a text participates in one or more genres but does not belong completely to them, its generic identity is in question. Bakhtin posed the same problem in relation to the novel, and a juxtaposition will be helpful. Bakhtin's point of reference is also, as opposed to Hegel and Lukács, the German Romantic theory of literature, although he views it in the context of Marxist philosophy. In "Epic and Novel," Bakhtin says: "All genres in 'high' literature . . . harmoniously reinforce each other to a significant extent; the whole of literature, conceived as a totality of genres, becomes an organic unity of the highest order. But it is characteristic of the novel that it never enters into this whole, it does not participate in any harmony of the genres . . . the novel gets on poorly with other genres. . . . The novel parodies other genres (precisely in their role as genres); it exposes the conventionality of their forms and their lan-

astronomers hypothesize. A black hole does not, strictly speaking, exist, if existence depends on being observable and measurable. Black holes cannot be observed because their gravity is so great no light emanates from them. That is why astronomers are so careful to remind us that no black hole has ever been observed. Black holes remain an unproved and perhaps unprovable hypothesis that explains certain observed celestial phenomena. Nevertheless, though it cannot be verified directly, a black hole may be inferred from matter's violent perturbation in its vicinity and the consequent emission of signals at various frequencies. Like black holes, the wholly others never manifest themselves directly. They give evidence of themselves in a variety of perturbations that can be registered.[93]

Perhaps my inner self, my conscience, presumed ground of my decisions and commitments, of all the speech acts I enunciate, may be "encountered" (though it is not really an encounter) as wholly other. Perhaps the wholly other might be an incomprehensible and unknowable otherness glimpsed when I come face to face with another person. Then perhaps the wholly other may be a power transcending cultural and personal difference, for example, the inscrutability of Apollo and the other divinities in *Oedipus the King* or the inassimilable irrational in Aristotle's *Poetics* and *Rhetoric*. Such others come, as they say, "from beyond the world." Death, finally (what could be more final than death?), may be wrestled with as something wholly other, as in Henry James's *The Wings of the Dove* and Wallace Stevens's "The Owl in the Sarcophagus." Death as other by no means necessarily presupposes the existence of some transcendence, the gods or God, nor does it presume some heaven or hell, some other place to which we go when we are dead. Death leaves those questions permanently open, since death is that bourn from which no traveler returns. The strength of Socrates' irony in the face of death in *The Apology* was his resolute insistence that since he knew nothing of death, he could not be afraid of it. Death, my death, the death that most matters to me and that I would most like to know, cannot be experienced. Death is not the object of any "I's" experience. It is wholly other.

Perhaps the wholly other may be a racial, national, class, or gendered other that is truly other and cannot be comprehended by analogy with my own knowledge of myself and therefore negotiated with. As I have said, today's "cultural studies," like the discipline of anthropology, often, though not always, presupposes that the cultural other can be understood and accommodated in some coalition subsumed under a common con-

guage; it squeezes out some genres and incorporates others into its own peculiar structure" (Bakhtin, 1981: 4–5). What Bakhtin expounds with regard to the novel is raised to the category of a general theory of literary writing by the Romantics (in a fragmentary way), by Derrida, and by deconstructive literary critics. This leads me to the second point.

If, according to Gasché, deconstruction must not be mistaken for an activity that neutralizes or annuls differences, of what then does deconstruction consist? "What does it do with the contradictions, aporias, and inconsistencies that it so eagerly points to in the formation of concepts or the argumentative and discursive structures of texts of all sorts? A first schematic answer is that deconstruction attempts to 'account' for these 'contradictions' by 'grounding' them in 'infrastructures' discovered by analyzing the specific organization of these 'contradictions.' . . . the very concept of infrastructure, as the *formal rule* that each time regulates differently the play of the contradictions in question, is an intrinsic part of [Derrida's] original contribution to philosophy" (Gasché, 1986: 142). Later on, Gasché tells us that by means of such infrastructures, deconstruction "accounts for the differences that fissure the discourse of philosophy, and any other discourse dependent on it" (ibid., 147). The "infrastructures" are quasi-concepts and have three fundamental features that Gasché explains brilliantly: "(1) their preontological and prelogical status, (2) their synthetic character, and (3) their economical and strategic nature" (ibid., 147). Hence, terms such as "inscription," "writing," or "text" must not be mistaken for the significations these words have in an empirical and common field. So, for instance, "*inscription,* or rather *inscription in general,* is the name for a *possibility* that all speech must presuppose—that marks all speech—before it can be linked to incision,

cept of culture. Suppose it was wrong about that? What would follow? Could there be a cultural studies of the wholly others? The critic treads on dangerous ground here, since this assumption about the wholly others may excuse much violence and injustice. The human instinct when confronted with an inassimilable other is to obliterate it, as the Europeans who colonized the New World did their best to kill Native Americans and destroy their cultures. Kurtz's idealism, in Conrad's *Heart of Darkness*, his desire to bring the light of civilization to darkest Africa, turns into what it has covertly been all along, a desire to "Exterminate all the brutes!"[94] Could there be a cultural studies of the wholly others that would avoid this, that would respect the others' otherness? If so, this would generate an organization of the university radically different from one that presupposes transparency, reconciliation, or consensus as goal.

The University of Dissensus

It follows from the more radical presumption about otherness that we should have a university of dissensus.[95] Such a university would institutionalize in its programs the various forms of unknowable otherness I have named. Two distinct notions of dissensus, corresponding to the two forms of otherness, may be identified. The word dissensus is a neologism. It sounds like a negative double of consensus, as "deconstruction" sounds like a negative double of "construction," though in neither case is this true. To assume that dissensus is the negative of consensus would lead one to believe that consensus is a horizon of total agreement to be reached beyond dissensus through a perhaps interminable dialogue, the rational give and take of conversation. Dissensus in this case is no more than a stage along the way toward agreement. For a time we disagree, but if we just go on talking long enough we shall come to agree. This notion of dissensus assumes that disagreement is posited on a ground of fundamental sameness. We are all rational human beings together. That sameness ultimately transcends differences of gender, sexual orientation, class, race, language, nation, ethnic culture, personal singularity, and so on. Though it is not quite the case—we are likely to think—that one culture is as good as another, at any rate they are all cultures. The one that happens to dominate, or the one to which I belong, has a plausible right to believe that those from other cultures, however much they are to be respected, should eventually come to be subsumed in the dominant one. It will make things

engraving, drawing, the letter—in short, to writing in the common sense of the term" (ibid., 157), or, "writing in Derrida's sense is not determined by what it is about, nor has it anything essentially in common with the signs present on the page, or with the (literary or philosophical) production of these signs. . . . Despite its quasitranscendental status, or precisely because of it, arche-writing is not essence" (ibid., 274).

To this, one might respond that, as we saw in the preceding chapter, in Miller's reading of De Quincey, neither "inscription" nor "writing" remains for Miller or De Quincey identified with inscription or writing in their material and ordinary sense, either. It would be absurd to assert that De Quincey was saying the same thing that Derrida would say later. But how has Derrida managed to reach the infrastructures? Such infrastructures appear either as a specific quality of the material text— whether literary or nonliterary—or through a specific type of reading. In both cases we must presuppose that the text—concrete and empirical— is disposed and organized in a way that allows us to read it in a concrete manner. Derrida has attained the infrastructures, or the infrastructures have arisen, in an ineluctable act of *reading* (whatever meaning we give to this word). Derrida has had to read Husserl, Saussure, Rousseau, Artaud, Mallarmé, Heidegger, Sollers, Kant, Marx, and others before composing his chain of undecidables, such as "différance," "dissemination," "hymen," "parergon," "supplement," and "specter." These words were in principle, and before the paleonymic displacement, inscribed materially on the text to be read. Derrida, in short, has had, paradoxically, to give a certain priority (so to speak) to the literary text. In "This Strange Institution Called Literature," he explains this as follows: "It is quite possible that literary writing in the modern period is more than one example among others,

so much simpler if we all come to share the same language, customs, and assumptions. American English, such a line of argument suggests, should be the official language of the United States. Dissensus is a momentary perturbation within a potential collective sameness guaranteed by a universal rationality that defines what it is to be human, defines "man" (and woman too) as the rational animal.

On the other hand, dissensus might be based on an otherness that goes all the way down. Perhaps this may be the radical otherness of another culture or its artifacts, perhaps the radical otherness of another person, possibly the result of a different gender or sexual orientation, but possibly also an otherness in other persons, of whatever gender or sexual orientation, that is the relay for an absolute otherness that speaks through them and makes demands on me for ethical commitment, decision, and act. If any of these possibilities were the case, then the imposition of consensus, even by a long process of rational discussion and compromise, would always be an unjustified coercion, violating something of infinite value in the other person or culture. If it were the case that otherness goes all the way down, then justice would demand a culture of dissensus made up of persons with irreconcilable values and goals.

Just what form would the humanistic side of the university take if cultural studies were to be based on the second notion of dissensus? It would mean, for one thing, a fuller shift from constative to performative models of cultural artifacts and of what happens in teaching and writing about them. It would also mean confronting the difficult task of creating a university of dissensus as a way of resisting the drift toward technologizing levelling.[96] A university of dissensus would be the locus of irreconcilable and to some degree mutually opaque goods. We should acquire as much understanding of other cultures as possible. We should do that, however, with an uneasy recognition that just as translation may be ultimately impossible, though we go on doing it, so the otherness of other cultures, like the otherness of other persons, may be ultimately unknowable, though we must go on trying to know it. That "must," however, should be accompanied by the realization that knowledge, too, can be a form of violence against other cultures. The demand made on us by other cultures is not just for understanding but, as Kwame Anthony Appiah has forcefully argued, for respect.[97] Respect is not a statement of knowledge, a constative assertion. It is a speech act, a pledge, an attestation: "Yes, I respect that. I respect its otherness. I want that otherness to persist." In this attestation,

rather a privileged guiding thread for access to the general structure of textuality, to what Gasché calls the infrastructure" (Derrida, 1992c: 71).

Let us imagine, for a moment, that Derrida (or, as we shall see later, de Man or, especially, Miller) had begun with a conception in which the text appears subordinated to the notions of "coherence" and "isotopy." These form, in part, the basis of the structuralist, semiotic, and linguistico-textual disciplines. They also constitute another way of naming the classical "metaphor of the organism." A. J. Greimas and J. Courtés tell us in their *Semiotics and Language: An Analytical Dictionary*: "(1) The term *coherence* is used colloquially to characterize a doctrine, a thought system, or a theory, all of the parts of which hold solidly together. (2) Some attempt can be made to define coherence negatively, as submission to the principle of noncontradiction, and positively, as the postulate upon which meta-logic is based and which also underlies all semiotic systems and all systems of constructed logic" (Greimas and Courtés, 1982: 35). Earlier, M. A. K. Halliday and R. Hassan asserted: "A text has texture and this is what distinguishes it from something that is not a text. . . . The texture is provided by the cohesive RELATION. . . . Cohesive relationships within a text are set up where the INTERPRETATION of some element in the discourse is dependent on that of another. The one PRESUPPOSES the other in the sense that it cannot be effectively decoded except by recourse to it" (Halliday and Hasan, 1976: 2–4). Let us further imagine that Derrida had begun with a notion of the text that is concrete and empirical, similar to the seventh type of ambiguity, the most radical of all, of which Empson spoke. A text, in short, is an assemblage of words in which a contradictory structure can appear "when the two meanings of the word, the two values of the ambiguity, are the two opposite meanings

however, the "I" as a pre-existing ethical agent is disarticulated. It becomes other to itself. The pledge is not made by a pre-existing "I" that remains the same after the affirmation of respect. The affirmation, as it responds to a call made by the other, dislocates, displaces, and recreates the self that utters it. Nor should the university of dissensus be thought of as made of pre-existing interest groups or communities that are unchanged by the teaching or writing performed by members of those groups: for example, those in women's studies, or in the different ethnic studies, or in gay and lesbian studies. It is a fallacy to think of each person as wholly defined by his or her participation in a given class, culture, or group. Each act of dissensus recreates the self of the one who makes it, for example, in teaching a given passage from John Milton or Toni Morrison. Moreover, each such act also implicitly recreates or alters the university.[98]

Institutionalizing dissensus in the university would be difficult but by no means impossible. The word "university" names not only the total-izing goal of the university, its aim to rationalize everything, but also the singleness of the university, "turning everything into one," as its etymology suggests. The university has always claimed to be the place of rational in-vestigation, teaching, and discussion in different fields with consensus as horizon, even though that claim may have always masked an actual hetero-geneity. Nevertheless, every time a work of literature is read or taught, this event may break the continuity and wholeness of the university commu-nity. Though such an event may not occur as often or as easily as Derrida suggests, when it does happen it cannot be assimilated into what was al-ready there as a pregiven set of assumptions and methodologies. In literary study, each act of reading or teaching of this sort is an encounter with the irreducible strangeness of works of literature. We have told ourselves that in teaching literature we are fulfilling our contract to provide more knowl-edge and to inculcate humanistic values in our students. That, however, is just the idea of the university that is being widely questioned now. Our task is to imagine and to bring into existence a university that will be a *com-munauté désoeuvrée*, in Jean-Luc Nancy's phrase.[99] Such an "unworked" or dismantled community will be an assemblage of groups, each other to the others and each working within a horizon of goals and purposes that cannot be reconciled with the others in some overarching principle of rea-son or idea of universal culture. Such a university would be decentered. It would be made up, to borrow Agamben's phrase again, of "peripheral singularities," not of people who have been educated by some universal-

defined by the context, so that the total effect is to show a fundamental division in the writer's mind" (Empson, 1949: 192).

If he had built on these assumptions, Derrida might have analyzed the *différance* within a word in a text that, in Gasché's words, "resists all hermeneutical solution" (Gasché, 1986: 134), or have discovered inequalities among the different parts of a text, as, for example: (1) between the preface of a text and its central body; (2) between the title of a text and its central body; (3) between two segments of a text divided by a blank; (4) between the explicit declaration of the author and the strategy he uses to prove such a declaration. Yet if he had begun with such assumptions he would have had no alternative but to interpret Saussure's "text" and his theory of the "difference" in a manner like that of such Saussurian linguists and semiologists as Nikolai Sergeevich Trubetzkoi, Eric Buyssens, André Martinet, Louis Prieto, the first Roland Barthes, Georges Mounin, and so on. In fact, Jean Cohen, commenting on the passages Saussure devotes to "difference," criticizes, the "negativist" interpretations of Deleuze and Derrida, as well as those of Jakobson: "But, if one can accept the total emptiness of the sign in what concerns its signifying side, connected to its functional "transparence," it is difficult to do the same thing for the signified side. How can one believe that the meaning of the word 'green' consists only in the fact of being neither blue nor yellow?" (Cohen, 1979: 42, my trans.).

If Derrida had started with such assumptions, he would not have been able to write, in developing his "deconstructive" strategy, a sentence like the following: "Once more, then, we definitely have to oppose Saussure to himself. Before being or not being 'noted,' 'represented,' 'figured,' in a 'graphie,' the linguistic sign implies an originary writing"

izing *Bildung* fulfilling the idea of a given nation's cultivated citizen. Nor, as I have said, would those singularities be defined by their participation in some pre-existing community, even some borderland community for whose predetermined good they are active.

Agamben, in a remarkable section of *The Coming Community* entitled "Tiananmen," shows how difficult it is to imagine a university of dissensus. Agamben, at least in this English translation, uses the phrase "whatever singularities" rather than "peripheral singularities." The word "whatever" translates the Latin *quodlibet* and the Italian *qualunque*. "Whatever singularities," Agamben explains, cannot be defined "by any condition of belonging (being red, being Italian, being communist) nor by the simple absence of conditions (a negative community, such as that recently proposed in France by Maurice Blanchot), but by belonging itself."[100] Though Agamben sees that all persons in the new globalized culture are turning into "whatever singularities" and that such singularities will join together to form "the coming community," he argues that such singularities and the communities they will form are "a threat the State cannot come to terms with": "What the State cannot tolerate in any way, however, is that the singularities form a community without affirming an identity, that humans co-belong without any representable condition of belonging" (87). The demonstrations in Tiananmen Square were an example of such a co-belonging: "Wherever these singularities peacefully demonstrate their being in common there will be a Tiananmen, and, sooner or later, the tanks will appear" (86). Though the State in one of its apparatuses, the university, is easily able to tolerate those identities that it can label as African American, Chicano or Chicana, and so on, the university of dissensus for which I am calling would be more like the co-belonging of "whatever singularities" Agamben describes. That makes the phrase "university of dissensus" an oxymoron. Institutionalized dissensus is profoundly alien to the traditional "idea of a university." Like the "democracy to come" the university of dissensus is a horizon, always something "to come."

That such a redefinition of the university would happen without resistance I am not so naive as to believe. More attainable might be a university of identifiable dissensual groups such as the one cultural studies may conceivably be bringing about, with here and there, now and then, some inaugural act of reading or teaching that could not be encompassed within the new boundaries. Such an event might pass unnoticed. It might

(Derrida, 1976: 52). Even less would he have been able to write, with regard to Mallarmé: "In the sentence that follows, the syntax—and the
carefully calculated punctuation—prevent us from ever deciding whether
the subject of 'reads' is the role ('*less than a thousand lines, the role, the one
that reads . . .*') or some anonymous reader ('*the role, the one that reads,
will instantly comprehend the rules as if placed before the stageboards . . .*')
Who is 'the one'?" (Derrida, 1981: 224). If Derrida had been talking of
Empsonian ambiguity, he would have spoken, as Françoise Rastier (1976)
did, of a systematic of the isotopy in which the figurative (pluri)isotopies
go together with the thematic (poly)isotopies. Greimas and Courtés comment in their dictionary on the analysis Rastier makes of a Mallarmé
poem: "In Mallarmé's poem 'Salut,' the figurative isotopies (banquet,
navigation, writing) as described by F. Rastier, are easily attached to corresponding thematic isotopies (friendship, solitude/escape, creation)"
(Greimas and Courtés, 1982: 164).

　　Since Derrida's readings discover discrepancies among the different strata of the argumentation of such works, we can hardly agree with
any claims for a regained coherence of the text. It is true that the tension
among the various strata does not lead to the elimination of differences.
That such differences remain contributes, however, not to the coherence
of the text—that would be a contradiction—but to a fissuring that does
not allow the reader to decide the unity of theme, syntax, or morphology.
This is why we must attend to a *trifurcation* (and not to a *bifurcation*) in
Derrida's discourse regarding the notion of text:

　　1. On the one hand, we have the material and concrete text as
　　seen from the viewpoint of a logic of identity and coherence (which

not appear to be something for which it is worth bringing in the tanks. But it might nevertheless be effective in bringing about change, at least in some minute degree. In number 216 of the *Atheneum Fragments*, Friedrich Schlegel asserts that "The French Revolution, Fichte's philosophy, and Goethe's *Meister* are the greatest tendencies of the age [*die größten Tendenzen des Zeitalters*]." *Tendenzen* here names an intervention that is materially effective in deflecting the course of history. In an admirably witty formulation Schlegel goes on to say: "Even in our shabby histories of civilization [*unsern dürftigen Kulturgeschichten*], which usually resemble a collection of variants accompanied by a running commentary for which the original classical text has been lost; even there many a little book, almost unnoticed by the noisy rabble [*die lärmende Menge*] at the time, plays a greater role than anything they did [*als alles, was diese trieb*]."[101]

The initiatory acts of reading, writing, or teaching I have described will have a performative as well as constative function. Only academic discourse that is a speech act as opposed to being just descriptive will make anything happen in the work toward fulfilling our unfulfillable obligation to the democracy to come. Only teaching or writing that is performatively effective will make anything happen institutionally and politically, as opposed to inadvertently supporting the status quo. One limitation of many descriptions of cultural studies, as well as of expressions of opposition to them—for example, those in the Bernheimer volume—is that they tend to be couched according to the traditional notion that the university is a place exclusively of *Wissenschaft*, a place where new facts are found as a result of "study," rather than a place where teaching and writing are to some degree also speech acts.

Even though the discourse of cultural studies may include graphic and even aural material, the basic medium will continue to be language. Whatever political effectiveness cultural studies has will come at least to a considerable degree through language, though pictures and music can also have powerful performative effects. Accounting for the latter calls for a radical revision of speech act theory. I have used the terminology of speech act theory to describe the work of dissensus within the new university. Such terminology, however, needs to be twisted, anasemically, as Abraham and Torok would say,[102] in order to name the use of language or other signs to bring about an event that will make a break in history rather than perpetuating what is already there. A performative use of language, in J. L. Austin's classic analysis in *How to Do Things with Words*,

corresponds to the classical metaphor of the organism and to the modern structuralist and linguistico-textual theories shared by János S. Pëtofi, A. J. Greimas, S. J. Schmidt, Teun Andreianus van Dijk, etc.).

2.   On the other hand, we have the material and concrete text that, in certain writings (and this reference to "certain writings" can only be a wager, as Paul de Man or J. Hillis Miller would admit), stands in opposition to the principle of noncontradiction. Such a text is composed in a nonsutured grafting that does not allow one to think of the text itself as simple presence. Elsewhere I have called this the theory of the text as *graft* (Asensi, 1990); Empson (1949) pays some attention to it in the course of his explanation of the seventh type of ambiguity.

3.   Finally, we have the quasi-concept of "arche-textuality," which does not correspond to any material, concrete, and present text. In fact, it constitutes the possibility of the material text. In a deconstructive strategy, however, the second notion of text is almost a condition of possibility for the third one. Between the two exists a type of order and a relation impossible to determine.

Gasché would have great difficulty in proving that, when Derrida writes the following in *Dissemination*, the words "dissemination" or "graft" do not refer to a level of the material text:

And to explain, with Mallarmé's text, why one is always at some pains to follow.

If there is thus no thematic unity or overall meaning to reappropriate beyond the textual instances, no total message located in some imaginary order, intentionality, or lived experience, then the text is no longer the expression or

depends for its efficacy on an elaborate context of protocols, rules, institutions, roles, laws, and established formulae. These need to be in place before the performative utterance is made. They remain in place just as they were after that utterance. The performative neither creates them nor alters them. It depends on their unaltered continuity. It is in itself a repetition of perhaps innumerable other utterances of the same speech act that also depend on the same context. The minister's or justice of the peace's utterance of the phrase "I pronounce you man and wife" is a classic example. It depends on the prior existence of the marriage ceremony, on ecclesiastical or civil sanctions that empower the minister or justice of the peace to marry people, and so on. These are operative before any given utterance of "I pronounce you man and wife." They remain operative and unchanged afterwards. The Austinian performative also presupposes the pre-existence of the perdurable self as agent, the ego or "I" who can say, "I promise," or "I decide," or "I pronounce."

The alternative kind of performative creates the norms and laws that validate it. Each such performative is unique and unrepeatable because it leaves everything different thereafter, in however small a way. It constitutes a happening that changes decisively the surrounding context. It responds to a call or demand from an "other" that can never be institutionalized or rationalized. Such a performative creates the "I" that utters it. As Derrida puts it, such a speech act is a catachresis that "while continuing to work through tradition emerges at a given moment as a *monster*, a monstrous mutation without tradition or normative precedent."[103] A university of dissensus should be the locus of a continual series of such mutations. The archiving of knowledge, however, also has its performative aspect, while those performative "mutations" also bring knowledge. The difficulty (in fact impossibility) of either sharply distinguishing or happily reconciling performative and cognitive language should not be underestimated, nor the resistance in the university to any performative goal, especially when that goal is stated overtly.

What should teachers and students do in this new situation? First, they should take stock of the changes in the university I have described and try to understand them. Second, they must begin to think out ways to justify what they do in the humanities to their various constituencies. This task will not be at all easy, especially since corporation executives and officials have probably had their ideas about the humanities formed by the attacks in the media on theory, "political correctness," women's studies,

representation (felicitous or otherwise) of any *truth* that would come to diffract or assemble itself in the polysemy of literature. It is this hermeneutic concept of *polysemy* that must be replaced by *dissemination*. (Derrida, 1981: 262)

One ought to explore systematically not only what appears to be a simple etymological coincidence uniting the graft and the graph (both from *graphion*: writing implement, stylus), but also the analogy between the forms of textual grafting and so-called vegetal grafting, or even, more and more commonly today, animal grafting. (Derrida, 1981: 202)

How many difficulties would arise, moreover, were we to compare Derrida's ideas on the irreducibility of syntax to semantics with the parallel ideas of Noam Chomsky? The latter also thinks, though from a very different viewpoint, that of generative linguistics, that grammar or syntax is independent of semantics, not only as a necessary methodology for approaching language, but also because grammaticality has nothing to do with signification (Chomsky, 1957). How could one, moreover, explain the possibility of a new Marxism, of a new political practice such as Derrida proposes in *Specters of Marx*, if Derrida were not at some level referring to a material text?

Derrida constantly moves between the second and third notions of text. Gasché's thesis in *The Tain of the Mirror* can be upheld only if one introduces just what he excludes—the second notion of text (derived from the Jena Romantics), which forms the basis of Derrida's evolution in reading theory and practice, as well as of those of de Man and Miller. But if that notion of text is included, then Gasché's thesis is disqualified for having excluded it. This assertion is independent of the fact that, from Derrida's point of view, "arche-writing" or *différance* is what, as nonorigin, nonconcept, nonsubstance, nonpresence, makes the rest of textuality

and multiculturalism. Academics often start out with two strikes against them. Moreover, many of these funding sources as well as the university bureaucrats who govern for them may have a predisposition to think that the humanities are primarily of use to teach communication skills. In the new research university rapidly coming into being it will be extremely difficult to justify what is done in the old way, that is, as the production of new knowledge, the *Wissenschaft* appropriate in the humanities, as new knowledge about living things is appropriate in biology. New "information" about *Beowulf,* Shakespeare, Racine, Goethe, Hugo, or even Emerson, William Carlos Williams, and Toni Morrison is not useful in the same way new knowledge about genes is when it leads to the making of a marketable medicine. Those corporation officers who will more and more control the university, along with legislators and administrators drawn from the sciences, are likely to say they admire the production of new knowledge in the humanities. Their reluctance to give money to support such research indicates that they may not really mean it. Most professors in the humanities these days know many brilliant, highly trained, and dedicated young humanists who have failed to find tenure-track positions, or sometimes any position at all. Most of a recent issue of the *ADE Bulletin* (Spring 1998, no. 119) is devoted to presenting the grim facts about current professional employment in English and other modern languages. The articles stress the rapid increase in part-time and adjunct faculty and report that only half of new Ph.D.'s in English and other modern languages can expect to get tenure-track jobs in the first year after receiving the Ph.D.

The product of value humanities professors and students make is discourse of a particular kind: new readings, new ideas. Nicholas Negroponte argues this forcefully for the research university in general in a recent essay in *Wired*.[104] Such ideas inaugurate something new, something unheard of before. Another way to put this is to say that the university is the place where what really counts is the ungoverned, the ungovernable. The ungovernable does not occur all that often. Most of what goes on in the university is all too easily governed. In fact it is self-governing, as when we say a machine has a "governor" that keeps it from running too fast. It just turns round at a moderate speed and keeps repeating the same. Nevertheless, the university ought to have as its primary goal working to establish conditions propitious to the creation of the ungovernable. Only if we can persuade the new corporate governors of the university that such work has

possible. It is also independent of the differences existing between Derrida, Miller, de Man, and others concerning the role assigned to literature within Occidental metaphysics.

What is to be concluded from what I have said in this chapter is that the following assertions by Gasché are unacceptable. They are unacceptable above all because by not taking into account the second notion of text to which I have referred, he relegates literary criticism and literature itself to what might be called pre-modern conditions. "Yet it must not be forgotten," says Gasché, "that although the philosophical and literary text may always fail to evacuate or minimize the encompassing power of language at the benefit of the signified, such is indeed the project of philosophy and literature; consequently, they must be studied from this point of view," that is to say, "literary criticism as the discipline that presupposes the decidability of meaning prior to the literary text" (Gasché, 1986: 261). I have shown in this chapter why, for Derrida at least, these assumptions must be challenged, as must the too rigid division between philosophy and literature on which Gasché tends to rely. The challenge is performed on the basis of the second and third Derridean notions of "text." These notions put in question the separation between literature and philosophy without denying its force within institutionalized disciplines. I have also shown that Gasché's reading of the Jena Romantics is distorted and how that is related to his mistaken claim that it is an error to appropriate Derrida for literary criticism. The development in this chapter of these two points—one relating to the interpretation of Friedrich Schlegel's proposals and the other relating to the three Derridean notions of "text"—returns me, by way of the third point (that is, the actual effects of deconstruction on literary criticism), to my main objective here: J. Hillis Miller's work.

indispensable utility are we likely to flourish in the new conditions. Doing that will take much patient thought and rhetorical skill.

I want now to make a small start at that by showing what I mean by saying works of literature are black holes. I shall do this through reading two works, Anthony Trollope's *Ayala's Angel* and Marcel Proust's *A la recherche du temps perdu*. I can imagine a reader at this point saying, "There he goes again, turning back to two of those dead white male authors." To this (perhaps imaginary) reproach I answer that this book justifies the continued study of those dead authors in the Western tradition by showing that, viewed from our present perspective, they seem extremely strange. They are especially powerful ways of encountering that unintelligible otherness I have defined above and am calling black holes. Though all writing makes a demand on me to read it, these authors do so with special urgency. They do so not because they are familiar, because I feel at home reading them, but for just the opposite reason. I was called to the study of English and European literature in the first place by a sense of how exceedingly peculiar are the things canonical authors say and how different these things are from what my teachers and much previous scholarship had prepared me to expect. I still feel that way, though the changes I have described in the first part of this book make these peculiarities even more salient. I leave to others who know the necessary languages the study of Native American, Japanese, Chinese, Korean, Arabic, Bengali, Hindi, Kiswahili, or Gikuyu literary works in their respective strangenesses.

2.

A Human Head with an Equine Neck

Viruses, Heterosemes, and Heterographs

What did *The Linguistic Moment* inherit—not only the book or the title but also the concept—from the eternal divisibility of any substance, material or mental, that was the basis of J. Hillis Miller's analysis of De Quincey? What does the critic do after *touching* literature and seeing that it melts in his hands? The answer could be the following: he went on to demonstrate that literary criticism, literary theory, and even literature itself are the story of a failure. This response, however, hides an enormous complexity. In what sense is this a story of failure? What did literary criticism intend to do? Why has literary criticism ended in failure? Here I refer neither to any ineffability of poetry, as expounded by idealist stylistics, nor to any supposed intellectual triumph of poetry or literature (as asserted, e.g., by Valéry). To clarify the significance of the last question is to explain what Miller understands by "deconstruction." What does Miller mean when he uses that term generally and applies it to literary activity? Let me begin with this quotation from the extended version of "The Critic as Host," first published in 1977:

The word "deconstruction" is in one way a good one to name this movement. The word, like other words in "de," "decrepitude," for example, or "denotation," describes a paradoxical action which is negative and positive at once. In this it is like all words with a double antithetical prefix, words in "ana," like "analysis," or words in "para," like "parasite." These words tend to come in pairs which are not

The Grounds of Love: Anthony Trollope's *Ayala's Angel*

Black Holes in the Internet Galaxy

Just what does it mean to speak of the need in the university for cata-chresic performatives as a response to a radical otherness? This otherness, I have said, cannot be directly confronted or named. Nevertheless, it generates an obligation that must be fulfilled, though it remains unfulfillable. Such formulations are forbiddingly abstract and at the same time distress-ingly contradictory. In order to explain what might be meant by them, I return to literature and to two examples: Trollope's *Ayala's Angel* and Proust's *A la recherche du temps perdu*. This essay began with a question about the justification of literary study at this moment in the university. I circle back to that question now to propose a quite different defense of literary study from the one Proust implicitly makes by way of the fractal mosaic figure. In place of that I put the figure of reading literature as the encounter with black holes in the Internet Galaxy.[1] By this I mean confronting some-thing radically alien, something that interrupts the continuity of all those

opposites, positive against negative. They are related in a systematic differentiation which requires a different analysis or untying in each case, but which in each
case leads, in a different way each time, to the tying up of a double bind. This
tying up is at the same time a loosening. It is a paralysis of thought in the face of
what cannot be thought rationally: analysis, paralysis; solution, dissolution; composition, decomposition; construction, deconstruction; mantling, dismantling;
canny, uncanny; competence, incompetence; apocalyptic, anacalyptic; constituting, deconstituting. Deconstructive criticism moves back and forth between
the poles of these pairs, proving in its own activity, for example, that there is no
deconstruction which is not at the same time constructive, affirmative. The word
says this in juxtaposing "de" and "con." (TNT, 168–69)

The choice of the term and the problem of the "parasite" is related
to the question provoked by "negative capability," that is, the identification between the critic and the text, between the critic and the consciousness embodied in the text. It continues the same preoccupation with
the metaphor of the critic, who is host in both the senses identified by
Miller, both the host who receives the poem as guest or parasite and the
host in its etymological sense, as hostile stranger who invades the poem,
becoming the parasite who inhabits the poem as house. The eternal divisibility in which the critic had participated in a movement of paradoxical
identification with the consciousness embodied in the text appears par excellence in the medium of language. The extensive fragment cited above
belongs to an essay whose first part (in the original version of 1977 in *The
Georgia Review*) is devoted to superimposing something like Piranesi's
Dreams or the theory of the palimpsest onto a word, a unique word, or
rather onto the prefix of a word, "parasite" or "para." Miller will show,
in the second part of the essay, that this word has an important literal
or figurative presence in Shelley's texts. He asserts that "deconstruction"
functions like "parasite" in that the prefixes "de" and "para" are oriented
toward contradictory significations: " 'para' is a double antithetical prefix
signifying at once proximity and distance, similarity and difference, interiority and exteriority, something inside a domestic economy and at the
same time outside it" (TNT, 144). Three features that can be abstracted
from this essay will constitute the framework for this chapter.

1. Language and its components, among which I distinguish the
categorematic and syncategorematic (i.e., linguistic particles that have
meaning versus those that do not), the semantic and nonsemantic, the
verbal and the pictographic, constitute the domain within which Miller's

wonderfully rational information highways the university, with help from governments, along with communications and technology corporations, is building. Reading literature also interrupts the assumptions that the more traditional and familiar historical context of the printed book carries with it. At this level of encounter, reading these works as printed books or as electronic phantasms makes little difference. The same meeting with otherness, I claim, will occur through carefully reading either form of a given text. The important difference is that reading *Ayala's Angel* in electronic form makes it perhaps easier to see what is genuinely strange about it. The familiar printed-book context encourages us to see it as belonging to us and to our tradition. Seeing it wrested from that context makes more visible the way it is to some degree alien to our present-day assumptions. The new context functions as a form of *Verfremdung* (alienation), as Bertolt Brecht would say, or "making it strange," as the Slavic formalists express it. Putting *Ayala's Angel* side by side with *Myst* or *Zen and the Art of the Internet* may perhaps allow the reader to see it as what it is: the expression

work takes place. Logically, his concept of "language" (which I shall call "hablantaje") and his way of "working" it do not coincide with those employed in structuralism, systematic linguistics, semiotics, and so on. As we shall see, his notion of "language" oscillates between verbality and non-verbality; above all, it is the limit beyond which it is not possible to go. (This does not presuppose the negation of referentiality as "operation," that is to say, as an effect of language and not as an entity preceding language.) "Undecidables" or Derridean "infrastructures," before belonging to the register of "quasi-concepts," have no alternative but to be inscribed in *language*. At least they cannot totally exclude their belonging to such "concepts," in the sense this word takes on in Heidegger's "A Dialogue on Language: Between a Japanese and an Inquirer." When the Japanese tells the Inquirer his concern about a "guiding concept in which we then bundle up everything" (Heidegger 1971: 25), the latter answers that it is not possible to avoid such a thing completely, given that "the mode of conceptual representation insinuates itself all too easily into every kind of human experience" (ibid.). In a similar way, de Man's opposition between rhetoric and grammar is already produced in each one of the pairs constituting the opposition, that is to say, in the heart of rhetoric and grammar themselves. I shall show that on this point, as on others, we attend a Millerian *reading* of Derrida and of de Man accomplished from the viewpoint of the matrix I referred to in the first chapter. This matrix, I claim, establishes the differences between them.

2. Certain types of texts (philosophical, political, but above all *literary*) put at stake the "undecidable" quality, present beforehand in language itself, which in certain stages of his work Miller terms "the linguistic moment." This conception has an "origin," clearly Heideggerian, though it goes back to Vico. When Heidegger states, for instance, that: "Poetry proper is never merely a higher mode (*melos*) of everyday language. It is rather the reverse: everyday language is a forgotten and therefore used-up poem, from which there hardly resounds a call any longer" (Heidegger, 1971: 208), he is drawing the picture within which Miller will move, although in a quite radical change from a Heideggerian milieu. That "linguistic moment" coincides with neither the defamiliarization of the Russian Formalists, the paradox of the New Critics, Jakobson's poetic function, nor the rhetorical function of Group m, because Miller's understanding of language comes from the philosophical and psychoanalytic

of a set of assumptions about human life as different from those common today, almost, as those of the alien cultures studied by anthropologists.

"Proportions, and Proprieties, and Unities"

Anthony Trollope's *Ayala's Angel* might not seem a likely choice to show that a literary work is a black hole. This late Trollope novel, published in 1881, just one year before the author's death, is a characteristic product of his genius. It returns with undiminished power to themes and narrative techniques that his forty-seven novels exemplify. Like all Trollope's novels, *Ayala's Angel* makes presuppositions about human life that might be compared to natural laws like gravity or the speed of light. They are taken for granted as the conditions within which all the characters live. Speaking in *An Autobiography* of the castle-building daydreams that were the genesis of his novel-writing, Trollope says: "Nor were these efforts in architecture spasmodic, or subject to constant change from day to day. For

field rather than from the linguistic one, although the influence of the latter cannot be denied.

3. Deconstruction is a characteristic of language, a result not of a movement of self-consciousness or reflexivity in language, but of how that characteristic is present in language in spite of itself and in spite of who uses it. It is produced both on a phonologico-morphological level and on a macrotextual one (to use a notion from text linguistics designed to describe the text as a whole). This is why Miller tells us that: "At the same time both word and counterword subdivide. Each reveals itself to be fissured already within itself" (TNT, 144). This is so not because of the word but of what in classical Greek was an adverb and in contemporary English is a prefix ("para," "ana," etc.). Furthermore, he tells us: "The present-day procedure of 'deconstruction,' of which Nietzsche is one of the patrons, is not, however, new in our own day. It has been repeated regularly in one form or another in all the centuries since the Greek sophists and rhetoricians, since in fact Plato himself, who in *The Sophist* has enclosed his own self-deconstruction within the canon of his own writing" (TNT, 152). One can speak of a "program" in this context. The self-deconstructive program, which functions on a phonologico-morphological level, reproduces itself in the discourse of the text: "A special version of the undecidable structure contained within the word 'parasite' operates in all these passages. One could say either that the word contains the passages in miniature within itself or that the passages themselves are a dramatization of the word" (TNT, 157). In a sense, one could argue that Miller is a linguist, a fact that would explain his peculiar interest in philology, rhetoric, and etymology.

Saussure, in expounding the relationship between the diachronic, synchronic, and pansynchronic study of language, links the issue of time in language with that of the dichotomy *langue/parole* and concludes: "*Everything which is diachronic in languages is only so through speech.* Speech contains the seeds of every change" (Saussure, 1983: 96–97). A scientific and systematic linguistics must privilege the study of *langue* and the synchronic cuts of language. Although the linguistics that came after Saussure, above all in its Prague version, would vary that proposal slightly, it has remained in force. Saussure defines *etymology*, assuring us that it is neither methodical nor systematic, as follows: "Etymology is thus first and foremost the explanation of words by investigating their connexions

weeks, for months, if I remember rightly, from year to year, I would carry on the same tale, binding myself down to certain laws, to certain propor- tions, and proprieties, and unities." [2] Trollope's novels too have fixed laws, proportions, proprieties, and unities. These justify speaking of those novels collectively as making a distinctive "world." This world is somewhat like, but not quite like, the real one in which I think I live.

The reigning laws of this Trollopean world operate, mutatis mutan- dis, in all his novels. *Ayala's Angel* is an especially good example because it so clearly shows what is most unclear—most problematic, opaque, dark, "other"—in this almost totally transparent world. One virtue of today's multicultural study is that it allows Americans or Europeans to see what is strange about earlier features of their own traditions. They can see better what is to some degree different in those traditions from the assump- tions they habitually make today. It is necessary to learn to read earlier works of Western culture as literary anthropologists: with respect for their strangeness and with an awareness of how difficult it may be to understand

with other words. Explaining means relating to terms already known. In linguistics, *to explain a word is to relate it to other words*, for there are no necessary relations between sound and meaning" (Saussure, 1983: 188). Curiously, in this definition Saussure himself links etymology with value and difference: "The conceptual part of linguistic value is determined solely by relations and differences with other signs in the language" (Saussure, 1983: 116). He adds: "Everything we have said so far comes down to this. *In the language itself, there are only differences.* Even more important than that is the fact that, although in general a difference presupposes positive terms between which the difference holds, in a language there are only differences, *and no positive terms*" (Saussure, 1983: 118).

Why this union between etymology and difference? A sign (a signifier, a signified, or a signifier-signified) can only be explained in relation to other signs, but the other signs that explain it, make it what it is, are necessarily both simultaneous and successive. Exigencies of methodology or of epistemological perspective might impel one to reduce the value of difference (its play) to the axis of simultaneity, but in a Derridean reading of difference as *trace*, as developed in *Of Grammatology*, the distinction between the two axes would make no sense. The same would be true of a Peircian perspective. If, as Umberto Eco has argued, the *interpretant* is *"another representation which is referred to the same 'object'"* (Eco, 1976: 68), or the interpretant is "the meaning of a sign-vehicle, understood as a cultural unit displayed through other sign-vehicles and thus showing its semantic independence from the first sign-vehicle" (Eco, 1976: 72), there is no reason to put aside an etymological explanation. Semiosis would be unlimited then, and in multiple directions. Logically, we do not mean that in order to explain the meaning of the word *berline* in the sentence "We went to the opera in Joseph's *berline*" it is necessary to refer to the name of the city of Berlin, where this kind of limousine was invented. We mean that another etymological signifier is inscribed in the word *berline*, in the manner of a "material" and metonymic palimpsest. In some contexts, that historical signifier-signified, registered and hidden in the present signifier-signified, is absolutely pertinent and necessary. This is so when psychoanalysis supposes a vertical or historical reemergence of the subject's past (say, memories or dreams). Very schematically, the basic principle of the interpretation of discourse in such a discipline is the *"relative autonomy of the signifier* under which slides a *signified*, which

them. This means no longer assuming that other cultures (for example, the nineteenth-century English one) can easily be turned into something assimilable to current ideas about human life.

Like all Trollope's novels, *Ayala's Angel* is characterized by a more or less complete transparency of the characters to themselves and to one another. This mutual transparency is shared with the reader through the narrator's discourse. The latter gives the reader constant access to the minds and hearts of the characters. Whatever they know about themselves and about those around them is transferred to the reader by the narrator. This storyteller has to an extreme degree the clairvoyance and ubiquity that are named by the term "omniscient narrator." Trollope's narrator also has the gift of a pellucidly simple and eloquent style. This matches a similar gift Trollope's characters generally have for expressing themselves clearly to themselves and to one another. The Trollopean narrator is not, however, wholly anonymous. His purity of language marks him as belonging to the same class as the characters whose story he tells. He speaks as a gentleman

is not necessarily included in the morpho-phonological unit such as it appears in the communicated utterance" (Kristeva, 1989: 269).

To join together etymology and difference presupposes reading Saussure, in spite of himself, along a line completely different from the one followed by linguistics or semiology and, above all, different from the discipline that has been called structuralist semantics. To attach "etymology"—and this name is useful only if it gives rise to a thorough effect of babelization—to difference and the sign implies reading Saussure just as the Joyce of *Finnegans Wake* or the Freud of *The Interpretation of Dreams* would do. Derrida does the same when, in the course of his reading of the name "Amon-Rē" and, more generally, of Plato's *Phaedrus* he warns us in a footnote: "The whole of that essay, as will quickly become apparent, [is] itself nothing but a reading of *Finnegans Wake*" (Derrida, 1981: 88). Miller reads Saussure in the same way he reads De Quincey—that is, he assumes that the sign or word is a palimpsest from which nothing belonging to the shifting, labyrinthine passages between present and past has been erased. This view is exactly the opposite of a conception in which the sememe, lexeme, or word is made up of features called *semes*, which are apportioned along a semic axis between oppositions (Greimas, 1966; 1984). It is the opposite of paradigmatic, syntagmatic, or syntagmatico-paradigmatic semantics, the opposite of some models that, already oriented toward the text or discourse as major unities, take into consideration both contextual and circumstantial selections (Eco, 1975; 1976; and 1979a; 1979b). Miller's deconstructive proposal lies in the following: both inside (or outside) the word and inside (or outside) the text exist semantic traces that, far from shaping a homogeneous or coherent field of homosemes or simply semes (a sine qua non of both the old structuralism and modern textual linguistics), form a heterogeneous, fissured tissue that does not know contradiction (what we could call *heterosemes*). "Each reveals itself to be fissured already within itself, to be, like *Unheimlich, unheimlich*" (TNT, 144). That is why, to the evident negative meaning of "parasitical" ("The parasite is destroying the host"; TNT, 144) is added the hidden, although not so hidden, positive meaning: " 'Parasite' comes from the Greek *parasitos*, 'beside the grain,' *para*, beside (in this case) plus *sitos*, grain, food. . . . A parasite was originally something positive, a fellow guest, someone sharing the food with you, there with you, beside the grain" (TNT, 145). The conclusion is inevitable: "If words in 'para' are one branch of the labyrinth of words in 'per,' the

talking to other gentlemen and ladies. Compared to Trollope's understated simplicity of statement, the flamboyance of Dickens's style may seem vulgar, lower middle class.

This echoing of eloquence from character to narrator in *Ayala's Angel* is exemplified in the representation of Tom Tringle. Of Tom's doomed love for Ayala, the narrator says: "He felt that there were words within his bosom which, if he could only bring them up to his mouth, would melt the heart of a stone. There was his ineffable love, his whole happiness at stake, his purpose, — his holy purpose, — to devote himself, and all that he had, to her well-being. Of all this he had a full conception within his own heart, if only he could express it so that others should believe him!"[3] Tom, in spite of the limitations of his intellect, has in fact pled his case with great eloquence to Ayala. He not only understands himself. He is able, like almost all Trollope's characters, to make himself understood by others. Here, however, the narrator speaks for him and gives him the words he has not fully articulated.

branch is itself a miniature labyrinth. 'Para' is a double antithetical prefix signifying at once proximity and distance, similarity and difference,
interiority and exteriority" (TNT, 144).

Miller refers this meeting of proximity and distance, in the same
place and time, to the relationship between the critic and the text, so that
"The Critic as Host" can be interpreted as a para-sitical commentary on
The Disappearance of God. Concretely in relation to De Quincey's reading, I identified a gap in that book between the declarative stratum of the
text (the necessity of identifying oneself with the consciousness embodied
in the work) and the demonstrative stratum (the meeting with a consciousness which dissolves and disintegrates in a multiplicity of particles
and in a palimpsest without end). Now "The Critic as Host" thematizes
that gap in terms of "undecidability." Who is the parasite but the critic—
the deconstructive critic, according to Wayne Booth and M. H. Abrams,
cited at the beginning of Miller's essay—who introduces himself surrep-
titiously, almost like a virus, into the artistic body of the author? Is not
that entry, sometimes incognito, sometimes openly, a perverse way of
identification with the other? I don't just identify with him; I am not *like*
Keats's sparrow pecking in the gravel, I *am* that sparrow; I live with him;
I feed on the same food. My identification with him is to a certain extent a sadistic way of being with the other, since I devour this other, even
at the risk of making him disappear. Miller asserts that "to call a kind of
criticism 'parasitical' is . . . strong language" (TNT, 145); with this type
of relation, there is no room for intersubjectivity or for dialogue. What
remains is only vampirization.

The basic Millerian matrix is still present, under another guise, in
this phase of his work, although things are not so simple. The question
"Who is the parasite?" apparently has a simple answer, but, as with the
morphology of the word, relations change and become contradictory.

What does it mean to live inside the text? What does it mean, all
things considered, to comment on it, criticize it, break it down, and re-
compose it? This question has no simple answer, either. On the one hand,
the critic and his discourse act as a parasite on the literary text, which
is his "host." The critic and his discourse enter, in some way or another,
into the literary text. They touch it. They adhere to it. This is the necessary principle of any approach to a literary work, or to an artistic work
in general. But, on the other hand, once "inside" the text, the critic discovers that the relation is reversed, that the "eater" is now "eaten," that

The Trollopean narrator can move through time and space to enter into the minds of any of the characters at any time. He shares their gift of language. He can transfer what they say, think, and feel to the reader. This may be explained in the curious metaphor Trollope uses in *An Autobiography* to describe the "all-important art of making meaning pellucid": "The language used should be as ready and as efficient a conductor of the mind of the writer to the mind of the reader as is the electric spark which passes from one battery to another battery" (A, 202). Demonstrations of electricity in Trollope's time were made by connecting two oppositely charged "batteries." A good writer's language penetrates the mind of the reader as naturally, as irresistibly, and as mechanically, as electricity sparks from battery to battery. Language becomes a transparent medium that carries thought and feeling from one person to another.

Much of *Ayala's Angel*, like Trollope's other novels, is made up of the narrator's reports, in indirect discourse, of what he finds when he enters into the characters' minds. The narrator then conveys to the reader, with

the Greek *sitéo* aims at an "I food," absorbed by the remaining textualities and commentaries—for instance, this one you are now reading, by
M. Asensi, which also acts as a parasite on Miller's *corpus*. Moreover, the
critic finds that he is not "inside" the text—which turns out not to be
a text, either. "Who, however, is 'Shelley'? To what does this word refer
if any work signed with this name has no identifiable borders, and no
interior walls either? It has no edges because it has been invaded from
all sides as well as from within by other 'names,' other powers of writing—Rousseau, Dante, Ezekiel, and the whole host of others, phantom
strangers who have crossed the thresholds of the poems, erasing their
margins" (TNT, 162–63). What does the critic's consciousness do once it
has been a parasite to that of the author? It warns that "the parasite structure obliterates the frontiers of the texts it enters" (TNT, 163). Miller's
choice of the terms "parasite" and "host" is not fortuitous. It is continuous with the problem of the alterity of literature, which always remains
itself absolutely other. What really happens is that this alterity, this secret
or encrypting, is subject to the double law or undecidability of touching
and not touching. Therefore: "The critic cannot unscramble the tangle of
lines of meaning, comb its threads out so they shine clearly side by side.
He can only retrace the text, set its elements in motion once more, in that
experience of the failure of determinable reading which is decisive here"
(TNT, 166).

Until now, I have spoken of Miller's direct or indirect readings of
Saussure. I have identified the important differences separating Miller
from other Continental movements. He himself explicitly refers to this:
"As is abundantly apparent in criticism at the present time, rhetorical
analysis, 'semiotics,' 'structuralism,' 'narratology,' or the interpretation of
tropes can freeze into a quasi-scientific discipline promising exhaustive
rational certainty in the identification of meaning in a text and in the
identification of the way that meaning is produced" (TNT, 167). Miller,
unlike Kristeva (1969a) or other semiotic, formalist, or stylistic traditions,
does not think that the text as practice is responsible for making language
strange, in an operation that questions language, changing or excavating
it through the work of the signifier. Miller does not distinguish between
the work as use value and exchange value, as merchandise produced and
put into circulation, and the work that means nothing, that points as a
mute, transformative production, prior to saying, communication, exchange, and sense. He does not demarcate semiotics (or linguistics) as

seemingly effortless simplicity, what the characters are thinking, feeling, and saying to themselves as well as to other people. About Trollope's flexible and easy use of indirect discourse there would be much to say. Its main feature is the change of what the character once said to himself or herself, or virtually said, in the first person present tense into what the narrator says the character said, now given in the third person past tense. An example is the full account of what is going on in Tom Tringle's mind as he walks through the rainy city after his last, failed attempt to persuade Ayala to marry him: "What should he do with himself? What else was there now left to him? He had tried everything and had failed." This is a translation into indirect discourse of: "What should I do with myself? What else is there now left to me? I have tried everything and have failed." Indirect discourse, however, is not quite so straightforward. Toward the end of this paragraph, Trollope's narrator observes that Tom did not exactly speak to himself in just these words: "Not exactly in those words, but with a full inward sense of the words, he told himself that Colonel Stubbs was

applying to the work in its social function from semiotics (or semanalysis) as applying to the work with that function suspended. All these differences lead to a demand for the "literary word," as Bakhtin frequently calls it, to be a crossing of textual surfaces, an intertextuality guided by its relation both to the historical and to the synchronic literary corpus.

For Miller, however, language is already, a priori, something strange or unknown, self-questioned, excavated in itself, mute, prior to saying, prior to the belonging of a communicative subject, and, of course, outside value. For Miller, language projects a double face. Language, like the parasite, is the familiar, the communicable, the rational and metaphysical, what the subject tries to dominate, the merchandise put into circulation. At the same time, however, it is the unknown, the irrational, the incommunicable and nihilist, that which speaks through the subject but that has no voice and is not put into circulation. After analyzing the words and prefixes present in "parasite" and "host," Miller writes about language: "This language is the expression of the inherence of nihilism in metaphysics and of metaphysics in nihilism. We have no other language. . . . The deconstructive procedure, however, by reversing the relation of ghost and host, by playing on the play within language, may go beyond the repetitive generation of nihilism by metaphysics and of metaphysics by nihilism. It may reach something like that *fröhliche Wissenshaft* for which Nietzsche called" (TNT, 153).

Intertextuality—let us accept this name for now, although it would be more advisable to call it *alterity*—is not just the patrimony of the literary word, but, as Miller's analysis proves, a characteristic of language itself, a characteristic that does not depend on a decision by the human subject. Miller continues to prove himself very Heideggerian. The critic cannot escape the "strange logic of the parasite," according to which one must "make the univocal equivocal in spite of oneself, according to the law that language is not an instrument or tool in man's hand, a submissive means of thinking. Language rather thinks human beings and their 'world,' including poems, if they will allow it to do so" (TNT, 148). This is quite like de Man's example of the conversation between Archie Bunker and his wife about the advisability of having his bowling shoes laced over or laced under: "The very anger he [Archie Bunker] displays is indicative of more than impatience; it reveals his despair when confronted with a structure of linguistic meaning that he cannot control and that holds the discouraging prospect of an infinity of similar future confusions, all

a gentleman,—whereas he acknowledged himself to be a cad" (420). The distinction in the first part of this sentence is an important one. The narrator gives words to a wordless inner sense that is nevertheless oriented toward exactly those words, just as, for a phenomenologist, our senses are directed toward objects that we "intend" even if we do not turn that intention into words. Here it is words themselves that are intended in this way. This allows the narrator to claim that in speaking for the character, he does no more than embody in the appropriate actual words the "full inward sense of the words" that Tom Tringle has.

This extraordinary translucence of one mind to itself and to others constitutes one of the great pleasures of reading Trollope, to those who find it pleasant. For me, to tell the truth, reading Trollope is wish fulfillment. When I read Trollope I enter into a world quite unlike the one in which I feel I actually live. I dwell for a time in a realm in which people have a marvellous understanding of one another. The grounds for this Trollopean transparency are several. Trollope assumes that each person has

of them potentially catastrophic in their consequences" (de Man, 1979: 10). Certain texts (literary or nonliterary) exploit that quality. As a system of differences, language leads into a polylogy or textual polygraphy: the word "host" leads Miller in "The Critic as Host" from contemporary English to the Old Norse, going through Middle English, Latin, Old French, and Slavonic as he identifies the way its antecedents and cognates mean both host and guest, or even hostile stranger.

Miller's analysis of Wallace Stevens's "The Rock" will help me in the next chapter to illustrate my three points. It will also put to the test the thesis that literature (which before the eighteenth century was not called "literature" but belonged to the field of the fable) has always yielded (except in certain cases like Mallarmé) to philosophy and has spoken its language. Later on, I shall be able to test whether even philosophy has yielded to philosophy.

Boustrophedonism: The Text as Surd

Eventually two key words, already used and defined in "The Critic as Host" (TNT, 168), appear in the title of a book published in 1985, which deals with nine poets. That title is *The Linguistic Moment.* Thanks to the adjective "linguistic," we would seem to be facing a concept belonging exclusively to the field of linguistics and literary criticism. Nevertheless, this "moment" is, according to Miller, a translation of Nietzsche's term *Augenblick,* which appears in the chapter "The Vision and the Enigma" of *Thus Spoke Zarathustra,* discussing the "eternal return." *Augenblick* means "glance" and also "moment, instant, while, interval." In the definition of "linguistic moment," all the significations of the German term participate: "This is a book, or at any rate, before it was written or while it was being written it was intended to be a book, about moments of suspension within the texts of poems, not usually at their beginnings or ends, moments when they reflect or comment on their own medium. I call this suspension the linguistic moment. It is a form of parabasis, a breaking of the illusion that language is a transparent medium of meaning. . . . The linguistic moment in poetry may take a wide diversity of forms, but in all the cases studied here it has such momentum that it tends to spread out and dominate the functioning of the whole poem" (LM, xiv). This explanation of the term gathers together all the topics we have considered in the section "Dirty Mirrors and Deconstructions." The "linguistic

more or less total access to his or her own thoughts, motives, and feelings. Trollope has little sense that his characters have unconsciousnesses or motives of which they are unaware. Nothing could apparently be further from Sigmund Freud's sense of layers beneath layers and depths within depths in the mind, buried secrets that are betrayed by anomalous features on the surface—slips of the tongue, puns, symbolic acts or locutions. Trollope's characters generally do not make slips of the tongue. What they want to say, they say clearly and without adornment. His men do not mistake the women they love for their mothers, nor do his young women love father surrogates, though they generally love and honor their fathers.

Each Trollopean character, moreover, has a fixed character that endures more or less unchanged through time. This selfhood is open to the knowledge of that self. Trollope's characters have an extraordinary degree of self-knowledge. Each might truthfully say, "I am what I am, and I know what I am." Even when in anger they assert that they will do something inconsistent with what they are, the reader is told that they know quite well

moment" originates in an act of self-reflection or parabasis (the reference to German Romanticism is obvious) that creates instants of vacillation within the poem with relation to its referent, as well as outside the poem with regard to the critic's ability to make decisions.

In *The Disappearance of God* we saw a gap between the explicit declaration of the text and its demonstration; here we confront two strategies, whether intentional or unintentional is of little importance. They are impossible to elude if the text is read attentively. First, the words Miller uses to define the "linguistic moment" are formed in contradictory semantic ways, by palimpsest. We must therefore ask, with regard to the concrete poems and their analyses, what the "reflexive" moment of the poem means, without interpreting such a notion and the process it denotes "literally." Second, Miller's explicit intentions are similar to the ones of *The Disappearance of God* in that he takes a phenomenological approach to the poetical text: "My attempt, following my great exemplar, Matthew Arnold, is in each case 'to see the object as in itself it really is.' I shall attempt to test out what the language of my poems really is, what it really says" (LM, xix). In the case of De Quincey, the author's intention of identifying himself was a failure (and it was not a failure at once) because of an infinite divisibility in the chiastic x. Now, readings of Stevens (which I shall follow more closely), Shelley, Hopkins, Yeats, and others necessitate bracketing the "being" or "being really" of the poem. Miller does the same thing when he uses and/or mentions Matthew Arnold. Miller is quite conscious of the paradoxical character of his formulations: having asserted that he will try to see what the poem is in itself, he warns us that: interpretation or literary criticism "is not the detached statement of a knowledge objectively obtained. It is the desperation of a bet, an ungrounded doing things with words: 'I bet this is a lyric poem,' or 'I bet this is an elegy.' . . . The realm of criticism remains a matter of winning or losing, and not a matter of knowing or not knowing" (LM, 26).

As a consequence, the following questions arise: How do we conjugate what the poem *is* with the catachresis, the "ab-surd," the chasm, and the *Abgrund*? How do we gather the "being" of the poem from a position that rests on the theory, the practice, and the subject of exemplariness? ("Nor can a series of such readings ever in other than a deluded and deluding way be organized as the support of a coherent historical story with beginning, middle, and end, a plot of history, though the history of criticism may be the history of a series of yieldings to that

they will never be able to carry out their threats. Of Sir Thomas Tringle, for example, the rich financier in *Ayala's Angel*, the narrator says Tringle knows he will not be able to sustain his anger towards his sponging son-in-law and towards the impecunious suitor for his other daughter's hand. The passage is a characteristic example of the self-transparency Trollope's characters have. This self-transparency has the further peculiarity of being effortlessly stretched out across time. There are few Proustian intermittencies of the heart or of memory in Trollope's world, almost nothing of Proust's assumption that each person is through time an almost infinite number of different persons. Trollope's characters can remember perfectly all their pasts. They often even have an accurate anticipation of the future. This temporal openness is a concomitant of the admirable continuity Trollope's characters have with themselves:

[Sir Thomas Tringle had] declared roughly that Mr Houston should not have a shilling of his money—as he had certainly been justified for doing; and his daughter, who had always been indulged in every kind of luxury, had at once concocted

delusion" [LM, xxi].) How can we relate what the poem really is in itself to a Nietzschean concept of philology? Miller claims to be a "philologist," with reference not to the strong European philological tradition of K. Vossler, L. Spitzer, or D. Alonso but to the philology that reads (again in quotation-translation, this time from Nietzsche) "slowly, deeply, looking cautiously before and aft, with reservations, with doors left open, with delicate eyes and fingers ('sie lehrt "gut" lesen, das heißt langsam, tief, rück- und vorsichtig, mit Hintergedanken, mit offengelassenen Tören, mit zarten Fingern und Augen lesen')" (LM, xix). As we can see, these first approaches to the notion of "linguistic moment" put at stake, in a clearly contradictory way, a great quantity of literary and theoretico-literary references. What connection exists between such a notion and those present in the works of the Russian Formalists, the New Critics, Czech structuralism, semiotics, and European philology or its associated literary criticism? It will also be necessary to decipher what, in that "linguistic moment," remains of Romantic reflexivity, and of Nietzsche, Heidegger, de Man, and Derrida.

Let us proceed, then, to the analysis of Wallace Stevens's "The Rock" (LM, 390–422). J. Hillis Miller might, though with a difference, have signed the words with which Harold Bloom opened *A Map of Misreading*: "There are *no* texts, but only relationships *between* texts" (Bloom, 1975: 3). His proposal would be more radical, however, for the entities put in relation are not even unitary texts. In "The Critic as Host" we have seen that, wondering who Shelley is, Miller answers that this name has no identifiable borders, that it is invaded by other powerful writings, that, in short, it is the name of a plurality (even that of a "cerologic subject," to use Kristeva's term for describing how the poetry of such writers as Mallarmé, Lautreamont, Rimbaud, and Baudelaire tends to delete the classical poetic subject and install in its place a poetic subject as erasure). Similarly, it is not possible to separate this poem by Stevens: (1) from other poems and writings by Stevens; (2) from the immediate tradition (in this case, the tradition of Whitman and Emerson); and (3) from the common language of poetry and philosophy (LM, 391).

From the beginnings of twentieth-century literary theory in the Russian Formalists, it has been clearly understood that poetic language can be perceived only in relation to other languages. For instance, Roman Jakobson (whom Miller explicitly cites in his chapter devoted to Hopkins) established in *Questions of Poetics* (1973) that poetic language is

a plot for running away from her home! As he thought of the plot it seemed to be wonderful to him that she should be willing to incur such a danger—to be ready without a penny to marry a penniless man—till he confessed to himself that, were she to do so, she would certainly have the money sooner or later. He was capable of passion, capable of flying out and saying a very severe thing to Septimus Traffick [his son-in-law] or another when his temper was hot; but he was incapable of sustained wrath. He was already aware that if Mr Traffick chose to stay he would stay—that if Mr Houston were brave enough to be persistent he might have both the money and the girl. As he thought of it all he was angry with himself, wishing that he were less generous, less soft, less forgiving. (283–84)

Another characteristic example of the self-awareness Trollope's characters have, including awareness of all their past lives, is the opening of chapter thirty-eight. In two and a half pages the narrator reviews the history of Frank Houston's relations to Gertrude Tringle and Imogene Docimer as they have been recounted in earlier chapters of the novel. This full awareness is ascribed in indirect discourse to Frank Houston himself.

perceived in relation to the current poetic tradition, to the common language, and to the poetic tendency governing this particular manifestation. The difference lies in that what prevailed in the Formalist proposal (if Formalism can be reduced to a proposal, which, strictly speaking, is impossible) was the idea of a "constructive function" (Tynianov, 1965: 123), which allows the material identity of the literary work to be ascertained as a system. What Miller proposes is closer to "intertextual" theories of literature (Bakhtin, Kristeva, Laurent Jenny, Barthes, Antoine Compagnon, etc.), although he does not agree completely with any of them, despite his allusions to "intertextuality": "single grand intertextuality system" (LM, 392), or "in formulations of the workings of intertextuality, the weavings of word with word, of figure with figure, in the canon of a writer" (LM, 393). But why does Miller speak of *intertextuality*?

To begin to answer this question, let us first look at how "intertextuality" has been defined. Kristeva does so thus: "Poetic meaning refers to different discursive meanings, so that various other discourses are legible in the poetic utterance. A multiple textual space, then, arises around poetic meaning, and it is possible to apply the elements of that multiple space to a concrete poetic text . . . paragrammatism, namely, the absorption of a multiplicity of texts . . . within the poetic message that . . . is presented as centered on a single sense" (1969: 66–67). By contrast, Compagnon's definition is: "The task of writing consists in rewriting, for it is about turning separate and discontinuous elements into a continuous and coherent whole, about joining them, about covering them . . . , that is to say, about reading them: . . . all writing is collage and gloss, citation and commentary" (Compagnon, 1979: 32).

In both definitions, the work of writing takes place as a reabsorption or reminiscence of other written or nonwritten, verbal or nonverbal texts. For this reason, Kristeva (1974) will come to prefer "transposition" to "intertextuality." Moreover, the result of that reabsorption or rewriting is an organized text, which is semantically closed, continuous, and coherent, in which the work of suture has erased the seams and the imprecise limits of each unity-collage. Therefore Lautréamont can thoroughly incorporate and deny a foreign text coming from Pascal, but this act denies neither the cohesive function of the new message nor its hyperassertive function (Kristeva, 1969a: 151). Michael Riffaterre suggests something similar in that from his *hypogrammatic* theory ("the production of the poetic sign is determined by *hypogrammatic derivation: a*

Houston, like Trollope's characters generally, exists as always aware not only of himself in the present moment but of all his past moments. Recapitulations of these pasts in the guise of telling the reader just what is going on at a given moment in a given character's mind are characteristic of Trollope's narrative technique. They serve as an improvised or prosthetic memory for the reader, in case he or she has forgotten. Trollope's novels move forward in time through constant retrospective recapitulations, like a wave that gathers and regathers all its bulk to advance on the shore. Trollope's narrator seems anxious to leave nothing out, to leave no corner of his story unilluminated. He tries to make sure the reader forgets nothing by presenting periodic recountings of what has already been told.

If Trollope's characters all tend to have a high degree of self-awareness and self-consistency over time, they are also to an extraordinary degree aware of what other people are thinking and feeling. Trollope takes this clairvoyance for granted. He does not give the reader much direct information about its source or much justification for it. Nevertheless, it is so

word or phrase is poeticized when it refers to . . . a preexistent word group";
Riffaterre, 1978: 23) one can infer a poetico-textual unity of significance
(Riffaterre, 1978: 31).

Miller would support the first part of those theories but not the
second. His reading of Saussure and Derrida has led him to recognize an
infinite and contradictory divisibility not only inside the words of a language (a language that, as a result of that divisibility, can never be *one*),
but also in the phonologico-morphological interior of language, and even
in the same trace or mark. Intertextuality, in Miller, stems at first from
particles considered in linguistics to be nonsignificative, though they
really mark directions of meaning. When he selects the word "absurd"
from the context "The sounds of the guitar / Were not and are not. Absurd," he not only analyzes it as a word in its syntagmatic and synchronic
dimension, but also splits it up into morphological segments, "Ab" (a prefix whose features are from "away, an intensive here") and "surdus" ("deaf,
inaudible, insufferable to the ear"). This leads to a "synchronic" run: "A
surd in mathematics is a sum containing one or more irrational roots of
numbers. . . . There is a square root of two, but it is not any number that
can be said, rationally. A *surd* in phonetics is a voiceless sound, that is
to say, a sound with no base in the vibration of the vocal chords." It is
followed by a "diacronic," babelic run: "The original root of the word
surd, *swer*, means to buzz or whisper, as in *susurration* or *swirl*. . . . The
Latin *surdus* was chosen in medieval mathematics to translate an Arabic
term that was itself a translation of the Greek *alogos*: speechless, wordless, inexpressible, irrational, groundless" (LM, 394). Perhaps not even
those phonologico-morphological elements or prefixes — "ab," meaning
"away" — are signifiers, phonemes, morphemes, or traces in their polygraphic dispersion.

Derrida warns us in *Glas* about GL: "GL / I do not say either the
signifier GL, or the phoneme GL, or the grapheme GL. Mark would be
better, if the word were well understood, or if one's ears were open to it;
not even mark then. / It is also imprudent to advance or set GL swinging
in the masculine or feminine, to write or to articulate it in capital letters.
That has no identity, sex, gender, makes no sense, is neither a definitive whole nor a part detached from a whole / gl remain(s) gl" (Derrida,
1986b: 119, right column). In the same way, the prefix "ab" and the word
"surdus" place us on the fringe ("away") of a logic of sense or roots. They
aim at the absence of sense, or rather, at the impossibility of making a

different from the relative opacity of people toward one another in the novels, say, of Jane Austen or of George Eliot, not to speak of "real life," as to constitute, even within the literary conventions of the Victorian period, a wish fulfillment. It is a paradisiac world of intuitive, almost angelic, insight by each person into those around. Or at least it is paradisiac in Trollope's world, though one should remember the mortal suffering to which such clairvoyance leads in George Eliot's somber novella "The Lifted Veil." Whether it is a good or pleasant thing to know what your neighbor is thinking and feeling depends on what that thinking and feeling are. For George Eliot it is a good thing we are "well wadded with stupidity" and are protected from clairvoyant insight into other people.[4]

The understanding Trollope's characters have of one another arises spontaneously, the reader may assume, from several factors. The characters all belong to the same class, race, and national community. They share the values and assumptions of a single inclusive culture. Problems of multicultural difference rarely arise in Trollope's novels, whatever may have been

decision, of talking ("speechless, wordless, inexpressible") about sense: "This disremembering annihilates everything that seems most vital in the poet's past, most solidly grounded. Such forgetting annihilates the past by uprooting it, by seeing its roots as nonexistent, 'alogical'" (LM, 394–95). Again one sees the paradox. The words I have just cited refer to the act of forgetting, which takes place in the person of the poet, poematic narrator, author, "author," or subject of the enunciation. He moves within the illusion of the past as it appears and disappears. ("In the final three stanzas the dismantled illusion is put together again"; LM, 395.) On this occasion, however, the critic does not seem to participate in the poet's obligatory amnesia. He apparently finds himself at the other extreme— forced to remember, to discover intertextuality, that "system of multiple connections" (Kristeva, 1969a: 239), in short, to act in a systematic, paradigmatic, and etymological way. He must remember the roots of the poem, above all because, as I have already said, those roots are the "program" of the poem. They anticipate its general strategy.

Nevertheless, what the critic remembers at the end, once he has arrived at Middle English, Latin, or Arabic, is: (1) that he cannot say anything, even to himself ("speechless, wordless, inexpressible, irrational, groundless"; LM, 394); (2) that he is telling us the impossibility of telling; (3) that he would say to us something like "I have never known how to tell a story" (Derrida, 1986a: 3). Wallace Stevens says:

> It is an illusion that we were ever alive,
> Lived in the houses of mothers, arranged ourselves
> By our own motions in a freedom of air
>
> . . .
> . . . The sounds of the guitar
> Were not and are not. Absurd. The words spoken
> Were not and are not. It is not to be believed.
>
> *(Stevens, 1954: 525)*

"It is a poem about forgetting," Miller asserts (LM, 394), about forgetting and about the remembering that remembers its remembering is an illusion among others. For this reason, we can ask whether Miller's critical literary discourse is a discourse about forgetting. Miller works his encyclopedico-linguistico-literary memory to find out that remembering remembers it has no voice, that it hardly buzzes, whispers (LM, 394).

Actually, to see the poem as it is in itself means to set forgetting

the actual situation in Victorian England. Trollope's characters, with few exceptions, belong to the British middle or upper class, even though distinctions both of birth and of money within these large categories are crucial to the stories he tells. For the most part Trollope's characters are all "gentlemen" and "ladies" together. Trollope's people are not "other" to each other in the way those belonging to another class or culture, in a multicultural nation like the United States, may have a pregiven opacity. Such opacity may be exceedingly difficult, if not impossible, for someone on the other side of a cultural divide to penetrate.

If class and race are not barriers to understanding the other person, of the three graces—class, race, and gender—that preside over present-day cultural studies (just as metaphor and metonymy, in Gérard Genette's witty formulation, were once the china dogs, the *chiens de faïence*, of rhetorical criticism), that leaves gender. Gender difference is what Trollope's novels are all about, since courtship and marriage are their main subjects. Trollope constantly makes careful notations about the differences between

against memory. More precisely, it is to oppose the memory of forgetting (yesterday as illusion) to the forgetting of memory (memory remembers its lack of ground [*groundless*]). To see the poem as it is means not to see it in order to see it again, in a constant game of visibility and blindness: "It contains a desire for illusion so great that the leaves come and cover that high rock of air, as the lilacs bloom in the spring, cleansing blindness, bringing sight again to birth, and so starting the cycle of illusion over again. Blindness is parallel to the deafness of absurd" (LM, 395). The critic is interpreting lines 28–31 of "The Rock":

> It is not enough to cover the rock with leaves.
> We must be cured of it by a cure of the ground
> Or a cure of ourselves, that is equal to a cure
>
> Of the ground, a cure beyond forgetfulness
> *(Stevens, 1954: 526)*

But why has it been said that the synchronic and diachronic, polylogic and polygraphic roots or rhizomes are the program of the poem's general strategy? Because the alternation between visibility and blindness represents a "cyclic" reading ("the periodic cycles"), a reading among others within the textual gene of the "speechless, wordless, inexpressible, irrational, groundless" process.

Other parts of the poem—for instance, the beginning of the second poem of "The Rock"—seem to be inclined not to the cyclical and to the oscillating but to stability. What kind of stability is this? What does a poem that prays for "a cure beyond forgetfulness" announce to us? "After the cure we would live in a permanent state of illusion known as illusion, therefore 'beyond forgetfulness.' This illusion would be known in such a way that the abyss, the *Abgrund*, would appear as the truth of the ground, without undermining the illusion, so that the illusion might never be forgotten" (LM, 395–96). Or "does Stevens mean that the cure beyond forgetfulness would permanently cover or solidify the abyss? Then the illusion might never again be scoured away and the abyss never again be seen" (LM, 396). The diachronic and systematic inquiry has filled up the particles thanks to their emptiness of sense. "Ab," away, comes to be:

   1. A *self-metatextual or self-metatheoretical "away"*: The impossibility of giving a semantic direction or directions that are more or less compatible with each other. ("The possibility of each of these alternatives is suggested by Stevens's often-cited adage: 'The final

men and women in his culture. He tends to express these differences as universal and absolute, not as culture-bound. An example is what he says apropos of Lucy Dormer's falling in love with Isadore Hamel: "A girl loves most often because she is loved, — not from choice on her part. She is won by the flattery of the man's desire" (154–55). Trollope's novels focus on the challenges to understanding that arise from such gender distinctions. The main gender difference in Victorian culture was that a woman's whole life was determined by her marriage, whereas only part of a man's fate was determined by his marriage. This seems strange and unjust to us today, but it is still the case in many traditional cultures around the world. Speaking of Frank Houston's failure to understand the woman from whom he has separated himself, Trollope says: "He had thought that to relieve herself from the burden of her love would be as easy to her as to him. In making this mistake he had been ignorant of the intrinsic difference in the nature of a man's and of a woman's heart, and had been unaware that that, which to a man at his best can only be part of his interest in life's concerns, will to a woman be everything" (365).

belief is to believe in a fiction, which you know to be a fiction, there being nothing else' "; LM, 396.)

2. A *textual "away" in the incipit* (the poem about forgetfulness): A spot on the fringe of the affectivity filling the things one remembers.

3. A *textual "away" as possible solutions to the incipit*: An "away" of forgetfulness through cyclic periods? An "away" of forgetfulness through an illusion that never disappears, even when it is conscious of being an illusion? An "away" of forgetfulness and of the abyss through an intervening covering over of what does not allow the feet any ground on which to rest?

Miller teaches us that the prefix "ab" resounds in "surdus," that "ab" interferes with "surdus" so that—in the gene and inside and outside the poem—the text, its author, and the chain of critics are taken *ab-ack* by that lack of original name. This does not allow us to escape "negative capability" and cease to remain in uncertainty, mystery, and doubt. Ernst Robert Curtius (1948, 1953) explains how from Greek poetry to Gracián and Calderón etymology was thought to be a pathway to truth and even action. (Curtius himself sees in etymology another possibility: the historical relationship between the real word and its history makes it possible to join both the word and its antecedents on the same syntagmatic level, a result that can produce events.) Although in the *Cratylus* Socrates begins by saying that syllables reveal things by imitating them, and that "the letter *rho*, as I was saying, appeared to the imposer of names an excellent instrument for the expression of motion" (Plato, 1963: 145i, 426d), by the end he also admits that possibly the name and the object named are two different things. Miller would support that last solution or self-deconstruction of the Platonic text. There lies the great difference between Miller and Heidegger regarding the use of etymology and diaphora (i.e., two words that are identical as signifiers, but absolutely different from the viewpoint of the signified). According to Arion L. Kelkel (1975), Heidegger admits the possibility of restoring the original figure of significations, the true original and historical meaning of words, whereas Miller would not. The infinite divisibility found already in De Quincey does not allow the recovery of any original, primitive, lost sense. The work of memory—intertextuality is, after all, an operation of re-cognition, repetition, and remembering—leads Miller to forgetfulness: "The lives these lived in the mind are at an end" (Stevens, 1954: 525).

In spite of this culturally determined difference between men and women, and in spite of the momentary misunderstandings to which it may give rise, Trollope's characters, men and women alike, have a high degree of insight into what the other person is thinking and feeling. The medium of this insight is partly the knowledge that the other person, though perhaps of the other sex, nevertheless belongs to the same culture and will in a given situation almost certainly be thinking and feeling what everyone else would think and feel in a similar situation. One important difference between men and women in Trollope's world is of course that his women do not feel sexual desire for other women or his men for other men. Consequently they have some difficulty understanding the desires of the other sex. Of homosocial affection only the most indirect and effaced references are made, usually in the form it takes of love between father and son or mother and daughter or between sisters. A fair degree of what Eve Sedgwick calls male homosociality exists in Trollope's novels, for example in Tom Tringle's friendship with Samuel Faddle in *Ayala's Angel*, or

The prefix "ab" and the stem "surdus," with their Middle English, Latin, Greek, and Arabic roots, are anything but "the greatest charge of initial and valid human perception," which Heidegger takes an etymological root to be (Steiner, 1978: 8). Though ancestral and common syllables, they are not replete with meaning. On the contrary, they are alogical, scarcely audible if heard at all; they imply no speaker and are not even words. Steiner further says about Heidegger: "By pondering intensely, and with a sort of vehement probing, the etymology and early history of a word, the thinker can compel it to yield its formidable quantum of illumination and energy" (Steiner, 1978: 8). Steiner's formulation places Heidegger within a venerable tradition of attempts to go from the name to the thing, from the *verbum* to the *res*. There he echoes such predecessors as Isidore of Seville, or Augustine's argument that Paul is called "the apostle of the people" because he is *minimus apostolarum*. In opposition to that tradition, though also within it, closer to Nietzsche and Derrida than to Heidegger and de Man, Miller encounters in the diachronic and synchronic labyrinth the impossibility of deciding, apropos light and energy, the absence or presence of an original name that foregrounds a determinate *res*.

Positively, with François Laruelle Miller could maintain that "the immanent essence of the a prioris, above all the *khōra*, suspends as a whole philosophical resistance and plunges the decision in the abyss of an unapproachable contingency. This is because the phenomenal content of the real or of the 'non-thetic' in general, which is more primitive than the Other, has the power of having suspended a priori the decision and the World" (Laruelle, 1989: 201). Here, the *khōra* and the "non-thetic" are equivalent to the lack of an original name. Catachresis, another version of such a lack, necessarily puts before our eyes the possibility of the real, since to have no name for something is a way of facing the impossible dimension of the real, the "thing." For Miller, the work of memory leads to what cannot even be, like Derrida's GL, a mark or trace, to what, in its minimal or ante-minimal figurativeness (in the sense of Lyotard's opposition between the figural—which has no reference or meaning and whose value arises from its materiality—and discourse, which works always within the problematic relationship between expression and content), amounts to an emptiness of sense. In this emphasis on the "thing," Miller's work can be seen as a postdeconstructive deconstruction. Of etymological grounding, he writes: "What is the status of these etymologies?

in the strong feelings of attraction and hatred among the various suitors for Ayala's hand. The latter is most evident in Tom Tringle's feelings about Jonathan Stubbs. Nevertheless, even the desires of the other sex can be understood. Of Lady Albury's difficulty in understanding why Colonel Stubbs is head over heels in love with something "so insignificant" as Ayala Dormer, the narrator says, with characteristic delicacy: "The speciality of the attraction is of course absent to the woman, and unless she has considered the matter so far as to be able to clothe her thoughts in male vestments, as some women do, she cannot understand the longing that is felt for so small a treasure" (340–41).

Of what might be problematic about the narrator's ability to understand the desires of his female characters, neither the narrator himself (he is clearly male) nor Trollope in his autobiography have any explanation or apology. It is taken for granted that a good male novelist can clothe his thoughts in female vestments. Henry James said Trollope made the English girl his special province.[5] That is certainly true. It is also true, how-

Identification of the true meaning of the word? Some original presence
rooted in the ground of immediate experience, physical or metaphysical? By no means. They serve rather to indicate the lack of enclosure of a
given word. . . . In any case, the effect of etymological retracing is not to
ground the word solidly but to render it unstable, equivocal, wavering,
groundless. All etymology is false etymology, in the sense that some bend
or discontinuity always breaks up the etymological line" (AT, 19).

Miller does not stop at combining a prefix ("ab") with a semantic
(anti)direction so as to place us "away." For him, it is no longer a question
of the *meaning* of these particles, morphemes, or words, but of the existence in a minute place on the material page (the most minute, the one
occupied by an "i") of marked heads, dots, hats, and tails, as the result
of the crossing between French, English, Latin, Greek, and Phoenician:
We can see this attention to what I call pictographic value, to materiality
as icon or mark, in what Miller writes of the *î* in *mise en abîme* (a phrase
that, incidentally, instantiates another form of "ab"):

Abyme is an older variant of the modern French *abîme*, from late Latin *abyssus*,
from Greek *abussos*, without bottom. The circumflexed *i*, *i* deprived of its head or
dot, and given a hat or tent instead, indicates a dropped *s*. This *i* is then dropped
in turn to be replaced by a *y*, *igrec*, Greek *i*. In fact the late Latin *y* was an equivalent both for Greek *u*, *upsilon*, "bare *u*," and for the *y*, or *u* with a tail, that is, an
i sound, as in French *ici*. The Greek *u*, which became Roman *y*, is only one of the
two letters deriving from the Phoenician *waw*, which is itself derived from *v*. The
other descendant is *f*, Greek *digamma*, "double gamma." The *gamma* is of course
also *y*-shaped. The word *abyme* is itself a *mise en abyme*, hiding and revealing the
hollow of the *u* by the masculine addition of the tail, but leaving no sign of the
absent *s*. The word *abyme* contains dropped letter behind dropped letter, in a
labyrinth of interchanges figured by the doubling shape of the *y*. (LM, 398)

The textual gene is a drawing or hieroglyph that oscillates between
a head and the lack of a head, between a tail (penis) and the lack of tail
(penis): the *y*, the *i*, the *v*, and the *f*. It is Ariadne's entangled ball of
thread, leading Theseus infinitely through Dedalus's labyrinth. (The passage just quoted might be interestingly compared with the ideas Maurice
Toussain develops in his *Contre l'arbitraire du signe*, 1983.) The conception of language with which Miller begins is not "linguistic" in the sense
of a systematic or antisystematic linguistics, but takes as its point of departure the idea of an emptiness that is hidden and then discovered, or,
alternatively, the idea of a language semantically built up and at the same

ever, of a long string of major English novelists, including William Makepeace Thackeray, George Meredith, and Thomas Hardy. Henry James himself made the American girl his special province. Such novels as *Vanity Fair*, *The Egoist*, *Tess of the d'Urbervilles*, and *Portrait of a Lady* or *The Golden Bowl* depend on the assumption that a male author can understand women. They know, in Freud's notorious phrase, what a woman wants.

Trollope's characters, in addition to the understanding of others they have on the basis of a shared culture, are granted a large degree of spontaneous hermeneutic skill. By "hermeneutic skill" I mean an ability to go accurately through signs to reach what they stand for. Trollope's characters can read correctly the speech, gesture, facial expression, and written language of the other person. Trollope's novels are full of passing notations assuring us of this skill's ubiquity. Of the way Sir Thomas Tringle speaks "with a deliberate courtesy" to the son-in-law he scorns, the narrator tells us that the son-in-law "perfectly understood" what that courtesy meant (329). Though Lucy says nothing in response to Isadore Hamel's ex-

time destroyed in the palimpsest. Both in the (real or mental) building and in its ruins, the signs and graphic forms are scarcely legible. We face another paradox, an undecidable icon, that of "ab" or that of the "i" with and without head, with and without tail, which relates by similarity, by participation, and by analogy to what happens later on in the major segments of "The Rock."

With that conception of language Miller comes to paint over (in a timid way?—no, definitively not) Stevens's poem. Over the *ab-surd* or *Ab-grund*, he paints the problematic and uncertain *i*. Perhaps he does so because the second part of "The Rock" is entitled "The Poem as Icon." The poem as (I)con. Or maybe not. Perhaps the critic, the ambiguous parasite settled in the "just as it is" of Stevens's text, also intervenes from a certain outside while still in the wake of the interior words. As Miller tells us, the "i" comes from a borrowing that illustrates what he has been saying about the abyss and the absurd: "Since it is a question here of the abyss, of the absurd and of the grounding or filling of that abyss, one may borrow from the French an untranslatable name for this impasse of language: *mise en abyme*" (LM, 398). This "illustrating" by means of borrowing not only anticipates one of Miller's most recent titles (*Illustration*, 1992), but also reveals the graphic element of his criticism, which appears on several occasions throughout the essay. "To illustrate" means "bringing to light, as a spelunker lights up a cave, or as a medieval manuscript is illuminated" (I, 61). By borrowing something seen as both from the outside (from French) and from an infinite inside where languages cross regardless of cultural or linguistic borders, the critic, like the poet-painters Henri Michaux and Apollinaire, draws an *i* or a *y* that covers the poem from beginning to end. What the critic brings to light is not itself light, but the play of letters that are seen and not seen. Miller is thus situated between Derrida and the painter Valerio Adami (about whom Derrida has written a brilliant essay; Derrida, 1987b: 149–82). The critic does not confine himself to analyzing the text by pursuing the Borgesian labyrinth of words, morphemes, phonemes, and traces. He does not confine himself to saying metalinguistically, regarding "The Rock," something about this semantics, this syntax, or this morphology.

The critic paints an "i" about which Derrida might have said:

A single drawing, once put on the rails, lends itself, without moving in itself, or almost, to a whole series of different readings, each time transformed through and through across the redistribution of the chromatic values [graphics of white

pressions of love, he can read her silence accurately: "There comes a time when no answer is as excellent eloquence as any words that can be spoken. Hamel, who had probably not thought much of this, was nevertheless at once informed by his instincts that it was so. 'Oh, Lucy,' he said, 'if you can love me say so'" (177). Of the letter Frank Houston sends to his real love, Imogene Docimer, after he has broken his engagement to Gertrude Tringle, the woman he had planned to marry for money alone, the narrator says, "It was a long rambling letter, without a word in it of solid clearly-expressed meaning; but Imogene, as she read it, understood very well its real purport. She understood more than its purport, for she could see by it,—more clearly than the writer did himself,—how far her influence over the man had been restored, and how far she might be able to restore it" (364).

Though Trollope does not write epistolary novels, letters exchanged among his characters play a crucial role in his novels. Each character has an inadvertent ability to expose his or her real character in a letter. The recipi-

and black, we would say here] and all the differential versions proposed by Adami. (Derrida, 1987b: 172–73)

Don't stop at that. Although it is not a transcendental (semantic or formal) element, *tr* gives itself up to analysis. Like any transformable conglomerate. Decompose the *tr*, vary its atoms, work substitutions or transfers, erase as Adami does when he's drawing. In a first picture, keep first of all the consonantal double, rub out the odd bar from the *t*, replace them with the traits of another consonant. For example, *f* (which is more or less the catastrophic reversal of the *t*), but for another journey, it could be *b, c, d, g, p, v*. (Derrida, 1987b: 174)

In the light of all these words, in the light of painting and graph, in the light of illustration, that the critic intended to see the poem as it is in itself cannot be other than a paradox. Instead, he sees through borrowed lenses that constantly change in gradation and angle.

But Miller paints on a painting, one more classical, more linguistic, more Mallarmean—that is, on the syntax of "The Rock." "There are other ways in which 'The Rock' is a *mise en abyme*. [That is, there are other elements the 'i' illustrates.] One is the sequence of phrases in apposition. This is a constant feature of Stevens's poetic procedure . . . : 'The blooming and the musk / Were being alive, an incessant being alive, / A particular of being, that gross universe'; 'They bud the whitest eye, the pallidest sprout, / New senses in the engenderings of sense, / The desire to be at the end of distances, / The body quickened and the mind in root'" (LM, 400–401). The possibility of a multiple reading, again stemming from the emptiness, reappears. Are the objects named by the poem elements which equal each other, given that they are "objects of the same verb" (LM, 401)? Are they progressive forms that, through repetition, reach the desired meaning ("reaching closer and closer to the desired meaning"; LM, 401)? Or, on the contrary, do the sequences and syntagms cancel each other out ("each new phrase cancels the previous one"; LM, 401)? Something similar happens with a word, the verb "being": "The sequence plays with various incongruent senses and grammatical functions of the word 'being'" (LM, 401). At this point the syntax and the word, as paintings and as verbalities, become—in a very graphic metaphor—"a snake with its tail in its mouth, or a snake almost succeeding in getting its tail in its mouth" (LM, 402).

The mutilated "i" or the "i" with attributes, the illegible graphico-pictorial "strength"—perhaps legible only in a way interminably anamor-

ent is granted an ability to see through the letter to the essential nature of the person who has written it. The narrator does not hide the characters' correspondence from the reader, just as he does not hide their other secrets. The narrator opens their private letters and makes them public, as if they were postcards that anyone could read. He characteristically says about a given letter exchanged between his characters something like: "It shall be given in its entirety." This reading of the characters' letters matches the way the narrator sees into their minds in a constant hidden surveillance. Think what it would be like to live in such a world, to have all one's letters read, to have one's most secret thoughts and feelings instantly recorded by an invisible but all-seeing, all-knowing spectator, who then publishes what he records where all the world may read it!

Trollopean Ideology

Little room seems left for any radical otherness in Trollope's novels. No black holes exist from which no signs emerge, no secrets that may not

phic (Miller says in one of his many references to painting, "The poem is like those paintings by Tchelitchev that are simultaneous representations of several different objects"; LM, 405) — reappears in another key word, "cure." This word appears on five occasions in four lines previously cited:

> It is not enough to cover the rock with leaves.
> We must be *cured* of it by a *cure* of the ground
> Or a *cure* of ourselves, that is equal to a *cure*
>
> Of the ground, a *cure* beyond forgetfulness.
> *(Stevens, 1954: 526, my italics)*

"What, then, of cure?" Miller wonders. Has it to do with those "new senses in the engenderings of sense"? Is it a case of phonetico-semantic repetition or, rather, an example of *distincto, diaphora,* or *antistasis*? Is it the "cum idem verbum repetiutur in contrario sensu" ("to repeat the same word with a different meaning"; Lausberg, 1960: vol. 2, 130)? Absolutely not. It is not that the word "cure," despite its identity as signifier, has three different explicit meanings in the first, second, and third lines. What happens is that the *antistasis* has already been produced inside the word, in its vertical and horizontal, its paradigmatic and syntagmatic axes, before a material repetition in the text of the poem comes to take place. It could be said, paraphrasing Umberto Eco, that the heteroseme or heterograph must appear as a virtual text, and that the text is no more than the expansion of a heteroseme or heterograph. This is one key in Millerian "deconstruction," what I will call, as I indicated in the introductory chapter, "deconstruction of the one."

Until now we have seen Miller practicing a kind of "microanalysis" that discovers the inexpressible and illegible on pictographic, verbal, and nonverbal levels of the text, so that we finally confront a minute and brief unity that is not a unity and re-produces in the poem as discourse. In the diagram of the *i* and/or the *y*, we find the structural and objective emptiness of an undecidability, and we also see how the poem is in itself in order to discover that there is no such "itself." De Man's "deconstructive" model does not follow this line. In the introduction to *Allegories of Reading*, de Man outlines the point of reference for the following chapters on Rousseau, Proust, Rilke, and others: "The grammatical model of the question becomes rhetorical not when we have, on the one hand, a literal meaning and on the other hand a figural meaning, but when it is impossible to decide by grammatical or other linguistic devices which of the

be penetrated by the senses and by the understanding. The almost total transparency of Trollope's characters to themselves, to one another, and to the reader through the narrator's undistorted report would appear to support the claim D. A. Miller makes, in *The Novel and the Police*,[6] that Trollope's novels are a puissant agent of the Victorian thought police. According to Miller, these novels express a sinister power of Foucauldian surveillance not unlike Bentham's famous panopticon. This surveillance, D. A. Miller holds, enforces a rigid, oppressive Victorian ideology of class and gender roles. The real police are almost totally absent from these novels because they are not needed. They are not needed because the narrator, who speaks for a collective community awareness, is an irresistible enforcer. Readers of Trollope's novels were coached into submission to this ideology, according to D. A. Miller, without being aware of what was being done to them. This coercion was all the more effective for being, like ideological restraints generally, invisible. Trollope's work was part of the subset of the ideological state apparatus that Althusser calls "the communications

two meanings (that can be entirely incompatible) prevails. Rhetoric radically suspends logic and opens up vertiginous possibilities of referential aberration" (de Man, 1979: 10).

For de Man, texts outline two readings that directly confront each other: grammar versus rhetoric, what is preached and what is done, the constative and the performative. In the last chapter of *Allegories of Reading*, "Confessions," de Man indicates that, although Rousseau explicitly declares that what he wanted was Marion's ribbon (a metaphor wherein the ribbon equals Rousseau's desire for Marion), his rhetoric of hyperbolical delight shows us that "what Rousseau really wanted is neither the ribbon nor Marion, but the public scene of exposure which he actually gets. The fact that he made no attempt to conceal the evidence confirms this" (de Man, 1979: 285). Declaration and demonstration, for instance, oppose and cancel each other. In de Man, the text is a (non)identity subject to a dual and negative tension never overcome or synthesized. From that follows his use of the controversial notions of "irony" and "parabasis." *Allegories of Reading* sums this up quite economically: "We call *text* any entity that can be considered from such a double perspective: as a generative, open-ended, non-referential grammatical system and as a figural system closed off by a transcendental signification that subverts the grammatical code to which the text owes its existence. The 'definition' of the text also states the impossibility of its existence and prefigures the allegorical narratives of this impossibility" (de Man, 1979: 270).

For Miller, instead, what is problematic is the distinction between the grammatical and rhetorical systems. For him, that distinction presupposes the absence of rhetoricity within grammar. Does the expression *mise en abyme* belong to rhetoric or to grammar? And what about the "i" with or without head, with or without tail—does it belong to rhetoric or to grammar? Is what cannot be named grammatical or rhetorical? In the context of Miller's essay, these questions are strange, because the *ab-yme* or the *ab-surd* or the *Ab-grund*, seen from a grammatical approach, is already rhetorical, already split at its origin, already "speechless, wordless, inexpressible." Grammar is subverted by *catachresis* (another key word in Miller's theoretical task), because the latter inhabits the very heart of the former's system of rules. Grammar, before coming to the text as discourse, as macrotextuality, has already been deconstructed. Furthermore, when the aporia exists on a semiotico-grammatical level, what is programmed is another aporia that will reproduce itself on the semantico-

ISA."[7] Watch out, because whatever you think, do, or feel, the Trollopian narrator is the agent of a real-life power that will be seeing and judging you, ready to punish you implacably for any deviance and reward you for submission, just as the characters in Trollope's novels are punished or are rewarded for obedience to ideological demands.

D. A. Miller does not much like Trollope, finds him tedious, and performs his own act of policing, by way of censorious judgment, in his essay. Perhaps he finds Trollope boring as a way of protecting himself from the novelist's ability to make his assumptions and those of his culture seem plausible. Better to find him boring than to take him seriously, since it might be dangerous to do so.[8] You might become subject to Victorian ideology, even at this late date. D. A. Miller has read, or at any rate refers to, only a few of Trollope's works, primarily the quite early novel, *Barchester Towers*. Nevertheless, what he says about Trollope, as about other writers, has its own force. It bores into the mind and sticks there.

One might think it possible to defend Trollope from D. A. Miller's

discursive level (to use Benveniste's terms). In de Man, deconstruction takes place in the text as discourse. In Miller, deconstruction takes place in the graphico-verbal component of the smallest unity. For him, when the text self-deconstructs, it is because the graph or the minimum feature, the heteroseme or heterograph, has already self-deconstructed.

When in *The Linguistic Moment* Miller approaches de Man's modus operandi, as he does in the essays on Hopkins or Wordsworth, in which a tension is supposedly maintained between the author's explicit declaration and his demonstration or rhetorical use, there always also appears an analysis that places itself prior to textuality or discourse, a hard look at the text that sees the picto-graphico-verbal: "If this is so, there is no word for the Word, only displaced metaphors of it. In the word lists in Hopkins' early onomatopoetic etymological speculations, each list goes back to an ur-gesture, action, or sound. In each case this is an act of division, marking, striking, or cutting. Here are examples of these lists: 'grind, gride, gird, groat, grate, greet,' 'flick, fleck, flake,' 'skim, scum, squama, scale, scale, keel' " (LM, 261). If Hopkins deconstructs himself, that is, if Hopkins deconstructs his own metaphysical position, his opposition of sensible and intelligible with regard to denomination and literal sign, it is because prior to his explicit declaration of that position the minimal element—the heteroseme, or heterograph, or heteroglyph—has already split without possibility of synthesis: "All these word lists lead back to an original sound or sound-producing act of differentiation. For Hopkins . . . the beginning is diacritical" (LM, 262).

If it is the beginning, if it is *at* and *during* the beginning, then deconstruction does not spring, on principle, from the dual and negative form of the macrotextual level. This explains why Miller does not thoroughly share classical theories of intertextuality. The declaration that several other discourses are legible in the poetic text leads Kristeva, for instance, to recognize two types of "partial" *grammé*: the written *grammé* (phonetic, semic, and syntagmatic; Kristeva, 1969a: 241, 1) and the read *grammé* (the foreign text as reminiscence and the foreign text as quotation; Kristeva, 1969a: 253, 1). In this exposition, elements with a delimiting and recognizable identity constitute the "origin" of the intertextual process (an origin within a chain, of course). Kristeva applies a clearly Greimasian criterion, a faith in the possibility of describing the structure of language's semantic level in scientific terminology, when she describes the semic writing *grammé* of specific passages from *Maldoror*, despite her

stern policing by arguing that Trollope brings clearly into the open Victorian assumptions about gender, proper behavior, and so on. Such clarity, it might be argued, constitutes an exposure of that ideology. Bringing an ideology so clearly out, one might claim, is not quite the same as simply enforcing it. It might be difficult, however, to make that claim persuasive. For the most part, the narrator of Trollope's novels and Trollope himself (for example, in letters and in nonfictional prose works) cheerfully re-affirms the main values endorsed by high Victorian ideology. This includes the racist ideology of British imperialism. A good place to see the latter is Trollope's books on South Africa, the West Indies, North America, Australia, and New Zealand.[9] If you want to know what Victorian ideology was, or at least one strong version of it, read Trollope. Moreover, as theorists of ideology like Althusser have persuasively argued, ideology critique in the form of an intellectual exposé, even in a powerful literary work, does not free you from that ideology.[10] Such freedom, if it comes through words at all, comes only through some performative use of language that leads to

recognition that the semes of common language and those of the poetic language function differently. The semes appear, then, listed and enumerated, as a limit beyond which the critic does not go. At the "origin" the written *grammés* are logically and mathematically identifiable; at the "end," the analyst needs another logic, because the poetic language is a negation of logic. What characterizes such poetic language is the intertwining of affirmation and negation, of being and nonbeing.

In Miller the opposite occurs: logic and rhetoric, common and uncommon, affirmative and negative, appear in the same space and time. For this reason, it is not possible to identify in the "origin" of the written *grammé* whatever type that *grammé* may be. The laws Kristeva sees as failing at the textual and discursive level in poetical language have already failed in common words, in the language of metaphysics that is nihilism, in the language of the parasite that is host and vice versa. There is not, then, any possibility of making in a mathematical or structuralist way a list of semes, phonemes, or syntagms, nor is there any possibility of distinguishing, strictly speaking, between what is writing and what is reading, for both would be two traces on the same heteroseme or heterograph. "What, then of *cure?*" Miller wonders. It is not a question of establishing columns of names first from a paradigmatic approach and then from a syntagmatic one. One does not place "cure" beside "rock," "ground," "leaves," "lilacs," "poem," and so on. Everything happens, everything has already happened, before that listing:

The multiple meanings of the word *cure*, like the meanings of all the key words and figures in 'The Rock,' are incompatible. They may not be organized into a logical or dialectical structure but remain stubbornly heterogeneous. They may not be followed, etymologically, to a single root that will unify or explain them, explicate them by implicating them in a single source. They may not be folded together in a unified structure, as of leaves, blossom, and fruit from one stem. The origin rather is bifurcated, even trifurcated, a forking root that leads the searcher for the ground of the word into labyrinthine wanderings in the forest of words. (LM, 397)

What is the logic that organizes or disorganizes the word "cure"? It is the logic that applies to the *ab-surdus* or to the *i* of the expression *mise en abyme*. It is the *i* with or without head, which does not support the critic and forces him to decompose in another graphico-verbal process—and does so in a violent way, in the *how it is* of the word-poem and in its *how it is not* ("products of a visible manipulation of verbal effects"; LM, 400).

changes in material conditions of existence. The question is whether Trollope's novels do that or even show it being done within the fictional stories.

Just what are the components of Victorian middle- and upper-class ideology as Trollope shows its power? Many of these components will seem to us as strange as those of some non-European society. I have already identified one of the most important features: the assumption that a woman's main business in life is to get herself as well married as possible, then settle down to having children and running a household with prudence and frugality. A woman's lot, in Trollope's England, is to marry and to bear children, lots of them. The narrator of *Ayala's Angel* speaks more than once of the way a newly married couple may expect a child once a year and will soon have many cradles in their nursery. Though we know from other evidence that the Victorians knew some forms of birth control, apparently it was inconceivable, at least in Trollope's novels, that a respectably married upper-middle-class couple would do anything to keep those babies from coming every year. Trollope is far too proper to say anything

Can the passivity of the critic who wants to see the poem as it is in itself and the activity of a manipulation which necessarily comes from outside, from "ab," from "away," live together? At this stage it is difficult to answer "no." Again, Miller is painting *on* painting.

The "a" in Latin *cura* is replaced by the "e" of English "cure," and so we find the medicine that cures ("making it vanish as a medicine cures a man of a disease by taking it away, making him sound again, or as an infatuated man is cured of a dangerous illusion"; LM, 396). Or Middle English "-uve" is replaced by Stevens's English "-ure," so that the "c-," like the "i," not only cures but "hides" ("a caring for the ground by hiding it"; LM, 397). There may be a kind of relation between the "c-" that cures and heals and the "c-" that hides or protects, but this is not necessarily so, because they are also opposed to each other in a radical way: to hide, to conceal, to repress, even to refuse is not a symptom of health. Perhaps the cure comes from the opposite, from bringing into the open, "a securing of it, making it solid, as one cures a new fiberglass hull by drying it carefully" (LM, 396). Or else Greek "-ios" is replaced by English "-re," Greek "ku-" replaced by English "cu-," the last having the same sound but not the same spelling. When we name the "Cur-iology," it is precisely a question of "writing." But of what type of writing? As in Plato's *Phaedrus*, suddenly the writing being discussed is not phonetic but hieroglyphic, and that is, necessarily, something very significant. What does "curiologic" mean? Miller cites the O.E.D.: " 'of or pertaining to that form of hieroglyphic writing in which objects are represented by pictures, and not by symbolic characters' " (LM, 397).

What Miller finds while he is painting is a form of painted writing, the hieroglyph (from *hieros*, "holy," and *gluphein*, "to engrave"): "Letters in the alphabetic sense are made of lines carved, stamped, or inscribed which turn back on themselves in one way or another to make a knot, a glyph"; "A hieroglyph is a fixed sign or character that cannot be deciphered only because the code has been lost" (AT, 8, 78). Perhaps this is why Tess d'Urberville misreads or reads naively Alec's figure and face: "an aged and dignified face, the sublimation of all d'Urberville lineaments, furrowed with incarnate memories representing in *hieroglyphics*, the centuries of her family's and England's history" (FR, 122, my italics). Of course, this is by no means the last time Miller finds himself with painted writing, a picture or drawing—suffice it to remember the work on "x" or "f" he accomplishes in *Ariadne's Thread* (24ff). In *The Lin-*

about whether his young heroines know the facts of sex. He does not say they do, and he does not say they don't. Henry James, in *The Awkward Age*, was not so discreet, perhaps because the society he describes was by then in rapid transition in this area. By the time of *The Awkward Age*, the assumption that a woman would go in innocence and ignorance to her marriage bed was becoming unworkable.

A man, by contrast, fulfills only part of his life by marrying well. He has, in addition, either some kind of professional position to uphold or an inherited position to maintain. He also hunts, spends time at his club, sometimes serves in Parliament, and in many other ways belongs to a male world of power and privilege. Women are for the most part excluded from this public world or can play only an indirect role there. While she is unmarried, Ayala hunts foxes as part of a primarily male group of hunters. Her riding to hounds, however, has its greatest importance for her as part of her courtship by Jonathan Stubbs. Marriage and filling those cradles with a new baby every year are as necessary for the moral good of men as

guistic Moment, where Miller's formalist fury is supposedly reaching its climax, this appearance of the pictorial is all the more conspicuous in showing that he is not reading Stevens's poem in a linear, eurythmical, or methodical way.

Let us see what he does do. He does not structurally divide into sections parts composing a stratified poematic line, in the style of Roman Ingarden. He does not point to semiotic levels of the text, in the style of Jurij Lotman, or to codes that foresee the decodification of the model or implicit reader, according to some proposals of Eco and Ingarden. He does not even arbitrarily divide the discursive segment into "lexias" (that is, into short units of meaning, as Barthes does in *S/Z*, though this concerned narration), or project stylematic considerations into the poem (as do Dámaso Alonso or Stanley Fish). There is no theory of poeticity in his writings, as there is in Jean Cohen. All this is so despite the fact that many concepts and metaconcepts originating in such methodologies resound in Miller's work. He does not seem to follow a specific order. He starts with the second part and afterwards goes to the first one. Then he comes back again to the second part in order to make his way to the third one, afterward coming back again to the first part. From Greek we go to Latin and from there to Middle English and, later on, to Phoenician. We can call this kind of reading by the very old name of "boustrophedon," borrowing it from what in Ancient Egypt was called "boustrophedonic writing." (And why not borrow it also from the character nicknamed *Bustrofedon* to whom Guillermo Cabrera Infante introduces us in *Three Sad Tigers*?) "Boustrophedonic" names a kind of writing that in its pictograms, phonograms, and determinatives could be read back and forth, from top to bottom and vice versa, "like the ox that goes back and forth when the plowman forces it to plow" and, curiously, like the electronic space of a computer (Jean, 1989: 28–29).

If reading is boustrophedonic, that is because writing also is (or continues to be) boustrophedonic. This is what Miller intends to say when he categorically asserts that "they [the multidirectional meanings of a word or of a whole poem] may not be organized into a logical or dialectical structure but remain stubbornly heterogeneous" (LM, 397). The boustrophedonic way that goes from *cura* to *cuuve* and finishes in *kurios* proposes to us, then, a type of reading that follows a principle of taxonomic disorder. What leads the critic from one place to another? Does Miller follow the same map or guide when he becomes immersed in Hopkins, Arnold,

for women. Speaking of one of the more problematic male characters in *Ayala's Angel*, Frank Houston, the narrator affirms: "It is hard to rescue a man from the slough of luxury and idleness combined. If anything can do it, it is a cradle filled annually" (625).

The central concerns of both men and women in these upper levels of Victorian bourgeois society are the preservation and redistribution of money. This happens by getting the unmarried young women properly married, in what might be called, in a locution not too unfair to the procedure, the redistribution of women. The two forms of exchange are of course closely related, since the redistribution of money takes place primarily, though not exclusively, through marriage. As in the world of Henry James's novels about England or Italy a little later, in *Portrait of a Lady*, for example, or *The Wings of the Dove*, or *The Golden Bowl*, what is strictly prohibited is for two members of this society to marry without money. It is no more proper for the impoverished artist Isadore Hamel to marry Ayala's equally poor sister Lucy than it is possible for Charlotte Stant to

and Stevens? Absolutely not. The absence of a methodological proposal, the lack of guide or *meta-hodos*, the boustrophedonism, the taxonomic disorder relate, first of all, to the "original" Millerian matrix, that is to say, to the rhapsodic attempt to be placed in a hearing position, in a position of abandonment into the hands of "language" (in the wide sense of this word), with the logically paradoxical aim of transmitting it like the Platonic *Io*. Contemplating the word "cure," for instance, we have found ourselves facing Greek *kuriology*: "use of literal expressions, speaking literally; from Kurios, as an adjective: regular, proper; as a noun: lord, master. A curiological cure of the ground would find proper names for that ground, make a mimetic icon of it, copy it exactly, appropriate it, master it" (LM, 397).

Does, then, the word "cure" have to do with the materiality of things (to cure, to hide) or with the relation between the word or icon and thing (the possibility that "the poem annihilates the rock, takes the place of it, and replaces it with its own self-sufficient fiction"; LM, 397)? In a "boustrophedonic" reading, not only is it possible to respond to this question (or any other), but one must insist on it. One must keep on projecting the calligraphy of the "i," slipping it, twisting it, lifting it, tracing its outline in the mass of air via a fleshly, slippery, sleight of hand (to paraphrase *Empire of Signs*, by Barthes, who refers there, like De Quincey, Derrida, and Miller, to a "palimpsest"). How do we move noiselessly from the curiology that paints and uses literal expressions to the "(i)con"? Is it possible to pass smoothly from pictorial writing to the expressive? Recent works on the iconic sign (e.g., Klinkenberg 1987) argue that it is not a sign subject to the binary relation of signifier-signified, but a sign subject to the triple relation between an *iconic signifier*, a *type*, and a *referent*. This triple relation invalidates, according to Klinkenberg, the traditional discussions around the question of motivation (Peirce, Charles W. Morris, Eco) and substitutes itself for a relation of "impossible visual translation." Yet this suggestion brackets out, whether voluntarily or involuntarily, the signification of that "translation."

Miller uses, not the concept of "iconicity," but the word "icon": the "i" alludes to "the contradictory meanings of the word *icon*" (LM, 404). Despite his admiration for William Wimsatt, Miller's use of "icon" has no more to do with Wimsatt's (1954) than with semiotic theories of iconicity. Rather, Miller insists upon one more movement, this time (bottom to top) from the Greek to the poem itself, from *kurios* to "The Poem as

marry Prince Amerigo in *The Golden Bowl*, or Madame Merle to marry Gilbert Osmond in *Portrait of a Lady*. Such assumptions are so different from our own today that it takes a considerable act of imagination to enter into Trollope's stories or James's.

James's social presuppositions in his novels are so like Trollope's presuppositions that it is not all that easy to figure out why things generally come out well for Trollope's characters, while things never come out well for James's characters. Trollope's characters almost always marry with sufficient money and live happily ever after. James's characters almost always lose the ones they love or live in misery with adulterous spouses. The adept reader of James knows beforehand that things are likely to turn out badly for the central figures in whatever novel he or she picks up, while the adept reader of Trollope can be almost certain of a happy ending. The description Frank Houston sardonically gives of the rose-colored world of the Victorian novel seems to fit Trollope's own work. "But then," writes Frank in a letter to Imogene, "in novels the most indifferent hero comes

Icon." Here is how "icon" occurs in this second part: "The fiction of the leaves is the icon // Of the poem"; "The icon is the man"; "His words are both the icon and the man"; "These leaves are the poem, the icon and the man." The "icon" serves as subject, as simple predicate, as double predicate, and as triple predicate. It is molded in a chiastic syntactic structure: The fiction of the leaves (a) is the icon (b) // The icon (a) is the man (b). Why is there this rushing about of "icon" in the syntax and in the space of the poem? The reason lies, once again, in the word itself as gene. The vibrations and fluctuations of the word are transmitted to the poem. The stir of the sign and graph reproduces within discourse. We enter the text "by way of the contradictory meanings of the word *icon*" (LM, 404). What does the poem propose from the iconic in relation to the "cure of ourselves"? What will the syntagm "its copy of the sun" mean when attached to "these cover the rock"?

We have arrived at one of the culminating points of the *mise en abyme*, of the "i," in short, of Miller's boustrophedonic reading. In order for "boustrophedonism" to exist, there must be a catachresis in writing and reading, a "necessity" for metaphor (Quintilian: "*catachresis* of which *abuse* is a correct translation . . . mean[s] the practice of adapting the nearest possible term to describe something for which no actual term exists" [Quintilian, 1966: 321, Bk. 6, chap. 6, 34]). Otherwise, the opposite tropes, that is to say those in which semantic exchange begins with a word's proper signification (metaphor, metonymy, synecdoche, etc.), would force us to always read in a single direction. The endless march means that "the poem as icon is both curiological, a mimetic copy of the whole, and at the same time a figure, similitude, or metaphor of the whole. The poem is an icon in both senses, in a coming and going between literal and figurative. This enigmatic interchange between proper and improper uses of language, in a bewildering multiplication of different chains of figurative terminology superimposed, juxtaposed, interwoven, is a final form of *mise en abyme* in 'The Rock'" (LM, 405). It happens, however—as we will see in the example Miller gives—that the participation or connection is not exclusively between the gene of the heteroseme or heterograph and the global poem-discourse, but also between these two and the position, interior-exterior, parasite-host, doubt-uncertainty, of the critic.

Boustrophedonism is made of the magnetizing mentioned earlier, that Heraclea stone Socrates refers to when he speaks with Io. The move-

out right at last. Some god comes out of a theatrical cloud and leaves the poor devil ten thousand a-year and a title. He isn't much of a hero when he does go right under such inducements, but he suffices for the plot, and everything is rose-coloured" (363).

Why this difference between Trollope and James? It might be possible to argue that the system still works in the mid-Victorian England of Trollope's novels, but is breaking down by the time it is chronicled in James's novels. The matter, however, is more complicated than that. Ultimately it has to do with basic presuppositions about human life that cannot fully be explained by historical context. The proof of that would be the large difference between Trollope's work and that of a contemporary like George Eliot. George Eliot's Tertius Lydgate, in *Middlemarch*, or her Gwendolyn Harleth, in *Daniel Deronda*, come out no less unhappy than James's Isabel Archer in *Portrait of a Lady* or Densher and Kate in *The Wings of the Dove*, whereas almost all Trollope's good people marry and live happily ever after. The same historical moment can give rise to radically different novels.

ment back and forth holds together a chain of heterogeneous elements
by a force passed from one to another. The poem, like the heteroseme
or heterograph, does not tell a story. It is the nonsynthesized mixture of
a series of stories. Is the poem either a poem or a virtual, minimal, sug-
gestive narration? What is this text in itself? Every time we say "poem,"
we are betting (as Miller points out). There are at least four different
scenes or stories in "The Rock," with corresponding terminology: (1) a
scene of love ("a scene of love, even a love story"; LM, 405); (2) a geometric diagram ("This diagram is described and analyzed with appropriate
mathematical and logical terminology"; LM, 405); (3) a natural scene with
a rock, a ground or soil, and a change of seasons ("Man shares in this
natural cycle as he eats of the fruit, or as he becomes himself a natural
body rooted in the ground"; LM, 405); and (4) a self-analysis, a "theory
of poetry, with an appropriate terminology" (LM, 405). This last scene or
story will give me the opportunity to discuss another paradox advanced at
the beginning of this section, the meaning of "self-reflexion," of "reflect,"
in short, of "linguistic moment."

   In the coming and going from one story to another, in the transfer
from one scene to another, the boustrophedon could wonder whether
he is confronting compatible or incompatible isotopic valences. Is there
another story, that of the man who remembers what happened seventy
years ago? Miller will solve this question later, referring to Whitman.
However, such a question would seem mischievously to insinuate that
there are more than four or five stories in the poem, that those four or
five stories named are just a minimum number of narratives. Do we not
see there a story of metamorphosis in the Ovidian style, a conversion
into leaves and fruits, into laurels? Story within story, scene within scene.
Is it the story of the imaginary, the affective, an identification between
two people, "an embrace between one desperate clod / And another in a
fantastic consciousness," something similar to or compatible with that
geometrical diagram of a "point A / In a perspective that begins again // At
B" ("The Rock," III: 11–13)? (Would Lacan say yes? Probably.) And what
about metapoetry—does the poem allude in one way or another to the
rock that "is the gray particular of man's life" or to something "as in vivid
sleep"? And what about the rock periodically covered by leaves, lilacs, and
fruits that the man eats—is it related at some point (point A or point B
that starts again) to the poem that describes itself as *"icon, copy, figuration,
imagery"* (LM, 405)? The questions, as the reader is aware, would be end-

Trollope's novels can end happily because the incompatible require-ments of enough money and genuine love can so often fortuitously both be obtained. If a young woman has money, in Trollope's novels, then she can expect to marry well, but may conceivably marry an impecunious suitor. The two daughters of Sir Thomas Tringle in *Ayala's Angel* are examples of that. If the young man has money, he may with impunity marry a woman who has no money, as Tom Tringle's desire to marry Ayala is approved by his family, though she has been left by her father completely portionless. Money in Trollope's novels is sometimes inherited money, such as that possessed by a rich nobleman with large estates. The Duke of Omnium in the Palliser novels, or Captain Batsby, with his safe income, in *Ayala's Angel*, are examples. Sometimes the money has been made, like Sir Thomas Tringle's millions gained in financial speculation. He has made money out of money, as Isadore Hamel bitterly observes. Only rarely are people in Trollope's novels shown doing any productive work, or even speculating successfully in the financial markets. If they were once in the army, like

244 A Human Head with an Equine Neck

less, and the responses would always fluctuate between yes and no, as the reader tries to discover what the relation, participation, or analogy among those four scenes consists in, tries to establish a hierarchy, a basis of reference. To put it another way, we would find ourselves in the pendular embrace of the osmotic *catachresis* or *inopia*.

To use Miller's own words: "The question, it would seem, is which of these scenes is the literal subject of the poem, the real base of which the others are illustrative figures. This question is unanswerable. Each scene is both literal and metaphorical, both the ground of the poem and a figure on that ground, both that which the poem is centrally about and a resource of terminology used figuratively to describe something other than itself, in a fathomless reversal. The structure of each scene separately and of all four in their relation is a dramatization, or articulation, or iconic projection of the uncanny relation, neither polar opposition, nor hierarchy, nor genetic filiation, between figurative and literal uses of language" (LM, 406). In fact, we encounter the problem in every literary text and even in every oral or written linguistic text. (Stanley Fish reflected on the same topic many years ago in "With the Compliments of the Author: Reflections on Austin and Derrida" [1982].) How can we know whether when someone wrote

> Lo giorno se n'andava, e l'aere bruno
> toglieva li animai che sono in terra
> da le fatiche loro; e io sol uno
> m'apparecchiava a sostener la guerra
> sì del cammino e sì de la pietate,
> che ritrarrà la mente che non erra.
> O Muse, o alto ingegno, or m'aiutate

Day was departing, and the dark air was taking the creatures on earth from their labors; and I alone was making ready to sustain the strife, both of the journey and of the pity, which unerring memory shall retrace. O Muses, O high genius, help me now! (Dante, 1970: 12, 13; *Inferno*, 2: 1–7)

he was doing it literally or allegorically, ironically or nonironically? Even if the text were explicitly to indicate "This is literal" we would not know, except in certain cases via contextual convention—and then it would be a problem of faith, not of verification—whether we should read it in a literal or in an ironical way.

According to Miller's (and de Man's and Derrida's) understanding

Captain Batsby, they did not fight. If they are in Parliament, like the Honorable Septimus Traffick, they do not govern, though something scornful is said in passing about Traffick's speech in Commons on the malt tax. (Trollope's Palliser novels do, of course, show politicians trying to govern the country.) Though Ayala's uncle, Reginald Dosett, is a clerk in the Admiralty, his clerking is hardly productive: "He spent six hours on six days of the week arranging indexes of a voluminous library of manuscript letter-books" (204). The chief reason to specify his occupation at all is to tell the reader exactly how poor, though respectable, he is. Though Sir Thomas Tringle much enjoys going to the city and looking after his millions, the process whereby he got the millions is not shown. It is not even so exactly shown as it is for Adam Verver in James's *The Golden Bowl* (and *that* is vague enough). Tringle is in this like Dickens's Cheeryble Brothers in *Nicholas Nickleby* or his John Jarndyce in *Bleak House*. Tringle's money has been made in financial speculation. His possession of his millions is, however, a given from page one of *Ayala's Angel*, just as much as are the thousands of pounds per annum a nobleman makes from his estates.

of deconstruction, as I demonstrated in the previous chapter with regard to the question of mimesis in De Quincey and in the Victorian novel, it is impossible to elude the literal reading of a text: "In one sense the description of all four of the scenes is entirely literal. They are icons in the sense of being mimetic pictures of things. . . . There really are rocks, leaves, flowers, fruit, and seasons of the year. . . . There really are geometrical diagrams. . . . [These are] a form of reference or mimesis, as realistic as a description of the weather" (LM, 406). De Man confirms this: Rousseau's "radical critique of referential meaning never implied that the referential function of language could in any way be avoided, bracketed, or reduced to being just one contingent linguistic property among others, as is postulated, for example, in contemporary semiology" (de Man, 1979: 207). Miller's "linguistic moment" is a suspension of referentiality, not its elimination, hence the great differences between Miller's proposal and those of the Russian or American formalists, such as John Crowe Ransom, Allen Tate, Cleanth Brooks, or William Wimsatt. The way in which John M. Ellis, in *Against Deconstruction*, understands the use deconstruction makes of the concept of "irony" is absolutely erroneous. He writes: "But imagine what happens if we commit ourselves to the ironic reading in all cases, indiscriminately. The first result is that irony loses its meaning. If everything is ironic, there is nothing left to give irony its distinctive quality— there is no irony" (Ellis, 1989: 91). This would be true only if Miller and de Man were using irony according to the classic postulate that defines this trope as the semantic movement of substitution of opposite meanings. But it is evident that what is in question is an irony that keeps the difference in itself, given that it implies keeping the two opposite meanings. How is it possible to deny the existence of irony, or of the irony of irony, when one is affirming that literal reading is unavoidable?

Nevertheless, one also cannot avoid "figurative" reading: "No reader of 'The Rock' can remain long under the illusion that it is a poem about the weather or indeed a poem about geometry or about love or about poetry" (LM, 406). The boustrophedon forces us to stop at every scene just as it is and immediately afterwards to continue from word to word, from syntagm to syntagm, from stanza to stanza, in order to read each one of them as a possible "figure" of the others. Wallace Stevens speaks of

> point A
> In a perspective that begins again
>
> At B: the origin of the mango's rind.

Trollope's novels characteristically begin, as does *Ayala's Angel*, with precise identification of the place each important character has in the social hierarchy. This includes specification of the income each has, exactly where the money comes from, just where each lives, what ages they all are, whether they are married or unmarried, whom they married, whether they are of noble birth or not, what rich or impecunious relatives they have, what expectations of inheritance they have, how many children they have, and what portions or inheritance they can give each. Whenever a new character is introduced in the course of the novel, the same kind of recapitulating history is given for that person. In Trollope's world, what a person is, all the way down to the bottom, so to speak, is to a large degree defined by this complex network of financial and social constraints.

The opening four pages of *Ayala's Angel* are a good example of this establishment of a determining social context for the main characters. Of Sir Thomas Tringle, for example, and his wife Emmeline, the narrator tells the reader the following:

> It is the rock where tranquil must adduce
> Its tranquil self, the main of things, the mind,
>
> The starting point of the human and the end.
> *(Stevens, 1954: 528)*

The word "point" appears in the first and last lines quoted. The sentence referring to the geometrical diagram is followed by a colon and, afterwards, a reference to the origin of the mango's rind. Immediately after that, an anaphoric "it" (necessarily anaphoric) reiterates one of the former elements, the diagram, the diagram as origin of the mango's rind or the mango's rind as origin, or the diagram that is the origin of the mango's rind. The anaphora introduces the rock, the calmness, the mind as the most important thing, the starting point of the human, and the end. (Like de Man, we could radicalize Empson, expanding his theory of ambiguity to the point where we can no longer resolve contradictions or realize where we are; de Man, 1983: 235–38. There, Empson merges with Derrida and Miller.) Should we understand that the geometrical diagram illustrates what happens with cyclical nature and with the mind? ("Point A" and "the starting point," is, as S. R. Levin would say, an odd coupling.) If this is so, then the geometrical diagram is not literally a geometrical diagram. It is the catachrestico-boustrophedonic figure that, like a recalcitrant Lacan, algebrizes nature and mind, but only for that purpose, for "making us see" through an analogy.

Or should we understand the mind and the mango's rind as possessing a common, subjacent system reducible to a geometrical or topological grammar, so that "the starting point of the human and the end," as well as "the mango's rind," are, as Michel Serres would say, like a locomotive and a nightingale reducible to or translatable in a formula? If this is so, then the geometrical diagram is a geometrical diagram, but neither the mango's rind nor the human mind are either rind or mind, but just the catachrestico-boustrophedonic figures that illustrate and make figurative by analogy such a mobile geometrical diagram. As for the rest, what is the function of the colon in a poem that has begun by talking about forgetfulness and finishes by talking about "midnight-minting fragrances"? Perhaps to tell us that what comes next explains what has just been said? But what has just been said ("point A / In a perspective that begins again // At B") is included within a sentence that includes what has just been said as complement: "The rock is the habitation of the whole, / Its strength and measure, that which is near, point A / In a perspective that begins

The elder [daughter of Reginald Dosett] had married a city man of wealth, — of wealth when he married her, but who had become enormously wealthy by the time of our story. He had when he married been simply Mister, but was now Sir Thomas Tringle, Baronet, and was senior partner in the great firm of Travers and Treason.[11] Of Traverses and Treasons there were none left in these days, and Mr. Tringle was supposed to manipulate all the millions with which the great firm in Lombard Street was concerned. He had married old Mr. Dosett's eldest daughter, Emmeline, who was now Lady Tringle, with a house at the top of Queen's Gate, rented at £1,500 a year, with a palatial moor in Scotland, with a seat in Sussex, and as many carriages and horses as would suit an archduchess. (1–2)

One of the most economically presented of these contextual constraints is a topographical one. Trollope can assume that his readers know the social mapping of London and the surrounding counties. Telling the reader just where a character lives is a powerful shorthand for identifying just who they must be. That Sir Thomas Tringle rents a house at the top of Queen's Gate at £1,500 a year,[12] not to speak of his moor in Scotland

again // At B:" (Stevens, 1954: 528). Can the boustrophedon revert to reading backwards, toward before the colon? Who explains whom from this last point of view? Each story or scene can be the "ground" of the others, but at the same time it is the "ab-ground": "Each scene is both ground and design on that ground, both literal and figurative. . . . As the reader tries to rest on each element in the poem or on a chain of elements forming a single scene, as he seeks a solid literal ground that might be the curiological basis of the other figurative meanings, that element or chain gives way. It becomes itself a verbal fiction, an illusion, an icon in the sense of similitude not in the sense of mimetic copy. The element becomes an *Abgrund*, not a *Grund*. The reader is forced then to shift sideways again, seeking to find somewhere else in the poem the solid ground of that figure, seeking, and failing, or falling, and seeking again" (LM, 407).

All this entails a complicated matter about which one can only draft the main points: to delimit different types of deconstructions in the heart of so-called deconstruction itself. When Derrida tells us in *Speech and Phenomena* that Husserl offers us the means of thinking against himself or, in *Of Grammatology*, that one must oppose Saussure to himself, it is necessary to presuppose a contradiction among the distinct strata (the declarative and demonstrative, title and main text, for instance) or, what is the same, affirm a position that later on in the course of writing contradicts itself. To give an example, it is necessary to accept that Saussure was speaking literally when he concludes: "A language and its written form constitute two separate systems of signs. The sole reason for the existence of the latter is to represent the former. The object of study in linguistics is not a combination of the written word and the spoken word. The spoken word alone constitutes that object" (Saussure, 1983: 24–25). Otherwise, there would be no possibility of deconstructing the opposition speech/writing in Saussure. We should not find this strange, since we are dealing with a theoretical text, the founding text of scientific linguistics. In order to notice later on the appearance of contradictions and aporias, we must similarly assume that Rousseau writes without irony in *The Social Contract*: "The social order is a sacred right which serves as a foundation for all other rights. Nevertheless, this right does not come from nature. It is therefore founded upon convention" (Rousseau, 1947: 141). The presence in such texts of affirmations that are contradicted later on explains why de Man asserts that "a deconstruction always has as its

and his seat in Sussex, while Reginald Dosett lives in Notting Hill and has a clerk's salary of £900 a year, tells the whole story of their social placement to any reader, even today, who knows London. The reader hardly needs to be told explicitly that "the difference between Queen's Gate and Kingsbury Crescent, — between Queen's Gate and Kingsbury Crescent for life, — was indeed great!" (8). When Ayala and her sister Lucy are shifted back and forth from one aunt or uncle to the other, like shuttlecocks, as Aunt Dosett says, they move from one social world to an entirely different one. They move from comparative poverty and pennypinching necessity to limitless luxury and wealth, or vice versa. The names of the two localities in London are enough to tell the reader exactly what the two milieux must be like. It is assumed that the reader has a mental map of London that will allow him or her to decode the meaning of an address. The novel is punctuated with detailed itineraries that depend for their understanding on knowing the social meaning of the parks and streets that are being named. An example is the exact specificity with which Lucy Dormer's

target revealing the existence of hidden articulations and fragmentations within assumedly monadic totalities" (de Man, 1979: 249). We might think we have in hand in *The Social Contract* a "political" text and that, since this is so, there is no alternative but to read certain assertions without a shadow of irony or allegory. Things, however, are not so simple. De Man warns us: "It may be just as difficult to decide upon the rhetorical status of theoretical texts such as the *Profession de foi* and the *Social Contract* as on a fiction such as the *Nouvelle Héloïse*. The difference between a fictional and a theoretical text carries very little weight in the case of Rousseau" (de Man, 1979: 247). Only in the case of Rousseau?

Let us for the moment leave this question unanswered and return to Wallace Stevens's text and to J. Hillis Miller's analysis. We have already been able to ascertain that when Stevens asserts, "The rock is the habitation of the whole, / Its strength and measure, that which is near, point A / In a perspective that begins again // At B," these words can be interpreted both as referential and as catachrestic or figurative. The assertions by Saussure, Husserl, Rousseau, and Wallace Stevens are not, therefore, considered from the same viewpoint in all the processes of deconstruction to which they have been subjected or self-subjected. Paul Valéry, as cited by Derrida, proposes that we should consider philosophy "as a 'particular literary genre,' drawing upon the reserves of a language, cultivating, forcing, or making deviate a set of tropic resources" (Derrida, 1982: 293). Derrida goes on to remark: "Perhaps I will be able to state further on how the critical necessity of this aesthetics, of this formalism or conventionalism, if adhered to otherwise than with controlled insistence and a calculated strategic reaction, would risk just as surely leading us back to the places in question" (Derrida, 1982: 294). Certainly, what is urged here—that is, back to basic philosophical questions like "What is reality?" or "What is liberty?"—neither confounds genres and discourses (saying that everything is literature) nor establishes impenetrable borders or impassable walls. We should remember that de Man also does not want to confound genres (though he speaks of rhetorical reading as a condition of possibility of the generic difference). Nor does Derrida want to keep anything absolutely separated. The problem is rather to wonder what a deconstructive reading of a text is. Is it different to read deconstructively texts that are literary, philosophical, political, religious, and so forth?

In *The Ethics of Reading*, Miller reads Kant more in the style of Derrida's *Of Grammatology* than in the style of his own *The Linguistic*

afternoon walks from her uncle's small house in Kingsbury Crescent, Notting Hill, to Kensington Gardens are described: "At some hour in the afternoon Lucy would walk from the house by herself, and within a quarter of an hour would find herself on the broad gravel path which leads down to the Round Pond. From thence she would go by the back of the Albert Memorial, and then across by the Serpentine and return to the same gate, never leaving Kensington Gardens" (31). It is on these walks that Lucy encounters Isadore Hamel, the man she ultimately marries. It is here also, in Kensington Gardens, that Kate Croy so repeatedly and so futilely meets Densher, in Henry James's *The Wings of the Dove*. The mentally inscribed topography of London is a resource on which generations of English novelists could depend. This is another example of the crucial difference between the meaning English literature has for an English man or woman and the meaning it has for an American. Place names and street names in London are less likely to have meaning for an American reader, though important aspects of *Ayala's Angel*'s purport depend on knowing

Moment. Derrida reads Mallarmé (in *Dissemination*) more in the style of Miller's *The Linguistic Moment* than in his own style in *Of Grammatology*. Perhaps it is because, as Derrida demonstrates with regard to Rousseau, "the philosophical text, although it is in fact always written, includes, precisely as its philosophical specificity, the project of effacing itself in the face of the signified content which it transports and in general teaches. Reading should be aware of this project, even if, in the last analysis, it intends to expose the project's failure. The entire history of texts, and within it the history of literary forms in the West, should be studied from this point of view" (Derrida, 1976: 160). Philosophical specificity that fails? A project that turns around on itself? In certain passages that we identify, correctly or incorrectly, with the name of deconstruction (the most philosophical or meta-philosophical ones, to which I do not assign any proper name), it seems as if the critic wanted to attribute to a certain type of texts a *position* with the aim of "deconstructing them." Texts that perhaps are not just positional, but positional and dispositional at once. Because, I ask again, what does this or that text consist in? Is reading a literary text different from reading a philosophical one?

In a brief essay that remained unfinished and unpublished at his death, "Comentario al 'Banquete' de Platón" (I. Qué es leer," 1946; "Commentary on Plato's *Symposium*," 1. "What Is Reading," 1962b: 145–71), Ortega y Gasset suggests that, although all words are not always misleading, they all can be. The same thing can happen to a sentence, since, when it is separated from the rest of the book, it does not have *one* meaning. Where then does sense lie, in the book as a whole? Surprisingly, Ortega does not yield at this point and claims that the book taken as a whole is misleading. But what book is Ortega talking about? About a literary book like *Don Quixote*? Or about a philosophical book? The fact that Ortega speaks of a "book" is already significant. We know, however, that he is referring to a book traditionally considered philosophical, the *Symposium* of Plato. Ortega comes to the conclusion that we do not know whether this book is written seriously or as a joke. In other words, we do not understand Plato (Ortega y Gasset, 1962b: 171).

This not knowing whether Plato intended his discourses seriously or as pure innocent pastime is connected with Schlegel's irony and with that of Kierkegaard. Kierkegaard tells us, concerning the words Abraham spoke to Isaac when the latter is to be sacrificed, "First and foremost he doesn't say anything, and that is his way of saying what he has to say. His

the social meaning of such topographical nomenclature. The relative thinness of American literature might be defined in part by saying we do not have any universally shared city. Neither New York nor Chicago, neither San Francisco nor Los Angeles, can play the role for us that London does for the English or Paris for the French.

If the major means of the redistribution of money is marriage, this explains the fascinated attention with which everyone in the community of characters in a Trollope novel watches an unmarried young woman to see whom she will eventually marry. Such a person is a wild card in the social game. She has infinite potential value, but no actual value, since she does not yet have a definite social role. Only marriage will give her that. Once she is married she is permanently set in a certain place in the social hierarchy and is no longer of much interest. There is no story to tell about her, unless she is tempted by adultery, as is, for example, Lady Glencora in *Can You Forgive Her?*

This fascination with the question of what marriage the young

answer to Isaac has the form of irony, for it is always irony to say something and yet not say it" (Kierkegaard, 1985: 142). (Concerning this line of thought—one that includes Melville's "Bartleby"—it would be interesting to invoke Derrida's analysis, as minute and subtle as always, in *The Gift of Death* [Derrida, 1995a]). Not knowing whether one speaks seriously (literally) or jokingly (figuratively) is the problem Miller poses at the beginning. Is this only with regard to literature? We shall see later on.

What can one infer from all this? That in that strange discourse provisionally called "literature" (as a result of its historical condition or context) *there is not any position* or, what comes to the same thing, though expressed more cautiously, *there cannot be any position*. I think this is a proper way, although not the only one, of interpreting Derrida's comment that "literature seemed to me, in a confused way, to be the institution which allows one *to say everything*, in every way. The space of literature is not only that of an instituted fiction but also a fictive institution which in principle *allows one to say everything*. To say everything is no doubt to gather, by translating, all figures into one another, to totalize by formalizing, but to say everything is also to break out of [*franchir*] prohibitions" (1992c: 36). One can *say everything* both in the fabulous and fictive universe—and here Derrida's words are explicitly limited to the modern epoch of literature, and are not meant to apply to medieval, Renaissance, or Counter-Reformation works. Saying everything applies also to the process whereby words, sentences, or literary discourses are written in an enigmatic or catachrestic way. The latter would presuppose a kind of historical generality in the definition of literature as saying everything and breaking prohibitions.

"Each of the scenes in 'The Rock' is, as a 'particular being,' the equivalent of all the others. Each holds an equivalent status as simultaneously both figure and ground," Miller asserts (LM, 408). This amounts to saying that this poem by Wallace Stevens (and not only this poem, although this nuance also belongs to the field of the bet) says everything equivocally, that is to say, in a literal and/or figurative way. The question, unavoidably, is: How does one deconstruct a text that has no position (*thesis*)? How does one move what a priori is already moved? Does Miller refer to this problem when he explains to us that "the deconstructive critic seeks to find, by this process of retracing, the element in the system studied which is alogical, the thread in the text in question which will unravel it all, or the loose stone which will pull down the whole building,"

woman will make and the development of a genre, the novel, to tell the story of courtship and marriage over and over again in different forms makes Trollope's England not entirely unlike a present-day traditional society like Nepal. As Sarah E. Miller has shown in a brilliant dissertation, everyone in Nepal (in upper-caste literate Brahmin extended families in Kathmandu at least) is deeply concerned with marriage negotiations and talks about them often.[13] Life for these Nepalese is to a considerable extent lived in terms of various repetitive narratives of such negotiations and their happy or unhappy outcomes. Victorian novels served a social purpose in Victorian middle-class society analogous to the social purpose served by these oral narratives in Kathmandu. I agree with D. A. Miller that this purpose was the enforcing of ideological assumptions about social behavior and role. By "ideological" I mean masking an arbitrary arrangement of power and roles, an arrangement that could be otherwise, as a natural, universal way of living. I differ from D. A. Miller, however, and agree with Althusser in not being so scandalized by this. It is hard to imagine a viable

or that deconstruction "annihilates the ground on which the building stands by showing that the text has already annihilated that ground, knowingly and unknowingly" (TNT, 126)? Does de Man refer to the same presupposition when, in his reading of Derrida's reading of Rousseau, he convincingly asserts, "There is no need to deconstruct Rousseau" (de Man, 1983: 139)?

These words are not easy to understand, for they by no means center on the critic's passivity. After all, any text can be presented as a positioning or can tend toward it. I think Derrida is referring to this when he speaks of the "specificity" of discourses. Faced with this specificity, the critic *distorts* (he is active, then) a textual screen behind which he discovers a pre-existing violence (therefore, he is passive *too*). However, the metaphor of the "loose stone" indicates less the structure evident in the text than a way of beginning the deconstructive reading. If we can assume anything from Miller's analysis of Stevens's text, it is precisely that within a text, sentence, word, or pictogram it is not possible to oppose the logical element to the illogical, the figure to the nonfigure, writing to reading, the local to the visitor, on the assumption that any one of those elements can be the tropologico-allegorical ground for the rest.

The position of the "deconstructive literary critic" must not be defined starting from the opposition passivity/activity, since he or she is neither totally passive nor totally active, though he or she shares both states. The critic's work consists in entering the textual door (participating, touching, identifying himself or herself, becoming immersed in) and in being conscious that, upon entering, he or she is already coming out (going away, knowing that he or she really never succeeded in touching, but went on seeing from the strangeness and alterity of the surface): "The reader must then seek the literal base elsewhere, in a constant lateral transfer with nowhere a resting place in the unequivocally literal, mimetic — the 'exact rock,' cured at last" (LM, 408). Gradually, in accordance with the folds that are appearing, the concept of the "linguistic moment" becomes more complex. Why? What does Miller name when, on defining this concept, he writes: "This is a book . . . about moments of suspension within the texts of poems, not usually at their beginnings or ends, moments when they reflect or comment on their own medium. I call this suspension the linguistic moment. It is a form of parabasis, a breaking of the illusion that language is a transparent medium of meaning" (LM, xiv)? Let us not be hasty in the interpretation of this passage.

culture without its ideology, nor one that does not use narratives of some kind to encourage people into taking that ideology for granted as god-given or natural. It is never a question of moving beyond ideology, only of moving to a perhaps better one, one more just and democratic. What is interesting in a writer like Trollope is the revelation, perhaps inadvertently, of cracks, fissures, and contradictions in the ideological construct he apparently endorses. These tensions led in later stages of British cultural history to this ideology's self-destruction. This self-destruction, it might be argued, is shown happening overtly in Henry James's novels—for example, in *The Awkward Age*. It is also foreshadowed in the most interesting aspects of Trollope's novels.

The crucial difference between present-day Nepal and Victorian England is that marriages in Nepalese Brahmin society are in principle entirely arranged. The woman has no power to choose her marriage partner. Love has nothing to do with it. She may refuse the one that is chosen for her, but that puts her in danger of becoming an old maid, the worst pos-

Its apparent simplicity is misleading, even more so when Miller's reader has moved from this definition to the examples, to Wallace Stevens and to the boustrophedon.

In "The Rhetoric of Blindness: Jacques Derrida's Reading of Rousseau," an essay originally published in 1971, Paul de Man sounds rather like Miller: "The text . . . accounts for its own mode of writing, it states at the same time the necessity of making this statement itself in an indirect, figural way that knows it will be misunderstood by being taken literally. Accounting for the 'rhetoricity' of its own mode, the text also postulates the necessity of its own misreading. It knows and asserts that it will be misunderstood" (de Man, 1983: 136). Gasché, in "Deconstruction as Criticism," concluded that: "If de Man calls 'literary,' in the full sense of the term, any text that implicitly or explicitly signifies its own rhetorical mode and prefigures its own misunderstanding as the correlative of its rhetorical nature, that is, of its 'rhetoricity,' then literariness, writing, and the text are understood according to the model of a conscious subjectivity, that is, of a self-reflexive presence. Consequently, it comes as a surprise when de Man still claims that it is precisely this self-reflexivity of the literary text that preserves it from metaphysics" (Gasché, 1979: 207). Some years later, in an interview with Stefano Rosso (published posthumously), Paul de Man answered this interpretation of Gasché in a subtly ironic way: " — my starting point, as I think I already told you, is not philosophical but basically philological and for that reason didactical, text-oriented. . . . I assume, as a working hypothesis (as a working hypothesis, because I know better than that), that the text *knows* in an absolute way what it's doing. I know this is not the case, but it is a necessary working hypothesis. . . . In a complicated way, I would hold to that statement that 'the text deconstructs itself, is self-deconstructive' " (de Man, 1986: 118).

Paul de Man is inviting us not to read in a literal way his assertion that the text knows what it is doing. In the interview, unlike the essay of 1971, the verb *knows* is italicized. It is rhetorical. It is, in effect, a case of personification or prosopopoeia. What does the assertion that the text *knows* mean? Actually, as de Man recognizes, the text knows nothing. It would be ingenuous (almost in the etymological sense of *ingenuus*, "noble, generous, naïve") to attribute to the text a function that does not correspond to it. It is a working hypothesis. And what does that mean? As Ortega y Gasset, in a footnote to the essay previously quoted,

sible fate in that society, the lowest rung in the social hierarchy. Though a good bit of marriage arranging certainly goes on among the adults in Trollope's England, nevertheless a young woman has much more freedom to choose a husband. Love has everything to do with it. Parents, relatives, and friends can put an eligible bachelor in a young woman's way. In the end, however, the choice is hers. A good woman will only agree to marry a man she loves. When Ayala refuses Jonathan Stubbs's first proposal, she is reported by the narrator to justify this by the simple fact that she does not love him: "When she was alone she considered it over all in her own mind. There could be no doubt that she was right. Of that she was quite sure. It was certainly a fixed law that a girl should not marry a man unless she loved him. She did not love this man, and therefore she ought not to marry him" (240). Later she justifies her refusal by asking her sister: "How is a girl to love a man if she does not love him?" (259).

Somewhat paradoxically, women had more social mobility in Victorian England, at least as Trollope shows it, than did men. That of course

explains it, we have to imagine Plato's body, his corporeal appearance, on the basis of his writing, as when in physics we use the hypothetical method (Ortega y Gasset, 1962b: 171). Yet the statement that the text is self-deconstructive is preceded by the sentence "In a complicated way, I would hold to." Why *in a complicated way*? Because (recalling a fruitful controversy) the way of understanding and facing metaphysical tradition and its relation to history and literature is distinct in Derrida and in Miller or in de Man. The example of the parasite and host gives an account of how Miller, unlike Derrida (a difference that in any case would have to be encompassed by a great number of protocols), understands the pairs metaphysics-nihilism, metaphysics-literature, and so on. To use a terminology peculiar to Ricœur, we would say that in Miller, as in de Man, the strategy *against* metaphysics takes an extended route, whereas in Derrida such a strategy follows, as in Heidegger, a shortcut. De Man and Miller refuse to see in Dante, Milton, Góngora, Rabelais, or Cervantes a monolithic transfer to metaphysics. "Inside" those textualities there exist—and we have already seen how complex this is—both metaphysics and its subversion. This is the reason why the Prior Saint Jean in Pater's "Apollo in Picardy," for instance (and then why not Ovid, Hardy, or Fernando de Rojas?), has experienced proleptically and anachronistically the end of the lineal book Derrida announces in *Of Grammatology* (AT, xii). Derrida and Gasché seem rather to be inclined to postulate an epoch, however—that of Mallarmé—that would suppose one of the "beginnings" of deconstruction in and from literature. I insist, nevertheless, upon the highly problematic character of this distinction.

If we return to Miller's readings, however, perhaps we shall understand better the bind we are dealing with. Gasché maintains: "The current notion of the text's autonomy and self-reflexivity only continues the claim of American formalism to a totalizing principle, to what is called the integrity of the literary form" (Gasché 1979: 182). But such an idea, attributed to someone like Miller, who is supporting, vis-à-vis the reading of a text, the necessity of a literal or referential interpretation ("the description of all four scenes is entirely literal" [LM, 406]), seems not to tally with Miller's kind of criticism. In relation to what is the text autonomous? In relation to history? To answer yes or no would be excessively simplistic. This issue will be discussed in the following section. In relation to philosophy? It is also not easy to answer whether Miller has performed the interpretation of Stevens's poem from within "the common language

did not make Victorian society less sexist or less oppressive of women. Whether women moved up or down the social ladder, they were still subordinate to men. Nevertheless, the male characters in *Ayala's Angel* are more or less permanently fixed in the roles they have at the beginning of the novel. Sir Thomas Tringle is a rich financier. His brother-in-law Reginald Dosett is a clerk in the Admiralty. And that is that. But the unmarried women in the novel can move far up or far down the social scale depending on whom they marry. Ayala has not a penny to her name. Her beauty and wit nevertheless make it possible for her to marry well. She can then look forward to a life of comparative luxury, as long as she plays obediently the social role assigned to her by marriage.

A fundamental contradiction, however, exists in Trollope's Victorian ideology of courtship and marriage. This is the contradiction between the purely economic calculation that uses marriage as a way of redistributing money within the hegemonic classes and the curious assumptions about love people in Trollope's novels hold. These are quite different from the

of poetry and philosophy" (LM, 391). In relation to a self-sufficient formalism? If this is so, what do the parasite and host have to do with this story? What does boustrophedonic reading have to do with it? In relation to the author? On many occasions, Miller precisely refers to the author by his name and profession in real life. Furthermore, he seems to enjoy himself in those references, as the chapter "The Narrator as General Consciousness," from *The Form of Victorian Fiction*, proves. Miller there attests: "Central in the young Dickens' suffering is his sense of being abandoned, cast away by his parents. He feels cut off from the community of family and friends within which he has earlier lived" (FVF, 57). We shall find this type of treatment again in *Fiction and Repetition*—for instance, in the chapter on *Tess of the d'Urbervilles*.

To affirm the autonomy of the literary text means to recognize in it an identity that Miller denies. How is it possible to speak of textual identity when, from heterosemes, heterographs, and pictographs to the macrotextual level there is a continuous circulation through Middle English, Latin, Greek, Phoenician, Milton, the Bible ("that eating, with its disturbing echoes of Milton and the Bible, is also a transgression with erotic and Satanic overtones" [LM, 404]), Whitman, Emerson, de Man, Derrida, Freud, Abraham and Torok, and so forth? How is it possible to speak of textual identity when the objective "structure" of the text avoids a delimitation of meaning by virtue of scenes, as in Stevens's poem, in which the roles of the literal and the figurative oscillate like a pendulum? Let us remember: "The multiple meanings of the word cure, like the meanings of all the key words and figures in 'The Rock,' are incompatible. They may not be organized into a logical or dialectical structure but remain stubbornly heterogeneous" (LM, 397).

Identity is lost because, as these words say, there is no transcendental poetry that eliminates the differences; they still remain. Here we find no trace of the space that erases, annuls, neutralizes, or cancels all the oppositions and particularities "present" in such a space. Nor do we find any principle of unity in connotations, ambiguities, and paradoxes, as happens in Cleanth Brooks's *The Well Wrought Urn* (Brooks, 1947). Rather, we find quite the opposite. The opposition between the literal and the figurative remains (they exchange their places, but never fuse); the frictions among the irreducible meanings are kept; the anamorphosis of the pictogram of the "i" looks at us from the text; the monad and the rock (the *Monadrock*) endure; the heteroseme and the poem are al-

assumptions most people hold today. We are somewhat more cynical and less credulous, though the ideology of romantic love still has great power today in the United States. We still tend to think of falling in love as a change in a person's essential self.

Ayala's Angel, like so many of Trollope's novels, makes a masterly use of multiple plots to give the reader a set of analogous stories. The stories are all versions of the theme of courtship and marriage. Ayala's story is the main plot. It is matched as a theme with variations by the love stories of five other women: Ayala's sister Lucy, their cousins Gertrude and Augusta (the two daughters of Sir Thomas Tringle), the Marchesa Baldoni's daughter Nina, and Imogene Docimer, Frank Houston's true love. These young women are measured by their capacity or lack of capacity to love one man and stick irrevocably to that commitment. All six of these young women are married by the end of the novel. Of this superabundance of marriages the narrator, or rather Trollope himself, since it is a characteristic wry parabasis breaking the illusion and speaking of the novel as a novel, can say: "If

ready broken a priori, and so on. Is there anything in Miller that allows any integrity of literary form or any totalizing principle? In what sense is Stevens's poem a whole? How do we propose any integrity in "the weavings of word with word, of figure with figure" (LM, 393)? In what sense does that "point A / In a perspective that begins again // At B: the origin of the mango's rind" constitute an organic totality? There is, in addition, a nuance in Miller that we must take into account. When he refers to textual self-dismantling he does not confine himself, like de Man, to using the trope of prosopopoeia *knowingly*, as an earlier citation I made shows de Man doing. Instead, he establishes the opposite possibility: "the text has already annihilated that ground, *knowingly or unknowingly*" (my italics). The text eliminates its own ground (position), knowingly or unknowingly. To put the point another way: what is important here is not whether the text knows it or not. What is important is not the model of self-consciousness, but the fact of that loss of identity, ground, or position. Knowing (*to know* or *knowingly*) always adopts the form of an uncertainty or doubt. Even when he touches the figure of the real author, when he mentions Stevens's knowledge, his competence in relation to the poem he himself created, Miller keeps the uncertainty through a question which, of course, leaves pending the impossibility of a response: "Stevens might even *have known* (why should he not have *known*?) the word curiologic" (LM, 397, my italics).

   For Hillis Miller, the text's "reflecting" or "commenting" on itself has to do, not with knowing, but with unknowing. Is it not strange that anyone should say that in such criticism a "fixed," "petrified" text knows its diachronic and synchronic links? If the "competence" of the author regarding his own products is already of little importance here, would it be logical to replace it by a "competence" of the text with regard to itself? That competence is inside and outside the text, like the critic who touches and loses contact, or like the preface that "is like a sign to a bridge . . . simultaneously at both ends of the bridge, or it is like a sign that has *Enter* on one side and *Exit* on the other" (LM, xiv). However, this loss of the text's identity with itself keeps Miller away from one of the basic postulates of New Criticism, as Gasché observes, that of the "organic unity" of the work. Barbara Johnson says something similar when, speaking of "difference" in Derrida and Barthes, she asserts: "In other words, a text's difference is not its uniqueness, its special identity. It is the text's way of differing from itself" (Johnson, 1980: 4). Miller refers to this self-differing

marriage be the proper ending for a novel, — the only ending, as this writer takes it to be, which is not discordant, — surely no tale was ever so properly ended, or with so full a concord, as this one. Infinite trouble has been taken not only in arranging these marriages but in joining like to like, — so that, if not happiness, at any rate sympathetic unhappiness, might be produced" (624).

In a way not unlike the extended families studied by Sarah E. Miller in Nepal, almost all the characters in *Ayala's Angel* belong either to the Dormer family or to the Albury family. *Ayala's Angel*, too, is the story of marriage negotiations between two extended families that are ultimately joined by a marriage. Any given character is almost certain to be related to many of the others, by blood or by marriage. Even Jonathan Stubbs is Lady Albury's cousin and so already a member of one of the two families. He is also the Marchesa Baldoni's nephew. His marriage to Ayala joins the novel's two chief families. This high degree of interrelation would be extremely difficult to make plausible in a novel about the present-day United

more than once. In the preface of *Fiction and Repetition*, for instance, he writes: "The New Criticism has great value in its assumption that every detail counts, but the accompanying presupposition that every detail is going to count by working harmoniously to confirm the 'organic unity' [another allusion to Wimsatt or to Wellek] of the poem or the novel may become a temptation to leave out what does not fit, to see it as insignificant or as a flaw" (LM, 19). Of course, what does not tally begins in the heterograph or pictogram and in the anamorphic painting of the analyst.

We can go even further. Ronald Schleifer, in an interesting essay entitled "The Anxiety of Allegory: De Man, Greimas, and the Problem of Referentiality" (Schleifer, 1985), proposes that the differences between Greimas and de Man result from the fact that whereas for Greimas the object of power and knowledge—in opposition to each other—is the world, "for de Man this is different: the opposite of knowledge is *ignorance*" (Schleifer, 1985: 233). In Greimas, "power" is related to "desire," whereas "knowledge" is related to the "object" or "referent." In de Man, "ignorance" is connected with "rhetoric" (self-contradictory, aporetic) and "knowledge" with "grammar" (self-consistent, significative). I would argue that Miller's paradigm differs not only from Greimas, but also from de Man, and more than Schleifer's conclusion (the reinscription of the referent in de Man's model) would suggest. Miller could not oppose "rhetoric" to "grammar," and therefore the opposite of "ignorance" would not be "knowledge." In addition, "catachrestic rhetoric" (grammar-rhetoric or rhetoric-grammar) entirely dominates an outline that has only one other equally complex pole: "power-ignorance." The reading of the lexical and syntactic chain of Stevens's poem forces us to formulate the following assertion, an assertion without real sense and without true end, which reminds us, to a certain extent, of Edward Lear's poems: "The icon is the man is the poem is the fruit is the sun is a theorem or geometrical design is the relation of love is . . . the rock" (LM, 408). What Stevens's poem effectively causes, as "power," is this comment by Miller or my own comment that, at the same time, Stevens's poem can be considered a "commentary on / deconstruction / of," among others, Whitman and Emerson: "From Whitman the reader moves back one further step to Whitman's immediate precursor, Emerson. The sequence forms its own *mise en abyme* of successive influence and misinterpretation, from Emerson to Whitman to Stevens" (LM, 411). The sequence reproduces the abyssal on the level of the concatenation or joining of the works, foreseen

States. Here marriage is likely to break up a person's family life by being with someone whose family is wholly unknown, often from a different race, religion, or culture. Marriage and the need for a job often lead newly-weds in the States to move thousands of miles away, completely out of the orbit of either of their two families. The notion of a closely knit extended family hardly makes sense any more for many people in the United States.

Being in love, for Trollope, is a metaphysical condition, not an animal attraction. To say "Jonathan Stubbs loves Ayala" or "I love you" is apparently for Trollope a constative statement, a statement of fact, not in any way a performative statement that creates what it names, as we might be inclined to view it today, if we even believe in love at all.[14] Trollope believes in it as an article of almost religious faith. Though Lucy Dormer has never spoken her love to Isadore Hamel and though he has said no more to her than a few words, the reader is told that "she held herself to be absolutely bound, as by a marriage vow, by such words as those,—words in which there was no promise" (159). The fact of being in love for Trollope seem-

in the pictogram of the "i." To sum up, Miller's textual conception can-not remain fixed in a paradigm because, as previously asserted, the text has no position.

What, then, is a "linguistic moment"? Despite its obvious connec-tions to concepts from other schools (cited by Miller himself), the lin-guistic moment has nothing to do with what Eichenbaum or Shklovsky (or even Jakobson, with his idea of "poetic function") call "defamiliar-ization," since it works neither to increase the difficulty and duration of perception nor, in its negative version, to destroy the automatism of per-ception—it does not attempt to make us sense objects. Shklovsky writes: "And art exists that one may recover the sensation of life; it exists to make one feel things, to make the stone *stony*. The purpose of art is to impart the sensation of things as they are perceived and not as they are known. The technique of art is to make objects 'unfamiliar,' to make forms dif-ficult, to increase the difficulty and length of perception because the process of perception is an aesthetic end in itself and must be prolonged" (Shklovsky, 1965: 12). This passage by Shklovsky is enough to make all merely formalist interpretations of Russian formalism disqualify them-selves, above all, because of Shklovsky's appeal to the "object," though I will not develop this idea here. What is important now is to notice that the "linguistic moment" is not a means of increasing perception of the poetic object. This is because Miller's essays lead us through an odd kind of thematic reading or, better, metathematic reading (even if only to make evident the impossibility of the simple theme). Therefore, they always take us beyond the poem itself: the forgetfulness, the cure, the cyclic, the stable, the fruit. Perception in Miller is concerned with the careful act of reading—of the poem (as objective and subjective genitive)—rather than with confronting an objectlike mode of the poem's being.

Above all, the "linguistic moment" does not allude to any way of making us feel the object as object; quite the opposite. It shows us that the object is perhaps not an object, but a figure. Rhetoric is not, as in Shklovsky, an instrument for "seeing" the object, but a tool that, aimed at the object, points it out as rhetoric—rather in the style of the cave paintings at Altamira—in a game of "showing-hiding." Miller's references to *aletheia* or to the Lethean river of forgetfulness in the analysis of the four scenes of the poem should not surprise us: "The structure of each of these scenes is the same. It is, in fact, the traditional metaphysical struc-ture of aletheia, the appearance of something visible out of the abyss of

ingly precedes the words for that fact. Love is for him a spontaneous movement of the whole substance of the self, down to its deepest foundational
levels, toward another person. Possession of that person will complete the
self or fulfill it. Unless you love me in return I cannot be wholly myself.
What I am is fundamentally characterized by my love for you. I give myself, body and soul, to you. Trollope's good characters could all say, "I love
you, therefore I am." Not everyone in Trollope's novels is capable of loving
in this way. It is, however, open to both sexes equally. Jonathan Stubbs and
Tom Tringle are as genuinely in love with Ayala as she is ultimately in love
with Stubbs. Tom's love for Ayala, the reader is told early in the novel, "had
been real, and was, moreover, permanent" (59). The novel is punctuated
by many circumstantial reports of his love's depth. His story is a moving
account of a possible disaster in Trollope's fictional world, the possibility
that a person, man or woman, may genuinely love another who does not
return that love. Jonathan Stubbs is as stubborn in his loving as Tom,
though more fortunate in the end. He tells Ayala that he will never give

truth. . . . The revelation or unveiling of what has been hidden brings the truth momentarily into the open, out of Lethean forgetfulness" (LM, 408). Catachresis causes us to have doubts about the object as an object, about the enunciation as an enunciation, and about the utterance as an utterance, in short about its "position": "Catachresis is the violent, forced, or abusive use of a word to name something that has no literal name. The word also means, in music, a harsh or unconventional dissonance. 'The Rock' seems based on the search for a name that would be an icon for the hidden truth, the figure for a covert literal. All the terms in the poem, however, are at once literal and figurative. [The last sentence removes from Miller the label "formalist" in the common sense of the word.] Each is a catachresis. According to the logic of a theory of language that bases meaning on the solid referentiality of literal names for visible physical objects, open to the light of the sun [this passage seems written in opposition to Shklovsky], the referent of a catachresis does not exist, was not and is not, absurd" (LM, 419).

If the "linguistic moment" arises when poems "reflect or comment on their own medium," it operates, not by making poems purely self-referential, but by emphasizing their lack of "position." For that reason the "linguistic moment" is a "suspension," "a breaking of the illusion that language is a transparent medium of meaning." That breaking of the illusion of the significative medium is the opposite of an oyster, which closes in on itself, with the nonreferentiality typical of a certain structuralism and of a certain semiotics; rather, again it is oscillation, *suspension*. If the "linguistic moment" (perhaps an erroneous denomination because of the insistence on the "linguistic" component) were mere transparent self-referentiality, it would make no sense to say that the poem does not attain itself as referent, does not give itself a sense, even if it is a polysemic sense. Another aspect that differentiates the "linguistic moment" from its supposed formalist affiliations is that such a notion gives rise, contrary to what happened in OPOIAZ or in the New Criticism, to a certain type of gnoseology, a theory of knowledge of the literary work, even though it is a negative one. This gnoseology is also present in Paul de Man. Christopher Norris sums it up in a book entitled *Paul de Man: Deconstruction and the Critique of Aesthetic Ideology*: "It is crucially by way of the aesthetic—a category too often simply assumed to reconcile the disjunct realms of sensous and cognitive experience—that critics have managed to maintain such a state of epistemological innocence. . . . It is

her up: "Does a man give up his joy,—the pride of his life,—the one only delight on which his heart has set itself! . . . I shall never give it up, Ayala" (489). When Ayala has accepted Jonathan, she tells him, "I want nothing else. I wonder whether there is anybody in all the world who has got so completely everything that she ever dreamed of wanting as I have" (630).

The difference between men and women is that loving demands of the woman absolute submission, whereas it is the man's place to give orders and be obeyed. Of course matters are not quite so simple in practice, as the example of Lady Glencora in Trollope's Palliser novels shows, or as is shown by the relative autonomy of a married woman like Lady Tringle in *Ayala's Angel*. Nevertheless, equality of the sexes by no means obtains.

A rigid hierarchy measures Trollope's various characters, not, as in Jane Austen, by intelligence and wit, but by degree of capacity for genuine love. Tom Tringle, though he is not all that smart, is just as authentically in love with Ayala as is the novel's hero, Jonathan Stubbs, while Gertrude Tringle's ability to shift easily from Frank Houston to Captain Batsby

therefore a major part of [de Man's] project to show how meaning cannot be reduced to any kind of phenomenal or sensory perception; how there always comes a point in the rhetorical study of texts where signifying structures no longer match up with any conceivable form of sensuous cognition (Norris, 1988: xiii). Opposition to this supposition of epistemological innocence, a supposition supported by aestheticist assumptions about the literary work, corresponds to what, by way of the futurist avant garde, influenced the project of Russian Formalism, as Eichenbaum recognizes: "The original group of Formalists was united by the idea of liberating poetic diction from the fetters of the intellectualism and moralism which more and more obsessed the Symbolists" (Eichenbaum, 1965: 106).

Miller holds that cognition and self-cognition embrace some negative characteristics, specifically the absence of whatever ground or position would have to be taken for granted in order for them to be accomplished. Cognition and self-cognition are also related to the common language of literature and philosophy to which our author referred at the beginning of his essay on Wallace Stevens, and which we shall have the opportunity to consider in detail in the following section. This concern for cognition is a part of the "meta-thematic" interest of the aspect of deconstruction closest to literary criticism.

Let me examine this briefly. In the first chapter of *The Linguistic Moment*, in the discussion of another poem by Wallace Stevens, "The Man with the Blue Guitar," we read the following concerning the narcissistic-cognitive moment of the poem: "For Stevens, the theory of poetry is the life of poetry, and nothing is more problematic than the theory of poetry. Stevens' poetry is not merely poetry about poetry. It is a poetry that is the battleground among conflicting theories of poetry. The poet tries first one way and then another way in an endlessly renewed, endlessly frustrated, attempt to 'get it right,' to formulate once and for all an unequivocal definition of what poetry is and to provide an illustration of this definition" (LM, 5). Stevens's is a meta-poetry, but problematic, a self-reflection, though interfered with (from the French *entre-férir*, battle and mutual wound). What is a reflexivity presented as a wound but a criticism of reflexivity? A poetry that talks about poetry but that neither in its utterance (distinct poetic theories) nor in its enunciation (the literal or figurative place from which it contemplates them) clearly "sees," a poetry that, perhaps, does not even "see" at all, is a poetry without position or solid standpoint. If it is without standpoint, from where does it

labels her as comically inferior because she is incapable of real love. Those who are capable of real love are justified in an obstinate fidelity, against all the arguments and coercions of those who try to cure them of their loves. One of the pleasures of reading Trollope is the pleasure of sharing vicariously in this justified obstinacy of the weak in defiance of the strong. One example among many is Lucy's defiance of her Aunt Emmeline's angry demand that she give up Isadore Hamel: "Of course you have a right to order, but I also have some right. You told me I was to drop Mr. Hamel, but I cannot drop him. If he comes in my way I certainly shall not drop him" (162).

It might appear from what I said at first that rational calculations of money and status would (and should) entirely determine who marries whom. Trollope's ideology of love inserts a discordant ingredient into this mix. However reasonable, prudent, and proper it is for a given young woman to marry such and such a man, however good a match he would be, however loud the chorus of friends and relatives telling her, attempting to persuade her, ordering her, cajoling her, to marry that man, she is

look at other things or from where does it look at itself? This idea now appears allegorized through a major intertextuality, the reproduction of the heteroseme or heterograph inherited from Whitman and Emerson.

Not only are the elements of nature (leaves, for instance, even hieroglyphics, and rocks) already present in Whitman, but so is the "I" that sees and absorbs everything: "I celebrate myself, and sing myself, / And what I assume you shall assume / For every atom belonging to me as good as belongs to you," say the first lines of *Song of Myself*. Of Emerson and Whitman, Miller writes: "For both Emerson and Whitman each self must affirm itself, if not in isolation, then as the axis of all, the incorporator of all" (LM, 414). Stevens's "The Rock" represents the crisis of the one who examines and self-examines. Miller tells us in parentheses that "of course both Emerson and Whitman had, each in his own way, already annihilated his own seemingly solid grounding" (LM, 413)—a logical consequence of the pictographic gene. Yet he wonders later: "Who, in contrast, is the 'we' of Stevens's 'The Rock,' the 'we' of whom the first two lines say, 'It is an illusion that we were ever alive, / Lived in the houses of mothers' (lines 1–2)? Husband and wife? Poetic *we*? The general collective first-person plural standing for all men and women together, all old folk of seventy?" (LM, 414)

If the poem "forbids thinking of it or feeling it as the autobiographical statement of a recognizable person" (LM, 414), how is it possible to accept the idea of an auto-biography of the poem? The "I" that attempts to look at itself and cannot is another indication that the poem suspends its relation to the outside in order to warn that it also does not have a clear relation to the inside. The "I" cannot be watched. Neither can the poem. The poem cannot be revised. Neither can the "I" or the "we." "This is a book . . . about moments of suspension within the texts of poems," Hillis Miller guarantees us; the linguistic moment "is a form of parabasis, a breaking of the illusion that language is a transparent medium of meaning" (LM, xiv). It happens, however, that that suspension not only involves the momentary breaking of transparency with regard to referential meaning, but also the breaking of transparency in relation to the poem looking at itself. Not just a parabasis of mimesis, but also a parabasis of self-reflexivity. If, from Descartes to Husserl, "philosophical reflection" designates the aspiration of endless self-grounding, self-foundation, self-position, and if poetic language is precisely a lack of position, could anyone say, strictly speaking, that Miller understands the text according

justified in refusing any suitor she does not love. "I don't understand," says Ayala, enunciating this law, "how anybody is to love any one or not to love him just because he is rich or poor" (549). A little earlier the Marchesa Baldoni had stated the same law as given and absolute in this society: "Nobody knows better than I do that a young lady is entitled to the custody of her own heart, and that she should not be compelled, or even persuaded, to give her hand in opposition to her own feelings" (503).

Since loving is to some degree unpredictable, irrational, and, in the most ethically admirable men and women, absolutely unalterable, once it has occurred, love introduces an element of unpredictability into Trollope's stories. This uncertainty constitutes their center of interest. Just who will Ayala come to love, so that she can marry, settle down, and cease to be the object of her whole community's fascinated curiosity? That is the central "subject" of *Ayala's Angel*. All the analogous subplots of other courtships are ancillary to her story, aids to understanding it by way of similarity or difference.

to the model of a conscious subjectivity or of a self-reflexive presence? Could anyone, once literature, writing, or the text have been read this way, say, without a feeling of uneasiness, that literature has simply yielded to the will of philosophy? Could anyone believe that the oxymoron of "as in a vivid sleep" ("like a voice of the voiceless, or like an ability to hear the soundless"; LM, 421) has voice and eyes to solve and be solved, to penetrate itself? Would anybody not realize that, in this sense, the revolution—a word whose use in the 1970s needs profound revision— of poetic language and its cerologic subject does not start with Mallarmé and Lautreamont, but already with Sophocles? What Miller says of the rhetoric of poetry would apply also, mutatis mutandis, to Sophocles.

At the beginning of this chapter, I noted that the "moment" of the "linguistic moment" translates Nietzsche's *Augenblick* from the chapter "The Vision and the Enigma" in *Thus Spoke Zarathustra*. That *Augenblick* is part of the riddle or parable (*Gleichnis*) Zarathustra tells to the sailors. What standpoint, ground, or perspective does the parable have? "A visionary riddle, like a parable, is an extended or narrative catachresis. Like catachresis it is neither literal nor figurative but both or neither at once. Such a form of language is the only mode in which what it says can be said and so does not substitute for any conceptual language that could be given, while at the same time it means more than it says. A parable or visionary riddle is a metaphor . . . and yet it does not substitute for any literal expression that could be presented" (LM, 427). Zarathustra says of his vision: "Thus I spoke more and more softly; for I was afraid of my own thoughts, and the thoughts behind my thoughts. Then suddenly I heard a dog howl nearby" (1978: 158). What is Zarathustra afraid of? Is he afraid of his underlying thoughts or of never being able to attain them? Are these two fears not the same thing? Is this similarity not the same as a steamy mirror? Is this not what Wallace Stevens hints in the following lines?

> The step to the bleaker depths of his descents . . .
> The rock is the stern particular of the air,
> The mirror of the planets, one by one,
> But through man's eye, their silent rhapsodist,
>
> Turquoise the rock, at odious evening bright
> With redness that sticks fast to evil dreams.
>
> *(Stevens, 1954: 528)*

How Do I Know I Am in Love?

I have said that being in love is a metaphysical condition. It involves the deepest substance of the self, taking substance both as what the self is made of and as its underlying base, its hypostasis, what stands beneath it to hold it up. How does my conscious self communicate with those deepest foundations of the self and tell whether a given impulse of loving is the real thing? A character might answer, "I know because I know," but, as Trollope shows in one of his most important novels, *He Knew He Was Right* (1869), it is possible to think you are right and nevertheless to be wrong. How can I know when I am in love? *Ayala's Angel* is a brilliant exploration of this question. It is in trying to answer it that the difficulties appear.

These difficulties can be demonstrated by looking more closely at Trollope's dramatization of Ayala's love for Jonathan Stubbs. It would be possible to argue that Ayala's story is no more than reinforcement by an

A rhapsodist whose eye makes out certain evil dreams, dreams erased from the face of the earth.

J. Hillis Miller: Who Is He?
Autoveilography (Aside)

J. Hillis Miller is a serious literary critic. We assume that his texts seriously explain and explore the difficulties of literary language. When he announces "My book will explore the ethics of narrative in its connection with the trope of prosopopoeia" (VP, 11), we trust him to try to fulfill his grave promise. He is speaking of ethics, after all, and besides, how could we interpret his words otherwise? Deep in our hearts, however, a suspicion perhaps might hide. Just for a moment. Who knows? My suspicion is not aroused when I realize how frequently Miller has changed his views on literature. It is not aroused when he arrives at the conclusion that we cannot decide the meaning of a given text, or when he states that we can no longer enter into dialogue with a consciousness present in the text. My suspicion is aroused when in an interview I read his brief answer concerning why he has changed his views on and approaches to literature (Heusser and Schweizer, 1991). I have already said something about this in the first chapter, but I cannot avoid returning to it. Miller's answer is: "It would be boring, I think, if you didn't change." I don't know if the "context" of an interview is less serious than the context of an essay on ethics. The brief answer is surely of little importance. Perhaps he is only joking, and I should not focus on it. Why, then, do I focus on it? On the one hand, because I was "shocked" by these "unimportant" words ("It would be boring") the first time I read them and decided to write about them; on the other hand, because I think that this brief answer inhabits the permanent center of the Millerian matrix, and this fact is remarkable. Miller changes. He does not want to get bored. I ask, therefore, "Who is J. Hillis Miller?" Of course, one might think I was asking after the empirical person called Joseph Hillis Miller, which would yield his biography (Oberlin College, Harvard, Johns Hopkins, Yale, Irvine, married, three children, heir of Poulet, polemic with Abrams, moderate or radical deconstructionist, concern with ethics, etc.).

    I first heard J. Hillis Miller's name in 1984, at a symposium entitled "Deconstruction: Theory and Practice" in Urbino. This sets up a curious

agent of the Victorian thought police of the idea that a young woman ought to put aside imaginary ideals and marry the most suitable man who presents himself and is approved of by her family, friends, and advisors. Ayala's reluctance to accept Jonathan Stubbs is, it may be, no more than feminine modesty, perhaps a virginal distaste for the physical side of marriage, expressed in her initial conviction that Jonathan is "hideously ugly" (149). Ayala's adventure is, however, much more interesting than that. It is more an investigation of Victorian ideological laws and even an interrogation of them than a blind, policemanlike enforcement of them.

Ayala's Angel, in a way unusual for Trollope, ascribes to its main character an obsessive idea. Ayala has read in the Bible that angels of light have come down from heaven and taken in marriage the daughters of men (Genesis 6: 1–2; the King James translation says "sons of God," not "angels of light"). She decides that only an angel of light would be a suitable mate for her:

paronomastic coincidence: the first time I heard his name was at Urbino, and the first time I saw him was at Irvine, in 1992. We met in "rb(v)n," where the only letters that change are "u" and "o," "i" (again the "i") and "e." While I was writing the preceding chapter, "Boustrophedonism: The Text as Surd," I could not help wondering if we and this book were not the result of those graphico-pictorial features, if we hinged on them. Obviously this is not so; it is only a simple pun. I am just playing with the signifier. But we know that we cannot simply say "playing with the signi-fier," since the signifier is the one that really plays. There is no need to re-call now the play of the signifier in order to realize that this paronomastic coincidence between Urbino and Irvine is more than a pun (though a pun is always more than a pun). What does Urbino mean? What does Urbino embody? I would say: urbanity. Another pun? "Urbino" and "urbanity." The signifier plays, but "urbanity" is very closely connected with the notion of "city," even if we are talking about the "urbane man-ner" or "urbane behavior." The only way to understand the meaning of "urbanity" is to think about the "city." Indeed, the words "urban," "urbane," "urbanity" come from the Latin word *urbis*, with the deriva-tive *urbanus*, meaning "city." Urbino, like many other European cities, embodies the city, the urban, the classical, the fact of having a center, of being organized around the center, European thought in art, politics, philosophy, and, above all, for me and for this book, in literary theory. We should remember that the "International Center of Semiotics and Linguistics" is located in Urbino.

By contrast, Irvine embodies the disappearance of the city (is it an invisible city, in the words of Italo Calvino?), the undecidable blend of nature and culture, the modern, the lack of center, a kind of organization based on no center, American thought and the way it assimilates and dis-rupts European thought (for example, the work of Derrida, who, along with other European thinkers, teaches at Irvine). The difference between Urbino and Irvine does not arise from geographical distance (this is not important in today's Internet world), but from their distinct traditions and constructions, to the extent that we could say, though this assertion is very naïve, that the cities are opposites, one excluding the other and vice versa. It is also true, however, that they are similar, and that the par-onomasia creates this similarity. I am not interested now in similarities that already exist—as, for example, and of course this is another easy pun, the urbanity one can find among Irvine's residents, or the well-known

Her ideas . . . about men, — or rather about a possible man, — were confined altogether to the abstract. She had floating in her young mind some fancies as to the beauty of love. That there should be a hero must of course be necessary. But in her day-dreams this hero was almost celestial, — or, at least, æthereal. It was a concentration of poetic perfection to which there was not as yet any appanage of apparel, of features, or of wealth. It was a something out of heaven which should think it well to spend his whole time in adoring her and making her more blessed than had ever yet been a woman upon the earth. (51–52)

Ayala measures all the men she meets, especially those who show an interest in her, by this abstract idea. One by one she finds them wanting. Her story, however, is not exactly, as one might expect, the narrative of her gradual growing out of this absurd idealization of the potential love object. This is so because Ayala's abstract idea is a version of the Victorian ideology of loving on which the whole society described by Trollope depends. Ayala discovers that Jonathan Stubbs is the very angel of light of whom she has dreamed. After she finally accepts him, the reader is told, "There

consequences of the "global village." I am interested in the resemblance that springs up in the effect of the paronomasia, in the moment in which we underline and paint the "u" upon the "i," or the "o" upon the "e."

This book is the result of that paronomastic movement, the result of joining one element to another (Urbino and Irvine) or of bringing one together with another in the same space and time, the result of hearing and seeing J. Hillis Miller at Urbino and Irvine (I[U]rb[v]in[o]e). This book is, in a sense, the continuation of this paronomasia and of this meeting. All this play is empirical (yes, I heard Hillis Miller's name for the first time at Urbino; I first saw him at Irvine) and, at the same time, textual (the paronomasia, the figure of the chiasmus that this book presents). These biographical facts were the basis for writing this book on J. Hillis Miller. But the opposite is also true: Miller's writing and reading were the basis for biographical facts, as, for example, my first meeting with him. I would say that the word was the cause. Why the word? The first time I heard Hillis Miller's name I was attending in Frankfurt Derrida's lecture on Joyce ("Ulysse gramophone: le oui-dire de Joyce"). I was twenty-four years old then and was very interested in deconstruction. Somebody sitting beside me said in an undertone that Derrida was dangerous (I knew it, I knew it, and not only this; it was one of the reasons that I liked Derrida, whatever the meaning of that adjective might be—"dangerous"). But immediately afterwards he added, "But there is another worse: Hillis Miller." Worse! Worse than Derrida! I had to read Hillis Miller. Like him, I was fascinated with the indigenous and abiding dimensions of literature and criticism. And later I met him.

Is J. Hillis Miller "dangerous"? I am not going to talk about private things. I am not Miller's biographer, and I do not have much knowledge of his private life. He is one of the most educated, urbane, respectful, and kind persons I have ever known. He will help you even if you wake him up at three o'clock in the morning. So the answer to the question "Is J. Hillis Miller dangerous?" is "No, he is not dangerous." It seems to me that he is not dangerous at all. But perhaps he *is* dangerous. When I asked Hillis Miller to collaborate in this peculiar book, my original idea was that he should write his own biography (an autobiography, maybe a noncanonical one). He, elegantly, refused this idea (with something like "I would prefer not to") and instead suggested writing on Proust, among others. I thought immediately that it would be very exciting to interpret that rejection. By what markers, for instance, can we decide whether his

was just a moment for her, in which to tell herself that the Angel of Light had come for her, and had taken her to himself" (535). Ayala's infatuation with her angel of light is an allegorization of the general ideology defining love as a metaphysical absolute on which *Ayala's Angel* and Trollope's other novels are based. Since Ayala's infatuation involves taking a verbal abstraction as a material reality, Ayala's angel fits with strict fidelity the definition of ideology as the confusion of linguistic with natural reality.[15]

Ayala's story brings into the open the workings of this ideology. It is, however, by no means intended, nor does it inadvertently function, as a critique of that ideology which might cure the novel's readers of being bamboozled by this ideological mistake. Nevertheless it does work, for a careful reader, to show what is peculiar about this ideology. This peculiarity lies in the impossibility of determining just when it is and how it comes about that Ayala falls in love with Jonathan Stubbs. When she first meets him, he orders her to dance with him. She assures herself that she is certain of one thing: Jonathan Stubbs, with his stubbly red hair, his wide

message was ironic or not? *A la recherche du temps perdu* is somehow like an autobiography, where the persistence of the "same" (between quotation marks) self and characters sustains the "coherence" of the "story." What attracted my attention regarding *La recherche*, however, was that this "autobiography" comes to light only when the author decides to disappear in order to recreate the memory of the impressions, when the narrator, at the very end of *Le temps retrouvé* quotes the passage from the Bible that says if we want to reap much grain, the wheat seed must die when it is sowed ("Thou fool, that which thou sowest is not quickened, except it die" [I Corinthians, 15: 36]). Even more, although we recognize the "I" of the narrator from *Du côté de chez Swann* until *Le temps retrouvé*, that "I" is agile, elastic, and solvent. It represents the distance within the coherent "self."

At the beginning of this book, I mentioned that when anyone writes about Miller's work, it seems obligatory to point out its changes and oscillations. I have just mentioned that, when asked about his changes, Miller has answered: "It would be boring, I think, if you didn't change." It would be boring to maintain all the time that reading is the "consciousness of the consciousness of another" (FVF, 2) or "that the critic's work is already done for him" (LM, 4). There are a lot of things to say about boredom, about the state of being bored; I will select only one of them. At first sight, this assertion seems to be frivolous. Is boredom a good, a logical reason for changing the perspective of your methodology in your research? We assume that Miller has not flipped his lid, that he is not being serious when he says such a thing, and that this frivolity is moored to the fact that his essays are very serious. But he is not the only one who says something about boredom. Boredom is worked up as a reading category by Barthes (following Kierkegaard) in his fragmentary book called *The Pleasure of the Text*. There he writes: "Text of pleasure: the text that contents, fills, grants euphoria; the text that comes from culture and does not break with it, is linked to a *comfortable* practice of reading. Text of bliss: the text that imposes a state of loss, the text that discomforts (perhaps to the point of a certain boredom), unsettles the reader's historical, cultural, psychological assumptions, the consistency of his tastes, values, memories, brings to a crisis his relation with language." According to Barthes: "Boredom is not far from bliss: it is bliss seen from the shores of pleasure" (Barthes, 1975: 14, 26).

Miller does not want to get bored; he does not want to remain

mouth, and his bristly red beard, is not her angel of light. In the course of the novel, Stubbs proposes to her three times and each time is refused on the ground that he is not the embodiment of her angelic ideal. Gradually she comes to understand and respect his high qualities and even ultimately to love him, though she refuses him one final time even after she knows she loves him, still on the ground that he is no angel of light.

There is a contradiction just here in the narrator's report. On the one hand, he asserts that she can only love Jonathan Stubbs when she gives up her infatuation with her idea about the angel of light. She can love him when the narrator can say: "The spirit had been wholly exorcised. . . . She never again spoke to herself even in her thoughts of that Angel of Light,— never comforted herself again with the vision of that which was to come!" (492–93). On the other hand, when she does become fully conscious of her love for Stubbs, she by no means gives up the idea of the angel of light. Rather, she comes to believe that Stubbs embodies the angel: "The Angel of Light had come for her, and had taken her to himself" (535). Her love

inside the repetition of the same grammar. His relation to literary and philosophical texts is, therefore, a relation of enjoyment because he is looking for a condition of loss, the abandonment of what he already has. He is unable to sustain the same theoretical point of view, or, what is the same: he is unable to sustain the same language. He needs to change. To be bored would mean keeping the same language, the same structure, the same grammar. When you are bored, nothing changes; it is as if you were within a process of endless repetition of the same, within an identity. Miller wants something unforeseen to happen. This is not in opposition to the "Millerian matrix," because this matrix is tied to the realm of otherness, of the beyond and abyss of literature. Miller's (non)position is located between cultural values and their loss. From the viewpoint of Barthes's terminology, Miller is doubly perverse since he participates at once in the deep hedonism of culture and in the de(con)struction of it.

On reflection, I am not sure how frivolous Miller's answer is. Nor am I sure how frivolous this frivolity is. The true source of my embarrassment consists in my ignorance concerning how to face frivolity in this area (literary theory, literary criticism, philosophy), an area in which we do not generally consider the frivolous to be worthy. This leads me to Derrida. In his *The Archeology of the Frivolous*, we read this definition, the last two sentences of which are cited from Condillac: "Frivolity consists in being satisfied with tokens. It originates with the sign, or rather with the signifier which, no longer signifying, is no longer a signifier. The empty, void, friable, useless signifier. . . . 'Useless is said of things which serve no purpose, are of no use. . . . If their utility bears only on objects of little consideration or worth, they are *frivolous*. As for *futile*, it adds still more to *frivolous* and is said chiefly of reasoning or arguments which bear on nothing' " (Derrida, 1980b: 118). In these terms, we can think that the statement "it would be boring" does not have an important aim or end, that it has nothing to say, or just a little. Derrida, still paraphrasing Condillac, continues: "The method for reducing the frivolous is method itself. In order not to be the least frivolous, being methodic suffices" (ibid.: 125), and "the frivolous instance results from a supplementary complication of the 'moving body' " (ibid.: 133).

At this point, we can only recognize that, from Condillac's point of view, Miller has been frivolous. He has not only changed his methodology (he is not methodical enough), which would suffice to reveal that he cannot reduce the frivolous, but he has also explained that his reason

for Jonathan is at once the exorcising of a bad spirit and the discovery of a material incarnation of that same spirit, now turned from bad to good. Which is the correct interpretation? The novel does not give the reader evidence to decide, though everything in the novel has led up to the necessity of deciding about this. It is the most important question in the novel. Any obvious way out of the impasse in interpretation is in one way or another unsatisfactory, for example by saying that we know she has been cured of her infatuation, while she does not. If she has not been cured, then her love is inauthentic, while everything in the novel seems intended to persuade the reader that Ayala's ultimate commitment of herself to Jonathan is the supreme example of authentic loving in this novel that ends with so many marriages.

The uncertainty about whether Ayala in loving Jonathan Stubbs is fulfilling her dream of the angel of light or being cured at last of an adolescent folly is related to an even more important one: the uncertainty as to just when Ayala began to love Jonathan Stubbs. When Stubbs is finally

for changing is his desire not to be bored. Obviously, this explanation turns on a motive of little worth. Perhaps he is joking, but he is joking about the reasons for having changed his approaches to literature. (Martin Heusser said in his interview of Miller: "You have always admitted to having changed your views on and approaches to literature" [HH, 155].) We come back to Derrida: if frivolity falls on the side of style, writing, the hollow, it must be linked to the figural deviation. Either the argument says nothing or something of no worth, or the argument deviates from itself. Really, there is no difference between these two possibilities: to say nothing or to say something of little worth both imply that the sign deviates in relation to its necessarily important referent or signified. One of the conclusions to be drawn here is that frivolity makes deconstruction possible: "Philosophy deviates from itself and gives rise to the blows that will strike it nonetheless from the outside. On this condition alone, at once internal and external, is deconstruction *possible*" (Derrida, 1980b: 132).

Leaving aside the steps of Derrida's strategy for bringing together frivolity and deconstruction, we find here some leads. For Miller, not to want to be bored implies refusing to remain inside literal meaning without moving, that is, always finding similar results in his procedures for reading texts. It implies, moreover, that we cannot recognize Miller in his abundant writing on literature, philosophy, and painting. In other words, Miller defaces himself as he changes methodology, language, and grammar, through the frivolity involved in the affirmation "it would be boring." Miller is, in fact, a textual moving body, a moving self. There is no way to control, to stop the metamorphoses of the "I" that speaks in his different essays. However, this is precisely what the Millerian matrix announces: the relationship between the critic (J. Hillis Miller) and the author (e.g., Thomas de Quincey) is the encounter between two selves who cannot be picked out and identified in the textual horizon. On the one hand, the consciousness of the author is an infinite divisibility, the impossibility of arriving at unity, at the figure of consciousness as a delimited entity, at the act of encompassing the one as one, even before the one could possibly exist. On the other hand, the critic, in his desire to place himself in a condition of loss, in his desire to enter into the beyondness and abnormality of literature and to do something new and unforeseen, as happens every time he touches literature, has to dissolve, to deface, to liquefy himself through the constant movement of his textual body.

accepted, the reader is told that "the Colonel did not quite understand the assertion" when Ayala whispered, "I always loved you" (536). It is not surprising that both Stubbs and the reader should not quite understand, since she has refused him so "pertinaciously" (538) and since the reader can find no trace in earlier parts of the novel of her having always loved him. If Trollope's characters are as transparent to themselves as I have claimed, she ought to have known, but if the reader looks back, for example, to reread the account of Ayala's first meeting with Stubbs, on the assumption that something must have been missed, all he or she finds is the following, as a report in indirect discourse of Ayala's judgment of Stubbs: "Nothing could be more unlike an Angel of Light than Colonel Stubbs" (150). After she has accepted him at last, both Stubbs himself and Lady Albury at different times ask Ayala why she has caused everyone so much trouble by refusing him again and again. Her answer is to assert once more that it was "love at first sight": "Lady Albury, I think I fell in love with him the first moment I saw him" (538). If that was the case, then why did she refuse him?

This critic does not admit to seriousness or to gravity, to having knowledge beforehand of what is going to happen in the act of reading. Miller's project is not compatible with boredom, because if he were to be bored, then it would be impossible to experience, to transform and disaggregate himself within literary space. For Miller boredom represents immobility, permanence, absolute identity, and an anodyne position. Here we have a key: "anodyne" comes from the Greek word *an* (without) *odunos* (pain). The mood in which we have no experience of pain produces an effect of not changing. If you don't experience pain and if you are all the time in a situation of well-being, then nothing happens to you; you have no experience. It's curious that "anodyne" is usually also used to designate what is uninteresting. It recalls Kierkegaard's notion of the "interesting" as an aesthetic category. (It seems that Miller, in using the category of "boredom," is not far from Kierkegaard.) The connection between boredom and the uninteresting may be the best witness of the consolidation of the "molar" self ("molar" in Deleuze's terms). This is the "self" Miller throws away. I begin to understand why Miller did not want to write an autobiography. We know that an autobiography, in its canonical sense, has to be based on a weighty "I." (I shall return to this later on).

I am not the one who underlines the relation between pain and the interesting. (Of course, this is the opposite of being bored). Kierkegaard does so, as I have sketched in the previous paragraph. In *Fear and Trembling* Kierkegaard asserts that the "interesting" is a fateful privilege, for which one pays the price of deep pain. Socrates embodies the most interesting life ever known; he is the most interesting man in history; and this is so because he suffered enormous calamity and pain. Moreover, Kierkegaard locates the category of the "interesting" between aesthetics and ethics. On the one hand, one now realizes that to speak of boredom is not untranscendental at all, which does not mean that boredom is a transcendental category. Here Miller does not agree with Kierkegaard, who claims that the "interesting" (and thus "boredom") is a transcendental category that depends on a consolidated self. Miller, however, works out "boredom" (and therefore the "interesting") as a category that requires disaggregating the "self" so as not to become bored. A consolidated self only leads to being bored. At least, this is what one infers from Miller's (a)position. But one sees that Miller, when talking about not being bored, is within the metaphysical tradition, even if he is within it in order to

"But why on earth did you give him so much trouble?" asks Lady Albury. "I can't tell you," answers Ayala, and in response to Lady Albury's further question, "Do you mean that there is still a secret?" Ayala answers that it is not a secret, but still she cannot tell: "I would tell you anything that I could tell. . . . But I cannot tell. I cannot explain even to myself" (536–37). She gives Jonathan the same answer when, in response to her saying, "Oh, I had loved you for so long a time!" he asks her a not unreasonable question: "Then why did you refuse me?" "Ah;" she says, "that is what I would explain to you now,—here on this very spot,—if I could" (544).

Ayala says there is no secret. There is none of the sort that she might know and keep from others. A secret, however, abides at the heart of *Ayala's Angel*. It is a secret of the more genuine kind, the kind that cannot be known by anyone and can never be revealed or penetrated, only responded to by some speech act like Ayala's "I always loved you."[16] Ayala's explanation to Lady Albury makes it even more evident that her "I always loved you" is a performative, not a constative utterance. Derrida, in the seminar

convert the literal meaning of the notions of that metaphysical tradition into an infinite figurativity embodied in irony and frivolity.

On the other hand, one can read Miller's strategy as an action both textual and extra-textual (the crossing between aesthetics and ethics). The person who wants not to be bored is the concrete and historical person Joseph Hillis Miller, and it is in this sense that we talk about his frivolity. But at the same time we are divining the consequences of that attitude in the formation of his texts. It would also be possible to say that we are divining the consequences of a textual formation in a virtual J. Hillis Miller biography. As a matter of fact, from the very beginning of this "aside" I have been confused about how to interpret the signals, tokens, and marks that surround this book. I have arrived at the conclusion that my confusion is the result of a constant mobility. Bringing together Irvine and Urbino by virtue of paronomasia, I have been obligated to run in two different directions, always keeping in contact the two poles of the rv(b)n's thread: the center and the absence of center, the city and the disaggregation of the city, the classical and the modern, and so on.

This center is also for me the "I" of J. Hillis Miller—his name, his place—in the same manner that the lack of center is the dissolution of Miller's self in an infinity of textual and extra-textual registers as a result of the fact that he does not want to be bored. Not to want to be bored is to be ironic in the Schlegelian sense in which Paul de Man uses this word in his lecture, given originally in 1977, "The Concept of Irony" (de Man, 1996: 163–84). De Man asks: "What if irony is always of understanding, if irony is always the irony of understanding, if what is at stake in irony is always the question of whether it is possible to understand or not to understand?" (de Man, 1996: 166). If this is the case, then irony and the ironic attitude are very dangerous. ("Irony would indeed be very dangerous"; de Man, 1996: 167). We find again the word "dangerous." I asked above, "Is Miller dangerous?" I was not going to talk about private things, but I could not resist answering, "No, I don't think so, and I have reasons for believing that." I have added, however, that perhaps Miller is dangerous, that yes, yes, Miller can be dangerous.

Paul de Man affirms throughout his lecture that irony and the impossibility of understanding are connected. Borrowing this definition from Schlegel and completing it, he says: "If Schlegel said irony is permanent parabasis, we would say that irony is the permanent parabasis of the allegory of tropes" (de Man, 1996: 179). "Irony is the permanent para-

mentioned in note 14, has persuasively argued that the bare statement "I love you" is already a speech act, not a statement of fact. When Ayala says, not "I always loved you," but "I think I fell in love with him the first moment I saw him," the "I think" indicates openly how much her assertion depends on her own deciding and saying. "I think" is an ambiguous locution. It may be the report of a fact about what is going on in one's mind, but it may also be a speech act reporting a decision, as when someone says, "I think I'll go swimming." Taking Ayala's "I think" in the second way would make "I think I fell in love with him the first moment I saw him" a sentence that brings about what it names. The final example of such a statement, made to Ayala's Aunt Margaret after she has been engaged for some weeks, has even more clearly the linguistic marks of a performative utterance: "I may say whatever I please about it now, and I declare that I always loved him" (616). To say "I always loved him" and to say "I declare I always loved him" are two quite different things. This is so not so much because "I always loved him" is not already a performative, but be-

basis" means that the task of irony is to interrupt, forever to disrupt any continuity, any kind of continuity, so that the break is brutal. In order not to get bored in doing literary criticism (it would be better to say, in writing), it is absolutely necessary to interrupt, to disrupt one's own methodology, one's own point of view, one's own language and "I." To say "Irony is the permanent parabasis of the allegory of tropes" involves, among other things, asserting that irony interrupts, disrupts the understanding based on the correlation between literal meaning and controlled figurative meaning, so that irony makes it impossible to understand. The consequence is that, if irony does not allow us to understand, then we discover, following Friedrich Schlegel and Paul de Man, that irony is the realm of error, madness, and stupidity. One says, "I change my approach to literature in order not to get bored," and immediately afterwards one is suspected of frivolity, nonsense, error, madness, and stupidity. But Miller (and here we have another way for defining the Millerian matrix) shifts from language to language, from methodology to methodology, from text to text; that is, he practices the brutal interruption of irony.

I can now understand why Miller did not want to write his autobiography. He would have become bored. Had he decided to write his autobiography, he would have had to maintain and support the weighty and anodyne "I." And he has no weighty and grave "I"; he has interrupted the continuity of his "I"; he has been ironic in relation to his "I," because the interruption and disruption of irony is the best way not to become bored. Irony, in breaking constantly, does not bore; it is joyful and slight all the time. The ironic man (the ironic "I") is the man (the "I") you cannot find, the man (the "I") absorbed into the veil. Before this vast open space, autobiography becomes autoveilography. Autoveilography is the gesture that makes possible and puts at stake Miller's ironic "I." Therefore, it is necessary to reject writing a biography, to reject becoming bored, since there is no unveiled and fixed "I." Miller has said more or less the same: "An inaugural performative, I claim, always exceeds its context, just as it is not amenable to being reduced to the deliberate act of consciousness, willing ego or 'I.' The 'I' that says 'I claim,' is created and made effective by the speech act it enunciates" (1, 55). If this is so, then neither we nor Hillis Miller can grasp his "I." Therefore, Miller cannot write his autobiography, because this autobiography is (de)constructed by the absolute interruption of the movement of the "I" in the different texts and languages in which that "I" appears. The only thing he can do is to

cause adding "I declare" makes verbally visible the speech act side of the sentence "I always loved him." A declaration is always a speech act of some kind, though like all speech acts it also contains a constative component. Its undecidability lies in the impossibility of deciding which of the two functions of language is dominant in a given case, just how the mixture works, whether it reports a fact or creates what it names. Ayala's loving may be the result of her declaration that she loves or it may simply be reported in that declaration, as when one makes a "customs declaration."

Just how Ayala came to love Jonathan Stubbs, just when it happened, just how firmly grounded her love is, and grounded on what, are matters the reader would like to be certain about. The narrator gives the reader little help in reaching that certainty. Presumably he would do so if he could. The original moment of Ayala's falling in love is a blank place in the novel. First she did not love him, and told herself clearly that she did not love him. Then later, at some mysterious and unascertainable moment, unascertainable because she is not shown as being aware of it when

invent another kind of auto-biography, or what he proposed to me: writing on Proust, perhaps in order to change his views again. This means to veil, to hide the "ego" in a plurality of "egos," all the time mastered by the graphic and by paronomasia. I insist: in Miller autobiography becomes auto-veilography.

Now for a warning: J. Hillis Miller is dangerous in the same way that irony is dangerous. Can we understand him? It is not easy to answer this question. Any essay or book by Miller uses, like Borges, clear language (earlier I called it Aristotelian language), which we can easily understand. What he is asking, for instance, in the opening words of *Hawthorne and History* is clear enough: "What is the present relation between literary theory and pedagogy in American colleges and universities?" (HH, 46). A contradiction appears, however, when one compares the theory about undecidability, the theory about consciousness, the theory about the ethics of reading, to the Millerian matrix in which all these theories dissolve. To give a provisional answer to my question, to the extent that the Millerian matrix subtends any of the different theories he uses at different times, we cannot understand J. Hillis Miller. No theory, even the most complex, will be able to control, to stop Miller's moving textual body. Here we encounter a veil. Which veil? No doubt, the most beautiful veil we have ever seen is literary language. This is why Miller has chosen the language of literature for veiling himself, for his auto-veilography.

Continuation: Changing Perspective

At this point we should, if possible, answer a question to which the response is apparently obvious. Is Miller a literary critic or not? From *The Form of Victorian Fiction* to *Ariadne's Thread: Story Lines*, the "objects" of his analysis have been narrators (novelists and storywriters, such as Trollope, Dickens, Hardy, Meredith, Goethe, Melville, James, Woolf, Borges, and Faulkner), and philosophers, critics, and essayists, such as Aristotle, Plato, Nietzsche, Kant, Benjamin, Wittgenstein, Kleist, de Man, and Derrida. Two disciplinary spaces, philosophy and literature, appear in Miller's work in a chiastic way: literature aims at and advances, in some way or another, philosophical "contents," while philosophy narrates or resorts to fictive stories. For the moment, this is not a problem of form, genre, or writing. It is not that philosophy and literature remain undifferentiated and without limits; rather, literature, as literature, poses in its own

it happens, she does come to love him. Then slowly, gradually, but at the same time in sudden bursts of self-intuition, she comes to realize that she already loves him. When she becomes fully aware of her love, then it seems to her as if it must date from the first moment she saw him. At any rate she declares, being free to say whatever she pleases about it now, that it does so date. Her present loving, as a performative commitment of herself to the other person, creates in retrospect an initiatory moment that was not there as something to be known and narrated when it occurred.

   The structure of Ayala's loving has that curious metaleptic temporal to and fro characteristic of trauma and of performative events generally. Falling in love, it could be argued, is, quite strictly speaking, a form of trauma. Such events do not occur when they occur. They occur only later on, in retrospect, at the moment when they are granted originating power by a speech act like Ayala's "I always loved you," or her "Lady Albury, I think I fell in love with him the first moment I saw him," or her "I declare that I always loved him." The reader is never given access, and cannot be

way problems similar to philosophical ones (though if so it is difficult to believe that literature is able to preserve its literary *being*), whereas philosophy, as philosophy, resorts to literary strategies. When this happens, it seems logical to think that the expression "philosophy as philosophy" becomes problematic.

In *Ariadne's Thread*, we hear that "ten years after *The Egoist* was published the second essay of Nietzsche's *On the Genealogy of Morals* followed a similar line of thought and of figuration. Nietzsche distinguishes, as Meredith does, between different forms of promising" (AT, 131). A line of thought is established and several distinctions are made in the novel in question, just as in philosophical discourse. As a result, Miller can claim that "Meredith's formulations function as a proleptic deconstruction of Nietzsche's male oriented or phallogocentric structure" (AT, 140). Yet we read in *The Ethics of Reading*, with regard to Kant's *Foundations of the Metaphysics of Morals*, that: "The reader has already encountered in the footnote itself one narrative element. I have respect not for a person but for a person as an example of some ethical value which is in turn an example of the law as such" (ER, 23). For that reason, "storytelling is the impurity which is necessary in any discourse about the moral law as such, in spite of the law's austere indifference to persons, stories, and history" (ibid.). For Miller, as for Derrida, such impurity is constitutive of each discipline. For instance, the terms and concepts used by literary criticism and literary theory, despite being differently minted and having different functions, are no different from those used in linguistics or in novels themselves: "The terminology of narrative may by no effort be compartmentalized, divided into hanks of different colored thread. The same terms must be used in all regions" (AT, 24). "A narrative dimension infects even the most abstract thought" (AT, 101).

Kant narrates a brief tale that illustrates, and perhaps unintentionally contradicts (though one cannot be sure about that), the idea of the representation of the law insofar as it is the determining basis of will. Meredith establishes a concrete theory about different types of "promise" through Clara's behavior regarding Willoughby. Fiction makes explicit, allegorizes, or dismantles ideas and concepts, whereas ideas and concepts adopt or call upon fictional forms. It is not that narrativity—to use a narratological term—is present in every type of discourse. Narrative texts are not among the basic forms of textual communication. Rather, fictional stories inundate other discourses, while fictions turn to the "other" of fic-

given access, to the moment of Ayala's falling in love. It is not something that can be known or confronted directly. As soon as she or anyone else—other characters, the narrator, the reader—is aware of it, it seems always to have happened already, at some time anterior to whatever time anyone is aware of it.

The impossibility of identifying the grounds of loving in a wholly satisfactory way constitutes the black hole in *Ayala's Angel* and therefore in the Internet Galaxy that contains *Ayala's Angel* as one of its stars. Or the novel might be thought of as a spectral and opaque angelic messenger, circulating at the speed of light around the World Wide Web. This impossibility justifies using for our relation to this unknowable center the portentous names of "aporia" and "undecidability." "Undecidability" is a proper word here for the impossibility of being sure, in a given case, whether the loving is genuine or not. "Aporia" is a correct name, in this case, not only for the form this uncertainty takes, but for the impossibility of making a way through from consciousness to the ground or lack of it that justifies

tion and question themselves as fictions. Miller writes in *Ariadne's Thread*: "It is impossible to tell where narrative stops, and something else—literary criticism, or philosophy, or some other form of 'non-fiction'—starts" (AT, 101). If this is Miller's starting point, how can we interpret titles like *The Form of Victorian Fiction* or *Fiction and Repetition*, or a subtitle like *Story Lines*? Should we think of them as names of peritexts that sum up the lessons of literary criticism? Or should we suspect that these titles, which promise to talk about fiction, feign, faithful to their etymon *fingere*, and therefore, like the paradox of the liar, are not fictions? Do they simulate or fabricate artifices in the manner of Borges's *Ficciones*? "Borges's stories are ostentatiously *ficciones*, fabricated artifices, *artificios*, that everywhere show the cunning hand of the artificer" (AT, 229). We cannot know where fiction stops or starts, which is not the same as saying that everything is fiction. Even when a literary author gives the title *Ficciones* to a collection of tales, we suspect a cunning hand behind it, perhaps a deceitful hand that indicates to us the possibility that all that fiction ("The Garden of the Forking Paths," "Death and the Compass," or, earlier, "Avatars of the Tortoise") does not limit itself to being a fiction. And if it does not limit itself to being a fiction, what, then, is a fiction? What exactly does Hillis Miller do when he writes titles that include the term "fiction"? Literary criticism? Philosophy, theory, or metatheory that utilizes the literary texts for its own concerns, as Loesberg (1991) says of Derrida or de Man? Is this a false promise that destroys itself within a short time? Or is it a promise that is kept until the end, making what Miller writes literary criticism and nothing but literary criticism?

In both Plato and Aristotle (understanding these two names as *corpora* forged by the historical tradition) one finds a double vision of the work of art. On the one hand, and this is the more evident, it appears to be a passive object of study, capable of being described and/or prescribed. Aristotle begins his *Poetics*: "I propose to treat of Poetry in itself and of its various kinds, noting the essential quality of each; to inquire into the structure of the plot as requisite to a good poem; into the number and nature of the parts of which a poem is composed; and similarly into whatever else falls within the same inquiry" (Aristotle, 1951: 7; 1447a). With this opening, three clear points of delimitation are established: (1) a separation between the subject of study (poetics as subordinated to the general principles of metaphysics or the first, transparent, literal philosophy) and its object (the *poietic* activities—tragedy, epic, and so forth,

a given affirmation of "I love you." An aporia is a blind alley in a logical sequence, an impasse that forbids going any further. This is so because a situation has been reached in which two contradictory statements seem to be equally true. Ayala's love is clearly genuine. We cannot verify that it is genuine. "Aporia" comes from a Greek word that means "no passageway." Just as it is impossible to confront astronomical black holes directly, though it seems they must be there, so it is impossible to find out the reason or the basis for Ayala's loving Jonathan or for the loving of the other characters. It is therefore impossible to know for sure whether a given case of loving is genuine. The good cannot be distinguished for certain from the bad. This is the case even though the reader knows well enough that Ayala is superior to Gertrude Tringle, who changes so easily from one lover to another. That knowledge, however, is rather an unverifiable faith in the superior authenticity of one "I love you" over another than knowledge of a sort that can be demonstrated irrefutably to be true or false. This kind of uncertainty is essential in all Trollope's novels, even though making dis-

the elocutionary, the metaphorical); (2) a detachment in the heart of the subject of study itself (*peri poietikēs autēs*), given that poetics is neither rhetoric, nor ethics, nor of course first philosophy, natural theology, or metaphysics; and finally, (3) a dissociation from the object of study, given that poetry is not history, Homer has nothing to do with Empedocles, and poetry is neither flute playing nor lyre playing, neither painting nor sculpture, neither philosophy nor dialectics. To sum up, we find the reduction of the artistic object and of its metatext (each one on its own level) to simple and passive present materials of study. On the other hand, the work of art is active insofar as it has negative (Plato) or positive (Aristotle) repercussions on those who perceive it. Pretense, mimesis, yields either more pretense (and therefore is contrary to virtue, in Plato's version) or catharsis (and therefore has good psychological effects, according to Aristotle). That is to say, the work of art has performative effects on, and even beyond, the reality in which it takes place.

In keeping with the "rhapsodic" or "listening" position Miller has adopted from the very beginning, he pays greater attention to the active dimension of literature and fable. In his work, all the theoretical tools used to prescribe, describe, and typologize work are put in the service of the following inversion. His criticism is not a metatext that speaks of a text, but a text that speaks of metatextuality and paratextuality, "world" and "life" included, in order to found and/or contradict, construct and/or deconstruct them. In *Versions of Pygmalion*, for instance, Miller asks, regarding *What Maisie Knew*: "Just how is the reader to evaluate Maisie's act? Is it ethically admirable? Should we try to emulate it in our own life?" (VP, 39). A few pages earlier, he says: "A book is a dangerous object, and perhaps all books should have warning labels. Strange things happen when someone reads a book" (VP, 21). Like Plato and the moralist critics of the seventeenth century (Gracián among them), Miller is worried about the effects fiction can have beyond itself. He is conscious that in fiction something more is at stake than simple enjoyment or aesthetic pleasure. Miller is a moralist, though we shall soon see what this assertion means. A book is or can be a dangerous object. Literature, more specifically narrative, is less the patient being x-rayed in an attempt to identify what its skeleton may have in common with other skeletons than the *agent* performing the x-rays, perhaps in order to come to odd or unknown conclusions, even with regard to *what it means to be an agent*.

Why, then, would it not be possible to compare a novel and a

tinctions among different acts of loving is, as I have said, the basis of their moral code. The major ethical yardstick distinguishing the good people from the bad in his novels is ability to love in the proper way and to have the courage to stick to that love through adversity.

The impossibility of knowing about this for sure means that it is impossible to tell, after all, whether a given character's "I love you" is constative or performative. This is so because no access is possible to the pre-existing grounds that would allow us to say for certain that it is constative. A constative statement is measured by its truth of correspondence to some pre-existing fact or state of things. A performative statement brings into existence the condition it names. Nevertheless, once the statement of love is made, as when Ayala whispers to Jonathan Stubbs, "I always loved you," it seems to depend on grounds that precede it. The statement "I always loved you" seems as if it must be true or false depending on whether or not it corresponds to an external fact, just as with a statement like, "It is raining today." It is either raining or not raining. It is true or not true that

philosophical or theoretical work with regard to their epistemological and practical functions, rather than to their genres? Why not consider the "formalizing" power of a literary text more effective than that of linguistico-theoretical or philosophical attempts? According to these premises, Meredith's *The Egoist* can be considered a deconstructive monument comparable to Nietzsche's *On the Genealogy of Morals*, Lyotard's *Discourse/Figure*, or Derrida's *Of Grammatology*: "Like all great works of deconstructive critique, *The Egoist* affirms as well as dismantles. If it brilliantly demonstrates the destructive potential of false assumptions about selfhood that are basic to the Victorian ideology of gender difference, marriage, property, class relations, as well as assumptions about the aesthetics and social function of novels at that time, *The Egoist* also proposes and puts in practice alternatives" (AT, 125). De Man expressed this in his own way by affirming: "Philosophers of science like Bachelard or Wittgenstein are notoriously dependent on the aberrations of the poets" (de Man, 1979: 17). We shall find this assumption in almost all Miller's work "on" narrative. It prevents his studies from being labeled "narratological." If, as Carlos Reis and Ana Cristina M. Lopes assert, "narratology intends . . . to describe in a systematic way the codes structuring narrative, the signs those codes include, centering, therefore, . . . on the dynamics of the productivity that governs the enunciation of the narrative texts" (Reis and Lupes, 1987: 227), Miller's works on narrative place him at the antipodes of such a project. This does not mean that on many occasions he does not use narratological terminology (mainly in regard to novelistic viewpoint, for the relation between the act of narrating and the thing or event narrated), although with quite different senses from those adopted in that field of study.

Miller always projects conceptualization, wherever it may come from (psychoanalysis, linguistics, deconstruction, philosophy, etc.), "inside" literature. The term "literature" covers a wide and undecidable discursive spectrum. What seems to come from the "outside," even the deconstruction of the polar pair inside/outside, is already found beforehand in the literary "inside." For Miller, literary writing possesses something of Writing, with a capital letter, of preprogramming. When Matthew narrates the arrest of Jesus, we read that one of the men with Jesus "stretched out his hand, and drew his sword, and struck a servant of the high priest's, and smote off his ear." Then Jesus says to the aggressor: "Put up again thy sword into his place. . . . Thinkest thou that I cannot now pray to

I always loved you. Such retrospective creation or revelation of its own grounds, however, and the consequent impossibility of deciding whether or not they were already there, is just what characterizes performative utterances of a certain anomalous though common sort. I say anomalous because these speech acts break the law that says the efficacy of a performative utterance depends on a stable context of institutions, laws, and social assumptions. This context is supposed to pre-exist the performative utterance and to remain unchanged through its occurrence and after it occurs. An example of such an anomalous speech act is the United States Declaration of Independence. It declares independence in the name of the "good people" or the "one people" of the United States: "When in the course of human events it becomes necessary for one people to dissolve the political bands which have connected them with another." The Declaration of Independence speaks in the name of that people when it says it declares independence "in the Name and by Authority of the good people of these Colonies." That people, however, is created by the Declaration itself. It did

my Father, and he shall presently give me more than twelve legions of angels? But how then shall the scriptures be fulfilled, that thus it must be?" (Matthew 26: 51–54). The passage differs interestingly from variants in the other Gospels. In Mark 14: 47–49, Jesus does not reprehend the aggressor and seems to include his action within the program. The scene as presented by Matthew represents the possibility that the program can fail to be fulfilled through the interference of something unexpected. Someone can avoid Jesus's arrest by force; someone can suddenly unprogram the foreseen. We do not know for certain if the aggression is an exception to the rule or included within it. Be that as it may, Jesus' answer indicates that everything must happen according to what is said in Holy Scripture.

Similarly, Miller asserts in *Fiction and Repetition* that "the words on the page act like a genetic pattern able to program the minds of those who encounter it" (FR, 62). To put this another way, the critic—or the reader in general—coincides with the literary work not because of the "encounter" of two consciousnesses, one of them having gone toward the other, nor because of the parasitical symbiosis of someone who has got into another textual organism, but because his behavior was already prescribed as a capacity to be programmed by the work. His coincidence is a potential precoincidence, the height of identification between work and reader. Unlike the scene in the Bible, however, and unlike the programming set forth in reception aesthetics (Iser's concept of the "implied reader"), the programming Miller talks about programs a disprogramming. One must then ask, Can a disprogramming be part of a program? Can the exception be programmed? Can boustrophedonism be programmed? How does a heteroseme, a heterograph, or a heteroglyph program? If we consider that, despite being part of the program (as when the message plays to James Bond, "This message will self-destruct in three minutes"), disprogramming disintegrates the program, in what sense does the reader coincide with the text? The following chapter will turn on this point, among others, and it will require once again a contradictory reading of certain texts by Miller.

The problem of the "program" gathers together the main motives that participate in Miller's vast work on narrative: time, repetition, ethics, prosopopoeia, performativity, example, the analogy between the inside and the outside of the text, and so on. The question concerning the "program" will permit us to inquire into two basic areas: the Millerian matrix announced at the beginning of this book and the question of whether

not exist prior to the Declaration. It is a case of lifting yourself by your own bootstraps. The efficacy of the Declaration of Independence then later on allows the United States Constitution to begin with the assumption of an accomplished fact: "We the people of the United States." [17]

Ayala's "I declare that I always loved him" may be similar to the Declaration of Independence, even though Trollope's fictional world seems so alien to such complications. The Declaration creates the "people" but depends on the prior existence of the people for its efficacy and justice. Ayala's "I always loved you," spoken finally to Jonathan Stubbs, creates or reveals the antecedent fact that validates it. It is impossible to know, however, which of these two it is, creation or revelation, even though nothing could be more important. The encounter through reading of this dark spot in the general transparency and intelligibility of *Ayala's Angel*, as of Trollope's fiction generally, constitutes an encounter with the otherness I am calling a black hole. It is a black hole also in our traditional idea of literature as the unequivocal reinforcement of a single culture's assumptions. This

or not Miller writes literary criticism. The "moralism" of this critic in relation to the impact of literature on life could make us think that he is very close to Paul Ricoeur. Like Ricoeur, he is critical of structuralism and concerned about the literary work's *action* and its *saying* about-being-about-the-world. Nevertheless, the question of the "program" and everything to which it gives rise will let us identify the great distance between them. Perhaps now Miller's comment that it would be boring not to change (school, methodology, language, face) is becoming clear. Whoever reads Miller's readings of Hardy, Melville, or Borges knows Miller does not get bored, or at least he gets bored very little, when he fulfills his act of writing-reading.

black hole is an unsatisfactory and unsatisfying enigma. The need to un-
cover this secret, though it turned out over and over to be impossible to do
so, may be what drove Trollope to write novel after novel until the day he
died. It may also explain why those who love Trollope read all those novels,
which seem so similar. Each new novel gives pleasure but it also leaves a
troubling uncertainty, and so we read another novel, and yet another . . .

Narrativity, Example (Exemplarity), Endlessness, Uncontrolled Performatives

Theory Out of Place: A Strange "Literariness"

In the introduction to *Fiction and Repetition*, Miller confesses: "The focus of my readings is on the 'how' of meaning rather than on its 'what,' not 'what is the meaning?' but 'how does meaning arise from the reader's encounter with just these words on the page?' I try to attend to the threads of the tapestry of words in each case rather than simply to the picture the novel makes when viewed from a distance. This necessitates my focus on details of language in each novel" (FR, 3). If we read in detail the readings included in *Fiction and Repetition*, this is a strange assertion. I will analyze the chapter devoted to Hardy's *The Well-Beloved*, with the aim of exploring this strangeness and finding out what this quotation says. In what sense is it strange? We might infer from it a typical semiotico-formalist position, a position now out of fashion. The position seems similar to the one taken by de Man when he writes, "Literary theory can be said to come into being when the approach to literary texts is no longer based

3.

Fractal Proust

In a sense it might even be said that our failure is to form habits.
— *Walter Pater*[1]

An entire epoch of so-called literature, if not all of it, cannot survive a certain technological regime of telecommunications (in this respect the political regime is secondary). Neither can philosophy, or psychoanalysis. Or love letters . . . . Refound here the American student with whom we had coffee last Saturday, the one who was looking for a thesis subject (comparative literature). I suggested to her something on the telephone in the literature of the 20th century (and beyond), starting with, for example, the telephone lady in Proust or the figure of the American operator, and then asking the question of the effects of the most advanced telematics [*la télématique la plus avancée*] on whatever would still remain of literature. I spoke to her about microprocessors and computer terminals, she seemed somewhat disgusted [*avait l'air un peu dégouté*]. She told me that she still loved literature (me too, I answered her, *mais si, mais si*). Curious to know what she understood by this.
— *Jacques Derrida*[2]

Putting Off Death's Coming On

If the new technological regime of telecommunications means the end of literature or at least of one epoch of literature, as well as the end of philosophy, psychoanalysis, and love letters, then surely it will also be the end of literary theory and of literary criticism "as we have known them." What would this mean? Why will the World Wide Web put an end to a certain mode of literary analysis? These chapters on Trollope and Proust are implicitly an exploration of that question. I cannot give answers so

on non-linguistic, that is to say historical and aesthetic, considerations or, to put it somewhat less crudely, when the object of discussion is no longer the meaning or the value [that is, the what] but the modalities of production [that is, the how] and of reception of meaning and of value" (de Man, 1986: 7). These are strange assertions—again, I emphasize the adjective *strange*—because of their appeal to "literariness." This appeal at times is explicit, as in this advice by Miller from "Is There an Ethics of Reading?": "My recommendation is that we should give up the attempt to transfer ethical themes directly from literature to life. It would follow that departments of literature should reduce their function to a kind of linguistic hygiene, that is, to a study of the rhetoric of literature, what might be called 'literariness'" (ITER, 99).

So, is "literariness" what de Man and Miller want to study, after all? The *literaturnost'*? Do they limit themselves to repeating Eichenbaum and Jakobson? According to Eichenbaum, "the object of literary science, as such, must be the study of those specifics which distinguish it from any other material. . . . Roman Jakobson formulated this view with perfect clarity: 'The object of the science of literature is not literature, but literariness—that is, that which makes a given work a work of literature'" (Eichenbaum, 1965: 107). Does deconstructive literary criticism mean the pursuit of what, after formalism, Barthes reserved as the task of literary theory in opposition to literary criticism—that is to say, not the production of sense but the question of how the production of senses in a literary work is possible? As I have formulated these questions, they presuppose specific concepts of "repetition," of "scientific language," of "theory," of "school," and of "methodology" that one should interrogate from the beginning in a cautious and wary way. This necessity seems to me evidence of a need for another way of reading the history and the texts of "theory" and "literary criticism." Earlier, I halted at what differentiates the "linguistic moment" from formalist proposals with regard to the problem of "self-reflexivity." Now we must interrogate the differences between for-

much as reach toward answers. One way to get an answer is to try to do literary analysis and see what happens. Suppose a surfer on the Internet were to encounter Proust's *A la recherche du temps perdu* as a database for searching in ARTFL?[3] Such a Netizen, as the new word has it, such a citizen of the Net, might want to use that availability as a test case for the effect of new communications technologies on literary study. The first thing to note is that, as in the case of Trollope's *Ayala's Angel*, such a testing cannot take place without reading the text in question. Reading on the monitor screen and reading on the printed page are different, though just how they are different is not all that easy to identify. In order to use the wonderful search capabilities of an on-line text, the user has to know useful questions to ask. In order to figure out what to ask, he or she must first have read the text or at least have some knowledge of what it might be useful to ask about it. The user of the Internet must already know, to some degree, what he or she is looking for in order to avoid becoming lost on what W. B. Yeats called the Hodos Chameliontos, the path of the chameleon, on which "image call[s] up image in endless procession." Hodos Chameliontos is a good description of the user's experience of the World Wide Web if it is just "browsed" without definite purpose.[4]

The reader might expect that Marcel Proust would have an even more radical sense of the other's otherness than that of a more conventional nineteenth-century novelist like Anthony Trollope. The critic must nevertheless keep that question open. To reach an answer it will be necessary to read patiently what Proust says about the other person. This is no easy task, given the inordinate length and complexity of *A la recherche du temps perdu*. As Paul de Man observes in an early essay, Proust's novel is written as if its author or narrator were already dead.[5] Why hurry when you are dead and have all the time in the world? De Man's later essay on Proust in *Allegories of Reading* replaces that comparison with a more appropriate figure, the figure of the incessant flight of time toward a death it never reaches while there is still time to go on writing. According to either trope, it is as if Marcel had infinite time at his disposal, along with the utmost urgency, time enough to follow every digressive inspiration and to develop every metaphorical analogy, but also the urgency of the shadow of death. Anyone who reads *A la recherche* for the story is likely to become frustrated and throw the book down in disgust. The forward movement of the action is often interrupted by pages and pages of digression, analysis, and memorial annotation. Or it might be said that the concept of digression is no

malism/semiotics and deconstruction with regard to theory, reading, and narration.

Is it true that "literariness" is out of fashion or that it has reached a crisis point? If we take into account movements like reception aesthetics, textual linguistics, pragmatics, and the New Historicism, this may seem to be so. All these trends have something in common: they all propose a leap from a synchrono-system to temporal positioning, and from temporal positioning to the contextual conditions that determine, complete, or construct it. Each trend makes that leap differently; each stresses different aspects. But in the end, all recognize that "literariness" is flawed by a relativism that results from several different factors (the socio-cultural field, the reader, the strategy between text and reader, the institution, etc.).
It is common knowledge, however, that all the properties that different schools claim are constitutive of literary being (strangeness, connotation, nonreferentiality) are not exclusive to literary work. They appear in other discourses, such as jokes, movies, and common language. It is not necessary to remember what led to the crisis of "literariness." In one way or another it has happened, and that is enough. Why, then, in the 1980's and 1990's does Miller continue to insist upon the necessity of approaching literature, and literary texts, from the viewpoint of the *literaturnost*? Why is somebody for whom the borders between the verbal and nonverbal, the seme and the pictogram, the literary and the nonliterary, Hardy and Derrida, cannot be clearly delimited—even though this delimitation was the obligatory presupposition among formalists, structuralists, and some semioticians—able to announce *aloud* and shamelessly that he is asking "How does meaning arise?" or warning of the need for a "linguistic hygiene"? Might Miller, like de Man, understand "literariness" differently from the critical tradition? In order to understand his notion of "literariness," might it be necessary to enter into the heart of the paradox and contradiction in his thinking, into "this other logic" (FR, 17) mentioned by John M. Ellis in *Against Deconstruction* (1989)?

longer pertinent to a work that is all digression, all a putting off of the moment of death, an *arrêt de mort*. This accords with a parallel to the *Arabian Nights* Marcel himself develops near the end of this huge work. This is the last of the long line of references to the *Arabian Nights* that punctuates the *Recherche*. These might be usefully "accessed" through a hypertext version of the *Recherche* that would serve as a prosthetic memory, or through the ARTFL database. "The idea of death," says Marcel, "took up permanent residence within me in the way that love [*un amour*] sometimes does. . . . In my awareness of the approach of death I resembled a dying soldier, and like him too, before I died, I had something to write.[6] . . . But I should need many nights, a hundred perhaps, or even a thousand. And I should live in the anxiety of not knowing whether the master of my destiny might not prove less indulgent than the Sultan Shahriyar, whether in the morning, when I broke off my story, he would consent to a further reprieve [*voudrait bien surseoir à mon arrêt de mort*] and permit me to resume my narrative the following evening" (F 4: 619–20; E 3: 1100–1101).[7]

One example, out of many, of these digressions within the one enormous detour on the way to death is the sequence in "La prisonnière" in which Marcel, the Baron de Charlus, and Brichot are kept waiting in suspended animation on the Verdurins' threshold while Marcel tells the reader all about Charlus at this stage of his life and about many other things too. The story makes here, as in so many other places, a potentially interminable sideways and backwards movement of narration that might exasperate a reader who does not understand that the story proper of *A la recherche* is perhaps no more than the occasion for Marcel's wonderful arabesquelike ruminations (F 3: 720–30; E 3: 211–26). As Mark Calkins has observed,[8] *A la recherche du temps perdu* is a monstrous example of what the old rhetoricians called *dilatio* or *copia*, dilation or copiousness as expansion but also as delay. In this case *copia* is the endlessly dilatory production of language and more language, postponing the end. This is so whether that end is thought of as the apparent goal of the *Recherche*, Marcel's discovery of his vocation as a writer, or as the more secret and properly improper goal, Marcel's (or Proust's) death. The *Recherche* is, like the *Arabian Nights*, the occasion of a virtually endless series of wonderful stories. It is also, like the *Arabian Nights*, haunted by a death that will happen when the storytelling stops. The writing of the *Recherche* was apotropaic. It was a way of holding off death. The apparent climax of Marcel's discovery of his vocation is only a cover for that. The *Recherche* takes place not after death but in the

In *Fiction and Repetition*, before asserting that he pursues the how and not the what of the literary work, Miller declares: "This book is not a work of theory as such, but a series of readings of important nineteenth- and twentieth-century English novels. The readings are more concerned with the relation of rhetorical form to meaning than with thematic para- phrase, though of course it is impossible in practice to separate these wholly" (FR, 3). As in the preface to *The Linguistic Moment*, Miller in- sists that his essays are neither wholly theoretical nor wholly practical. They are slow, detailed, philological readings in the Nietzschean sense. How can a work or a collection of essays *that are not theoretical* propose a study of "literariness," which requires in one way or another a high de- gree of generality and, therefore, of theory? What kind of "literariness" is it whose analysis not only fails to be considered theory but asserts that "the possibility of doing literary theory, . . . is by no means to be taken for granted" (de Man, 1986: 7)? To speak of the failure of criticism to find an end to the process of interpretation, "since no movement back- ward through the woven lines of the text will reach a starting place with explanatory power to run through the whole chain" (FR, 173), is to be situated almost at the opposite extreme from the "independent science of literature which studies specifically literary material" Eichenbaum names (1965: 103). Even if we accept, following de Man, the idea that the para- digm for all texts is a figure or system of figures and their deconstruction (Miller does so, for instance, in AT, 242), we are obliged to recognize that it is a matter of drawing boundaries, rather than of a specific peculiarity of literature. Literary criticism exists within boundaries, as a discipline, as part of literary studies. Notice that the formula speaks of "texts" and not of "literary texts." This applies particularly to Miller, for whom de- construction is an intrinsic property of language considered from a verbal and pictographic viewpoint.

Why, then, should we retain the concept of "literariness" instead of substituting for it other nouns—for example, "emptiness," "gap," "ab-

brief interval between life and death, or, as Wallace Stevens puts it, "in the syllable between life / And death."[9] Stevens's word "syllable" is appropriate for the *Recherche*, since language is what makes that brief but interminable moment of delay possible. Language holds open indefinitely the instant between life and death.

I shall return later to the question of what it might mean to speak of the *Recherche* not as written from beyond death, but as written on the brink of death, in that infinitely expandable, dilating, or dilatable moment just before death, within which we all live so long as we live. At this point it may be said, however, that the usual opposition between a Marcel who puts off taking up his vocation as a writer from day to day, from month to month, and from year to year, in lazy procrastination, and the Marcel beyond the end of the *Recherche* who has found his vocation at last and is going to sit down, on the next day beyond the end of the book, to begin writing the *Recherche*, is a false one. Doing nothing and writing the endlessly unfinished and unfinishable *Recherche* amount to the same thing or are mirror images of one another. Both are forms of suspension, delaying the moment of death.

A large problem, at least for some readers, in accounting for the *Recherche* is the intervening screen of so much distinguished criticism. Confronting this might lead the critic to his or her own procrastination. Ever since its publication, Proust's great work has stood like a high mountain in the landscape of "modernism," along with the mountains named "Joyce," "Faulkner," "Mann," "Musil," and so on. One by one the masters of various critical strategies have tried to climb Mount Proust and stand in sovereignty on its summit. From work by Ramon Fernandez through Samuel Beckett, Georges Bataille, Georges Poulet, Walter Benjamin, Maurice Blanchot, Emmanuel Levinas, Gilles Deleuze, Roland Barthes, René Girard, Jean-Pierre Richard, Gérard Genette, and Paul de Man, down most recently to books by the Althusserian Marxist Michael Sprinker and by Luzius Keller (a Swiss critic of consciousness), the "philosophical reading" of Vincent Descombes, and a substantial book by Julia Kristeva, critics of many kinds have had their say about Proust, not to mention the voluminous work of those who have given their lives to specialist studies on Proust—studies textual, biographical, and formal.[10] Even Jacques Derrida, who had hardly ever before written or lectured on Proust, to my knowledge, has recently included in his seminars "Questions of Responsibilities" an exuberantly penetrating discussion of the deaths of Bergotte and Swann

sence," "abyss," or "secret," terms that are often used by Miller, de Man, and Derrida, and that seem to be more in harmony with the deconstructionist style? This retention should be a warning to those who see in deconstruction a destruction of literary studies. It indicates the necessity of severe rigor in reading texts. This rigor must necessarily pass through the text and through all the complexity it contains. Not by chance do both de Man and Miller call for "philology." To take for granted that the "context"—political, institutional, historical, economic, racial—*determines* the "text" and therefore to interpret the text from the coordinates of context involves forgetting, to paraphrase de Man, that contextual materiality should be interrogated from the linguistic viewpoint, carefully remembering all the problems of borders (Derrida has interrogated this in "Living On: Border Lines," 1979) and the performativity—political, historical, and so forth—that the text achieves. The criticism of Formalism made by Galvano della Volpe (1967: 139–55) and Trotsky (1957) (criticism that would, with variants, be repeated concerning structuralism) could make sense because in some of its most radical stages Formalism attempted to reduce the poetic text to a simple formal signifier and the methodology that analyzed it to empirical technicality. But to make such accusations of deconstruction would be an unforgivable anachronism, since from the beginning Miller (like de Man and Derrida) has consistently proposed studying the text as a force that establishes or creates history, ethics, politics, or different types of values—at least as a factor that is rhetorically linked to them.

The "literariness" Miller (or de Man) refers to is a way of circumscribing the necessary steps through the complex, sophisticated reading of a text, since without that prior attention to textual mechanisms there is no way of understanding, for instance, such nonliterary texts as Marx's *The German Ideology* or *The Communist Manifesto*. To put it another way, only by reading rhetorically can one understand any type of text. This "difficulty [of reading] may well stem from the use of such thematic terms

in relation to the themes of mortality, lying, and literature in Proust. One might imagine a more or less comprehensive seminar on twentieth-century French literary theory that would have on its syllabus exclusively works about Proust. Reading these might delay even further coming to terms with Proust, in an inadvertent mimicking by the reader of Proust's own delay.

The matter is made more complicated by the fact that Proust was himself a distinguished literary critic and theorist, though a polymorphous one. His writings contain the program for more than one kind of literary criticism that was later on institutionalized. Proust's work has been influential in the development of such diverse literary theories that it seems impossible they could all be true to their Proustian heritage. If Georges Poulet saw in Proust one origin for a criticism of consciousness, Walter Benjamin assimilated him to his theory of allegory; Paul de Man's essay on Proust is a crucial statement of the impossibility of reading, the endless failure of sign and meaning to come together in an achieved "truth"; Gérard Genette made Proust the test case for narratological analysis, and so on. Each critic makes Proust paradigmatic for his or her kind of criticism.

In this shrewd situation, it is probably best to try to go around all those intervening lesser foothills of secondary work, while keeping their contours in mind. You must read Proust for yourself. Or, according to my figure, you must climb the big mountain, on the presumption that "you cannot imagine what it is like up there unless you have been there yourself." Many strange things are found within the covers of *A la recherche du temps perdu*. Even the contradictory richness of what these great critics say hardly prepares the reader for them.

What do I find when I try to read *A la recherche du temps perdu* for myself? The fundamental generative given of the *Recherche* is the distinction between the writing Marcel and the written Marcel, along with the hidden distinction between either of these and Marcel Proust himself. This structure may be opposed to that of *Middlemarch*. In Eliot's novel the "omniscient" narrator has sovereign and equal knowledge of all the characters' interior lives. She (or "he," since the narrator may be imagined to take the masculine name and gender of Marian Evans's nom de plume, George Eliot) can move at will from one character's mind to another, taking always a global perspective, as if, according to one of the narrator's images, he (the narrator) were like the angel "Uriel watching the progress of planetary history from the sun." [11] An omniscient narrator is likely to be implicitly mas-

as 'political' or 'religious,' as if their referential status were clearly established and could be understood without regard for the rhetorical mode of
their utilization" (de Man, 1979: 246). Miller's or de Man's "literariness"
neither erases nor sets aside political, religious, institutional, or racial
problems, but emphasizes the problem of their referential status considered as something independent of the text, at the same time that, from
within the text, the limits of intratextuality are questioned. Consequently,
we do not confront some recalcitrant formalism, but an adjustment or
displacement in the viewpoint from which we must consider the relation
"text / outside the text." That is not the same thing as erasure or denial.
Derrida asserts that deconstruction "attacks not only the internal edifice,
both semantic and formal, of philosophemes, but also what one would
be wrong to assign to it as its external housing, its extrinsic conditions
of practice: the historical forms of its pedagogy, the social, economic or
political structures of this pedagogical institution. It is because deconstruction interferes with solid structures, 'material' institutions, and not
only with discourses or signifying representations, that it is always distinct
from an analysis or a 'critique' " (Derrida, 1987b: 19). From the viewpoint
of Miller or de Man, this can only be accepted after a deconstruction of
the opposition inside/outside and, above all, after the act of reading and
analysis, though this act means—and if it *does*, it is better to know it—
coming to realize the impossibility of analysis and reading.

The "literariness" Miller refers to is, precisely, a reservation concerning or contention with movements and trends that tend to avoid this
reading and analysis. A paragraph from *Illustration* (1992) referring to
"cultural studies" makes this clear:

The political aspect of cultural studies is the noblest and most attractive. Who
could oppose the righting of injustice and the enfranchising of the disenfran-
chised? Who would not be attracted by the idea that he or she is not just reading
this or that work, but furthering the cause of universal justice? The problem is
to know you are really doing that, or at least to know as much as can be known

culine, an example of paternal authority as such, even when the novel, as in this case, is written by a woman. Memory is not a problem for the narrator of *Middlemarch*. "Omniscience," for him, means not only ubiquity in space but also total recall. *Middlemarch* is written in the past tense, but it is a peculiar past tense. It is the past tense of an immediate total presence to everything all the characters once thought and felt. The omniscient narrator of *Middlemarch* (and of other Victorian novels in this mode) really is like a god: all-knowing, present everywhere at all times, granted an internal knowledge of others that he can then share with the reader.

The originating presuppositions of *A la recherche du temps perdu* are quite different. The "writing Marcel," that is, the "I" that is writing down the words we read, has no supernatural ubiquity. He has internal access through memory only to the mind and feelings, the past sensations and perceptions, of the "written Marcel," that is, of himself at earlier stages of his life. The writing Marcel has only indirect access, by way of what the written Marcel knew, to other people. Each other person is for the written Marcel, as for the characters in *Middlemarch*, a cluster of signs to be interpreted. No verification of that interpretation by way of direct access to the other person's internal consciousness is ever possible, either for the writing or for the written Marcel. This is a given of the narration, just as the narrator's "omniscience" is a given for *Middlemarch*.

Furthermore, the writing Marcel is limited in his account of the written Marcel's life to what he, the writing Marcel, can remember. Memory, even that magic affective memory resurrecting the past by linking two times together through a similarity in sensation and feeling, is, for Proust, intermittent and distorting. It is perhaps most distorting when it is beguiled by the false identities of affective memory. For Marcel, not everything is remembered, and nothing is remembered perfectly. The powers and limitations of human memory are one of the chief themes of the *Recherche*, as everyone knows, whereas memory is not a problem in *Middlemarch*. It is not a problem, at least, for the narrator, who hovers with a smiling gravity over all the times of all the characters. George Eliot's narrator has the all-knowing surveillance of a perfectly working Benthamite panopticon.

The *Recherche* has seemed to many readers structured around the copresence in every sentence of the writing Marcel's achieved wisdom and the ignorance of the written Marcel. That wisdom, however, as Paul de Man recognized,[12] is a never-achieved horizon rather than a given of the

about why you cannot know. Theoretical reflection may be essential to this—or perhaps may keep it from happening. That is the question. Since what cultural studies produce is discourse, whatever effect they have will, properly speaking, be performative, that is, a way of doing things with words. That effect will, therefore, be subject to linguistic constraints on the relation between power and knowledge in discourse. (1: 18)

This preservation of "literariness" departs from the circumscribed path of the verbal object—language, poem, tale, novel—the critic describes, in the boustrophedonic sense we suggested earlier. Miller, moreover, applies "textualist" criteria to *The Sun of Venice: Going to Sea* or *Ulysses Deriding Polyphemus*, by J. M. W. Turner. *Illustration* is a book entirely devoted to the "concrete" reading, not of a book, but of a collection of pictures and illustrations—to the hard task of reading in general. As Miller writes humorously: "De Man or Derrida make such extravagant demands on the mere act of reading a poem, a novel, or a philosophical text that it makes one tired just to think of it. Surely reading cannot be all that difficult! Or require such self-consciousness, such hesitations" (ITER, 80). To put it briefly, Miller's "literariness" does not refer to any specificity of the literary fact, much less to a cutting off of the artistic object from the "world," but to an unavoidable and ineluctable necessity, to the responsibility of the critic as against that of the man of letters, of "metalanguage" as against "language": in short, of *reading*. It is, according to all these preliminaries, a really strange *literaturnost'* (although we should not write this name in Russian any more), which keeps on leading the reader to unknown, and sometimes not very pleasant, places. (I am aware that as I write these lines Miller is preparing two or three books more.) But in those places one solves what is, according to Ortega y Gasset, a terrible spiritual need: not to be bored to death.

Reading, however, is an unknown quantity, an *x* we must find, because it is far from clear what Miller understands by *the act of reading*. I shall return later to the relation between text and context, but now it is

narration. This is true in spite of the way the narration is punctuated by a refrain asserting: "Then I thought so and so. Later on I came to know I was wrong." In the naïveté of this claim to knowledge may be glimpsed the effaced presence of a third silent figure, that of Marcel Proust himself. It would be a mistake to identify Proust the author with even the most advanced stages of what the writing Marcel says he knows. As Proust said in a letter of February 7, 1914, to Jacques Rivière: "And so I am forced to depict errors, but without feeling bound to say that I hold them to be errors. So much the worse for me if the reader believes I hold them to be the truth. [*Je suis donc forcé de peintre les erreurs, sans croire dire que je les tiens pour des erreurs; tant pis pour moi si le lecteur croit que je les tiens pour la vérité.*]"[13] Proust does not say, as might have been expected, "So much the worse for the reader." He says, "So much the worse for me." He means, I suppose, that the errors he has been forced to depict as the only way to get at the truth will be ascribed to him, and he will be falsely taken to be in error. That has certainly happened. Those errors have been taken by readers not only as Proust's truth but as a truth to which the critic can give allegiance. The long tradition of recuperative criticism of the *Recherche*, criticism that gives the work an unequivocal happy ending in an achieved wisdom and a triumphant vocation, shows that Proust was right in his foreboding. The writing Marcel has, by an almost irresistible error, been taken as the equivalent of Proust himself.

Another salient formal feature of the *Recherche* may be related to this incessant failure of the three persons ever quite to coincide. This feature is so obvious and so much taken for granted that it is difficult to reflect on its implications for meaning. *A la recherche du temps perdu* is a monster, in several senses of that word. It is a huge work, over three thousand pages long. Far from being a shapely whole, it is unfinished. It is an enormous fragment or collocation of fragments. Perhaps it was in principle unfinishable, or it may be that the contingent event of Proust's death left it incomplete. That remains to be investigated. The *Recherche* is also a monster in its transgression of traditional novelistic conventions. The reader is not surprised to learn that Proust at first had trouble getting it accepted for publication. He had to publish the first parts at his own expense. As with Joyce's *Finnegans Wake* or Musil's *The Man Without Qualities*, genre expectations are exploded because the work does not so much break generic laws as carry them to the point of hyperbole. *A la recherche du temps perdu*, like any monster, is sui generis. It is a genus unto itself. It is not

necessary to identify what the activity of reading means for Miller in relation to the problem of the program and to the inversion of the relation between literary text and critical text. To do so, we must return to the question "How does meaning arise?," which is the contrary of the question "What is the meaning?" That "how" has to do, we have been told, with rhetoric, and rhetoric, for Miller, is closely connected with a basic trope: catachresis. It also has to do with another aspect, literary *saying*, in which many lines of connection and disconnection are intermingled. Whereas the subtitle of Miller's chapter on *Tess of the d'Urbervilles* in *Fiction and Repetition* is "Repetition as Immanent Design," the chapter on *The Well-Beloved* is subtitled "The Compulsion to Stop Repeating." The "how" Miller mentions does not prevent him from writing: "All good readers of *Tess* would agree that Tess suffers and even tend to agree that she does not wholly deserve her suffering, and it is because all good readers of *Tess* share in the narrator's sympathy and pity for that suffering, that we care about the question of why Tess suffers so" (FR, 119). Confronting a novel like *Tess* or like *The Well-Beloved*, Miller cannot avoid talking about its characters as if they were real people, "seen perhaps through that glass [the narrator's language] and perhaps distorted by it" (AT, 29). If there *are* real people in a novel, though this is a reality created by prosopopoeia, then Plato is right to take fables very seriously, to the extent of wanting to watch them politically. In Augustinian terms, we would say that since the function of the novel is to pretend, to feign, to be fiction, not to be inclined to the *mendax*, the lying, but to the *fallax*, the deceitful, the novel is *real* in its own way. The contradictory *being-true* of the outward appearance (the fiction accomplished as fiction) legitimizes to a certain extent attitudes like the reader's compassion for the character. Perhaps this way of reading is unavoidable, but Miller is conscious that the being-true of fiction, for the same reason that it leads to the real, also leads to the marrow of its being-fiction. We will later move from this oxymoronic structure to a chiastic one.

fully to be explained by any of its genealogical filiations—for example, to traditional autobiography or to traditional first-person fictive narration.

How can one define and explain the *Recherche*'s monstrosity? Is it no more than the sign of self-indulgent aestheticism on the part of an effete bourgeois author who had lots of time and money? Since he could if necessary pay for publication, he could go on filling notebook after notebook without any concern for the reader's patience or for the work's "marketability." [14] Since the work has turned out to be a masterpiece of "modernism," self-indulgence can hardly be a sufficient explanation, though the reader, as he or she moves across this vast surface, like an ant across a flowerbed, may sometimes be tempted to think so.

An investigation of the *Recherche*'s writing and "final" form will help explain further the work's monstrosity. A large secondary literature has investigated in detail the making of the *Recherche*. Though the story of this making is extremely complex, its main outlines can be stated briefly. The novel was born, oddly enough, out of the explanatory narrative material introduced here and there in a work of literary theory, the unfinished *Contre Sainte-Beuve*, though the unfinished novel of the 1890's, *Jean Santeuil*, already contains germs of many episodes, characters, and themes in the *Recherche*. [15] As late as 1914 Proust, in the letter to Rivière, still thought the novel would consist of three volumes, the just-published *Swann's Way*, then two more to be entitled *The Guermantes Way* and *Time Regained*. Such a three-volume work would have had a neat, almost dialectical, symmetry: thesis, antithesis, synthesis. As time went on, however, the project got longer and longer. More and more volumes were added. The most significant fact, for my purposes here, is that the additions were interpolations, not extrapolations. More and more long narrative segments were inserted between that famous first sentence, "Longtemps, je me suis couché de bonne heure" (For a long time I used to go to bed early; F 1: 3; E 1: 3), and the final equivocal affirmations of *Time Regained*. This large-scale accretion by interpolation is matched on a smaller scale by the way parts already written were continuously and interminably expanded by the addition of new material. "The manuscript of *The Fugitive*," say the editors of the first Pléiade edition, "like all Proust's Notebooks, is swelled with additions: little strips of paper [*bequets*] added to the manuscript, small sheets folded and glued on, that tripled or quadrupled the length of the original text." [16] The handwritten notebooks were first typed. The typed version was then inordinately revised and augmented. Finally the manuscript

Miller's formula could be summed up as follows: the being-true of fiction implies that fiction is real in a double sense, that is, in the sense of being an accomplished fiction and in the sense of being a fiction that allegorically speaks of its truth as fiction. Fiction in this sense is used for foreseeing (or foreseeing and questioning at once) something of the *other truth*, the truth of philosophy or dialectics. If this is so, and fiction is *fallax* rather than *mendax*, the Augustinian formula forces Miller to move constantly between these different kinds of "truth" or, what is the same, makes him unable to confine himself to a literal, Aristotelian, or narratological reading of a narration. For this reason, some incursions into the *what* of the novel appear close to the question "How does meaning arise?" Furthermore, a title like "*The Well-Beloved*: The Compulsion to Stop Repeating" appears to assume dominion over the reader's compassion for the protagonist. This title alludes to one of the central concepts of Freud's essay *Beyond the Pleasure Principle*: the repetition compulsion. Miller explicitly refers to this concept in the essay on *Tess* when he talks about trauma: "For Freud, the first episode is sexual but not understood as such at the time. The second event is innocuous, but is experienced as a repetition of the first, liberating its traumatic effect. The trauma is neither in the first nor in the second, but in the relation between them" (FR, 136). The title as such does not sum up anything. It is a conditional response rather than a conviction, without need of the usual syntax of a condition. About the title and about the response, about the title as the response to what it itself promises as title, we could say what Derrida asserts about a passage from *Beyond the Pleasure Principle*: " 'If I were asked, then, perhaps, I might answer that . . . But what? . . . that I am no more convinced of them than I am engaging anyone else to believe them.' He does not say that he is convinced, but he does not say the opposite, he does not say that he does not believe them. And above all he does not seek to convince anyone else, to involve, to enroll, to recruit, to enlist" (Derrida, 1987: 378). We could apply Derrida's words to Miller's title be-

was set in proof. Proofs were not just corrected. In fact, Proust was careless about that. The proofs were instead monstrously augmented with new
material: "The 'additions' covered the margins of the proofs, then over-
flowed on blank pages which, pasted on slips and to one another, ended
by forming interminable strips, what Françoise [Marcel's servant in the
novel] called *paperoles*" (1st Pléiade ed., 1: xxv, my trans.). "But it is a new
book!" cried the N. R. F. editor Copeau when he confronted the returned
proofs of *A l'ombre des jeunes filles en fleurs* (ibid., 1: xxv, my trans.). Finally,
the work was printed, not at Proust's own command, but by the arbitrary
decision of the printer, who laid down the law without any authority from
Proust and without any valid evidence that the work was finished. The
printer, not Proust, said *bon à tirer* ("ready to print"). Like Balzac, Proust
was the despair of typesetters and publishers, as he is still the despair of
editors. The relative neatness and finished look of the standard Pléiade editions and of the English translation cover over a near chaos.

When Proust died on November 18, 1922, his magnum opus had only
been published through *Sodom and Gommorah II*. At his death he had only
revised *La prisonnière* up to page 73 of the third volume of the Pléiade edition of 1954. As the editor says: "Death had not permitted him to continue
that final revision [*revision sûpreme*] beyond line 3 of our page 73" (ibid., 3:
1057, my trans.). To speak of *revision suprême* is an absurdity. It was the last
only because Proust died. That long syllable between life and death finally
ended. The Sultan of Death stopped giving reprieves. As long as Proust
was alive, there could in principle have been no end to the revisions. These
took the form of insertions rather than of additions after the end. *Gonflé* is
the right word. The *Recherche* was swelled, dilated, by new interpolations
that left the overall contours more or less the same, as a balloon keeps the
same design on its surface when it is blown up to different larger sizes.

The editor of the first Pléiade edition uses a different figure to name
this structure in a note on the text in the first volume. The work, he says,
was like a tree that still has sap and therefore puts forth new branches, but
also, contradictorily, he says it is like a process of endless grafting (ibid.,
1: xxv). Which is it? If it is like a tree, then the additions are organically
connected to and similar to the parent trunk. A tree is a classic example
of a fractal in nature: "Each . . . branch, however small," says Hans Lauwerier in *Fractals: Endlessly Repeated Geometrical Figures*, "can in its turn
be considered the trunk of a complete tree, a scaled-down copy of the entire figure."[17] If the interpolations were grafted in, on the other hand, they

cause the title is not only about Freud and psychoanalysis, but also about "repetition" as a philosophical problem (for instance, not going too far afield, about Kierkegaard's repetition—as in his *Either/Or* [Kierkegaard, 1959]—which counters Hegel's memory and Schopenhauer's will) and, of course, about repetition as a linguistic and semiological problem and as a problem of the literary text (intertextuality, etc.). I speak of "repetition" without taking into account what Miller states in the introduction to *Fiction and Repetition* about the two types of repetition, about repetition in Plato, Nietzsche, Benjamin, Deleuze, Proust, Derrida. The subtitle "The Compulsion to Stop Repeating" sums up the contradictory links between the narration-fable and the philosophical problem of repetition. In the introduction to *Fiction and Repetition*, Miller does not resort to linguistic theories of repetition (Henning Brinkmann, Klaus Brinker, A. J. Greimas, Samuel Levin) but to philosophical ones, if it is possible to continue to maintain the difference: to Plato and repetition as identity and copy; to Nietzsche and repetition as difference and transformation.

The subtitles I have cited refer to a crossing in which philosophy falls back on narration, narration falls back on philosophy, and both of them fall back on com-passion and sym-pathy. *The Well-Beloved* "asks why it is impossible to stop a chain of repetitions. What is it, the novel implicitly asks, that compels Jocelyn, like the protagonists of Hardy's other novels, to repeat the pattern of a love doomed to cause suffering and dissatisfaction, even if he more or less deliberately attempts to avoid doing the same thing over and over?" (FR, 158). This question is psycho-analytic: Does Jocelyn perhaps manifest some repetitive symptoms that are the result of some psychic trauma, and does his self attempt to control the excessive tensions that are caused by such a trauma? It is philosophi-cal: Are his repetitive acts caused by a search for the ideal model? It is semiological: In that model behavior, how does Jocelyn interpret the signs that appear to him incarnate in women's bodies? It is narrative: A male artist seeks the "well-beloved" in different women of three generations

may have been from a different species and have had a different shape from the parent trunk. A lot hangs, for our concept of the overall form of *A la recherche du temps perdu*, on which figure we see as more appropriate.

The material base of the *Recherche* depended, in the particular form it took, on Proust's still living in the era of the manuscript notebook, the typed copy, the book set by linotype with proofs to correct and add to (as already in Balzac's prelinotype time). This era is already as far away from us as the steam locomotive or the paddlewheel riverboat. With a text composed on a computer, all this work of revision for the most part vanishes without a trace. I have repeatedly revised and augmented this present text here, as I am still doing right at this moment. (I leave it to the reader to figure out the referent of "right at this moment.") All trace of this long process has vanished. When a text is stored on a computer's hard disk, deletions disappear without a trace (though they can sometimes be retrieved for a time). Augmentations are not distinguishable from what was written in the first draft. This book I am now writing does not yet exist as final hard copy. It exists as ghostly invisible electro-magnetic rearrangements of the electrons on my hard disk. Such a text is not immaterial, but it has an exceedingly odd material form. As I said earlier apropos of the electronic version of *Ayala's Angel*, I call it "ghostly" or "angelic" because what I have written is not phenomenally visible as a text or indeed in any other way until it has undergone a long relay of technological transformations that turn the series of virtual o's and 1's in invisible material form on the hard disk into readable form on the monitor screen or as printed out by the printer attached to the computer.[18]

In a computer-generated text evidence of the various stages of composition tend to be permanently erased. In Proust's day, on the contrary, the various stages of composition, setting, printing, and revision left traces that are intimately connected to the historical moment of modernism, the final moment of the printed book's domination. The mode of composition and production of the *Recherche* belongs to what seems a quaint, bygone era. Today, this way of composition seems more and more archaic. Its hegemony was already, as Proust's novel testifies, being disturbed by telephone, telegraph, and cinema. The way these new means of telecommunication also destabilized the self and its relations to others is one important theme of the *Recherche*. The fact that we are rapidly entering a new era, a "new technological regime of telecommunications," means that it is perhaps easier to see what is distinctive about earlier regimes. Of course many

and finally presents a project to block up the old natural wells of his home village, called the Street of Wells, because of the risk of pollution. The act is an emblem of his wish to cut himself off from the sources of the repetition compulsion. These questions arise when the text is read, and when it is read in a particular way. The fact that the single question of repetition impinges on all those disciplinary fields does not mean that psychoanalysis, philosophy, semiology, and literature are able to take charge of the narration and to close it off, but quite the opposite. It means that none of those points of view can touch the narration, whereas the narration can touch them. The novel questions. It does not do so, of course, explicitly or methodically. In some passages, someone directly mentions an immanent will. Toward the end of the novel, Jocelyn says to Marcia: "And so the island ruled our destinies, though we were not on it. Yes—we are in hands not our own" (Hardy, 1975: 203). However, the question Miller poses remains implicit, just as when the idea of "world" or the object "world" appears under the pretense of the character's "world" in Calderón's *El Gran Teatro del Mundo* (*The Great Theater of the World*).

The question about repetition means that an action or function (in the narratological sense) is never simply an action or a function. Furthermore, we can never be sure what a given action means as such, or even if it is an action. We might ask whether, within the so-called logic of actions (Bremond, 1973), Jocelyn pursues the well-beloved according to the pattern Propp describes as the beginning of a folk tale: "A tsar gives an eagle to a hero. The eagle carries the hero away to another kingdom" (Propp, 1968: 19). Could we say quietly, according to the Greimasian proposal, that Jocelyn is the actant Subject that desires an object called the well-beloved? To say about something or about someone that it or he is an actant presupposes, in spite of the aim of formalizing grammatical functions, that there is somebody or something that acts and that fulfills a function as agent of the action. This is problematic for two reasons. First, the action of the subject can be denied by the text itself, in harmony with

people still today write in longhand and have their work typed by others, as Proust did and as did many other writers of his time, though few took or take such advantage of the possibilities of endless revision. It might nevertheless be said that Proust's way of composition anticipated before the fact the way composition on the computer makes it so easy to add and revise that no text ever seems quite finished. The difference is that in Proust we have a much more complete record of the stages of composition than will any longer be likely with texts of any kind written on the computer. It is necessary to go to much trouble and to have more vanity than most people have to save all the stages recording the composition of something written on the computer. On the other hand, it would be entirely possible to have a hypertext version of *A la recherche du temps perdu* that would contain all the successive drafts of a given passage or episode one behind the other in hyperstacks. Such an incorporation of the *Recherche* into the new "regime of telecommunications" would, to put it succinctly, turn the novel from a masterpiece of modernism into the "postmodern" masterwork it always secretly was, *avant la lettre*, thereby confounding the neat historicizing that has such power: first modernism and then postmodernism. The *Recherche* was modernist only so long as it was submitted, artificially, to the old constraints of the printed book that determined what "literature" was according to certain ideas of wholeness, completeness, and unity.

Interminable Reading

Proust made extravagent use of the opportunities for revision available to him. This caused some disquieting features of the *Recherche*. Both the standard English translation by C. K. Scott Moncrieff and Terence Kilmartin and the first French Pléiade edition of 1954 give a spurious appearance of unity and completion to the work. This is so even though both give some examples of alternate versions or of passages left out of first published versions. The new Pléaide edition of 1987 gives a much better idea of the *Recherche*'s actual state at Proust's death. The variants and drafts take up almost as much space as the main text. The reader learns, if she takes the trouble to read the "Esquisses," that a given passage in the *Recherche* is likely to exist as a long series of drafts. Many of these contain things of great interest that never made it into the "final" version—final, that is, in the sense that it is what got printed in the early editions. Reading these drafts and variants is disturbing to the traditional sense that a

the Nietzschean criticism of the "I" as identity. We have already seen that Jocelyn says, "We are in hands not our own." "The inner world, the world of the 'I,' is like the external world man has constructed for himself in the primeval joy of his artistic shaping. The inner world too, the world of 'thoughts, feelings, desires (*Gedanken, Gefühlen, Begehrungen*),' is phenomenal. It is an appearance, a fiction, a work of art," Miller writes in *Ariadne's Thread* (39). Second, the action, even when it is referred to a nonpsychological actant like those "hands not our own," is expressed in rhetorical terms (in terms, specifically, of prosopopoeia), which aim at a parabolic-allegorical dissonance difficult to control. What, exactly, would constitute an objective actant in *The Well-Beloved*? Do we hold to the literariness of words ("hands not our own") or go further, knowing that what we have before us is a rhetorical expression? And if we go further, where to?

On the basis of the evidence, we can guess where that "further" aims. The fictitious actions of the narrative evolution implicitly give rise to *theoretically* deconstructive strategies. Here, the adverb "theoretically" is italicized because the fable can be theoretical only in a certain sense. The novel does not confine itself to embodying ideas and concepts. If this were so, in what sense would it be different from a medieval or baroque allegory? In what sense would it be different from the Horatian prescription *docere-delectare*, to teach by pleasing? On the one hand, by means of the example, it would amuse us, and, on the other, it would teach us something that is sheltered in the example and overpowers it. Instead, theoretically narrative functions like a meta-metatheory whose purpose is to question the rules and theory it applies inside itself and that support it from outside. Unlike linguistic, logical, or mathematical meta-metalanguages, narrative's goal is neither to formalize its own metalanguage nor to found its conditions of possibility, but to dissolve both itself as such meta-metalanguage and, in like manner, the metalanguage, at the same time as it practices them. When one links the noun "narrative" to

literary work ought to exist in a fixed, definitive form. Even the most stable aspects of the narrative swim before the reader's eyes. The reader is told that the proper names and occupations of important characters were sometimes changeable. Charlie Morel, for example, often appears in the manuscripts for the posthumously published last volumes as Bobby Santois. He is sometimes not a violinist, but a flutist or a pianist. The list of the notebooks, manuscripts, typescripts, proofs, and paper slips glued on or floating free that make up the archive for the *Recherche* in "Le Fonds Proust de la Bibliothèque nationale" runs for twenty closely printed pages in small type in the new Pléiade edition.

The reader of that new edition may breathe a sigh of relief and say, "Now at last I have access to something like the original *Recherche* in all its monstrous, wonderful, provocative amplitude and disorder!" Alas, no. No sooner had I acquired the new Pléiade edition than I encountered, by good or bad luck, a distinguished Proust scholar, Anthony Pugh. He was one of the first to be allowed to work, years ago now, with the Proust manuscripts, typescripts, and proofs. He cheerfully informed me that the transcriptions in the new Pléiade edition, especially in the later volumes (the ones that at the moment most interest me), are often unreliable. Even if much more of the proliferating disorder of what Proust actually wrote is present in this new edition, the reader can still never be sure, for any word or sentence from one end of the text to the other, that she is reading what Proust actually wrote. The printed testimony, there on the page, may be a lying witness. The situation is a little like that of Marcel in the *Recherche* when he tries to get proof positive that Albertine does or does not indulge in lesbian practices. Whatever evidence he gets, even the most circumstantial and documentary, is always suspect. It is always open to being challenged as in one way or another not giving reliable proof. This, as I shall explain more completely later, is because such proof is a performative speech act rather than a statement verifiable by indubitable cognition.

It is a source of anxiety, at least to me, to realize that even the most authoritative scholarly printed text, such as the second Pléiade edition of the *Recherche*, has an element of performative imposition as opposed to cognitive validity. It is as if each sentence in the four big volumes were prefaced implicitly with: "Trust me. I swear the following is what Proust really wrote." To test this out would mean going back to the originals and doing the work all over again for yourself. Even then, how could you be sure you could trust the testimony of your eyes and have read the text right? As the

the adjective "meta-metatheoretical," one creates an antithesis, one that accurately names what happens. Narrative is always a wider ensemble that, by denying the logic of noncontradiction, includes in itself all possible connections that could theoretically deal with or become manifest in it. Narrative is always divided by and confronted with its other, while remaining an alterity (which always remains absolutely other) for the critic. This is not, in fact, a categorical way of distinguishing between theory and literature, for as Miller and de Man have proved, criteria similar to the ones we are applying to narrative discourses can also be applied to theoretical or philosophical discourses. What Miller finds in Hardy can also be found in Aristotle or in Kant. What de Man explored in Proust is analogous to what was explored by him in Poulet and in Lukács. This neither confuses nor differentiates theory and literature, since in each case the reader is conscious of different discursive strategies that attempt to guide the text.

This wider ensemble (or, to put it in a semiotic key, this infinite a-code), identified with literature, reveals the true strength or power of language. That power is to establish and dissolve, to limit and remove limits. Following Miller closely, this power could be described as the place where the deconstructive property of language appears in the most virulent way. This framework helps us understand Miller's words from *Ariadne's Thread* (whose program and dis-program are already inscribed, without doubt, in *Fiction and Repetition*) concerning "the impossibility of distinguishing analytical terminology, the terms the critic needs to interpret novels, from terminology used inside the novels themselves. Any novel already interprets itself. It uses within itself the same kind of language, encounters the same impasses, as are used and encountered by the critic. . . . Similar blind forks or double binds are encountered in the attempt to develop a general 'theoretical' terminology for reading prose fiction and, on the other hand, in the attempt to eschew theory, to go to the text itself and, without theoretical presuppositions, to explicate

"Note on the Text" of the first Pléiade edition asserts, "One has also to have a lot of experience with Proust's handwriting to be able to distinguish his 'a's,' his 'e's,' and his 'o's.' [In one place in *Les jeunes filles en fleur*] Proust speaks very clearly of 'a crown closed [*fermée*] by a French peer's bonnet.' All the editions read *formée* ['formed']" (1st Pléiade ed., 1: xxv, my trans.). The editor says the "o" is clearly an "e," but we have only his word for it.

The accuracy of a transcription, it can be seen, comes down to the materiality of the letter. This is the level where an "o" may be an "a" or an "e," and where these letters may be distinguished from one another only according to initial presuppositions about what Proust is likely to have written, the regularities of his stylistic habits, his usual handwriting, the surrounding words, and so on. If meaning is generated by phonemic differences that make *fermée* distinguishable from *formée*, our reading of the vowel in a given ambiguous manuscript word is determined by expectations set up by the surrounding letters and words. It all depends on initial presuppositions that may be mistaken or whose validity is forever unverifiable.

Proust, as it happens, has in a number of important passages inscribed the situation of the reader of *A la recherche du temps perdu* in the situation of the characters within the novel. The novel abounds in letters and telegrams. Examples are the two contradictory telegrams Albertine sends Marcel just before she dies in an accident, if it was really an accident. (She is thrown from her horse against a tree, but may have deliberately sought her death.) The reading or misreading of all these telegrams repeats the reader's situation in Marcel's. One passage crucial for the interpretation of what is at stake in Albertine's lies has to do with anacoluthons in her speech. She hides her possible lesbianism, while implicitly revealing it, by shifting in the middle of a sentence from the first to the third person. This shift turns what may have been the beginning of a confession into an objective statement about someone else. I say "possible" and "what may have been" in order to be faithful to Marcel's long, agonized, and unsuccessful attempt, an attempt continued even after Albertine's death, to find out for sure whether or not she is (or was) a lesbian. The point of all this section of the book is to show, as Marcel says, that "nous ne le savons pas, nous ne le saurons jamais" (one does not know, and one will never know; F 3: 653; E 3: 143). Why this is so I shall try to explain later.

In another episode Albertine stops an obscene phrase in the middle, "me faire casser. . . ." Marcel adds later on, in a sudden horrifying intu-

its meaning" (AT, 23). Certainly, the terminology is the same, but that is not the same thing as using it in exactly the same way it has been used in five hundred years of disciplinary history. Fiction and theory use the same terms in different ways. Nevertheless, "Jocelyn's series of repetitive loves embodies in his emotional life what might be called the 'theory of signs' which is presupposed in Hardy's writing" (FR, 149). If in *The Disappearance of God* words embody mental states, in *Fiction and Repetition* the amorous ups and downs of the protagonist embody a theory, specifically, a "theory of signs" (using the word "theory" with all the cautions mentioned above). What is embodied is a theory that is established and dissolved. This theory is not a critic's suspicion or unmasking (we shall see later the consequences of this for a theory of interpretation), but an inscription objectively installed in the narrative text.

When Jocelyn looks at the new moon, it is hard to close our eyes to all the marks converging in that passage. In Miller's essay, this fragmentary citation, the first quotation from Hardy's novel, appears just after the subtitle, "The Compulsion to Stop Repeating," as the first chapter epigraph: "He was subject to gigantic fantasies still. In spite of himself, the sight of the new moon, as representing one who, by her so-called inconstancy, acted up to his own idea of a migratory Well-Beloved, made him feel as if his wraith in a changed sex had suddenly looked over the horizon at him. In a crowd secretly, or in solitude boldly, he had often bowed the knee three times to this sisterly divinity on her first appearance monthly, and directed a kiss toward her shining shape" (FR, 147). After this passage from Hardy, in the second epigraph Shelley appears, via a fragment from a poem titled "To the Moon." This citation also speaks of the lunar divinity as a sister who looks at him. By means of these two quotations, the essay's opening denies its title, beheads it. Whereas the title denies the *Wiederholungzwang*, the repetition compulsion, the epigraphs affirm it. Repetition is inevitably produced. There is no way of stopping it. Jocelyn's story "is not so much, like *Tess of the d'Urbervilles*, the demon-

ition, the words *le pot*, which make the phrase a reference to anal sex ("to go and get my pot broken"). By a complex reasoning on Marcel's part, her use of this phrase is proof positive, so he briefly thinks, that Albertine is "Gomorrahan." Reading, in such cases, whether of spoken or of written words, requires an active intervention by the reader. For this hermeneutic intervention the reader must take responsibility, even though it happens spontaneously, like the flash of intuition that gives Marcel the words Albertine never actually said but may have been going to say: *le pot.*

Paul de Man's essay on Proust in *Allegories of Reading*, "Reading (Proust)," not only discusses a specific scene of reading, in both the restricted and the extended senses of the word. It is also notorious for claiming that the *Recherche* is really about "Reading," from one end to the other. De Man's essay is also notorious for asserting that "according to the laws of Proust's own statement it is forever impossible to read Reading."[19] Just what these sentences mean will take considerable reading of passages in the *Recherche* to figure out (however "unreadable" those passages may be). I shall return to de Man's assertions later. One thing they do *not* mean is the vulgar and erroneous clichés that for so-called "deconstruction" "it's all language," and that reading is a free-for-all in which the subjective bias of the reader determines the meaning that is freely read into signs.

One striking passage in *La fugitive* deals directly with reading in the most literal sense. The passage comes in the episode of Marcel's trip to Venice. This episode will be one of my main focuses here. While in Venice, Marcel receives an astonishing telegram that he reads as coming from the presumably long-dead Albertine: "My dear friend, you think me dead, forgive me, I am quite alive. I long to see you, talk about marriage [VOUS PARLER MARIAGE], when do you return? Affectionately [TENDREMENT]. Albertine" (F 4: 220; E 3: 656; Proust's French gives the telegram in full caps, as Marcel would have received it). The most amazing thing about this telegram is that Marcel thrusts it into his pocket and tries to forget about it. Far from reviving his love for Albertine, it finishes the process of his falling out of love with her. Now he no longer cares whether she is dead or alive. For him she is dead, because he has become a different person, someone who no longer loves Albertine. Marcel's reaction to the supposed telegram from Albertine is a striking confirmation of Jacques Derrida's apparently ironic or frivolous claim that the new communications technologies will put an end to love letters. You cannot, it appears, make love by telegram. A telegram that apparently contains all the right words to make

stration of an unwilled compulsion to repeat, as it is a dramatization of the futility of a more or less deliberate attempt to stop repeating and so win what Hardy in 'Wessex Heights' calls '*some* liberty' " (FR, 151; Miller's italics). Everything starts with Hardy's own text, which repeats, in the middle of a play of identity and difference, certain texts by Shelley: "*The Well-Beloved* takes from Shelley the theme of a brother-sister love, or of a narcissistic loving of oneself in the beloved. . . . Like Shelley, Hardy explores the relation of this theme to the problem of writing or the creative imagination, and to the problem of transcendent origin" (FR, 148).

In this repetition of "theme" (again the unavoidable *what* of the text), Miller, unlike Harold Bloom, does not see a subversion of Shelley's supposed Platonic "idealism": "Shelley was already as much a skeptic as Hardy, a fact which Hardy well understood" (FR, 148). This leads to an interestingly paradoxical implication. The thesis that Hardy bitingly subverts Shelley's idealism would imply that the relation between texts (historically and synchronically) is a relation between compact identities. A skeptical text opposes an idealistic text, a realistic text opposes a skeptical one. For Miller, however, the relation between texts is a relation between identities and differences, so that an idealistic and/or skeptical text reproduces in another one something equally idealist and/or skeptic. What really changes is the tactic a text uses to carry out the conscious or unconscious, voluntary or involuntary affirmation of opposites that remain forever opposite. The relation between metaphysics and nihilism does not substantially change throughout Western history, for the text of metaphysics always leads to the text of nihilism and vice versa. No age of metaphysics has not also been an age of nihilism. No age of construction has not also been an age of deconstruction. Yet the repetition in identity and difference must be both the same and not the same, if that program is not to constitute a deprogramming. In the evolution of literary works, identity is at once affirmed and denied. This is not a thesis but a wager, one with far-reaching consequences for the history of literature and com-

it a love letter kills love in its recipient and even strikes the lover, its sender, dead. Albertine is finally really dead for Marcel when he receives what he thinks is a telegram from her expressing the most tender affection. About making love by computer I shall say little. Suffice it to say that erotic relations are radically transformed when they take place in cyberspace and become virtually real rather than really real. The "really real" is suspended, interrupted, made less possible. To return to the *Recherche*: later on, just as he is leaving Venice, Marcel receives a letter from Gilberte, his first love, the woman he had loved long before he loved Albertine. This letter lets him figure out that he and the telegraph operator had completely misread the earlier telegram. It was actually from Gilberte announcing her coming marriage to Marcel's friend Robert de Saint Loup. This leads Marcel, not so much the "written Marcel" of the time of the episode as the "writing Marcel" of the time beyond the end of the book, the indeterminate "now" of the narration, to reflect on the hazards of reading at the level of deciphering the letters on the page.

How can he have gotten the letter so completely wrong? It happened by a process exactly analogous to the one that led the editors of the *Recherche* to see *formée* rather than *fermée* in Proust's manuscript scribble, or vice versa. Marcel's sudden shift from seeing the telegram as from the dead Albertine resurrected to seeing it as from Gilberte is like those shifts in perception that make us see unstable figures, such as the famous Gestaltist duck-rabbit, first as one thing and then as another, by an abrupt transformation. Marcel gives his mistake, or rather that of the telegraphist (another anacoluthon there, shifting from the first to the third person in laying the blame!), in reading "Albertine" for "Gilberte," the widest applicability to the entire human situation, even when we are not, literally speaking, "reading" at all. The fatal propensity to read any "text" of literature or of life according to an original mistake is inveterate and incurable:

All of a sudden I felt in my brain a fact, which was installed there in the guise of a memory, leave its place and surrender it to another fact. The telegram that I had received a few days earlier, and had supposed to be from Albertine, was from Gilberte. As the somewhat labored originality of Gilberte's handwriting consisted chiefly, when she wrote a line, in introducing into the line above it the strokes of her *t*'s which appeared to be underlining the words, or the dots over her *i*'s which appeared to be punctuating the sentence above them, and on the other hand in interspersing the line below with the tails and flourishes [*les queues et arabesques*] of the words immediately above, it was quite natural that the clerk who

parative literature. Recently, Pierre Brunel and Yves Chevrel wrote about comparatism: "Literary studies lead straightway to the texts. Now, a text is not always pure. It gives rise to foreign elements" (Brunel and Chevrel, 1989: 29). Actually, a text does not give rise to foreign elements. A text is always made of foreignness, and the foreignness begins with the impossibility of distinguishing between what is the text itself and what is alien. Though it is possible to identify in practice the features of an author (which indeed call for a re-cognition), those features do not constitute themselves except by starting from the other they bring with themselves. It would follow that a text has neither a beginning nor an end.

This last assertion is profoundly anti-Aristotelian, since it implicitly denies that: "Tragedy [or any literary work] is an imitation of an action that is complete, and whole, and of a certain magnitude. . . . A whole is that which has a beginning, a middle, and an end" (1450b; Aristotle, 1951: 31). When Aristotle defines poetry not according to its technical aspect but as the imitation of an action, he is establishing the basis of a certain contradiction: "People do, indeed, add the word 'maker' or 'poet' to the name of the meter, and speak of elegiac poets, or epic (that is, hexameter) poets, as if it were not the imitation that makes the poet, but the verse that entitles them all indiscriminately to the name. Even when a treatise on medicine or natural science is brought out in verse, the name of poet is by custom given to the author; and yet Homer and Empedocles have nothing in common but the meter, so that it would be right to call the one poet, the other physicist rather than poet" (1447b; Aristotle, 1951: 9). From a technical point of view—the line, the rhyme, the black letters on the white paper—one can consider that a work has a beginning, a middle, and an end, although from the viewpoint of the story line this division is not possible. In *Oedipus the King*, it is obvious that the fundamental action (Oedipus's assassination of his father, Oedipus's marriage to his mother and the engendering of sons-brothers and daughters-sisters) has already taken place. The action has already begun somewhere else by

dispatched the telegram should have read the loops of *s*'s or *y*'s in the line above as an "-ine" attached to the word "Gilberte." The dot over the *i* of Gilberte had climbed up to make a full stop [*point de suspension*]. As for her capital *G*, it resembled a Gothic *A*. The fact that, in addition to this, two or three words had been misread [*mal lus*], had dovetailed into one another (some of them indeed had seemed to me incomprehensible), was sufficient to explain the details of my error and was not even necessary. (F 4: 234–35; E 3: 671)

As the reader can see, it all comes down to the level of the word or rather to the materiality of the letter within the word. All meaning depends on some material substratum for its existence and transmission. This is as true of digitized as of printed texts, of spoken as of written language, since spoken language is not transmitted through a vacuum but as modulations of air, and a digitized text, however "angelic," must have some material base through all its transformations. As Proust intimates, all other sign systems must also have a material base: for example, our reading of another person's inner thoughts and character by means of gesture or facial expression. This might be phrased by saying that there is no such thing as direct testimony of meaning. Meaning must always be mediated by some technical means of transcription, whether that be handwriting, a printed text, or, more recently, such advanced communication technologies as telephone, telegraph, video, television, computer monitor, or laser printer attached to a computer. None of these, even the most apparently immediate, gives the "reader" direct access to meaning or truth, though each imposes its own matrix of possibility and expectation. The generation of meaning depends, therefore, on our faith that we have the correct key to an accurate reading. All of these testimonies to meaning are indirect. This is as true of the video of Rodney King being beaten as of any transcription by printed word or tape recording of an eye-witness account. It is true also of the Pléiade edition of Proust's *Recherche*, or of its transcription into the ARTFL electronic archive. In all these cases the record is mediated by some technical means. It consequently must be read according to some set of initial presuppositions about these, even though these presuppositions may differ from one technological means of recording to another. What the reader makes of the text always comes down to what she makes of those little marks on the manuscript, the printed page, or on the computer screen. Is it an *a*, an *o*, or an *e*?

Proust's (or Marcel's) account of this process is contradictory, as is the vocabulary for describing the act of reading throughout the *Recherche*.

the time Oedipus leaves the palace and addresses a group of citizens with these words:

> Children, young sons and daughters of old Cadmus,
> why do you sit here with your suppliant crowns?
> The town is heavy with a mingled burden
> of sounds and smells, of groans and hymns and incense.
>
> *(Sophocles, 1973: 11)*

The beginning is not really a beginning but one link in a chain that began previously and that gives rise to other actions. The beginning is a middle situated at an uncertain place on a chain that has neither beginning nor end. Likewise, when the chorus recites

> You that live in my ancestral Thebes, behold this Oedipus,—
> him who knew the famous riddles and was a man most masterful;
> not a citizen who did not look with envy on his lot—
> see him now and see the breakers of misfortune swallow him!
> Look upon that last day always. Count no mortal happy till
> he has passed the final limit of his life secure from pain.
>
> *(Sophocles, 1973: 76)*

this end is not an end, since we know that the collection of misfortunes, and therefore the action, continues in a small village of Attica (specifically, in *Oedipus at Colonus*). The end of *Oedipus The King* is another middle. But is it possible to keep talking about "middle" when there is neither "beginning" nor "end"?

The denial of the compact structure of beginning-middle-end (a denial thematized, intentionally, in many twentieth-century novels) can be situated on a level distinct from that of the action and characters. Clearly neither Jocelyn, nor Avice Caro, nor Marcia appears as such in Shelley. Nor do they appear in the work of subsequent authors. The denial of the beginning-middle-end structure can be located, rather, in the field of the characters' or narrator's attitudes, as well as in the themes of

The contradiction lies in how the account hovers between epistemologi-cal, cognitive language, a language of truth and lie, error and correctness, on the one hand, and, on the other hand, the language of performative speech acts. Proust's words in the passage I have quoted make it sound as if mistakes in reading could be corrected by a recognition of what the text "really says," just as the Pléiade editor says the word Proust wrote was "very clearly" *fermée*: "The telegram that I had received a few days earlier, and had supposed to be from Albertine, was from Gilberte." Nevertheless, distinctly present behind this reassuring theory of reading as often in error but in principle corrigible by a verifiable reading is another possibility. According to this other possibility, Proust's words "error" and "mistake" are not to be opposed to a "true reading" or to a "correct initial hypothesis." They name rather the way any reading requires an initial performative leap on the basis of unwarranted and unwarrantable presuppositions. These are not the result of some corrigible or incorrigible subjective bias, but follow from the reader's necessary prior incorporation in some system of reading or other, each of which has its own complex horizon of expectations. We can call such reading expectations "ideological," even though the literary criticism of a given historical period, for example, is conspicuously rami-fied and nontotalizable. That is true of ideology in general. Ideology is always heterogeneous to itself. Such fissures, cracks, and inconsistencies are a regular feature of ideologies, one evidence that they are what they are. A change in the regime of telecommunications, such as we are going through now, is almost certain to change the ideological assumptions about mean-ing that will determine the way we read. That is what Derrida means by saying literature will not survive such a change as is taking place now with ever-accelerating rapidity, a change that was already happening by way of telephone and telegraph in Proust's day.

Each one of that long line of distinguished critics of Proust, from Fernandez and Beckett down through Poulet and Richard to Barthes, Ge-nette, de Man, and Kristeva, reads Proust according to some set of initial presumptions. Without such assumptions, what Marcel calls "an initial error" or "an original mistake in our premises," it is impossible to read at all. The alternative to an original mistake is not an original correct pre-supposition but another, different original mistake, since "mistake" names not a corrigible error but the necessary blind leap into a text to make sense of it. It is impossible to get out of this situation. It is impossible to read

the novel, which come, not necessarily from another novel, but from a distinct semiotic system, whether that be, for example, a collection of works different in genre, a single poem, or social reality itself understood as text (as in Bakhtin, 1968, 1981, 1984b). Bakhtin sees the birth of the novel in an assimilation of the carnivalesque festivals of the Middle Ages, among other things. *The Well-Beloved* makes explicit this semiotic dimension of repetition: "The similarity to Shelley is scarcely surprising in a novel which not only draws its epigraph from *The Revolt of Islam* but also contains citations of *Prometheus Unbound* and *Epipsychidion*, as well as another quotation from *The Revolt of Islam*. Hardy's work is steeped in echoes of Shelley. *The Well-Beloved* is so much under the aegis of Shelley that it might be defined as a parody of him, or as an interpretation of his work, or as a subterranean battle to combat his influence" (FR, 148). The "theme" not only reproduces itself, but also inscribes in itself everything that tangentially or directly touches it. An example is the references to the moon. It is impossible to close our eyes to the multiple possible inscriptions contained in the allegorical element here, its being legible as allegorical of *x*. Consciousness "sees in the moon a sisterly image of itself. The moon's inconstancy is the reflex of the beholder's" (FR, 147). This mirroring makes the moon masculine as well as feminine, and thus is like the way it was interpreted in Egyptian mythology: as masculine element, divine star considered to be Ra's and Horus's left eye, representing the symbol of rejuvenation and renovation.

Jocelyn kneels before the moon and sends her a kiss, since he sees in her a sister or brother. Is this a sister or brother of rejuvenation and renovation? Toward the end of the novel's second part, in the chapter "A Grille descends between," we witness the following dialogue between the second Avice and Jocelyn:

> "Yes, I would, sir [be married to him]."
> "What! You would? You said you wouldn't not long ago."
> "I like you better now! I like you more and more!"

without unverifiable assumptions that are not just personal but also cultural and ideological. This may be one of the things, though not the only thing, as I shall show, de Man means when he says it is impossible to read Reading. Reading is a spontaneous performative event, not a passive cognitive activity. It is made possible by an implicit speech act that says "I declare this word is 'Albertine,' " but could just as well have said, "I declare the word is 'Gilberte,' " and then could return back to "Albertine" again, in an unstillable oscillation between duck and rabbit. This is what Marcel means when he says reading is a matter of guesswork and creative "reading into," though he still uses the terms "mistake" and "error," which would allow another way of reading what he says (duck for rabbit again), this time a reading governed by the possibility of definitively correcting the "mistake":

How many letters are actually read into a word by a careless person who knows what to expect [*une personne distraite et surtout prévenue*], who sets out with the idea that the message [*la lettre*] is from a certain person? How many words in the sentence? We guess as we read, we create; everything starts from an initial error; those that follow (and this applies not only to the reading of letters and telegrams, not only to all reading), extraordinary as they may appear to a person who has not begun at the same starting-point, are all quite natural. A large part of what we believe to be true (and this applies even to our final conclusions) with an obstinacy equalled only by our good faith, springs from an original mistake in our premises [*d'une première méprise sur les prémisses*]. (F 4: 235; E 3: 671)

Reading, according to Marcel, is not a verifiable epistemological activity. It is a matter of faith and belief. Reading is a speech act in the sense that every reading is implicitly prefaced by the statement, "I believe this to be true," or "I posit the following protocols of reading." Like all leaps of faith, reading is ultimately unverifiable, nor can it easily be proved to be wrong. Marcel not only emphasizes the way a reading is necessarily founded on initial premises that are always in error: "We guess as we read, we create; everything starts from an initial error." He also stresses the way this initial mistake leads "quite naturally" and inevitably to a long chain of further mistakes. He emphasizes in addition the obstinacy with which we stick to the initial error and follow out all its apparently natural and correct consequences even to the limit of the final conclusions we draw. Reading in this too is like ideology. It is exceedingly difficult if not impossible to talk someone out of his or her error. We are obstinate because of the naive good faith in which we believe that the reading our initial error leads to

Pierston sighed, for emotionally he was not much older than she. . . .
When was it to end—this curse of his heart not ageing while his frame moved
naturally onward? Perhaps only with life." (Hardy, 1975: 139–40)

Hardy—why not call this an intersection of writings?—reads the Egyptian tradition ironically. Heart and emotion are rejuvenated and renewed, but inside a body that gets older and older. The contrast between the soul and the body gives rise to the tragic or to the ridiculous, since there is no Tot who, with his saliva, could attach a youthful body to Jocelyn's young heart, as happens in the Egyptian myth. The narrator also emphasizes physical aging in describing the once-beautiful Marcia after she removes "beautifying artifices": "The cruel morning rays—as with Jocelyn under Avice's scrutiny—showed in their full bareness, unenriched by addition, undisguised by the arts of colour and shade, the thin remains of what had once been Marcia's majestic bloom. She stood the image and superscription of Age—an old woman, pale and shriveled, her forehead ploughed, her cheek hollow, her hair white as snow" (Hardy, 1975: 201). Hardy's moon, Jocelyn's moon, the moon of their evolution and history, is more in harmony with the Tartessian tradition, that of the earliest culture in Andalusia, which Lorca resumes and in which the moon represents death, in a religion whose gods are immanent within nature and in which to die is as natural and desirable as to be born. "Before but the relic of the Well-Beloved, she had now become its empty shrine" (Hardy, 1975: 153), notes the narrator, echoing Jocelyn's feelings.

If, as Miller says, "*The Well-Beloved* takes from Shelley the theme of a brother-sister love, or of a narcissistic loving of oneself in the beloved," it is necessary to recognize that the chain not only goes analeptically (toward and away from Shelley) but also proleptically; the past not only becomes present, but the present takes place in the future. An example of this constant prolongation is offered by Proust: "Marcel Proust, with his characteristic brilliance as a critic, recognized the importance of *The Well-Beloved*. He saw that it is exemplary of the repetitive symmetries of

is a correct one. It is founded, we think, not on error but on an accurate perception of what is actually said by the marks on the telegram, on the written or printed page, or on the computer screen, on the video tape— on any material witness of meaning. We say, "It is a duck, not a rabbit; an *e* not an *o*." Everything follows from that, by an implacable law imposing on us a logically consistent reading as the price of sanity.

Self-Similarity of the Second Kind

This disquieting assumption about reading applies also to my reading or to any other reading of the *Recherche*. Moreover, it can be demonstrated that this assumption pervades the *Recherche* in one form or another from beginning to end. In the light of this concept of reading, can one say anything further of the overall form of *A la recherche du temps perdu* as we have it now? The *Recherche* is a text with a definite beginning and ending set in place quite early in the process of composition. Between these two limits stretches a line of words that could be ceaselessly augmented by further interpolations going all the way from a single word to the addition of whole blocks of narrative not envisioned in the initial plan. The reader's assumptions about form will determine the validity or invalidity of the synecdochic procedures that are a necessary recourse when writing about any work of literature, but especially about one as inordinately long as *A la recherche du temps perdu*. Any discussion of this immense novel must make the part stand for the whole.

The form of the *Recherche*, I claim, may be understood by analogy with the graphing of fractals, discussed already in relation to Proust at the beginning of this book. A fractal is a simple formula that can be represented geometrically, though in a paradoxical or non-Euclidean form. The formula can, that is, be used to generate a spatial design, when numbers are chosen to fill in the various parameters and it is graphed iteratively. These spatial designs have peculiar properties. The Pléiade editor's figure of the tree that still has sap and can put forth new branches is one such natural fractal design. The well-known Mandelbrot set, as it exists, for example, in a familiar computer screensaver, is more useful for my purposes. The chief peculiarity of fractals, as I said in the discussion of Proust's image of France as a polygon filled to the borders with tiny polygons each repeating the design of the whole, is their property of "self-similarity." This means that smaller and smaller parts of the whole repeat the pattern of

Hardy's work as a whole, and he saw also the way it can be seen as a clue to the meaning of those symmetries. Proust's reading of Hardy comes in the passage in 'La prisonnière' in which Marcel explains to Albertine his notion that a great writer or artist, a Vermeer, Stendhal, Dostoevsky, or Hardy, creates the same work over and over throughout his life" (FR, 152). As we can see, the chain reaches not only to Proust but to all the authors mentioned (even beyond them—for example, to the unfortunate relation of narcissistic love between Quentin and Caddy, brother and sister, that Faulkner narrates in *The Sound and the Fury*). Not only does each creator write or paint the same thing throughout his or her life, but, as Marcel explains to Albertine, speaking of Vermeer's paintings: "You must have realized that they're fragments of an identical world, that it's always, however great the genius with which they have been recreated, the same table, the same carpet, the same woman, the same novel and unique beauty, an enigma at that period in which nothing resembles or explains it, if one doesn't try to relate it all through subject matter but to isolate the distinctive impression produced by the colour" (Proust, 1982: 384).

The most peculiar thing about literature is a feature of the signifier's materiality. As material traces, according to Derrida, signifiers can have neither origin nor end. They are part of an endless chain leading backward and forward in time. Since literature, too, is made of material traces, letters on the page, this means that fable, mimesis, and imagination, as types or aspects of literature, also cannot have identifiable origins or ends. This means that it is impossible to depart from an *infinite remaining in the middle*. Here "middle" does not point to one part of a triad that also contains "beginning" and "end," but indicates at once the impossibility of a beginning and an end and a middle that includes and enables them. The middle, as we have seen, constitutes the condition of possibility of beginnings and ends. If the sentence "A person who differed from the local wayfarers was climbing the steep road which leads through the sea-skirted townlet definable as the Street of Wells" (Hardy, 1975: 28), with

the whole, down to the infinitely small. "A fractal," says Lauwerier, "is a geometrical figure in which an identical motif repeats itself on an ever diminishing scale."[20] Even unimaginably small parts of the whole still repeat the pattern of the whole.

Strictly speaking, "similarity" means an exact repetition of a pattern at a different scale, as geometers say two triangles are "similar" if they have the same angles at their three corners but sides of different lengths. In the case of the most interesting fractals, however, an aleatory element has been introduced into the formula. In this case, the smaller part repeats the pattern of the whole, but with a difference. Surprising discontinuities and unpredictabilities appear, which link fractal geometry with chaos theory. I spoke earlier of the way my 420 feet of the Maine coast repeat the pattern of the whole coast. This self-similarity is, however, a statistical or stochastic one. "In reality," says Lauwerier, "coastlines are created by the whims of nature; chance is at work in this creative process. If we interpret self-similarity not in the exact sense, but statistically, we get more realistic fractals. [He means they look like natural forms: a tree, a shoreline, a landscape.] To do this we require each part of the fractal to have the same statistical properties of form" (104). Lauwerier goes on, in a chapter called "Chance in Fractals," to show how stochastic fractals can be generated by so-called "Monte Carlo methods," which modify fractals "by a kind of controlled randomness" (104). This controlled randomness, as Lauwerier shows, is related to what is called "deterministic chaos." In the case of a sequence of random numbers, "Everything is fixed by the choice of the first number. So the sequence is deterministic, but it gives the impression of being chaotic" (106). A fractal incorporating "deterministic chaos" into the formula it graphs will involve both a high degree of statistical self-similarity and also a high degree of unpredictability and discontinuity. A tiny difference introduced into the numbers setting the parameters of the generating formula will sometimes produce large unexpected differences in the resulting geometrical figure when it is graphed on a computer screen. The graph of any given fractal will have unexpected and unpredictable irregularities. "Self-similarity," at ever reducing scales stretching down toward infinity, but of course never reaching it, "statistical similarity," "chance," "deterministic chaos"—these are the key concepts necessary to define fractals. I shall now identify more exactly the pertinence and the limitations of fractals for understanding *A la recherche du temps perdu.*

The *Recherche* is like a fractal in another way than in possessing an

which *The Well-Beloved* starts, is the beginning of this novel, that results from its placement in the middle in relation to Shelley, Proust, and
so forth. This quality of being in the middle prevents us from thinking
about comparative literature as "comparison" between compact, unitary texts organized according to the three stages of beginning, middle,
and end.

Regarding this point, another aspect of Miller's essay powerfully at-
tracts our attention. If, according to Bakhtin, one of the semiotic systems
at the root of the modern novel is the carnivalesque festival, a system of
lived organization and social play assimilated by the verbality of the novel,
Miller insists now upon the same relation in the opposite direction. If at
the start a verbal textual system assimilates a vital textual system, at the
end a verbal textual system provokes (and has effects on) a vital textual
system. Not only is *The Well-Beloved* extended by *A la recherche du temps
perdu* (in the same way as *The Well-Beloved* builds upon Shelley's *The
Revolt of Islam*), but that development is carried out by a vital textual system, that of Proust. This expression "vital *textual* system" echoes Derrida's
assertion concerning Rousseau in *Of Grammatology*: "In what one calls
the real life of these existences 'of flesh and bone,' beyond and behind
what one believes can be circumscribed as Rousseau's text, there has never
been anything but writing" (Derrida, 1976: 159). As Miller notes, the
bringing together of the mother, daughter, and granddaughter (Odette,
Gilberte, and Mlle de Saint-Loup) in Proust's novel reflects the previous
meeting of the three Avices (the mother, daughter, and granddaughter) in
Hardy's novel, although Proust is at the same time fictionalizing a similar
unification in his own life:

No doubt, for example, Proust would have written *A la recherche du temps perdu*
if he had never read *The Well-Beloved* (which he did in 1910), but his novel would
not have been quite the same, nor perhaps would his life have been the same.
The great scene of the Princess de Guermantes' matinée at the end of Proust's
novel brings together in Odette, Gilberte, and Mlle de Saint-Loup the mother,
daughter, and granddaughter whom Marcel has loved or may yet love. Gilberte

ambiguous self-similarity at different scales. On the one hand, a fractal is generated by the graphing, on x and y axes, of a relatively simple formula that yields an iteration when numbers are put in place of the placeholders a and b. The iteration extends in principle down to infinity, so that there are "innumerably," as the mathematicians say, smaller and smaller versions of the large pattern. That is why the visual graphing is ambiguous. The finer details can never be completely shown. A fractal is attracted, so to speak, by an infinity it can never reach, but each fractal has its own infinity. This infinity is defined by the possibility of drawing ever smaller and smaller stochastically similar versions of a given pattern, ad infinitum. Infinity is infinity, but there appear to be innumerable ways to approach closer and closer to it. In that sense, at least, it may be said that infinity is multiple, "others" rather than "other." To put this another way, each asymptotic structure may have its own infinity. Since infinity is by definition unknown and unknowable, it would be impossible to be sure whether it is always "the same" infinity that is approached by different routes. It may be or it may not be. If a fractal is one way to approach infinity without ever reaching it, *A la recherche du temps perdu* may be another. Each, however, may reach out toward its own private infinity. In one sense a fractal is a spatial pattern fixed there on the computer screen. In another sense it is temporalized by being an iteration, an operation repeated over and over through time. A fractal is a temporal series governed by its infinitely delayed approach to infinity. The computer image arbitrarily stops the iteration at a certain point.

Something similar (no doubt stochastically similar) can be said of the *Recherche*. As its name suggests, it is a search, a research, a reiterated effort carried on through time to recover lost time. This research is governed, however, not just by the retrospective attempt through affective memory and the power of writing to recover as much as possible of lost time. As the *Recherche* itself makes abundantly clear, it is also governed by its prospective attempt to reach a goal in the future. This goal may be defined as the converging point of three imaginary personages, the written Marcel (the Marcel then, who had all these thoughts and experiences), the writing Marcel (the Marcel now, who is writing these experiences down and so is engaged in a *recherche* to recover lost time), and the author Marcel Proust (who has effaced himself behind his allegorical representative, the writing Marcel). The future goal of the *Recherche* is the converging point where the truth of the written Marcel's experiences is fully recuperated by

offers to introduce her daughter to Marcel, just as the second Avice introduces
her daughter, the third Avice, to Jocelyn. . . . Moreover, the real Marcel Proust
loved both Mme Arman de Caillavet and, later, her daughter. He wrote, probably in 1910, the year he read *The Well-Beloved*, a witty, impertinent letter to the
mother about his love for the daughter. . . . Both Proust's life and his novel seem
to have been intermittently taken possession of by patterns from Hardy. (FR,
172–73)

In this quotation, Miller points to the phenomenon of a repetition without beginning and end that hurtles in several directions. Naturally, remaining in the middle implies repetition, and repetition implies
analogy and contamination. "It is as though Proust had become willy-
nilly subject to a compulsion to repeat like that of Jocelyn, like that of the
narrator of *The Well-Beloved*, or like that of Hardy himself" (FR, 173). The
Millerian matrix appears again, this time formulated in terms, not of an
identification between consciousnesses (the critic and the author), but of
an analogy between textual mechanisms, both verbal (or pictographic)
and vital. Miller here does not talk about a critic who goes to meet an author, but about a reader-author-critic who finds himself impelled by the
text he reads. We witness the contact between two textual mechanisms
distant from one another and start to enter into the question of the performativity of literature, that is to say, of its active role. On the one hand,
literature does not limit itself to being a passive object to be contemplated
or studied, but has the ability to engender history, that is to say, more
writing, whatever its type. On the other hand, the effects of analogy are
a mixture of participation and nonknowledge of what is going to happen
as a result of the very fact of participating. Graziano Ripanti, speaking
of analogy, comments that when an object cannot be known directly it
can be indirectly known by means of another known object with which
it maintains some relations (Ripanti, 1984: 49). In other words, the problem of the "contact" between critical text and literary text, like Keats's

the writing Marcel at some point prior to the hour of his death. This point can never be reached. Another name for it is the black hole of death. The highest consciousness of truth will only be reached beyond the absolute loss of consciousness in death. Death is another name for the infinity that draws the *Recherche* from a prospective horizon. Paul de Man says this in his own way in the admirable concluding sentences of "Reading (Proust)." His formulation is made apropos of the phrase "plus tard, j'ai compris" (later on I understood). That phrase punctuates the *Recherche* as a claim that the writing Marcel came eventually to understand all those truths that were hidden from the written Marcel. Here is what de Man says:

This formulation, "plus tard, j'ai compris," is very familiar to readers of the *Recherche*, for it punctuates the entire novel like an incantation. Literary criticism has traditionally interpreted this "later on" as the moment of fulfillment of the literary and aesthetic vocation, the passage from experience to writing in the convergence of the narrator Marcel with the author Proust. In fact, the unbridgeable distance between the narrator, allegorical and therefore obliterating figure for the author, and Proust is that the former can believe that this "later on" could ever be located in his own past. Marcel is never as far away from Proust as when the latter has him say: "Happy are those who have encountered truth before death and for whom, however close it may be, the hour of truth has rung before the hour of death." As a writer, Proust is the one who knows that the hour of truth, like the hour of death, never arrives on time, since what we call time is precisely truth's inability to coincide with itself. *A la recherche du temps perdu* narrates the flight of meaning, but this does not prevent its own meaning from being, incessantly, in flight.[21]

This passage raises many questions for the thoughtful reader. Just why is an allegorical figure "obliterating"? Just why is it that we can never know the truth before the hour of our death? Why is it that what we call death is another name for the convergence at an unattainable infinity of truth and the consciousness of truth? What kind of truth is it that de Man and, it may be, Proust have in mind, a truth that can never coincide with itself? Just what does this have to do with time, a time which is always "out of joint," as Hamlet says, a time in which the most important event never arrives on time, but always too late or too early? What would it mean if truth were to coincide with itself? Does not truth always coincide with itself, in a kind of tautological circularity or superimposition: "The truth is what is true," or "What is true is the truth." "The truth is the truth is the truth." Why does de Man say "what we call time is" rather than just

negative capability, is an undecidable that gathers yet does not merge identification-knowledge and being in doubt. Miller aims in the same direction in this essay: by remaining in the middle, reading the text mixes the knowledge (the locutive-constative level of discourse) that results from contact with the text and its effect, and nonknowledge and doubt (the illocutive-performative level of discourse) as to what will happen as a result of that knowledge.

In fact, what will happen when Proust yields to the compulsion to repeat acts of Jocelyn, the narrator, or Hardy must remain a question mark. Marcel's object of analysis in *The Captive* (a very subtle analysis, indeed, as subtle as a deconstructive suspicion performed by a super-erudite Archie Bunker, but also a super-irritated one, irritated by irony and the irreconcilable splitting of language) is Albertine's lies: "But I knew beforehand that her answers would be fresh lies" (Proust, 1982: 178). This evasiveness he terms the "being-fugacious" of this woman. Her fugacity drives both his loving jealousy toward her and its reverse, his coldness and murderous instincts. Marcel constantly talks about abandoning Albertine and leaving for Venice, as well as about her "disappearance." He says to her: " 'I beg of you, my darling girl, no more of that trick riding you were practising the other day. Just think, Albertine, if you were to have an accident!' Of course I did not wish her any harm. But how delighted I should have been if, with her horses, she had taken it into her head to ride off somewhere, wherever she chose, and never come back to my house again" (Proust, 1982: 116). Albertine is ultimately killed in a fall from her horse, in fulfillment of the wish Marcel denies. In this way Marcel repeats the narcissistic love Jocelyn feels toward the different Avices or, apparently, at the start of the novel, toward Marcia. The objects of Jocelyn's analyses are not the actions or acts of the beloved women, but something that is beyond them, something that is really in himself. In fact, Jocelyn is blind, for he does not see the corporeal evidence, the signs that successively appear to him. The result is that he himself is the one who

"time is"? Could it be because the word "time" is, like the word "death," or the word "truth," or the word "meaning," a performative catachresis imposed on something unknown and unknowable, something, like "infinity," wholly and irremediably other? Whether or not this is the case for Proust, or rather for the text he wrote, can only be determined by actually reading the *Recherche*, segment by segment, a virtually endless task. It can be seen now, however, that only the hypothesis of a wholly other would make it plausible to speak of meaning as being perpetually in flight. That flight of meaning would include the meaning of the work that narrates the flight of meaning. If "death," "truth," "time," "meaning" are names we give to an unknowable other, then that other, like the infinity toward which a fractal moves without ever being able to reach it, would be the unattainable horizon of the potentially unending iterations that make up the *Recherche*.

Far from taking place within the endless leisure of death, as de Man asserts about the *Recherche* in that earlier essay, Proust's novel takes place in time. What Proust calls time, however, is defined as the agonizing failure of truth ever to coincide with itself. The cleft within which truth fails to coincide with itself is figured in the unbridgeable gap between Proust and Marcel, between the invisible author and his obliterating allegorical figure. To put this another way, that fissure is the narrowing space between the hour of death and the forever postponed hour of truth that never comes on time, in an incessant fleeing away of a meaning that we nevertheless continually approach. This painful movement in place is not at all like the endless leisure of the dead. It is more like something de Man elsewhere uses as a figure to define the flight of meaning: the experience of being caught in a revolving door.[22] Witnessing the endless iterations of a fractal on ever-reducing scales that lead only to new versions with a difference of where we were at larger scales is also something like being caught in a revolving door. This similarity returns me to the initial image for the *Recherche* in my title: "Fractal Proust." Reading Proust is something like watching the sequence of randomly chosen blowups of ever smaller and smaller segments of the Mandelbrot fractal on the computer screen in the After Dark screensaver.

What relevance, if any, does understanding fractals have to understanding *A la recherche du temps perdu*? The analogy between the two is only an analogy. Like all metaphorical similarities, it will lead to error if taken literally. Taking it literally would mean making the aboriginal linguistic error of mistaking a metaphorical likeness for an identity. On the other hand, the comparison of the *Recherche* to fractals may possibly allow

changes his orientation with regard to the well-beloved, for example, in a simple encounter: "Pierston here gave in brief the history of his revived comradeship with Avice, the verge of the engagement to which they had reached, and its unexpected rupture by him, merely through his meeting with a woman into whom the Well-Beloved unmistakably moved under his very eyes—by name Miss Marcia Bencomb" (Hardy, 1975: 57). To put it briefly, we cannot predict the effect of a repetition. For this reason, though the text programs future behaviors by readers and writers, it does not prescribe them. It does not program them in the way suggested by reception aesthetics (see, for instance, the notion of "implied reader" in Wolfgang Iser's work; Iser, 1974), but according to a programming that is accomplished and undone at once.

Derrida has referred to this aporia in speaking about Europe:

Neither monopoly nor dispersion, therefore. This is, of course, an aporia, and we must not hide it from ourselves. I will even venture to say that ethics, politics, and responsibility, *if there are any*, will only ever have begun with the experience and experiment of the aporia. . . . That is not easy. It is even impossible to conceive of a responsibility that consists in being responsible *for* two laws, or that consists in responding *to* two contradictory injunctions. No doubt. But there is no responsibility that is not the experience and experiment of the impossible. As we said just a moment ago, when a responsibility is exercised in the order of the possible, it simply follows a direction and elaborates a program. It makes of action the applied consequence, the simple application of a knowledge or know-how. (Derrida, 1992a: 41, 44–45)

Miller invokes such contradictory laws or injunctions with regard to the effect or the remaining in the middle of the literary text. In one way or another, the commentary identifies itself with (and is provoked by) the commented-upon. It uses the text's own terms. It touches it, encrypts itself inside it, but that ipseity and that encrypting at the same time cause (and are in fact) a result that is already outside the text. This result continues the chain, in a repetition that engenders unlike possibilities with-

the identification of features of the former that might not otherwise have been noticed. How is Proust's *Recherche* like a fractal? The *Recherche*, like a fractal, is organized according to a principle of self-similarity. It is, however, self-similarity of the second kind, that is, similarity with a difference, with unexpected and unpredictable irregularities. It might be better to call it "self-dissimilarity." The stories that organize the large-scale patterns of Marcel's life—for example, his love first for Gilberte and then for Albertine—are echoed, though never exactly, in ever-reduced versions (for example, in Swann's love for Odette), down to small-scale episodes like the death of Bergotte followed by Albertine's lie to Marcel about having talked to Bergotte when in truth he was already dead, or like the sequence of episodes that make up Marcel's trip to Venice. At a lower level still would be all the brilliant metaphorical comparisons that make up so much of the stylistic texture of the *Recherche*, or the complex structure of recurrent syntactical patterns that make up Proust's notoriously long sentences. Lower still is the level of word echoing word, beneath that again the level of the letter. At the level of the letter, the reader encounters something similar to Marcel's inability ever to be sure whether or not Albertine is lying, whether or not she is lesbian. Since lying is performative rather than constative, it is impossible ever to check it against the truth, as I shall show later on. This corresponds on a larger scale to the impossibility of being sure whether Proust wrote an *a*, an *e*, or an *o*. We have no access to the referent that would verify that Albertine lies or that it is in fact an *o*. To say, "We guess as we read, we create; everything starts from an initial error" is true at any of these levels and in all the versions at any given level. Nevertheless, the statement is true in a different way in every case. Each example is a singularity.

What is misleading about Proust's image, discussed at the beginning of this book, of France as a polygon filled to the brim with millions of little polygons, that is, Frenchmen, is that it suggests that the analysis of any one of these little polygons will give you proleptic knowledge of all the rest and also of the large polygon that is the French nation. You can understand politics by studying human nature. This would be the case if France exhibited fractal self-similarity of the first kind, the exact repetition on a smaller scale of a larger pattern. Marcel's own narrative demonstrates what is dubious about this assumption. Not only, he finds out, is each person unique. Each such unique person is also inhabited from time to time by a thousand different selves, each different from all the others, though exhibiting a statistical self-similarity to the others.

out beginning or end. Among those semiotico-textual effects we find the motives or themes of a literary work, "shared" viewpoints, shared "experiences," and, of course, commentaries and readings.

Miller terms ends that follow each other without interruption, in an iterative way the "aporia of interminability":

> Any reader, or anyone who writes a critical essay on *The Well-Beloved*, is momentarily the last in this line. He is no more able than any of the other links in the chain to put an end to it. He cannot provide a definitive explanation of the novel which will stop the passing on of its compulsion to repeat itself. What the critic says also in its own way keeps the generative force alive. This might be called the aporia of interminability. . . . Each explanation both hides and reveals the lack of sufficient reasonable explanation, the failure of that 'principle of reason' which is the basis of metaphysical thinking in the West. (FR, 173)

Jocelyn is compelled to repeat throughout his life, a life that Hardy sums up synecdochally in three sections—when he was twenty, when he was forty, and when he was sixty—the same behavior, the same type of search, the same attempt to find and possess definitively an image embodied in a woman. What he pursues, once he finds himself before the mother-Avice, the daughter-Avice, and the granddaughter-Avice, is always the same thing. However, that "sameness" is Jocelyn's whole problem. He was not able to recognize the first one—she is not the *first one* actually—though he might have married her. He either recognized her too late, or destiny played a dirty trick on him. When Avice the First dies, Jocelyn comes to visit her daughter and, though he notices some differences ("The voice truly was his Avice's; but Avice the Second was clearly more matter-of-fact, unreflecting, less cultivated than her mother had been" [Hardy, 1975: 96]), he does not fail to recognize the image he was looking for, "the Idea, in Platonic phraseology" (Hardy, 1975: 118):

> "How old you are?" he asked.
> "Going on nineteen."

The result of this high degree of statistical self-similarity at different scales in the *Recherche* is a curious kind of synecdoche. The part is like the whole and like other parts. It is, however, not so much like them that the analysis of one part will allow the reader to make valid generalizations about the other parts or about the whole. Reading one part does not release the reader from the obligation to read the other parts. In such a case the choice of an example is crucial. It preprograms the conclusions that can be drawn from it. Each example is sui generis. In spite of its similarity to other examples, it gives the reader a slightly different result when it is used as a way of talking about the whole. This is true even when the part is used by Marcel as the occasion of a reflection about the questionable value of synecdoche or of universal conceptualizations in general. That too is only one aspect of the truth. Another way to express this singularity of each part of the *Recherche* is to say that each part is made of the particularities of language, not of the visible spatial designs that make up a graphed fractal. The analogy with fractals is with something incommensurable with language. The comparison of literary works with spatial designs is beguiling, as I have here been beguiled, but misleading if fundamental differences are not also taken into account.

The comparison of the *Recherche* with stochastic fractals nevertheless gives the reader a way of understanding why an attempt to write about the *Recherche* does not lead to complacency except in those who are able to fool themselves, as Marcel is so inveterately fooled, for example, into assuming that Albertine must be either lesbian or not lesbian. If you know the *Recherche* at all well, when you are presenting a reading of one episode or passage (and there is no reading of any worth that does not single out individual passages for analysis) you are always uneasily aware that if you had chosen another equally salient passage you would have gotten a significantly different result.

The comparison with fractals also indicates why the incomplete state of the *Recherche* did not result from the contingent accident of the author's death. The *Recherche* was in principle unfinishable. It would always have been possible to add more material, more short or long interpolations. These would not have repeated anything already said. They would have fitted in with it in the odd, mind-twisting way each part of a stochastic fractal fits the whole. To use the figure of the fractal, as I have done in this section, is, since fractals are part of the new computer space, an example of the way new kinds of telecommunication transform our sense

It was about the age of her double, Avice the First, when he and she had strolled together over the cliffs during the engagement. (Hardy, 1975: 96)

This possible liaison is also blocked, however, so that later on he recognizes "that the desire to make reparation to the original woman by wedding and enriching the copy—which lent such an unprecedented permanence to his new love—was thwarted, as if by set intention of his destiny" (Hardy, 1975: 120).

This repetition confirms the existence in Avice the Second of a body with neither soul nor idea that Jocelyn can reach, a signifier without signified, outside Jocelyn's sphere. The same thing will happen with Avice the Third. So we find ourselves moved little by little from the tragic to the ridiculous. From classic mythology we pass to parodic baroque mythology. The repetition, of which the text is conscious (if I may say so), only engenders corruption, dissemination, irony. I stress that the text is conscious from the outset that it establishes a global correspondence between the world of love and the world of arts. If the idea of the Well-Beloved is not found in the different bodies of the women who appear to Jocelyn, the idea of beauty also escapes from the works of art the latter sculptures. Jocelyn's father "had been persistently chiselling for half a century at the crude original matter of those shapes" (Hardy, 1975: 72), whereas Jocelyn "had been modelling and chipping his ephemeral fancies into perennial shapes" (ibid.). In Miller's words: "The same drama is enacted in a different way in the other mode of Jocelyn's island-bred tendency to fantasy. Like his series of erotic fascinations, Jocelyn's sculpture takes the form of a potentially endless sequence of statues of the goddess. Each statue, as it is completed, becomes mere stone once more, an empty sign, and so Jocelyn must begin another statue" (FR, 163).

This is precisely how Miller considers narrative to be meta-meta-theoretical, with all the nuances we have introduced regarding this word. If in Aristotle's *Metaphysics* emptiness of meaning is considered to be an

of literature by giving us new models for the formal properties of literary works. In an earlier age, organic unity was the natural model for a good literary work. Those who dwell in cyberspace are more likely, it may be, to notice hitherto unnoticed features of textual form and meaning in older works. Or the *Recherche* takes on new features when it comes to inhabit cyberspace by being digitized or put online. These features were always there, but they now become accessible in a new way. In the case of *A la recherche du temps perdu*, this new sense of the strange form the novel takes leads us to see the work as not fitting older ideas about what a good work of literature is like. This may be part of what Derrida means by saying literature will not survive the new regime of telecommunications. We may now value the *Recherche* more, however, for having an unfinished and unfinishable quality, for being undecidable in meaning, as well as for being inhabited by a built-in reaching toward an infinity it can never reach, than we would if it could be shown to be organically unified, to be logocentric in the way good literature was defined in the long regime of the codex book from Aristotle to the New Critics. Logocentric in this case means delimited by a beginning, middle, and end, all governed by an underlying and pervasive logos that rules the whole and binds it into a unity. *A la recherche du temps perdu* does not fit that paradigm. Nor, for that matter, it may be easier now to see, does *Oedipus the King*.

The Two Synecdoches

The testimony of the *Recherche* is ambiguous in the two main examples of self-similarity that it gives. This is appropriate for a work that comes at the historical moment when one set of communication media was being replaced by another. The two chief examples of self-similarity in the *Recherche* are, first, the character of a person at different times in his or her life, and, second, the relation to one another of works by the same painter, musician, or poet. Much is at stake in getting Proust's ideas about persons and artworks right: not only the right reading of the *Recherche*, but also the possibility of giving a valid reading of the whole book by way of reading parts. A detailed reading of the whole *Recherche*, page by page, would produce another monster, a monster about a monster. It would be an impossible critical essay, one perhaps thirty thousand pages long. This assumes each page could generate at least ten pages of nonredundant commentary. Some form of representative choice is necessary. On what basis

inhuman monstrosity (1006a.30; Aristotle, 1963: 69), if in the Christian interpretation allegory is always allegory of something, and if analysis and criticism (metatheory and theory) are founded on the possibility of decision regarding that something and that fullness of meaning, then narrative, this particular narration by Hardy, questions those assumptions at the same time as it recognizes we need them. This is why Hardy speaks of "The Compulsion to Stop Repeating" by means of a significative and performative diaspora: the text narrates a story or collection of stories but also sets forth in that narration a semiotic theory of stories, a theory aimed at the premises on which the possibility of literary criticism and literary theory is based. The semiotic proposal of Hardy's narration warns us about the emptiness of the signifier, or, what is the same, about the allegory of the impossibility of reading, as de Man would say. Thus what the narration says is a blank, a double and empty saying that carries out a double movement. It recognizes a tendency toward "padding" the signifier and escapes from the facticity of that padding, so that the implicit theory of the novel turns back on itself in an eternal movement that is in itself pure repetition. The chiasmus closes. Narration speaks mimetically of something that is beyond narration, but that mimetic speech is its way of being theoretically reflexive. Narration proposes an (anti)semiotic theory that speaks of itself as theory and of the theory supporting it, but that reflexivity is only in the mimesis of something that is beyond narration. "*The Well-Beloved* superficially obeys, as do Hardy's earlier novels, the conventions of nineteenth-century realism" (FR, 149). In that "superficiality" is inscribed the chiasmus to which I refer.

Miller writes: "In such an experience of disillusionment the once-beloved becomes no longer the sign of a spiritual plenitude, but the sign of an absence, of nothing at all. She becomes an empty emblem, a nest from which the bird has flown, 'a language in living cipher no more.' . . . Jocelyn's erotic fantasies are an occasion for experiencing a linguistic problem, the incompatibility of meaning with the signs for it and the

can such a choice claim validity? How can a responsible critic write re-sponsively and responsibly about *A la recherche du temps perdu*?

What the *Recherche* says about this crucial issue is riven by a basic contradiction, though "contradiction" in its usual sense is not quite the right word for it. The alternative to one assertion in this case does not take the form of a determinate negation, that is, saying the opposite of what the first assertion said, "contra-dicting" it. Neither side can be generated as the simple negation of the other. In this case, to borrow Nietzsche's for-mulation, "one may doubt . . . whether there are any opposites at all."[23] Moreover, the statement of one side is not possible without also shadow-ing the other. The word "contradiction" must be understood here "ana-semically," as Nicolas Abraham and Maria Torok put it, that is, against the grain of its usual meaning.[24] In the *Recherche* each side of the "contra-diction" is a catachresis for an unknowable alterity that calls forth both assertions, just as Marcel is drawn by the hour of his death, the hour that will also be the time when truth will be revealed. Only by stressing one or the other side of the contradictions have critics been able to propose a consistent reading of Proust. This has often presupposed a happy end-ing for *Le temps retrouvé*. Such an ending would be a revealed truth that would coincide with Marcel's realization of his vocation to write the book that will reveal that truth to others. This will turn out to be the book the reader has been reading for over three thousand pages. It is always possible to show that any such univocal or logically consistent reading is incom-plete, even when it is based on a close and persuasive reading of passages that are clearly important. Nevertheless, careful readings of other equally salient passages will "contradict" it, and vice versa. But the heterogeneity of the *Recherche* is not even quite so simple as that, as I shall show.

As Proust says, "par la commodité du récit" (for narrative conve-nience) (F 3: 659; E 3: 150), for the sake of making a coherent story out of it, the heterogeneity of what Proust wrote may be explained by way of synecdoche's two horizons. Synecdoche stands uneasily between metaphor and metonymy. On the one hand, the part may really be like the whole. If so, it is a form of metaphor. In that case, knowing the part will be a valid way of knowing the whole. A sample of grain from a sack will tell you what all the rest of the grain is like. A smaller part of a fractal of the first kind is an exact image of the whole. On the other hand, the part may be just a contingent part of a heterogeneous whole, so that knowing it gives no valid knowledge of the whole. This would be a metonymical synecdo-

emptying out of belief in a transcendent referent when this incompatibility is recognized" (FR, 162). This sign of an absence causes a chain
of repetitions doomed never to stop and destined to produce unpredictable effects: Jocelyn as lover and sculptor, Hardy as writer, Hardy
as fictitious narrator, the novel in relation to other novels, the critic as
theoretician and/or commentator: "The structure is repeated again in
the relation of *The Well-Beloved* to other works by Hardy. It is once more
repeated, though not in quite the same way, in the novel's relation to
works by other writers before and after" (FR, 158). It seems evident, therefore, that Miller reads *reading* in *The Well-Beloved* in the broad sense of
this word. Miller reads a story: he wonders, for instance, about Tess's or
Jocelyn's sufferings; he focuses on Hawthorne's veils, on Bartleby's retro-
fetal silences. He reads a theory, making us notice, as Deleuze did for
Proust in *Proust and Signs* (Deleuze, 1972), that Hardy's narration reflects
on signs. Finally, he reads critical commentaries or essays, and he reads
them both inside and outside the novel. He begins again the back and
forth movement of boustrophedonic reading, about which we now know
something more: it consists not only in a pluridirectional reading of the
text, but also in a multidimensional reading that obliges us to recognize
that Miller is a literary critic whose reading realizes the impossibility of
literary criticism (as Lacan speaks of the impossibility of desire).

In a double movement of affirmation and denial, Miller is and is
not a literary critic. As a philologist he is a literary critic, but as a philologist he is not. His thorough attention to the literary text makes him a
literary critic and at the same time negates him as such. How can a real
literary criticism or a real literary theory exist whose place is both inside
and outside the text and whose assumptions are questioned? How can
a literary criticism whose target, literature, is constantly threatening its
own literary being exist? ("The possibility of doing literary theory, which
is by no means to be taken for granted," de Man writes [de Man, 1986:
7].) How can a literary criticism that can only decide the impossibility of

che. The sack of grain may be made up of layers or regions of grain quite different from one another in quality. Each grain may be different from all the others. Moreover, the sack itself is not at all like the grain, even though we say, "Bring me that sack," when we mean the sack filled with grain. To say "sail" for "ship" or "milk" for "bottle of milk" might lead to erroneous conclusions for anyone who assumed the sail or the milk was like the whole of which it is a part. Synecdoches of container for thing contained, thing contained for container, or other forms of inside/outside substitutions are crucial in Proust,[25] as de Man has shown in "Reading (Proust)." Such figures are a converging place for the "contradiction" that is not exactly a contradiction, as I am attempting to reveal and define.

The synecdochic assumption underlying Marcel's assertion that, since France is filled to the brim with little polygons repeating the large one on a smaller scale, so the study of individual psychology will yield political wisdom, recurs in one way or another in many places throughout the *Recherche*. Marcel's desire to "know" Albertine, to know once and for all whether she has lesbian proclivities, presumes that Albertine has a fixed and consistent personality that remains the same through time. It also assumes that "being lesbian" is a stable essence, like belonging to a given species, being a lion rather than a tiger, to use one of Marcel's own figures.[26]

The assumption of permanent, essential selfhood, however, appears most frequently, or at any rate seems to appear, in Marcel's assertions about art. It may be difficult or even impossible ever to know another person well enough to verify one way or the other the hypothesis that he or she has a fixed, essential, perdurable personality. In the case of works of art in relation to their makers, however, the hypothesis can perhaps be verified by experiencing a series of works by the same artist. Nonartists may remain opaque. Works of art give us access to the hidden depths of the artist, a core of self that is unique and that remains the same through all the variety of the artist's works: "As the spectrum makes visible to us the composition of light, so the harmony of a Wagner, the color of an Elstir, enable us to know that essential quality of another person's sensations [*cette essence qualitative des sensations d'un autre*] into which love for another person does not allow us to penetrate" (F 3: 665; E 3: 156). The whole program of Georges Poulet's "criticism of consciousness" is founded on this assumption. Poulet more than once paid homage to Proust as one of the precursors of his kind of criticism. One example of a Pouletian passage in Proust is the eloquent speech in which Marcel explains to Albertine that all artists — painters, mu-

deciding exist, or, in other words, how will it be able to decide only on a meta-metatheoretical level? This problem is emphasized in the following words, whose assertion Miller repeats throughout his work: "Criticism of a given novel or body of novels should therefore be the following of one or another track until it reaches, in the text, one or another of these double blinds, rather than the attempt to find a presupposed unity. Such a unity always turns out to be spurious, imposed rather than intrinsic. This can be experienced, however, only through the patient work of following some thread as far, deep into the labyrinth of the text, as it will go. Such an effort to read is not the 'deconstruction' of a given novel. It is rather a discovery of the way the novel deconstructs itself in the process of constructing its web of storytelling" (AT, 23). In this quotation, one must emphasize the last words, which encompass in one process, one gesture, the deconstruction and construction of the plot. They confirm what has been hazarded here—namely, that the fictitious actions of the narrative evolution are inevitably accompanied by strategies that are *theoretically* deconstructive. To narrate and to deconstruct go together. This assertion may seem strange, but it constitutes the background against which Miller's proposals are developed. It means that the example resists, that literature as example, fiction, or fable or "as if . . ." escapes from the frame of theory and/or literary criticism as it was derived from the works of Plato, Aristotle, and Horace.

If we come back to the problem of the relation between repetition and the structure of beginning-middle-end, we notice that the questioning of such a structure proceeds not only from what has been called contamination or participation among texts (the Millerian matrix), a flowing over from one text to another of narrative attitudes and characters' actions, reproduction of themes, and so on, but also from the heart of the narration. Until now we have spoken of definite numbers. There are *three* Avices, *three* generations, just as with Proust. There is *one* narration. Yet it

sicians, and writers alike—Elstir, Vermeer, Vinteuil, Hardy, Dostoevsky, Stendhal, or Barbey d'Aurevilly, create the same work over and over. "The great men of letters," he says, like the great painters and composers, "have never created more than a single work, or rather have never done more than refract through various media an identical beauty which they bring into the world [*n'ont jamais fait qu'une seule oeuvre, ou plutôt réfracté à travers des milieux divers une même beauté qu'ils apportent au monde*]" (F 3: 877; E 3: 382). A moment earlier, apropos of Vinteuil's music, he had spoken of "this unknown quality of a unique world which no other composer had ever yet revealed [*cette qualité inconnue d'un monde unique qu'aucun autre musicien ne nous avait jamais fait voir*]" (F 4: 877; E 3: 382).

On the one hand, there are intellectual resemblances, deliberately and rationally concocted, between one part of a work and another or between works. On the other hand, there are inadvertent similarities, achieved when the artist is trying his hardest to create something new, trying to be different from himself. This difference is analogous to that distinction, of which Georges Poulet makes so much in his reading of Proust and in his account of memory generally, between an intellectual memory, the deliberate repetition within my mind of something that I once felt or saw, what the Germans call *Gedächtnis*, and the happiness of involuntary affective memory, what the Germans call *Erinnerung*. The famous cases in the *Recherche* are, for example, the intensely happy memories that overwhelm Marcel when he once more tastes madeleine cake dipped in tea or when he steps on uneven paving-stones in the Guermantes courtyard, which bring back the uneven pavement before Saint Mark's Cathedral in Venice. Marcel makes the parallel explicit at the climax of *Le temps retrouvé*:

As I moved sharply backwards I tripped against the uneven paving-stones in front of the coach-house. And at the moment when, recovering my balance, I put my foot on a stone which was slightly lower than its neighbor, all my discouragement vanished and in its place was that same happiness [*la même félicité*] which at various epochs of my life had been given to me by the sight of trees which I had thought that I recognised in the course of a drive near Balbec, by the sight of the twin steeples of Martinville, by the flavor of a madeleine dipped in tea, and all those other sensations of which I have spoken and of which the last works of Vinteuil had seemed to me to combine the quintessential character [*synthétiser*]. (F 4: 445; E 3: 898–99)

has remained quite clear that those three loves within a narration constitute not only a repetition but an unstoppable one. As a whole, *The Well-
Beloved* reproduces Shelley in the same way Proust reproduces Hardy. But
the repetition that *deconstructs* the structure beginning-middle-end is exposed and told by the narrative sequence itself, now without the need to
call upon other, apparently exterior textualities. On the one hand, Miller
recognizes that "the basic plot of *The Well-Beloved* can scarcely be said
to be 'realistic' in the ordinary sense" (FR, 149). What does this mean,
" 'realistic' in the ordinary sense"? It means maintaining "the illusion that
[the events] are imitated from some extralinguistic reality. They present
themselves as a species of history. They are, moreover, committed, at least
in their apparent form, to the notion that the stories they tell have definite contours, a beginning, a middle, and an end" (FR, 153). We should
not forget that we are speaking of a nineteenth-century novel, of a realistic novel, and not of Borges, Beckett, Duras, Onetti, or Robbe-Grillet.
The realistic convention, that is, the referential, mimetic convention,
cannot be eluded, since it forms a part of the orientation of the text.
This referential mimesis would be present in any case, even though it
might not be the main orientation of the text, as in the case of certain
twentieth-century works (as the preceding chapter showed us with regard
to Wallace Stevens, one of the most contradictory poets of this century
on the subject of textual referentiality). Yet despite the presence of those
conventions, conventions that will never be erased, merged, or destroyed,
"*The Well-Beloved* anticipates Fowles or Borges. . . . [It] brings into the
open those subversions of the idea of a single ending which were already
latent in one way or another in Victorian fiction" (FR, 156). To put the
point another way: "The problem of endings [and beginnings] is thematized in the story" (FR, 156).

The novel begins with "A Supposititious Presentment of Her."
Where does or did she begin? Until now we have spoken of three Avices;
however, there are at least two moments in the narration at which we be-

A curious and perhaps important fact may be noticed in what Proust says here. Marcel notes the extreme specificity of the experiences that in their repetition generate the replacement of "discouragement" by "happiness." What could be more unique than the taste of madeleine cake dipped in tea? Nevertheless, Marcel also stresses the fact that the happiness in all these cases is "the same happiness." How could it be that such different sensations produce the same elation? What does Marcel's careful registration of this "sameness" mean? I shall return to these questions later.

Against all these assertions of some profound unity that art or sensation can reach must be set those passages where Marcel entertains the other hypothesis. This is the possibility that these seeming unities are factitious. No two experiences are the same. Works of art give us only the illusion of access to some profound unity. Both I myself and all the people I know are a thousand different persons by turn as time passes. The word "hypothesis" is a key word in the *Recherche*, as a search of the ARTFL database will show. Marcel uses the word repeatedly, for example, to name his contradictory suppositions about Albertine, his agonized speculations about whether or not she is lying to him, whether or not she engages in lesbian practices. He uses the word "hypothesis" also to name the two possible sources of the great pleasure certain details in artworks give him. A phrase in Vinteuil's septet, for example—"evoking the joyful clanging of the bells at noon [*la joie titubante des cloches de midi*]" (F 3: 875–76; E 3: 380), at first seems to him ugly but eventually becomes his favorite, "either because I had grown accustomed to its ugliness or because I had discovered its beauty. This reaction from the disappointment [*la déception*] which great works of art cause at first may in fact be attributed to a weakening of the initial impression or to the effort necessary to lay bare the truth—two hypotheses which recur in all important questions about the truth [*la réalité*] of Art, of Reality, of the Immortality of the Soul; we must choose between them [*c'est un choix qu'il faut faire entre elles*]; and, in the case of Vinteuil's music, this choice was constantly presenting itself under a variety of forms" (F 3: 876; E 3: 380–81).

We must choose, but we cannot choose. A hypothesis, as its etymology suggests, is a presupposition that is tentatively laid down in order to be tested out. The Greek word *hupothesis*, "proposal, suggestion, supposition," comes from *hupotithenai*, "to place under," propose, suppose, from *hupo*, "under," plus *tithenai*, "to place." The Indo-European root is *dhe*, to set, to put. The English word "do" has the same root. *Tithenai* is

come aware that Avice the First, the one really called Avice Caro, is just
one of many urns that have contained the idea of the Well-Beloved. Both
the narrator and Avice herself refer to this. After Jocelyn's meeting with
Avice (toward the end of the first chapter), following many years without
seeing her, the narrator, speaking from within Jocelyn's mind, says: "His
affection for her was rather that of a friend than of a lover, and he felt by
no means sure that the migratory, elusive idealization he called his Love
who, ever since his boyhood, had flitted from human shell to human
shell an indefinite number of times, was going to take up her abode in
the body of Avice Caro" (Hardy, 1975: 31). Although Jocelyn does not expect it, although the "ups and downs of life" have an apparent and rapid
power to dissolve his loves, the Well-Beloved is incarnate for good in the
body of Avice Caro, whence it does not really move anymore, since it is
transmitted to her descendants. It is evident, however, that (as the narrator notices) this incarnation is just a repetition, for the beginning of
the Well-Beloved goes back to the childhood of the protagonist. Jocelyn's
doubts about Avice Caro occur precisely because the Well-Beloved has
iteratively reappeared before that encounter. In what before? We do not
know. According to the first version of the novel, Jocelyn has difficulty
burning his old love letters. Those old sendings open the story backwards.
They are the evident signs of some actions that have taken place, that we
know only indirectly and partially, and that tell us that the beginning
of this story is not a beginning, but another middle. Something similar
to what happened when Alec d'Urberville raped Tess happens now. The
narrator of *Tess of the d'Urbervilles* comments: "Doubtless some of Tess
d'Urberville's mailed ancestors rollicking home from a fray had dealt the
same measure even more ruthlessly towards peasant girls of their time"
(Hardy, 1978: 108). The *same* behavior of Tess's male ancestors toward
peasant girls of their time now inevitably happens to Tess. This behavior (in the same way Oedipus's murder of Laius is outside the action of

a reduplicated form, as though one were to say, "put put." [27] A hypothesis is a peculiar kind of speech act. You put something down to see what will happen, as a basis for further investigation. Marcel's hypotheses are the peculiar sort of doings, puttings, or suppositions that cannot be verified one way or the other, just as the existence of black holes cannot be verified in the usual way, even though from one time to another we have experiences that seem to confirm one or the other of the hypotheses.

The results of positing first one and then the other of these two hypotheses, which correspond to the two kinds of synecdoche, confirm that while much of importance—Art, Reality, and the Immortality of the Soul—hangs on proving one hypothesis or the other, neither hypothesis can be verified. This uncertainty fuels the writing of the *Recherche*, guarantees its endlessness, and justifies the name *recherche* in the title. It justifies, that is, Proust's use of an academic word that names the attempt to verify hypotheses in science, social science, or the humanities, as when we speak of a "research university." In the research university a hypothesis in any of these fields is of no use, cannot possibly lead to more *Wissenschaft*, unless it can be disproved if false. Marcel, it may be, instinctively uses or misuses this word to hide from himself that he is not in a situation assimilable to this scientific model. He urgently needs to believe it is possible to ascertain the facts about Albertine's hidden life, just as it is possible to verify or disprove a scientific hypothesis or a hypothesis about some historical event.

A good example of Marcel's use of the term "hypothesis" occurs when he returns from the Verdurins' party and quarrels with Albertine. The two hypotheses between which he hovers are the assumption that everything Albertine tells him is true and the assumption that she lies, that she hides from him her love of women and wants to leave him: "I continued to live by the hypothesis which accepted as true everything that Albertine told me. But it may be that during this time a wholly contrary hypothesis, of which I did not wish to think [*une hypothèse toute contraire et à laquelle je ne voulais pas penser*], never left me" (F 3: 848; E 3: 353, trans. slightly altered). The contrary hypothesis is of "the presence in her of a sentiment which she concealed and which might lead her to form plans for another life without me" (ibid.). Of this other hypothesis he says, it "explained far more things and had also this to be said for it, that if one adopted the first hypothesis the second became more probable, for by allowing myself to give way to effusions of tenderness for Albertine, I obtained from her nothing but irritation (to which moreover she assigned

Oedipus the King) is not portrayed in the novel, however, just as Jocelyn's many earlier love affairs are not shown.

In this way, the novel makes evident that the "presentation" is just an arbitrary cut (though a significant one) in the middle of an action whose origin either has disappeared or is impossible to narrate. In addition, the novel proclaims that there is no beginning that could be narrated, only middles that function as beginnings. Not only is a human action simulated, but a beginning is, as well. The beginnings—and, as we shall see in a moment, the ends—are lost in what Borges calls a "universe (which others call the Library) . . . composed of an indefinite and perhaps infinite number of hexagonal galleries, with vast air shafts between, surrounded by very low railings" (Borges, 1964: 51). What will critical discourse be able to do before that vast extension and that powerful discourse but become another link in the chain, a footnote swallowed up by the omnivorous library or the novel that gobbles up everything like a Pantagruelian Saturn? Criticism could say, with Avice at the other moment in Hardy's novel when the principle of endless repetition is manifest: " 'I see—I see now!' she whispered, 'I am—only one—in a long, long row!' From the white sheets of paper round about her seemed to rise the ghosts of Isabella, Florence, Winifred, Lucy, Jane and Evangeline—each writer from her own bundle respectively—and Maud and Dorothea from the flames. He hardly knew what to say to the new personality in the presence of the old" (Hardy, 1975: 219). If we take notice of these words, we cannot agree with Proust when, in the passage from *The Captive* that refers to *The Well-Beloved*, he asserts that the protagonist of *The Well-Beloved* is a man who "loves three women" (Proust, 1982: 383). The thing Jocelyn loves is subject to an infinite iterability and divisibility. For this reason, Miller correctly writes: "Far from being a beginning, Avice, like Tess, is only an intermediate digit somewhere in the midst of a long series stretching before and after into misty vagueness. Of this series neither the beginning nor the end is given nor can in principle be given. The ante-

a different cause)" (ibid.). The reader can see how Marcel here is twisting the normal use of the word "hypothesis" as well as the normal idea of what it means to lie.

These passages show how the two hypotheses about Albertine are so oddly imbricated in one another that the adoption of one makes the other more probable. Why does this happen? It must be because hypothesis, in Marcel's odd use of the word, is not simply an epistemological presupposition subject to rational verification or disproof. It also has a performative dimension. It puts the one who holds the hypothesis in a different position. It makes him act differently. It works thereby on the person about whom the hypothesis is held to make her act differently, namely, in a way that makes the second hypothesis more probable, without by any means definitively proving or disproving it. In all this hypothesis making, followed by vain attempts to prove or disprove one or the other of them, Marcel remains cut off from access to what Albertine really is, what she does behind his back, what she is thinking and feeling at any given time. As Marcel says, his intuitive conviction that she is betraying him may "alter Albertine's intentions instead of making them plain [*les démêler*]" (F 3: 850; E 3: 355). Marcel says that even now, when he is remembering all this and writing it down much later in time, he finds it "difficult to say" (ibid.) one way or the other whether or not it was really the case that he altered Albertine's intentions. Everything takes place within Marcel's mind and feelings. Everything is reported by his language, according to the basic narrative law of the *Recherche*. This law says the reader is perpetually imprisoned within Marcel's (possibly mendacious) account of what he experienced, thought, and felt: "So that what probably existed in me was an idea of Albertine entirely contrary to that which my reason formed of her, and also to that which her own words suggested [*dépeignaient*], an Albertine who was none the less not wholly invented, since she was like a prophetic mirror [*un miroir intérieur*] of certain impulses which occurred in her, such as her ill-humour at my having gone to the Verdurins'" (F 3: 848–49; E 3: 353). "Not wholly invented" here does not mean that Marcel has any direct access to Albertine's thoughts and feelings. Far from it. It means that the other Albertine can be constructed by Marcel on the basis of some symptoms that can be objectively recorded, in this case her irritation. Of what that irritation is a sign Marcel can never know for certain. He can only make hypotheses. According to a mathematical figure Marcel himself uses, Albertine's hidden nature is the unknown x of an algebraic

cedent items in the row do not disappear. They remain, both in Tess and in *The Well-Beloved*, as written records which inhibit the possibility of action initiatory or free" (FR, 157).

If remaining in the middle cuts the ground out from under the search for identifiable originary principles, it does the same for the search for ends. Putting endings in question is a favorite motivation for twentieth-century narrative experiments and a prolongation of the games present at the birth of the modern novel (Cervantes, Sterne). Miller has told us that Hardy proposes already, for instance, what Fowles or Borges will dramatize later on. What does Yu Tsun exasperately call for, regarding the novel of his ancestor Ts'ui Pên, in Borges's story "The Garden of Forking Paths," one of the texts Miller refers to in this essay on Hardy? Yu Tsun explains to the sinologist and involuntary transmitter of information Stephen Albert: " 'We descendants of Ts'ui Pên,' I replied, 'continue to curse that monk. Their publication was senseless. The book is an indeterminate heap of contradictory drafts. I examined it once: in the third chapter the hero dies, in the fourth he is alive' " (Borges, 1964: 24). Further on, Albert explains to his interlocutor that his irritation at this multiple structure results from a linear and unitary conception of time different from Ts'ui Pên's: "In contrast to Newton and Schopenhauer, your ancestor did not believe in a uniform, absolute time. He believed in an infinite series of times, in a growing, dizzying net of diverging, convergent, and parallel times. This network of times which approached one another, forked, broke off, or were unaware of one another for centuries, embraces *all* possibilities of time" (Borges, 1964: 28). Miller would, then, be asserting that Hardy too advances a notion of time that embraces all possibilities. This is confirmed in the way the New Wessex Edition (unlike others, including the Spanish translation of 1934) prints jointly the two versions (both the one of 1892 and that of 1897). Pages 153 and following of Miller's essay give a thorough account how the novel has two

equation that has too many variables, too many unknowns, ever to be solved. The equation can never be more than "approximate": "The approximate equation of that unknown quantity [*L'équation approximative à cette inconnue*] which Albertine's thoughts were to me had given me, more or less, the following" (F 3: 850; E 3: 355).

The Other as Unknown X

Proust's assumption throughout the *Recherche* is that what the people we love really are, as opposed to the selves that we invent for them on the basis of their behavior (what they say and do in our presence, their facial expressions and gestures), remains forever unknown and unknowable. Each other person is an x, a black hole. Since Marcel can never prove or disprove either of the hypotheses he holds about Albertine, he can never bring his *recherche* about her to an end. It continues interminably, even when she has left him and when he begins to think he no longer loves her. His research continues even after she is dead. He goes on trying to get objective proof that when she was alive she indulged in lesbian practices.

This implacable law of perpetual ignorance is formulated succinctly apropos of Swann's ignorance of Odette's succession of lovers: "he knows nothing [*il ne sait rien*]"; "he can never find out [*il n'en peut rien savoir*]" (F 3: 804; E 3: 303). In order to understand these assertions better, the passage within which the phrases occur must be cited:

These lovers M. de Charlus began to enumerate with as absolute a certainty as if he had been reciting the list of the Kings of France. And indeed the jealous lover, like the contemporaries of an historical event, is too close, he knows nothing, and it is for strangers that the chronicle of adultery assumes the precision of history, and prolongs itself in lists which are a matter of indifference to them and become painful only to another jealous lover, such as I was, who cannot help comparing his own case with that which he hears spoken of and wonders whether the woman he suspects cannot boast an equally illustrious list. But he can never find out; it is a sort of universal conspiracy, a "blindman's buff" [*une brimade*] in which everyone cruelly participates, and which consists, while his mistress flits from one to another, in holding over his eyes a bandage which he is perpetually trying to tear off without success, for everyone keeps him blindfold, poor wretch, the kind out of kindness, the cruel out of cruelty, the coarse-minded out of their love of coarse jokes [*vilaines farces*], the well-bred out of politeness and good breeding, and all

versions. The ways Jocelyn decides to commit suicide by drowning in the sea, and/or that Avice the Third decides the same in order to avoid break-ing off her engagement to Jocelyn, and/or that Jocelyn decides to remain alive, to marry Marcia (for their friendship), and to block up the wells of the Street of Wells, and/or that Jocelyn contracts marriage with Avice the Third, according to the narrations of the different versions, are simi-lar to the chaotic novel by Ts'ui Pên in which the hero first dies (thereby apparently bringing the novel to an end) and later on is alive again.

We can correctly say that between the death and life of the protago-nist all possibilities are included, as in Borges's story. From a narrative viewpoint, the life and death of the protagonist represent the opposite extremes, for which remaining in the middle functions as closure. This closing is not true closure since, with Tess, her death seems to engen-der a new repetition in the figure of her sister, who has taken her place beside Angel Clare: " 'Justice' was done, and the President of the Im-mortals, in Aeschylean phrase, had ended his sport with Tess. And the d'Urberville knights and dames slept on in their tombs unknowing. The two speechless gazers bent themselves down to the earth, as if in prayer, and remained thus a long time, absolutely motionless: the flag continued to wave silently. As soon as they had strength they arose, *joined hands again*, and went on" (Hardy, 1978: 449, my italics). The protagonist's life—Oedipus's life, for instance—lets fiction go beyond the borders de-limited by the blanks and blacks of the text. The protagonist's death—the death of Jocelyn, Tess, or Yu Tsun—yields, in like manner, to the possibility of the fiction's continuation by virtue of a species of vampir-ism transmitted to other similar characters. As Proust observes: "Isn't the Dostoievski woman (as distinctive as a Rembrandt woman) with her mys-terious face, whose engaging beauty changes abruptly, as though her ap-parent good nature was only play-acting, into coarse ferocity (although at heart it seems that she is more good than bad), isn't she always the same,

alike respecting one of those conventions which are called principles. (F 3: 804; E 3: 303)

This remarkable passage turns on the distinction between historical knowledge and immediate, living knowledge. Historical knowledge is rational memory, *Gedächtnis*. This is the cold, exterior memory we may have of our own pasts on the basis of external evidence. My birth certificate tells me I was born in such and such a place on such and such a date as the child of such and such parents. I have no reason to doubt that, but I have no memory to confirm it. I cannot ratify it from my own experience. As Proust's novel abundantly testifies, much of our past life is no longer available to us as living testimony. Only those rare and fortuitous moments of affective memory give us back (or appear to give us back, since their authenticity is unverifiable), with all the warmth and immediacy of inwardly confirmed living experience (*Erinnerung*), a precious few of the past moments we lived through. Most French citizens are able, or used to be able, to recite the names of the kings of France with ready accuracy, since they had been forced to learn them by rote at school, just as a United States citizen is taught at school the succession of presidents from George Washington down to the latest victor in the media sweepstakes. Both are cases of external rote knowledge, based on books. Charlus has no direct knowledge of Louis XIII or of any other French king, nor have I any direct knowledge of George Washington. Charlus knows the names of Odette's lovers in the same way as he knows the names of the kings of France, through an external and rationalized knowledge in which he has no personal investment. This does not mean that historical knowledge is inauthentic or unverifiable. On the contrary. It is the only knowledge of the past that is objectively verifiable. The paradox is that the object of historical inquiry is knowable and verifiable just because we are outside it, indifferent to it, not personally involved in it. This might give those committed to cultural studies pause, since their "studies," insofar as they fit the university's definition of verifiable research, may cut them off from intimate knowledge of what they want to preserve and make effective. Swann, on the other hand, can never know his wife's infidelities because he is too close to her. Nor can Marcel ever find out whether or not Albertine has lesbian lovers. The lover is blindfolded by the strength of his love. He feels his way helplessly, like a man playing the game of blindman's buff: "And indeed the jealous lover, like the contemporaries of an historical event, is

whether it's Nastasia Philipovna writing love letters to Aglaya and telling her that she hates her, or in a visit that's absolutely identical with this . . . Grushenka, as charming in Katerina Ivanovna's house as the latter had supposed her to be terrible, then suddenly revealing her malevolence by insulting Katerina Ivanovna" (Proust, 1982: 384). As we shall observe, the mixture of identity and particularity or difference underlined by Proust constitutes one of the possible bonds of repetition.

According to Miller, "The full meaning of the novel emerges only through the juxtaposition of the two versions." If the aporia of interminability aims at the idea that "each explanation both hides and reveals the lack of sufficient, reasonable explanation" (FR, 173), how can a "full meaning" exist? What is this trying to say? If it concerns a movement through which the critic comes to possess the meaning of the text, we would find ourselves before a contradiction. Stephen Albert tells Yu Tsun: "In all fictional works, each time a man is confronted with several alternatives, he chooses one and eliminates the others; in the fiction of Ts'ui Pên, he chooses—simultaneously—all of them" (Borges, 1964: 26). The critic who is contaminated by (and identifies with) the text attains the "full meaning" insofar as that "full" includes every alternative beginning and end, not just one set of them, because otherwise the critic could not account for the fact that Jocelyn decides both to commit suicide and to get married. On the diegetic level, it is not possible to make a decision: "The presence of two quite different endings for the novel, either one of which makes a plausible conclusion, forbids the reader to interpret the novel in terms of a necessary momentum toward a single conclusion" (FR, 154). On the metadiegetic level, it is possible to decide that "the concept of the definite text does not correspond to anything but to religion or to weariness" (Borges, 1980: 181). Therefore, the critic must make the decision of indecision. On a meta-metadiegetic level, *The Well-Beloved* is the agent (and the patient) that makes possible the undecidability of the other two

too close, he knows nothing, and it is for strangers that the chronicle of adultery assumes the precision of history." It would seem that the contemporaries of a historical event, like the man who is drawn close by love to his beloved, would know most, would be best able to convey knowledge, but he is too close, he knows nothing. He can only bear witness.

Bearing witness, as Jacques Derrida in his recent seminars has tirelessly borne witness, is not a cognitive but a performative event. Witnessing is a matter of demanding credence. The witness says, "Believe me. This is what I saw with my own eyes." Swann and Marcel would be satisfied only with this direct knowledge, but their mistresses and all their acquaintances conspire to keep them from it. The comedy of Marcel's jealousy is that it shows Marcel suffering greatly from a mistake. He confuses a performative with a cognitive situation. He wants to know, once and for all, whether Albertine is a lesbian, but this he can never know. He can never know whether or not Albertine or other witnesses he enlists are lying.[28] I shall return later to the all-important question of lying in the *Recherche*.

The opposition between Charlus's knowledge of Odette's lovers' names in their sequence and Swann's nonknowledge may be clarified by another historical parallel. Books about military history can diagram the Battle of Waterloo as a matter of massed troops led by this or that commander moving across a map. Through such accounts we get knowledge about the Battle of Waterloo. Chapters three through five of Stendhal's *The Charterhouse of Parma*, on the other hand, describe the Battle of Waterloo as witnessed from close up by Fabrice. Far from being comprehensible, it is for Fabrice a bewildering series of incomprehensible events. As the narrator says of the hero after the battle is over and he gets to Amiens: "So many and profound were the reflections he made on the things that had recently happened to him that he became another man [*comme un autre homme*]. He had remained a child upon one point only: Was what he had seen a real battle? And, if so, was that battle Waterloo? For the first time in his life he found some pleasure in reading; he was always hoping to find in the newspapers, or in published accounts of the battle, some description or other which would enable him to identify the ground he had covered with Marshal Ney's escort, and later with the other general."[29]

Literature, as Stendhal and Proust show, gives not historical knowledge, but the nonknowledge of those who are too close. The same thing can be said of the knowledge given by literary criticism, such as this essay. This does not mean that verified historical knowledge about literature

levels, that is to say, the novel is its own main deconstructive agent. The "full meaning" Miller talks about is precisely the expression of the whole that covers all (or none of) the possible meanings and not the expression of achieving a key meaning to the novel.

What has Miller done? How has he read texts by Hardy, Brönte, Woolf, and so on? Few people will miss that this reading has a great deal to do with the notion of "iterability" Derrida deals with in "Signature Event Context" (1982: 309–30, esp. 326–27). We should not stop even here. In "Thomas Hardy, Jacques Derrida, and the 'Dislocation of Souls,'" Miller says of a quotation from Derrida's "Telepathy": "It almost seems, as I have said, that these sentences were written with a kind of retrospective prevision of their appropriateness as a commentary on Hardy's 'The Torn Letter,' or as if 'The Torn Letter' had been written with foresight of Jacques Derrida's meditations on July 9, 1979, though so far as I know Derrida had not then and has not yet read Hardy's poem. Even so, Hardy's poem, which is a 'letter' in the first person written to an unnamed 'you,' has found its proper recipient at last in the unwitting Derrida. Derrida has become its reader without even knowing it" (TPP, 173–74).

What can these words, applicable both to Hardy's poem and to his novels, imply but the power of literature? The power of what and for what? This is precisely the key to Miller's specific reading. Boustrophedonism—that is, the attempt to cover all possibilities in the sense of Ts'ui Pên's novel—supposes that Miller verifies (rather than just names) a triple reading. De Man, in reply to a question from Stefano Rosso about the differences between him and Derrida, says: "Derrida's text is so brilliant, so incisive, so strong that whatever happens in Derrida, it happens between him and his own text. He doesn't need Rousseau, he doesn't need anybody else; I do need them very badly because I never had an idea of my own, it was always through a text, through the critical examination

cannot be given, just as the date of the Battle of Waterloo can be given and verified. We can know much about Proust's life, about the dates and circumstances of the *Recherche*'s composition, about the "originals" of his characters. We can know a great deal about surrounding historical circumstances at the time, for example about the Dreyfus case, or about the social situation of homosexuals in Proust's France. Nevertheless, that kind of ascertainable knowledge covers much less of literary criticism's domain than many people think or than might be wished. What we call "readings" of literary works are more like the second kind of nonknowledge gained by those who are too close. A factual list of Odette's lovers would not be literature. The story of Marcel's inability to find out the truth about Albertine is literature. One evidence for this curious status of literature is the perpetual wild divergence of opinion about what literary works mean. If literary knowledge were verifiable we would long since have heard the last word about *Hamlet*. We would be able to pass on a single, settled, universally agreed upon knowledge of what *Hamlet* means. Luckily, this will never happen. A "reading" of *Hamlet*, or of *The Charterhouse of Parma*, or of *A la recherche du temps perdu* is more like a performative act of bearing witness than like a verifiable cognition, more like Stendhal's account of Fabrice's bewilderment than like reading a historical account of the Battle of Waterloo. The phrase "literary history" has always been a species of oxymoron. The literary critic says, "Believe me, this is what I found when I read Proust's *Recherche*. I promise you that if you read it yourself you will find the same thing."

The passage from Stendhal turns on an opposition between historical knowledge and immediate nonknowledge similar to that Proust establishes between Charlus's knowledge and Swann's nonknowledge of Odette's adulteries. The irony is that Fabrice's "profound reflections" do not amount to much, whereas the childish doubt he has about whether he has really been at the battle of Waterloo is truly profound. His desire to get things straight by reading the newspapers or historical accounts is like the fatuous assumption by the narrator of Henry James's *The Aspern Papers* that he can get intimate knowledge of Jeffrey Aspern's life if he can just read Aspern's private papers.

It might be argued, nevertheless, that just as what Fabrice saw he unequivocally knew and could testify to, as an eye witness, even though what he saw did not allow him to know whether or not he had been in the Battle of Waterloo or even in a battle at all, so, in the same way, if Marcel were

of a text" (de Man, 1986: 118). It is as if de Man were saying that Derrida reads the texts from outside because the power of his own text (a philosophical power?) is enough for him, whereas de Man needs to read from inside because he lacks his own text. Perhaps, however, de Man's words should be read ironically.

If we compare Miller's way of reading with Derrida's and de Man's, I would say that Miller is the critic who constantly moves between his own text (differentiating him from de Man) and the text he analyses (differentiating him from Derrida). This makes him Aristotelian (when he reads the narration in a referential and diegetic way, e.g., when he wonders about Tess's undeserved suffering or about Jocelyn's repeated mistakes), anti-Aristotelian (when he keenly analyzes the way in which that diegesis is broken in the impossibility of completing an Aristotelian reading), and, in addition, boustrophedonic, when his reading becomes a discourse on the conditions of reading. Just as "The Garden of Forking Paths" is at once a story about spies and a (meta-meta)theoretical proposal (being two things at once, jointly and separately), Miller's essay analyzed here reads the story and reads the reading in order to discover why the reading is not viable. Story and metastory are kept apart and, at the same time, interact. What Miller would answer to de Man and Derrida is that, whatever way you look at it, literature cannot be touched, penetrated, or examined, yet we are under an obligation to touch it, to penetrate it, and to examine it in a philological way. Shall we be surprised at Miller's passing from this impasse to the problem of an ethics of reading?

As if . . .

For many centuries, institutions and their representatives (whether philosophical, religious, political, etc.) suspected that behind poetical

to get evidence with his own eyes that Albertine has been lying to him, the blindfold would be removed. He would know for sure at last. Proust, however, firmly denies that possibility, or has Marcel do so. This happens in the important pages of reflection by Marcel that follow the episode of the death of Bergotte. I have discussed these pages in a separate essay.[30]

If certainty about people we love is impossible, it might nevertheless seem from many things Marcel says that works of art give us real knowledge of the artist. This is a knowledge not possible with those who are not artists, unless, perhaps, they are, like Albertine, mistresses of the art of lying. Marcel, however, entertains two contradictory hypotheses about art, parallel to those he holds about other people. Between these two ideas about art he hovers, unable to decide which is true. On the one hand, Marcel says, apropos of his experience of Vinteuil's music: "It is inconceivable that a piece of sculpture or a piece of music which gives us an emotion that we feel to be more exalted, more pure, more true, does not correspond to some definite spiritual reality, or life would be meaningless [*ne corresponde pas à une certaine réalité spirituelle, ou la vie n'aurait aucun sens*]" (F 3: 876; E 3: 381). On the other hand, it is possible that life *is* meaningless. The appearance of a profound unity in the work of great artists may be the result of a mere fabricating power. Marcel asserts this as an alternative hypothesis apropos of Wagner, even though he has just been praising those artists—Balzac, Hugo, Michelet, and Wagner himself—who discover retrospectively a unity in their own work that they did not know it had. "But then," says Marcel, "no less than by the similarity I had remarked just now between Vinteuil's phrase and Wagner's, I was troubled by the thought of this Vulcan-like skill. Could it be this that gave to great artists the illusory aspect of a fundamental, irreducible originality, apparently the reflection of a more than human reality, actually the result of industrious toil [*l'illusion d'une originalité foncière, irréductible, en apparence reflet d'une réalité plus qu'humaine, en fait produit d'un labeur industrieux*]?" (F 3: 667; E 3: 158–59).

This other hypothesis, the hypothesis of a fundamental disunity that may take on the illusory appearance of unity, the hypothesis that life is after all meaningless or has only such meanings as we may attribute to it by some unauthorized speech act, is entertained no less frequently and expressed no less eloquently by Marcel than the hypothesis of a profound unity. It is entertained even in relation to the knowledge we get of the

or literary "feigning" there was something more than feigning, something that came very close to a certain profound truth. For this reason, poetic works were under strict surveillance before their publication (as in the European phenomenon of the Holy Office or the book-burning episode in *Don Quixote*). In response, works sometimes circulated anonymously, without the author's signature, or texts were phrased in symbolic or enigmatic ways, so that things were both said and not said at once. (An extreme example, already considered as an aesthetic category, is the Gracian doctrine of *concept* ["wit," which he defined as "the art of squeezing correspondences between words and things"].) On the part of the critical reader, a prescriptive criticism, a commentary that judged with ethical and metaphysical criteria the form and the content of the work, became necessary. All this was independent of the effects of the poetic work with regard to its internal or external repetition. To put this briefly in narratological terms: At particular moments in history (or in histories, given that chronologies in different languages and countries obviously do not coincide), the "possible world" of poetic fiction comes to possess something more than a simply textual existence. It has political power, to be allowed, or sometimes feared and repressed. Perhaps as a result of this, Derrida speaks of literature as a

historical institution with its conventions, rules, etc., but also this institution of fiction which gives *in principle* the power to say everything, to break free of the rules, to displace them, and thereby to institute, to invent and even to suspect the traditional difference between nature and institution, nature and conventional law, nature and history. Here we should ask juridical and political questions. The institution of literature in the West, in its relatively modern form, is linked to an authorization to say everything, and doubtless too to the coming about of the modern idea of democracy. Not that it depends on a democracy in place, but it seems inseparable to me from what calls forth a democracy, in the most open (and doubtless itself to come) sense of democracy. (Derrida, 1992c: 37)

artist by way of his art. This other hypothesis, as I have suggested, is expressed most often in what Marcel says about the continuity of character in people who are not artists, for example, himself and Albertine. A cascade of such passages, eloquent in their rhetorical power, punctuates the *Recherche*. I cited in an earlier part of this book the sentences near the end of the *Recherche* in which Marcel says he needs "not the two-dimensional psychology [*la psychologie plane*] which we normally use but a quite different sort of three-dimensional psychology [*une sorte de psychologie dans l'espace*]" (F 4: 608; E 3: 1087). Marcel needs this new kind of psychology to record the multiple changes through time both of himself as center of experience in the *Recherche* and of the other people to whom he has been related. His figure for this, you will remember, is the motion of planetary bodies around their own axes, through their own orbits, and in relation to one another: "Each individual therefore—and I was myself one of these individuals—was a measure of duration for me, in virtue of the revolutions which like some heavenly body he had accomplished not only on his own axis [*autour de soi-même*] but also around other people [*autour des autres*], in virtue, above all, of the successive positions which he had occupied in relation to myself" (ibid., trans. slightly altered). This passage was cited earlier as a demonstration that pre-computer-age texts like *A la recherche du temps perdu* already have virtually a hypertext structure in the intricate system of repetitions and cross-references that link each part of the text with others. In the present context the passage may be taken to indicate the way time, for Marcel, is the fundamental dimension of human existence. Temporality, however, is a dimension of perpetual change and discontinuity, change both of Marcel and of all the others to whom he is related. The figure of planetary revolutions, however, still too much suggests the solid continuity through time of selves that rotate in complex dances in themselves and in relation to one another.

Proust's immense novel ends with another and more grotesque figure, that of each person as augmented monstrously through time. All men and women are like people "perched upon living stilts which never cease to grow [*vivantes échasses, grandissant sans cesse*], until sometimes they become taller than church steeples, making it in the end both difficult and perilous for them to walk and raising them to an eminence from which suddenly they fall" (F 4: 625; E 3: 1107). Marcel's vocation is to describe these monsters created by the slow passage of time:

That "authorization to say everything" is a complex expression whose meaning in relation to a given story, even the most recent one, is not easy to determine. It is not strange that Derrida himself says that he initially understood "in a confused way" (Derrida, 1992b: 36) that literature authorizes saying everything. In any event, it seems certain that, paraphrasing S. R. Levin's thesis in "Concerning What Kind of Speech Act a Poem Is," the possibility of literature would be inscribed in all the uses of language that imply an illocutive power of the type "I imagine myself in and invite you to conceive a world in which . . ." (Levin, 1976: 150). Literature in the specifically modern Western sense of the word arises with the appearance of democratic nation-states, but it has always been a possible way to use language, a way authoritarian regimes must censor or suppress.

The confused concept of imagination so fashionable in certain contexts of literary theory does not purport to establish a sharp difference or opposition between imagination and reality, between *mythos* and *logos* (see Lacoue-Labarthe and Nancy, 1970), or between the form and content of a text, although of course it is not possible (or advisable) to avoid all the implications that follow from such oppositions. In fact, on the basis of Aristotelian assumptions, everyone would be willing to accept, on principle (to mention the two texts that will be my point of reference), that Kant's *Foundations of the Metaphysics of Morals* is a nonfictitious text that wants to speak of what *is*, or more specifically of what *must be*, whereas Melville's "Bartleby, The Scrivener" is a fictitious text whose aim, let us suppose for the moment, is to tell us something that could be or could have been but that does not and did not really exist. Why then, does Miller, a well-known *literary critic*—let us call him that although we have already seen the restrictions of such an attribution—who has been accused of turning deconstruction into a simple method of reading (as if the methods of reading in question were really *simple*), deal first, when speak-

But at least, if strength were granted me for long enough to accomplish my work, I should not fail, even if the results were to make them resemble monsters [*resembler à des êtres monstrueux*], to describe men first and foremost as occupying a place, a very considerable place compared with the restricted one which is allotted to them in space, a place on the contrary prolonged past measure [*sans mesure*] — for simultaneously, like giants plunged into the years, they touch epochs that are immensely far apart, separated by the slow accretion of many, many days — in the dimension of Time [*entre lesquelles tant de jours sont venus se placer — dans le Temps*]. (F 4: 625; E 3: 1107)

Several "artifacts of translation" [31] have crept into the English here. These make the translation say something somewhat different from what the French says. Proust wrote *êtres monstrueux*, "monstrous beings," rather than "monsters." The French tips the balance in the direction of saying these temporalized beings are simply very large, but still with an overtone of "monstrous" in the sense of unlawful, grotesque, outside the norms of the species to which they appear to belong. *Sans mesure* is even stronger than "beyond measure." The French suggests that temporalized human beings are inordinate, immeasurable, not just too big to measure, but incompatible with any form of measurement, *sans mesure*. As such, temporalized human beings are implicitly sublime or uncanny in their resistance to being measured, like the Titanic man in Goya's *The Colossus* (or *Panic*, as it is also called). Human beings cannot be encompassed by human perception, reason, or language.

Time, in Proust's French, finally is not a "dimension" but just itself, *le Temps*. *Le Temps* is a strange medium that eventually turns every human being into a monstrous being. The analytic language Marcel uses in this climactic image, moreover, is incompatible with the image itself, just as figuring human beings in their interrelation as revolving planets is incompatible with the conceptual language Marcel uses. The figure of stilts suggests a slowly growing appendage or expansion of the self, an expansion that is continuous, homogeneous, and finite. The stilts may be higher than church steeples and lead ultimately to the death of the one who is forced to walk on them, but any such stilts would still be measurable. As all the thousands of pages that precede this ultimate one would confirm, not to speak of the words *monstrueux* and *sans mesure* in this last sentence, the stilts in question are neither continuous nor homogeneous. No yardstick can measure them. They are *sans mesure*. The figure helps the reader to "think" something that is incompatible with the figure and that is,

ing of the "ethics of reading," with certain passages from Kant's *Meta-physics of Morals*? Similar questions might be asked regarding the motive that guides his interest, as a literary critic, in de Man, Derrida, Benjamin, Turner, or Kleist. But our interest should first turn toward Kant. Why is Kant, in a book that thematizes the problem of exemplarity, the example that opens a book entitled *The Ethics of Reading*? Perhaps the reason is that Kant, in the *Metaphysics of Morals*, faces, from a metaphysical view-point, the question of ethics. That is true. Why not interrogate, regarding the ethics of reading, a classic book on ethics, in spite of an "extremely dense, complex, and thick history [that] stands between us and Kant like an opaque mist or like an impenetrable thicket of thorns around the sleeping beauty, forbidding direct access to Kant" (ER, 15)? Reading Kant would be preliminary to an ethical reading of literature. Finally the de-constructionists would face up to one of the black holes of their theory: the context (in the broad sense) of literature, specifically ethics. Or would it be another deconstructionist ruse, reminiscent of the assertion by de Man (the second example in Miller's book) that "the ethical category is imperative (i.e., a category rather than a value) to the extent that it is linguistic and not subjective. Morality is a version of the same language aporia that gave rise to such concepts as 'man' or 'love' or 'self,' and not the cause or the consequence of such concepts. The passage to an ethical tonality does not result from a transcendental imperative but is the refer-ential (and therefore unreliable) version of a linguistic confusion. Ethics (or, one should say, ethicity) is a discursive mode among others" (de Man, 1979: 206).

For Miller, the *literary* text, without edges, at once centered and de-centered, full of fissures and eager to cover them, subject to the aporia of interminability, a power that (de)programs from inside the deprogram-ming that will take place in the sequence of—literary or nonliterary— commentaries it causes, is, pardon the paradox, an absolute verbality, if

strictly speaking, unthinkable. Such figures may, in Proust's own terminology, be called allegories. What Proust stresses in his analysis of allegory
in the two discussions in the *Recherche* of Giotto's Virtues and Vices in
the Arena Chapel at Padua is the incompatibility between the allegorical
image and its meaning. If Charity were not labelled KARITAS, the viewer
would not know she is charity, since the figure does not look charitable.
The angels painted on the blue ceiling of the Arena Chapel do not look
like supernatural beings. They look like some extinct earthly species or like
airplanes doing the loop-the-loop. Another label for such figures is "catachresis," since what we call catachreses are figurative names for something
unknown and unknowable. If the monstrous extension of human beings
through time is really *sans mesure*, measureless, then it cannot be measured, that is to say, represented—for example, by any figure, neither by
that of the man on stilts as high as a church steeple nor by that of planetary revolution, nor by any other of the spectacularly inventive metaphors
that make up so much of the *Recherche*'s linguistic texture.

"Ce pouvoir simili-électrique"

Just what is it about human beings that makes them seem to Marcel
êtres monstrueux and *sans mesure* when their temporality is taken into account? I have already defined the law of ignorance that makes other people,
at least those who matter most to Marcel, unknown and unknowable.
Exactly why that is so and what consequences it has remains to be "re-
searched." In order to begin that task, four closely intertwined assumptions about human beings must be added to the presupposition of their
unknowability. Marcel expresses these repeatedly in slightly different ways,
according to the pattern of self-dissimilarity I have identified:

1. The incoherent multiplicity of selves in Marcel himself.
2. The incoherent multiplicity of selves in other people, for example,
Albertine.
3. The way each person does not have a fixed or even evolving personality in the ordinary sense, but is an empty matrix that holds the
possibility of innumerable inconsistent selves.
4. The presumption that other people, most significantly the ones
we love, are, like works of art, mediators of an impersonal otherness we
glimpse through them.

we can describe what lacks identity as being "absolute." Perhaps, however, its strength comes precisely from its "emptiness," from its "infinite" meta-metatheoricity. Along the same lines, de Man wrote, "The reading is not 'our' reading, since it uses only the linguistic elements provided by the text itself" (de Man, 1979: 17). To make of the text, of its rhetoric and grammar, of its complex and unbounded utterances an enveloping reality that avoids a movement or strategy alien to it is a way of turning textual self-reading into something all-powerful and, therefore, a way of avoiding a process of interpretation in which the critic says and does whatever he wants with the text. Although Miller does not completely share de Man's position, although he maintains, in different ways (according to the various works he discusses) the existence of *his* reading, we also find in him a devotion to the literary text as an enveloping and absolute reality, in spite of, as he will tell us in relation to the ethics of narrative, the similarity of the critic's work to Pygmalion's. This "in spite of" complicates matters. It returns us, so to speak, to the Millerian matrix, to the relation, in short, between reading and text, between exterior and interior. These words from *Versions of Pygmalion* express it succinctly: "My book will explore the ethics of narrative in its connection with the trope of prosopopoeia. But we have already learned something a little unsettling. Though none of us, of course, would take a statue as a real person, in order to 'read' the *Metamorphoses* it is necessary to yield to its basic narrative personifications, by a certain willing suspension of disbelief. We must think of Pygmalion, Galatea, Cinyras, Myrrha, and even Venus to some degree *as if* they were real persons, not just black marks on the page" (VP, 11–12, my italics).

The text I read—Ovid's *Metamorphoses*, Kant's *Metaphysics of Morals*, or Melville's *Bartleby*—is an object that is dead (black marks on the inanimate page), but we see it as if it were enveloping and absolute, animate, though that "as if" seems to encompass many things, among them

Notations of the first two of these assumptions recur throughout the *Recherche*, like Wagnerian leitmotivs. In *Albertine disparue*, for example, reflecting on the way the part of him that is still comfortably *chez soi* in his blue satin armchair, closely associated with his possession of Albertine, does not yet know that Albertine has left him, Marcel defines that part as "one more of those innumerable and humble 'selves' [*moi*] that compose our personality [*qui nous composent*] which was still unaware of Albertine's departure and must be informed of it" (F 4: 14; E 3: 437). Albertine herself, as Marcel recognizes repeatedly in *La prisonnière*, is not one single person, about whom he might get irrefutable information, once and for all. She is a multitude of Albertines, a swarming legion of heterogeneous selves. These different Albertines are discontinuous. They do not add up to a coherent moving picture. They are, rather, a series of separate and disconnected snapshots. "For I possessed in my memory," says Marcel, "only a series of Albertines, separate from one another, incomplete, a collection of profiles or snapshots [*instantanés*], and so my jealousy was restricted to a discontinuous expression, at once fugitive and fixed, and to the people who had caused that expression to appear upon Albertine's face" (F 3: 655; E 3: 145–46). (He means the expression he interprets as being desire for some woman or other.)

Marcel's jealousy is at once fugitive and fixed. It is fixed because it is always the same jealousy. It reforms itself again and again in identical anguish as soon as he thinks he has assuaged it. At the same time it is fugitive, since it is constantly changing its focus by shifting to the particular new person with whom he thinks Albertine may be sleeping: Mlle Vinteuil, Andrée, any woman she looks at with interest on the street, and so on. Each imagined betrayal gives Marcel a snapshot of a different Albertine.

A glimpse of the worst Albertine of all is given when she begins and then breaks off the phrase *me faire casser*, which Marcel later completes with *le pot*, so filling in the missing words of a vulgar cliché:

Albertine was several persons. [*Albertine était plusieurs personnes.*] The most mysterious, most simple, most loathsome of these revealed herself in the answer which she made me with an air of disgust, and the exact words of which, to tell the truth, I could not quite make out (even the opening words, for she did not finish her sentence). I did not succeed in reconstituting them until some time later when I guessed what was in her mind. We hear things retrospectively when we have understood them. [*On entend retrospectivement quand on a compris.*] (F 3: 840; E 3: 343, trans. slightly altered)

a programming that deprograms my behavior in connection with reading. This implies a strange and unsettling (Miller's words) incest: "But a relation in which there is no otherness, in which the same mates with the same, is, precisely, incest" (VP, 11). If we really accept that reading is the relation of a thing with itself, of a text with itself (according to de Man's thesis), of the same thing with the same thing, then why would it be necessary to pose the problem of the ethics of reading or of the ethics of narrative? For an ethical question to arise, something must exist in relation to another thing. There must be a text and also another thing different from the text (even if it is inside and not outside the text, in the heart of the text itself). It is impossible to avoid postulating that my reading is, somehow, *my* reading in relation to a text that is *other* if we want to set forth what happens when I, as a reader or as a critic, encounter Ovid, Kant, or Melville. One solution is to use the linguistic elements the text gives us. A quite different one may result from the way such linguistic elements are used. One solution is that we just rely on the text, and a quite different one is what we do with that text, which is the only thing we possess. Miller points out as one of the features of the "ethical moment" that it is "a response to something, responsible to it, responsive to it, respectful of it. In any ethical moment there is an imperative, some 'I must' or *Ich kann nicht anders.* I must do this. I cannot do otherwise. If the response is not one of necessity, grounded in some 'must,' if it is a freedom to do what one likes, then it is not ethical, as when we say, 'That isn't ethical'" (ER, 4).

Here Miller explores a double question. On the one hand, our reading is *ours* insofar as the literary space is the space of alterity, the space of the other in relation to whom I pose problems of behavior, as when Kant says: "The shortest but most infallible way to find the answer to the question as to whether a deceitful promise is consistent with duty is to ask myself: Would I be content that my maxim . . . should hold as a universal

Here is another and perhaps even more disturbing example of the failure to know a present experience. The only evidence Marcel has of this most mysterious and most loathsome Albertine is something she says. He does not actually hear it when she speaks it, since she does not finish the sentence and since he does not even quite make out the words she does speak.

We recognize the words in a sentence, we make sure they are these words and not others that sound much like them, primarily by placing them in syntactical patterns. When the syntax is still incomplete, the words may be this or they may be that. We cannot know for sure. Only later on, retrospectively, in this case by guessing at the missing two words, *le pot*, does Marcel give a meaning to the words he heard Albertine say. His filling out of the sentence, however, is only a guess. It is a guess both at the missing words and also at the words he actually heard but heard so indistinctly as not to be quite sure what they were. The example is like that of the mistaken reading of the telegram apparently from Albertine but really from Gilberte: "We guess as we read. All begins with an initial mistake." This act of retrospective assigning of meaning now allows Marcel to hear at last, but of course without actually hearing, what he did not hear when it was there to be heard: "We hear things retrospectively when we have understood them [*compris*]." But "understanding," literally "taking in [*comprendre*]," is here invention in its double sense of making up and finding out. It is impossible for Marcel to verify his projection and discovery of meaning. It is impossible to tell whether it is invention in the sense of projection, or whether it is invention as discovery, a response to what was already there.

Albertine is certainly not going to tell him. Even if she were to tell him, she might be lying, as she lies when she gives him a thousand innocuous explanations of the words she said: "She gave me endless versions, none of which tallied in the least [*mais qui ne cadraient nullement*], not simply with her words which, having been interrupted, remained obscure to me, but with the interruption itself and the sudden flush that accompanied it" (F 3: 840–41; E 3: 343). Testimony, affirmation on oath, may always be a lie, as is apparently the case when Albertine says of her innocent explanations of *me faire casser*: "I swear to you that was all [*je vous jure que c'est cela*]" (F 3: 841; E 3: 343). I say "apparently" because it cannot be verified one way or the other. I shall return to this later on. The Albertine who wants anal sex is "mysterious" as well as "loathsome" because that Albertine can only be known indirectly, inferred from always uncertain signs, by unverifiable hypotheses. This is also true of all the other Albertines. Even the hypothesis

law for myself as well as for others?" (Kant, 1969: 22). The relation between the critic and the text (or between the narrator and character, etc.) must be a privileged place for ethical problems to arise: "Is it possible . . . to say that our respect for a text is like our respect for a person, that is, it is respect not for the text in itself but respect for a law which the text exemplifies?" (ER, 18). Logically, if the text exemplifies a law, that is because it embodies the other in relation to my reading. This alterity of literature, which always remains absolutely other, makes me suppose a priori that my reading is *mine*. Yet my reading cannot be an action alien to the text itself; it is related to it somehow. That gives the possessive "my" a different nuance. Before I can set forth an ethical question in relation to the other, the other must be present in myself. I must recognize it, be recognized by it, determine it and be determined by it, as when Kant warns us about the negative isolation of the self in ethical decision: "I immediately see that I could will the lie but not a universal law to lie. For with such a law there would be no promises at all" (Kant, 1969: 22).

Before one can ask about an ethics of reading, the text as an alterity must appear through the "my" of my reading, barred by the "my" of reading, whereas the "my" appears barred by the text. How, from this viewpoint, might anybody who has read ("it does not occur all that often," says Miller regarding the act of reading; ER, 3) Miller's texts be able to assert that deconstructive literary criticism is a discourse in which the critic freely says whatever he or she wants about the text (assuming, besides, that there exists something like what the critic says, namely Kant's words)? Who could dare describe Miller's works as "nihilist" and immoral? Whoever reads them may discover contradictions and, on that basis, be able freely to adopt one position or another, but he or she will not find an ungrounded writing. Miller recognizes that this is one of the reasons that has led him to set forth the question of the ethics of reading: "Deconstruction, such (mis)readers of it claim, asserts that the reader,

of the multiple and fugitive Albertines is unverifiable. For all Marcel knows there may be a hidden "real" and permanent Albertine whom he can never be certain he has glimpsed. The impossibility of knowing for sure torments him and keeps him fascinated by her. If he could know her and possess her completely, if she were fully transparent to him, she would be boring, without interest, as he repeatedly asserts, for example when, shortly before she leaves him, he says, "I felt that my life with Albertine was on the one hand, when I was not jealous, nothing but boredom, and on the other hand, when I was jealous, nothing but pain [*souffrance*]" (F 3: 895; E 3: 400).

The notion that I myself and the others I desire to know and possess are not unified and self-similar over time but *ondoyant et divers*, as Montaigne puts it, is by no means a new idea in modernist literature. The concept of the self's fugitive discontinuity and inconsistency has a long history in the West, particularly in French writing, as Georges Poulet's brilliant studies of French writers from Montaigne to Proust have abundantly demonstrated. Much less a received idea, however, is Proust's conception of the framework or ground (neither of these figures is quite right) within which or over which the interminable series of different selves displays itself. To that I now turn.

Speaking of his sense of himself, Marcel asserts that the only constant in the endless series of disconnected selves he becomes is an indifferent, undifferentiated, impersonal matrix. This "apparatus" is to be defined as no more than the possibility of becoming this or that Marcel. This is a terrifying vision of the self's ghostly anonymity. Marcel has to look at himself in the mirror to reassure himself that he has a substantial embodied existence. In a passage relegated to a note in the Pléiade edition, Marcel plans to buy an expensive yacht for Albertine. He thinks that when several years hence he has spent almost all his money on Albertine, he will leave the remainder to her and kill himself. That decision leads to a moment of self-reflection:

[It] made me think of *myself* [*à moi*]. Now, since one's ego [*le moi*] lives by thinking incessantly of all sorts of things, since it is no more than the thought of those things, if by chance [*par hasard*], instead of being preoccupied with those things [*au lieu d'avoir devant lui ces choses*], it suddenly thinks of itself, it finds only an empty apparatus, something which it does not recognise [*un appareil vide, quelque chose qu'il ne connaît pas*] and to which, in order to give it some reality, it adds the memory of a face seen in a mirror. That peculiar smile, that untidy moustache [*Ce drôle de sourire, ces moustaches inégales*]—they are what would disappear from the face of the earth. (F 4: 1059–60; E 3: 1116)

398   Narrativity, Example, Endlessness, Uncontrolled Performatives

teacher, or critic is free to make the text mean anything he wants it to mean. The implicit or explicit reproach is that this is immoral. . . . I want to demonstrate that this line of thought, whether expressed in the mass media or in academic circles, is a mistake" (ER, 9).

In making this demonstration, Miller focuses, through the question of the ethics of reading, on some of the main concerns guiding his work. He foregrounds his key *leitmotiv* (what we have been calling the Millerian matrix), that is to say, the problem of the relation between the critic and his discourse and the author and his text. If we notice at all, we find ourselves wondering whether an ethical moment of reading, which obliges respect for the text, means inquiring into the relation of touching and not touching between text and commentary, commentary and text, between the parasite and his host, whether, in short, it means an insistence on emphasizing the strange duality (a "my" that is and is not mine) implicit in the act of reading. How do text and commentary relate when the text embodies a law (or the law) the commentary should respect? Does respect for the text mean that the commentary allegorizes my behavior or not? Does it mean that the text controls me or that I transgress it? Can I do with it whatsoever I wish? Can I use it or interpret it or skillfully make it say what it does not say?

I can touch the text and identify myself with it as if I respected it, as if I were linked to it by a categorical imperative. Otherwise, the text might seem to be just a pretext for me, a means for saying something else, as if the only thing that linked me to it was a hypothetical imperative. Alternately, and given that ethics implies or necessitates concrete action, reading stages the ability to act, the text's ability to create an uninterrupted chain of effects, or, rather, reading raises the difficult question of the text's "performativity," not parasitic, mimetic, or fictitious performativity, but real performativity. This does not necessarily mean having grounds outside the linguistic act itself, since Miller's constant concern is

This extraordinary passage defines the self in relation to its prospective death. Confrontation of death is a way to get down to the bare bones of the ego, since the inevitability of dying essentially defines the self. I am a being who is not only capable of dying but who is certain one day to die. Just what is it that disappears when I die? The ego, *le moi*, in this passage so Cartesian in its terminology if not in its doctrine, lives only by way of that about which it thinks. The ego is no more than the thought of those things. But those things are external and contingent. "I" am not those things about which I think. I am rather the possibility of thinking about all those things. When, by chance, the self suddenly detaches itself from those external things it thinks, that possibility of thinking is revealed to be no more than "an empty apparatus." Such a moment of self-reflection can only happen "suddenly," "by chance," *par hasard*, since it is a senseless and contingent interruption of the ongoing current of my life, just as my death will someday be. Thinking of oneself is a foretaste of death. It is a little death that punctuates my life at unforeseen moments, in anticipation of the real death that will one day come.

The thought of the ego and the thought of death are alike in being "most strange." "Accordingly," says Marcel, "this thought of my death, like the notion of my ego, seemed to me most strange [*singulière*]" (F 4: 1060; E 3: 1116). The strangeness lies in the fact that if the ego is like death, then what should, one would assume, be the most intimate and familiar part of myself, my ego, turns out to be the most alien, like death itself. The *moi* is a completely empty and indeterminate possibility of thinking. It is a piece of unliving machinery, like a computer whose "random access memory" will manipulate, with sublime impersonality, whatever is put into it. This lifeless apparatus lives only by thinking. Its life is loaned to it entirely by what comes to it from the outside.

This insight is so strange and, to tell the truth, so frightening that the ego, in a desperate move to give the empty apparatus some reality, adds to it the memory of a face seen in a mirror, not "my face," but, as Proust puts it, "a face [*une figure*]," not that face seen here and now, but the memory of it, and not the perception of the face itself, since I cannot look at my own face, but, in a double remove, the memory of the mirrored reflection of that face. That reflection is a simulacrum, with left and right reversed, of what we look like to other people. Here is an adult "mirror stage." This mirror stage, however, is not associated with the child's accession to the symbolic order, as in Lacan's essay "Le stade du miroir,"[32] but

with the effect of literature on "life." Finally, the ethics of reading, understood so that "there is a necessary ethical moment in that act of reading as
such, a moment neither cognitive, nor political, nor social, nor interpersonal, but properly and independently ethical" (ER, 1), leads to another
constant in Miller's thought: his concern for the rhetorical, catachrestic,
prosopopoeic dimension of the literary text, to the extent that he asserts
that "without storytelling there is no theory of ethics" (ER, 3). What can
the relation between ethics and rhetoric, or between ethics and narrative,
be? Is it just one example among others? Kant says to us in the *The Metaphysics of Morals*, "Nor could one give poorer counsel to morality than to
attempt to derive it from examples (*Beispielen*)" (Kant, 1969: 29).

The initial formula, hypothesis, or bet remains: Every text—
narrative, poetic, dramatic, political, or otherwise—has a momentum
intrinsically ethical. At the same time, every discourse on ethics, every
philosophico-metaphysical discourse on ethics, needs tales, narrations,
suppositions, examples, and so forth, not only to illustrate its ideas, but
also, and above all, for its own internal structural constitution. If we
pause over these words, we shall observe that the two parts of the formula presuppose each other. The formula could be reduced to another,
more synthetic expression, one in which ethics and narrative are mutually implicated: "Ethics and narration cannot be kept separate, though
their relation is neither symmetrical nor harmonious" (ER, 2). This does
not mean that there is no difference in genre or strategy—though certain modern and medieval texts still deny this—between philosophical
discourse on ethics and narrative discourse. This is stated explicitly in
the introductory passage, "Reading Doing Reading," of *The Ethics of
Reading*: "I have said that there is a special appropriateness of narrative
examples for an investigation of the ethics of reading, but the reasons
for this must not be misunderstood. It is not because stories contain the
thematic dramatization of ethical situations, choices, and judgements

with the grownup's confrontation of what cannot be confronted or seen face to face, his or her own particular death.

Since the empty apparatus of thinking is already dead, what will disappear from the face of the earth when I die is not that mechanism but no more than what is most external to it, what other people see: that peculiar smile, that untidy moustache. The *moi* itself, the empty apparatus for thinking, will not disappear because it has always already disappeared. It has no sensible qualities that would ever allow it to appear, any more than death can appear as something open to sensation, perception, or experience.

If Marcel's own self is not even a succession of discontinuous selves, but rather the empty possibility of being all those selves by thinking about this or that, what about the selves of other people as they are comprehended by Marcel? What is it that underlies all the different selves Albertine is for Marcel? What Proust has Marcel say in one crucial place about this is surprising, extreme, hyperbolic. It goes well beyond the relatively banal idea that the other person is difficult to know because she is an endless succession of different selves. The passage in question occurs in the episode at the end of *Sodome et Gomorrhe* when Albertine changes her mind at the last minute and agrees to go back to Paris with Marcel. Marcel reflects on the detachment between the now-familiar furniture of his room in the hotel at Balbec and all the different events in his life that have "taken place," as we say, within it: "the diversity of the acts performed [*joués*] beneath the same ceiling, between the same glazed bookshelves, the change in one's heart and in one's life which that diversity implies, seem to be increased still further by the inalterable permanence of the setting, reinforced by the unity of the scene [*du lieu*]" (F 3: 510; E 2: 1164). The room with its glazed bookshelves, Marcel thinks, may be "an intellectual world, which was the sole reality," while his feelings for Albertine may have no more reality than the factitious emotion caused by reading episodes in a novel ("quelque chose comme celui que donne la lecture d'un roman," ibid.).

This leads Marcel to think of a more radical detachment, one that is like the detachment of a room from what is experienced within it, and yet is also fundamentally different, less easily thinkable. The false parallel between the two detachments nevertheless helps him to think the second one. The false analogy is like a catachresis. It is a figure carried over from what is known to give a name to what remains unknown. The new

that they are especially appropriate for my topic, but for a reverse reason, that is, because ethics has a peculiar relation to that form of language we call narrative. The thematic dramatizations of ethical topics are the oblique allegorization of this linguistic necessity" (ER, 3). Although the two parts of the formula are reciprocally presupposed by their summation in a single expression, their effects separately and in their different discursive genres follow distinct paths and must be analyzed one by one, in spite of their copresence at certain points of Miller's investigation. This nuance explains why Miller devoted two books, *The Ethics of Reading* and *Versions of Pygmalion*, to the second and first parts of the hypothesis, respectively. Let me first focus on the second part of the formula, on the way in which philosophical discourse on ethics needs narrative, for its structural internal constitution and not just to illustrate ideas or theses. Kant repeatedly says quite the opposite throughout the *Metaphysics of Morals*. Since it is, for Kant, a question of arriving at the law as such, beyond any concrete experience or tendency, "by no means could it [the example] authoritatively furnish the concept of morality" (Kant, 1969: 29). A few lines later, Kant says: "Imitation has no place in moral matters, and examples serve only for encouragement. That is, they put beyond question the practicability of what the law commands, and they make visible that which the practical rule expresses more generally. But they can never justify our guiding ourselves by examples and our setting aside their true original which lies in reason" (Kant, 1969: 29). To what extent is it possible to avoid examples?

In the preceding paragraph, Kant relates imitation to the example, a well-established relationship. In the Latin etymon *exemplum*, he gathers at least the meanings "example," "model," "copy," "reproduction," and "sample," as well as others coming from the terms that gave rise to *exemplum*, namely, *eximere*, "to take out," "to extract," and *emere*, "to take." This linking of imitation and example foresees their association with lit-

distinction is between Marcel's love for his various mistresses, including Albertine, and those mistresses themselves. The latter, says Marcel, are not the "image" (F 3: 511; E 2: 1164) of the former. Just as the room and what happens within it are distinct, the one just the *lieu* where the other takes place, so Marcel's love is distinct from the faces, the voices, the bodies of the women he loves. The relative solidity of the two sides of the distinction has changed place, in a chiasmus, between the first form of detachment and the second. Though Marcel's room with its glazed bookshelves, its shutters opening on the sea, may be "an intellectual world, which was the sole reality," nevertheless that room has a satisfying solidity, "the unalterable permanance of the setting reinforced by the unity of the scene [*la permanence immuable du décor, renforcé par l'unité du lieu*]." In the case of Marcel's love and his mistresses, however, the mistresses are as tangible and real as those glazed bookshelves, whereas his love is a response to something that remains the same through all the succession of mistresses, but is imageless, unknowable, without any apparent materiality at all. His love is a response to an implacable demand made on him by something that entirely exceeds any temporary object of love and is only mediated by them all. This something is unthinkable, invisible, colorless, odorless, tasteless. It can only be named in a sequence of inadequate and inconsistent figures, as a "virtue," as a "quasi-electric power," as "invisible forces," as "obscure deities," as "occult forces" to which or to whom Marcel must make sacrifice and utter contradictory incantations in an effort to find the right performative formula that will induce those deities to appear. Though he may touch, hold, and possess woman after woman, the obscure deities never appear, in spite of the fact that they determine his love with irresistible force. The passage expressing this is perhaps the most explicit statement anywhere in Proust naming the incompatibility between the actual women Marcel loves and the forever invisible power that motivates that love:

That love was genuine [*vrai*], since I subordinated everything else to seeing them [my mistresses], keeping them for myself alone, and would weep aloud if, one evening, I had waited for them in vain. But it was more because they had the faculty [*propriété*] of arousing that love, or raising it to a paroxysm, than because they were its image [*qu'elles n'en étaient l'image*]. But when I saw them [his mistresses], when I heard their voices, I could find nothing in them which resembled my love and could account for it. And yet my sole joy lay in seeing them, my sole anxiety in waiting for them to come. It was as though a virtue [*une vertu*] that had no connection with them had been artificially attached to them by nature, and that this

erature in both Platonic and Aristotelian registers. In *Passions*, Derrida asserts: "Something of literature will have begun when it is not possible to decide whether, when I speak of something, I am indeed speaking of something (of the thing itself, this one, for itself) or if I am giving an example, an example of something or an example of the fact that I can speak of something, of my way of speaking of something, of the possibility of speaking in general of something in general, or again of writing these words, etc." (Derrida, 1995b: 142–43). We should note the form of Derrida's utterance. He does not speak of "literature" and does not identify a possible "literary being." Rather, he mentions an indeterminate and imprecise "something (*quelque chose*)" of literature that starts at a determinate time, a time that, nevertheless, cannot be pointed out with certainty. This approach tallies with the conditional tense Aristotle uses in order to characterize the poet's task: "not . . . what has happened, but what may happen" (1451a; Aristotle, 1951: 35). The traditional interpretation of Aristotle's words seems not to have taken sufficiently into account that the Aristotelian definition does not agree with the Parmenidian opposition between being and not-being. The question of what "would be able to" happen does not tell us anything about whether what poetry has told us is or is not. We are still uncertain as to whether it is or it is not.

The "would be able to" does not affirm that poetry talks about something that is, rather than a general and universal example or a model free from accidents and the particular. If it is more universal than history, this results, not so much from effacing the being of what it tells, as from departure from that being through an uncertainty that cannot be decided. The result is that the expression "possible world" is contradictory when fictionality is its defining feature. Fiction, as non-being, should, strictly speaking, belong to the field of the "impossible" world. From the moment we speak of "possibility," we question the being of literature

virtue, this quasi-electric power [*ce pouvoir simili-électrique*], had the effect upon
me of exciting my love, that is to say of controlling all my actions and causing all
my sufferings. But from this, the beauty, or the intelligence, or the kindness of
these women was entirely distinct. As by an electric current that gives us a shock
[*comme par un courant électrique qui vous meut*], I have been shaken [*secoué*] by
my loves, I have lived them, I have felt them: never have I succeeded in seeing
or thinking them [*jamais je n'ai pu arriver à les voir ou à les penser*]. Indeed I am
inclined to believe that in these relationships (I leave out of account the physical pleasure which is their habitual accompaniment but is not enough in itself to
constitute them), beneath the outward appearance of the woman, it is to those
invisible forces [*à ces forces invisibles*] with which she is incidentally accompanied
that we address ourselves as to obscure deities [*comme à d'obscures divinités*]. It is
they whose good will is necessary to us, with whom we seek to establish contact
without finding any positive pleasure in it. The woman herself, during our assignation with her, does little more than put us in touch with these goddesses [*avec
ces déesses*]. We have, by way of oblation [*comme des offrandes*], promised jewels
and travels, uttered incantations [*prononcé des formules*] which mean that we adore
and, at the same time, contrary incantations [*des formules contraires*] which mean
that we are indifferent. We have used all our power to obtain a fresh assignation,
but one that is accorded to us without constraint [*sans ennui*]. Would we in fact
go to so much trouble for the woman herself, if she were not complemented by
these occult forces [*complétée par ces forces occultes*], considering that, once she has
left us, we are unable to say how she was dressed and realise that we never even
looked at her? (F 3: 511; E 2: 1164–65)

Exploiting the traditional use of religious figures to name the lover's
"adoration" of the beloved, Marcel here asserts that it is not the beloved
whom we adore, nor is it she to whom we offer sacrifices and utter magic
formulas designed both to coerce and to implore the satisfaction of our
love, or perhaps to feign our indifference. Rather, we adore plural forces,
like electric currents, forces that we only for convenience personify as goddesses, since we have never succeeded in seeing them or even in thinking
them. They are invisible and unthinkable. What Marcel stresses is the complete dissimilarity between the actual women who are the accompaniment
(not the vehicle) of these occult forces and those forces themselves. One is
by no means the image of the other. So irrelevant are the actual features
and dress of the woman we implore to give us an assignation that afterwards we cannot even remember how she looked or how she was dressed.
The occult forces have only been artificially and arbitrarily connected to

with regard to its being or non-being. The poetical meaning does not affirm the being of non-being (Kristeva, 1969a), but remains undecidable with regard to the being or non-being of what it says or narrates, or else asserts at the same time that being and non-being. In this sense, Derrida neither speaks of literature (since this would suppose attributing to it a place in the opposition being/non-being) nor expresses himself in terms of a decision. Quite the opposite: something (*quelque chose*) of literature will have started (*aura commencé*) when it will not have been possible to decide (*quand il n'aura pas été possible de décider*). This undecidability concerning what "is" in literature allows questions that, as Miller writes, call for inquiry into "a possible analogy between the ethical choices of characters within novels and the ethical acts of readers of novels. That is one version of the double genitive in 'ethics *of* reading.' Does the ethical act of the protagonist inside the book correspond to the ethical acts the reading of the book generates outside the book?" (ER, 2). If on the one hand, literature effaced completely the being of what it says or tells, if it fit in with the opposition reality/fiction, if, in short, the narrative world were merely textual, how would anybody be able to argue for an analogy between the world of fiction and the world of reality? On the other hand, if literature corresponded to the being of what it tells or says, if it were to be thought under the authority of the real, if, in short, the narrative world were referential in an absolute or even metaphorical way (Ricoeur, 1977), why would anyone suggest that fiction might be *analogous* to reality?

Let us term an *entry* of literature the entry of something (*quelque chose*) of literature. In this hazy borderland—the place and non-place of literature—the possibility of literature takes place. Derrida writes: "What I have just said about speaking on some subject does not require utterance [*la parole*], i.e., a discursive statement and its written transcription. It is valid for every trace in general, whether it is preverbal, for example, or a mute deictic, the gesture or play of an animal" (Derrida, 1995b: 143).

women from whom they are entirely distinct and which they only "incidentally [*accessoirement*] accompany."

Only a lover who, like Marcel, is promiscuous, who shifts from one woman to another, would be able to make the discovery recorded in this paragraph. A man who loves only one woman and remains faithful to her might make the idolatrous mistake of thinking that the one woman he loves is the sole and adequate image of those obscure deities. "Idolatry" is the proper term here. One could say that Proust has in this paragraph transposed the Mosaic prohibition against graven images into the realm of fleshly love. It is idolatry to think that the woman I love bears any resemblance to the all-powerful force to which I respond when I fall in love.[33] If I love many woman in sequence, I am able to detach the electric shock of what really motivates my love from the trivial conduit, let us say the copper wire, that transmits that shock. I can then see that they are entirely distinct. What Marcel records here is an experience to which he bears witness as though he were swearing on oath: "I have lived them, I have felt them: never have I succeeded in seeing them or thinking them." I shall return later to the importance of this testamentary aspect in Marcel's discourse.

What Marcel testifies to here might be expressed as the breakdown of metonymic similarity in its particular form of the relationship between container and thing contained. Just as Marcel's hotel room bears no similarity to the various events it has contained, so the women Marcel has loved bear no similarity to what he has experienced through them. What he has experienced is not even something contained in these women. It is just accidentally attached to them, from the outside. He has submitted to the irresistible demand from invisible and hidden forces for a response. To those invisible forces or obscure deities I would give the name "the others." They are a spectacular example of that other other I discussed above, the other that can never be returned to the same and that always appears as a plurality, in many voices, *à plusieurs voix*.[34]

"Une patrie inconnue"

Does anything like Marcel's record of the way his loving is a response to something other than any of the women he loves appear in his account of the effect on him of works of art—painting, music, literature? It would appear not. Marcel's discussion of art, as I have said, seems to be organized around the opposition between the hypothesis that the artwork is a facti-

Precisely because he speaks of an *entry* of literature and not of literature itself as specificity, identity, or closed circle, Derrida can assert that that "something" does not necessarily identify itself with the verbal, but can refer to a dumb deictic or to an animal's game. The gesture without words also imitates (as in Aristotle's *Poetics*, 1447a; Aristotle, 1951: 7), just as the animal plays, though Aristotle would have denied to animals the power to make a literary gesture. Perhaps the space of the word, the space of the poem or novel, is the privileged place where literature enters more profoundly, but that does not mean that literature is exclusively there. If, on the one hand, technical elements like meter, rhyme, or the title of a novel habitually function as signs that prove that what is there is literature, on the other hand, Aristotle says that those technical factors are not the basic ones that identify poetical facts since medical or physical contents as well as poetical ones can be cast in this form (1447b; Aristotle, 1951: 9). If I talk about Aristotle, it is not to conclude that Derrida and Miller are saying the same thing, but to suggest that a reading of Aristotle can aim in this direction. Derrida speaks of the entry of literature in a way analogous to what Miller ascribes to Kant: "We must, he says, perform a little experiment, enter in imagination into a little fiction, an 'in such a way' or 'als so' " (ER, 28). According to Miller, literature, narrative, and fiction put in an appearance just when the "as if" appears, and the "as if" is identified, in its turn, with imagination. All this has great import for literary theory or literary criticism, for two basic reasons.

    1. It implies the disintegration of the literary fact (not only because of the well-known crisis of literariness). It turns from essentialist assumptions about literature to the notion of an *entry* of literature, literature, moreover, not as a delimited object. In such an entry converge the historical-contextual factors to which the iterability of the notion of entry or "as if" gives rise (e.g., what the

tious assemblage of pieces technically arranged around an illusory center and the opposed hypothesis that the artwork does in truth give us what we can get in no other way, knowledge of the artist's hidden self. The artist's self, according to this alternative hypothesis, really exists. It remains the same through all the vicissitudes of the artist's life. If this is so, artists would appear to be different, for Marcel, from all other people, for example, the various women he loves.

To be certain this is what Proust really says, I propose to look a little more closely at an important segment of the *Recherche*. This passage is one of the high-water marks of Proust's art. It describes Marcel's experiences and meditations as he listens to Vinteuil's septet at the Verdurins' evening party. The passage is a spectacular example of Proust's notoriously elaborate prose. It is all too easy to take it as a kind of tone poem in words and therefore not bother to read it with close attention to detail. The passage is a curious kind of mimesis. "Ekphrasis" is the name given to the description in words of a real or imaginary painting or sculpture. Homer's description of Achilles' shield and Keats's "Ode on a Grecian Urn" are paradigmatic examples. Theorists of ekphrasis quite properly distinguish between descriptions of paintings, sculptures, or pots that really exist and descriptions of imaginary ones, such as the two examples I have given. Auden's "The Fall of Icarus" and Ashbery's "Self-Portrait in a Convex Mirror" describe (though that is of course not quite the right word; "read" might be better) paintings by Breughel and Parmigianino, respectively. These paintings do really exist and can be set beside the poems. Vinteuil's septet, like Vinteuil himself, is imaginary. So far as I know, no word exists to name as a separate genre descriptions in words of music. This genre may by a species of catachresis also be called an ekphrasis. Other distinguished examples are E. M. Forster's description of Beethoven's Fifth Symphony in *Howards End* or Mann's description of Adrian Leverkuhn's compositions in *Dr. Faustus*. Though Proust may to some degree have had César Franck's music in mind as a model for Vinteuil's work, nevertheless Vinteuil, unlike Beethoven, and like Leverkuhn, is a fictive composer. His sonata and his septet can be encountered nowhere but in the pages of *A la recherche du temps perdu*. One evidence for this is the way Proust kept changing the form of the imaginary work in successive drafts. Sometimes it was a symphonic piece, sometimes a quartet, sometimes a sextet, sometimes a piece for ten instruments, and then finally a septet, though exactly for which instruments is not specified.

chain of writing understands by "as if" in Horace, Dante, Cervantes, Mallarmé, Proust, or Nabokov). We have always to take into account that, as Miller has shown, repetition belongs both to the "inside" and to the "outside" of the literary text.

2. A literary theory needs the example and has special dealings with that example. Perhaps, moreover, it is able to function itself as an example, as when the teacher gives an example to the students (and what I am saying now is just another example) of *how* a set of words would be an analysis of a narrative text from the viewpoint of structuralism or psychoanalysis. For instance, when Miller examines certain passages from Kant's *Metaphysics of Morals*, he comes to the conclusion that the choice "of examples in the course of an argument . . . are not only not innocent (no example is innocent) but . . . in open or covert ways pose a fundamental challenge to just the conceptual formulations the examples are apparently meant to exemplify and support. The example undermines that of which it is posed as an example" (ER, 30).

Given that literary theory, like any other human "science," is interested in the relation between the universal and the singular, and given that, as Derek Attridge says, "this question of the singular and the universal raises a number of issues of importance in any consideration of literature" (Derrida, 1992c: 17), statements like those by Miller must attract the attention of the reader and worry him or her.

Kant's text is an excellent point of reference. What stands out most in Miller's exploration of certain passages of Kant's essay are the ways through which literature enters, puts in an appearance, within the purest, according to Kant's own claim, conceptual discourse. Miller neither brings up the question of the "form" of philosophy nor maintains the suspicion that, at its core, philosophy is no more than literature. Such

Learning this from the drafts and notes has an unsettling effect, at least on me. It brings home the complete dependence of this music on Proust's language for its existence. You cannot ever hear it played at any concert. Proust could change it at will from symphony to chamber music. Keats asserts, apropos of the music being played by the musicians carved on the Grecian urn, "Heard melodies are sweet, but those unheard/Are sweeter" (ll. 11–12). Vinteuil's septet is one of those sweeter works condemned to be eternally unheard. To the importance of this I shall return later.

At first the passage about Vinteuil's septet seems to confirm the understanding of Proust's ideas about art I have suggested above. Marcel, as he listens to Vinteuil's septet, until now unknown to him, is persuaded again of the uniqueness of Vinteuil's genius. Marcel calls this, in a paradoxical phrase, the "permanent novelty [*durable nouveauté*]" of his work (F 3: 758; E 3: 256). This durability consists in the fact that each time Vinteuil's work is played, the unique world of his music is opened up again. It does not ever cease to be new: "The revolution that their apparition has effected . . . is unleashed, it explodes anew, when, and only when, the works of the once-for-all-time innovator are performed again [*quand on rejoue les oeuvres du novateur à perpétuité*]" (F 3: 758; E 3: 255). The innovation occurs once and once only. It is an inaugural event. Once it has occurred, however, it is durable, sempiternal, as long as the music goes on being replayed or even goes on being capable of being replayed. The novelty consists in the fact that all Vinteuil's works, however different superficially from one another, reveal "profound similarities [*similitudes profondes*]" and "disguised, involuntary resemblances [*ressemblances dissimulées, involontaires*]" (F 3: 760; E 3: 257).

The word *involontaires* points to a distinction discussed above. This distinction is parallel to the better-known one Proust makes between voluntary memory, which is superficial and inauthentic, and affective memory, which is involuntary and gives back the past in all its sensible immediacy. In a similar way, the "deliberate resemblances [*ressemblances voulues*]" (ibid.) between one part of a work and another or between one work and another by Vinteuil are "the work of [Vinteuil's] intellect, necessarily superficial" (ibid.). But when Vinteuil tried hardest to be different from himself, those disguised, involuntary resemblances revealed the profound unity from which all his works arose: "for then Vinteuil, striving to do something new, interrogated himself, with all the power of his creative

a contradiction would be foreign to Miller's discourse. The question does not refer to whether philosophy is, after all, literature, but to the way literature (as *entry*, in the sense Derrida names) enters philosophy as philosophy. Can the literary entry be present in a discourse in which, as Kant argues, it is necessary "to construct a pure moral philosophy which is completely freed from everything which may be only empirical and thus belong to anthropology" (Kant, 1969: 5) or, as he puts it elsewhere, a "completely isolated metaphysics of morals, mixed with no anthropology, no theology, no physics or hyperphysics" (Kant, 1969: 31)? For this reason, Miller tells us, "Readers of Kant will know the importance of this notion of purity. It means the removal of everything contingent, empirical, local, such as the moral codes of a particular time, place, class, country, or culture, in order to leave the absolutely universal, abstracted from all particularity" (ER, 16). There are at least two places in Kant's text, however, where he shows that precisely because it is a question of a pure moral philosophy, it is not possible to confront the law as such face to face, to take it for granted. So, in the chapter "Transition from the Popular Moral Philosophy to the Metaphysics of Morals," we read: "We have also clearly exhibited the content of the categorical imperative which must contain the principle of all duty (if there is such)" (Kant, 1969: 49). And in the last chapter, "Transition from the Metaphysics of Morals to the Critical Examination of Pure Practical Reason," Kant says, "We have finally reduced the definite concept of morality to the idea of freedom, but we could not prove freedom to be real in ourselves and in human nature. We saw only that we must presuppose it if we would think of a being as rational and conscious of his causality with respect to actions, that is, as endowed with a will" (Kant, 1969: 76).

The Kantian inferences could not be more consistent. If it is true that the law as such should be free of all accidents, particularities, or models, then the expression "law as such" neither names nor subsumes any-

energy, reached down to his essential self at those depths [*atteignat sa propre essence à ces profondeurs*] where, whatever be the question asked, it is in the same accent, that is to say its own [*le sien propre*], that it replies" (F 3: 760; E 3: 258). Marcel does not say "essential self," as the translation has it, but "essence," which is not quite the same thing. The involuntary sameness in everything Vinteuil composed, evidence of an absolute singularity at the source, is, says Marcel, proof of the existence and individuality of the soul: "The impression conveyed by these Vinteuil phrases was different from any other, as though, in spite of the conclusions to which science seems to point, the individual did exist [*l'individuel existait*]" (F 3: 760; E 3: 257); "it is indeed a unique accent, an unmistakable voice, to which in spite of themselves those great singers [*chanteurs*] that original composers are rise and return, and which is a proof of the irreducibly individual existence of the soul [*une preuve de l'existence irréductiblement individuelle de l'âme*]" (F 3: 761; E 3: 258). It is also a proof of a quasi-immortality of the soul, since, as Marcel says, "Vinteuil had been dead for many years; but in [*au milieu de,* that is, "by means of," or "through the medium of"] the sound of these instruments which he loved, it had been given to him to go on living, for an unlimited time, a part at least of his life" (F 3: 759; E 3: 256).

These assertions would seem to be definitive evidence that, for Marcel, at least at this time of his life, the irreducible individuality of the soul is the rock bottom origin, so to speak, of the unique accent perceptible everywhere in the work of a great composer like Vinteuil. Such assertions would seem to be supported by equally eloquent affirmations elsewhere in the *Recherche,* as when Marcel tells Albertine that Hardy, Dostoevsky, and Stendhal have each brought a novel and unique beauty into the world. If we look a little closer, however, with another increase in magnification, at what Marcel actually says about the sources of the singular note that persists in all Vinteuil's work, something else appears. This something other contradicts or fundamentally modifies the idea that the individuality of the self is a solid origin.

According to this other hypothesis, it is not so much that for Marcel the self is an abyss rather than a ground, as that the self for him is a kind of tunnel, like Alice's rabbit hole. That tunnel leads down to an unknown, unknowable world, unique to each artist and inexpressible by any direct means. That world is not something possessed or lived in now that can be described. The artist's work rather prays or solicits that world to reveal itself. Such appeal is a "hope" or a "promise," not a command. If

thing like the law as such. The latter must remain unnamable, without face, without phenomenality, without possibility of being known, veiled, absent, inaccessible: "Freedom is a mere idea, the objective reality of which can in no way be shown according to natural laws or in any possible experience. Since no example in accordance with any analogy can support it, it can never be comprehended or even imagined. It holds only as the necessary presupposition of reason" (Kant, 1969: 89). The law as such would be something like the absence of the book, text, or writing. And if Kant gives examples, tells stories, formulates hypotheses about particular cases, he aims to prove that the law as such cannot be inferred from such stories or narrations. Yet the latter proliferate in *The Metaphysics of Morals*. We have, for example: the merchant who does not deceive an inexperienced customer by charging him too much money; the man who, after having suffered many setbacks, decides to go on with his life and not commit suicide; the well-to-do man who thinks about improving his fellow man's condition; someone who suffers from gout; a man who makes a promise intending not to keep it; a story of loyalty in friendship; the saint in the Gospels; the doctor who cures versus the poisoner who kills, and so on. These brief narrations or acts of imagination appear whenever Kant argues *a contrario*, that is, with a negative value. They are bad examples, negative but also necessary. This necessity, as Miller correctly observes, opens a huge field of possibilities. The specific focus of *The Ethics of Reading*, Miller says, is on narrators' or authors' acts of reading their own texts: "I have chosen to concentrate on . . . passages where an author reads himself. In such passages the ethics of reading is manifested in one of its most revealing versions, that is, in places where the author and the reader are the same. At such moments an author turns back on himself, so to speak, turns back on a text he or she has written, re-reads it, and, it may be, performs an act which can be called an example of the ethics of reading" (ER, 15).

the novelty and singularity of Vinteuil's work is an "apparition," that is, something like a ghost in broad daylight, that work must, like a ghost, be invoked by the composer if it is to become manifest. The initial musical phrases in each work are such an invocation. They call upon the work to appear. It is as if the work were something already existing somewhere waiting to be summoned into hearing by the right magic formula. The terminology of such speech acts as invocations, prayers, supplications, promises, hopes, or incantations, runs all through these pages. The word translated as "singers" in the phrase "those great singers that original composers are" is *chanteurs* in the French original. The word means "singers," but with overtones of song as chant, as incantation, as enchantment. The term, or its cognates, is used repeatedly to keep before the reader's mind the magical aspect of music. In Vinteuil's sonata, a timid question is responded to by the "little phrase" about which so much is made earlier in the novel, just as much is made, in the episode of Bergotte's death, of the "little patch of yellow wall" on the right side of Vermeer's *View of Delft*. These small parts are the equal of or even greater than the whole of which they are a part, the contained containing the container. This is a version of the fractal logic I discussed earlier.[35] In the septet, the opening is not a timid question but rather a "breathless supplication to find the fulfilment of the strange promise" of the opening (F 3: 759; E 3: 256). In both the sonata and the septet the beginning is like an appeal: "Do please come!" A little later Marcel opposes the "brief calls" of the sonata to the "restless, urgent, imploring" "medley of scattered fragments" of the septet, but affirms that it is in both cases nevertheless "the same prayer" (F 3: 759; E 3: 257). In Marcel's figure, the opening motifs of the two works are performative invocations. They are calls or prayers that cause the rest of the music to appear. What appears is the magical little phrase in the sonata, or, in the septet, the brilliant tonal colors that rise to a climax in the "lurching, riotous clangor of bells [*la titubation de cloches retentissantes et déchaînées*]," "the material representation of the coarsest joy" (F 3: 755; E 3: 252). Though the first call is necessary to set the music in motion and is initiated by the composer, the implication of Proust's figure is that the rest of the music already exists somewhere waiting to appear, like the ghost of Hamlet's father. It is not really "composed" by Vinteuil. It is discovered by him. It is "invented" in the primary sense of encountered, come upon, or made to manifest itself out of its hiddenness.

Marcel's recurrent figure for such incantatory invocations is the first light of dawn that heralds the appearance of the day. These appeals occur

We will leave aside the question, which Miller also raises, whether or not an author gives himself or herself away more in footnotes than in the main text, or the question whether we can really differentiate between main text and footnote: "Footnotes, as any astute reader will know, are often places where an author gives himself away in one way or another in the act of fabricating a protective cover. A footnote often reveals an uneasiness, identifies a fissure or seam in an author's thought by saying it is not there" (ER, 15). But what need dictates rereading and the footnotes that result? Why does Kant reread himself? Why does he retrace his steps? Miller identifies the context of that self-reading as being when Kant speaks of the law as such and of pure respect for the law: "Nothing remains which can determine the will objectively except the law, and nothing subjectively except pure respect for this practical law. This subjective element is the maxim that I ought to follow such a law even it thwarts all my inclinations" (Kant, 1969: 20). From the objective purity, or law as such and subjective purity, or respect for that law, it follows, as I shall show, that this "purity," whether objective or subjective, is inexpressible and inaccessible. This purity, perhaps because of its purity, because of remaining suspended in the emptiness of the mere supposition, is infected with a vagueness (characteristic of everything that is inexpressible) that makes it unrecognizable.

Kant thereupon returns to what he has already said and explains what he understands by "respect" in a footnote. That note begins: "It might be objected that I seek to take refuge in an obscure feeling behind the word 'respect,' instead of clearly resolving the question with a concept of reason" (Kant, 1969: 20). Is it possible to resolve in a rational concept what has neither a definite name nor a face? How might one express this inexpressible law? "The reader would like to know. He would like to have access to [the law], to confront it face to face, to see it written down somewhere, so he can know whether or not he is obeying it. Well,

at the moment before the coming of daylight, as the sun rises from its dark sojourn beneath the earth: "Whereas the sonata opened upon a lily-white pastoral dawn, dividing its fragile purity only to hover in the delicate yet compact entanglement of a rustic bower of honeysuckle against white geraniums, it was upon flat, unbroken surfaces like those of the sea on a morning that threatens storm, in the midst of an eerie silence [*un aigre silence*], in an infinite void, that this new work began, and it was into a rose-red daybreak that this unknown universe was drawn from the silence and the night to build up gradually before me" (F 3: 754; E 3: 251–52).

As is the case with most versions of incantation, an odd contradiction inhabits Marcel's formulations. On the one hand, the day is going to appear in any case. Nothing I say or do will keep the sun from rising or make it rise any sooner. To put this in quasi-theological terms, the god will come or not come as he pleases. My invocations do not coerce him. On the other hand, it seems as if my prayers are a necessary prelude to the god's epiphany. The matutinal cooing of a dove or the cockcrow that precedes dawn are invocations required to make the new day come. In the case of the septet the cockcrow is an initial "song of seven notes, but the strangest, the most remote from anything I had ever imagined, at once ineffable and strident [*à la fois ineffable et criard*]" (F 3: 754; E 3: 252). This is the presunrise call. Vinteuil makes it up. The rest of the septet is the response. Vinteuil does not make up that remainder. It just manifests itself. The first invocative call returns, however, at the end of the work. It comes back as now the most material auditory incarnation of the unknown world Vinteuil's music brings to this earth: "In the end the joyous motif was left triumphant; it was no longer an almost anxious appeal addressed to an empty sky [*un appel presque inquiet lancé derriére un ciel vide*], it was an ineffable joy which seemed to come from paradise" (F 3: 764–65; E 3: 262). In strange reversal, what seemed at first to be the only part of the work that was autonomously "composed" by Vinteuil turns out to be itself already a "gift" from those obscure and profound sources of Vinteuil's music. The magic incantation would not work if it did not already come from the realm it is used to invoke, though we may think that we have made it up on our own. If you use the wrong command or the wrong password, nothing will happen.

This already moves what Marcel says about art in the direction of what he says about love. One important evidence that Marcel makes little distinction between the generation of love in response to unknown and

Kant cannot tell you exactly what the law as such is, in so many words, nor can he tell you exactly where it is, or where it comes from. The law, as Jacques Derrida puts it, gives itself without giving itself. It may only be confronted in its delegates or representatives or by its effects on us or on others" (ER, 20). Miller focuses on a later sentence in the footnote: "Respect is properly the conception of a worth which thwarts my self-love. Thus it is regarded as an object neither of inclination nor of fear, though it has something analogous to both" (Kant, 1969: 21). Later on, Kant explains how respect is analogous to inclination and fear.

In reading this sentence, Miller follows the same protocols as in his analysis of Stevens's poem. In the poem, the reader could not know which was the literal level (love, the geometric diagram, the rock, nature) and which the figurative. This was because the poem was without ground, *Ab-grund* or *Ab-ground*, and therefore all the narrations present there, beginning with that of the seventy-year-old man who remembers and finishing with that of the mango's rind, were catachreses, ways of naming what has no name. Boustrophedonically, Miller inscribes on *Foundations of the Metaphysics of Morals* (*Grundlegung zur metaphysik der Sitten*) an *Ab-Grundlegung*, an *Ab*, like the "i" without tail and sometimes without head, of *abyme*. The aim of the *Grundlegung*'s discourse can only be supposed; because of its unapproachability, it has no basis, is *Ab-grund*. The title, then, is to a certain extent contradictory. The promise of giving a foundation (*Grundlegung*) remains unfulfilled and is shown to be impossible by Kant himself, who offers us a de-foundation, an *Ab-Grundlegung*. The title is a promise that Kant does not keep, perhaps even a promise he made intending not to keep.

What is at stake from then on is a special variant of analogy: "Respect for the law is said to be analogous to just those two feelings which it has been said not to be: inclination and fear. The name for this procedure

unknowable forces that exceed any object of love, on the one hand, and the generation of the artwork out of a response to an "unknown world," on the other, is Marcel's use of the same figurative terminology to describe both. An example is his using in both cases some version of the "solar myth" that dominates the *Recherche*.[36] I shall return to this solar myth later. I promise to do so.

Marcel in the passage I have been discussing draws an explicit parallel between the septet as the climax of Vinteuil's composing career and Marcel's love for Albertine as the climax of his serial loves. His love for Albertine is only heralded by his earlier loves and even by his first tentative responses to Albertine, just as everything before the septet is only a timid promise of it: "Vinteuil's sonata and, as I later discovered, his other works as well, had been no more than timid essays, exquisite but very slight, beside the triumphal and consummate masterpiece now being revealed to me. . . . so, if I now considered not my love for Albertine but my whole life, my other loves too had been no more than slight and timid essays that were paving the way, appeals that were clamouring [*des appels qui réclamaient*], for this vaster love: my love for Albertine" (F 3: 756–57; E 3: 253–54, trans. slightly altered). Moreover, just as all Marcel's loves, including even his love for Albertine, are not responses to the woman herself but to something beyond any of them, something that makes imperative demands on him by a sort of electric shock, so Vinteuil's works are not grounded on his selfhood but are responses to something that is profoundly hidden within him, at unknown depths, while at the same time utterly exceeding him. Marcel uses the same figure of the electric shock to define Vinteuil's discovery of violent new colors in an orchestral piece. He is said to have derived, "from the colors he had just hit upon, a wild joy [*une joie éperdu*] which gave him the strength to discover, to fling himself upon others which they seemed to call for, enraptured, quivering as though from the shock of an electric spark [*comme au choc d'une étincelle*] when the sublime came spontaneously to life at the clang of the brass, panting, intoxicated, unbridled, vertiginous" (F 3: 759; E 3: 256). This passage, as the reader can see, emphasizes not only the violence of the act of composition but its spontaneity, its involuntary aspect. The new colors come at the call of the first ones which he "had just hit upon," by luck, not by design. The result is an explosion of tonal color.

of naming by figures of speech what cannot be named literally because it cannot be faced directly is catachresis or, as Kant calls it in paragraph fifty-nine of the *Critique of Judgement*, 'hypotyposis (Hypotypose).' Kant's linguistic procedure in this footnote is an example of the forced or abusive transfer of terms from an alien realm to name something which has no proper name in itself since it is not an object which can be directly confronted by the senses" (ER, 21). Kant writes: "We have finally reduced the definite concept of morality to the idea of freedom, but we could not prove freedom to be real in ourselves and in human nature. We saw only that we must presuppose it if we would think of a being as rational and conscious of his causality with respect to actions, that is, as endowed with a will" (Kant, 1969: 76). We can only suppose that here we confront the dilemma (the undecidability) of either opting for something (the law itself) that is prior to its catachresis or opting for something that is an effect of that catachresis, since it did not exist before. Which of these two it is cannot be determined, though nothing in the realm of ethics more urgently needs determining.

Before dealing with that important undecidability, we must specify that catachresis is expressed in terms of narrativity, or at least in terms of an implicit narrative, however short it may be. This is because, although the law as such and the respect for that law cannot be inferred from experience or from examples, the latter are, after all, the support that guides particular concrete actions, of which Kant, as we have already seen, gives a good account. Something truly problematic begins to take shape there from the moment when the catachresis of the pure law, of the law as such, is nothing more than the narration of a particular case, of an example: "The reader can watch a shadowy narrative and the inadvertent demonstration of the necessity of narrative in any account of ethics slowly emerge as Kant develops his concept of respect. Even when it is defined as pure practical reason, ethics involves narrative, as its sub-

"L'étrange appel"

The unknowability and inexpressibility of the world Vinteuil's music opens up are named in a group of striking figures not yet identified. One name for the unknown world from which Vinteuil's music comes is death, that horizon toward which all the *Recherche* precipitously moves, as it hangs in the syllable between life and death. Our need to communicate in words is perhaps a result, Marcel thinks, of a wrong turning mankind took. This was the turn away from a line that might have developed something like music rather than language as a means of "communication between souls": "And, just as certain creatures are the last surviving testimony to a form of life which nature has discarded, I wondered whether music might not be the unique example of what might have been—if the invention of language, the analysis of ideas had not intervened—the means of communication between souls" (F 3: 762–63; E 3: 260). Such communication would approach the immediate intuition of what the other is thinking and feeling that we imagine is enjoyed by the angels. Since music is a testimony to such angelic communication, it is as incompatible with human language as the realm of death: "the question that [Vinteuil] put to himself in so many forms, his habitual speculation, [was] as free from analytical forms of reasoning as if it were being carried out in the world of angels, so that we can gauge its depth, but no more translate it into human speech than can disembodied spirits when, evoked by a medium, they are questioned by him about the secrets of death" (F 3: 760; E 3: 258). If death is that bourn from which no traveler returns, if it is the realm of the wholly other, and if art comes from sources as profound as death, then those sources are as deep, as unknowable, as much incompatible with articulation in language, as secret, in the strong sense of the word "secret," that is, forever undiscoverable, as are the secrets of death. The peculiarity of Marcel's assertion, the reader can see, is that it disqualifies just what Marcel is doing—translating Vinteuil's septet into human speech. He is doing what he says it is as impossible to do as to say anything about the secrets of death. Those secrets are a name for the unknowability of the sources of Vinteuil's art.

What forbids saying anything about death and the origin of art at the same time as it enables it? The key to an answer lies in the elaboration of a figure I have already used. This figure is fundamental to Marcel's vocabulary here. Vinteuil's music does not come from his selfhood. It comes from a profound and unknowable "world" that is special to him and that

versive accomplice. Storytelling is the impurity which is necessary in any discourse about the moral law as such, in spite of the law's austere indifference to persons, stories, and history. There is no theory of ethics . . . without storytelling and the temporalization (in several senses of the word) which is an intrinsic feature of all narrative" (ER, 23). Kant's footnote is a significant confirmation of this: "All respect for a person is only respect for the law (of righteousness, etc.) of which the person provides an example. Because we see the improvement of our talents as a duty, we think of a person of talents as the example of a law, as it were (the law that we should by practice become like him in his talents), and that constitutes our respect" (Kant, 1969: 21). The story of the person of great talent is often told in literature. (Proust is a good example.) It is told again by Kant himself in the second chapter of his text. In addition, the person-to-person relation is one of the keys of every narrative, both in the relation between the narrator (point of view, perspective, vision, focalization, field restriction, etc.) and the protagonist, and in the relation between one character and another: "It might be the basic story, for example, so fundamental to the novel as a genre, of the relation between the narrator and the protagonist whose story he tells as an example for himself and for the reader" (ER, 24).

We find again the theoretical (or meta-metatheoretical) power raised to the literary text's power of infinity. In this case that power is narrative, since it is about knowing the other person. This has a three-fold aspect.

I. On the one hand, if, as Kant has written, "All respect for a person is only respect for the law (of righteousness, etc.) of which the person provides an example" (Kant, 1969: 21), such an action depends on our ability to interpret, on our knowledge of the signs that person shows voluntarily or involuntarily. How is that knowledge possible? Kant himself is conscious that: "It is in fact absolutely impossible by experience to

is different from that of any other artist or person. Marcel speaks of this "world" in quasi-Platonic terms as a lost "fatherland [*patrie*]." Vinteuil does not know or remember this homeland, though he was its sole original inhabitant. This is what makes Marcel's idea only quasi-Platonic, since for Plato or for the Christian-Platonic tradition we were all originally inhabitants of a single fatherland, the same for all of us. For Marcel each artist has a different lost homeland: "Each artist seems thus to be the native of an unknown country [*une patrie inconnue*], which he himself has forgotten, and which is different from that whence another great artist, setting sail for the earth [*appareillant pour la terre*], will eventually emerge" (F 3: 761; E 3: 258). Vinteuil's music is not the product of an actual memory of the lost fatherland. He cannot remember it, though his music may gradually become "more adapted [*adéquate*] to his memory of his inner homeland" (F 3: 761; E 3: 259). The word "memory" here, however, names a haunting nostalgia for something that cannot really be remembered in the way, for example, we remember our own names. A moment later Marcel denies that Vinteuil's homeland is remembered in the ordinary sense of that word. It is a memory without memory. Vinteuil's music rather is the product of a prayer, call, or invocation that brings musical forms here that are in secret resonance with that homeland: "Composers do not actually remember this lost fatherland, but each of them remains all his life unconsciously attuned to it [*inconsciemment accordé en un certain unisson avec elle*]; he is delirious with joy when he sings in harmony with his native land" (F 3: 761; E 3: 259). Attunement, harmony, resonance, vibration at a distance: these are the only relations between the artwork and its source.

Each human being, artist and nonartist alike, belongs to a unique and singular homeland, special to him or her alone. Those of us who are not artists have no way to communicate that singularity to others. Marcel calls this "the residuum of reality which we are obliged to keep to ourselves, which cannot be transmitted in talk, even from friend to friend, from master to disciple, from lover to mistress, that ineffable something [*cet ineffable*] which differentiates qualitatively what each of us has felt" (F 3: 762; E 3: 259). The artist alone finds a magical way to externalize or materialize something that is attuned to his secret homeland. As a result, so it seems, only by way of the work of a true artist like Vinteuil can we get outside ourselves and discover one or another of those hidden worlds of the others. "The only true voyage of discovery," says Marcel, "the only really rejuvenating experience [*le seul bain de Jouvence*], would be . . . to see the

discern with complete certainty a single case in which the maxim of an action, however much it may conform to duty, rested solely on moral grounds and on the conception of one's duty . . . , for, when moral worth is in question, it is not a matter of actions which one sees but of their inner principles which one does not see" (Kant, 1969: 27). Although Kant earlier states that the nonexistence of precedent does not imply the nonexigency of duty in general to every human being, how can a person embody the moral worth of righteousness if basically we cannot see anything that could make us sure about that? How would we make up our minds about the moral quality of another person and therefore about the behavior we ourselves should adopt in relation to him or her? (As we shall see, this is the problem that confronts the narrator of "Bartleby, The Scrivener.") Should we, then, take moral worth for granted in any person, whatever he does or shows, given that the signified of that external signifier remains unknown? If so, our situation could be an ironic one. An apparently bad action could really be an honest gesture with regard to the inner reality or the intentions of its author, whereas an apparently good action could be an immoral gesture in that inner reality. "There is," Miller writes, "already a latent story in that confrontation. It implies the story of their interaction or mutual influence or growing knowledge of one another" (ER, 23–24).

2. On the other hand, that knowledge or nonknowledge of one's fellow man makes the narratological problem of perspective or narrative modalization into something nontechnical, not in the sense of giving it a particular type of ideology (though that is not excluded), but rather by leading to the recognition of a literary power (a narrative power) according to which "the thematic dramatization of ethical topics in narratives are the oblique allegorization of this linguistic necessity" (ER, 3).

3. Furthermore, precisely because the relation of knowledge or nonknowledge between narrator and protagonist, or between character and

universe through the eyes of another, of a hundred others, to see the hundred universes that each of them sees, that each of them is; and this we can do with an Elstir, with a Vinteuil" (F 3: 762; E 3: 260). Our knowledge of these other worlds is owing to the artworks such creators have invented (both made up and discovered) for us.

In a curious way, nevertheless, these unknown worlds are not dependent for their existence on the works of art that open them up, even though we can know them only through the works. Marcel specifies this in what he says about the origin of the score for Vinteuil's septet. This origin is a good example of the constant entanglement in Proust's novel of what might be called the theoretical level with the level of Marcel's life story. Vinteuil's daughter's lesbian alliance with her governess had led the two women to desecrate Vinteuil's photograph, in spite of their actual veneration for the father. This event is described much earlier in the novel, when Marcel sees the women through a window as they make love and spit on the photograph. Now Marcel is haunted by the fear that Albertine will meet Vinteuil's daughter and her companion to carry on her own secret lesbian life. The same woman, however, Vinteuil's daughter's friend, perhaps out of guilt for having darkened Vinteuil's last years, has devoted herself after his death to deciphering his indecipherable manuscripts. Without her work the world would have known only Vinteuil's comparatively inferior sonata, not his glorious masterpiece, the septet: "Indecipherable they may have been, but they had nevertheless been in the end deciphered. . . . By spending years unravelling the cryptic scroll [*le grimoire*] left by him, by establishing the correct reading of those illegible hieroglyphs [*ces hiéroglyphes inconnus*], she had the consolation of ensuring an immortal and compensatory glory for the composer over whose last years she had cast such a shadow. . . . Mlle Vinteuil's friend had disentangled, from papers more illegible than strips of papyrus dotted with a cuneiform script, the formula, eternally true and forever fertile, of this unknown joy, the mystic hope of the crimson Angel of the Dawn" (F 3: 765–67; E 3: 263–64).

Marcel's stress on the illegibility and indecipherability of Vinteuil's notes is important. They must be both unreadable and readable: unreadable because they are notations of something like the conversation of angels or the secrets of death, that is, something wholly other, wholly unknowable; readable because only by being turned into notations that musicians may actually play can they bring into material existence, as audible sounds, the artwork that is in resonance with Vinteuil's forever unknowable home-

character, constitutes the basic bond of narrative, the latter sets itself up as one of the privileged places where I may encounter the concrete (and, at the same time, because of its literariness, also universal) ethical situations which, according to Kant, are an example of the law as such. Therefore, as Miller goes on to say: "If I know the person well enough to know that he is an example of the law, there must be a story to tell about our relation" (ER, 24). Playing with analogies but going beyond simple paradigmatic association, Miller asks: "Is it possible, I ask first, to add another analogy to those Kant proposes and to say that our respect for a text is like our respect for a person, that is, it is respect not for the text in itself but respect for a law which the text exemplifies?" (ER, 18). Obviously the answer is yes, although a "yes" in quotation marks. The "yes" brings with it the problem of deciding which is the literal basis of this analogy and which the figurative (the text or the person), as well as the problem of knowing whether the text (or person) can really serve as foundation and basis of a law as such according to which one is able to take a decision—if, that is, in life or in reading it is possible to make a division of this sort.

In fact, these two problems cannot be kept separate. Important results follow from the observation that the catachrestic narrative, used as an analogy for what can only be supposed (the law as such), lends its voice and its face to what is neither exemplifiable, nor conceivable, nor cognizable. Since the law as such and its main basis, freedom, can only be supposed, the only way to make suppositions is by means of what Derrida denominates "quelque chose de la littérature" ("something of literature") and that Miller calls an "act of imagination." To suppose this or that about the law as such, however, means straying from the concrete and troubled being of things, and entering deeply into the field of fictionality. This is so even though, as has been pointed out before, such fictionality must ultimately link back to the concrete and troubled state of things. The only way to reach the law as such is to imagine an "as if,"

land. The music does not create that homeland. It is nevertheless the only means we have of knowing anything about it. If the septet had not been deciphered, the homeland would still have existed but would have remained unknown. Marcel draws a parallel between this contingency and what would have happened if Wagner or Hugo had died when they had written only their comparatively insignificant early works. What Marcel says of Hugo, if he had died without having written a line of the *Legend of the Centuries* or the *Contemplations*, would apply also to Vinteuil's septet if Mlle Vinteuil's friend had not done her laborious work of decipherment: "What is to us his real achievement would have remained purely potential [*virtuel*], as unknown as those universes to which our perception does not reach, of which we shall never have any idea" (F 3: 768; E 3: 265). Those incommensurable universes always already exist. They exist prior to the works that bring them down to this earth. They would continue to exist even if every copy of Vinteuil's septet, Wagner's *Tristan*, Hugo's *Contemplations*, or Proust's *Recherche* were destroyed. A parallel may be drawn between what Marcel says here and two analogous assertions. Henry James, in the preface to *The Golden Bowl*, says that what he calls "the clear matter" of the novel exists independently of his notation of it in the actual words of the novel. Jacques Derrida, in "The Time of a Thesis: Punctuations," says that the realm a literary work refers to precedes that work and would go on existing even if all copies of the work were destroyed.[37]

I have included Proust's name along with those of Vinteuil, Wagner, and Hugo. What Marcel says about Vinteuil can also be taken as an allegory of Proust's own work. Marcel himself indicates the parallel, at least the parallel with his own hypothetical, as yet unwritten work. The impression made on Marcel by the opening phrase of the septet, like the little phrase in the sonata, is said to be analogous to the impressions made on Marcel at crucial moments in his life by something he sees, "the sight [*l'impression éprouvée*] of the steeples of Martinville, or of a line of trees near Balbec" (F 3: 765; E 3: 262–63). Marcel asserts that "those impressions which at remote intervals I experienced in my life" were "starting-points, foundation stones [*comme les points de repère, les amorces*] for the construction of a true life" (F 3: 765; E 3: 262). That "true life" will be of course the one he will create or rather discover in his own artwork, the novel that remains yet to be written on the tomorrow just beyond the final page of the *Recherche*. These "impressions," of which the opening of Vinteuil's septet is, according to Marcel, one of the strongest he has felt, are "the strange

that is to say, to allow the *entry* of literature. The law enters with literature and literature enters with the law. Kant and Miller, each with his own language, with almost diametrically opposed aims (though this should not matter to textuality and rhetoric), and within their different spatio-temporal coordinates, come to similar conclusions. Let us examine them together. Kant's conclusion is very close to the brief "concluding remark" that closes *The Metaphysics of Morals*: "Thus the question, 'How is a categorical imperative possible?' can be answered to this extent: We can cite the only presupposition under which it is alone possible. This is the Idea of freedom, and we can discern the necessity of this presupposition. . . . But how this presupposition itself is possible can never be discerned by any human reason" (Kant, 1969: 91). The law as such, the objective categorical imperative of the law as such, freedom, and so forth can only be presupposed, and, furthermore, it is the nature of such presuppositions that we can discern them only in an ineluctable way. In other words, to presuppose (that is, to narrate as the *entry* of literature) freedom means recognizing that the only thing we can do is just that: presuppose, narrate, perform "as if." Miller puts it this way: "One glimpses here a curious relation between the necessity of narrative in any discourse about ethics and the necessity of using analogies or figures of speech in place of an unavailable literal or conceptual language. Narrative, like analogy, is inserted into that blank place where the presumed purely conceptual language of philosophy fails or is missing" (ER, 24).

Kant does not name literature, he does not want to name or resort to it, but in spite of this he resorts to it, he names it. I am not sure whether narrative is inserted into the blank place where the conceptual language of philosophy disappears or fails, or into the blank place where the conceptual language of philosophy is erected and raised. These two are not quite the same thing, but the second possibility has the advantage of showing us a narrative *engraved* in the generic language of philosophy

summons [*l'étrange appel*] which I should henceforth never cease to hear, as the promise and proof that there existed something other [*qu'il existait autre chose*], realisable no doubt through art, than the nullity [*le néant*] that I had found in all my pleasures and in love itself" (F 3: 767; E 3: 264–65). Proust's word "other [*autre*]" justifies my use of the word "others" to name the unknown worlds, wholly other to this one, that Marcel's does not know or ever have the possibility of knowing. He rather receives each as a performative summons, as an irresistible call saying "Come here!"

Just as Vinteuil's septet exists only in Marcel's description of it and is an unheard and unhearable piece of music, like the music played on pipe and timbrel by the silent figures on Keats's Grecian urn, so the realm of otherness to which the *Recherche* takes us depends for our knowledge of it on all those notebooks, proofs, little slips of paper, *paperoles*, and *becquets* that Proust scribbled on in those interminable thousand and one nights in his cork-lined room. If he had died before writing them (and he lived always, even more than most people, in the shadow of imminent death), Proust would have been known as a minor French author of the turn of the century, the author of a few essays, translations, parodies, and an incomplete work of fiction, *Jean Santeuil*. The world of the *Recherche*, in the words I have already cited from what Marcel says about Wagner or Hugo, "would have remained purely potential, as unknown as those universes to which our perception does not reach, of which we shall never have any idea."

Proust too has had, in the indefatigable labor of manuscript scholars and editors, those who have played the same role in relation to his work as Mlle Vinteuil's friend played in relation to Vinteuil's indecipherable scribbles. Without their work we should never have had all that part of Proust's work that has been published posthumously. In a small and no doubt secondary way, the same thing may even be said of this present essay. As Marcel asserts, Vinteuil's music only takes on material reality when it is played, just as the *Recherche* remains merely virtual as long as it is not read. But just as Marcel's description in words of Vinteuil's septet brings it into material, earthly existence in another way (in this case, paradoxically, in the *only* way—since it is unheard and unhearable, it exists only in Proust's words), so this present essay, like other critical work on Proust, if it is at all successful, brings into existence not exactly the "world" of the *Recherche*, but, through a combination of citation and commentary, something analogous to it, in resonance with it at a distance.

itself. Either way, the necessity of narrative has something to do with the rhetoric of philosophical enunciation. Kant asks: "What kind of law can that be, the conception of which must determine the will without reference to the expected result? Under this condition alone the will can be called absolutely good without qualification" (Kant, 1969: 21). To which he replies: "I should never act in such a way *that I could not also will that my maxim should be a universal law* [ich soll niemals anders verfahren, als so, *daß ich auch wollen könne, meine Maxime solle ein allgemeines Gesetz werden*]" (Kant, 1969: 21).

The analysis is not now determined by content. Miller does not stop at what Kant says, but looks at how he says it, at the rhetorical form of his utterance. We find ourselves again before that assertion that the critic does not pursue the what of meaning but the how of its appearance, taking into account that we are not arbitrarily applying a methodology of literary criticism to a nonliterary text. We are following a necessity dictated by the philosophical text itself. We should underscore this: Miller does not deal with Kant's text, a philosophical text on ethics, as though it were literature in order to come to the conclusion that "everything is writing or literature." Whoever says this either has not taken the trouble to read or has read blindfolded. Quite the opposite is true. The logic of Kant's discourse, the logic according to which the presupposition is a necessity, leads necessarily to an expression of that "presupposition" that can only exist, not in some infrastructural purgatory but in a particular textual reality. A rigorous reading of *The Metaphysics of Morals* forces us to stop at the sentence and at the details through which the main thesis of the book is expressed, the assertion of the categorical imperative. To apply a rhetorical reading to a philosophical text is neither more nor less than to follow the internal demand of such a text. That is why Miller comments on Kant's words: "I must act in such a way (*als so*) that it is as if I

"Le mensonge, le mensonge parfait"

A parallel exists between the magical charm of Albertine's art of lying and the novelist's art as exemplified by the *Recherche*. Demonstrating this will allow an insight into Proust's (or Marcel's) theory of the lie, as well as a further understanding of what he thinks about art. Lying is an "art," not just a "skill," as the translation mendaciously puts it in a phrase about Albertine's penchant for lying. That lying is an art, one of the fine arts, means it can, paradoxically, be added to the series that includes literature, painting, and music as another one of the ways to reach or "take in," in the sense of *apprendre*, "apprehend, appropriate, make one's own," the unique otherness at the heart of another person.[38] Since all men and women, even those who are not artists, lie, the universal human capacity for lying means a breakdown of the firm distinction Marcel apparently makes elsewhere in the *Recherche*. This is the difference between the unknowable otherness of all people who are not artists and the exceptional opportunity the music of Vinteuil, the paintings of Elstir, or the writings of Hardy, Dostoevsky, or Balzac offer us to glimpse the unique otherness of each. That otherness is the unknown homeland of the artist, the source of each work's singularity. Lying, surprisingly, works in the same way.

In an extraordinary passage not about Albertine's lying but as part of an apparently peripheral reflection on the way great artists or writers like Bergotte are likely to marry inferior and ill-tempered women who lie to them, Marcel ascribes to the universal human penchant for lying the same power to reveal unknown worlds that the works of great writers, painters, or composers have. The careful reader will note that the passage is an example of the anacoluthon or failure in grammatical consistency that Proust elsewhere associates with the way Albertine's presumed lies are betrayed in sentences she begins in the first person and ends in the third person. She does this spontaneously in order to disguise the confession she was perhaps almost about to make of her love for women. In this case, Marcel's assertion of the way we can discover unknown worlds as much through the lies of others as through listening to Vinteuil or reading Hardy shifts in the middle of the passage to the way one's own lies are a means of discovering unknown worlds. The third-person plural used to designate liars in the first sentences ("women," "his mistresses") abruptly shifts back to the "we" of the last sentence:

were assuming that to be the case. In that 'in such a way' a whole fictive narrative is implicit" (ER, 26).

Strictly speaking, the formula through which Kant's fundamental thesis is expressed has a double characteristic, one well designated by the classical rhetorical system. First, it is a comparison (*comparatione*) based on the *locus a maiore ad minus* aspect, since it accounts for the least by way of the most, the former being included in the latter (Lausberg, 1960). My concrete acting (the particular and, for this reason, the least) has to be done so that or *as if*—this is the term of the comparison—I wanted my maxim to become universal law (the general, that is, the most). It goes without saying that the universal law (the most) includes or should include that particular case (the least). Now, in the sense we have been developing the relationship of ethics to narration, given that the law in itself can only be presupposed and is not directly accessible, one could argue that we are also, in fact, in a *locus a minore ad maius* case in which the most is explained or becomes credible by the least. Kant recognizes this in these words, which I quote again: "Thus the question, 'How is a categorical imperative possible?' can be answered to this extent: We can cite the only presupposition under which it is alone possible. This is the Idea of freedom, and we can discern the necessity of this presupposition" (Kant, 1969: 91).

The fact that the presupposition is unavoidable explains why the most has to become credible through the least, why the universal law and/or the categorical imperative can only be shown or explained in an invented story of the sort: "May I, when in distress, make a promise with the intention not to keep it?" (Kant, 1969: 21). When we understand that with this formula we are within a field of comparison based both on *locus a maiore ad minus* and on *locus a minore ad maius*, the next step is to recognize that this is a *comparatione* that uses the *locus a fictione*. The necessity of the presupposition in relation to the categorical imperative

This may indeed explain to a certain extent [since, as Marcel has just said, we act blindly (*à l'aveuglette*), but choose, like animals, the plant that is good for us] why men like Bergotte generally surround themselves with women who are inferior, false and ill-natured [*méchantes*]. Their beauty is sufficient for the writer's imagination, and excites his generosity [*exalte sa bonté*], but does not in any way alter the nature of his mistresses, whose lives, situated thousands of feet below the level of his own, whose improbable connections, whose lies, carried further and moreover in a different direction from what might have been expected [*les mensonges poussés au-delà et surtout dans une autre direction que ce qu'on aurait pu croire*], appear in occasional flashes [*par éclairs*]. The lie, the perfect lie [*Le mensonge, le mensonge parfait*], about people we know, about the relations we have had with them, about our motive [*notre mobile*] for some action, formulated by us in totally different terms, the lie as to what we are, whom we love, what we feel with regard to people who love us and believe that they have fashioned us in their own image [*nous avoir façonnés semblables à lui*] because they keep on kissing us morning, noon, and night—that lie is one of the few things in the world that can open windows for us on to what is new and unknown, that can awaken in us sleeping senses for the contemplation of universes that otherwise we should never have known [*puisse nous ouvrir des perspectives sur du nouveau, sur de l'inconnu, puisse ouvrir en nous des sens endormis pour la contemplation d'univers que nous n'aurions jamais connus*]. (F 3: 721; E 3: 213)

As in what Marcel says about Vinteuil's music, so in what he says here about the lie: the "universes that otherwise we should never have known" are plural, singular, and distinct. They are realms of "others," each separated from all the others, rather than of a heterogeneous single "otherness." Each unknown world seems to be located in a different place, a place not contiguous to any of the others. According to a contradiction or indecision characteristic of Proust, Marcel sometimes, as in this passage, seems to give priority to language in the invention and discovery of new worlds, whereas sometimes he affirms that a single unknown world is the private property of each person. Even here, however, what seems to be meant by "the perfect lie" is a lie that goes to the roots of the person who utters it. The perfect lie is not just a superficial fib. It is a "lie as to what we are," just as Vinteuil's music springs from profound sources that make him the unique artist he is.

Moreover, lies are like artworks in yet another way. According to a paradox of performative language or other signs that Derrida has explored,[39] the unknown world is in both art and lying "invented" in the double sense of being made up and discovered. When it has been made up it seems as if what is made up has been there all along waiting to be in-

makes it obligatory to admit the *entry* of literature or fiction. What are the stories of the merchant who does not deceive an inexperienced customer by charging him too much money, someone who suffers from gout, or a man who makes a promise with the aim of not keeping it, if not fictions? "*Fictio* consists . . . in the . . . creation of an exemplary case that, with the *loci*'s help, can be treated in a partial sense better than in an authentic case. Immediately afterward it must be shown that the exemplary case and the authentic case are similar, in order to infer by means of analogy the juridical consequences" (Lausberg, 1960: 124).

Heinrich Lausberg, like me, is speaking of *fictio* within rhetorical argumentation and not within poetics. The only difference between his words and the object we are dealing with is that, whereas he points out a difference between the exemplary case and the authentic case, in Kant's formula there is room only for the exemplary case. The exclusion of examples posed by Kant at the beginning of *The Metaphysics of Morals* turns into the necessity of including them, or, what is the same, the necessity of using aesthetic figures. The example, narration, or story is, as Miller recognizes, "the impurity which is necessary in any discourse about the moral law as such" (ER, 23). The presupposition, example, or story is established where philosophical discourse wishes to reach the purity of the universal maxim, that is, where examples and tales should not be. It is possible to subvert the sense of Kant's italics, to read them in another direction, so that the utterance "*that I could not also will that my maxim should become a universal law*" is not so much emphasis—to stress what is really basic in my concrete and particular act—as the appearance of the fictitious other in the philosophical utterance. Read in this way, these italics mark the entry of the literary entry.

Or, perhaps, it might be a question of what Deleuze and Guattari have called "conceptual personae": "The conceptual persona is not the philosopher's representative but, rather, the reverse: the philosopher

vented in the sense of discovered. Vinteuil's music offers a glimpse of the unknown homeland that is the source of his music and that is unique to him. It is unique because it is a homeland with a single inhabitant. That homeland pre-exists Vinteuil's music. It is revealed by the music as something always already there rather than something created by it. Nevertheless, the inventive, performative power of the music is necessary to release any knowledge, indirect and mediated though it is, of that homeland. In an analogous way, "the lie, the perfect lie" does not create a factitious or fictitious world, wholly imaginary, as might seem to be the case in what Marcel says about Albertine's "charming skill in lying naturally [*l'art charmant qu'elle avait de mentir avec simplicité*]" (F 3: 694; E 3: 187). Each perfect lie functions rather as an art of invention in the sense of discovery. It opens a window on a new and unknown world that was always latently there, though our sleeping senses were not awake to it. That world would have remained there waiting to be discovered even if the appropriate lie had never been uttered to unlock it. It would still remain if every trace of the lie that "invented" it were to disappear. To each such lie belongs a different universe. Without the charming power of many lies we should never have a chance to know all those different and incommensurate universes.

The disquieting impasse here, however, lies in the fact that knowledge of these universes created by lies and by works of art in no way gives that knowledge of the other person the jealous lover wants. All Marcel can know is the charming worlds created by Albertine's lies, lies he can never even be sure are lies, just as knowledge of Vinteuil's unique homeland does not tell us anything about what was going on in Vinteuil's mind when he composed his great septet. The knowledge given by lies and by art is curiously impersonal. What the jealous lover wants is verifiable, personal, and intimate knowledge of the beloved. Is she lying to me? Is she lesbian? Does she love someone else, perhaps a woman? These things he can never know, and so his jealousy is forever unassuageable.

The most spectacular, and at the same time the most hidden, example of the charming art of lying with simplicity is *A la recherche du temps perdu* itself, the novel I am at this moment reading to find out Proust's (or Marcel's) idea of the perfect lie. So powerful is the charming or enchanting force of the novel that the reader almost irresistibly thinks it must be based on real life. The reader identifies Marcel with Proust and imagines that there must have been "originals" for Albertine and the other characters, originals that Proust more or less straightforwardly copied. If Proust's bi-

is only the envelope of his principal conceptual persona and of all the other personae who are the intercessors [*intercesseurs*], the real subjects of his philosophy. Conceptual personae are the philosopher's 'heteronyms' " (Deleuze and Guattari, 1994: 64). According to these authors, it is necessary to make a distinction between a conceptual persona and an aesthetic figure: "The difference between conceptual personae and aesthetic figures consists first of all in this: the former are the powers of concepts, and the latter are the powers of affects and percepts. . . . Art and philosophy crosscut the chaos and confront it, but it is not at the same sectional plane; it is not populated in the same way. In the one there is the constellation of a universe of affects and percepts; and in the other, constitutions of immanence or concepts. Art thinks no less than philosophy, but it thinks through affects and percepts" (Deleuze and Guattari, 1994: 65–66). Therefore, whereas Descartes's concept of self "has three components—doubting, thinking, and being" (Deleuze and Guattari, 1994: 24), Kant's concept of *universal Law* seems to have the following five: universality, duty, pure will, action, and inaccessibility. In the end, the entry of fiction (the entry of affections and percepts) takes place as a result of the translation into components of the concept. The component of duty necessitates translation into the space of the fiction that embodies, translation into someone who suffers from gout or into someone whose action "was done neither from duty nor from direct inclination but only for a selfish purpose" (Kant, 1969: 16). That fictitious embodiment is as compulsory in Kant's text as in Descartes's doubting, thinking, and being, for the situation of doubt is also a narrative at some level. Deleuze and Guattari correctly indicate the general valences of the different types of discourse (philosophy, concepts; science, prospects; art, affects and percepts), but they do not sufficiently take into account the reciprocal relations of dependence between the constitutions of immanence and the constellation of a universe, what we could call an *aporetic structural consti-*

ographers are to be believed, however, Proust loved men, not women. Like Charlus transposing the gender of the women in traditional love poetry, or like Albertine lying so charmingly that Marcel says he would see things and people according to that lie, in defiance of ocular proof, Proust has constructed a novel that is a gigantic lie from one end to the other. This is so at least in the way it imagines a heterosexual penchant in its hero and thereby transposes Proust's own feelings and experience to a different register. Proust's big lie, a lie thousands of pages long, is invisible because it is spread all over the text, like the large letters on a map in Poe's figure for the invisibility of the purloined letter. If you want to hide something, put it well out in the open, as Proust did, for example, in giving Marcel's loves transposed male names: Gilberte, Albertine, Andrée.

The effects of learning or remembering Proust's perfect lie, "the lie as to what we are, whom we love, what we feel with regard to people who love us and believe that they have fashioned us in their own image," are multiple. On the one hand, seeing the lie as a lie contributes powerfully to the destabilizing of gender and identity that is one of the main themes of the *Recherche*. It demonstrates that gender and sexual orientation are ideological or linguistic constructions, performative projections, not natural facts. One evidence for that is the way such hypnotically effective and bewildering lies can be told about gender and sexual preference. This recognition makes the reader see in a strange ironic light many passages in the novel. One example is Marcel's lyrical description, as he remembers watching Albertine sleeping, of the female body as far superior in beauty to the male body with its awkward handle, like the metal bracket that holds up an antique statue in a museum. The reader is left in a dizzy oscillation between thinking of the *Recherche* as a great novel about homosexuality told from a heterosexual perspective and thinking of it as a closeted novel written secretly from a homosexual perspective. The impossibility of deciding between those two ways of reading leads the reader to recognize that these two previously distinct perspectives are unstable constructions. This shows in a new way the folly of Marcel's attempt to find out whether Albertine is truly and essentially lesbian, or of any corresponding attempt in the real world, for example the attempt to label Marcel Proust as essentially straight or essentially gay.

On the other hand, recognizing Proust's big lie shows the reader that what is revealed in the *Recherche* can be encountered nowhere but in the pages of the novel. The novel does not correspond mimetically to some

tution or, in the texts we are dealing with, "the entanglement of narration and ethics" (ER, 25). In other words, the philosophical concept is a gap. With no extensional or intentional reference, it arises when a narrative catachresis fills it in. This fact will immediately lead us to the problem of creation (a crucial issue in Deleuze and Guatari's work) in relation to performativity.

Between the concept and the component, in their own possibility of relation in the middle of emptiness, between the law as such and the particular act that embodies it, the bridge (*their* bridge) is the entry of literature or fiction in the form of narrative. Saying this takes for granted that we are no longer speaking of a narrativity identified with such particular genres as the novel, tale, or poem, but of narrativity as a "fundamental activity of the human mind" (ER, 28), or as a power that is supported by itself beyond any concrete or abstract declaration. When, in *Expression in Philosophy: Spinoza*, Deleuze writes, "The question of what a body can do makes sense taken alone, since it implies a new conception of the embodied individual, of species, and of genera," he must resort, like Kant, to the "as if," to fiction, to a little parable: "If someone happens to encounter a body that can combine with his own in a favorable relation, he tries to unite with it. When someone encounters a body whose relation is incompatible with his own, a body that affects him with sadness, he does all in his power to ward off the sadness or destroy the body" (Deleuze, 1990: 257–58). In this gesture, the concept is translated into affection, the philosophical discourse into "composition": "Composition is the sole definition of art. Composition is aesthetic, and what is not composed is not a work of art" (Deleuze, 1994: 191). The gap of the concept in the philosophical text's form of enunciation shapes a vacancy that can only be filled in by the entry of literature, which Miller denominates a "species of artwork": "This chasm too can only be bridged by a species of artwork, though one not openly defined as such by Kant. Across the gap between

historical, nonlinguistic world. It evokes a special and unique world that is created and at the same time revealed as an eternally pre-existing possibility by just these lying words, though these words only give indirect and lying knowledge of it. Proust's novel, like any perfect lie, "awaken[s] in us sleeping senses for the contemplation of universes that otherwise we should never have known." The prefigurative matrix or pre-existing world that the novel "represents," like what I have called the black holes of the others, or like Plato's *khōra* in Derrida's reading of it, or like the indifferent, impersonal, and ungendered "empty apparatus" of the self's many selves as Marcel understands it for himself or for Albertine, is prior to gender differentiation. It may therefore be figured with equal validity and equal invalidity by alternative gender constructions. It is perhaps best figured by destabilizing oscillations of gender and identity such as those of Proust's *Recherche*.[40]

"L'ensoleillement tortueux et frais d'une grappe de raisin"

Earlier in this book, discussing the availability of Proust's work on the Internet, I promised to turn ultimately to the sun in *A la recherche du temps perdu*. I have already briefly touched on that in a reference to the way Paul de Man speaks of Proust's "solar myth"[41] and in an analysis of Marcel's use of sunrise as a figure to describe Vinteuil's septet. What is that solar myth? What does it have to do with Marcel's jealousy and Albertine's lies? "Myth" is an unusual word in de Man's vocabulary. As a search by way of ARTFL reveals, the word *soleil* recurs often in Proust's work. Perhaps this is to be expected in a novel that, like many novels, often describes the weather. The recurrence of *soleil* may be a trivial fact. It is necessary to read the novel to find out. A chief motivation for my readings of Trollope and Proust is to show that though having literary texts available on the Internet changes in important ways our procedures of reading, nevertheless it does not remove the task of reading. Nor does the electronic version suddenly become transparent "information" flowing back and forth on the Infobahn. The computer will not do the reading for you. This is true in spite of the extensive use of a reading metaphor in computer jargon, as in "ROM" or "Read Only Memory" for basic operating programs that are inscribed unchangeably on a computer chip, or as in "CD-ROM" for compact disks that also have "Read Only Memory" that can be "read" by

the law as such and the immediate work in the real world of the practical reason must be cast a little fictional narrative. This narrative must be on both sides of the gulf at once, or lead from the one to the other. It must be within the law as such, and it must at the same time give practical advice for the choices of the pure will in a particular case in the real work of history, society, and my immediate obligations to those around me" (ER, 28).

These works by Miller accomplish a double movement in relation to the classical notion of "literature": its dissolution (or deterritorialization) as a space defined and delimited by a tradition of poetics that lasts until modern structuralism, and its nonessentialist redefinition (or reterritorialization), such that literature can be seen to people the most varied places, each time in a different way. This double movement can be perfectly seen in relation to Kant. What Kant rejects in the form and reference of his discourse (the example, fiction) is precisely what he needs to constitute that discourse. Here again one finds a starting point in de Man, who, in his analysis of Rousseau's *The Social Contract*, writes: "What the *Social Contract* keeps doing however is to promise, that is, to perform the very illocutionary speech act which it has discredited and to perform it in all its textual ambiguity, as a statement of which the constative and the performative functions cannot be distinguished or reconciled" (de Man, 1979: 275–76). This is not an affirmation that Kant "does literature" or that the differences between philosophy and literature enter a chemical state of liquefaction. De Man and Miller indicate that the internal and external constitution of philosophical discourse needs the "entry of literature," at the same time as the internal and external constitution of literary discourse claims an "entry of philosophy." Of course, we are indebted to Miller for developing the idea or concept of the entry of literature, an idea which, though defined by its fictionality, is not purely and simply "literature." Miller certainly accepts de Man's formulation, but in his hands it

a computer, that is, called up to appear on its monitor or played on its audio system, but not changed.

What de Man meant by Proust's "solar myth" requires a little explanation. "Reading (Proust)" discusses several solar passages in the *Recherche*. The sentence in which the phrase "solar myth" occurs makes reference to a specific myth, the myth of Iris. It appears in the context of an iridescent discussion of the spectrum's iridescence as it is alluded to by Proust: "The solar myth of *A la recherche du temps perdu* would then be condensed in the scarf of Iris."[42] A further clue to what this might mean and to a connection of the sun with Albertine is given in a passage in "Albertine disparue" de Man does not discuss. This passage confirms that de Man was on the mark, as usual, when he associated the Proustian sun with the rainbow of refracted colors, the scarf of Iris.

Long after Albertine's death, Marcel laments to himself that though someone must exist who could tell him the truth about Albertine, just as he has been able to tell Bloch the truth about the Princesse de Guermantes or about Mme Swann, the lover is never able to get such testimony: "such a person exists always . . . but we never come across him. . . . I said to myself: 'If I could have known such and such witnesses [*témoins*]!' — from whom, if I had known them, I should probably have been unable to extract anything more than from Andrée, herself the custodian of a secret which she refused to surrender" (F 4: 131–32; E 3: 562). The realization of this sad imprisonment in ignorance leads Marcel to recognize that now that Albertine is dead, the only women that attract him, "whether or not I could learn anything from them" (F 4: 132; E 3: 562), are those who are associated in some way with Albertine's milieu or with women who might have attracted Albertine. This leads Marcel to elaborate a law of substitution by association or contiguity. A desire to know and possess, to know by possessing or possess by knowing, a desire that might be called an unassuageable, concupiscent curiosity, leads the lover to substitute by a species of metonymy things near to the central object of desire, in ever-receding degrees of proximity, for the beloved herself or himself. Freud called these substitutes "festishes." If the lover can possess the substitutes, he or she may by indirection come to know and possess the central object of desire they replace.

Two important and to some degree surprising features of Proust's way of expressing this must be stressed. Albertine is not, as might be expected, the original desired object for which the others are substitutes. The desire to possess her is itself a substitute for the desire to possess Balbec: "I

remains the interrogation and development of a performativity that cannot be reconciled with cognition (nor is it in de Man). The strange form of the *entry* of literature is Miller's addition.

If, as de Man persuasively demonstrates in his essay on Rousseau (paraphrasing Nietzsche, as he himself recognizes), "all laws are future-oriented and prospective; their illocutionary mode is that of the promise" (de Man, 1979: 273), then the story narrated by Kant as an example about the man who makes a false promise ("Let the question, for example, be: May I, when in distress, make a promise with the intention not to keep it?"; Kant, 1969: 21) is not one story among others, or one example among others. In fact, it cannot be compared, in its relation to the universal law and the discursive maxim that enunciates it, with the story of the man who suffers from gout or with that of the merchant who does not deceive the inexperienced customer. In other words, not only is the use of example that Kant rejects in his initial hypothesis essential for the constitution of the pure maxim on pure law, but now we discover among his examples one—the example of the promise (*Versprechen*)—that is not like the rest, insofar as it seems to define the positing of what fills in the gap in the philosophical and/or ethical concept. A third term appears inside and outside the Kantian maxim on respect. The maxim needs the entry of literature, but what literary entry? The promise. A chain linking universal law, fiction, and the promise is then established. The promise becomes fiction and fiction becomes the promise; the universal law becomes both promise and fiction. De Man points out: "Every promise assumes a date at which the promise is made and without which it would have no validity; laws are promissory notes in which the present of the promise is always a past with regard to its realization" (de Man, 1979: 273).

The fact that every promise assumes the future of its promise gives rise to fiction or the entry of literature. The future of the concrete present of the promise cannot but adopt the form of a narration that cannot be

had had in the past the illusion of recapturing Balbec, when in Paris Albertine came to see me and I held her in my arms, and similarly I established some contact, restricted and furtive though it might be, with Albertine's life, the atmosphere of workrooms, a conversation across a counter, the spirit of the slums [*l'atmosphère des ateliers, une conversation de comptoir, l'âme des taudis*], when I embraced a seamstress [*une ouvrière*]" (F 4: 132; E 3: 563). A strangely reversible trope of figure and ground operates here. It is a variant of the tropes of person and milieu, or name and place, that pervade the *Recherche*. These tropes are analyzed indefatigably by the writing Marcel as a major source of the written Marcel's mystifications. He loves the Duchesse de Guermantes because to possess her would be to possess her estate, the church on the Guermantes estate he so much admires, and the whole illustrious history of her family, just as seeing a Titian at the Louvre is a substitute pleasure for going to Venice, where the painting originally hung, while possessing the working girl Marcel meets in Venice and then taking her back to Paris would be like possessing a Titian for himself.

Submission to the powerful illusions generated by synecdoche is the occasion of marvelous flights of eloquence by Marcel. The passage I shall cite is one of almost innumerable examples. But such submission by the "written Marcel" is always accompanied, for those who have eyes to read, by a discreet deconstruction of that illusion by the writing Marcel. Since Marcel first saw Albertine outlined like the rising or setting sun against the horizon of the sea at Balbec, she stands for Balbec: "Was she not, after all. . . . , the girl whom I had seen the first time at Balbec, beneath her flat cap, with her insistent laughing eyes, a stranger still, slender as a silhouette projected against the waves [*mince comme une silhouette profilée sur le flot*]?" (F 3: 575–76; E 3: 61). To possess Albertine is to repossess Balbec, just as to possess Albertine's working-class milieu by embracing a working girl is a way of repossessing Albertine, even after she is dead. You can possess and know the landscape by way of the figure in it, or vice versa, but the head of the chain here is Balbec, not Albertine. As Marcel says, "desire always springs from an initial glamour [*un prestige préalable*]," a "charm" that confers a magic attraction (F 4: 132; E 3: 562). Albertine's charm for Marcel derived initially from her association with Balbec. She was a substitute pleasure for Balbec. Balbec is for Marcel one figure or another outlined against the wide vista of the sea into which the sun sinks each day. Those figures, whether it is the church at Balbec, the frieze of *jeunes filles*

verified (except in a deferred future no longer the present of the promise). Such a narration tells, according to its consonance with *a* law or with *the* law, what will or should happen in the future. Logically, that "will happen" hides a "would be able to happen if this promise is fulfilled," and that "would be able to happen" is, in fact, a "would be able to be," that is, the fundamental attribute Aristotle confers on the fable. In conclusion, without fable the promise cannot exist, and without promise the law cannot exist. Or, vice versa, the law implies the promise and the latter, in turn, involves fiction. Of course, among the law as such, promise, and fiction there is a relation of anacoluthon or of self-deconstruction: "Kant says something other than what he means to say. This something betrays a hidden flaw in his argument and makes that argument a non sequitur or an anacoluthon, a failure in following" (ER, 36).

The concept of universal law is necessarily empty. A short fable must fill it in, providing the promise of a future, a prospection or prolepsis, a performative action, in short, an inaugural act. For this reason, writes Miller: "The story I must tell myself ["The shortest but most infallible way to find the answer to the question as to whether a deceitful promise is consistent with duty is to ask myself: Would I be content that my maxim . . . should hold as a universal law for myself as well as for others?"; Kant, 1969: 22] is a miniature version of the inaugural act which creates a nation, a people, a community. I must act as though my private maxim were to be universal legislation for all mankind. In the fiction of this 'in such a way' universal and particular, public and private, the law as such and a particular code of behavior, are bridged, and I become myself an example of the moral law, worthy of respect. The implied story in such an *als so* is the grand historical story of the divinely sanctioned lawgiver or establisher of the social contract, Moses, Lycurgus, or the framers of the Declaration of Independence or of the Rights of Man" (ER, 29). According to the aporia of interminability, de Man repeated (or is an

en fleur outlined against the sea, or Albertine herself as the synecdochic representative of all the girls, are substitutes for the sun. The figure that Marcel uses to express the receding series of substitutions, each further away than the last from the central object of desire, is a solar one. It is the figure of Iris's scarf, the rainbow of refracted colors around a central solar blazing radiance. This is what de Man calls Proust's "solar myth":

Andrée, and those other women, all of them in relation to Albertine—like Albertine herself in relation to Balbec—were to be numbered among those substitute pleasures, replacing one another in gradual declension [*de ces substituts de plaisirs se remplaçant l'un l'autre en dégradation successive*], which enable us to dispense with the pleasure to which we can no longer attain, a trip to Balbec or the love of Albertine, pleasures which (just as going to the Louvre to look at a Titian consoles us for not being able to go to Venice where it originally was), separated one from another by invisible gradations [*nuances indiscernables*], convert one's life into a series of concentric, contiguous, harmonic and graduated [*dégradées*] zones, encircling an initial desire which has set the tone, eliminated everything that does not combine with it, applied the dominant color (as had, for instance, occurred to me also in the cases of the Duchess de Guermantes and of Gilberte). (F 4: 132–33; E 3: 563).

A trip to Balbec means being able to see the broad vista of the sea after the sun has set. Embracing Albertine in Paris is a substitute for that pleasure. That an association of Albertine with a hidden sun is not an ungrounded extrapolation is indicated by a passage early in *La prisonnière* in which Marcel looks at Albertine's naked body: "her belly . . . was closed, at the junction of her thighs, by two valves with a curve as languid, as reposeful, as cloistral as that of the horizon after the sun has set" (F 3: 587; E 3: 74). Focusing on Albertine is like choosing one color out of the rainbow of possible colors. That color then tints everything that can be taken as a substitute for it. As long as Marcel is infatuated with Albertine, all his other desires are for replacements for her, just as she was initially a replacement for the central object of desire. This center is in the passage about "substitute pleasures" covertly named, without being explicitly named, in the figure of the sun, the blazing focal radiance around which the "series of concentric, contiguous, harmonic and graduated zones" organizes itself. A computer search using ARTFL would not turn up the lengthy passage cited above, since the word "sun" does not appear in it. That is a good proof that you must read for yourself, and read more than just the citations the computer search finds, even if the possibility of such searching

effect of) Rousseau, and now Miller repeats (or is an effect of) de Man, who reminds us that: "Since [the *Social Contract*] implicitly and explicitly denies, in chapter 7 of book 2 ('Du législateur') and again in the related chapter 8 of book 4 ('De la religion civile'), any form of divine inspiration for itself, it is clear that Rousseau does not identify himself with any of the major legislators, be it Moses, Lycurgus, or Christ; instead, by raising the suspicion that the Sermon on the Mount may be the Machiavellian invention of a master politician, he clearly undermines the authority of his own legislative discourse" (de Man, 1979: 275). The deconstruction of the authority of a legislative discourse leads unavoidably to the intimate fictionality that creates history as a connected narrative: "It creates history. It is the prolepsis of a story not only with a beginning but with a middle and an end" (ER, 29).

Miller emphasizes such fictionality. If the law is a gap that promises a future with a lonely hypothetical existence, it is not strange that literature (now not only the entry of literature, but genres specifically literary) resembles a trying out (George Eliot's "experiments in life") and that "we read novels to see in a safe area of fiction or imagination what would happen if we lived our lives according to a certain principle of moral choice. We take the novel as potentially an example of the moral law as such and as the basis of a legislation for all mankind" (ER, 30). The Millerian matrix appears again. Indeed, for reading novels in this way to be possible, the reader must "touch" and enter into character or into the consciousness that embodies particular moral situations, while, at the same time, keeping the basic distance of alterity. This alterity of the text always remains absolutely other in relation to reading.

Between nearness and distance, fictionality deconstructs the law in two directions. On the one hand, the law as such, by depending on the example of the promise, shows that its foundation is not prior but subsequent to some narrative in words. The entry of literature or of literariness is one feature of the new telecommunications regime that changes forever the concept of "literature."

The reader will remember the passage I discussed earlier in which Marcel asserts that all the women he has loved have been no more than the medium of an invisible, occult, all-attracting object of desire with which they have nothing in common. Marcel's experience of substitute pleasures by no means hides from him the way the substitutes are not really substitutes in the sense of a synecdochic part for whole based on similarity. None of the women Marcel loves, including Albertine, is at all like the "occult forces" artificially attached to them, any more than the working girl Marcel embraces is like Albertine, or Albertine like the sea at Balbec after the sun has set. The chain is made up of metonymic contiguity, "concentric, contiguous, harmonic and graduated zones." These zones are the simple side-by-sideness of things fundamentally different from one another. Just as important, they are things that are not at all like the always invisible and unattainable central object of desire. The sun itself is only one more substitute for that.

The relation between all these figures—the women, the sun, the Titian—and what they substitute for is, properly speaking, allegorical. I use here the definition of allegory in Marcel's discussion of Giotto's frescoes in the Arena Chapel at Padua. What Marcel emphasizes, the reader will remember, is the way Giotto's figure of Charity does not look at all charitable and would not be identifiable as such if she did not have a label, KARITAS, to tell the beholder that is what she stands for (see F 1: 80–81; E 1: 87–88). The passage I have been discussing ends with an elegant formulation of this law of metonymic substitution. This law is expressed as a ratio: A is to B as C is to A. The C in this case is not a person but an object that has been permeated and made what it is by the sun. It is therefore able to function as a displaced representative of the sun. The word "sun," or rather one of its representatives, appears here in the word *ensoleillement*, translated as "sun-drenched." Neither Albertine nor the sun is the head of the chain as what is outside it and controls the whole sequence of substitutions. Each is a substitute for the others, the sun for Albertine, Albertine for the sun, and each of these is only a substitute for the nameless, invisible, and unattainable otherness that motivates the whole endless drama of substitute desire: "Andrée and these women were to the desire, which I knew I could no longer gratify, to have Albertine by my side, what had been, one evening, before I knew Albertine by sight and felt that she could

gives a groundless foundation to the law as such. This entry "is not just any act. It is a specifically linguistic act" (ER, 32). The literary entry is the *i* without tail, the *ab-grund* of the law as such. It is a question of naming the law as an entity existing a priori, but a question of delineating it in a linguistic act that projects it into an uncertain future. However, if the law as such comes to thought as a promise that inaugurates a face that did not exist before, no one can assert that that promise will be kept in the future time that the promise itself promises. This is "the possibility that it will be impossible ever to confirm with certainty whether the form of language in the performative makes happen what it promises will happen" (ER, 32). The promise makes something happen in a state of fictionality. This fictionality does not relate to what it is (reality) or to what it is not (fiction), but to what it would be able to be, that is to say, to an infinite deferral that opens an endless chain of linguistic-literary acts. So, if "Kant's example therefore does not exemplify that of which it is meant to be an example" (ER, 36), if there is a lapse there in Kant's discourse or language, it is because the space of fiction (deterritorialized and reterritorialized by Miller) is capable of being analyzed, not only with regard to what constitutes externally and internally the law as such and the maxim enunciating it, but also—and this means a return to the starting thesis—with regard to what Miller has called the "specific ethics of narrative." What could the metaphysics of morals say about the literariness called the "specific ethics of narrative" or about de Man's formula that "*Die Sprache verspricht (sich)* ('Language promises [itself]'; also: 'Language misstates.')" (de Man, 1979: 277)?

J. Hillis Miller's Galatea

It seems natural that someone so concerned about the law should be able to write: "The right reading of 'Bartleby, The Scrivener' depends

never be mine, the writhing, sun-drenched freshness of a cluster of grapes [*l'ensoleillement tortueux et frais d'une grappe de raisin*]" (F 4: 133; E 3: 563)

"Du gouffre interdit à nos sondes"

A further step in understanding Proust's solar myth may be made by turning to a passage in *Le temps retrouvé*. Almost the last time Marcel sees his friend Robert de Saint Loup before Saint Loup is killed in the trench battles of the First World War, he expresses his nostalgia for the conversations they used to have together when Saint Loup was in barracks at Doncières. " 'Do you remember,' I said to him, 'our conversations at Doncières?' " Saint Loup confirms this nostalgic remembrance by way of a citation from Baudelaire:

Ah! those were the days! What a gulf [*Quel abîme*] separates us from them! Will those happy times ever re-emerge

> du gouffre interdit à nos sondes,
> Comme montent au ciel les soleils rajeunis
> Après s'être lavés au fond des mers profondes?
> *(F 4: 340; E 3: 782)*

The citation comes from Baudelaire's "The Balcony," slightly altered at the beginning.[43] Baudelaire wrote *d'un gouffre*, "from *a* gulf," not *du gouffre*, "from *the* gulf." Saint Loup's memory universalizes a gulf that is, in Baudelaire's poem, perhaps just one among many, just as the rejuvenated suns, in the poem, are plural. Saint Loup's version may be translated: "from the unfathomable gulf [more literally: "from the gulf forbidden to our sounding-lines"], / As rejuvenated suns rise in the sky, / After having washed themselves in deep seas?" Baudelaire's poem is spoken in apostrophe to his mistress and in memory of their *serments, parfums*, and *baisers infinis*, that is, not just "conversations," as Marcel puts it, but lover's oaths, erotic perfumes, and kisses infinite, kisses presumably infinite in number as well as in intensity.

Saint Loup, if not Marcel himself, here makes one of the silent transpositions from heterosexual to homosexual love like those the Baron de Charlus used to practice when he was at school in order to understand heterosexual love poetry. By this time in the novel Marcel knows all about Saint Loup's homosexuality and about his infidelity to his wife Gilberte. He seems somewhat embarrassed by what Saint Loup says and quickly

on answering these questions right or on showing that they are unanswerable" (VP, 156). Miller should be able to speak about what is right and do it twice: a right reading and a right answer to these questions. To decide whether a reading is right or not is a gesture characteristic of medieval hermeneutics (one could say, of any hermeneutics). It is also one of the basic concerns of the pragmatic and receptionist theories of literature. However, in Miller's assertion there is something uncanny. A right reading of a text (in this case "Bartleby, The Scrivener") depends on answering certain questions right or on showing that it is not possible to do so. If this second possibility were to be the case (and for Miller this is often so), we would confront the following syllogism. (1) A right reading depends on the possibility of answering certain questions. (2) Since it is not possible to answer them, then the only right reading is to recognize the impossibility of a right reading: "In the case of Melville's story, the narrator's inability to fulfill his responsibility to Bartleby is analogous to our interpretation based on what the text says" (VP, 175). (3) The right reading is that there is no right reading. Of course this is paradoxical, almost an oxymoron. At the same time, it is necessary to take into account something quite obvious. In the sentence "the right reading is that there is no right reading," two levels mix. The right reading or the misreading belongs to a metatextual level, whereas saying that the right reading is the impossibility of the right reading belongs to a meta-metatextual level. The aim of *Versions of Pygmalion* is precisely to interrogate that paradoxical sentence in relation to two further questions: the question of Ovid's story of Pygmalion and Galatea and that of the ethics of narrative.

If in Kant's ideas on the metaphysics of morals we discover that the law as such is an empty concept (thus catachrestic), a blank that can only be filled in by a narration, what happens when we have a text that presents itself as a literary narrative? Or, rather, what happens when we take as a starting point *this* particular narrative text? These questions fore-

changes the subject to a discussion of military strategy, one topic of their old conversations. Nevertheless, this is one of the places where the homosexual or at least "homosocial" aspect of the long friendship of Marcel and Saint Loup most explicitly emerges, even though it is by way of parts of Baudelaire's poem that are not cited. Since Marcel's pleasure, early in the novel, in Saint Loup's company and conversation is presented as innocent of any erotic side, his nostalgia may be for a time of male friendship that was ignorant of the homosexual overtones he now understands so well. In Marcel's experience of their friendship, or at any rate in his presentation of it in the *Recherche*, their relation was homosocial rather than homosexual. Now he knows about Saint Loup's proclivities. Saint Loup's citation of Baudelaire's explicitly erotic but heterosexual poem is far from innocent. It redefines the nature of their past friendship.

The speaker in "The Balcony" boasts that he has the power to raise the dead, to bring back to life lost happy times: "Je sais l'art d'évoquer les minutes heureuses" (l. 17). Presumably poetry is that art, though the poem is spoken directly to the woman and asserts that only when he is in her arms again can he recover those *minutes heureuses*. The poem mimes and repeats, through its verbal power of "evocation," a recovery that occurs by way of the body: "Car à quoi bon chercher tes beautés langoureuses / Ailleurs qu'en ton cher corps et qu'en ton coeur si doux? (For what is the point of seeking your langorous beauties anywhere but in your dear body and in your heart that is so soft?)" (ll. 19–20). By way of his citation Saint Loup asks whether the happy conversations he had with Marcel can ever be reborn, as the sun is reborn each day from its immersion in the sea. The answer is "no," not in real life. Nevertheless, Proust's (or Marcel's) art of evoking past happy times has in the long course of the *Recherche* recovered in words and made available for us as readers, from the depths of time past, all those happy conversations at Doncières so innocently enjoyed by Marcel. This parallels Baudelaire's art of raising the dead through poetry or through lovemaking. Every reader brings those conversations at Doncières back to life each time the *Recherche* is read.

What is most important for my purposes, however, is Proust's use of a solar figure. This figure is borrowed from Baudelaire, but echoes all the other suns in the *Recherche*. Taken together, these make up Proust's solar myth. Once again, as in the other solar passages I have cited, the relation between persons is figured by way of the sun. Vinteuil's septet is troped as a sunrise that brings from perpetually hidden depths echoes of a singu-

ground those examples Kant tries to eschew and that at the same time
are necessary for his discourse. What happens when we are before *this* example, "Bartleby, The Scrivener"? What occurs when *that* protagonist
constantly answers, "I would prefer not to"? Perhaps we would prefer not
to answer. In a sense, Miller prefers not to answer. He adopts a position
very similar to Bartleby's. He says something that infinitely defers the act
of delimiting, deciding, criticizing the problem that takes place in the
confrontation between the analyst and the literary text. Whereas other
theoreticians of literature have quickly answered these questions, Miller
answers without answering: "What happens is something always fortuitous and unpredictable, something surprising, however many times the
book in question has been read before, even by me. One way to define
this unexpected quality of true acts of reading is to say that they never
correspond exactly to what other readers tell me I am going to find when
I read that book" (VP, 20). What happens or what will happen when we
put ourselves before this particular narrative text is something we cannot describe beforehand, because it is unpredictable. In the same manner
that the performative enunciation of a promise (or of *the* law or of *a* law)
does not tell us anything about its future fulfillment or nonfulfillment, we
cannot say anything either about the text/analysis relation except that the
ethical response to reading provokes other textual acts: "What do I mean
by 'ethics' in the phrase 'the ethics of reading'? I mean more or less what
Henry James means in that preface to *The Golden Bowl*, when he says
that 'the whole conduct of life consists of things done, which do other
things in their turn.' If James is correct to say that writing, say writing
The Golden Bowl, is a thing done that does other things in its turn, my
question is concrete and specific. In what sense is reading novels, poems,
or philosophical texts, teaching them or writing about them a thing done
that does other things in its turn?" (VP, 15).

The strategic position of "ethics" in Miller's work implies by defini-

lar homeland that belongs to Vinteuil alone or rather that he belongs to, though it remains as unknown to him as to everyone else. In a similar way, the old friendship between Marcel and Saint Loup, so tenderly celebrated in earlier episodes of the *Recherche*, now belongs to the lost abysses of time past. An implacable interdict prevents us from plumbing those depths. The sun, however, rises each day fresh and new after bathing all night in the fathomless sea. This happens according to a figure that goes back at least to the Pre-Socratics in the Western tradition and that sometimes was expressed, for example by Heraclitus, as the notion that a new sun rises each day.[44] This may be taken to justify the plural, *soleils*, in "The Balcony." It is not the sun but suns that rise rejuvenated in Baudelaire's poem, a different sun every day. This daily resurrection is a promise, in spite of the recognition that time past is time past, that the past may after all be recaptured, "regained," *retrouvé*, most signally by an artistic effort like the *Recherche* itself.

Yet the solar figure is only a figure, and an impossible one at that, from the perspective of its referential validity. The sun does not really sink into the sea, nor do fire and water mix. Imagining the suns washing themselves (Baudelaire's phrase is a reflexive: *s'être lavés*) at the bottom of deep seas is a powerful, but factitious, personification. My word "impossible" here is an allusion to a footnote in Paul de Man's "Reading (Proust)."[45] The footnote condenses de Man's entire essay on Proust in fractal miniature. In the footnote de Man analyzes another solar passage, one that occurs in the episode of Marcel's excursion from Venice to see the Giottos at Padua. Having entered the cool semi-darkness of the chapel from the bright, warm sunlight outside, Marcel compares the blue of Giotto's chapel vault to "these brief moments of respite that interrupt the most beautiful days when, without having a single cloud, the sun having turned its eye elsewhere [*le soleil ayant tourné ailleurs son regard*] for a moment, the blue of the sky softens and turns darker" (F 4: 227, de Man's translation; Moncrieff and Kilmartin say: "the sun has turned its gaze elsewhere," E 3: 663). De Man focuses on the inside/outside chiasmuses that make up the tropological rhetoric of this passage: from the warm sunlight outside to the cool, sunless interior of the chapel, but with exchanges back and forth from one to the other. This form of chiasmus is essential to de Man's understanding of tropological exchange systems generally.

At the end of the footnote, however, de Man moves to a different register. He recognizes that in the passage he has quoted this system of re-

tion a specific behavior in some concrete situation. Such "situationality" directs Miller's theoretical and literary reflection, despite its textualist orientation, to a level where textual exteriorities engage responsibility, context, history, and society. The passage just cited, however, proves that Miller does not identify such aspects of particular works as pre-existing givens. Quite the contrary: he affirms that it is impossible to do so. The behavior of the literary critic confronting a particular literary text is subject to contingency, singularity, and adventure (Barthes, 1981: 40), though that of course does not exclude responsibility. Rather, it forces discussion of an "inaugurative responsibility" that emerges as a result of a promise (or law, or ethical commitment) that has no grounds or basis when it is made: "Performative praxis can be thought of as inaugural, as bringing something hitherto unheard of into the world. For this the bringer must take responsibility. This responsibility cannot be grounded in anything that preceded the performative art of the artist or scholar, though it must at the same time be faithful to what it transforms" (1, 55).

That the outside of the text (whatever these words may mean) cannot be circumscribed does not mean that we cannot take responsibility for what happens or for what is going to happen. Rather, it means that this behavior does not find any ground or support, that it may even occur by accident: "Imagine a situation in which by accident I take a certain book down from the shelf or spot an open book on someone's desk. If I know the language, I may be said to read it whether or not I want to do so. And I must take responsibility for the consequences of that act. . . . This accidental encounter may have the most extensive ethical consequences in my own life, and in those of others, as my act of reading causes other things to be done in their turn. My own reading of the criticism of Georges Poulet, for example, occurred in just this fortuitous way. It was nevertheless decisive for my professional career as teacher and critic, even for my personal life" (VP, 18).

ciprocal substitutions breaks down. Since Marcel does not make use of the simple natural analogy of having a cloud obscure the sun, the phrase "the sun having turned its eye elsewhre," as de Man says, "becomes pure nonsense from the naturalistic point of view that the logic of the passage, structured as a nature/art dialectic, demands."[46] Proust's use of non-naturalistic analogy in this passage, like the personification of the suns bathing themselves in the sea (not discussed by de Man), undoes "Genette's model of happy totalization" reconciling metaphor and metonymy.[47] The use of non-naturalistic analogics also undocs "thc cntirc notion of tropology as a closed system."[48] It does this undoing by introducing something irreducibly other to that system, that is, by a locution that makes sense as allegory but is nonsense as a referential statement.

The last two sentences of de Man's remarkable footnote are characteristically elliptical, condensed, hyperbolic, and even "unreadable," though of course knowledge of the rest of *Allegories of Reading* and of de Man's other work helps the reader try to read them. De Man concludes his footnote by saying that closed tropological systems

depend on the necessary link between the existence and the knowledge of entities, on the unbreakable strength of the tie that unites the sun (as entity) with the eye (as the knowledge of the entity). The sentence "the sun having turned its eye elsewhere" is therefore, from a tropological point of view, the most impossible sentence conceivable. Its absurdity not only denies the intelligibility of natural metaphors but of all tropes; it is the figure of the unreadability of figures and therefore no longer, strictly speaking, a figure.[49]

The reader will note that de Man has here appropriated Proust's figure to his own purposes. In Proust's formulation it is the sun that is endowed with an eye able to turn its sovereign look elsewhere and momentarily darken the sky. The look is sovereign because the sun's gaze illuminates everything. It is the condition of our own seeing and therefore of our knowledge. In de Man's formulation, however, the eye in question becomes the eye of the beholder, which knows the sun by seeing it. He uses the example of the sun and the human eye that knows the sun as a demonstration of how tropology as a closed system depends on an unquestioned referentiality in language. In order for there to be tropes, literal language must first exist, language based on the knowledge of the thing named, as when we look at the sun and say, "That is the sun." De Man's example of the sun as entity that is beheld by the eye, so bringing about knowledge

Miller accidentally encountered Georges Poulet's work. Our reading of a narrative like "Bartleby, The Scrivener" can be accidental too, even if someone has forced us to read it. In any event what is true—according to Miller—is that the consequences of this reading cannot be programmed. For this reason, they contradict both theoretical-literary metalanguages and particular criticisms (the allusion to de Man is evident, since this is one form of the resistance to theory): "Reading is always the disconfirmation or modification of presupposed literary theory rather than its confirmation. . . . A book is a dangerous object, and perhaps all books should have warning labels. Strange things happen when someone reads a book" (vp, 21). Before accepting these assumptions one must ask: What in the text makes the critical act unpredictable? If "ethics" in its primary sense implies a specific behavior by the critic, who nevertheless finds no support for a programming or verification of his hypothesis, that absence of support should be somewhere. Naturally, that *somewhere* is the text. The literary text may perhaps be defined as the place par excellence of the lack of "thetic" position. We find in this fact the second sense of "ethics."

Ethics does not correspond only to a level of behavior situated outside the text (the relation between text and critic, text and context, text and history, etc.). Ethics is also a dimension inside the fable itself. Furthermore, internal and external ethics maintain a relationship doomed to uncertainty, to questioning, among other things, the internal/external opposition. Why is the text the place where the "thetic" position is lacking? "Thetic position" is, in fact, a redundant expression. It alludes to the presence of a decision or directional point of view (monosemic or polysemic), to an absence of irony. Kant's text intends a thetic position. Indeed, in some way or other it has one, but that thetic position is divided and, from the perspective of reason, unsteady.

In order to ask "Why does the literary text lack a thetic position?," we must explain the complex system of relations that Miller puts at stake.

of the entity, already contains a latent contradiction or "impossibility." The sun cannot be looked in the eye. To try to do so is to be blinded, to lose ocular access to intelligibility. Nevertheless, on the basis of referential sentences like "That is the sun," it is possible to exchange and transfer names within an indefinitely extendable system of tropes. The phrase "the sun having turned its eye elsewhere" undoes this system by showing how it is possible to make a phrase that is grammatically correct but that is not grounded in phenomenal intuition or knowledge. You can never see the sun in a cloudless sky turn its eye elsewhere. Nevertheless you can say it. The phrase is "from a tropological point of view, the most impossible sentence conceivable," even though "turn its eye elsewhere" reminds the reader that trope means turning. It is an impossible sentence, nevertheless, because, from a tropological point of view, all tropological sentences must be rooted in a phenomenal knowledge whose archetype is eyesight, seeing the thing with your own eyes. From an allegorical point of view, however, the sentence is perfectly possible, since allegory depends on the discrepancy between the phenomenal entities used and the meaning that is given to them. Allegory freely manipulates the names or other representations of entities in defiance of their naturalistic and intelligible features. The example de Man gives is Giotto's Charity, who does not look charitable.

Another example, not referred to by de Man, occurs a moment after the passage about the sun turning its eye elsewhere. Marcel says the flying angels with which Giotto has peopled his sky give him "the same impression of actual movement, literally real activity, that the gestures of Charity and Envy had given me" (F 4: 227; E 3: 663). The reference is to a passage already referred to near the beginning of the whole immense novel, in *Swann's Way* (F 1: 80–81; E 1: 87–88). Just as the down-to-earth verisimilitude of Giotto's Charity, who looks like a cook handing up a corkscrew, does not correspond to its allegorical meaning, so Giotto's angels do not look like supernal messengers. They look rather like "winged creatures of a particular species that had really existed [*volatiles d'une espèce particulière ayant existé réellement*], that must have figured in the natural history of biblical and apostolic times," or they look like aviators practicing the loop-the-loop (F 4: 227; E 3: 663). Since all tropes and all tropological systems are grounded on at least one figure that, like the sun turning its eye elsewhere, or like the nonangelic angels, comes from outside the realm of what can be known by the senses in nature, "the intelligibility" not only of "natural metaphors but of all tropes" is "denied" by the absurdity of

Let us take a concrete example, "Bartleby, The Scrivener." The title of the essay Miller devotes to Melville's narrative ("Who is he? Melville's 'Bartleby, The Scrivener'") is taken from the text itself. It appears the first time the narrator hears about Bartleby after having left him and moved to a new office. A "perturbed-looking stranger" asks the narrator about his relationship with Bartleby. The narrator replies that he has nothing to do with him. Finally the stranger exclaims, "In mercy's name, who is he?" Both this question and the title constitute a suitable clue to understanding the book called *Versions of Pygmalion*. Ovid's *Metamorphoses* are in their turn excellent material for Miller's conceptual and analytical creation. On the one hand, ethics, understood as a way of doing things that provokes other things, is properly allegorized in the Ovidian text. In this book one story is always linked up to another, not only in the sense that one fable implies another, but also in the sense that the consequences of an action, as in the Pygmalion story, take place in later stories. (Remember what happens to Pygmalion's granddaughter Myrrha.)

On the other hand, Pygmalion, with his own hands and with Venus's help, brings to life what was just a marble statue, Galatea. To bring a statue to life is like filling in what was empty before, like putting words where only silence existed. In short, Pygmalion literally enacts the figure of speech known as prosopopoeia: "If most of the metamorphoses in the *Metamorphoses* go from human to inhuman, life to death, animate to inanimate, the coming alive of Galatea goes the other way. The name for the figure of speech of which this metamorphosis is the literalizing allegory is *prosopopoeia*. This trope ascribes a face, a name, or a voice to the absent, the inanimate, or the dead" (VP, 3–4). The connections between prosopopoeia and Freud's *Unheimlich* are evident. But insofar as the activity of the critic and that of the reader have to do with Pygmalion, the *Unheimlich* must concern us, as a passage I have already cited affirms: "Though none of us, of course, would take a statue as a real per-

a phrase like "the sun having turned its eye elsewhere" or like "the suns having bathed themselves in the deep ocean." Such phrases are unintelligibly torn between their impossibility as referential assertions and their grammatical and allegorical possibility. They are an uncrossable limit for the mind. The mind oscillates between comprehending and not comprehending such phrases. This oscillation may, strictly speaking, be called an "aporia," since it is an impasse beyond which the mind cannot go. This aporia is mimed by the difficulty we have in "reading" or understanding de Man's formulations here. They boggle the mind, as when de Man says the sun turning its eye elsewhere "is the figure of the unreadability of figures and therefore no longer, strictly speaking, a figure." It is no longer, strictly speaking, a figure because, strictly speaking, a figure depends on the consonance between the referential meaning and the tropological meaning. In this case the two have split apart. Such a figure figures the unreadability of figures since it brings into the open the way all tropological systems are constructed over the abyss of a dissonance between reference and allegorical meaning. All figures secretly fissure in this way, even those that seem most securely grounded in referentiality. "Readability" is by de Man implicitly defined as the transparent harmony between referential meaning, grounded in phenomenal intuition, and an elusive allegorical meaning. I call it elusive because it is, strictly speaking, not intelligible. We can know the trope but not what the trope stands for, just as Giotto's angels give us no knowledge of celestial messengers.

De Man formulates this nonconsonance and the consequent abyss of unreadability in a climactic and elegantly intransigent statement near the end of his essay:

According to the laws of Proust's own statement it is forever impossible to read Reading. Everything in this novel signifies something other than what it represents, be it love, consciousness, politics, art, sodomy, or gastronomy: it is always something else that is intended. It can be shown that the most adequate term to designate this "something else" is Reading. But one must at the same time "understand" that this word bars access, once and forever, to a meaning that yet can never cease to call out for its understanding.[50]

These sentences are to some degree misleading. They give ammunition, when they are misunderstood, to those who reproach so-called "deconstruction" for saying "it is all language." They are misleading, however, only if "Reading" is mistakenly taken in the narrow sense of understanding

son, in order to 'read' the *Metamorphoses* it is necessary to yield to [their] basic narrative personifications, by a certain willing suspension of disbelief. We must think of Pygmalion, Galatea, Cinyras, Myrrha, and even Venus to some degree as if they were real persons, not just black marks on the page" (VP, 11–12). That is to say, the reader should be like the student Nathaniel in Hoffmann's "The Sandman," who mistakes the doll Olympia for a human being, but he must not come to believe it completely. Nathaniel must be rational, not in a psychotic state. He must see in Olympia a doll and a real person at once. To construct a prosopopoeia while being conscious that it is a prosopopoeia is a difficult task indeed.

Pygmalion animates what is inanimate. The reader takes black marks on the page to be real people. The narrative and/or the example gives a face to the Law. These three cases share a common matrix: something empty and inanimate becomes full or animate. The concept is flooded by fables, Galatea by movement, the text by life. When Miller explains, "My book will explore the ethics of narrative in its connection with the trope of prosopopoeia" (VP, 11), we should understand a linkage between ethics, narrative, and prosopopoeia. The last is the procedure by which the second deconstructs the possibility of the first understood as law, program, theory, and/or criticism. After all, prosopopoeia reveals that what precedes it is dead, unknown, or empty. Kant writes: "We cannot show with certainty by any example that the will is here determined by the law alone without any other incentives, even though this appears to be the case. For it is always possible that secret fear of disgrace, and perhaps also obscure apprehension of other dangers, may have had an influence on the will" (Kant, 1969: 42). In this way he settles the basic principle of nonknowledge and the accompanying impossibility of acceding to the other. If the other, my neighbor, my fellow man, the text, the law, and so forth are unknown, then what remains beyond myself (of course including the beyond that exists in myself) is too much like the

language printed in books and not seen as an allegorical trope for an always frustrated desire to "read" oneself, other people, natural objects, politics, and so on. This desire to read includes the whole of human life, not just the relatively narrow corner of it that involves reading books. Moreover, as the passage makes clear, the word "Reading" is for de Man a catachresis that at once names and covers over, therefore bars access to, the meaning it names, just as "Marcel," in de Man's formulation at the end of his Proust essay, is an "allegorical and therefore obliterating figure for the author."[51]

Even more, however, must be said, more than de Man says, about his example in the footnote demonstrating the impossibility of reading Reading. The sun is not just one entity among others, chosen as a convenient example of the necessary link between the existence and the knowledge of entities, the sun and the eye that knows that sun. The sun that turns its gaze elsewhere has links to all the other suns in the *Recherche* I have been discussing. Even this sun, for example, is not without its covert erotic associations. These associations are deeply buried in the successive layers of the drafts for the *Recherche*. Proust spent much time elaborating an episode involving Marcel's assignation at a hotel in Padua with Mme Putbus's chambermaid. He then decided to leave out not only the episode itself but almost all lateral traces of that episode. This episode would have connected the solar associations of Padua with another displaced figure for the sun: the chambermaid. Moreover, the sun, as I have said, cannot be looked in the eye. It is therefore not only a traditional figure for the head, chief, sovereign, the patriarchal top of the chain of representations, as in Plato. Its invisibility, as the one entity that cannot be made intelligible by being looked at, though it is the source of all possibility of seeing, also makes it an appropriate image of the unreadability of figures. If you cannot read Reading, neither can you read the sun, allegorical figure here for unreadability. Furthermore, as the passage citing Baudelaire makes clear, the sun's diurnal vanishing beneath the waves and reappearance again at dawn makes it a powerful figure for the unsoundable gulfs into which it plunges. To put this another way, the sun that has turned his eye elsewhere is a catachresis for the unknown and unknowable gulfs that I am calling the realm of the "others." The sun, rising or setting, is a manifestation without manifestation of the realms it visits when it is not visible. That the sun can turn its eye elsewhere cuts us off from the circuit of communication with those gulfs in the sea in which it bathes itself each day. The notion that the sun turns its eye elsewhere is a brilliant figure for the power the sun espe-

emptiness and death that can only be filled in by a linguistic face, by a prosopopoeia that will never say more than that it covers up something. It is like the black veil the minister in Hawthorne's tale puts over his face, for reasons no one will ever know. Since prosopopoeia attributes a "material" superficiality, that is, a face, open to the senses, to what is absent, dead, or unknown, such an attribute can operate only by means of some presupposition and in a state of conditionality. Otherwise, it would make no sense to say that Pygmalion's gesture is autoerotic: "Ovid's description of the anthropomorphizing of Galatea strongly emphasizes the autoerotic side of this process. Autoeroticism is a region of human experience in which prosopopoeia appears to be least verbal, most bodily, tactile, and affective" (VP, 6).

The presupposition and its conditionality are, similarly, the means by which the critic works in relation to the literary text, if it is true that the text does not offer a sound basis for verifying one or another interpretative hypothesis. The presupposition and conditionality also constitute the medium within which Bartleby's narrator moves. To maintain this way of looking at the relation to the literary other, to preserve the text as the place of the unknown, the repetition from the Ovidian corpus (in this case the fable of Pygmalion and Galatea) must remain in a constant state of transformation or deformation: "The word 'versions' in my title is meant to suggest not only different tellings of the same story, but also deflections, or one might even say 'metamorphoses,' of that story" (VP, 7). As a confirmation of this point, it is sufficient to juxtapose how Gongora treats the story of Galatea in the seventeenth century with the way Melville treats the same story in the nineteenth century.

Miller's analysis of Melville's narrative could be summed up, though inadequately, as follows: someone (the homodiegetic narrator) tries to give life, to apply a prosopopoeia, to a character whose most characteristic feature is to constantly show himself as unknown (*Unheimlich*). At-

cially has to illuminate this world but also to turn to an unknown world we shall never see. The sun that turns its gaze tropes itself, makes itself into an allegorical figure. By anthropomorphizing the sun, by making the sun into an eye that can look at us or not look at us, as opposed to simply illuminating us and making it possible for us to know other entities, the sentence at once humanizes the wholly other and at the same time seals its perpetual separation from us, as the sun's gaze turns elsewhere.

Finally, the image of the sun turning its gaze elsewhere is, as de Man does not bother to say, a personification, as are most catachreses. The figure is an unauthorized name for the unknown and unknowable. The sun is not a person and does not have an eye, any more than the sun bathes in the sea. To ascribe such human attributes to the sun in an act of prosopopoeia is an unwarranted performative positing, not the report of an achieved knowledge. The phrase saying "the sun having turned its eye elsewhere" frustrates comprehension. Two irreconcilable functions of language, the referential and the performative, clash within it. The referential sustains tropological systems. The performative personifies by naming things in catachresis as substitutes for the unknowable realm of the others. Catachresis is not nonreferential, but it can be called referential only against the grain of the word, since it refers to what cannot be phenomenally known. Catachresis refers only by performatively constituting what it names, for example, by ascribing to the sun a gaze, in response to that demand from the others Proust names a "strange call."

I return now, after this tropological turning away or digression, to Baudelaire's "The Balcony" and to Proust's use of it. As in the case of the sun turning its look elsewhere, the promise of a recovery of the past in "The Balcony" takes place only in a sentence that is naturalistically and therefore tropologically impossible. It takes place, that is, in the milieu appropriate to art, a site appropriate to myth or allegory. The suns rise in the sky rejuvenated after having washed themselves in the sea's depths. Baudelaire's word *interdit*, interdicted, in "interdit à nos sondes," names a verbal ban. This is consonant with the implication that the sounding line in question is some forbidden formula of words. Such words would form just that poetic art of "evocation" the speaker in "The Balcony" boasts of having. But Baudelaire's poem asserts that no formula of words will succeed in sounding these depths. Such words are interdicted, meaning, literally, "spoken against," as by an irrevocable decree. If the depths are "interdit à nos sondes," they are unfathomable. The poet can "evoke." He

tempting to be Pygmalion, that someone becomes passive, since what he tries to animate turns him into something inanimate, that is to say, into Galatea. Melville's text reverses Ovid's fable. It tells how somebody becomes Galatea as she was before she was brought to life, a statue of marble or salt. The narrator is a quiet and stable lawyer who notarizes "conveyances," documents that convey property from one owner to another. The writing of title deeds must be extremely correct in order for them to fulfill their function. The narrator-lawyer has three copyists with fixed habits who work with him to copy and collate different documents. Bartleby, the new copyist, interrupts all this (vital, professional, operative) mobility by answering to every demand, "I would prefer not to." As time goes on, this expression becomes more and more radical. Bartleby ends up denying his own life. The play of this tale, explains Miller, lies in projecting mobility and immobility into the same space.

Miller's reading derives, not from a "thematic" analysis, but from the material and linguistic side of the "thematic," even from certain linguistic details, details apparently alien to the course of the plot. Miller is deconstructively attentive in his interpretation of details. The subtitle of "Bartleby, The Scrivener," for example, is "A Story of Wall-Street." "Wall Street" is a proper name. It is therefore a trope worn away, a transparent signifier that erases its origin in the very act of being pronounced or written, but that hides "an embodied oxymoron. The name combines in itself the two motifs of mobility and fixity that organize 'Bartleby, The Scrivener.' No doubt it is only an accident that the great center of legal and financial activity in the United States is called 'Wall Street,' but the name seems uncannily appropriate as a general name for the place where money and property flow back and forth as on a great financial boulevard, while at the same time being the place where the buck may stop, hit the wall. More particularly, the name 'Wall Street' is a perfect encapsulating figure for the opposition between dialectical and narrative mobility, on

can call forth the happy minutes of the past, just as Glendower, in Shakespeare's *Henry IV, Part One*, 3.1.54, claims that he can call spirits from the vasty deep. It seems uncertain, however, whether or not the minutes will appear, any more than the spirits were certain to appear for Glendower. "But will they come when you do call for them?" asks Hotspur.

The sentence Saint Loup quotes is interrogative in the poem, as is Proust's appropriation of it. In the next to the last stanza Baudelaire's speaker claims he knows the art of evoking happy minutes. In the last stanza this claim is put in question when he asks whether or not these lover's oaths, perfumes, and infinite kisses will be reborn from interdicted gulfs as suns rise rejuvenated from their bath in the profound sea: "Renaîtront-ils?" They may be reborn or they may not be. The poem ends hovering on that unanswered question. Proust's appropriation of Baudelaire's version of the "solar myth" supplements the passage about the concentric circles of Marcel's substitute desires. It universalizes this pattern in cosmic terms. Proust's citation of Baudelaire makes clear that the gulf from which all these substitute objects of desire arise remains something wholly other, something unknowable and unattainable. It is as unattainable and unknowable as the place the sun goes when it sets was for the old cosmology. What rises each day is no more than another substitute for those forever interdicted depths. The sun itself is only one more trope of substitution, not the literal object for which Albertine, Balbec, all those other women, the sundrenched grapes, the Titian, Vinteuil's septet, and so on, are figures, in an endless chain, or in an endless series of concentric, progressively degraded circles around an absent center. That the sun itself is a figure is attested to by the absurdity, from a referential point of view, of what Baudelaire and Proust say about the sun. If it is true that Proust's *Recherche* is organized around a solar myth, the myth in question is an allegorical one. This scarf of Iris is not an iridescent figurative band around a central literal sun. The sun itself, rather, is one more allegorical figure representing an unknown homeland. An unbreakable interdict prevents us from ever confronting that otherness face to face. We can only encounter it by way of its substitutes. No attainable original exists for which the substitutes substitute.

the one hand, and dead fixity on the other, the impasse face to face with the wall" (VP, 150–51). Wall Street is named for a wooden wall the early Dutch settlers put up there to protect their settlement from the Native Americans.

That wall is prolonged inside the text in the topography of the lawyer's chambers: one window looks onto a white wall, and the other window looks onto a black wall: "White wall against black wall" (VP, 151). One way or another, the oxymoron of a minimum paratextual (*parergonic*) element of the paratext (since the analysis of "Wall Street" is not about the title but about the subtitle, a fold or nuance of the general title) gives rise in its heteroseme, in its minimal semantic universe, to what organizes the whole of a text that will be described as aporetic. This kind of procedure reveals that Miller continues to practice (as he did in *The Linguistic Moment*) a nonlinear analysis of a narrative text which structurally is not linear either. On the syntagmatic horizontal of the action he imposes a vertical, an axis that leads to the perception of parasites, which are a sine qua non of the text. The reader will find other important details analyzed by Miller in his essay on Melville: the fact that Bartleby may have worked in the Dead Letter Office; the name of the carriage — a "rockaway" — in which the narrator runs away from Bartleby; the mute bust of Cicero, and so on.

What interests me now is the sentence-bomb that accompanies Bartleby's undefinable behavior: "I would prefer not to." Derrida has written of this sentence: "Bartleby's 'I would prefer not to' takes on the responsibility of a response without response. It evokes the future without either predicting or promising" (Derrida, 1995a: 74–75). Miller gives a detailed account of the range of contradictory meanings (just as contradictory as those for "Wall Street") that comprise both the words ("prefer," "not") and the temporal modality ("would") of this disconcerting, sinister, tragic, and comic sentence. He concludes: "Even this neutral or

"O sole mio!"

My last solar passage is perhaps the most extraordinary of all, and the most complex. It comes at the end of the "Séjour à Venise."[52] This section is presented as the third stage in Marcel's "nearing total indifference with regard to Albertine" after her death (F 4: 1108; E 3: 637; this sentence is relegated to a footnote in the new Pléiade edition). Marcel's account of his visit to Venice has a complex, three-dimensional existence. It is complicated both in the sequence of its episodes and in the layers of previous drafts that underlie each episode. It has the three-dimensional depth in space and time that Marcel says, in a passage already discussed from *Le temps retrouvé*, he wants for the novel he is going to write. That passage uses, the reader will remember, a figure of planetary revolution to describe the way Marcel is related to his past selves and to the various characters who have figured in his life.

The intricate structure of final text, variants, and drafts is also a good indication of how useful a hypertext version of the *Recherche* would be. Even with its appendixes of notes, variants, and drafts, the Pléiade edition preserves the illusion that the ideal for a printed book is a single line of words leading from the first word to the last, to be read in that order. The variants and drafts were steps toward the achievement of a final univocal, linear order. They can be jettisoned now that order has been achieved. On the contrary, what the reader is given, particularly in the posthumous volumes, is a construction by the editors, with many arbitrary editorial decisions hidden under the apparent coherence of the finished product. A hypertext version would suggest more truthfully that the *Recherche* exists only factitiously as a completed whole. It is actually a vast, mobile, unfinished assemblage of words. This assemblage is not even adequately imaged as a spatial movement like that of planets around the sun, since words are not things and are not related to one another as things are related. A hypertext version of the *Recherche* would allow the reader to move by a series of mouseclicks back through the layer on layer of drafts that accumulated through time, like layers of snow on a glacier, from the earliest existing version down to the "finished" text. Or the reader could move sideways through the drafts of the various episodes that existed at a given moment in time. Or the variants of a given phrase or word could be called up instantly on the screen, rather than laboriously searched for in the notes. A multi-dimensionality like that Marcel wanted for his novel could be real-

passive-active motionless motion in the word 'prefer,' which can turn the tongue of the man who happens to hear it, is disabled of such force as it has by the incomplete conditional in Bartleby's 'would,' by the negative in 'not,' which says not that Bartleby would prefer to do this or that, but that he would prefer not to do . . . whatever his employer has asked him to do. The final word, 'to,' is the beginning of a prepositional phrase left hanging in the air, presumably by the ellision of the words that would complete it: 'to . . . do what you have just asked me to do.' 'I would prefer not to': he does not say he will and he does not say he won't" (VP, 155). "I would prefer not to" is an irony in Kierkegaard's sense: by being neither active nor passive, by being active and passive at once, by saying neither yes nor no, by moving and immobilizing both itself and what is outside it, it does not actually say anything. This is why it leads Bartleby's narrator into a situation where it is almost impossible for him to decide.

Before weighing the terrible effects of that simple and singular phrase, however, one must take into account to whom it is addressed. One must take into account the narrator, since it is he who gives us the text to read, who functions as the framework of the text as offered. Can we imagine the narrator and protagonist of Bret Easton Ellis's *American Psycho* confronting Bartleby and receiving the answer "I would prefer not to"? The effects of "I would prefer not to" are only possible given the particular characteristics of the narrator in "Bartleby." Even before Bartleby appears, the narrator already intends to hint to Turkey that he need not come to his chambers to work after twelve o'clock because of his inflamed ways after that hour: "As he was in many ways a most valuable person to me, and all the time before twelve o'clock, meridian, was the quickest, steadiest creature too, accomplishing a great deal of work in a style not easy to be matched—for these reasons, I was willing to overlook his eccentricities, though indeed, occasionally, I remonstrated with him. I did this very gently, however, because, though the civilest, nay, the bland-

ized in a new technological model of which Proust could have had no
inkling. He lived rather in the now distant era of the telephone, the telegraph, and the typewriter, of "aerial navigation and wireless telegraphy" (F
4: 239; E 3: 676). Nevertheless, what he produced calls out for translation
into the new electronic medium and already anticipates it.

The "Séjour à Venise" is, in its episodic form, a fractal miniature
of the whole novel. It treats of love, gastronomy, diplomacy, landscape,
or rather, urbanscape, art, the magic of names, Marcel's relation to his
mother, memories of Combray, Marcel's fading recollections of Albertine,
the law of substitution that governs desire, and so on. Its roots go deep in
Proust's creative life. The trip to Venice already figures in the notebooks
that became *Contre Sainte-Beuve*, written before *A la recherche du temps
perdu* was even conceived. Each episode and theme of the Venice visit
would merit a long analysis—the opening comparison of morning sunlight in Combray and in Venice; sightseeing with his mother or alone; visits
to Saint Mark's, full of Ruskinian echoes; Marcel's solitary walks and gon-
dola excursions in Venice; his discovery at night of a vast moonlit *campo*,
hidden in the labyrinth of Venetian streets and canals, a magic place that
he can never find again by daylight; the wonderfully comic episode of
Norpois's meeting with Prince Foggi and Norpois's magic speech act that
creates a new Prime Minister of Italy: "And has no one mentioned the
name of Signor Giolitti?" (F 4: 215; E 3: 650); Marcel's visit to the Arena
Chapel at Padua, already discussed; the episode of the telegram from Gilberte mistakenly read as coming from an Albertine brought back from the
dead; Marcel's pursuit of Venetian women as substitutes for Albertine; the
climactic episode of his refusal to join his mother on her departure from
Venice; the final scene in the train when Marcel and his mother read the
last letters they received in Venice and Marcel discovers that his telegram
was not from a resurrected Albertine but from Gilberte announcing her
forthcoming marriage to Robert de Saint Loup. The Venice sojourn forms
a miniature version of the whole novel. It is a small masterpiece within the
greater one that cunningly mirrors the whole.

One curious feature of the trip to Venice is more or less invisible in
the finished novel. Proust, as I have already mentioned, worked during a
considerable period, in five different notebooks, on an episode that was in
the end excluded: the story of his assignation at Padua with the Baroness Putbus's chambermaid. "Putbus" was "Picpus" in the early drafts, an
even more grotesque name. The suppressed story remains covertly present

est and most reverential of men in the morning, yet in the afternoon he was disposed, upon provocation, to be slightly rash with his tongue, in fact, insolent" (Melville, 1984: 637–38). Nevertheless, Turkey will insist upon continuing his afternoon work, interpreting his inflamed ways in a quite different way from the narrator. For Turkey it is not a question of inflamed ways but of gallantry: " 'In the morning I but marshal and deploy my columns; but in the afternoon I put myself at their head, and gallantly charge the foe, thus!'—and he made a violent thrust with the ruler" (ibid.: 638). To that, the narrator will reply (in a more practical interpretation of the facts): " 'But the blots, Turkey,' intimated I" (ibid.). Turkey does not flinch, however, and goes on with his ideal interpretation, in addition, identifying himself with the narrator: "True,—but with submission, sir, behold these hairs! I am getting old. Surely, sir, a blot or two of a warm afternoon is not to be severely urged against gray hairs. Old age—even if it blot the page—is honorable. With submission, sir, we *both* are getting old" (ibid.). Turkey turns the narrator's reasoning against him: a blot on the paper is not something negative, but an honorable sign of old age, which comes to all. Because the narrator has both ears and sensibility, he cannot but succumb to Turkey's syllogistic strategy: "This appeal to my fellow-feeling was hardly to be resisted. At all events, I saw that go he would not. So, I made up my mind to let him stay" (ibid.). The narrator is a man of peace and quiet, disgusted by violence, someone who listens to others to the extent of letting himself be imposed upon by them. To give another example, he will turn a blind eye to a certain "little business at the Justices's courts" (ibid., 634) in which Nippers is involved, looking for another excuse (the fact he dresses well), to keep Nippers at his chambers. Not only does the narrator listen, he may listen too well.

    This feature of the narrator makes him especially susceptible in the extraordinary situation with Bartleby. He not only hears that upsetting phrase, he also sees an amazing mode of gesturing. Miller develops this

in the way Marcel's reading in the register of guests expected at his hotel the notation "Mme Putbus and attendants" triggers his refusal to join his mother for the train trip back to Paris. Nothing, in the final version, tells the reader that one of those attendants would have been Mme Putbus's chambermaid. As a result, the intensity of Marcel's refusal to leave Venice in the final version seems more than a little unmotivated. If the affair with the chambermaid had been included, his desire to stay would have been explicable. What can one say about the relevance to our reading of an episode that was almost, but not quite, suppressed?

The Pléiade editors compare this episode to a scaffolding that is necessary for the construction of a building but is then removed when the edifice is complete (F 4: 710). A literary work, however, is not made of wood, bricks, and plaster, but of words. A better comparison might be with the secrets that Albertine eternally keeps from Marcel, sealed ultimately with the silence of death, an enclosure like the Piombi, or lead-lined prison cells in which Venetian political prisoners were incarcerated and which Marcel imagines imprisoning his memories of the dead Albertine deep within him.[53] Marcel, too, it would appear, has secrets he keeps from his readers. A better way to put this would be to say that Proust attempted to keep this episode secret from readers. In any case, the final text of the novel has its secrets. These secrets are true secrets. They are impenetrable. They can never be revealed, but in a peculiar sense in this case. Just as it is impossible ever to know whether the coin the protagonist of Baudelaire's "Counterfeit Money" gives the beggar was or was not counterfeit,[54] so it is impossible ever to know whether the reader should or should not use fortuitous knowledge of the omitted episode about Baroness Putbus's chambermaid. If it was left out, it was left out. The novel has closed seamlessly over the effaced secret, like a door over a lead-lined prison cell. To take it into consideration is illicit, impertinent, unwarranted. The episode is not part of the finished book. Yet all those drafts of the omitted episode have now been exposed, the door of the prison cell opened. What use should the reader make of those drafts? No answer other than an arbitrary one can be given. What might justify a choice remains secret.

My chief interest here, however, is in the solar resonances of the Venice sojourn's final episode. As the reader will see, this episode too has something to do with secrets. After his mother, accompanied by all his belongings as well as hers, sets off for the train station, Marcel, now a guilty and disobedient child, impelled by "that old desire to rebel against

when, speaking of what the narrator knows about Bartleby, he writes: "As the reader learns later, the last thing in the world one would expect to find anywhere would be letters or diaries written by Bartleby. He is not the letter-writing sort. He is rather the place where all letters written by others stop. It turns out that the narrator does not mean 'written documents' by 'original sources.' He means ocular proof. The only original source for trustworthy knowledge of Bartleby is the testimony of the eyes" (vp, 145). Bartleby's physical behavior is gentle, peaceful, hermetic, mechanical, inhuman. There is not "any thing ordinarily human about him," says the narrator (Melville, 1984: 643). To that behavior is added the terrible sentence "I would prefer not to." The effects the lawyer feels result from the combination of a particular bodily behavior with a particular way of speaking. His emotions oscillate between irritation ("had there been any thing ordinarily human about him, doubtless I should have violently dismissed him from the premises"; "for a few moments I was turned into a pillar of salt"; ibid., 643, 644), sympathy ("there was something about Bartleby that not only strangely disarmed me, but in a wonderful manner touched and disconcerted me"; ibid., 644), and, of course, pity and compassion. Yet Bartleby does deny himself. Although the sentence vibrates in an ironic movement that does not say anything, his acts accompany the sentence with a peculiarly passive denial. Derrida writes, following in Miller's wake: "But in saying nothing general or determinable, Bartleby doesn't say absolutely nothing. *I would prefer not to* looks like an incomplete sentence" (Derrida, 1995a: 75). The incomplete sentence contrasts with the complete movement of Bartleby's gestures. What the narrator hears is a "neutral or passive-active motionless motion" (vp, 155) in the sentence. What the narrator sees is a body that is actively doing nothing, that is denying itself.

   In Bartleby, the lawyer witnesses not deferral but negative performance, stubborn resolution, impatience, pure presence. The conflict

an imaginary plot woven against me by my parents" (F 4: 230; E 3: 666), stays behind. He orders a drink to be brought to him on the hotel terrace overlooking the canal and settles down there to watch the sunset. From a boat that has stopped in front of the hotel, a musician sings "O sole mio." Marcel's misery at causing his mother trouble and his sense of solitude bring about a curious transformation in his perception of his surroundings. Just as he is alienated from himself, torn between his desire to go and his desire to remain, his fidelity to his mother and the imaginary pleasures of staying, so he is alienated from his surroundings. The link between person and scene that is so important a presupposition of the *Recherche* is broken. The result is a disintegration of the scene. The word "Venice" is detached from Venice. Venice is detached from the mendacious dream of the magical city that has motivated so many of Marcel's desires to travel. Before Marcel's eyes Venice is dismantled, or, one might even dare to say, "deconstructed." Marcel recognizes that "Venice" has been no more than a fiction imposed by will or habit on a meaningless substratum. Venice is reduced to its material base. It becomes no more than hydrogen and oxygen fortuitously combined to make water and adjacent heaps of stones, "the stones of Venice" in a sense not absolutely different from the meaning Ruskin gave that phrase. All the elements that are usually combined in one inextricable whole, the person, the name, and the place, are separated from one another and lie side by side in alien proximity:

The town that I saw before me had ceased to be Venice. Its personality, its name, seemed to me to be mendacious fictions [*fictions mensongères*] which I no longer had the will to impress upon its stones [*le courage d'inculquer aux pierres*]. I saw the palaces reduced to their basic elements, lifeless heaps of marble with nothing to choose between them, and the water as a combination of hydrogen and oxygen, eternal, blind, anterior and exterior to Venice, oblivious of the Doges and of Turner. And yet this unremarkable place [*ce lieu quelconque*] was as strange as a place at which one has just arrived, which does not yet know one, or a place which one has left and which has forgotten one already. I could no longer tell it anything about myself, I could leave nothing of myself imprinted upon it [*se poser sur lui*]; it contracted me into myself until I was no more than a throbbing heart and an attention strained to follow the development of "O sole mio." (F 4: 231; E 3: 667, trans. slightly altered)

In this admirably eloquent passage, the disintegration of elements that are normally held together in a unit joining figure to scene in an act

arises precisely as a result of the joint presence of two semiotic systems that at once cohabit and exclude each other: verbality and gesture. Both codes are indecipherable, each in its own way: the verbal code, as a result of its ironic combination of nuances and semantic modalities; the gestural one, because it moves in a sinister way between life and death. "The narrator," Miller writes, "tries or considers a series of strategies for dealing with Bartleby. Much of the black comedy of the tale consists in the narrator's report of his frantic attempts to do something about Bartleby, this 'cadaverous' presence, this 'incubus' or 'ghost' who 'haunts' his office like an 'apparition,' and who 'like a very ghost, agreeably to the laws of magical invocation, and at the third summons,' appears when the narrator calls him by name" (VP, 162). Though both codes oppose, include, and exclude each other, each also holds inside itself a heterogeneity of close and irreconcilable fragments. Here we find again the interminability Miller had already found in De Quincey or in his analysis of the term "parasite." How does somebody who *does not do* (collate, write, eat, etc.) utter a sentence that defers patiently and interminably any type of action, a sentence that also has the strange virtue of repeating itself in a relevant-irrelevant way? Bartleby exemplifies Derrida's law of iterability with a vengeance.

The lawyer makes a demand: "'The copies, the copies,' said I hurriedly. 'We are going to examine them. There'—and I held towards him the fourth quadruplicate" (Melville, 1984: 644). To this, Bartleby replies, "I would prefer not to," then disappears behind the screen. The exchange can be considered a "dialogue"—a peculiar dialogue, but a dialogue after all. The lawyer then asks, "*Why* do you refuse?" To which Bartleby replies, "I would prefer not to" (ibid.). This is a dialogue in the style of Ionesco's *The Bald Soprano*. I am not asking you to do anything; I am asking you why you refuse to do it; and you go on answering, "I would prefer not to." What does "I would prefer not to" mean in this case? Is it an ironic way of saying that Bartleby is not going to copy? Or is it a brusque way

of intimate inculcation or superposition causes a radical paralysis of will. It is as though Marcel were hypnotized. Though he knows that if he waits much longer he will miss all chance to join his mother and catch the train, he can do nothing but listen to the singer repeat once more and yet again the banal words of "O sole mio." These have now come to be identified with his paralysis. The song almost seems to be causing his delay and his suffering. It even seems to be causing the disintegration of Venice into a heap of stones:

And it was perhaps this melancholy [*cette tristesse*], like a sort of numbing cold, that constituted the despairing but hypnotic [*fascinateur*] charm of the song. Each note that the singer's voice uttered with a force and ostentation that were almost muscular stabbed me to the heart. When the phrase was completed down below and the song seemed to be at an end, the singer had still not had enough and resumed at the top as though he needed to proclaim once more my solitude and despair. (F 4: 233; E 3: 669)

Why "O sole mio"? Why did Proust choose just this song to have Marcel listen to with fascinated attention as he sits hypnotized on the terrace watching the sun sink toward the horizon? "O sole mio" is a popular Italian love song in Neapolitan dialect. It is the "You Are My Sunshine" of Italy. Anyone who has listened to a Luciano Pavarotti concert will, most likely, have heard him "bellow" (Proust's word) the song, in a fashion not unlike the way the reader imagines Proust's Venetian boatsinger to have sung it. In the song the sovereignty usually ascribed to the sun is transferred to the beloved. Her face becomes the source of radiance for all the world. Here are the words in dialect, followed by an approximate translation: "Che bella cosa 'na iurnata'e sole, / n'ària serena dopo 'na tempesta! / pe' ll'aria fresca pare già 'na festa. . . . / Che bella cosa 'na iurnata'e sole. / Ma n'atu sole cchiù bello, ohi ne', / 'o sole mio sta nfronte a te! / O sole, sole mio sta nfronte a te, / sta nfronte a te! [What a beautiful thing a sunny day (is), calm air after a storm! Because of (or, in) the fresh air it already looks like a feast. . . . What a beautiful thing a sunny day (is). But another sun, a more beautiful one, my sun, is in your face! My sun, my sun, is in your face, is in your face!]." [55]

"O sole mio," the reader can see, is, like the passage from Baudelaire Saint Loup quotes, another version of Proust's "solar myth." Here the power usually ascribed to the sun is transferred to a substitute, according

of saying that he is not going to answer any question the lawyer asks him? What, exactly, would he prefer not to do? This situation reveals an astonishing automatism, more characteristic of a machine than of a human being, despite the fact that this kind of dialogue is very human. Bartleby creates an impenetrable veil, and neither the narrator nor the reader can know what is hidden behind it. Perhaps another type of man, another type of actant, less receptive, with duller eyes and ears, would have behaved more expeditiously in regard to Bartleby. But the veil would have remained impenetrable. That Bartleby's narrator listens too well makes the situation tragicomic. Miller asks: "And what of Bartleby's first word, 'I'? 'I' have shown that there is doubt that the question 'who is he?' can be answered in reference to Bartleby. By what authority, then, in the name of what ego or subjectivity, does Bartleby get his authority to speak in such a sinister and subversive way the 'I' that is a necessary part of all performative utterances, even when it remains merely implicit, as when I sign my name? What 'I' beyond all limited, circumscribed, and therefore efficacious 'I's' speaks through Bartleby as the bringing to a halt of all felicitously operative 'I's'?" (VP, 155).

Is that "I" not perhaps in the same position as the law, history, context, and so on? If Bartleby's "I" is veiled by its speech and gesticulation, just as the law in Kant's text (or in Kafka's parable) has no face because it cannot be embodied in any concrete example, then the veil is the sign of the unknown that it covers over. Bartleby is an opaque, gloomy, and inaccessible character by virtue of what under "normal" circumstances should constitute a medium of transparency and accessibility: word and gesture. Moreover, importantly, Bartleby only exists (if we admit that he exists) thanks to speech and gesticulation, which hide something strange and unknown—in short, are empty. The veil has a double and contradictory function: to hide and at the same time to put a prosopopoeia in place. What is secret is manifest through a material surface that hides it.

to the Proustian law of substitute desire I have identified. Since Marcel's hearing of the song comes at a moment when he has finally forgotten or has almost forgotten his love for Albertine and is shifting rapidly from one substitute to another, to various Venetian working girls, to various other women, mostly from Austria, he meets at the hotel, and since the conflict between these momentary infatuations and his abiding love for his mother has been brought into the open by his refusal to join her in leaving Venice, he is, for the moment, demystified. He can see all these objects of desire as factitious substitutes for one another and all these as replacements for a personified sun that now no longer has the power to dominate everything with its light. The sun stands amazed as it listens to a song that now is explicitly said to dismantle Venice. The song also deprives the sun, verse by verse, of its kingship. Marcel's experience comes to a climax in another of those solar sentences that is impossible because in it the referential and the allegorical separate out, just as all the other usually combined elements of the scene have been detached from one another. In this case the shift of the sun's power so that it now "stands [*sta*]" in the face of the beloved paralyzes the sun, as Marcel is paralyzed. This defiance of the sun causes it to stand still in the sky, as the sun stood still when Joshua commanded it to do so, against all naturalistic possibility (Josh. 10:12–13).[56] The sun watches in amazement, by the light of its own fading, the disintegration of the scene. This disintegration is figured, at the end of the passage, in the way the elements of the once-golden Venetian scene have now become an "equivocal" alloy of baser metals artificially combined. If the sun remains fixed in the sky it will never be able to set. Therefore it will never be able again to bathe itself in those profound gulfs where lies that lost homeland the sun gives fresh news of every day:

I was gripped by an anguish that was caused me by the sight of the Canal which had become diminutive now that the soul of Venice had fled from it, of that commonplace [*banal*] Rialto which was no longer the Rialto, and by the song of despair which "O sole mio" had become and which, bellowed [*clamé*] thus beside the insubstantial [*inconsistants*] palaces, finally reduced them to dust and ashes and completed the ruin of Venice; I looked on at the slow realization of my distress, built up artistically, without haste, note by note, by the singer as he stood beneath the astonished gaze of the sun arrested in its course beyond San Giorgio Maggiore [*par le chanteur que regardait avec étonnement le soleil arrêté derrière Saint-Georges-le-Majeur*], with the result that the fading light was to combine for ever in my

In the Millerian vein, the veil must be always linguistic and/or pictorial. Because that graphic or pictographic veil, by covering over what is unknown, comes to stand in for it, the veil structurally implies an *entry* of literature, a fictionality. This is what Miller means when he relates the text-context relation to figuration: "The relationship between text and context is always figurative. Any conceivable vocabulary you have to talk about it is some figure of speech or other" (HH, 152).

If the unknown (law, history, the referent, etc.) is perceived thanks to the graphic or pictographic veil, what the veil forms is an effect and never a cause. What can a cause be whose effect cannot be known? This claim that the veil is an effect is the crux of the discussion between Miller and cultural studies. Historicism (in the sense of New Historicism), pragmatism, and reception theories attempt to explain the text starting from an assumption brought in from outside it, even when the outside of the text is also considered "text." The problem is that in order to be able to explain the text from outside it, one must cross two minefields. First, it is necessary to know what remains outside the graphic or pictographic veil; second, the point of reference used (history, context, psychology, etc.) must allow access to the text, that is, allow it to be read or make it legible. This is opposed to all we have seen here: the veil is shown in order to give name or face to what has neither name nor face: "The veil is the type and the symbol of the fact that all signs are potentially unreadable, or that the reading of them is potentially unverifiable" (HH, 97). Here the paradox is born: the veil is legible (since it gives a face or a voice to what, in fact, has none) to verify that legibility is impossible (since the function of the veil is to hide). Thus the literary text and the critico-literary text—which at this point are not essentially different—are more performative than constative. Every prosopopoeia has an effect, insofar as it is a graphic gesture that has risen from nothing. At the same time, what the veil does not

memory with the throb of my emotion and the bronze voice of the singer in an equivocal, unalterable and poignant alloy [*alliage*]. (F 4: 233; E 3: 669)

This passage is the nadir in all Proust's work, the low point beneath which it is impossible to sink. The self, for once, confronts what is "really there," something wholly inimical to continued human life. Everything that is normally integrated is separated out into disconnected regions. The external world becomes a heap of stones. The self, deprived of all the usual fictions that have constituted it, is without will to impose its ordering power on the external world, on other people, and on itself. Time stops. All contact with the hidden homeland of otherness is lost. Even the sun will no longer go to those depths on its diurnal rounds.

At that prolonged lowest moment, a moment that might, it seems, continue for an eternity, suddenly, out of nowhere, what Proust here calls "habit" reasserts itself. Time begins again, the will to action is restored, the power to impose fictions returns, the sun moves again, Venice is once more Venice, and everything returns to normal:

But suddenly, from caverns [*antres*] darker than those from which flashes the comet which we can predict—thanks to the unsuspected defensive power of inveterate habit [*de l'habitude invétérée*], thanks to hidden reserves which by a sudden impulse it hurls at the last moment into the fray—my will to action [*mon action*] arose at last; I set off in hot haste [*je pris mes jambes à mon cou*] and arrived, when the carriage doors were already shut, but in time to find my mother flushed with emotion and with the effort to restrain her tears, for she thought that I was not coming. (F 4: 233–34; E 3: 670)

The reader will see what is extraordinary and unexpected about this passage. Marcel's recovery of an active will is ascribed to habit. "Habit [*habitude*]" here names all the superficial and baseless fictions that give the self and its environment a semblance of interconnected wholeness. Marcel asserts that the break in his paralysis is caused by "l'insoupçonnable puissance défensive de l'habitude invétérée." Habit has a power to defend us from the vision of what is "really there," here, a senseless heap of stones with abundant hydrogen and oxygen in chemical combination sloshing around them. For Pater, whose dictum about our failure being to form habits is cited as an epigraph for this chapter, habit is a barrier against living, as we should do, in proximity to the eternal moment of unique sensation that is all there is. For Proust, on the contrary, in a way more

allow to be seen guarantees the failure of literary theories and of readings that try to remove the veil.

What does Bartleby's narrator see? In the Millerian matrix, what the narrator of the text sees is the same thing we see. The critic remains automatically and a priori identified (notice that I do not say "identifies himself") with the narrator's viewpoint. Alongside the syntax, morphology, temporality, and so forth, of a narrative text, one must place ethics as one more element. In "Bartleby" ethics is located in the relation that joins the narrator's point of view with the figure of Bartleby. In other examples — for instance, in the other texts analyzed in *Versions of Pygmalion* — this placement varies. What does Bartleby's narrator see? He sees something that does not allow him to see or to know. The lawyer tries to "vivify," to control, to "animate" Bartleby by every possible means. The first time he describes him, he does so in the following terms: "In answer to my advertisement, a motionless young man one morning, stood upon my office threshold" (Melville, 1984: 641). Bartleby presents himself as motionless, and he will continue that way. The narrator feels forced to take an ethical decision toward such an attitude, but: "How can one feel and act charitably toward someone about whom one knows nothing? The divine injunction is to love your neighbor, but Bartleby is a ghost, a walking dead man, a living statue, a kind of zombie possessed by who knows what malicious spirit. The idea of befriending or of loving Bartleby as one loves ones's neighbor is absurd. But dealing with him harshly and ordering him to do his duty as hired help does not work either. He neither refuses nor agrees to do what he is asked to do. His power lies in this neutrality, in the impossibility of arousing any anger in him in response to one's own anger" (VP, 165).

In fact, Miller's position is not wholly alien to Iser's postulates in *The Implied Reader*, though with a twist. Iser writes of an implicit reader who delimits the possibilities of interpretation. Miller also writes of an

Nietzschean than Paterian, it is impossible to live with a clear vision of what is really there, so Proust's definition of habit is quite different from Pater's. *Habitude* is a key word in Proust's vocabulary. A search by way of ARTFL brings up fifty uses of the word in *Albertine disparue* alone, many of great interest, but this passage gives the clue to its Proustian meaning.

Habit for Proust, surprisingly, has its source in the dark depths, the lost and unknown homeland, unique to each person, that gives its force to lies and to works of art like Vinteuil's septet. Habit is grounded in the realm of otherness the sun visits when it sinks into the sea. Just as each great artist, Elstir or Vinteuil, Vermeer or Hardy, has his or her own unique accent, nostalgic echo of each artist's singular lost homeland, and just as each person, Albertine, for example, has his or her own special way of lying, a way that gives us unique access to "unknown worlds," so "habit" is Marcel's name for the special way each person, artist and non-artist alike, organizes himself and the circumambient world in perdurable patterns that make continued life possible. "Habit" names both the power and what the power makes. No doubt there is much irony in calling this constructive and constructed energy "habit," since the word admits what is superficial and factitious about what holds each human life together. Habit, however, or rather the will to action, habit's "hidden reserves" that form habits, is not baseless. It comes "from caverns darker than those from which flashes the comet which we can predict."

Proust perhaps knew that there are two kinds of comets, parabolic and hyperbolic ones. Parabolic comets, for example Halley's comet, return in predictable periods in their rotation around two centers, far distant from one another, one the sun, the other, perhaps virtual, a point in space. Hyperbolic comets flash once around the sun and then speed off forever, never to return. In either case, however, the comet's trajectory is lawful and predictable. The comet's trajectory is here negatively compared to the will to action. The latter has "darker" sources. A comet is analogous to the sun in its regularity and in its swinging into unsoundable gulfs. Moreover, a comet is governed by the sun. This passage is another oblique version of Proust's "solar myth."

Marcel's will to action, however, the defensive power of inveterate habit, comes from caverns darker than those gulfs from which a comet comes and into which it plunges again. They are darker in the sense of being unknown and unknowable. Those caverns are what I have been call-

implicit reader ("the narrator's need can be seen as the presence within the text of an allegory of the reader's own need to dominate the story by interpreting it"; VP, 162), whose function is to point out the impossibility of interpretation. A narration in which the narrator tells us the impossibility of telling a narration, a narration in which "our inability to read this text in the sense of providing a satisfactory interpretation based on what the text says" (VP, 175) is prefigured, turns the story of Pygmalion inside out. This narrative reverses the prosopopoeia, since the impossibility of telling a story or the impossibility of verifying any interpretative hypothesis turns the narrator and the reader into statues of marble or salt.

All of us have been turned into statues by the sinister Ovid that is Bartleby—Bartleby as both character and text: "But if Bartleby is the statue and not the sculptor, his immobility has a power to immobilize the narrator, to turn him at least momentarily to stone" (VP, 177). In the end, Miller has redoubled or displaced the matrix that has guided him from the beginning: to accede to the text, to the other, to the other consciousness, to the prosopopoeic illusion. Once there, he has suffered the anguish and the pleasure of becoming a marble Galatea who never stops writing.

ing the realm of the "others." This means that the return of the power of action is unpredictable, in its form and in its time of coming. In this it is like the invention of a lie or of a work of art, even though, when the will to action has asserted itself again, it can be seen to take patterns that are characteristic of the person's whole life.

Coda: The Excess of Reading

"Coda" means tail. This coda returns me to my beginning. That makes "Black Holes" not boustrophedonic but a species of ouroborous, the snake with its tail in its mouth, however far from my beginning I may seem to have strayed, like an errant comet. My trajectory has been more like that of an elliptical comet, with the contemporary research university and the "others" as twin focuses, determining my orbit. That figure, however, like Proust's planetary trope, is still too rational. If the university is the sun and the black hole of the "others" the second focus, that black hole would exert such force as to draw the comet in or to whirl it off on a new, more eccentric orbit. It would be possible to extend my discussion of Proust indefinitely or to read a virtually interminable series of additional examples from literature. Only "par la commodité du récit," as Proust puts it, can I bring my story back to its starting place.

We may call this exorbitancy the excess of reading, taking the "of" as both a subjective and an objective genitive: an excess intrinsic to reading and something that exceeds reading. W. B. Yeats, in spite of his lifelong commitment to the cause of Irish liberation, and in spite of his at least partial agreement with the statement by Thomas Mann cited as an epigraph to a late poem, "Politics" ("In our time the destiny of man presents its meaning in political terms"), in the poem itself defies Mann and asks: "How can I, that girl standing there, / My attention fix / On Roman or on Russian / Or on Spanish politics?" (ll. 1–4). Yeats records, in an adjacent poem, "The Circus Animals' Desertion," that he became more interested

in action and character in his plays than in the allegorical or political meaning the plays had: "Players and painted stage took all my love, / And not those things that they were emblems of" (ll. 30–31).[1] In a somewhat similar way, my readings of Trollope and Proust have exceeded their function as examples of themes developed in the first part of this book. I have found the challenge of reading these two works interesting and absorbing in itself. Each solar example, in my reading of Proust, has led to another, and each has demanded extensive and responsible reading. My reading has been excessive or exorbitant in the sense that it has led me on a long journey in search of something elusive that these works, each in a different way, allow me to glimpse. In Proust's case, this is figured as the place the sun goes when it sets. For Trollope it is the ground of ethical decision or commitment. The phrase "excess of reading" names the way reading exceeds initial theoretical presuppositions, the use of literary works as examples of a conceptual argument, and any attempt to encompass a work by its historical or cultural contexts. Each work gives knowledge (or nonknowledge— an experience of the limits of knowledge) that is singular and unique, attainable in no other way. If this were not the case, if the work could be completely accounted for by its context, then there would be no reason beyond aesthetic titillation to go to all the hard work necessary to read it. Everything it tells us could be known by studying its context. The work would be an empty placeholder for its circumambient culture. Reading the "of" in the second way, moreover, so that "the excess of reading" names what exceeds reading, gives yet another sense. It deploys the phrase to designate the "elusive something" that is the motivation of reading, its forever unattainable horizon. I have called that elusive "center on the horizon"[2] the realm of the wholly others. This realm is always in excess of reading.

I began this book by saying that radical changes are occurring in the research university today. I related those changes to the end of the Cold War, the decline of the nation-state, the rise of multicultural study, the concomitant waning of the independent discipline of English literature, and the globalizing of economies and of university research. This globalizing has happened in part under the influence of new communications technologies, without which it would have been impossible. All these changes put us in a new place, from which we can turn back to take a fresh look at literary works. The fresh look is facilitated by these changes. The changes wrest literature from the familiar institutional contexts in which our reading of it has often been enclosed. The danger, however, is that lit-

erature will come to be seen as just one more form of historical "information" like any other. "Information technologies" have created a powerful new paradigm redefining every form of sign as so many bits and bytes of "information." These may be stored, manipulated, transferred, and translated in all these marvelous, but disquieting, new ways I have discussed. Such technologies are related to the new forms of cultural studies, of which this present book is in its own way an example. The new telecommunications and what I have called "cultural studies" are different aspects of the same epochal change. Those technologies, however, not only give the illusion of mastery over whatever can be "digitized." They also produce an "alienation effect" that may facilitate new readings. My readings of works by Trollope and Proust, in my encounter in each case with something radically "other" in the work, have been presented as examples of the way literary works are strange comets that come from "dark caverns," or, according to my title metaphor, are black holes in that great galaxy of global information we shall more and more have at our fingertips, no more than a mouseclick away. These black holes are not linguistic. They are not made of language. Nor is language the only medium in which such black holes may be indirectly glimpsed, since, as reading Trollope and Proust suggests, painting, music, photography, as well as more recent media like cinema, the duplicities and opacities of the other person or of oneself, the sun setting over the ocean—any of these may function, as well as assemblies of words, as allegorical figures for such unknowable places. We may call those black holes whose indirect manifestations appear in literary works "the others of language." The "of" in this sentence must be taken in both senses—once more both as a subjective genitive and as an objective genitive. These black holes both belong to language and are other to it.

What does this encounter with the other of language have to do with the university of dissensus, the call for which was the endpoint of the first section of this book? I claim the encounter with "others" in literature is exemplary, with all the ambiguities of "exemplarity" in this case. How can the irreducibly particular be exemplary of anything but itself? It is just in the encounter with singularity that reading a work like *Ayala's Angel* or *A la recherche du temps perdu* is exemplary. A university of dissensus would, I said, be based on respect for the otherness of the others, the otherness of the other person, the otherness of those belonging to other cultures, the otherness of cultural artifacts, including works of literature. Reading *Ayala's Angel* or *A la recherche du temps perdu* is exemplary of what that

means. It is exemplary of the aporias of the ethico-political situation in which we all live.[3]

Either Trollope's novel or Proust's, when I read one or the other, demands to be understood. Reading either work makes me in one way or another responsible for it—responsible to teach it or to write about it, to account for it, to explain it to others, to pass judgment on it, even if I keep that judgment to myself. Such a responsibility can never be completely fulfilled, though that does not make it any less exigent. Responsibility, as Derrida has forcefully argued, must be, if it is to exist at all, always excessive, always impossible to discharge. Otherwise it will risk being the repetition of a program of understanding and action already in place.[4] In reading both *Ayala's Angel* and *A la recherche du temps perdu* I have encountered, in a different way in each case, a core of incomprehensibility. I have named this, figuratively, a black hole. The effect of such an encounter is to dispossess my self of its seemingly secure self-possession. This illusory self-possession may, in this case, have taken the form of a program for literary study or of expectations established by the already-existing criticism of the work in question. The encounter with the unpredictable otherness of a literary work puts "me" in a situation beyond anything that can be defined as the encounter of a pre-existing subjectivity with something it has an obligation to know and account for. The "I" is created by the encounter. It is created as something fragile and unstable, always liable to be created anew by another reading, even of the same work. In this the subjecthood of the reader is like the multitudinous selves of Marcel and Albertine in Proust's *Recherche* or like Ayala in Trollope's novel, who cannot re-establish her continuity with herself after a falling in love of whose originary moment she was not aware and cannot now recover. My responsibility in each reading is to decide and to act, but I must do so in a situation where the grounds of decision are impossible to know. As Kierkegaard somewhere says, "The moment of decision is a madness." The action, in this case, often takes the form of teaching or writing that cannot claim to ground itself on pre-existing knowledge or established tradition but is what Derrida calls "l'invention de l'autre [the invention of the other]."[5] This is another double genitive naming the way "I" both create and discover the other, both make it and find it, but at the same time am made by it, in an experience of dispossession or displacement. My reading also, in however small a way, remakes the institution, for example the univer-

sity, within which the reading or teaching takes place and is authorized. Reading, when it happens, like other encounters with otherness, remakes, though perhaps in an almost imperceptible a way, the self and all its institutional, interpersonal, social, and political contexts. That is our chance. To that chance I give the name: the university of dissensus to come.

Reference Matter

Works Cited for 'J. Hillis Miller; or, Boustrophedonic Reading'

Abrams, M. H. (1953). *The Mirror and the Lamp.* New York: Oxford University Press.

Alonso, Dámaso (1950). *Poesía española: Ensayo de métodos y límites estilísticos.* Madrid: Gredos.

Aristotle (1951). *The Poetics.* Trans. S. H. Butcher. In *Aristotle's Theory of Poetry and Fine Art.* New York: Dover.

——— (1963). *Metaphysics.* Trans. Richard Hope. Ann Arbor: University of Michigan Press.

Asensi, Manuel (1990). "Crítica límite / El límite de la crítica." In M. Asensi, ed., *Teoría literaria y deconstrucción.* Madrid: Arco.

——— (1991). *La teoría fragmentaria del círculo de Iena: Friedrich Schlegel.* Valencia: Amós Belinchón.

——— (1992). "La otra filología: Paul de Man, J. Hillis Miller y la lectura lenta." *Glosa,* no. 3, 63–92.

Ayrault, Roger (1961–76). *La genèse du romantisme allemand.* 4 vols. Paris: Aubier-Montaigne.

Notes to 'Black Holes'

CHAPTER I: LITERARY STUDY IN THE TRANSNATIONAL UNIVERSITY

1. The best discussion of this is by Bill Readings in *The University in Ruins* (Cambridge: Harvard University Press, 1996). I have learned much from this important book, the best of the many current books about the transformation of the Western university. Readings's death in a commuter plane crash in the fall of 1994 was a major loss to humanistic study. My dedication of this book to him indicates a little my own debt to him, both as a friend and as a colleague.

2. See Robert Young, "The Idea of a Chrestomathic University," in Richard Rand, ed., *Logomachia* (Lincoln: University of Nebraska Press, 1993), 99–116, for a discussion of Newman's book as a stage in the development of the British university from the eighteenth century to the present.

3. George Eliot, *Middlemarch* (Harmondsworth: Penguin Books, 1974), 375.

4. See J. Hillis Miller, "Teaching *Middlemarch*: Close Reading and Theory," in Kathleen Blake, ed., *Approaches to Teaching Eliot's 'Middlemarch'* (New York: The Modern Language Association of America, 1990), 51–63.

5. Marcel Proust, *A la recherche du temps perdu*, ed. Jean-Yves Tadié, Pléiade ed. (Paris: Gallimard, 1989), 4: 350; *Remembrance of Things Past*, trans. C. K. Scott Moncrieff (New York: Vintage, 1982), 3: 795.

6. All these features of fractals are discussed in Hans Lauwerier, *Fractals: Endlessly Repeated Geometrical Figures*, trans. Sophia Gill-Hoffstädt (Princeton: Princeton University Press, 1991). Hans Lauwerier was until his retirement Professor of Mathematics at the University of Amsterdam. I mention this to indicate that his book is based on professional knowledge of the mathematics of fractals.

7. *Middlemarch*, 591.

8. The advice *"Get 'Geist'"* is given to the English people by Arminius, Matthew Arnold's imaginary German philosopher, in the first letter of *Friendship's Garland* (1871). See Matthew Arnold, *The Complete Prose Works*, ed. R. H. Super, (Ann Arbor: University of Michigan Press, 1965), 5: 42. "[I]n Berlin," Arminius explains to Arnold, "we oppose 'Geist,'—*intelligence*, as you or the French might say,—to 'Ungeist.' . . . We North-Germans have worked for 'Geist' in our way, by loving knowledge, by having the best-educated middle and lower class in the world. . . . France has 'Geist' in her democracy, and Prussia in her education.

Bakhtin, Mikhail (1968). *Rabelais and His World*. Trans. Helene Iswolsky. Cambridge: M.I.T. Press.

—— (1981). *The Dialogic Imagination*. Ed. Michael Holquist. Trans. Carol Emerson and Michael Holquist. Austin: University of Texas Press.

—— (1984a). *L'oeuvre de François Rabelais et la culture populaire au Moyen Age et sous la Renaissance*. Paris, Gallimard. Orig. pub. 1970.

—— (1984b). *Problems of Dostoevsky's Poetics*. Ed. and trans. Caryl Emerson. Minneapolis: University of Minnesota Press.

Barthes, Roland (1974). *S/Z*. Trans. Richard Miller. New York: Hill and Wang.

—— (1975). *The Pleasure of the Text*. Trans. Richard Miller. New York: Hill and Wang.

—— (1981). *Camera Lucida: Reflections on Photography*. Trans. Richard Howard. New York: Hill and Wang.

—— (1982). *Empire of Signs*. Trans. Richard Howard. New York: Hill and Wang.

—— (1987). *Criticism and Truth*. Trans. Katrine Pilcher Keuneman. Minneapolis: University of Minnesota Press.

Benjamin, Walter (1973). *Der Begriff der Kunstkritik in der deutschen Romantik*. Ed. Hermann Schweppenhäuser. Frankfurt am Main: Suhrkamp.

Where have you got it?—got it as a force, I mean, and not only in a few scattered individuals. Your common people is barbarous; in your middle class 'Ungeist' is rampant; and as for your aristocracy, you know 'Geist' is forbidden by nature to flourish in an aristocracy" (40–41). See Jacques Derrida's discussion of Arnold's ironic *"Get 'Geist'* " in a long footnote in *De l'esprit: Heidegger et la question* (Paris: Galilée, 1987), 114–16.

9. Vincent Cable, "The Diminished Nation-State," in *What Future for the State? Daedalus* 124, no. 2 (Spring 1995), 23–53. This issue has essays by social scientists with titles like "The New World Order, Incorporated: The Rise of Business and the Decline of the Nation-State," by Vivien A. Schmidt. According to Schmidt, the result of the "liberalized new world order" is "a strengthening of business, with transnational corporations less tied to nations and national interests, and a weakening of the nation-state overall, in particular of the voice of the people through legislatures and nonbusiness, societal interests" (76). The shift in funding from government agencies to transnational corporations is making major changes in United States universities.

10. Cable, "Diminished Nation-State," 26.

11. Richard O'Brien, "Global Financial Integration: The End of Geography," in *Chatham House Papers*, Royal Institute of International Affairs (London: Pinter, 1992), 7.

12. Cable, "Diminished Nation-State," 26.

13. Wallace Stevens, *Opus Posthumous* (New York: Knopf, 1957), 165.

14. Cable, "Diminished Nation-State," 26.

15. See, for example: Samuel Weber, *Institution and Interpretation* (Minneapolis: University of Minnesota Press, 1987); Bernard Bergonzi, *Exploding English: Criticism, Theory, Culture* (Oxford: Oxford University Press, 1990); Peter Elbow, *What Is English?* (New York: The Modern Language Association of America; Urbana: The National Council of Teachers of English, 1990); Jacques Derrida, *Du droit à la philosophie* (Paris: Galilée, 1990); Gerald Graff, *Professing Literature: An Institutional History* (Chicago: University of Chicago Press, 1987) and *Beyond the Culture Wars: How Teaching the Conflicts Can Revitalize American Education* (New York: Norton, 1992); Jaroslav Pelikan, *The Idea of the University: A Reexamination* (New Haven: Yale University Press, 1992); Alfonso Borrero Cabal, *The University as an Institution Today* (Paris: UNESCO and the International Development Research Center, 1993); Ronald A. T. Judy, *(Dis)forming the American Canon: African-Arabic Slave Narratives and the Vernacular* (Minneapolis: University of Minnesota Press, 1993); Antony Easthope, *Literary into Cultural Studies* (London: Routledge, 1991); Bruce Wilshire, *The Moral Collapse of the University: Professionalism, Purity, and Alienation* (Albany: SUNY Press, 1990); Peggy Kamuf, *The Division of Literature; or, The University in Deconstruction* (Chicago: University of Chicago Press, 1997). Many of these are discussed by Readings.

16. See Brook Thomas, "Parts Related to Wholes and the Nature of Subaltern Opposition," *Modern Language Quarterly* 55, no. 1 (March 1994): 79–106. The quoted phrase is used on 79.

Blanchot, Maurice (1959). *Le livre à venir*. Paris: Gallimard.

———— (1969). "L'Athenaeum." In *L'entretien infini*. Paris: Gallimard. 515–27.

———— (1993). *The Infinite Conversation*. Trans. Susan Hanson. Minneapolis: University of Minnesota Press.

Bloom, Harold (1975). *A Map of Misreading*. New York: Oxford University Press.

Blumenberg, H. (1981). *Die Lesbarkeit der Welt*. Frankfurt am Main: Suhrkamp.

Borges, Jorge Luís (1962). *Ficciones*. Trans. Anthony Kerrigan et al. New York: Grove Press.

———— (1964). *Labyrinths: Selected Stories and Other Writings*. Trans. Donald A. Yates et al. New York: New Directions.

———— (1980). "Las versiones homéricas." In Borges, *Prosa completa*. Barcelona: Bruguera. 1: 182–86.

Bosanquet, Bernard (1910). *A History of Aesthetic*. 3d ed. London: Swan Sonnenschein.

Bremond, Claude (1973). *Logique du récit*. Paris: Seuil.

Brooks, Cleanth (1947). *The Well Wrought Urn: Studies in the Structure of Poetry*. New York: Harcourt, Brace.

Brunel, Pierre, and Chevrel, Yves (1989). *Précis de littérature comparée*. Paris: Presses Universitaires du France.

17. Erich Auerbach, *Mimesis: The Representation of Reality in Western Literature*, trans. Willard R. Trask (Princeton: Princeton University Press, 1953).

18. See note 15, above.

19. As Readings puts this in a comment on Judy's *(Dis) Forming the American Canon*: "I am concerned to introduce a transitional step into the passage from the modern German University of national culture to the bureaucratic University of excellence, one which positions the American University as the University of a national culture that is contentless" (*University in Ruins*, 201).

20. Franklin Court, *Institutionalizing English Literature: The Culture and Politics of Literary Study* (Stanford: Stanford University Press, 1992); Robert Crawford, *Devolving English Literature* (Oxford: Clarendon Press, 1992). One chapter of Crawford's book is entitled "The Scottish Invention of English Literature" (16–44).

21. Gauri Viswanathan, *Masks of Conquest: English Literature and Colonial Rule in India* (New York: Columbia University Press, 1989).

22. F. O. Matthiessen, *American Renaissance: Act and Expression in the Age of Emerson and Whitman* (London: Oxford University Press, 1941); Charles Feidelson, *Symbolism and American Literature* (Chicago: University of Chicago Press, 1953); R. W. B. Lewis, *The American Adam: Innocence, Tragedy, and Tradition in the Nineteenth Century* (Chicago: University of Chicago Press, 1955); Perry Miller, *The New England Mind: From Colony to Province* (Cambridge, Mass.: Harvard University Press, 1953); Roy Harvey Pearce, *The Continuity of American Poetry* (Princeton: Princeton University Press, 1961); Sacvan Bercovitch, *The Puritan Origins of the American Self* (New Haven: Yale University Press, 1975); Harold Bloom, *Figures of Capable Imagination* (New York: Seabury Press, 1976).

23. See F. R. Leavis, *The Great Tradition* (Garden City, N.Y.: Doubleday, 1954).

24. Harold Bloom's *The Western Canon: The Books and Schools of the Ages* (New York: Harcourt Brace, 1994) is wider in scope and more ecumenical. I am speaking of Bloom's earlier essays on American authors, for example, those in *Figures of Capable Imagination*. There, in "The Native Strain," Bloom says: "There are a myriad of figures to illustrate American Orphism, but I want to confine myself here first to our very best poets (or those who seem best to me) — Whitman, Dickinson, a certain aspect of Stevens, and Hart Crane — and then to my own contemporaries I admire most, A. R. Ammons and John Ashbery" (75).

25. See Carolyn Porter, "What We Know That We Don't Know: Remapping American Literary Studies," *American Literary History* 6, no. 3 (Fall 1994): 469–526. Important work in this area includes: Paul Lauter, ed., *Reconstructing American Literature: Courses, Syllabi, Issues* (New York: Feminist Press, 1983); A. LaVonne Brown Ruoff and Jerry W. Ward, eds., *Redefining American Literary History* (New York: Modern Language Association, 1990); Virginia Yans-McLaughlin, ed., *Immigration Reconsidered: History, Sociology, and Politics* (New York: Oxford University Press, 1990); Donald Pease, ed., *Revisionary Interventions into the Americanist Canon* (Durham: Duke University Press, 1990); Philip Fisher, ed., *The New*

Cabrera Infante, Guillermo (1971). *Three Trapped Tigers*. Trans. Donald Gardner and Suzanne Jill Levin. New York: Harper & Row.

———— (1981). *Tres tristes Tigres*. Barcelona: Seix Barral.

Cervantes, Miguel de (1950). *Don Quixote*. Harmondsworth, Middlesex: Penguin.

Chomsky, Noam (1957). *Syntactic Structures*. Cambridge: M.I.T. Press.

Cohen, Jean (1979). *Le haut langage: Théorie de la poéticité*. Paris: Flammarion.

Compagnon, Antoine (1979). *La seconde main, ou le travail de la citation*. Paris: Seuil.

Curtius, Ernst Robert (1948). *Europaische Literatur und lateinisches Mittelalter*. Bern: A. Francke.

———— (1953). *European Literature and the Latin Middle Ages*. Trans. Willard R. Trask. Bollingen Library. New York: Pantheon.

Dante Alighieri (1955). *La Divina Commedia*. Ed. Natalino Sapegno. Florence: La Nuova Italia Editrice.

———— (1970). *The Divine Comedy: Inferno*. 1: *Italian Text and Translation*. Trans. Charles S. Singleton. Bollingen Series 80. Princeton: Princeton University Press.

Deleuze, Gilles (1968a). *Spinoza et le problème de l'expression*. Paris: Minuit.

American Studies (Berkeley: University of California Press, 1991); Gustavo Pérez Firmat, ed., *Do the Americas Have a Common Literature?* (Durham: Duke University Press, 1990); Amy Kaplan and Donald Pease, eds., *Cultures of United States Imperialism* (Durham: Duke University Press, 1993); Donald Pease, ed., *National Identities and Post-Americanist Narratives* (Durham: Duke University Press, 1994); Paul Lauter, *Canons and Contexts* (New York: Oxford University Press, 1991); and the new *Cambridge History of American Literature*, ed. Sacvan Bercovitch and Cyrus Patell, of which two volumes of the eight planned have been published (Cambridge: Cambridge University Press, 1994, 1995). John Carlos Rowe helped me with this list. In the fall of 1996, Rowe convened a residential research group on postnational American studies at the Humanities Research Institute of the University of California. The goal was to work toward institutionalizing the new American studies in the University of California and other universities. See Alan Liu's *The Future Literary: Literary History and Postmodern Culture* (Stanford: Stanford University Press, forthcoming) for a brilliant and fascinating discussion of the influence of computer technology and its graphic layouts on the presentation of new multicultural American literary histories or anthologies such as Paul Lauter, general ed., *Heath Anthology of American Literature*, 2d ed. (Lexington, Mass.: D. C. Heath, 1994), and *American Mosaic: Multicultural Readings in Context*, compiled by Barbara Roche Rico and Sandra Mano (Boston: Houghton Mifflin, 1991). Paul Lauter's essay in the "Teacher's Manual" of the *Heath Anthology* is a good description of the changes now taking place in American literature and American studies. I shall discuss in more detail later the effect of new communication technologies on literary study.

26. This is a schematic summary of the complex argument made in the seventh of Fichte's *Reden an die Deutsche Nation*, "Noch tiefere Erfassung der Ursprünglichkeit, und Deutschheit eines Volkes." See Johann Gottlieb Fichte, *Reden an die Deutsche Nation* (Hamburg: Felix Meiner, 1955; orig. pub. Berlin: In der Realschulbuchhandlung, 1808), 106–24, and, for a translation, *Addresses to the German Nation*, ed. George Armstrong Kelley (New York: Harper and Row, 1968), 92–110. For a discussion of Fichte's views on Germanness, see Jacques Derrida, "Privilège," in *Du droit à la philosophie*, 51–53, and "La main de Heidegger (*Geschlect* II)," *Psyché: Inventions de l'autre* (Paris: Galilée, 1987), 416–20.

27. See Jacques Derrida, *De l'esprit: Heidegger et la question* (Paris: Galilée, 1987: 112–16). For Heidegger, German is even better than Greek for speaking of the highest spiritual things. As Derrida paraphrases this: "German is therefore the only language, in the final analysis, that can name that highest or superlative excellence (*geistigste*), which it does not share in the end except to a certain point with Greek" (113, my trans.). Philippe Lacoue-Labarthe, *La fiction du politique* (Paris: Christian Bourgois, 1987), trans. Chris Turner as *Heidegger, Art and Politics: The Fiction of the Political* (Oxford: Basil Blackwell, 1990), gives the best account of Heidegger's "national aestheticism," with its roots in German Romanticism and its sinister links to the atrocities of National Socialism.

28. According to Bettina J. Huber, in "The MLA's 1993–94 Survey of Ph.D.

———— (1968b). *Différence et répétition*. Paris: Presses Universitaires de France.

———— (1970). *Proust et les signes*. Paris: Presses Universitaires de France.

———— (1972). *Proust and Signs*. New York: G. Braziller.

———— (1990). *Expression in Philosophy: Spinoza*. New York: Zone Books.

———— (1994). *Difference and Repetition*. New York: Columbia University Press.

Deleuze, Gilles, and Guattari, Félix (1991). *Qu'est-ce que la philosophie?* Paris: Minuit.

———— (1994). *What Is Philosophy?* New York: Columbia University Press.

della Volpe, Galvano (1967). *Critica dell'ideologia contemporanea: Saggi di teoria dialettica*. Rome: Editori Riuniti.

De Man, Paul (1979). *Allegories of Reading: Figural Language in Rousseau, Nietzsche, Rilke, and Proust*. New Haven: Yale University Press.

———— (1983). *Blindness and Insight: Essays in the Rhetoric of Contemporary Criticism*. 2d ed. Minneapolis: University of Minnesota Press.

———— (1986). *The Resistance to Theory*. Minneapolis: University of Minnesota Press.

———— (1996). *Aesthetic Ideology*. Minneapolis: University of Minnesota Press.

De Quincey, Thomas (1985). *Confessions of an English Opium-Eater and Other*

Placement: The Latest English Findings and Trends through Time," *ADE Bulletin*, no. 112 (Winter 1995): 48, only 45.9 percent of those who received a Ph.D. in English in 1993–94 got tenure-track jobs. See also Cary Nelson, "Lessons from the Job Wars: Late Capitalism Arrives on Campus," *Social Text* 13, no. 3 (Fall/Winter 1995): 119–34, and his "Lessons from the Job Wars: What Is to Be Done," *Academe* 81, no. 6 (November–December 1995): 18–25. Two other essays from the same issue of *Academe* also discuss the job market and the conditions of graduate study: Michael Bérubé, "Standard Deviation: Skyrocketing Job Requirements Inflame Political Tensions," 26–29, and Stephen Watt, "The Human Costs of Graduate Education; or, The Need to Get Practical," 30–35. For the job outlook for new Ph.D.'s in the physical sciences, see, in the same issue of *Academe*, Arthur S. Brill and Daniel J. Larson, "Are We Training Our Students for Real Jobs?," 36–38. The academic job market has by no means improved in the years since 1995.

29. See Thomas Keenan, "Live from . . . / En direct de . . . ," in Elizabeth Diller and Ricardo Scofidio, eds., *Visite aux armées: Tourismes de guerre / Back to the Front: Tourisms of War* (Caen: Fonds Régional d'Art Contemporain de Basse-Normandie, 1994), 130–63. "Comprehensive media coverage," says Keenan, "has not just changed the conduct of military operations—images and publicity have become military operations themselves, and the military outcome of the operation cannot easily be distinguished from the images of that operation" (143).

30. Giorgio Agamben, *The Coming Community*, trans. Michael Hardt (Minneapolis: University of Minnesota Press, 1993), 81–82.

31. See Louis Althusser, "Ideology and Ideological State Apparatuses (Notes Towards an Investigation)," in *Lenin and Philosophy and Other Essays*, trans. Ben Brewster (New York: Monthly Review Press, 1972), 127–86.

32. Robert H. Atwell, "Financial Prospects for Higher Education," *Policy Perspectives*, The Pew Higher Education Research Program 4, no. 3 (September 1992): Sec. B, 5B.

33. The division of humanities at the University of California at Irvine, for example, suffered $1,215,035 in budget cuts in the years 1992–95. No one seems to expect that support to return. A recent memorandum from the Dean of Humanities at Irvine quotes two recent statements by experts on American higher education in the 1990's. Donald Kennedy, former president of Stanford University, says: "It is inconceivable that our societal commitment to the support of knowledge acquisition will be maintained at historical levels. That circumstance alone signifies that university leaders are facing a period of resource restraint unlike any they—or their faculties—have ever experienced" ("Making Choices in the Research University," *Daedalus* [Fall 1993]: 130). David Breneman, an economist and specialist on higher education, declares: "Higher education is moving into a new era of permanently diminished financial support. . . . The 'comprehensive college or university' may be an eduational luxury that can no longer be supported in a meaningful way." "Having lost ground in the jockeying for state revenue, colleges and universities will find it hard to increase their share of appropriations. . . . [California's] budgetary prospects continue to be bleak, particularly for higher

Writings. Ed. Grevel Lindop. World's Classics ed. Oxford: Oxford University Press.

Derrida, Jacques (1973). *Speech and Phenomena and Other Essays on Husserl's Theory of Signs*. Trans. David B. Allison. Evanston: Northwestern University Press.

——— (1974a). *Glas*. Paris: Galilée.

——— (1974b). "Mallarmé." In *Tableau de la littérature française*. Paris: Gallimard. 3: 368–79.

——— (1976). *Of Grammatology*. Trans. Gayatri Spivak. Baltimore: The Johns Hopkins University Press.

——— (1978a). *La vérité en peinture*. Paris: Flammarion.

——— (1978b). *Writing and Difference*. Chicago: University of Chicago Press.

——— (1979). "Living On: Border Lines." In Harold Bloom et. al., *Deconstruction and Criticism*. New York: Seabury Press.

——— (1980a). "La loi du genre." *Glyph*, no. 7, 176–201.

——— (1980b). *The Archeology of the Frivolous: Reading Condillac*. Trans. John P. Leavey, Jr. Pittsburgh: Duquesne University Press.

——— (1981). *Dissemination*. Trans. Barbara Johnson. Chicago: University of Chicago Press.

education. . . . My conclusion is that higher education in California is in a state of emergency." (The first two sentences come from David Breneman, "Higher Education: On a Collision Course with New Realities," *Association of Governing Boards of Universities and Colleges*, AGB Occasional Paper no. 22, n.d. [a paper originally published in 1993 by American Student Assistance], 6, 13. The second two sentences are cited from David W. Breneman, "Sweeping, Painful Changes," *The Chronicle of Higher Education*, section 2 [September 8, 1995]). The Irvine dean's response to this is to begin discussions of "Possible Academic and/or Administrative Reconfiguration of the School of Humanities." The reconfiguration is driven not just by the budget crisis but also by changing priorities resulting from a new definition of the university's mission. That mission will no longer be "knowledge acquisition" but service to the global economy. The study of European languages and literatures, for example, will be likely to have a lower value in the new university, especially in one situated strategically on the Pacific Rim.

34. *UCI News* (January 24, 1996), 3.

35. Press release of January 3, 1996, and policy statement of January 1997.

36. See Jean-François Lyotard, *La condition postmoderne: Rapport sur le savoir* (Paris: Minuit, 1979); *The Postmodern Condition: A Report on Knowledge*, trans. Geoff Bennington and Brian Massumi (Minneapolis: University of Minnesota Press, 1984).

37. See Frank Aydelotte, *Materials for the Study of English Literature and Composition: Selections from Newman, Arnold, Huxley, Ruskin, and Carlyle* (New York: Oxford University Press, 1914). Significantly, Aydelotte was a Rhodes Scholar and wrote a history of the Rhodes Scholarships in the United States, *The American Rhodes Scholarships: A Review of the First Forty Years* (Princeton: Princeton University Press, 1946). The Rhodes Scholarships were originally endowed for the purpose of spreading British culture and British values to British colonies or former colonies.

38. See Paul de Man, "The Return to Philology," in *The Resistance to Theory* (Minneapolis: University of Minnesota Press, 1986), 21–26, for a discussion of this as it was taught in Benjamin Brower's Humanities 6 course at Harvard in the 1950's.

39. Jacques Derrida, "Mochlos ou le conflit des facultés," in *Du droit à la philosophie*, 424; "Mochlos; or, The Conflict of the Faculties," trans. Richard Rand and Amy Wygant (Lincoln: University of Nebraska Press, 1992), 22–23.

40. De Man, *Resistance to Theory*, 121.

41. J. L. Austin, *How to Do Things with Words*, 2d ed. (Oxford: Oxford University Press, 1980), 22.

42. Rey Chow, "In the Name of Comparative Literature," in Charles Bernheimer, ed., *Comparative Literature in the Age of Multiculturalism* (Baltimore: The Johns Hopkins University Press, 1995), 112.

43. A specific example is the addition in the 1995 edition of Frank Lentricia and Thomas McLaughlin, eds., *Critical Terms for Literary Study* (Chicago: University of Chicago Press, 1995) of new entries for: "Imperialism/Nationalism";

——— (1982). *Margins of Philosophy*. Trans. Alan Bass. Chicago: University of Chicago Press.

——— (1986a). *Mémoires for Paul de Man*. Trans. Cecile Lindsay, Jonathan Culler, and Eduardo Cadava. New York: Columbia University Press.

——— (1986b). *Glas*. Trans. John P. Leavey, Jr. and Richard Rand. Lincoln: University of Nebraska Press.

——— (1987a). *The Post Card: From Socrates to Freud and Beyond*. Trans. Alan Bass. Chicago: University of Chicago Press.

——— (1987b). *The Truth in Painting*. Trans. Geoff Bennington and Ian McLeod. Chicago: University of Chicago Press.

——— (1988). "Telepathy." Trans. Nicholas Royle. *Oxford Literary Review* 10, nos. 1–2: 3–41.

——— (1991). *A Derrida Reader (Between the Blinds)*. Ed. Peggy Kamuf. New York: Columbia University Press.

——— (1992a). *The Other Heading: Reflections on Today's Europe*. Trans. Pascale-Anne Brault and Michael B. Naas. Bloomington: Indiana University Press.

——— (1992b). "Some Statements and Truisms about Neo-logisms, Newisms, Postisms, Parasitisms, and Other Small Seismisms." Trans. Anne Tomiche.

"Desire"; "Ethics"; "Diversity"; "Popular Culture"; and "Class." In the first edition of 1990, these were not yet "critical terms for literary study." Now they are important enough to warrant doing the book over. The tendency to guide thinking by appeal to a list of slogan words or "buzz words" is characteristic of these new developments. An example is the list of "terms for a new paradigm" Antony Easthope gives in *Literary into Cultural Studies* (London: Routledge, 1991), 129: "institution; sign system; ideology; gender; subject position; the other." Easthope goes on to say of this list of abstractions that "others could be easily added to them if required" (130). They do not form a closed system. They are just a list of what cultural studies happens to be interested in. Easthope, like others in cultural studies, is anxious not to close the door on the inclusion of further topics. "Culture" in "cultural studies" becomes a term progressively emptied of meaning by coming more and more to include everything in human life. Another good example of this is the last paragraph of a letter to *The New York Times* of August 5, 1994, from Conrad Atkinson, Professor of Art at the University of California at Davis. Defending the proposed Disney theme park five miles from the site of a major Civil War battle at Manassas, Virginia, on the ground that opposing it is the same kind of snobbism that attacked rock music and Elvis Presley, as well as on the ground that visual experience can be as sophisticated and subtle as experience of verbal meanings (with which I agree), Atkinson says: "Remember: You never know where culture is gonna come from; you never know what culture is gonna look like; you never know when or where you're gonna need culture; you never know what culture is gonna do, and you never know what culture is for" (*The New York Times*, Tuesday, August 16, 1994, A14). In this quite extraordinary statement, culture becomes a magic invisible elixir, an omnipotent cure-all, or, to put this another way, culture becomes a synonym in its ubiquity, power, and invisibility for ideology as it is defined by Louis Althusser as "a 'representation' of the imaginary relationship of individuals to their real conditions of existence" (Althusser, *Ideology and Ideological State Apparatuses*, 162). Culture, for Atkinson, is everywhere, and it is by definition unknowable. Cultural studies must then study an object not open to study, since everything under the sun may possibly be culture. You can never know what it is, what it does, and what it is for. Or perhaps Atkinson means that you can never know beforehand what is going to turn out to be culture, so you should suspect everything of being culture and therefore study it. Anything in the world might be culture and therefore is worth study by cultural studies. This refusal by cultural studies to limit the definition of culture returns in the Bernheimer Report on "Comparative Literature at the Turn of the Century," discussed below.

44. Alan Liu, *The Future Literary: Literary History and the Culture of Information*, p. 2 of draft MS.

45. Rey Chow, "In the Name of Comparative Literature," 110–11: "already, in myriad forms for an extended period of time, the very disciplinary structures that we seek to challenge have been firmly established in the pedagogical practices related to non-Western languages and literatures, . . . 'qualifications' and 'expertise' in so-called other cultures have been used as the means to legitimate entirely con-

In David Carroll, ed., *The States of "Theory": History, Art, and Critical Discourse*. New York: Columbia University Press. Rpt. 1994. Stanford: Stanford University Press. 63–94.

———— (1992c). *Acts of Literature*. Ed. Derek Attridge. New York and London: Routledge.

———— (1992d). "Donner la mort." In Jean-Michel Rabaté and Michael Wetzel, eds., *L'éthique du don: Jacques Derrida et la pensée du don*. Paris: Métailié-Transition.

———— (1993). *Passions*. Paris, Galilée.

———— (1995a). *The Gift of Death*. Trans. David Wills. Chicago: University of Chicago Press.

———— (1995b). *On the Name*. Ed. Thomas Dutoit. Stanford: Stanford University Press.

Eco, Umberto (1968). *La struttura assente*. Milan: Bompiani.

———— (1975). *Trattato di semiotica generale*. Milan: Bompiani.

———— (1976). *A Theory of Semiotics*. Bloomington: Indiana University Press.

———— (1979a). *Lector in fabula. La cooperazione interpretativa nei testi narrativi*. Milan: Bompiani.

servative institutional practices in hiring, tenuring, promotion, reviewing, and publishing, as well as in teaching."

46. Bernheimer, ed., *Comparative Literature in the Age of Multiculturalism*, 42. The citation is from the report of the committee.

47. In Carlyle's translation: Professor of Things in General at the University of Don't Know Where.

48. See René Wellek, *A History of Modern Criticism: 1750–1950*, 8 vols. (New Haven: Yale University Press, 1955–92).

49. Bernheimer, ed., *Comparative Literature in the Age of Multiculturalism*, 44. The citation is from the committee report.

50. See "The Legs of Sense," the introduction to Tom Cohen, *Anti-Mimesis: From Plato to Hitchcock* (Cambridge: Cambridge University Press, 1994), 1–8. Cohen uses the phrase "ferocious abjection" (4) to describe the repudiation of Paul de Man's work after the wartime writings were discovered. This particular abjection has been an essential moment in the story I have been following, for example, in Charles Bernheimer's version in the introductory essay "The Anxieties of Comparison," *Comparative Literature in the Age of Multiculturalism*, 1–17. Bernheimer does me the honor of citing an essay of mine as an example of the sort of thing the revolt against theory revolted against (5–6). A little later he says: "History, culture, politics, location, gender, sexual orientation, class, race—a reading in the new mode has to try to take as many of these factors as possible into account. The trick is to do so without becoming subject to Miller's criticism, without, that is, suggesting that a literary work can be explained as an unmediated reflection of these factors" (8). That is the trick all right.

51. I speak of the United States and from my "subject position" in the here and now of 1998.

52. Stevens, *Opus Posthumous*, 176.

53. See Stephen Greenblatt, "Fiction and Friction," in *Shakespearean Negotiations: The Circulation of Social Energy in Renaissance England* (Berkeley: University of California Press, 1988), 66–93. Greenblatt's goal in this essay, it should be said, is to help us understand Shakespeare better, here *Twelfth Night*.

54. David Simpson's phrase. See his *Romanticism, Nationalism, and the Revolt Against Theory* (Chicago: University of Chicago Press, 1993), esp. 172–88.

55. Jon Katz, "Birth of a Digital Nation," *Wired* (April 1997), 184. The essay is also available online at www.wired.com/5.04/netizen/. A more recent essay by Jon Katz modifies somewhat, on the basis of a Merrill Lynch Forum and *Wired* poll, some of his generalizations about the "digital young." See Katz, "The Digital Citizen," *Wired*, 5, no. 12 (December 1997): 68–82, 274–75. "Where I had described [the digital citizen] as deeply estranged from mainstream politics," says Katz, "the poll revealed that they are actually highly participatory and view our existing political system positively, even patriotically" (71).

56. I have discussed this and related issues in *Illustration* (Cambridge: Harvard University Press, 1992), 37–43. See George P. Landow, *Hypertext: The Convergence of Contemporary Critical Theory and Technology* (Baltimore: The Johns Hopkins

———— (1979b). *The Role of the Reader: Explorations in the Semiotics of Texts.* (No trans. indicated.) Bloomington: Indiana University Press.

———— (1990a). *I limiti dell' interpretazione.* Milan: Bompiani.

———— (1990b). *The Limits of Interpretation.* (No trans. indicated.) Bloomington: Indiana University Press.

Eichenbaum, Boris (1965). "The Theory of the 'Formal Method.'" In Lee T. Lemon and Marion J. Reis, eds., *Russian Formalist Criticism: Four Essays.* Lincoln: University of Nebraska Press. 99–139.

Ellis, John M. (1989). *Against Deconstruction.* Princeton: Princeton University Press.

Empson, William (1949). *Seven Types of Ambiguity.* 2d ed. New York: New Directions.

Finlay, Marike (1988). *The Romantic Irony of Semiotics: Friedrich Schlegel and the Crisis of Representation.* Berlin: Mouton de Gruyter.

Fish, Stanley E. (1970). "Literature in the Reader: Affective Stylistics." *New Literary History* 2, no. 1: 123–62.

———— (1982). "With the Compliments of the Author: Reflections on Austin and Derrida." *Critical Inquiry* 8: 84–112.

University Press, 1992), for the best book so far on hypertext and humanistic study. A hypertext version of this book, "*Hypertext* in Hypertext," is available from The Johns Hopkins University Press on 3.5 inch diskette for either MS Windows or Macintosh—another sign of the times.

57. Eduardo Cadava, *Words of Light: Theses on the Photography of History* (Princeton: Princeton University Press, 1997), xx.

58. The present tense in this sentence refers to the first draft of this part of *Black Holes*, written in the summer of 1994.

59. Jacques Derrida, "No Apocalypse, Not Now (full speed ahead, seven missiles, seven missives)," trans. Catherine Porter and Philip Lewis, *Diacritics* 14, no. 2 (Summer 1984): 20–31.

60. Joe Clark, "Plug in to the Internet," *MacUser* 10, no. 9 (September 1994), 87.

61. I owe this insight to Matthew H. Miller.

62. These problems are recognized by John Browning in "There's No Place like Cyberspace: New Worlds Require New Ideas, not Old Metaphors," *Scientific American* (October 1995), 44–46. After putting in question the various ways "virtual reality" attempts to represent the relations of things in cyberspace, Browning's little essay ends by asserting that "if the old symbols are borrowed to represent new ideas, confusion is likely to result. If there is a 'nonspace of the mind,' it must look like no space we have ever seen—if it is seeable at all."

63. See Borges's description, in "The Analytical Language of John Wilkins," of the *Celestial Pantomime of Benevolent Knowledge*: "animals are divided into a) those that belong to the Emperor, b) embalmed ones, c) those that are trained, d) suckling pigs, e) mermaids, f) fabulous ones, g) stray dogs, h) those that are included in this classification, i) those that tremble as if they were mad, j) innumerable ones, k) those drawn with a very fine camel's hair brush, l) others, m) those that have just broken a flower vase, n) those that resemble flies from a distance" (Jorge Luis Borges, *Other Inquisitions, 1937–1952*, trans. Ruth L. C. Simms [New York: Simon and Schuster, 1964], 103).

64. See note 24, above. The large "hypertext archive" of British poetry from 1780 to 1910 being assembled for the Web by Jerome McGann at the University of Virginia (http://www.lib.virginia.edu/etext/britpo/britpo.html) is an exception to this diminishment of poetry's place.

65. William Wordsworth, *The Prelude*, ed. Ernest de Selincourt and Helen Darishire, 2d ed. (Oxford: Oxford University Press, 1959), 1805, 5: 45–49, p. 138.

66. Georges Poulet, *Les métamorphoses du cercle* (Paris: Plon, 1961).

67. Jon Carroll, "Guerrillas in the Myst: From Garage Start-up to the first CD-ROM superstars—Robyn and Rand Miller," *Wired* (August 1994), 2.08:69.

68. Marcel Proust, *Time Regained*, trans. Andreas Mayor, F 4: 608; E 3: 1087, trans. slightly altered.

69. See Northrop Frye, *Fables of Identity: Studies in Poetic Mythology* (New York: Harcourt, Brace & World, 1963), especially "Myth, Fiction, and Displacement," 21–38, and "The Structure of Imagery in *The Faerie Queene*," 69–87, for

Flaubert, Gustave (1980). *Correspondence*. Ed. Jean Bruneau. Ed. de la Pléiade. Vol. 2. Paris: Gallimard.

Fortunati, Vita, and Franci, Giovanna (1989). "Prefazione" and "Nota Bio-Bibliografica." In their trans. J. Hillis Miller. *L'etica della lettura*. Modena: Mucchi. 9–30; 193–205.

Freud, Sigmund (1970). *Beyond the Pleasure Principle*. New York: Liveright.

Gadamer, Hans-Georg (1960). *Wahrheit und Methode*. Tübingen: J. C. B. Mohr.

—— (1988). *Truth and Method*. Rev. ed. Trans. William Glen-Doepel. Trans. ed. Garrett Barden and John Cumming. Revisions of trans. by Joel Weinsheimer and Donald Marshall. New York: Continuum.

Gasché, R. (1979). "Deconstruction as Criticism." *Glyph*, no. 6, 177–215.

—— (1986). *The Tain of the Mirror: Derrida and the Philosophy of Reflection*. Cambridge: Harvard University Press.

Genette, Gérard (1982). *Palimpsestes: La littérature au second degré*. Paris: Seuil.

Greimas, A. J. (1966). *Sémantique structurale: Recherche de méthode*. Paris: Larousse.

—— (1984). *Structural Semantics: An Attempt at a Method*. Lincoln: University of Nebraska Press.

examples of Frye's spatializing habit of mind. See also Joseph Frank, "Spatial Form in Modern Literature," in *The Widening Gyre* (New Brunswick, N.J.: Rutgers University Press, 1963), 3–62, and T. S. Eliot, "Tradition and the Individual Talent," *Selected Essays: 1917–1932* (New York: Harcourt Brace, 1932), 3–11.

70. Katz, "Birth of a Digital Nation," 184.

71. Walter Benjamin, *Gesammelte Schriften*, ed. Rolf Tiedemann and Hermann Schweppenhäuser, 7 vols. (Frankfurt am Main: Suhrkamp, 1974–89), 1: 478.

72. In Walter Benjamin, *Illuminationen* (Frankfurt am Main: Suhrkamp, 1955), 148–84; *Illuminations*, trans. Harry Zohn (New York: Schocken, 1969), 217–51.

73. From a recent, unpublished seminar on witnessing and questions of responsibility, my trans.

74. See above, "*Get 'Geist'*: The Crisis in Representation," for a discussion of how suspect synecdochic representation has become to those in the new American studies.

75. At least they understand culture as it is embodied in the United Kingdom, a class society very different from the social structure of the United States. In the United States race, gender, and ethnic particularity are much more important than class in the European sense in determining the hierarchy of power and privilege. That does not mean the United States is not a class society, but that class membership in the United States is much more difficult to define. Leonard Bast, in Forster's *Howards End*, has little hope of rising out of his class, whereas Fitzgerald's Jay Gatsby, in *The Great Gatsby*, or Faulkner's Thomas Sutpen, in *Absalom, Absalom!*, are exemplars of the American myth of upward mobility.

76. See Judith P. Butler, *Bodies That Matter: On the Discursive Limits of "Sex"* (New York: Routledge, 1993); Judith P. Butler, *Gender Trouble: Feminism and the Subversion of Identity* (New York: Routledge, 1990); Diane Elam, *Feminism and Deconstruction: Ms. en Abyme* (London: Routledge, 1994). For forceful critiques of cultural studies, see Michael Sprinker, "We Lost It at the Movies," *MLN* 112 (1997): 385–99, and Tom Cohen, *Ideology and Inscription: "Cultural Studies" after Benjamin, de Man, and Bakhtin* (Cambridge: Cambridge University Press, 1998).

77. These presuppositions about the other are constant themes in Levinas's work, for example, in *Humanisme de l'autre homme* (Montpellier: Fata Morgana, 1972), or in *Autrement qu'être ou au-delà de l'essence* (The Hague: Martinus Nijhoff, 1974); *Otherwise than Being, or Beyond Essence*, trans. A. Lingis (The Hague: Martinus Nijhoff, 1981), or in *Hors sujet* (Montpellier: Fata Morgana, 1987); *Outside the Subject*, trans. Michael B. Smith (Stanford: Stanford University Press, 1994). For the best single essay by Levinas on his concept of the "other," see Emmanuel Levinas, "La trace de l'autre," *Tijdschrift voor Philosophie* (September 1963): 605–23; "The Trace of the Other," trans. A. Lingis, in Mark C. Taylor, ed., *Deconstruction in Context: Literature and Philosophy* (Chicago: University of Chicago Press, 1986), 345–59. The citation in the previous sentence comes from "The Trace of the Other" (357). For the best book on Levinas, see Jacques Derrida, *Adieu à Emmanuel Levinas* (Paris: Galilée, 1997).

Greimas, A. J., and Courtés, J. (1979). *Sémiotique: Dictionnaire raisonné de la théo-rie du langage.* Paris: Hachette.

——— (1982). *Semiotics and Language: An Analytical Dictionary.* Bloomington: Indiana University Press.

Group Mu (1970). *Rhétorique Général.* Paris: Larousse.

——— (1981). *A General Rhetoric.* Baltimore: The Johns Hopkins University Press.

Halliday, M. A. K., and Hasan, R. (1976). *Cohesion in English.* London: Longman.

Hardy, Thomas (1975). *The Well-Beloved.* London: Macmillan.

——— (1978). *Tess of the d'Urbervilles.* London: Macmillan.

Hegel, G. W. F. (1975). *Aesthetics: Lectures on Fine Art.* Trans. T. M. Knox. 2 vols. Oxford: Clarendon Press.

Heidegger, Martin (1971). *On the Way to Language.* New York: Harper & Row.

Heusser, Martin, and Schweizer, Harold (1991). "The Authority of Reading: An Interview with J. Hillis Miller." In J. Hillis Miller, *Hawthorne and History.* Oxford: Basil Blackwell.

Hölderlin, Friedrich (1980). *Poems and Fragments.* Trans. Michael Hamburger. Bi-lingual ed. Cambridge: Cambridge University Press.

78. See John P. Muller and William J. Richardson, eds., *The Purloined Poe: Lacan, Derrida, and Psychoanalytic Reading* (Baltimore: The Johns Hopkins University Press, 1988).

79. See Jacques Lacan, "Le séminaire sur 'La Lettre volée," in *Ecrits* (Paris: Seuil, 1966), 11–61; "Seminar on 'The Purloined Letter,' " trans. Jeffrey Mehlman, *Yale French Studies*, no. 48 (1972), 39–72.

80. See Jacques Derrida, "Le facteur de la verité," in *La carte postale* (Paris: Aubier-Flammarion, 1980), 441–524; "Le facteur de la verité," *The Post Card*, trans. Alan Bass (Chicago: University of Chicago Press, 1987), 413–96. See also Jacques Derrida, "Pour l'amour de Lacan," *Résistances de la psychanalyse* (Paris: Galilée, 1996), 55–88.

81. Jacques Derrida, "Apories: Mourir—s'attendre aux 'limites de la verité,' " in *Le passage des frontières* (Paris: Galilée, 1994), 317. Also available as *Apories* (Paris: Galilée, 1996); *Aporias*, trans. Thomas Dutoit (Stanford: Stanford University Press, 1993), 22.

82. Jacques Derrida, "Il faut bien manger," in *Points de suspension: Entretiens*, ed. Elisabeth Weber (Paris: Galilée, 1992), 269–301; " 'Eating Well,' or the Calculation of the Subject," trans. Peter Conner and Avital Ronell, *Points . . . : Interviews, 1974–1994*, ed. Elisabeth Weber (Stanford: Stanford University Press, 1995), 255–87; Jacques Derrida, "Psyché: Invention de l'autre," in *Psyché: Inventions de l'autre* (Paris: Galilée, 1987), 11–61; Jacques Derrida, *Apories*; Jacques Derrida, "Tout autre est tout autre," in *L'éthique du don: Jacques Derrida et la pensée du don*, ed. Jean-Michel Rabaté and Michael Wetzel (Paris: Métailié-Transition, 1992), 79–108; *The Gift of Death*, trans. David Wills (Chicago: University of Chicago Press, 1995), 82–115. I have discussed these essays in "Derrida's Others," in Julian Wolfreys, ed., *Applying: To Derrida* (London: Macmillan, 1996).

83. Jacques Derrida, "Deconstruction and the Other," in Richard Kearney, *Dialogues with Contemporary Continental Thinkers: The Phenomenological Heritage* (Manchester: Manchester University Press, 1984), 123–24.

84. Nicolas Abraham and Maria Torok, *Cryptonymie: Le verbier de l'homme aux loups*, introd. Jacques Derrida (Paris: Aubier-Flammarion, 1976); *The Wolf Man's Magic Word*, with Foreword, "Fors: The Anglish Words of Nicolas Abraham and Maria Torok," by Jacques Derrida, trans. Barbara Johnson (Minneapolis: University of Minnesota Press, 1986).

85. Derrida in "Fors" refers to a then-unpublished essay by Nicolas Abraham, "Le fantôme d'Hamlet ou Le Vᵉ Acte" (*Cryptonymie*, 47).

86. See Frantz Fanon, *The Wretched of the Earth*, trans. Constance Farrington (New York: Grove Weidenfeld, 1991), and Edward Said, *Culture and Imperialism* (New York: Vintage, 1994).

87. Jean-François Lyotard, *Peregrinations: Law, Form, Event* (New York: Columbia University Press, 1988), 44. See also Jean-François Lyotard, *The Differend: Phrases in Dispute* (Minneapolis: University of Minnesota Press, 1988).

88. See Maurice Blanchot, *La communauté inavouable* (Paris: Minuit, 1983);

Ingarden, Roman (1973). *The Cognition of the Literary Work of Art*. Evanston: Northwestern University Press.

Iser, Wolfgang (1972). *Der Implizite Leser: Kommunikationsformen des Romans von Bunyan bis Beckett*. Munich: Wilhelm Fink.

——— (1974). *The Implied Reader: Patterns of Communication from Bunyan to Beckett*. Baltimore: The Johns Hopkins University Press.

——— (1976). *Der Akt des Lesens: Theorie ästhetischer Wirkung*. Munich: Wilhelm Fink.

——— (1978). *The Act of Reading: A Theory of Aesthetic Response*. Baltimore: The Johns Hopkins University Press.

Jakobson, R. (1973). *Questions de poétique*. Paris: Seuil.

Jakobson, R., with Halle, M. (1980). *Fundamentals of Language*. The Hague: Mouton.

Jean, Georges (1989). *L'écriture, mémoire des hommes*. Paris: Gallimard.

Jenny, Laurent (1976). "La stratégie de la forme." *Poétique* 27: 25–39.

Johnson, Barbara (1980). *The Critical Difference: Essays in the Contemporary Rhetoric of Reading*. Baltimore: The Johns Hopkins University Press.

Kafka, Franz (1955). *The Trial*. Trans. Willa and Edwin Muir. Harmondsworth, Middlesex: Penguin.

Jean-Luc Nancy, *La communauté désoeuvrée* (Paris: Christian Bourgois, 1986); William Readings, *The University in Ruins*; Diane Elam, *Feminism and Deconstruction: Ms. en Abyme.*

89. In V. N. Volosinov, *Freudianism: A Marxist Critique*, trans. I. R. Titunik (New York: Academic Press, 1976), 93–116, esp. 98–106. See Tom Cohen's admirable discussion of this passage, " 'Well!': Voloshinov's Double-Talk," *SubStance* 21, no. 2 (1992): 91–101.

90. This essay is included, along with other late essays, where what de Man called the "materiality" of language is constantly at stake, in *Aesthetic Ideology*, ed. Andrzcj Warminski (Minneapolis: University of Minnesota Press, 1996), 129–62. The citations come from 132.

91. See, for one example, Paul de Man, "Phenomenality and Materiality in Kant," *Aesthetic Ideology*, 70–90, esp. 87–90.

92. Jacques Derrida, "Deconstruction and the Other," in Richard Kearney, *Dialogues with Contemporary Continental Thinkers*, 118.

93. For an authoritative account of black holes by a distinguished physicist, see Kip S. Thorne, *Black Holes and Time Warps: Einstein's Outrageous Legacy* (New York: W. W. Norton, 1994). Astrophysicists have recently become more willing to assert the indubitable existence of black holes, but they still often hedge what they assert by saying something like "A massive black hole *may* lie at the center of the galaxy." Recent work in quantum mechanics even suggests that the information in matter sucked into a black hole may not be wholly lost. See Leonard Susskind, "Black Holes and the Information Paradox," *Scientific American* (April 1997), 52–57.

94. This terrifying admonition is scrawled at the bottom of Kurtz's idealistic essay on "The Suppression of Savage Customs."

95. What is said here about a university of dissensus develops ideas I proposed in a brief essay published in *The Times Literary Supplement* in the summer of 1994. A funny thing happened to that essay on the way to the printer. It was cut and elegantly revised by the *TLS* editor, Alan Jenkins. I was given the opportunity to read and approve this new version. At some later point, however, the word "dissensus," still present in the final version I approved, was changed to "dissent." The word "dissenter" was then used in the title invented by someone at the *TLS*: "Return Dissenter." This change made my essay say the exact opposite of what I intended to say. "Dissent" names a resistance to some hegemonic orthodoxy, as the dissenters in England resisted the established Church of England, or as Matthew Arnold makes fun of what he calls the "dissidence of dissent." "Dissensus," on the other hand, presupposes a situation in which no dominant orthodoxy exists from which to dissent, only decentered and nonhierarchical communities made of "peripheral singularities," as Bill Readings called them, borrowing the phrase from Giorgio Agamben. I do not suppose that the change from "dissensus" to "dissent" was the result of a conspiracy by the *TLS* to subvert what I was trying to say. Some copy editor or perhaps even some computer program was probably offended by the word "dissensus" and replaced it with a word in the *TLS*'s vo-

Kant, Immanuel (1969). *Foundations of the Metaphysics of Morals*. Indianapolis: Bobbs-Merrill.

Keats, John (1970). *Letters*. Ed. Robert Gittings. Garden City, N.Y.: Anchor, Doubleday.

Kelkel, Arion Lothar (1975). *Heidegger*. Paris: Seghers.

Kierkegaard, Søren (1959). *Either/Or*. Trans. David F. Swenson and Lillian Marvin Swenson, with revisions and a Foreword by Walter Lowrie. 2 vols. Garden City, N.Y.: Anchor, Doubleday.

——— (1985). *Fear and Trembling: A Dialectical Lyric: By Johannes de Silentio*. Trans. Alastair Hannay. Harmondsworth, Middlesex: Penguin.

Klinkenberg, Jean Marie (1987). "El signo icónico: La retórica icónica: Proposiciones." In *La crisis de la literariedad*. Madrid: Taurus. 8–29.

Kofman, Sarah (1984). *Lectures de Derrida*. Paris: Galilée.

Kristeva, Julia (1969a). *Sémiotique: Recherches pour un sémanalyse*. Paris: Seuil.

——— (1969b). *Le langage, cet inconnu*. Paris: Societé Géneral pour la Publication.

——— (1974). *La révolution du langage poétique*. Paris: Seuil.

——— (1984). *Revolution in Poetic Language*. Trans. Margaret Waller. New York: Columbia University Press.

cabulary. The subversion of my meaning was a striking example of the massive power of ideological assumptions as they work in the apparently neutral form of a journalistic "house style." It is apparently just not possible within the *TLS*'s style to say what I was trying to say. The present book attempts to get it said.

96. The final chapter of Bill Readings's *The University in Ruins* is entitled "The Community of Dissensus" (18–193). That chapter has much aided my thinking about this topic. See also Diane Elam, *Feminism and Deconstruction*, especially the last two chapters, on what Elam calls "groundless solidarity."

97. In a lecture given in New York on March 4, 1994.

98. Jacques Derrida, in "Mochlos," speaks eloquently of this transformative power in teaching. See "*Mochlos*—ou le conflit des facultés," *Du droit à la philosophie*, 422–24; "Mochlos," trans. Richard Rand and Amy Wygant, in Rand, ed., *Logomachia*, 21–22.

99. See Nancy, *Communauté désoeuvrée*.

100. Agamben, *Coming Community*, 84. Agamben is referring to Blanchot, *Communauté inavouable*.

101. Friedrich Schlegel, *Kritische Schriften* (Munich: Carl Hanser, 1964), 48; *Philosophical Fragments*, trans. Peter Firchow (Minneapolis: University of Minnesota Press, 1991), 46.

102. See Nicolas Abraham and Maria Torok, *L'écorce et le noyau* (Paris: Aubier-Flammarion, 1978); Nicolas Abraham, "The Shell and the Kernel," trans. Nicholas Rand, *Diacritics* 9, no. 1 (Spring 1979): 19–28.

103. Jacques Derrida, "Deconstruction and the Other," in Kearney, *Dialogues with Contemporary Continental Thinkers*, 123. According to Derrida, "the founding concepts of metaphysics — *logos, eidos, theoria*, etc. — are instances of *catachresis* rather than metaphors. . . . In a work such as *Glas*, or other recent ones like it, I am trying to produce new forms of catachresis, another kind of writing, a violent writing which stakes out the faults [*failles*] and deviations of language, so that the text produces a language of its own, in itself" (ibid.). Tom Cohen's *Anti-Mimesis* brilliantly builds on de Man and Derrida but goes beyond them in its focus on United States literature and film and in its demonstrations of what materialist, interventionist writing and reading are. Another theoretically exigent example is Walter Benjamin's materialist historiography. In his essay on Eduard Fuchs, Benjamin says, "cultural history only seems to represent a deepening of insight; it does not present even the appearance of progress in dialectics." Benjamin means by "dialectics" the active work of materialist historiography. He describes in the seventeenth of the "Theses on the Philosophy of History" the way a "historical materialist" sees "a revolutionary chance in the fight for the oppressed past" when he (or she) finds a way to "blast [*herauszusprengen*] a specific era out of the homogeneous course of history—blasting a specific life out of the era or a specific work out of the lifework" (Walter Benjamin, *Illuminations*, trans. Harry Zohn [New York: Schocken, 1969], 263; Walter Benjamin, *Illuminationen* [Frankfurt a. M.: Suhrkamp, 1955], 278). In order to change the future we must change our grasp of the past. Only something like Benjamin's *Heraussprengung* will make cultural studies an effective interven-

———— (1989). *Language: The Unknown: An Initiation into Linguistics.* Trans. Anne M. Menke. New York: Columbia University Press.

Lacoue-Labarthe, Philippe, and Nancy, Jean-Luc (1970). "La fable (littéraire et philosophie)." *Poétique*, no. 1, 51–63.

———— (1978). *L'absolu littéraire: Théorie de la littérature du romantisme allemand.* Paris: Seuil.

———— (1988). *The Literary Absolute: The Theory of Literature in German Romanticism.* Trans. Philip Barnard and Cheryl Lester. Albany: State University of New York Press.

Laruelle, François (1989). *Philosophie et non-philosophie.* Liège: Pierre Mardaga.

Lausberg, Heinrich (1960). *Handbuch der literarischen Rhetorik: Eine Grundlegung der Literaturwissenschaft.* Munich: Max Hueber Verlag.

Leitch, V. B. (1983). *Deconstructive Criticism: An Advanced Introduction and Survey.* New York: Columbia University Press.

Levin, Samuel R. (1962). *Linguistic Structures in Poetry.* The Hague: Mouton.

———— (1976). "Concerning What Kind of Speech Act a Poem Is." In Teun A. van Dijk, ed. *Pragmatics of Language and Literature.* Amsterdam: North-Holland. 141–60.

tion. Benjamin spent the last part of his life developing a method of criticism that would be materialist in this way. The use of theory, in such thinkers as these, turns out paradoxically not to be its contribution to knowledge but its power to facilitate politically and institutionally transformative praxis and, moreover, to exemplify it.

104. Negroponte claims that research universities will have a crucial role in the new situation, where companies rather than governmental agencies increasingly support universities. The companies will need the universities as the place where new ideas in all fields are developed. Quite correctly he sees the process as expensive, given that not all new ideas pan out. According to him, however, the pedagogical mission of the university (producing educated students) will support that crucial innovative role: "companies have realized that they cannot afford to do basic research. What better place to outsource that research than to a qualified university and its mix of different people? This is a wake-up call to companies that have ignored universities—sometimes in their own backyards—as assets. Don't just look for 'well-managed' programs. Look for those populated with young people, preferably from different backgrounds, who love to spin off crazy ideas— of which only one or two out of a hundred may be winners. A university can afford such a ridiculous ratio of failure to success, since it has another more important product: its graduates" (*Wired* 4, no. 1 [January, 1996]: 204). What Negroponte says is as true for the humanities as for the sciences. The challenge is to persuade those in charge that new ideas in the humanities are also valuable.

CHAPTER 2: THE GROUNDS OF LOVE

1. "Galaxy" is a name for a World Wide Web search program used by the Mac-Web browser for finding sites on the Internet.

2. Anthony Trollope, *An Autobiography*, World's Classics ed. (London: Oxford University Press, 1961), 36. Further references will be to this edition, indicated by "A," followed by the page number.

3. *Ayala's Angel*, World's Classics ed. (London: Oxford University Press, 1960), 418. Further references will be by page numbers in the text to this edition.

4. This citation comes from a remarkable passage in *Middlemarch*, near the beginning of Chap. 20, about "the roar on the other side of silence." See George Eliot, *Middlemarch* (Harmondsworth, Middlesex: Penguin, 1974), 226. This passage makes explicit George Eliot's particular sense of otherness. For a discussion of this, see my "The Roar on the Other Side of Silence," *Edda* (3/95), 237–45.

5. "Trollope settled down steadily to the English girl; he took possession of her, and turned her inside out" (Henry James, "Anthony Trollope," *Literary Criticism: Essays on Literature: American Writers; English Writers* [New York: The Library of America, 1984], 1349–50). James's essay was first published in *Century Magazine* (July 1883), and then reprinted in *Partial Portraits* (1888).

6. See D. A. Miller, "The Novel as Usual: Trollope's *Barchester Towers*," in *The Novel and the Police* (Berkeley: University of California Press, 1988), 107–45. The real police, it so happens, do play a role in *Ayala's Angel*. They appear in the serio-comic episodes of Tom Tringle's drunken assaults, first on a policeman and then,

Levinas, Emmanuel (1968). *Totalité et infini: Essai sur l'extériorité*. The Hague: Martinus Nijhoff.

———— (1969). *Totality and Infinity: An Essay on Exteriority*. Trans. Alphonso Lingis. Pittsburgh: Duquesne University Press.

Loesberg, Jonathan (1991). *Aestheticism and Deconstruction: Pater, Derrida, de Man*. Princeton: Princeton University Press.

Lotman, Jurij M. (1977). *The Structure of the Artistic Text*. Trans. Ronald Vroon. Ann Arbor: (Dept. of Slavic Languages and Literature), University of Michigan.

Lyotard, Jean-François (1971). *Discourse, Figure*. Paris: Klincksieck.

Melville, Herman (1984). "Bartleby, The Scrivener: A Story of Wall-Street." In *Pierre, Israel Potter, The Piazza Tales, The Confidence-Man, Uncollected Prose, Billy Budd*. Ed. Harrison Hayford. New York: The Library of America. 635–72.

Mounin, Georges (1970). *Introduction à la sémiologie*. Paris: Minuit.

Münster, Reinhold (1987). "Con hermosa anarquía." Introduction to the Spanish trans. of Friedrich Schlegel, *Lucinda*. Valencia: Natán. i–xxxiv.

later, on his rival Jonathan Stubbs. The real policing of Tom Tringle and the other characters, however, is done by community restraints such as those D. A. Miller describes. These powers, not the police, get Tom in the end. He settles down to his destiny as the son of a rich financier, marries a suitable wife, and has a house in the country and one in London.

7. See Louis Althusser, "Ideology and Ideological State Apparatuses," 127–86, esp. 141–48.

8. As D. A. Miller recognizes, when he expands on his comment that "When I read Trollope, it is all I can do not to be bored": "Far from the simple reflex-response to banality, boredom hysterically converts into yawning affectlessness what would otherwise be outright panic" (*Novel and the Police*, 145).

9. See Anthony Trollope, *The West Indies and The Spanish Main* (London: Chapman and Hall, 1859); *North America*, 2 vols. (London: Chapman and Hall, 1862); *Australia and New Zealand*, 2 vols. (London: Chapman and Hall, 1873).

10. See Louis Althusser, "A Letter on Art in Reply to André Daspré (April 1966)," in *Lenin and Philosophy and Other Essays*, 221–27. See also my discussion of this in *Topographies* (Stanford: Stanford University Press, 1995), 353–54.

11. Such motivated names are characteristic of Trollope's practice. They tell the reader that Sir Thomas's firm got its start by working crossways against the grain of the law and by financial practices that were treasonous.

12. The top is better than the bottom because nearer to Kensington Gardens, to which Queen's Gate leads on the north.

13. Sarah E. Miller, "Twice-Born Tales from Kathmandu: Stories That Tell People" (Ph.D. dissertation, Cornell, 1992).

14. Or as Jacques Derrida viewed it in a superb seminar on the phrase "I love you," given at the University of California at Irvine in the spring of 1993.

15. This is Paul de Man's definition in "The Resistance to Theory," in *The Resistance to Theory* (Minneapolis: University of Minnesota Press, 1986), 11: "What we call ideology is precisely the confusion of linguistic with natural reality, of reference with phenomenalism."

16. Jacques Derrida has devoted a whole series of seminars to the exploration of this other kind of secret. See *Donner le temps 1. La fausse monnaie* (Paris: Galilée, 1991) for a preliminary exploration of this impenetrable secrecy.

17. See Jacques Derrida, "Déclarations d'Indépendence," *Otobiographies* (Paris: Galilée, 1984), 13–32.

CHAPTER 3: FRACTAL PROUST

1. Walter Pater, "Conclusion," in *The Renaissance*, ed. Donald L. Hill (Berkeley: University of California Press, 1980), 189. Pater goes on to explain what he means: "for, after all, habit is relative to a stereotyped world, and meantime it is only the roughness of the eye that makes any two persons, things, situations, seem alike" (ibid.). I shall ultimately come round to what Proust means by habit. It seems not so different from what Pater means, but it would be well to remember

Nietzsche, Friedrich (1978). *Thus Spoke Zarathustra: A Book for All and None.* Trans. Walter Kaufmann. New York: Penguin Books.

——— (1988). *Also sprach Zarathustra.* Kritische Studienausgabe. Ed. Giorgio Colli and Mazzino Montinari. Berlin: Walter de Gruyter.

Norris, Christopher (1982). *Deconstruction: Theory and Practice.* London: Methuen.

——— (1988). *Paul de Man: Deconstruction and the Critique of Aesthetic Ideology.* New York: Routledge.

Novalis (Friedrich von Hardenburg) (1968). *Die Dichtungen.* Heidelberg: L. Schneider.

Ortega y Gasset, José (1962a). "Miseria y esplendor de la traducción." In *Misión del bibliotecario.* Madrid: Revista de Occidente. 97–128.

——— (1962b). "Comentario al 'Banquete' de Platón (I. Qué es leer)." In *Misión del bibliotecario.* Madrid: Revista de Occidente. 145–71.

——— (1992). "The Misery and the Splendor of Translation." Trans. Elizabeth Gamble Miller. In Rainer Schulte and John Biguenet, eds., *Theories of Translation: An Anthology of Essays from Dryden to Derrida.* Chicago: University of Chicago Press. 93–112.

that it is only the roughness of the eye that makes any two persons or what they say seem alike.

2. Jacques Derrida, "Envois," in *La carte postale* (Paris: Aubier-Flammarion, 1980), 212, 219; *The Post Card*, trans. Alan Bass (Chicago: University of Chicago Press, 1987), 197, 204.

3. See the discussion of ARTFL in the section of this book called "Literature in Cyberspace," above.

4. W. B. Yeats, *The Autobiography* (Garden City: Doubleday, 1958), 181.

5. Paul de Man, "Montaigne and Transcendence" (1953), trans. Richard Howard, in *Critical Writings: 1953–1978*, ed. Lindsay Waters (Minneapolis: University of Minnesota Press, 1989), 11: Proust's "temporal perspective is necessarily that of the past, which has frozen into the immobility of the irrevocable, and his book is actually written from the point of view of Death—of a man who is already dead."

6. This sentence is not in the new Pléiade edition, which has instead: "Moi, c'était autre chose que j'avais à écrire, de plus long, et pour plus d'une personne. [As for me, it was something different I had to write, longer, and for more than one person.]" (F 4: 620, my trans.).

7. Marcel Proust, *A la recherche du temps perdu*, ed. Jean-Yves Tadié, Pléiade ed. (Paris: Gallimard, 1989); *Remembrance of Things Past*, trans. C. K. Scott Moncrieff and Terence K. Martin (New York: Vintage, 1982). References to the novel will appear in the text and will refer to these editions, designated "F" and "E."

8. A Ph.D. dissertation "A la recherche de l'unité perdue," at the University of California, Irvine.

9. Wallace Stevens, "The Owl in the Sarcophagus," in *Collected Poems* (New York: Knopf, 1954), 432.

10. See Ramon Fernandez, *Proust* (Paris: Nouvelle Revue Critique, 1943); Samuel Beckett, "Proust," in *Proust; Three Dialogues* (London: John Calder, 1965), 9–93; orig. pub. 1931); Georges Bataille, "Proust," *La littérature et le mal* (Paris: Gallimard, 1957), 141–57; Georges Poulet, "Proust," *Etudes sur le temps humain* (Paris: Plon, 1953), 364–404; Poulet, *L'espace Proustien* (Paris: Gallimard, 1963); Poulet, "Proust," *Mesure de l'instant* (Paris: Plon, 1968), 303–35; Walter Benjamin, "Zum Bilde Prousts," *Illuminationen* (Franfurt a. M.: Suhrkamp, 1969), 355–69; Benjamin, "The Image of Proust," *Illuminations*, trans. Harry Zohn (New York: Schocken, 1969), 201–15; Maurice Blanchot, "L'expérience de Proust," *Faux Pas* (Paris: Gallimard, 1943), 53–58; Blanchot, "L'expérience de Proust," *Le livre à venir* (Paris: Gallimard, 1959), 18–34; Emmanuel Levinas, "L'autre dans Proust," *Noms propres* (Montpellier: Fata morgana, 1976), 149–56; Levinas, "The Other in Proust," trans. Seán Hand, *The Levinas Reader*, ed. Seán Hand (Oxford: Blackwell, 1989), 160–65; Gilles Deleuze, *Proust et les signes* (Paris: Presses Universitaires de France, 1971); Deleuze, *Proust and Signs*, trans. Richard Howard (New York: George Braziller, 1972); Roland Barthes, "Proust et les noms," in *To Honor Roman Jakobson* (The Hague: Mouton, 1967), 1: 150–58; René Girard, *Mensonge romantique et verité romanesque* (Paris: Grasset, 1961); Girard, *Deceit, Desire, and the Novel: Self and Other in Literary Structure*, trans. Yvonne Freccero (Baltimore: The

Pease, Donald (1983). "The Other Victorian at Yale." In Jonathan Arac et al., *The Yale Critics: Deconstruction in America*. Minneapolis: University of Minnesota Press. 66–89.

Plato (1963). *The Collected Dialogues*. Ed. Edith Hamilton and Huntington Cairns. Trans. Lane Cooper et al. Bollingen Series 71. Princeton: Princeton University Press.

Poulet, Georges, et al. (1967). *Les chemins actuels de la critique*. Paris: Plon.

Propp, Vladimir (1968). *Morphology of the Folktale*. 2d ed. Trans. Laurence Scott. Austin: University of Texas Press.

Proust, Marcel (1982). *Remembrance of Things Past*. Trans. C. K. Scott Moncrieff and Terence Kilmartin. Vol. 3. New York: Vintage.

Quintilian, Marcus Fabius (1966). *The Institutio Oratoria*. Trans. H. E. Butler. Loeb Classical Library, vol. 3. Cambridge: Harvard University Press.

Rastier, Françoise (1976). *Essais de sémiotique poétique*. Paris: Larousse.

Reis, Carlos, and M. Lopes, Ana Cristina (1987). *Dicionário de narratologia*. Coimbra: Almedina.

Ricoeur, Paul (1975). *La métaphore vive*. Paris: Seuil.

Johns Hopkins University Press, 1965); Jean-Pierre Richard, *Proust et le monde sensible* (Paris: Seuil, 1974); Gérard Genette, "Proust palimpseste," *Figures* (Paris: Seuil, 1966), 39–67; Genette, "Proust et le langage indirect," *Figures II* (Paris: Seuil, 1969), 223–94; Genette, "Métonymie chez Proust" and "Discours du récit," *Figures III* (Paris: Seuil, 1972), 41–63; 67–273; Genette, *Narrative Discourse: An Essay in Method*, trans. Jane E. Lewin (New York: Cornell University Press, 1972); Paul de Man, "Reading (Proust)," *Allegories of Reading* (New Haven: Yale University Press, 1979), 57–78; Michael Sprinker, *History and Ideology in Proust: A la recherche du temps perdu and the Third French Republic* (Cambridge: Cambridge University Press, 1994); Luzius Keller, *Proust lesen* (Frankfurt a. M.: Suhrkamp, 1991); Vincent Descombes, *Proust: Philosophie du roman* (Paris: Minuit, 1987); Descombes, *Proust: Philosophy of the Novel*, trans. Catherine Chance Macksey (Stanford: Stanford University Press, 1992); Kevin Newmark, "Ingesting the Mummy: Proust's Allegory of Memory," in *Beyond Symbolism: Textual History and the Future of Reading* (Ithaca: Cornell University Press, 1991), 106–41; Julia Kristeva, *Le temps sensible* (Paris: Gallimard, 1994); Kristeva, *Proust and the Sense of Time*, trans. Stephen Bann (New York: Columbia University Press, 1993).

11. George Eliot, *Middlemarch* (Harmondsworth, Middlesex: Penguin, 1974), 448. I had, by the way, lost the page reference for this citation and was able to find it in two minutes using the "Find" command in my word processor to search the complete text of *Middlemarch* I have "downloaded" from the Internet into my computer hard disk. In order to look for it, however, I had already to know that it was there, that is, I had to have read *Middlemarch*. Nevertheless, having *Middlemarch* "on line" changes fundamentally the conditions under which I now read it or write about it. Even if I read it in a printed book version, I know that an infinitely manipulable digitized version is available to me at any moment. My sense of the text's mode of existence is now different in ways that are difficult to calculate.

12. De Man, *Allegories of Reading*, 78. I shall discuss later what de Man says in this passage.

13. Marcel Proust, *Correspondance*, ed. Philip Kolb (Paris: Plon, 1970–93), 13: 100, trans. Catherine Chance Macksey, in Vincent Descombes, *Proust*, 5.

14. "1913,—Laborious and vain applications to various publishers, N.R.F., Mercure de France, Fasquelle and Ollendorff, for the publication of the novel, *A la recherche du temps perdu*. Grasset agrees to publish it at the expense of the author" (Marcel Proust, *A la recherche du temps perdu*, ed. Pierre Clarac and André Ferré, 1st Pléiade ed. [Paris: Gallimard, 1954], 1: xli–ii, my trans.).

15. "Scholars who have studied Proust's notebooks describe the way in which this essay [*Contre Sainte-Beuve*] was taken over by bits of narrative originally intended as illustrations supporting its theses. Thus the meditation of *Time Regained* was not added to the narrative, as an afterthought, in order to bring out its meaning. What happened was the reverse: the novel was born of a desire to illustrate the propositions of the essay" (Descombes, *Proust*, 5).

16. First Pléiade ed., 3: 1091, my trans. *Bequet* means literally "little beak." *Bequet* is an alternative for *languette*, meaning "shaped like a little tongue." Either

———— (1977). *The Rule of Metaphor: Multidisciplinary Studies of the Creation of Meaning in Language.* Toronto: University of Toronto Press.

———— (1983). *Temps et récit.* Vol. 1. Paris: Seuil.

———— (1984a). *Time and Narrative.* Vol. 1. Trans. Kathleen McLaughlin and David Pellauer. Chicago: University of Chicago Press.

———— (1984b). *Temps et récit: La configuration du temps dans le récit de fiction.* Vol. 2. Paris: Seuil.

———— (1985a). *Time and Narrative.* Vol. 2. Trans. Kathleen McLaughlin and David Pellauer. Chicago: University of Chicago Press.

———— (1985b). *Temps et récit: Le temps raconté.* Vol. 3. Paris: Seuil.

———— (1988). *Time and Narrative.* Vol. 3. Trans. Kathleen McLaughlin and David Pellauer. Chicago: University of Chicago Press.

Riffaterre, Michael (1978). *Semiotics of Poetry.* Bloomington: Indiana University Press.

Ripanti, Graziano (1984). *Le parole della metafisica.* Urbino: Quattroventi.

Rousseau, Jean-Jacques (1947). *The Social Contract.* 18th-c. trans. rev. by Charles Frankel. New York: Hafner.

word names the tongue- or beak-shaped strips of paper that one pastes to a manuscript or printer's proof.

17. Hans Lauwerier, *Fractals: Endlessly Repeated Geometrical Figures*, trans. Sophia Gill-Hoffstädt (Princeton: Princeton University Press, 1991), 3.

18. The first Pléiade edition of the *Recherche*, as I have already noted, exists in scanned form in ARTFL, the huge database of French literary and philosophical materials available on the World Wide Web. The text of the *Recherche*, as I have also said, is not available from this electronic archive to be downloaded on the user's computer. ARTFL is rather a searchable database that produces on the computer screen all the passages in a given text containing a key word or words. This database, like the digitized version of *Middlemarch*, radically changes the mode of existence of *A la recherche du temps perdu*. It makes it enter the new cyberspace I have tried to map in the chapter on *Ayala's Angel*.

19. De Man, *Allegories of Reading*, 77.

20. Lauwerier, *Fractals*, ix.

21. De Man, *Allegories of Reading*, 78. De Man's citation is from the first Pléiade edition of the *Recherche*, 3: 910.

22. "But is it possible to remain, as Genette would have it, *within* an undecidable situation? As anyone who has ever been caught in a revolving door or on a revolving wheel can testify, it is certainly most uncomfortable, and all the more so in this case since this whirligig is capable of infinite acceleration and is, in fact, not successive but simultaneous" (Paul de Man, "Autobiography as De-Facement," in *The Rhetoric of Romanticism* [New York: Columbia University Press, 1984], 70).

23. "Man darf nämlich zweifeln . . . ob es Gegensätze überhaupt giebt" (Friedrich Nietzsche, *Jenseits von Gut und Böse, Kritische Studienausgabe*, ed. Giorgio Colli and Mazzino Montinari [Berlin: Walter de Gruyter, 1988], 5: 16; *Beyond Good and Evil*, trans. Walter Kaufmann [New York: Vintage, 1966], 10).

24. See chap. 1, note 102.

25. Another synecdoche there! Calling the work by the name of its author.

26. The figure is employed by Marcel to describe M. de Charlus's lack of jealousy for the women Morel loves: "It was of men alone that M. de Charlus was capable of feeling any jealousy so far as Morel was concerned. Women inspired in him none whatever. This is indeed an almost universal rule with the Charluses of this world. The love of the man they love for a woman is something else [*quelque chose d'autre*], which occurs in another animal species (a lion leaves tigers in peace, does not bother them, and if anything reassures them)" (F 3: 722–23; E 3: 214).

27. These etymologies come from *The American Heritage Dictionary* (New York: American Heritage Publishing Co., Inc., 1969).

28. Any assertion that Albertine is or is not lesbian will be an act of bearing witness, therefore a speech act. What it might mean to say that the assertion "Albertine is a lesbian" is a performative, not a constative, utterance presupposes a concept of speech acts different from that of J. L. Austin or John Searle. For this difference see the discussion of performative language at the end of the first section of this book. See also Jacques Derrida, *Limited Inc*, trans. Sam Weber (Evanston:

Saussure, Ferdinand de (1981). *Cours de linguistique générale.* Ed. Tullio de Mauro. Paris: Payot.

———— (1983). *Course in General Linguistics.* Trans. Roy Harris. London: Duckworth.

Schlegel, Friedrich (1958a). *Kritische Schriften.* Munich: Carl Hanser.

———— (1958–95). *Kritische Ausgabe.* Ed. Ernst Behler, Jean-Jacques Anstett, and Hans Eichner. 35 vols. Munich: Ferdinand Schöningh.

———— (1971). *Lucinde and the Fragments.* Trans. Peter Firchow. Minneapolis: University of Minnesota Press.

———— (1991). *Philosophical Fragments.* Trans. Peter Firchow. Minneapolis: University of Minnesota Press.

Schleifer, Ronald (1985). "The Anxiety of Allegory: De Man, Greimas, and the Problem of Referentiality." In Robert Con Davis and Ronald Schleifer, eds., *Rhetoric and Form: Deconstruction at Yale.* Norman: University of Oklahoma Press. 215–38.

Schmidt, S. J. (1973). "Théorie et pratique d'une étude scientifique de la narrativité littéraire." In C. Chabrol, ed. *Sémiotique narrative et textuelle.* Paris: Larousse.

Northwestern University Press, 1988); Derrida, *Psyché: Inventions de l'autre* (Paris: Editions Galilée, 1987), 58–61; Paul de Man, "Promises (Social Contract)," in *Allegories of Reading*, 246–77; de Man, "Pascal's Allegory of Persuasion," in *Aesthetic Ideology*, ed. Andrzej Warminski (Minneapolis: University of Minnesota Press, 1996), 51–69; J. Hillis Miller, "History, Narrative, and Responsibility: Speech Acts in 'The Aspern Papers,'" in Gert Buelens, ed., *Enacting History in Henry James* (Cambridge: Cambridge University Press, 1997), 193–210; also in *Textual Practice* (Summer 1995), 9, no. 2, 243–67. For use of this concept of speech acts in feminist thinking, see Judith P. Butler, *Bodies That Matter: On the Discursive Limits of "Sex"* (New York: Routledge, 1993); Judith Butler, *Gender Trouble: Feminism and the Subversion of Identity* (New York: Routledge, 1990); Diane Elam, *Feminism and Deconstruction: Ms. en Abyme*, (London: Routledge, 1994).

29. Stendhal, *La Chartreuse de Parme*, in *Romans et Nouvelles*, Pléiade ed., ed. Henri Martineau (Paris: Gallimard, 1952), 2: 93; Stendhal, *The Charterhouse of Parma*, trans. Margaret R. B. Shaw (Harmondsworth, Middlesex: Penguin, 1958), 88.

30. J. Hillis Miller, "'Le Mensonge, le Mensonge Parfait': Théories du mensonge chez Proust et Derrida," trans. Yasmine van den Wijngaert, reviewed by Chantal Zabus and Cécile Hayes, in Michel Lisse, ed., *Passions de la littérature* (Paris: Galilée, 1996), 405–20.

31. I am thinking of the way, for example, a computer-generated telescope image produces what are called "artifacts," that is, elements of the image that are not there in the outer reality to which the image corresponds.

32. Jacques Lacan, "Le stade du miroir comme formateur de la fonction du Je," *Ecrits* (Paris: Seuil, 1966), 93–100.

33. Proust's ultimate repudiation of Ruskin was defined in similar terms. It was a rejection of Ruskin's idolatry of art works, a rejection of his false belief that a work of art is the true image of the spiritual reality to which it appears to give us access. See Gary Wihl, "Idolatry in Ruskin and Proust," in *Ruskin and the Rhetoric of Infallibility* (New Haven: Yale University Press, 1985), 109–55, for a brilliant discussion of Proust's rejection of what he saw as Ruskin's idolatry.

34. Derrida's phrase. See *Psyché*, 61.

35. Jacques Derrida has discussed this "logic" from a different perspective in a recent seminar on the episode of Bergotte's death in the *Recherche*.

36. Paul de Man's phrase. See *Allegories of Reading*, 69.

37. See Henry James, "Preface," *The Golden Bowl* (New York: Augustus M. Kelley, 1971; rpt. of the New York Edition), 1: xiii–iv; Jacques Derrida, "Ponctuations: le temps de la thèse," *Du droit à la philosophie* (Paris: Galilée, 1990), 443–44; "The Time of a Thesis: Punctuations," trans. Kathleen McLaughlin, in Alan Montefiore, ed., *Philosophy in France Today* (Cambridge: Cambridge University Press, 1983), 34–50. I have discussed both of these elsewhere, the first in "Re-Reading Re-Vision: James and Benjamin," in *The Ethics of Reading* (New York: Columbia University Press, 1987), 110–22, the second in "Derrida's Topographies," in *Topographies* (Stanford: Stanford University Press, 1995), 297–301.

Schuwer, Camille (1949). "La part de Fichte dans l'esthétique romantique." In Albert Béguin, ed., *Le romantisme allemand*. Paris: Les Cahiers du Sud. 833–74.

Serres, Michel (1974). *La traduction*. Paris: Minuit.

Shklovsky, Victor (1965). "Art as Technique." In Lee T. Lemon and Marion J. Reis, eds., *Russian Formalist Criticism: Four Essays*. Lincoln: University of Nebraska Press. 3–57.

Silva, Vítor Manuel de Aguiar e (1969). *Teoria da Literatura*. Coimbra: Almedina.

Sophocles. *Oedipus the King* (1973). Trans. David Grene. In *Sophocles I*. Ed. David Grene and Richmond Lattimore. Chicago: University of Chicago Press.

Steiner, George (1978). *Heidegger*. London: Fontana/Collins.

Stevens, Wallace (1954). *The Collected Poems*. New York: Alfred A. Knopf.

——— (1957). *Opus Posthumous*. New York: Alfred A. Knopf.

Todorov, Tzvetan, ed. (1965). *Théorie de la littérature: Textes des formalistes russes*. Trans. Tzvetan Todorov. Paris: Seuil.

Toussain, Maurice (1983). *Contre l'arbitraire du signe*. Paris: Didier Erudition.

Trotsky, Leon (1957). *Literature and Revolution*. New York: Russell & Russell.

38. Jacques Derrida spoke eloquently, in his seminar on lying in Proust, of Marcel's untranslatable use of the word *appris*. It is untranslatable not just because "learned" is an inexact equivalent, but because the French word *appris* carries the resonance of the adjacent family of words in *-prendre*, a family that has no exact equivalents in other languages: *prendre, comprendre, reprendre,* etc.

39. Jacques Derrida, "Psyche: Invention de l'autre," in *Psyché*, 11–61, esp. 58–61, and elsewhere, for example, in what he says about literature in "Ponctuations: le temps de la thèse."

40. See Jacques Derrida, *Khôra* (Paris: Galilée, 1993), esp. 91–92; Jacques Derrida, *Khōra*, trans. Ian McLeod, in *On the Name*, ed. Thomas Dutoit (Stanford: Stanford University Press, 1995), 87–127, esp. 124–25. See also Tom Cohen's comment on this, apropos of a similar configuration in Hitchcock's films, in *Ideology and Inscription: "Cultural Studies" after Benjamin, de Man, and Bakhtin* (Cambridge: Cambridge University Press, 1998), 167–68.

41. De Man, *Allegories of Reading*, 69.

42. Ibid.

43. See Charles Baudelaire, *Oeuvres complètes*, ed. Y.-G. le Dantec, ed. de la Pléiade (Paris: Gallimard, 1954), 110–11.

44. "The sun . . . is new each day," Heraclitus, fr. 6, in G. S. Kirk and J. E. Raven, eds., *The Presocratic Philosophers* (Cambridge: Cambridge University Press, 1966), 202.

45. De Man, *Allegories of Reading*, 60–61.

46. Ibid., 61.

47. Gérard Genette's model is proposed in "Métonymie chez Proust," *Figures III* (Paris: Seuil, 1972), one of de Man's main targets in this essay.

48. De Man, *Allegories of Reading*, 61.

49. Ibid.

50. Ibid., 77.

51. Ibid., 78.

52. This segment is printed in the new Pléiade edition as chapter three of *Albertine disparue*, the new name for the fifth section of *A la recherche du temps perdu*. The fifth section was called *La fugitive* in the old Pléiade edition, *The Fugitive* in the Moncrieff/Kilmartin translation.

53. "Sometimes at dusk as I returned to the hotel I felt that the Albertine of long ago, invisible to my eyes, was nevertheless enclosed within me as in the *Piombi* of an inner Venice, the tight lid of which some incident occasionally lifted to give me a glimpse of that past [*une ouverture sur ce passé*]" (F 4: 218; E 3: 654).

54. See Jacques Derrida's admirable discussion of "Counterfeit Money" in *Donner le Temps; 1, La fausse monnaie* (Paris: Galilée, 1991), 40–217; *Given Time: 1. Counterfeit Money*, trans. Peggy Kamuf (Chicago: University of Chicago Press, 1992), 31–172. Derrida makes this particular secret the emblem of a universal connection of literature to unfathomable secrets.

55. I am grateful to Anna Pfeiffer for providing a copy of the words and music, to Georgia Albert for the translation, and to Wendy Hester for help with "Piombi"

Tynianov, J. (1965). "De l'évolution littéraire." In Tzvetan Todorov, ed., *Théorie de la littérature*. Trans. Tzvetan Todorov. Paris: Seuil. 120–37.

van Dijk, T. A. (1980). *Text and Context: Explorations in the Semantics and Pragmatics of Discourse*. London and New York: Longman.

Wimsatt, William K. (1954). *The Verbal Icon: Studies in the Meaning of Poetry*. Lexington: The University Press of Kentucky.

Wimsatt, William K., and Brooks, Cleanth (1957). *Literary Criticism: A Short History*. London: Routledge & Kegan Paul.

and other details of Marcel's Venice sojourn. The music for "O sole mio" is by Eduardo di Capua (d. 1917), from an original melody by Alfredo Mazzucchi (1879–1972). The words are by Giovanni Capurro (d. 1930). Albert says she does not know what to do with "ohi ne'," except to assume that it is probably an interjection. If she, who has fluent Italian, does not know, neither do I.

56. An earlier reference to Joshua's miracle appears thousands of pages earlier, at the beginning of *Du côté de chez Swann*, in an odd passage about the strange psychological effects of insomnia and the way it puts time out of joint when sleep comes at odd hours: "Suppose that, towards morning, after a night of insomnia, sleep descends upon him while he is reading, in quite a different position from that in which he normally goes to sleep, he has only to lift his arm to arrest the sun and turn it back in its course [*il suffit de son bras soulevé pour arrêter et faire reculer le soleil*]" (F 1: 5; E 1: 5).

CODA

1. W. B. Yeats, *The Variorum Edition of the Poems*, ed. Peter Allt and Russell K. Alspach (New York: Macmillan, 1977), 631, 630.

2. Wallace Stevens's phrase, in "A Primitive like an Orb" (l. 87), *The Collected Poems* (New York: Knopf, 1954), 443.

3. See Thomas Keenan, *Fables of Responsibility: Aberrations and Predicaments in Ethics and Politics* (Stanford: Stanford University Press, 1997), for an admirably rigorous account of these aporias and of the chances they provide for the democracy to come.

4. "The surplus of responsibility of which I was just speaking will never authorize any silence. I repeat: responsibility is excessive or it is not a responsibility. A limited, measured, calculable, rationally distributed responsibility is already the becoming-right of morality; it is at times also, in the best hypothesis, the dream of every good conscience, in the worst hypothesis, of the small or grand inquisitors" ("Eating Well, or, The Calculation of the Subject: An Interview with Jacques Derrida," in Eduardo Cadava, Peter Connor, and Jean-Luc Nancy, eds., *Who Comes After the Subject?* [New York: Routledge, 1991], 118).

5. See Jacques Derrida, "Psyché: Invention de l'autre," in *Psyché: Inventions de l'autre* (Paris: Editions Galilée, 1987), 11–61, and my "Derrida's Others," in John Brannigan, Ruth Robbins, and Julian Wolfreys, eds., *Applying: To Derrida* (New York: St. Martin's Press, 1996), 153–70.

Cultural Memory | *in the Present*

Library of Congress Cataloging-in-Publication Data

Miller, J. Hillis (Joseph Hillis).
Black holes / J. Hillis Miller. J. Hillis Miller ; or,
Boustrophedonic reading / Manuel Asensi ; translated by
Mabel Richart.
      p.   cm. — (Cultural memory in the present)
The Asensi portion of the book is a translation from an
untitled and as-yet-unpublished manuscript in Spanish.
Includes bibliographical references.
ISBN 0-8047-3243-4 (cloth : alk. paper). —
ISBN 0-8047-3244-2 (pbk. : alk. paper)
1. Criticism.   2. Difference (Psychology) in literature.
3. Trollope, Anthony, 1815–1882. Ayala's angel.   4. Proust,
Marcel, 1871–1922. A la recherche du temps perdu.
5. Miller, J. Hillis (Joseph Hillis), 1928– —Contributions
in criticism.   I. Asensi, Manuel, 1959–   J. Hillis Miller; or,
Boustrophedonic reading.   II. Title: J. Hillis Miller; or,
Boustrophedonic reading.   III. Title: Boustrophedonic reading.
IV. Title.   V. Series.
PN81.M527   1999
801'.95—dc21   98-41706

Original printing 1999
Last figure below indicates year of this printing:
08   07   06   05   04   03   02   01   00   99